P9-DUV-723

DATE DUE

JE 5'00			
NO 13 01			

An Odyssey in Learning and Perception

LDCC **Learning, Development, and Conceptual Change**
Lila Gleitman, Susan Carey, Elissa Newport, and Elizabeth
Spelke, editors

Names for Things: A Study in Human Learning, John Macnamara, 1982

Conceptual Change in Childhood, Susan Carey, 1985

"Gavagai!" or the Future History of the Animal Language Controversy,
David Premack, 1986

*Systems That Learn: An Introduction to Learning Theory for Cognitive and
Computer Scientists*, Daniel N. Osherson, 1986

From Simple Input to Complex Grammar, James L. Morgan, 1986

Concepts, Kinds, and Cognitive Development, Frank C. Keil, 1989

Learnability and Cognition: The Acquisition of Argument Structure,
Steven Pinker, 1989

Mind Bugs: The Origins of Procedural Misconception, Kurt VanLehn, 1990

Categorization and Naming in Children: Problems of Induction, Ellen M.
Markman, 1990

The Child's Theory of Mind, Henry M. Wellman, 1990

The Organization of Learning, Charles R. Gallistel, 1990

Understanding the Representational Mind, Josef Perner, 1991

An Odyssey in Learning and Perception, Eleanor J. Gibson, 1991

An Odyssey in Learning and Perception

Eleanor J. Gibson

A Bradford Book
The MIT Press
Cambridge, Massachusetts
London, England

This book was set in Palatino by Asco Trade Typesetting Ltd., Hong Kong, and was printed and bound in the United States of America.

Library of Congress Cataloging-in-Publication Data

Gibson, Eleanor Jack.
  An odyssey in learning and perception / Eleanor J. Gibson.
     p.   cm.—(Learning, development, and conceptual change)
  "A Bradford book."
  Collection of articles in perception published from the 1930's to the present.
  ISBN 0-262-07133-9
  1. Perception—History. 2. Perceptual learning—History. 3. Learning, Psychology of
—History. 4. Psychology—History. I. Title. II. Series.
  BF311.G478   1991
  153.7—dc20   90-19541
                                                                          CIP

Contents

Series Foreword

This series in learning, development, and conceptual change will include state-of-the-art reference works, seminal book-length monographs, and texts on the development of concepts and mental structures. It will span learning in all domains of knowledge, from syntax to geometry to the social world, and will be concerned with all phases of development, from infancy through adulthood.

The series intends to engage such fundamental questions as

The nature and limits of learning and maturation: the influence of the environment, of initial structures, and of maturational changes in the nervous system on human development; learnability theory; the problem of induction; domain-specific constraints on development.

The nature of conceptual change: conceptual organization and conceptual change in child development, in the acquisition of expertise, and in the history of science.

Lila Gleitman
Susan Carey
Elissa Newport
Elizabeth Spelke

Foreword by *Elizabeth S. Spelke*

This volume portrays a scientist and her science. We learn about Eleanor J. Gibson and her field, experimental psychology, both through the scientific papers that she has collected here and through the personal essay that weaves these papers together by highlighting the questions and concerns that guided and animated her work.

There are many things to gain from this book. First, the reader will learn a good deal about the nature and development of perception and action from Gibson's classic papers. Some of these papers have influenced experimental psychology so profoundly that they may seem familiar, even commonplace, to first-time readers. What psychologist in the 1990s could doubt, for example, that learning can bring changes in what we *perceive*, not just changes in how we *respond* to what we perceive? Yet psychology owes this insight, and the defeat of vigorous arguments to the contrary, largely to Eleanor and James Gibson's studies of perceptual learning.

Other papers describe findings that go against deeply ingrained beliefs about the nature and development of psychological capacities. For example, consider Gibson's demonstration, as an undergraduate, that learning to act on an object with one hand immediately transfers to the other hand. This experiment shows quite clearly that what one learns, when one learns a new and appropriate action, is not a response contingency (such as "flex this finger when you hear this tone") but what Gibson calls an "affordance": a property of the environment with consequences for the perceiver/actor (such as "after the tone, this plate gives off a shock"). Gibson's finding should give pause to those engaged in the long-standing effort to understand action in terms of elementary responses and their concatenation.

Another finding that experimental psychology cannot quite digest is Gibson, Walk, and Tighe's demonstration that young animals of a wide range of species, including humans, avoid visually specified drop-offs as soon as they are capable of locomotion. Elegant experiments with animals that locomote at birth, and also with animals reared in the dark, reveal that the capacity to perceive a three-dimensional surface layout can develop in the absence of any visual experience or trial and error learning. Perceptual systems appear to be built to bring animals information about the layout and its affordances, contrary to empiricist theories of space perception.

The reader of this book also will learn something about the flourishing of experimental psychology in twentieth-century America. Gibson's papers portray a discipline coming into its own, focusing on fundamental questions about perception and action, gathering insights into the nature and development of these functions, and raising new questions for the next century of psychology to pursue.

Consider, for example, the progress that has been made in the study of perception and action in infancy. With her studies of the visual cliff, Gibson was one of the founders of that field of research in the late 1950s. Lacking her own laboratory, she was not able to continue her studies of infants at that time. Research on infant perception continued in other laboratories in the 1960s. Nevertheless, the fundamental questions about perception and perceptual development—how perceivers apprehend a layout of surfaces, objects, and events; how the various perceptual modes work together to produce an experience of a unitary world; how perceptual systems serve to guide effective and adaptive action—were raised consistently only by Gibson's unofficial students, T. G. R. Bower and Albert Yonas. Then, in 1975, Eleanor Gibson was for the first time in a position to establish her own infant study laboratory. The papers collected here show what has happened to the field of infant perception since that time: Gibson's studies of surface perception, event perception, perception of intermodal relations, and perceptual guidance of action have helped bring the study of infant perception into its own. Her contribution, during the four years that she was both a member of Cornell's active faculty and the director of her infant laboratory, is incalculable. Those years of work provide as good an example as any of the progress that can be made in experimental psychology when a gifted scientist is given the freedom and the resources to pursue her science.

During much of her career, Gibson did not enjoy this freedom. Her first goal was to become a comparative psychologist. With her training in perception, and with her theoretical disposition to view perception and action as interconnected functions, each adapted to the environment of a particular species, Gibson could have undertaken a lifelong comparative and ecological study of perception and perceptually guided action. She was prevented from achieving this goal each time she tried: as a new graduate student, rejected from her psychology department's only laboratory of comparative psychology because of her sex; as a technical assistant in a different laboratory, charged with incompetence after making a discovery that the director of the laboratory later published as his own; as a mature scientist, but without an academic appointment, her attempts to conduct research at her university's laboratory thwarted by the sudden removal of the animals she had been rearing and observing in an extended longitudinal project.

Eleanor Gibson's career has not greatly suffered from these reverses, thanks to her indomitable spirit, but science has. The most basic questions about surface, object, and event perception in most nonhuman species remain unanswered, even unasked. The lack of a vigorous, comparative study of perception and action has had serious consequences not only for psychology but for two of its surrounding disciplines: neurobiology and evolutionary biology.

Eleanor Gibson's career has coincided with a tremendous growth of research in neuroscience, most of it conducted with laboratory animals and much of it exploring the neural structures and processes subserving perception and action. Her career has also coincided with a blossoming of zoological studies of behavior in its adaptive, evolutionary context. Both these fields are in need of a comparative psychology of perception and action. Reason and experience suggest that progress in neuroscience will only occur if investigations are grounded on a solid understanding of the functions that neural structures serve. Moreover, the right ecological and evolutionary analysis of species-typical behavior requires an appreciation not just of an animal's physical environment but of its perceived environment as well.

The comparative, experimental psychology of perception has been so little developed, however, that some neuroscientists and evolutionary biologists appear to have convinced themselves that the field is not needed: that studies of neurobiology at one end, and of evolution at the other, will suffice to unravel the secrets of mind, brain, and behavior. Since this conclusion threatens to hamper progress in the brain and behavioral sciences for years to come, one can only hope that future scientists and teachers with Eleanor Gibson's gifts, education, and goals will come along and that they will be allowed to build the research discipline she envisaged.

A third reason to read this book is to learn about Gibson herself. Reading this personal account of her life and work is an exhilarating experience. Despite the obstacles in her path, hers is a story of success. Her professional life was devoted to work on problems that engaged her from the beginning. Her work afforded insight into many of these problems and raised new problems to challenge her. We learn from Gibson's life that professional status and material resources do not make a scientist, however necessary they may be to a scientist's work. The most important ingredients of a good scientist are the personal qualities Gibson exemplifies.

What are these qualities? Some are gifts at which most of us can only marvel: the prodigious intelligence that enabled her to complete all her graduate training short of the thesis in one year; the extraordinary eye for phenomena that allowed her to recognize in a common observation (for example, that newborn goats don't fall off stools) the germ of experiments of major consequence. Others are qualities that we may emulate: the courage to espouse and defend original views in the face of opposition or indifference; the judicious combination of flexibility, ingenuity, and determination that allowed her to face obstacles and prevail; the generosity and patience she displayed with students, giving of her time and wisdom whenever it was needed to anyone with any curiosity and willingness to learn.

For me, Gibson's most striking quality is her nearly magical blend of firmness and openness. The firmness has been felt by everyone who has ever disagreed with her, and it is evident throughout this book: She has had the strength, conviction, and integrity to develop and maintain her own enduring conception of mind and action. At the same time, Gibson is always wholly open to change. Her openness is exemplified at many points in this book. Note, for example, the readiness—almost delight—with which she now criticizes some of her earlier theories of reading and many of her early claims about infant perception. This openness is characteristic and deep. Gibson has always tried to find things out, not to vindicate previously held opinions. She has changed her ideas again and again in response to new experimental findings. A major part of her genius, I believe, lies in her ability to remain open to further development and change while maintaining a conception of her subject that is strong and systematic and rich enough to serve as the source and framework for all her work.

What is this conception? This book is an extended answer to that question. Gibson's conception can be felt in the earliest papers in this collection; it emerges enriched and deepened, but not fundamentally changed, in the papers that follow. Her conception cannot be identified with any particular period in the history of psychology: it was never fashionable in the past, and it is not antiquated now. I tend to doubt that Gibson's approach will solve all the mysteries that psychology seeks to unravel. When we are face to face, however, I cannot help wondering whether she might not be right about everything. Eleanor Gibson sees the problems of perceiving, acting organisms so clearly, and she has always had such a firm sense of how to practice psychology as a science.

Introduction

When I was asked to put this book together, I wondered if a collection of papers, some of them written as long as fifty years ago, would be of interest to today's psychologists (many of whom disavow that title, preferring something like "cognitive scientist"). But as I reread the old papers and recollected the spirit of the times when they were written, I discovered that this kind of journey into the past was of real value to me, and so it could be for others. However diverse the topics, I found that there were common problems and continuing threads running through them. Questions about learning and about perception were there from the start, sometimes viewed from a behaviorist's approach, sometimes from a comparative approach, sometimes from a practical cognitive approach (in the case of the research on reading), but always pointing ahead to the need for a good theory of perceptual learning and development. We didn't know we needed it in the thirties; it began to be apparent during the war years; and then in the fifties it emerged as an acknowledged need. Some early tries were rediscovered and new ones proposed. Once a need is acknowledged, relevant data begin to accumulate, new theoretical efforts appear, and confrontations of views sharpen the issues. All these things happened.

We saw Lashley, Hebb, and Brunswik in the vanguard, followed by Bruner, Piaget, and some Russian psychologists. Strange bedfellows, one might say, but similar questions were being asked by all of them. Progress was made toward a theory of perceptual learning, and I think I helped. But the job isn't finished. A good, complete theory is still needed. Viewing new leads with the successes and mistakes of the past in mind helps keep the enterprise in perspective. In behavioral development, we typically see hints and brief previews of what's ahead, a precursor forecasting the full-blown accomplishment. Perhaps this is a natural course for development of anything, including a theory. There comes a time when important transition points stand out and a new kind of question can be asked: What motivating force or dynamism was responsible for the changes? We are reaching that point just now in perceptual development, and theory should take a new spurt. There was a strong developmental approach in psychology before 1950 (for example, Gesell and Piaget). In the upsurge of infant psychology, it was lost as we admired the feats of the "competent infant" disclosed with our new technology; and now the time has come for a renewed and strong developmental approach leading to an understanding of what moves perceptual development.

In putting this book together, I chose papers that seemed significant in their time, and in accompanying text I have explained the occasion for writing them and considered what significance they have now. Are the old questions still with us in new clothing, or have we formulated new ones? Is there progress and continuity in a scientific history, or even in one person's living of it?

I have divided the papers into six sections and arranged them in a roughly chronological order. A consistent chronological order won't do, because accidents intervene in a lifetime and upset the consistency of one's advance toward a goal. Yet, there is an underlying focus. In my case, it began with these concerns—an interest in animal behavior and development, in learning, and gradually in perception—and these wove themselves together over time. My aim for this book, since I believe that a developmental approach is the most fruitful one, is to show how changes take place, where the transition points lie, and where the current is heading. I'd like to think I'd shown, too, how much fun it can all be.

To whom is this book addressed? Principally to today's graduate students and young researchers. I had them in mind, because I thought they might find encouragement in the early reverses that befell me which, however discouraging at the time, left channels that led on to interesting work. My own graduate students have read it, they said with profit. Naturally, I hope anyone in search of a theory of perceptual learning, or a way of thinking about cognitive development and the origins of knowledge, will read it. And I hope it fills in a few details of the history of psychology.

I
Experimental Psychology in the Thirties (1932–1942)

Introduction to Part I

In the 1930s psychology was a lusty young science. The American tradition of functionalism, made memorable by James and Dewey, flourished as a strong conviction of evolutionary theory and a lot of research on animals; the shade of Titchener survived in the thriving enterprise of psychophysics; behaviorism was not just a legacy but a fact. Psychology laboratories (all universities had one and so did any self-respecting college) were full of activity and an air of excitement. Here was a new science, bursting with discoveries to be made, fields to be mined, theories to be destroyed or constructed. The brightest young academics were attracted to the scene, so the company was good and the competition challenging. Learning was the big topic of the day, as befit the functional tradition, but there were plenty of other tempting ones, such as motivation and psychoanalysis for the daring, and psychophysical research pursued under the most stringent rules for the less imaginative. University faculties accepted psychology as a biological science and even allowed science credit to introductory courses with laboratory sections, which nearly every department of psychology offered.

This was where I came in. The hardheaded atmosphere promising new findings from laboratories focused on behavior was incredibly appealing, and I was won over before I was twenty years old. Clinical psychology and testing were already looming large, but it was the laboratory scene that dazzled. Nearly sixty years and more than sixty experiments later I can easily capture the stirring moments. It seems worth describing the psychology of that era as it struck a student of the times, illustrating it with papers of the era. They are my own (often with a collaborator to make things more interesting). I explain what motivated me at the time, and how times changed as psychology (and I) grew up through the rest of the twentieth century. I begin with a sketch of the psychology of the 1930s, as it existed in the laboratory, and follow with a brief sketch of my introduction to it.

The Functional Tradition

The functional tradition was particularly strong at Columbia and Chicago universities, and at many colleges too. "Sensory control" of maze-learning was a popular topic for research. There were numerous investigations of the role of vision, olfactory cues, "floor cues" (related to what we would now call echolocation), and so on. Maze-learning theories were couched in sequences of turns (left, left, right, etc.) and how they were rewarded, influenced by Thorndike's connectionism, soon to be expanded and formalized by Clark Hull. In recent years these problems have resurfaced, but we speak of information for perceptual control of action, and finding the way in foraging and homing, putting a stronger emphasis on how an animal adapts its behavior to its environmental niche. The line of descent extends back to functionalism, however.

There was research with other animals too, with a major interest in other primates. The primate research was descended from psychologically minded followers of Darwin like Romanes and Hobhouse and was cognitively oriented. Lashley had a hand in it, and of course Yerkes, who superintended colonies of chimpanzees at Orange Park and Yale. Problem solving and communication were favored topics for research. Köhler's *Mentality of Apes* (1925) fanned the flames, but he never had an animal laboratory in this country.

Functional psychology also supported a developmental approach, a natural outcome of Darwin's evolutionary theory. Darwin, in fact, wrote an infant biography of his own son. Romanes, in his book, *Mental Evolution in Man* (1889), provided a chart comparing phylogenetic and ontogenetic development that, however fanciful, remains fascinating. "Child Psychology" thrived with Gesell at Yale, but it was more concerned with norms than theory. It didn't hold the excitement of a laboratory where theories were put to the test. Developmental psychology really came into its own in the sixties, a tale to be told later.

The Psychophysical Enterprise

Titchenerian introspection was conspicuously absent by 1930, but psychophysics was alive and well, the flame kept alight by E. G. Boring at Harvard. Boring's *Physical Dimensions of Consciousness* (1933) was a bible for graduate students and anyone else who wanted to do research in perception. Nowadays I wouldn't call what the psychophysicists did perception, but it was what the Establishment allowed in America in those days, and it was admired for being rigorously scientific as opposed to the perception psychology of the Gestalt psychologists, which was considered "soft," phenomenological, and weak on measurement. As the term psychophysics indicates, it was dualistic, aiming to match up physical dimensions of frequency, intensity, and so on with mental scales of judgment. It was nonfunctional, dry, even inhuman, but a strong technology was spawned and it had its uses, making possible applications to industry and other sciences. Graduate students had to learn all the psychophysical methods and the mathematics that evolved to support them. In a later section I turn to psychophysics with outdoor studies of distance perception. The methods were also useful in studies of perceptual learning, later on a major interest of mine. To become a psychophysicist, one went to Harvard, where Boring reigned.

Learning in the 1930s

Learning was the great topic of the day. It might be studied as verbal learning or as "memory," where the big names were E. S. Robinson, author of *Association Theory Today* (1932), and followers of his such as John McGeoch and Arthur Melton; or it might be centered around the conditioned response. Clark Hull, at Yale, epitomized the hardheaded learning theorist, basing his theory on conditioning. He considered himself a functionalist, however. I was inspired as a young student by his *Psychological Review* papers on conditioning, especially "A Functional Interpretation of the Conditioned Reflex" (1929), in which he strove to interpret various manifestations of conditioning as adaptive behavior. The four papers in this series are classics, clear and insightful. They predated his papers composed as miniature logical systems and the books on learning theory, where the stress was placed on mechanism and deductive rigor. Whether Hull really achieved rigor or not, he had vigor and his laboratory was an exciting place, seething with activity.

Hull was not the only functionalist concerned with learning theory. There was his arch-rival, Tolman, at Berkeley. How a rat learned a maze was as interesting to Tolman as it was to Hull, but although he eschewed the words and only described behavior, Tolman was at heart a cognitive psychologist. The rat learned the maze because it discovered what led to what and formed a cognitive map of the layout and what it afforded. One of the joys of a meeting of the American Psychological Association in those days was seeing Hull and Tolman with their respective followers holding forth in the same room, everyone arguing excitedly (and good naturedly).

The Impact of the Thirties on a Student

I attended Smith College as an undergraduate, a great place for a young woman to be introduced to science. As a women's college, Smith had a strong female faculty in science and the arts, because that was where a woman scholar could find honor and promotion. There were truly great women at Smith, for example Marjorie Nicholson, the world's expert on science and imagination. I first encountered psychology in a year-long introductory course that included a weekly laboratory (I later taught it). My second course was called Animal Psychology, taught by Margaret Curti, a Chicago-trained functionalist. It was entrancing, because we students were permitted to run an experiment ourselves. The animals were rats, of course, and they learned a maze.

The real excitement came my senior year when I had a year-long course in advanced experimental psychology with James Gibson, a young assistant professor fresh from Princeton. There were eight students in the class (four of them later obtained Ph.D.s). We worked in pairs and performed an experiment per month, setting up apparatus, obtaining and running our own subjects, researching the background, and writing it all up. Every experiment was a novel problem and we covered a wide field, with experiments on reaction time, learning, memory, perception, adaptation to prisms—the gamut of the field at the time. It was one way that a young professor who wanted to do research could keep his hand in, despite teaching two or three courses a term. Many papers came out of the work begun in that course. I was proud that an experiment of mine with Gertrude Raffel Schmeidler (later a Columbia Ph.D.) was published in the *Journal of Experimental Psychology*. The experiment was on bilateral transfer of a conditioned reflex. We had a functional interpretation of the CR of our own (see following paper), ahead of its time.

That course taught me the thrill of doing experiments and the great satisfaction of discussing problems daily with colleagues. Smith had an excellent course on history and systems of psychology, taught by a Ph.D. of Boring's, and by the time I was a senior, Kurt Koffka was giving a course on Gestalt Psychology, which I attended. Later, when I was a graduate student, I regularly attended Koffka's seminar as most of the Smith psychology faculty did. It was the local forum for debate, despite Koffka's rather authoritarian style. I was never much attracted to Gestalt psychology, as I have ever been uneasy with a phenomenological approach, a fact that undoubtedly influenced my choice of Yale for graduate school.

Smith College was very supportive and encouraged its students to go on to graduate work. I stayed on at Smith for two years after graduation as a teaching assistant and obtained a master's degree there. My thesis (done with James Gibson) was on retroactive inhibition in verbal learning, very much in a functional tradition. It was deep depression times and there were few fellowships for women. When I went to graduate school at Yale, Smith gave me a small fellowship, but Yale contributed nothing.

At Yale, I intended to specialize in comparative psychology and work in Yerkes's laboratory, not so much because of Yerkes's ideas but for the glamor of working with chimpanzees (a poor reason, I fear). That expectation was not fulfilled. Yerkes informed me, none too graciously, that he allowed no women in his lab—a real shock after the nurturing atmosphere of Smith. Clark Hull accepted me as a graduate student, however. He was deep in his enterprise of building logicodeductive systems. He allowed me to choose my own topic, but I was required to back it up by a theoretical presentation with formally stated premises, deductions, etc. I managed to do it, but with a bit of tongue in cheek. I wanted to work on verbal learning and forgetting, and to show that remembering and forgetting depended on differentiating content into meaningful units that did not confuse with one another in an incoherent melange. I could borrow my main concepts, differentiation and generalization, from the conditioned response literature, which made them very respectable at the time. But the terms held commonsense psychological meanings for me, perceptual meanings I would have said later. No one at Yale worked on perception or was in the least interested in it.

I performed my thesis experiments, except the one on generalization in a reaction time experiment, at Smith, where I returned as an instructor after a year at Yale. I had a very busy year at Yale getting through all the many requirements, including a proseminar for all the new students. It was a showcase for the professors, each of whom had a few weeks to display his ideas (all were men, of course). Yale was generous in letting me take a degree with only one year's residence credit. I took Clark Hull's enormous memory drum back to Smith and worked there on my dissertation. Smith retained me on its faculty and kept me so busy that, except for directing a few master's theses, I got little further research done. It was after World War II before the scene really changed for me, as it did in many ways for psychology in America.

1

Bilateral Transfer of the Conditioned Response in the Human Subject

James J. Gibson, Eleanor G. Jack, Gertrude Raffel

This paper is a functional treatment of the conditioned response, emphasizing its adaptiveness as a response of the whole organism rather than an isolated reflex as Pavlovians would have it. The discussion emphasizes this point:

> *Our hypothesis would have it that in the adult, organized habits of withdrawing or pulling away have been developed for all parts of the body which have come in contact with painful stimuli. We can suppose then that in our experiment, the conditioned stimulus has become effective not only for the particular withdrawal response in connection with which it was learned, but also for this entire repertory of avoiding reactions.*

This point was supported in later experiments by Wickens (Wickens 1939 a and b) in which finger withdrawal was conditioned with the hand in normal position and then reversed so that a flexor rather than extensor movement had to be performed if transfer occurred. It did. In part II, an experiment that I performed much later with goats as subjects leads to a similar conclusion, so it was not only human adult subjects for whom avoidance to shock is not a simple reflex. When we come to part VI, I show how the much later concept of affordance fits these cases, which are basically similar to the response to "looming" presented there.

It is interesting to find Hilgard and Marquis in their classic work, Conditioning and Learning, *referring to our results and Wickens's as "insightful behavior in typical conditioning experiments" (Hilgard and Marquis 1940, 243). They also say "in these cases the equivalence is obviously learned." I wouldn't be so sure about that. I think we have discovered since then that behavior is organized originally in larger synergies that involve patterns of postural activities that can be broken down or individuated into smaller ones, rather than the opposite—not a learned "equivalence" of smaller pieces as Hilgard and Marquis supposed in 1940. The elementarism of early behaviorism died hard (if it has).*

Journal of Experimental Psychology, 1932, 416–421.

However, these two important critics of their time did raise many doubts about building a theory of behavior on reflexes that could only widen the domain of acting by being "conditioned" to whatever stimuli chance and opportunity happened to juxtapose with them.

During the course of an experiment on the conditioned withdrawal response of the hand to an electric shock, the opportunity presented itself to test for transfer of this conditioned response from the trained right hand to the untrained left hand. The subject sat at a table with the palm of the hand resting on one large brass electrode and the middle finger on another smaller one. The hand was not strapped down or constrained in any way. The apparatus and electrical circuit were essentially the same as in Watson's research,[1] except that the arrangement for graphically recording the responses on a kymograph drum was not employed. One of the Es simply sat at the side of S and recorded the finger movements as they occurred. In order to keep the attention of S off the experiment, and to lessen any anticipatory fear of the electric shock, S was required to read aloud during an experimental sitting. The conditioned stimulus was the sound of an electric buzzer lasting for one second and starting approximately $\frac{1}{10}$ sec. before the shock. This timing was accomplished by using a double contact key which, when depressed, first completed the buzzer circuit and then the shock circuit.

The procedure was as follows. After S was seated with the right hand on the electrodes, and had begun to read aloud, the buzzer was sounded alone. For several subjects who were suspicious or fearful, the sound by itself was adequate to produce a withdrawal movement. Although this response always disappeared after one or two repetitions of the buzzer stimulus, the records of such subjects have been omitted from the data on transfer. After the above test, combined stimulations of buzzer and shock were given at irregular intervals varying from 3 to 20 seconds. When 10 repetitions had been completed one of two procedures was used. (1) In the first, the buzzer was sounded alone and any conditioned withdrawal movement was noted. If none appeared, another series of reinforcements was given and a second test for the conditioned response made. When the latter made its appearance, a final series of reinforcements was given and then S was told to shift over and place the *left* hand on the electrodes, with the middle finger on the far electrode as before. The buzzer was now sounded alone and any withdrawal movement noted. (2) In the second procedure, instead of waiting for the conditioned response to appear in the right hand, E made a test for the transferred response in the left hand immediately after the first 10 combined stimulations. If none appeared, S was required to shift back to the right hand and more reinforcements were given, after which another test for transfer was made. As a check on the transferred response when it occurred, a final test for the conditioned movement in the *right* hand was subsequently made.

Results

Twenty subjects were used in the experiment. Of these, 19, or 95 percent, were successfully conditioned to withdraw the finger of the right hand when the buzzer was sounded alone. From 10 to 52 repetitions of the combined stimuli were necessary to establish the response. (The one subject who failed to become conditioned had undergone electrical treatments for a year, and showed a very weak withdrawal response even when the shock administered was much stronger than that usually employed. At the end of 200 repetitions no conditioned response had occurred and the experiment was stopped.) Of the 19, 6 showed some indication of responding to the buzzer alone before the experiment was begun, and their results have accordingly not been considered. Thirteen subjects remain for whom the data on transfer of the conditioned response seem valid. Although at no time did any subject in this group receive a shock with the left hand, 8, or 62 percent made definite withdrawal responses of the finger when the left hand was placed on the electrodes and the buzzer alone was sounded. Three of this group had given evidence of a conditioned response of the right hand before the left hand was tested, whereas 5 showed the response in the left or transfer hand first and subsequently in the right.

It is possible that a larger number of subjects might have manifested transfer if the experiment had been continued longer. No more than 100 combined presentations of buzzer and shock were given to any one subject. If by that time no indication of transfer had shown itself the attempt was abandoned. This was done in part out of consideration for the subject for whom the experiment was naturally somewhat uncomfortable, and in part out of a desire to investigate other problems in addition to the transfer phenomenon during the experimental sitting.[2]

The appearance of the conditioned withdrawal response in the right hand itself was found to be somewhat irregular and unstable, this finding being in accord with the results of previous experiments.[3] In 2 subjects, only one definite conditioned response could be elicited, all attempts thereafter being negative. These subjects were apparently surprised and somewhat chagrined to find that they had reacted to the sound of the buzzer alone, and thereafter set themselves "not to be fooled more than once." They constitute two of the group for whom transfer could not be demonstrated. In general the reports of subjects indicate that various attitudes such as timidity towards shocks, a desire to appear indifferent, a desire not to be tricked into responding, and the like, played a large part in the experiment, and were the probable explanation of much of the irregularity with which the conditioned response showed itself. In view of this instability of the response in the right hand it is not surprising that the transferred response in the left hand could not always be demonstrated.

Discussion

In a significant number of cases (62 percent) the establishing of a conditioned withdrawal response of the right middle finger is accompanied by the formation of a similar conditioned response of the corresponding finger of the other hand. From this fact alone little can be concluded with certainty. Chiefly it suggests the need for further research on such questions as the extent of transfer to other (unsymmetrical) fingers of the same and the opposite hand, the latent periods of transferred responses as compared with the latency of the primary conditioned and unconditioned response, the possible occurrence of implicit movements in the transfer hand, and the like. But it also suggests a possible explanation towards which further experiments may be oriented.

It is clear in the first place that the conditioned withdrawal movement can scarcely be considered a single isolated reflex, or even a conditioned reflex, if by the term we mean a response limited to a specific muscle or muscle group. This latter criterion is frequently regarded as definitive for the true reflex. The hypothesis is suggested that the conditioned withdrawal to shock involves, or perhaps is itself, a generalized habit of avoiding or withdrawing when the buzzer is heard, which may be evoked from another part of the body than that in which the response was learned. Unfortunately no systematic data were obtained as to transfer of the response to other fingers. It was, however, informally determined with several subjects that the conditioned response did readily transfer to the index finger of the same hand. The extent to which a general avoidance response to the buzzer was set up can only be inferred. But from the above evidence and from what is known of transfer of learning to symmetrical and unsymmetrical parts of the body[4] it is possible to suppose that the withdrawal response could have been elicited in the other fingers and perhaps even in other parts of the body.

It should be noted that the conditioned response which is concurrently established in the untrained hand, is really a latent or potential response. It becomes actual and overt only when the finger of the untrained hand is for the first time resting on the electrode. Our hypothesis would have it that in the adult, organized habits of withdrawing or pulling away have been developed for all the parts of the body which have frequently come in contact with painful stimuli. We can then suppose that in our experiment, the conditioned stimulus has become effective not only for the particular withdrawal response in connection with which it was learned, but also for this entire repertory of avoiding reactions. Furthermore when any part, say a finger, is in a potentially painful situation (e.g., resting on an electrode) we may conceive that the appropriate withdrawal response for that finger is in a state of readiness—perhaps of sub-activation. It is this particular finger, therefore, which is withdrawn under such circumstances, rather than any other. Consequently the difference between the latent or potential conditioned response and the actual one depends on the presence of a specific preparatory set aroused by the situation.

On the conscious side, in so far as these activities are represented in consciousness, the above formulation would run as follows. The conditioned stimulus has become during training a general signal to withdraw. Together with this habit, there is present (normally) a definite preparatory set to withdraw the particular finger which is resting on the electrode. Hence when the finger of the untrained hand is placed in that situation, the sound of the buzzer sets off the proper response.

The introspective reports given by the subjects indicated not only that the set or attitude was an important factor in the experiment but also that the responses, both conditioned and unconditioned, could not be classed as definitely either voluntary or involuntary. They were not completely voluntary in the sense of being intended, as, e.g., a finger movement in the reaction time situation is intended. The conditioned responses were usually accompanied by a feeling of surprise. On the other hand, they were not wholly involuntary in the sense of being automatic as is the knee jerk. The conditioned responses could have been inhibited had the subject wished to inhibit them. The cases of the two subjects who set themselves not to be fooled more than once are in point. That the unconditioned response itself could be inhibited in large part was shown by one subject who took the instructions to forget about the finger on the electrode so far as possible, as meaning that he should not respond voluntarily. The finger was so successfully "forgotten" that the only response to the shock was a slight trembling or twitching movement, even when the stimulus was painfully strong. From the above evidence it appears even more clear that avoidance to shock is not a reflex. It is rather a response high enough in the scale of complexity to be in part dependent on a voluntary set.

Since a conditioned response can be formed between a stimulus and a response which was never overtly made during the conditioning process, the inadequacy of the simple diagram or physiological schema used frequently in explaining conditioning is once more demonstrated. Any real physiological explanation of the present facts would have to be based on an adequate theory of the physiological basis of bilateral transfer. Such a theory has not yet been formulated. It is possible that further research on transfer of the simple type of learning here described will contribute to this problem.

Notes

1. For the original research on this subject, see J. B. Watson, The Place of the Conditioned Reflex in Psychology, *Psychol. Rev.*, 1916, 23, 89–116.

2. These additional problems had to do with the fact of so-called 'sensory irradiation' (Pavlov) and the establishing of differential responses to buzzers of different pitch.

3. J. B. Watson, The Place of the Conditioned Reflex in Psychology, *Psychol. Rev.*, 1916, 23, 89–116. G. Humphrey, The Effect of Sequences of Indifferent Stimuli on a Reaction of the Conditioned Reflex Type, *J. Abn. and Soc. Psychol.*, 1927, 22, 194–212.

4. See for example C. W. Bray, Transfer of Learning, *J. Exp. Psychol.*, 1928, II, 443–467.

2

Retention and the Interpolated Task
Eleanor J. Gibson, James J. Gibson

This paper is a condensation of my master's thesis at Smith College. James Gibson was my thesis sponsor (he became my husband while I was working on the thesis). Verbal learning and memory, in the Chicago tradition, was much in vogue (note the reference to E. S. Robinson, one of the Chicago group). The material employed in these experiments was typically letters, digits, or nonsense syllables. Retroactive inhibition was a popular notion for explaining forgetting, and similarity of interpolated material to whatever was originally presented for learning was considered critical. But the similarity was generally content oriented, and referred to likeness between individual items, consistent with the elementarism of the thirties. My functional-mindedness led me to the hypothesis that the task engaged in, which is oriented toward process rather than content, must be of equal importance. It makes me think now of the later information processing terminology, emphasizing "processing" of "alphanumeric characters." But of course that would be twenty-five years later.

The experiment varied both content and task with respect to original and interpolated task relations. "The similarity of two tasks, then, will be expressed in terms of the significant features *which the two tasks have in common." The features chosen were the "material" and the "operation" performed on it. As the experiment demonstrated, both so-called features had the effect of reducing retention when they were presented separately in an intervening task, but detrimental effects when they were combined were greater than the sum of the injury done by the two separately. I suppose that one could say that "processing" numbers is not the same task as "processing" letters, whatever the operation. This experiment led me to think further about retroactive inhibition and consequently was the forerunner to my Ph.D. thesis.*

American Journal of Psychology, 1934, 46, 603–610.

The similarity problem in retroactive inhibition arises from the fact that the integrity of retention of memorized material is a function of the similarity between the learning and the interpolated activity. According to the Skaggs-Robinson theory,[1] the function is of the following nature. The curve of retention starts at a high level with maximum similarity, which Robinson took to mean that the interpolated task is identical with, or a continuation of, the original learning. The curve falls as the similarity of interpolated material is "reduced from identity" until retention reaches a minimum at the stage which, presumably, other investigators have called a "similar" interpolation. The curve then rises until, at the stage of dissimilar or rest interpolation, retention is at the level usually considered normal.

The latter portion of this curve embodies the type of results usually obtained in experiments on the similarity problem. The first part, showing decreasing retention with decreasing similarity, has been verified by Robinson[2] and Dreis[3] with two experiments wherein the interpolations consisted of varying amounts of rehearsal to which were added complementary amounts of new memorization. The greater the proportion of rehearsal, the greater was the similarity of the interpolated activity to the original learning. These experiments, along with some others,[4] arose from Robinson's tentative assumption that *improvement through practice* and the *disintegrating effect of interpolation* are related phenomena; in other words, that *practice-effect* passes over into "interpolation-effect" without break.

It should be noted that, in this attack on the similarity problem, the interpolated activity is not a single *task*, as it can be only if it is separate and distinct from the original learning task. In other words, the interpolations of Robinson and Dreis were not activities having an effect (either facilitatory or inhibitory) on the integrity of retention of the primary learning. They were instead continuations of the primary learning in varying amounts, combined with new learning. Likewise, the retention which was measured in these experiments was not retention of a primary learning, but of that *plus* some continuation of it.

The position can be taken, of course, that the retroaction problem need not be defined in terms of discrete primary and secondary tasks. The interpolated activity does not have to be a separate and unique task, the argument might run, since it is precisely the factor of indistinctness and confusion between tasks which is most likely to be the explanation of retroactive inhibition. This hypothetical argument, however, begs the question in favor of a radical form of the "transfer" theory of retroaction. There is as yet no proof that it is the single and complete explanation of the phenomenon.

The theoretical approach of the experiment to be described differs from that expressed by the Skaggs-Robinson function in that retroaction is thought of as one of the problems of the interrelations of tasks—that problem dealing with the effect of a second task on the tested retention of a first. This emphasis on task-characteristics carries with it its own mode of dealing with the similarity factor in retroaction. Two tasks are designated as similar with reference to definite features which the two have in common. Such features would not be independent elements but aspects by means of which two tasks could be compared. There are undoubtedly many such which could be used as a basis of comparison, but certain features of a task will stand out as being more important than others for a genuine description of it and consequently for a significant statement of similarity. The similarity of two tasks, then, will be expressed in terms of the *significant features which the two tasks have in common.*

The two most obvious features of a task are the *operation* which the subject is instructed to perform and the *material* with which he must perform it. The term *operation* will be used to mean that aspect of a task best indicated by the word *Aufgabe,* and the term *material* will be used to indicate what could be called the perceptual data. These two features are not distinct components. They are at least partly interdependent, since a change in the material of a task would be accompanied by some change in the operation, and vice versa. For example, the operation in memorizing nonsense syllables is not the same as in memorizing nonsense forms, although both are "memorial" in nature.

This distinction is not new. There have been related ones ranging from the distinction between act and content to Tolman's characterization of behavior as goal-seeking and as involving "behavior-supports."[5] Robinson himself, in an earlier experiment, distinguished between the "process" and the "content" of a task and found that "the degree of retroactive inhibition is a function of similarity of process as well as similarity of content."[6] He further demonstrated that another feature, which he called "form of presentation," was important for retroactive inhibition. His data, however, did not show that these features were independently capable of causing retroaction. As a consequence, perhaps, he did not follow up this line of thought in his subsequent research. With the exception of this experiment of Robinson's, all researches on the similarity factor have worked with similarity of material alone. When variations in the operation of the interpolated task have been included in an experiment, this factor has not been specified nor has its effect been isolated and measured. Little is known, then, about the influence of operational or functional similarity on retroaction.

The Experiment

In the experiment to be described, our problem was to decide upon a set of interpolated tasks which would enable us to isolate and compare the decrements in retention separately caused by similar *operation* and by similar *material*. The relative importance of the two factors for retroaction could thus be determined. Specifically, we wished to compare degrees of retention of the primary learning in the following cases: (1) when the secondary task is like the primary task in both operation and material; (2) when it is like in operation but different in material; (3) when it is different in operation but like in material; (4) when it is different in both operation and material.

In order to make the above comparisons it was necessary to select a primary learning task and four kinds of interpolated tasks fulfilling the above requirements. On the basis of a preliminary experiment, learning a list of paired consonants was chosen for the primary task. The interpolated tasks were (1) learning another list of paired consonants, (2) learning a list of paired digits, (3) cancelling a specified pair of consonants whenever it appeared in a sheet of pied type, and (4) cancelling a pair of digits in the same manner. A fifth interpolated task, of the sort generally employed as a control or 'rest' condition, was also included. It consisted of looking at pictures (moving-picture 'stills') and it was believed to differ from the primary task even more than did cancelling digits—in fact it was designed to be as different a task as possible. Among other features, it lacked the motivational or 'work' characteristics of the other four tasks.

For the sake of simplicity, we shall call the tasks, in order, *Learning Letters, Learning Numbers, Cancelling Letters, Cancelling Numbers,* and *Pictures*. The following schema designates by capital letters the arrangement of tasks in the five interpolated conditions. There were 5 groups of Ss, one group corresponding to each condition.

Interpolated Condition (Group)	Primary Learning	Secondary Task
I	LL	LL
II	LL	LN
III	LL	CL
IV	LL	CN
V	LL	P

Experimental materials

For primary learning, all groups studied a list of 10 pairs of consonants. No pairs were included which made familiar abbreviations (such as PM); no pair consisted of consecutive letters of the alphabet; and nearly all the consonants of the alphabet were used in one list. For the secondary task, Group I learned another list of consonants made up like the one just described, Group II learned a list of 10 pairs of digits. No digit appeared with disproportionate frequency, nor did consecutive pairs contain a digit more than once. Group III had to read through a sheet of pied consonants striking out the combination KS whenever it appeared. The combination occurred about three times in every two lines. Group IV cancelled a digit combination in the same manner. The pictures secured for Group V were photographs (8 × 11 in.) of dramatic situations obtained from a motion picture distributor.

Procedure

Five laboratory sections of a large course in psychology served as the 5 groups of Ss. They averaged about 26 Ss each. In view of the absence of any selective factor in the assigning of students to sections, the groups were probably as nearly equal in ability as any that could be found. The experiment was administered in the manner of a group mental test with the reading of definite instructions by the E and emphasis on careful adherence to them. The material for each group was bound in pamphlet form and passed out to the Ss. The first sheet contained a warning not to open, the second sheet had on it the list for primary learning, the third was blank, the fourth contained the material for the interpolated task, the fifth had a column of 10 short lines for the written recall of the primary list, and for Groups I and II the sixth had another set of lines for the recall of the inter-polated list. The pictures for Group V could not be incorporated in the booklets, so they were placed face down on the Ss' tables before the experiment began.

The experiment was run off in the same way for all groups, apart from the differences in the interpolated activity. Two minutes were allowed for the study of the primary list with a view to reproducing it, in correct order, later. Ss then turned to the blank page for 30 sec., during which they were given instructions for the interpolated task. Three minutes were allotted to the interpolated task; then the Ss turned to the fifth sheet and, after brief instructions, wrote as many pairs of consonants from the first list as they remembered during $1\frac{1}{2}$ min. Finally, for Groups I and II, the Ss turned to the sixth page and reproduced the secondary list. The time-intervals allowed for primary learning, for interpolated task, and for recall, were determined after preliminary experimentation.

Scoring

The following system was used in scoring the recalls written by the Ss. One credit was given if a consonant-pair was reproduced correctly in the same position which it occupied in the primary list, or if it was reproduced correctly in its relatively correct position (i.e. relative to the pair of consonants which preceded it on the list). One-half credit was given if a pair was correctly reproduced in a position one place removed from its correct position (relative or absolute). One-half credit was given if one-half a pair was reproduced in its correct position. No other recall received credit.

Results

Table 2.1 is a summary of the results, showing the number of Ss in each group, the range of the individual recall scores in each group, the average number of consonant-pairs recalled, and the probable errors of the aver-ages. As one would expect, Condition I, learning a second list of con-sonants, results in poorer retention than any of the other interpolated conditions. Conditions II and III show about the same average number of pairs recalled. The loss resulting from either common operation alone, or

Table 2.1
Summary of Results

	Group				
	I LL-LL	II LL-LN	III LL-CL	IV LL-CN	V LL-P
No. Ss	27	22	25	30	28
Range	0–9	0.5–10	0.5–10	3–10	4–10
Av.	3.7	6.2	6.3	7.6	8.6
P.E.$_{av.}$	±.28	±.36	±.38	±.25	±.21

common material alone, seems to be about the same, i.e. similarity of operation and similarity of material are apparently of about equal importance in determining decrements of retention.

In Condition IV (LL-CN), where neither operation nor material is like that in the first task, recall is better than it is in the two conditions in which one of these features is similar. This improvement is manifest in both the average recall and the range of the individual scores. Condition V (P), where the interpolated task was simply looking at pictures, gives the best recall of all 5 conditions. Both the average recall and the range of the individual scores show that there is an improvement even over LL-CN, where neither operation nor material were common to the first and second tasks.

Fig. 2.1 shows graphically the different percentages of the total possible recall which resulted from the 5 interpolated tasks. It should be remembered that the maximum possible recall was 10 consonant-pairs. Using these percentages, we may make the comparisons indicated as the purpose of our experiment. Condition IV (LL-CN) was different from the primary task in both material and operation, and 76% of the maximum recall was obtained by this group. Condition III (LL-CL) was like IV, except that the material was similar to that used in the primary task. Its recall was 63%. Subtracting this from 76% we find a difference of 13 units. Hence we may say that *similarity to the primary task in material only* causes a loss in retention, in this situation, of 13 units of percentage. Condition II (LL-LN) was like IV (LL-CN) in material, but in operation was similar to the primary task. The average recall for this group was 62%. Subtracting from 76% (recall for IV) we find a difference of 14 units. Hence in this condition we may say that *similarity to the primary task in operation only* causes a loss in retention of 14 units of percentage.

Now, if it were assumed that a task is made up of two actually independent and separable components, material on the one hand, and an operation on the other, it might then be expected that with an interpolated task having both operation and material similar to the first task, the loss

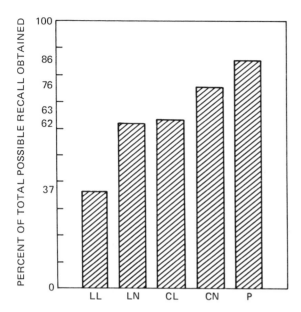

Figure 2.1
Effect of different interpolated tasks on retention of a list of 10 paired consonants. Reading from left to right, the five interpolated tasks are LL (learning a second list of letters), LN (learning a list of numbers), CL (cancelling letters), CN (cancelling numbers), and P (looking at pictures).

would be a sum of the losses caused by these two independently. Since there is a loss of 13 with similarity of material and 14 with similarity of operation, the sum of the losses, in this case, might be supposed to be about 27. Actually, however, comparing Condition I (both material and operation in common) with Condition IV (neither in common) the loss is 39 units of percentage. The presumption is that the effect of an interpolated task in which similarity of material and operation is combined is greater than the sum of the effects of two tasks each similar in one of these features respectively.[7] If this inference is correct, it would indicate that the material and the operation within a single task interact, each enhancing to some extent the effect of the other. Consequently one can be separated out only with violence to the other, and in varying them independently, as we have done, the remaining common feature is no longer *as similar as it would be if both remained the same.*

In Condition V (P) the interpolated task was different from the first task in a variety of features. The percentage recalled (86) was greater than in Condition IV (CN), where the interpolated task was different in operation and in material. The gain in V as compared to IV suggests that there are other features than these two with reference to which comparisons may be made, and that one or more of these features, e.g. the 'work' attitude, remained common to the primary and interpolated tasks in IV, but not in V.

The above comparisons can be made, with at least equal logic, by examining *gains* in retention as a function of *non-resemblance* of the interpolated task. The gains are 25 units with a difference in material only, 26 units with a difference in operation only, and 39 units with a difference in both. As before, the non-additive character of the latter gain can be explained by supposing material and operation to be interdependent.

Summary

Our experiment shows that comparison with reference to *features* of two tasks is useful in understanding the relation between similarity and retroactive inhibition.

It has been demonstrated that under the conditions of this experiment the interpolation of a task which is similar to the primary learning either in *operation* or in *material* results in poorer retention than does the interpolation of a task similar in neither. In this situation, the two features *operation* and *material*, seem to be about equally important in the effect on retention.

Operation and *material* were chosen as the two most obvious features or characteristics by means of which two tasks might be compared. That these are not the *only* features on which a comparison may be based is suggested by the fact that Condition V, which differed in other respects, gave better retention than Condition IV which differed in the two features of material and operation.

Finally, the original suggestion that features of a task are interdependent seems to be upheld by the probability that the sum of decrements due to *operation* and *material* does not equal the loss caused by similarity in both.

Notes

1. See E. S. Robinson, The 'similarity' factor in retroaction, this JOURNAL, 39, 1927, 297–312. For Skagg's earlier formulation, see E. B. Skaggs. Further studies in retroactive inhibition, *Psychol. Monog.*, 34, 1925, (no. 161), 1–60.

2. E. S. Robinson, *op. cit.*

3. T. A. Dreis, Two studies in retroaction, *J. Gen. Psychol.*, 8, 1933, 157–172.

4. L. Harden, A quantitative study of the similarity factor in retroactive inhibition, *J. Gen. Psychol.*, 2, 1929, 421–432; and N. Y. Cheng, Retroactive effect and degree of similarity, *J. Exper. Psychol.*, 12, 1929, 444–449.

5. E. C. Tolman, *Purposive Behavior in Animals and Men*, 1932, 10 f.

6. E. S. Robinson, Some factors determining the degree of retroactive inhibition, *Psychol. Monog.*, 28, 1920, (no. 128), 28.

7. This line of reasoning is valid only if the average retention scores (or percentages) being compared are close enough to the middle of the range of possible scores to be relatively unaffected by the distorting effect of the limits of this range, i.e. if the average scores are really proportional to the average degrees of retention. The experimental difficulty in obtaining averages which are proportional is a great source of error in research on retroaction. The writers believe, from an inspection of the distributions of individual scores and the ranges of these scores (Table 2.1), that the averages for Conditions I and IV are not sufficiently distorted to invalidate the above inference.

3

Sensory Generalization with Voluntary Reactions
Eleanor J. Gibson

This experiment was the first of several undertaken for my dissertation research at Yale University. My dissertation sponsor, Clark L. Hull, generously gave me his notebooks to peruse over a long weekend, thinking I might find a project that appealed to me among a number roughly outlined there. He was in the habit of writing a sort of diary every Sunday morning, noting down events of the week just past, especially ideas that had occurred to him, including ones for new experiments. Reading the notebooks was fascinating, but I returned them with the conviction that I had to formulate my own problem and that I would continue in the vein of my master's thesis, working on verbal learning and forgetting with human subjects. Hull greeted my decision without much enthusiasm. If I wanted to work with him, I had to stay in his territory. He told me to write up my ideas as a proposal, and he would consider them. A previous student of Hull, W. M. Lepley, had published a monograph on serial learning and forgetting based on conditioned reflex principles. Hull called this work to my attention thinking I might do something similar.

Lepley had proposed that rote learning might be thought of as a series of conditioned responses, with each item in the series serving as a stimulus for a later response, either a simultaneous conditioned response for the nearest item, or as conditioned trace responses for later ones. The latter would lead to anticipatory intrusions, which would have to be suppressed and would give rise to "inhibition of delay." Hull (1935) spun this idea into an elaborate deductive model and showed that a number of typical phenomena of rote learning could be accounted for. Although the ideas and reasoning were clever, they somehow did not convey a feeling of what one actually does in a learning situation. However, Hull was insistent on the importance of extending analogies with conditioning to other learning situations. Two other conditioning phenomena, generalization and differentiation, appealed to me as reasonable candidates, fortunately. Generalization

Journal of Experimental Psychology, 1939, 24, 237–253.

was analogous (perhaps) to similarity, which had turned out to be important in retroactive inhibition and might conceivably provide a base for interference theories of forgetting, which were becoming fashionable. Differentiation between lists and between items seemed to be a requirement for successful learning and retention. I set out to formulate a kind of minimodel of verbal learning using these concepts.

It seemed to me that analogies with the conditioned response in human learning situations required some proof that conditioning phenomena could be replicated with so-called voluntary responses. Would generalization occur along a dimension, distributed in a gradient like "irradiation" spreading from a source in conditioned reflex experiments? If irradiation was a function of indistinguishability of a signal from the original one presented for learning, it might be a reasonable expectation that a gradient of generalization would be apparent in an analogous situation with human subjects instructed to respond to a particular signal. I chose a reaction time situation mainly because it was traditional for investigating simple instructed responding, but also for a semipolitical reason. Hull had purchased an expensive Dunlap chronoscope, equipped with a voice key, several years before, and it had never been used. He was eager to make use of it. Ergo, I used it. It broke down frequently and gave me much trouble, but it did have the advantage that I could use a verbal response, supposedly more akin to verbal learning than a key press. The choice of vibrators as stimuli was also influenced by Hull, he being partial to them because he had used them in an experiment demonstrating a "gradient of irradiation in man" (Bass and Hull 1934).

The experiment worked out very well and produced nice gradients of frequency of generalized responses. "False" reactions, as the generalized responses would be called in a reaction time experiment, seem to be the result of confusing a "false" stimulus with the instructed one. Confusion of items, as a source of generalization, pleased me and fit well with the concept of generalization as lack of distinguishability, which I was leaning toward. But attitudes adopted by the subject complicated what might have been a simple gradient in more traditional conditioning situations. The attempt to relate similarity and generalization, begun at this time, continued for many years. When my dissertation was finally published, I received a postcard from E. G. Boring (it was typical of him, an enthusiastic correspondent, to send one to a new Ph.D., even one unknown to him). He wrote, "So you want to equate similarity with generalization? Well, why not?" But I think I had my doubts, even then. Years later, I wrote a short paper for the Psychological Review called "A re-examination of generalization" (Gibson 1959) in which I argued that recognition of similarity is not the same as failure to discriminate.

Theoretical contributions to the problem of learning have recently been characterized by a new series of attempts at linking the facts of conventional learning experiments with the conditioned response. The method of these systematic studies has been to use the empirical laws of the conditioned response as deductive principles in other learning situations. Maze learning (11, 12), discrimination learning (19, 20), and rote learning of verbal material (13, 14) are some of the fields for which detailed predictions have been made by this method. As a parallel to these attempts, it seemed worth while to apply the principles of *generalization* and *differentiation* to verbal learning (7). If it is assumed that generalization occurs among the cue or stimulus items during the learning of verbal lists, and that blocking of the right response occurs in proportion to the strength of the tendency to generalize, then differentiation must occur as an integral part of the learning. From these, and a few other related assumptions, a number of detailed predictions can be made with reference to the learning of single lists, interference, and retroactive inhibition. The only sure way of testing such a hypothesis is to make an experimental test of all the predictions which can be derived from the deductive principles or postulates. But this is a lengthy and laborious process. If certain of the underlying assumptions appear to be vulnerable and subject to relatively direct empirical test, it may be economical to begin the experimental program with an examination of them. The investigation to be reported consists of an experimental examination of an assumption underlying the application of the principle of generalization to verbal learning.

All the studies mentioned above must necessarily assume that the principles which are exploited operate not only with conditioned responses, but also with so-called voluntary reactions. Several of these laws have already been tested in connection with certain voluntary reactions (e.g. experimental extinction (18), and the importance of the temporal factor in determining direction (21)). It was, of course, entirely possible that the phenomenon of generalization might be peculiar in some respects to that type of learning situation from which the concept was originally derived. Although conditioned responses themselves do not appear to be confined to reflex mechanisms, there are good indications that conditioned voluntary reactions are not in every way functionally similar to conditioned involuntary reactions (15). We therefore desired to discover whether the phenomenon of generalization (and especially the typical gradient of generalization) would occur not only with conditioned responses, but also with reactions commonly described as voluntary ones. Accordingly, an experiment was planned with the purpose of discovering whether or not a series of stimuli known to give a gradient of generalization in a typical conditioned response situation would also do so when the response was not a reflex, but a voluntary verbal reaction. It was felt that positive results in this experiment would give some psychological justification for developing a system of the sort suggested, whereas negative results would necessarily mean abandoning the notion of relating conditioning and verbal learning by way of the concept of generalization.

A series of tactual stimuli placed at varying distances on the skin was chosen as being a stimulus dimension recognized as giving a gradient of generalization in a conditioning experiment.[3] The reaction time situation was employed, since it has been the traditional way of studying simple voluntary responses. The subject reacted verbally with a nonsense syllable. He was instructed to respond to a designated stimulus, and was given practise in so doing. Later the other stimuli were introduced to see whether they would be responded to in the same way as the practised stimulus. If there were a gradient of generalization analogous to that found with conditioned reactions, the generalized or "false" responses should be more frequent, the nearer the stimulus to the practised one in the skin dimension.

Apparatus and Procedure

Apparatus   Four vibratory stimuli of the type described by Bass and Hull (2) were applied to the subject's back. Each vibrator was mounted in a large rubber sponge, and the four sponges were secured in a tight cloth jacket provided with straps. Two straps extended over the subject's shoulders and two others around his chest. The vibrators were four inches apart in a straight line, and the series could be made to extend either across or up and down the subject's back. The device when worn resembled a cork life-preserver. The subject could not feel the vibrators except when they were electrically activated. The plunger of each vibrator stimulated the skin through two layers of cloth—the covering of the jacket and the subject's shirt.

Reaction time was measured by means of a voice key in circuit with a Dunlap chronoscope. The chronoscope was the regulation one sold by Stoelting, driven by a tuning fork. The voice key was the standard type which breaks a contact at the sound of the subject's voice. The preparatory intervals were regulated by a contact on a revolving drum which was stopped between trials. The drum was driven by a motor which was started at the beginning of a trial; after a variable interval, the contact was made, activating relays which simultaneously closed the vibrator circuit and started the chronoscope. The subject's reaction broke the voice-key circuit, stopping both vibrator and chronoscope. The vibrators were wired in parallel circuits and separate switch keys were mounted on the experimenter's control board, so that the appropriate one could be selected for each trial.

The subject was seated comfortably in front of a large screen, the only visible apparatus being the voice key. All other apparatus and the experimenter were concealed behind the screen.

Procedure   The following instructions were given the subject to read at the beginning of the experiment:

This is a reaction time experiment. That means that whenever a certain signal occurs, you are to react as quickly as you can with a particular response. The signal will be a vibratory stimulus on the (lower, upper, right, or left) part of your back which will be demonstrated to you in a minute, and the response will consist of speaking DUT into this voice key. Whenever you feel the vibrator, say DUT immediately. The noise of the apparatus starting will serve as a ready signal so you can get prepared to respond in a hurry. You will be given some practise trials before your reaction time is recorded. You are to respond *only to the demonstrated stimulus*. Later in the experiment there will be other extraneous stimuli. These stimuli will be other vibrators located in different places on your back. You are *not* to respond to any except the demonstrated stimulus on the——part of your back.

Experiments on reaction time show that you can go faster if you keep your mind on the response you are to make, so keep a motor attitude, that is, be prepared to say DUT the instant this vibrator stimulates you.

When the subject finished reading the instructions, the vibrator to which he was to respond was demonstrated to him. This vibrator was always at one end of the series (extreme right, extreme left, top, or bottom). Then 50 trials with the stimulus to which he had been instructed to respond (the "practised" stimulus) were given. Reactions were taken at a rate of about one in 20 seconds. At the beginning of a trial, the experimenter started the drum (the sound of which served as a ready signal), a variable interval of from $\frac{1}{2}$ to $2\frac{1}{2}$ seconds intervened, the stimulus occurred, the subject responded, the drum was stopped, and the chronoscope reading taken by the experimenter.

A practise series of 50 trials was given first with the designated stimulus. Then 100 more trials were given during which the 3 "prohibited" stimuli were interspersed at random intervals among trials with the designated stimulus. Each of the 3 prohibited stimuli occurred 9 times during the 100 trials.

The order of the prohibited stimuli was varied with each subject according to a prearranged plan so that order of occurrence did not favor any one stimulus when a group of subjects was considered together. This precaution was taken in case there should be a tendency for false responses to decrease with practise.[4] A group of 9 subjects was required to balance the order. Eighteen subjects (Group I) were run with the vibrators placed vertically up and down the back (half with the practised stimulus at the top of the series, the other half with the practised stimulus at the bottom); 18 more subjects (Group II) were run with the vibrators arranged horizontally across the back (again half practised at each extreme).

The subjects were all students at Yale University and were paid for their services.

Controls   Following the experiment proper, the subjects were given two brief series of tests, one to check on the relative intensity of the stimuli, and the other to check on their localizability. The intensity of the vibrators was controlled mechanically in so far as possible, in that the vibrators, their wiring, and mounting were identical; as a further precaution, each subject was put through a series of judgments of comparative intensity of the stimuli, in case there should be a tendency for more false responses to occur to a stimulus of stronger intensity and thereby distort the curve of fre-

Table 3.1
Judgements of Relative Intensity of Vibrators

	Percent of Time Judged Stronger than Standard		
	Nearest Stimulus	Next Stimulus	Farthest Stimulus
Group I A	22%	49%	32%
Group I B	88%	54%	74%
Group II B	88%	86%	65%

quencies. Paired comparisons of the stimuli were used, and the subject was asked to give a judgment of the relative intensity. The designated or practised stimulus was used as a standard, and was paired with each other 8 times, in a random order. Data for 3 of the 4 sub-groups are presented in Table 3.1 (the control was not thought necessary until several subjects had already been run). An examination of the percentage of time each stimulus was judged stronger in comparison with the standard shows some small differences in intensity within each group. But it is significant that the intensity differences vary in no particular direction, as the differences in frequency of response will later be shown to do. In other words, there was not the slightest tendency for the intensity variations noted to correspond with relative frequency of response to the prohibited stimuli. It may therefore be concluded that differential intensity played an insignificant part in determining the gradient of response to the prohibited stimuli.

The second control test was given to determine whether or not the four vibratory stimuli could be absolutely localized. Since the vibrators were spaced four inches apart, they were readily discriminable when one was presented for immediate comparison with another.[5] But it is often the case that two stimuli which can be easily discriminated when presented for comparison cannot be absolutely identified. Since in our experiment a stimulus was presented alone with a period of 20 seconds intervening between stimuli, something approaching an absolute localization was required, and the question arose whether or not generalization was occurring as a result of the subject's inability to identify surely the designated point. Therefore, each vibrator was presented separately to the subject, and he was asked to give an absolute judgment of its spatial location by identifying the stimulus; a card bearing the numbers 1, 2, 3, and 4 in the same plane as the vibrators was placed in front of the subject to facilitate the naming response. Each vibrator was presented for identification 3 times, in a random order.

In the case of the 18 subjects who had the series of stimuli distributed *across* the back (Group II), only 1 confusion of points 0 and 1 occurred out of 108 chances (less than 1 percent).[6] No confusion of point 0 with any

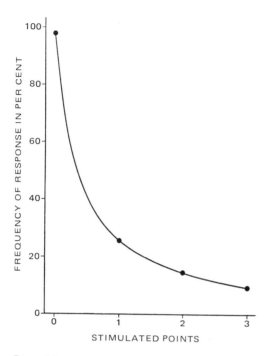

Figure 3.1
Frequency of response to vibrators as a function of proximity to practised point (Group I, vibrators placed *vertically*). Frequency of response in percentage is represented on the ordinate, and stimulated points in order of proximity on the abscissa.

other point occurred. When the vibrators were distributed *up and down* the back, more errors of identification occurred. Points 0 and 1 were confused 14 times out of 108 chances (13 percent). Again, 0 was not confused with points 2 and 3. It is quite in keeping with the facts of skin sensitivity that the vibrators placed vertically should be harder to localize, since spatial thresholds are higher when stimuli are applied in a longitudinal direction on the skin than when they are applied transversely. It is clear, however, that any generalization found in Group II, at least, can hardly be due to mistaken localization of stimuli.

Results

The main question of the experiment was whether or not generalization was more apt to occur in proportion as the prohibited stimulus approximated spatially to the practised one. This question was answered by the relative frequency of response to the prohibited stimuli. These results are best presented graphically. In Fig. 3.1 are presented combined results for the 18 subjects who had the series of vibrators placed up and down the back. The practised stimulus is designated as 0, and the others are designated 1, 2, and 3 in order of proximity to it, regardless of whether the 0 stimulus was at top or bottom. The 0 stimulus is almost invariably responded to (98 percent). False responses are made to the closest prohibited vibrator 25 percent of the time, to the next closest 14 percent of the time, and to the farthest 9 percent of the time. In general, the curve shows a continuous gradient from point 0 to point 3, in accordance with the expectation that a process analogous to generalization of conditioned responses occurs with voluntary responses.[7] The differences between the frequencies at the four points have very satisfactory critical ratios (44.2 to 2.67), with the exception of the difference between point 2 and point 3 which has a critical ratio of only 1.48.[8] The continuous downward trend, however, is unquestionable. Furthermore, when the data for the two sub-groups of 9 subjects each are plotted separately, the resulting curves are both similar to the one above, showing a continuous slope from 0 to 3.

The results for the 18 subjects who had the vibrators placed across the back are given in Fig. 3.2. Here the slope from point 0 to point 2 resembles

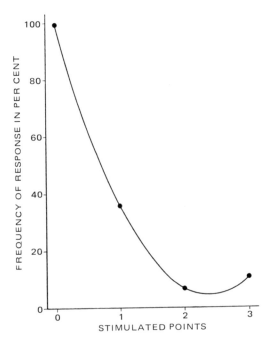

Figure 3.2
Frequency of responses to vibrators as a function of proximity to practised point (Group II, vibrators placed *horizontally*).

closely the slope in Fig. 1, but the upturn at point 3 is not typical of the usual curve of generalization. It must be remembered, however, that the vibrators here were distributed horizontally, and points 0 and 3 were consequently *symmetrical*. Perhaps the symmetrical location is responsible for the higher degree of generalization at point 3 than at point 2. Anrep (1) reports that symmetry is an effective cause of generalization; he found, in fact (with dogs as subjects), that stimulation of the point symmetrical with the 0 point was equally as effective as stimulation of the 0 point itself. The difference in this group between points 2 and 3 has a statistical reliability of only 1.16 times its standard error. But when the data for the two subgroups are plotted separately, they resemble the curve drawn from combined data, showing an upturn at 3. It seems unlikely that this is a mere chance resemblance. It is notable, also, that in Fig. 3.1, where there were no symmetrical points, no such upturn occurred.

It is interesting to compare percentages of generalization at point 1 in Groups I and II keeping in mind the fact that stimuli 0 and 1 were accurately localized by Group II but not invariably by Group I. It might be expected on common sense grounds that less accurate localization should accompany a greater number of false responses, but such is not the case. For Group II, the frequency at point 1 is 36 percent, while in Group I it is only 25 percent; more false responses occurred when the vibrators were easily identified. Generalization of responses, therefore, can hardly be explained by the inability of the subject to identify the correct stimulus.

A second difference is that between response to stimulation at the 0 points themselves in the two cases. Figure 3.1 shows a slightly lower percentage of response at this point than does Fig. 3.2 (98 percent as compared with 100 percent).[9] Again frequency of response was lowered when absolute localization was poorer. This fact suggests that the difficulty of discriminating points 0 and 1 in Group I induced a strong inhibitory attitude in the subjects—i.e., caused them to react with greater "caution." If this was the case, reaction time should be increased. An examination of the times reveals that it was. Taking the first 50 practise trials as a control, and comparing with them all the trials with the o stimulus *after the prohibited stimuli had been introduced*, an average increase in latency is found in the latter case of 63 ms. in Group I, and 42 ms. in Group II. It is significant that the greater average increase in latency occurs in Group I.

The invariable increase in latency after introduction of prohibited stimuli is interesting. It is related, for one thing, to the difference always found between simple and discrimination reactions in the reaction time experiment. Furthermore, it suggests the analogous situation with Pavlov's dogs when a previously differentiated stimulus is introduced among trials with a conditioned stimulus. An inhibitory process occurs which 'spreads' or leaves an after-effect serving to depress the ensuing conditioned responses.

It should be pointed out that the possible influence of fatigue has not been controlled in the above comparison of the first 50 reactions with later reactions. It is most improbable, however, that the increase in latency is even partially due to fatigue. For one thing, practise effects would normally continue after 50 reactions and balance any fatigue; furthermore, the effects of fatigue in the reaction time experiment are very slight (see 4, p. 46).

The reaction times were analyzed to see whether the gradient of frequency of response to the four stimuli was accompanied by a correlative gradient of speed. Superficial consideration might lead to the expectation of a negative correlation between frequency and latency, since positive evidence of such a correlation in the case of simple conditioned responses is available (3, 9). But such a correlation has never been demonstrated for *generalized* responses in the conditioning situation. Furthermore, in the present situation two factors are present which cut across the expected correlation—in fact, work in opposition to it. In the first place, there is voluntary inhibition of long-latency false responses. The effect of such inhibition would presumably be to allow only the *fastest* potential responses to occur. Since the subject does not inhibit responses to the designated or practised stimulus when they are slow, no selection of fast responses would occur for this stimulus. Simply averaging the times of all responses made to each of the four stimuli would, therefore, show an artificially *decreased* latency of response to the prohibited stimuli; whereas the superficial prediction was that latency of these responses should be greater than those to the designated stimulus, since frequency of response is lower.

Table 3.2 shows the average latency of response to the four points of stimulation in both groups. The average latency at point 0 is calculated from all the responses to that stimulus *after* the introduction of the false stimuli (it will be remembered that reaction times for the preceding practise responses were shorter). The results show that the average latencies by no means increase from point 0 to point 3, as they should if a negative correlation between frequency and latency exists; on the contrary, there is a *decrease* in latency as the stimulus is displaced from the practised point. Our assumption of voluntary inhibition of long-latency false responses is therefore probably correct.

Table 3.2
Average Latency of Response to the 4 Vibrators in Ms

	Vibrator 0	Vibrator 1	Vibrator 2	Vibrator 3
Group I (Vertical distribution)	233	219	149	151
Group II (Horizontal distribution)	170	161	106	122

The second complicating factor is the slight tendency for the subjects of Group I to confuse points 0 and 1. It has already been pointed out that frequency of response at these points was lower than in Group II, probably because of "caution" or a strong inhibitory attitude. It is as if the subject had to make a discrimination reaction between two confusable stimuli; and, as is well known to be the case,[10] the reaction time lengthened accordingly. The average latency at points 0 and 1 for Group I may be seen to be abnormally high in comparison with the rest of the figures.

The first of these two complications may possibly be eliminated by the following procedure. For each point, the times of only the fastest 6 percent of the total number of *possible* reactions may be averaged. The hypothesis is that the whole distribution of possible responses should be slightly faster, the greater the frequency of reaction produced by the stimulus (or the nearer the stimulus to the designated point). By taking the top 6 percent of the potential responses, we include only reactions which were fast enough to slip by (above the threshold of voluntary inhibition), and avoid the difficulty. There is no way of avoiding the influence of the second complicating factor in presenting the results.

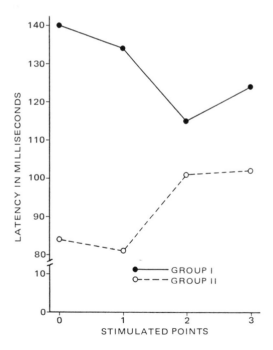

Figure 3.3
Average latency of the fastest 6 percent of responses at the four stimulated points .

Figure 3.3 shows the curves of latency of response to the four stimuli when only the fastest 6 percent of the potential responses are included in each case. Curves for both Groups are plotted on the same axes. If there were a perfect inverse relationship between frequency and latency, the curves should show a constant upward slope. A glance at them does not indicate much tendency for an increase in latency to accompany spatial displacement from the 0 point, as does decreasing frequency. But if points 0 and 1 for Group I are discounted (for the reasons given above), there will be seen to be a rough upward trend. A perfect slope, even aside from the two discounted points, could hardly be expected considering that 6 percent of the potential reactions in the case of the three prohibited stimuli includes only 10 responses at each point. Therefore, although it cannot be concluded that speed is correlated with frequency under the present circumstances, it may be suggested that such a trend is not entirely absent when the complications introduced by difficult localization and voluntary inhibition are considered.

Discussion

Several references have already been made to the reaction time literature pointing out parallels between the present experiment and the discrimination reaction time experiment. Some other facts from this source seem to be relevant. The "false" reaction, an event generally found but so far as we know never studied, would seem to be understandable in many cases as an example of generalization. With reference to some recent attempts to condition voluntary responses in a reaction time set-up, it has been suggested by Gibson (5) that what were taken to be conditioned voluntary reactions were more likely generalized reactions. The fact that generalized responses have been demonstrated to occur in a voluntary situation lends plausibility to this suggestion.

Furthermore, phenomena reported in studies of the effect of a distracting stimulus on speed of reaction to a given stimulus can be interpreted in the light of our approach. Evans (4) found that distraction was particularly effective when the distracting stimulus belonged to the same sense department as the stimulus to be responded to. That is, if the distracting stimulus was an intermittent flash of light, while the designated stimulus was a flash of light of different intensity coming from a slightly different place, the increase in reaction times was greater than if the distracting stimulus had been a tone or a touch. Our data likewise show that reaction time increases significantly when other stimuli of the same dimension as the practised stimulus are introduced, especially when the new stimulus is not easily discriminated from the practised one. It may be tentatively suggested that in such situations a type of inhibition is set up comparable to the inhibitory after-effects reported by Pavlov (17, p. 125) and by Anrep (1) when a differentiated stimulus is introduced among trials with a conditioned stimulus. But such a possibility must be explored in an experiment especially designed for the purpose.

The results of this experiment have a certain bearing on the relation between conditioned and voluntary responses. In common with the experiments specifically directed at the study of this relationship, the results show both similarities and differences. Generalization and the gradient of generalization appear under both conditions. But the instructions which were necessarily introduced in the "voluntary" situation apparently produce a set or attitude of caution which has the effect of shortening reaction times of the few responses made to the false stimuli. It is a question whether generalized responses in the conditioning situation would show an increase or a decrease. It seems possible that the latencies of generalized responses would be *longer* while the discrimination is being built up, and *shorter*, as in the present situation, when the frequency of generalized responses has been lowered by differential reinforcement. That is, establishment of differentiation would inhibit false responses in most cases; the few which occurred might be faster than normal responses, as in the present situation. Such cases might be produced by disinhibition, for instance. But investigation, rather than speculation, is obviously called for by this problem.

A new line of experimentation is suggested by the probability that false reactions to a prohibited stimulus do not occur simply because the subject cannot tell the difference between this stimulus and a designated one. Similarities of a superthreshold nature appear to play a part. The exact nature of the relationship between generalization and perceptual "similarity" and identity is an unanswered problem, and one which should yield to a technique combining psychophysical methods and methods designed for the study of conditioned responses.

Summary

Subjects were instructed to respond verbally as quickly as possible to a designated vibratory stimulus, but not to respond in this way to other stimuli. Practise was given in responding to the designated stimulus. Later other vibratory stimuli, distributed either longitudinally or transversely on the subject's back, were introduced, to see whether generalized or "false" responses would occur and whether they would be more frequent, the nearer the stimulus to the designated one on the skin. The following conclusions may be drawn.

1. Frequency of response to the prohibited stimuli showed a gradient of generalization analogous to the gradient found in the condi-

tioned response experiment, when the vibrators were distributed longitudinally.

2. When the vibrators were distributed transversely, an upturn at the end of the curve of response resulted. This upturn was probably caused by the symmetrical relations of the point stimulated and the designated point.

3. Introduction of prohibited stimuli apparently produced an increase in latency of response to the designated stimulus. This increase was particularly noticeable when one of the prohibited stimuli was not easily discriminable from the designated stimulus.

4. The average latency of response to the prohibited stimuli was less than that to the designated stimulus, probably because the long-latency false responses had been inhibited.

5. When the differential effects of voluntary inhibition were avoided, there was some indication that speed was positively correlated with frequency of response.

6. With reference to the problem of the relation between conditioned and voluntary responses, the present results suggest that similarities exist, but that differences due to the instructions introduced in the voluntary situation are to be expected.

Notes

1. The writer wishes to express gratitude to Professor Clark L. Hull for encouragement and advice during the progress of this research. The experiment is one of a series of studies presented to the Faculty of the Graduate School of Yale University in partial fulfillment of the requirements for the degree of Doctor of Philosophy in Psychology.

2. This experiment was reported before the Eastern Branch of the American Psychological Association in 1937 (6).

3. Generalization gradients have been demonstrated with this stimulus dimension by Anrep (1) and by Bass and Hull (2).

4. Such a tendency did occur. About 70 percent of all false responses came during the first half of these 100 trials.

5. Myers (16) gives the two-point threshold in the region of the spine as 5.4 cm when the stimuli are distributed longitudinally.

6. The designation 0 is used to refer to the stimulated point which the subject was instructed to respond to. The numbers 1, 2, and 3 refer respectively to the vibrator nearest, next, and farthest from that point.

7. For a similar negatively accelerated curve of generalization in the conditioned response situation see Hovland (10).

8. Reliabilities were calculated with the formula given by Yule (22, p. 269) for the standard error of the difference between two proportions.

9. Although small, the difference is statistically reliable, its critical ratio being 3.67.

10. Henmon (8) found that the smaller the difference between two stimuli, the longer the reaction time to the difference.

References

1. Anrep, G. V., The irradiation of conditioned reflexes, *Proc. Roy. Soc.*, 1923, 94, Series B, 404–425.
2. Bass, M. J. and Hull, C. L., Irradiation of a tactile conditioned reflex in man, *J. Comp. Psychol.*, 1934, 17, 47–65.
3. Campbell, A. A. and Hilgard, E. R., Individual differences in ease of conditioning, *J. Exper. Psychol.*, 1936, 19, 561–571.
4. Evans, J. E., The effect of distraction on reaction-time, with special reference to practice and the transfer of training, *Arch. of Psychol.*, 1916, 37, pp. 106.
5. Gibson, J. J., A note on the conditioning of voluntary reactions, *J. Exper. Psychol.*, 1936, 19, 397–399.
6. Gibson, E. J., Sensory irradiation with voluntary responses, *Psychol. Bull.*, 1937, 34, 511–512.
7. Gibson, E. J., *A Systematic Application of the Concepts of Generalization and Differentiation to Verbal Learning*, Dissertation, Yale University, 1938.
8. Henmon, V. A. C., *The Time of Perception as a Measure of Differences in Sensations*, New York: Science Press, 1906.
9. Hilgard, E. R. and Marquis, D. G., Acquisition, extinction, and retention of conditioned lid responses to light in dogs, *J. Comp. Psychol.*, 1935, 19, 29–58.
10. Hovland, C. I., The generalization of conditioned responses: I. The sensory generalization of conditioned responses with varying frequencies of tone, *J. Gen. Psychol.*, 1937, 17, 125–148.
11. Hull, C. L., The goal gradient hypothesis and maze learning, *Psychol. Rev.*, 1932, 39, 25–43.
12. ———, The concept of the habit-family hierarchy and maze learning, *Psychol. Rev.*, 1934, 41, 33–52; 134–152.
13. ———, The conflicting psychologies of learning—a way out, *Psychol. Rev.*, 1935, 42, 491–516.
14. Lepley, W. M., A theory of serial learning and forgetting based upon conditioned reflex principles, *Psychol. Rev.*, 1932, 39, 279–288.
15. Marquis, D. G. and Porter, J. M., Differential factors in conditioned voluntary and conditioned involuntary responses, *Psychol. Bull.*, 1937, 34, p. 772.
16. Myers, C. S., *A Text-Book of Experimental Psychology*, Cambridge: University Press, 1928, pp. xiv + 344.
17. Pavlov, I. P., *Conditioned Reflexes*. Translated and edited by G. V. Anrep, Oxford University Press, 1927, pp. xv + 430.
18. Peak, H. and Deese, L., Experimental extinction of verbal material, *J. Exper. Psychol.*, 1937, 20, 244–261.
19. Spence, K. W., The nature of discrimination learning in animals, *Psychol. Rev.*, 1936, 43, 427–449.
20. ———, The differential response in animals to stimuli varying within a single dimension, *Psychol. Rev.*, 1937, 44, 430–444.
21. Stephens, J. M., The conditioned reflex as the explanation of habit formation. III. The operation of two higher order reactions in close succession, *J. Exper. Psychol.*, 1936, 19, 77–90.
22. Yule, G. Udny, *An Introduction to the Theory of Statistics*, London: Charles Griffin and Co., Ltd., 1922, pp. xv + 415.

4

A Systematic Application of the Concepts of Generalization and Differentiation to Verbal Learning

Eleanor J. Gibson

The centerpiece of my dissertation was this attempt to use the concepts of generalization and differentiation to deduce a number of phenomena characteristically found in paired associate learning studies of the time, such as transfer, interference, and retroactive inhibition. To please Hull, I used concepts indicating phenomena found in conditioned response learning situations, but as I thought of them, the concepts actually referred to perceptual aspects of the learning process. However, one didn't speak much of perception in public in those days, so there is a kind of surreptitious meaning smuggled in. I wanted to emphasize structural features of items to be learned, rather than sheer association. Perceptual differentiation, preliminary to association with another unit, whatever it might be, was promising as the process that must be involved. The term predifferentiation *evolved in the process of constructing the model and pulling out deductions. It became a popular term and was the focus of considerable research (for example, Arnoult 1953).*

In preparing this paper, I tried to follow Hull's lead (Hull 1935) presenting definitions, assumptions (called "postulates," in emulation of a geometrical proof), and then deductions that could be tested experimentally, with the complete argument given. It now seems to me somewhat labored and pretentious, as does Hull's work. Spelling everything out, with explicit definitions and predictions, has its merits. Even so, incomplete definitions that allow unvoiced assumptions to creep in can occur, although it is remarkable how often they go unremarked. I find a few now in my own model and wonder why no one pointed them out at the time.

This "miniature system," as well as Hull's miniature and more major ones, are long since passé for most psychologists, but it seems that that doesn't include everyone who is concerned with models of behavior or cognition. A few years ago I gave a seminar at the University of Pennsylvania whose participants included promotors of Artificial Intelligence and roboticists. I asked them to read, as historical background, the paper that follows and a sample of Hull's work. To my astonishment, they considered it a revelation, exciting and promising!

Psychological Review, 1940, 47, 196–229.

Introduction

A recent trend in experimental and theoretical psychology has been the attempt to systematize the facts of a given field on the basis of empirical principles derived from study of the conditioned response (14, 15, 21, 39, 16).[1] It is reasonable to expect that the same general laws hold from one learning task to another, in so far as the situations are similar, and it is possible that the greater the simplicity of the learning, the better are the chances of laying bare mechanisms which operate in all learning.

It is necessary, however, to guard against the chance that the principles chosen for systematic exploitation are artifacts of the experimental situation from which they were derived, and have no importance as general characteristics of learning. Hull has suggested a procedure for testing the value of a theory built on such concepts (14). The essentials of such a test are the development of a clear-cut hypothesis, exploration of the hypothesis for all its derivatives, and experimental test of such derivatives as have received no direct substantiation or disqualification. The theory must stand or fall with the experimental evidence for or against the predictions which it makes.

The following account is an attempt to develop a theory relating various facts of verbal learning (such as transfer, interference, certain intra-list effects and retroactive inhibition), to two experimentally defined characteristics of the conditioned response—generalization and differential inhibition. The theory will be explored for deductions of known facts as well as for implications yet to be tested, since it has been undertaken principally in the hope of systematizing many of the facts already known. That transfer, interference, and retroactive inhibition are related has long been suspected, as the so-called "transfer" theory of retroactive inhibition implies (2, p. 427 ff.). The hypothesis to be presented is likewise classifiable as a "transfer" theory, but it aims to make as explicit as possible the mechanisms assumed to be responsible for the transfer, which is itself a phenomenon as poorly understood as retroactive inhibition.

The hypothesis will first be stated in a brief, informal fashion. Then, for the benefit of the reader who wishes to make a more scrupulous examination, the terms used will be explained, assumptions stated, and arguments for various predictions presented in detail.

Statement of the Hypothesis

The hypothesis asserts that a major necessity of verbal learning is the establishment of *discrimination* among the items to be learned, and that this process of discriminating is actually a fundamental part of what is called generally the learning process. If no discrimination between the items already exists, then the early part of the learning process will see an *increase* in the tendency to confuse the items, followed by the development of discrimination. Learning time should be at a maximum in this case. If such discrimination already exists, learning time should be at a minimum. Positive transfer will occur in situations where the nature of a second task permits discrimination acquired in a previous task to be beneficial. Negative transfer will occur when generalization with a previous task occurs, but where the situation is such that discrimination *between some aspect of the two tasks themselves* is required, as well as learning of the second. Retroactive inhibition will occur, similarly, if a second task generalizes with one already learned, and if the situation is such that discrimination between some aspect of the two tasks must be produced before the first can be recalled adequately.

The reader familiar with the facts of conditioned responses will see immediately the possibility of stating these assumptions in terms of *generalization* and *differentiation*.[2] The hypothesis will be stated as it applies to verbal learning by the paired associates method. It is assumed that when a list is being learned by this method, generalization may occur between the various stimulus items, so that a response learned to one tends to occur, as a response to other stimulus items in the list also. Figure 4.1 represents a list in which generalization is occurring. The dotted lines represent generalization tendencies and the solid arrows represent connections with the "right" responses, which are to be learned. In such a list as this, where the generalizing stimulus items all have different responses, those responses occurring or tending to occur by virtue of generalization will block the right responses in proportion to the strength of the tendency to generalization. In order to reduce the strength of the generalizing tendencies (to increase the differentiation), differential reinforcement through practice must be applied. It is assumed, that varying degrees of generalization may occur between one item and others in a list, and consequently that lists may vary as to the average strength of generalization occurring in the list. The

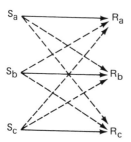

Figure 4.1

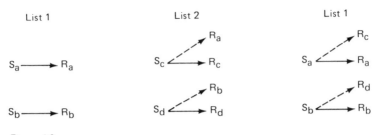

Figure 4.2

necessity for greater differentiation will then serve to make the learning more difficult in lists where a high degree of generalization occurs than in ones where less generalization occurs; and it will also be responsible for poorer retention, since the differentiation, especially with lower degrees of learning, decreases over a period of time, allowing spontaneous recovery of the generalization. If the above hypothesis is correct, the generalization in either case should be apparent in actual confusion of responses.

Furthermore, in any two-list situations such as the ones used to study interference and retroactive inhibition, it is assumed that inter-list generalization may occur. When a first list is followed by a second one which includes stimulus items similar to ones in the first, stimulus items in the second list will tend to produce responses from the first; and likewise when list 1 is again presented for recall and relearning, response members from list 2 will tend to recur. Figure 4.2 represents responses from list 1 tending to occur by generalization in list 2, and ones from list 2 occurring by generalization when list 1 is again tested. In each case, the generalizing tendencies will block the right excitatory tendencies in proportion to the strength of the generalization. Again, the generalization should be evident in actual confusion of responses—in this case, errors of "reversion" to the wrong list.

The degree of learning of any list cannot be predicted from the number of practice repetitions alone, according to this hypothesis, since the amount of differential reinforcement or practice required to reduce generalization to a given strength increases with the *degree* of generalization between stimulus items. The extent of differentiation achieved as a result of a given amount of differential reinforcement will vary, then, with this factor. Moreover, the extent of differentiation must be calculated also in terms of time elapsing since differential reinforcement has been discontinued, since spontaneous recovery will eventually occur. Pavlov has shown that spontaneous recovery occurs more slowly, the farther differential inhibition has been carried 33, p. 123). Temporal intervals between learning and recall thus assume importance in the light of the hypothesis, and together with

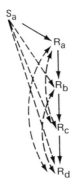

Figure 4.3

degree of learning, must be taken into account in predicting inter-list effects.

The hypothesis has been stated in terms of lists learned by the method of paired associates, but the same logic will apply throughout to lists learned by any method which allows a stimulus-response analysis. Figure 4.3 represents a list being learned by the *anticipation* method. Item S_a functions only as a stimulus and must produce the next item, R_a, as its response. But when this item actually appears, it functions as a stimulus. The dotted lines represent generalizing tendencies within the list. The hypothesis cannot be so easily applied to other verbal learning situations, since in most of them the subject's performance is not so controlled as to allow a detailed S-R analysis. Such would be the case with the method of complete presentation, for instance. However, there seems no good reason to suppose that the hypothesis *cannot* hold with such a method. In the sections which follow, evidence will be quoted without comment when it has been obtained by the paired associates or anticipation method, but where any other method has been employed, this fact will be specifically referred to.

The role of the *responses* in determining ease of learning a single list or in transfer situations is not specifically delineated by the present hypothesis. It is conceivable that something analogous to generalization of stimulus items might occur among response items, especially since every response is in a sense a stimulus as well. Müller's substitution hypothesis develops this possibility (30). According to Müller, "active" substitution was said to occur when idea *a* was connected with idea *b*, and idea *A*, which was similar to *a*, also produced *b*. This description follows the pattern of sensory generalization which has been described here. But Müller also described "passive substitution"; *B* might be substituted for *b*, when *B* was similar to *b* but not associated with *a*. This, in terms of the present hypothesis, would amount to generalization of response items, if it occurred. Confusion errors would result in either case, and *a priori* might be due to either type of generalization. But recent work of Thorndike (41) suggests that the stimulus items of a list are chiefly effective in producing such errors. He found that stimulus members of a very long list evoked responses made to *other stimuli like them* nearly twice as often as they evoked responses connected with unlike stimuli. But a stimulus member evoked a word which was *like the response* connected with it little or no oftener than it evoked unlike responses.

An experiment by McGeoch and McGeoch (28) seems also significant in this connection. In a retroactive inhibition experiment, stimulus members of corresponding paired associates in a list 1 and a list 2 were synonymous; or response members were synonymous; or both members were synonymous; or neither were. When the stimulus members were synonymous, there was a consistent increase in retroactive inhibition over the condition where neither member was synonymous, but this was not the case when response members were synonymous. Furthermore, when both members were synonymous, there was no consistent increase in retroactive inhibition as compared with the condition where stimulus members only were synonymous. On the basis of these results, the present hypothesis will confine itself to the exploitation of the concept of sensory generalization as originally stated.

Relation to Other Systems

There has been in the past at least one rather ambitious attempt to systematize some of the facts which are being considered, and there are contemporary theories which apply to the same realm. The earlier attempt referred to is that of G. E. Müller and his students. Müller and Pilzecker (30), besides presenting an enormous mass of experimental data based on a thorough-going exploitation of the *Treffermethode*, posited a number of kinds of inhibition (e.g., associative inhibition, retroactive inhibition) to explain their results. Their substitution hypothesis, which rose from an exhaustive analysis of errors, in a sense foreshadows the present theory. Müller's theories, naturally, rose out of his results; and though his terminology has left a lasting impression on the literature, it seems antiquated today, because the foundation laid by these earlier investigations makes it possible to develop a more comprehensive theory which may even suggest the psychological processes or mechanisms underlying his types of inhibition.

A systematic attempt to explain various facts of memory and learning is being made at present by Gestalt psychologists, and has given rise to experimental work, notably by Köhler and his students (20, 33, 32, 35). The essence of the theory is that the Gestalt laws of spatial organization hold also in the field of memory; by analogy with their laws of perceptual organization, the Gestalt psychologists predict such effects as difficulty in learning homogeneous series, retroactive inhibition, and proactive inhibition. For instance, the 'law of similarity in spatial organization' is assumed to hold for memory, and is demonstrated in a series of experiments by von Restorff (35), in which retention of homogeneous series of items is compared with retention of heterogeneous series. An item in a heterogeneous series is said to be in a better position to be retained than the same item in an entirely homogeneous series, since by the law of similarity there is *aggregation* of the traces of the homogeneous items, thereby causing any single item to lose its identity. Also, an 'isolated' item in one series may lose its superiority if a second series follows which is composed of items similar to it (retroactive inhibition), while an isolated item in a second series will have no advantage if the series preceding it is made up of similar items (proactive inhibition). The theory is characterized by Koffka as a 'dynamic trace theory' and has been elaborated in his book (19). It could probably be restated in terms of discrimination, and in this sense is similar to the theory presented in this paper. The chief difference lies in the concepts on which the two theories are based, and the methods by which they are developed.

A third theory, advanced by James (17) to explain interference, rests like the present theory on Pavlovian concepts. His theory differs considerably from the present one, however, in that the key concept is external inhibition, rather than differential inhibition. The theory is extended to cover retroactive inhibition, but it is unfortunately not developed to the extent of predicting experimental results or specific tests. No experimental work seems to have followed it. The theory could consistently supplement the one suggested in this paper.

The present-day associationists have assembled a number of "laws" which bear some relation to the central notions of the present hypothesis. In Robinson's book (36), a *Law of Assimilation* is included which is very similar to the notion of generalization. It is stated as follows: "Whenever an associative connection is so established that an activity, *A*, becomes capable of instigating an activity, *B*, activities other than *A* also undergo an increase or decrease in their capacity to instigate *B*." The law is extended to cover "assimilation of instigated processes" as well. The *Law of Acquaintance*, suggested in the same work, is superficially similar to a principle of discrimination. But the law apparently means by acquaintance mere isolated repetition of a given item; "acquaintance" is relevant to the present theory only in so far as it produces discrimination from other items. Mere acquaintance does not seem to increase efficiency of learning (Waters, 42). Much closer to the notion of discriminability of stimulus items is Thorndike's *Law of*

Identifiability, which states that "connections are easy to form in proportion as the situation is identifiable, distinguishable from others ..." (40, p. 87). In general, these laws seem to name results, rather than to form a coherent and interrelated system.

Explanation of Terms

The following terms are crucial to the hypothesis and are consequently explained in some detail. Illustrations will be presented when necessary.

1. *Generalization:* the tendency for a response R_a learned to S_a to occur when S_b (with which it has not been previously associated) is presented.[3] A *generalization gradient* is said to be formed when a number of stimulus items show decreasing degrees of generalization with a given standard stimulus. The hypothesis need make no assumption as to the type of stimulus continuum which will yield a generalization gradient, but it is consistent with it to suppose that such a gradient will be yielded by a group of stimuli which can be arranged along *any dimension or scale* with respect to the presence of some discriminable quality or aspect—in other words, stimuli which would be considered to vary in degree of *similarity.* Experimental evidence proves that not only simple dimensions such as pitch and intensity (11, 12) yield generalization gradients. Yum (44) found that when nonsense syllables, words, or visual patterns were stimuli in a learning series, different but similar stimulus items would in a test series elicit the responses learned, the strength of the tendency varying with the degree of similarity between test item and original stimulus item; and Gulliksen (10) found that similarity of test figures to a training figure correlated significantly with tendency to give the training figure's response. Razran (34) has recently demonstrated generalization on the basis of synonymity of words.

2. *Multiple generalization:* the tendency for responses which are being learned to members of a *series* of stimulus items to occur as generalized responses to members other than their "right" associate. The situation employed in Yum's experiment (44) was such as to yield multiple generalization. Gulliksen's experiment (10) provides a transition between simple generalization and multiple generalization, since a choice between two antagonistic responses, each of which had been learned to a standard stimulus, was possible.

3. *Right response:* the response paired with a particular stimulus item in a list presented by the paired associates method, or the response immediately following a particular stimulus item in a list presented by the anticipation method.

4. *Learning:* a list is said to be completely learned when the right response item is given in each case upon presentation of the stimulus item. A given *degree of learning* or criterion of learning means that a certain percentage of right responses is reproduced upon presentation of the stimulus items.

5. *Differentiation:* a progressive decrease in generalization as a result of reinforced practice with $S_a \rightarrow R_a$ and unreinforced presentation of S_b.

6. *Reinforcement:* a process which occurs during verbal learning when a subject sees a response as he anticipated it and thinks "that's right." Differential reinforcement designates the situation wherein a right response is reinforced and a generalized response is not reinforced.

7. *Excitatory tendency:* tendency for a particular stimulus to evoke a particular response in a degree greater than zero.

8. *Meaning:* a characteristic of a verbal or visual item which serves to differentiate it from other items.

Statement of Postulates

A number of postulates are basic to the hypothesis and should be made evident at the outset. In some cases these principles have been empirically demonstrated in the conditioned response situation; in other cases they are incapable of empirical demonstration, and must rest on confirmation of the relationships which they predict in combination.

1. When lists are learned by a paired associates or anticipation method, S-R connections are set up between certain of the items (between members of a pair in paired associates, and one and the next in the anticipation method).

2. If there is a right excitatory tendency and also a generalized one between the same S and R, the resultant excitatory tendency will be stronger than either one alone; if a right excitatory tendency and a generalized one are aroused by the same S but lead to different R's, they will interfere, the weaker tending to block the stronger in proportion to the strength of the weaker.

3. Stimulus items which generalize when presented for learning in a single list will also do so when they are presented in the form of two lists, and with the same *relative* degree of generalization.

4. Generalization will increase to a maximum or peak during the early stages of practice with a list, after which it will decrease as practice is continued. (This assumption has been confirmed by the author in an experiment to be reported, 7.)

5. In list-learning, all decrease in generalization is due to differential reinforcement.[4]

6. The amount of reinforcement required to reduce a generalizing tendency to a given strength will increase with increasing strength of the generalizing tendency. (This postulate is an "empirical" one, in the sense that it has often been demonstrated in the conditioned response situation, 33.)

7. After the cessation of practice, differentiation will decrease over a period of time, leading to an increase ("spontaneous recovery") of generalization. (This, again, is an "empirical" postulate, 13, 33.)

8. Spontaneous recovery will occur more slowly, the more differential reinforcement has been applied. (Demonstrated in the conditioned response situation, 33.)

9. If differentiation has been set up among a number of stimulus items, it will be easier to differentiate them again later, even though they are paired with different overt responses than those learned when the original differentiation was set up. (This assumption might be called "transfer of differentiation.")

10. If differentiation has been set up among a number of stimulus items, there will be less tendency for them to generalize with new stimulus items or for new stimulus items to generalize with them, the decrease in generalization being proportional to the amount of differential reinforcement given. (Analogous to this are the cases reported in Pavlov (33), of dogs who, having once learned to differentiate a circle from an ellipse, found it easier to differentiate between the circle and other ellipses of different ratio. A common sense analogy would be the case of a child who, after at first generalizing all the animals he sees, learns that cats are not dogs; after this, he does not have equal trouble in learning that rabbits are not dogs. He would not have to see every animal in the world in order to differentiate dogs from other animals.)

Some Propositions that Follow from the Hypothesis

A number of propositions which may be predicted from the hypothesis just presented will be stated. These will not be formally derived in the strictest logical sense, but for each one the argument will be indicated as clearly as possible, with reference to the definitions and postulates on which it depends. Examples will follow the argument when any clarification seems necessary, and evidence for or against the proposition will be reported. In some cases, the propositions are familiar facts of verbal learning. For the convenience of the reader, the propositions will be given titles and grouped under traditional headings.

Similarity

Similarity will be considered, in the present instance, as that relationship between stimulus items which can be indicated and measured in terms of their *tendency to generalize*. A priori, this is a reasonable criterion of similarity, since a group of stimuli among which generalization occurs would, according to usual standards, be considered similar (e.g., a series of tones, or of spots along the fore-leg). Yum (44) found that judges' ratings of perceptual similarity of visual patterns and synonyms to their respective standards coincided with the degree to which the forms or synonyms were capable of producing a response originally learned to the standard. Furthermore, it seems obvious that a common way of speaking of similarity is in terms of discriminability, or tendency *not* to generalize.

A complication in terminology is introduced by the fact that generalization will vary with other factors than "original" generalization tendency. As has already been pointed out, it will vary also with degree of learning and with the time interval since learning was left off. These two factors are in a sense secondary determiners of degree of generalization, and "original" generalization tendency" will be used therefore to denote the degree of generalization apparent before differentiation has been set up through differential reinforcement. Under the heading of "similarity," then, will be included propositions which have as their major variable the degree of original generalization of stimulus items.

I. *Intra-List Transfer and Concept Formation*

> If multiple generalization occurs during the learning of a list, and if the list is constituted so that the generalizing stimulus items are paired with the same responses, learning should be easier in proportion to the degree of generalization.

The argument for this proposition would be as follows: Suppose that a list is to be learned in which multiple generalization may occur, and suppose that those stimulus items which are similar (i.e., generalize to a high degree) actually have the *same* responses to be learned to them. The generalizing excitatory tendency and the right excitatory tendency, in this case, will coincide. According to postulate 2, if there is a right excitatory tendency and a generalized one between the same S and R, the resultant excitatory tendency will be stronger than either one alone. Now, according to the definition of generalization, generalization may exist in different degrees, so that the aggregate generalization in a list may vary from low to high. Then, in the present case, the higher the degree of generalization in the list, the stronger will be the resultant excitatory tendencies after the same amount of practice, and the easier will be the learning.

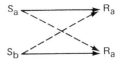

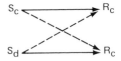

Figure 4.4

An example of such a list is presented in Fig. 4.4. As the broken arrows indicate, items S_a and S_b generalize, and items S_c and S_d generalize; and both items of a pair have the same response. The higher the degree of generalization between the groups of items having the same response, the easier the list will be to learn. The important thing about this situation is that the arrangement is the one commonly employed in studying concept formation, which suggests that the process called concept formation is related to the process of verbal learning, since both depend upon differentiation and generalization. Since control lists where little generalization occurs are not usually included in concept experiments, the above prediction has not been checked.

II. *Inter-List Transfer*

If generalization occurs from a first list to a second list, and if the generalizing items have the same responses, list 2 will be easier to learn as the degree of generalization between the two lists increases.

Suppose that a list 1 of paired associates is to be followed by a list 2 so constituted that generalization occurs from list 1 to list 2. It is assumed (postulate 3) that stimulus items which generalize when presented for learning in a single list will also so do when they are presented in the form of two lists, and with the same relative degree of generalization. Now suppose further that the generalizing items in the two lists have the same responses. The reasoning given for the above proposition will then apply, and the greater the degree of generalization, the easier list 2 will be to learn.

An example of this situation, obviously a transfer one, is given in Fig. 4.5. The broken arrows in list 2 represent generalizing tendencies from list 1. But since the generalizing and the right responses coincide, positive transfer should result. It must not be forgotten that internal generalization

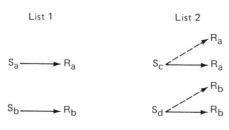

List 1   List 2

$S_a \longrightarrow R_a$ $S_c \rightleftarrows \begin{matrix} R_a \\ R_a \end{matrix}$

$S_b \longrightarrow R_b$ $S_d \rightleftarrows \begin{matrix} R_b \\ R_b \end{matrix}$

Figure 4.5

will also occur to some extent in both lists; but it should not interfere with the transfer, since a control group learning merely list 2 would have the same internal generalization to contend with, and would only lack the beneficial generalization from list 1.

No evidence obtained under these precise conditions is available, but an experiment of Bruce's (3) is relevant. He found positive transfer when the responses of two lists were the same, and the stimulus items very similar (two letters in common). Less transfer occurred when stimulus items had no letters in common.

III. Retroactive Facilitation

If generalization occurs between two lists, and if the generalizing items have the same responses, recall or relearning of list 1 will be facilitated as the degree of generalization between the two lists increases.

The situation is essentially that described in the above proposition, except that retention of list 1 is to be tested following the learning of list 2. The argument above will apply.

This situation might be dubbed *retroactive facilitation* (Fig. 4.6). Retention of list 1 should be facilitated increasingly as generalization between the two lists increases, since learning list 2 should strengthen proportionally the excitatory tendencies already developed in learning list 1.

A retroaction experiment by Bunch and Winston (4) contained one condition in which response syllables from the first list were retained intact in the second, while the stimulus syllables were different. Inhibition, rather than facilitation, resulted during recall and relearning of list 1. This evidence is apparently not in harmony with the present theory. But degree of generalization of stimulus members was not varied or specified. A further test should be made where the stimuli are quantified according to generalizing tendency, so that several degrees of inter-list generalization may be employed. Relative degree of facilitation would be expected to follow the above prediction.

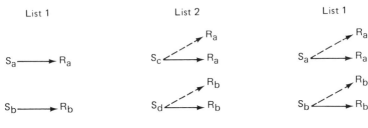

Figure 4.6

IV. Intra-List Interference or Difficulty of Learning Homogeneous Lists

If multiple generalization occurs during the learning of a list, and if the list is constituted so that the generalizing items have different responses, an increasing number of repetitions will be required to reach a given criterion of learning as the strength of the generalizing tendencies increases.[5]

Suppose that a list in which multiple generalization may occur is so constituted that the generalizing stimulus items have different responses. The generalizing excitatory tendency, and the right excitatory tendency, in this situation, will conflict (see Fig. 4.1). Two cases requiring slightly different arguments may result.

Case 1: If, in the above situation, the generalizing tendency is stronger than the right excitatory tendency after a few repetitions, it is obvious that the generalizing tendency will have to be reduced in strength, since learning is defined as giving the right response., But a decrease in generalization must be obtained through differential reinforcement (postulate 5), and the amount of reinforcement required to reduce any generalizing tendency to a given strength will increase with increasing strength of the generalizing tendency (postulate 6). Therefore, in this case, an increasing number of repetitions will be required to reach a criterion such as complete learning as the strength of the generalizing tendency increases.

Case 2: If, in the same situation, the right excitatory tendency is the stronger tendency after a few repetitions, it is nevertheless weakened in proportion to the strength of the generalizing tendency (postulate 2). By postulates 5 and 6, it is clear that an increasing number of repetitions will in this case also be required to reach a given criterion of learning, as the strength of the generalizing tendency increases.

In a list of the sort described, every right excitatory tendency will be interfered with more or less, according to either case 1 or case 2. Therefore, putting these two cases together, it may be said that an increasing number of repetitions of the list will be required as the strength of the generalizing tendencies within it increases.

This prediction is checked in detail in an experiment done by the writer (7), in which the lists compared are quantified according to degree of generalization. The evidence is conclusively positive. In so far as the generalizing tendencies are actually stronger than the right excitatory tendencies and above threshold strength, overt errors of confusion should occur during the learning. These did occur in the experiment reported, and with a much higher frequency in the higher-generalization series.

V. *Retention of Homogeneous Lists*

Difficulty in recalling or relearning a list will be proportional to the degree of original generalization, if time has been allowed for spontaneous recovery to occur.

In a situation similar to the one described above, the differentiation which was established during learning will decrease over a period of time, leading to "spontaneous recovery" of the generalization (postulate 7). The generalizing tendencies will again interfere with the right excitatory tendencies, in proportion to their strength (postulate 2), so that retention will be impaired in proportion to the degree of original generalization.

Positive evidence for this prediction may be found also in the writer's experiment (7). Retention of high-generalization lists was poorer than retention of low-generalization lists after one day, even though the former lists were given more than twice as many learning repetitions.

VI. *Learning of "Isolated" Items*

A stimulus-response pair which is a member of a list containing other stimulus items having a strong tendency to generalize with it will require more repetitions to be learned than would the same pair as a member of a list whose stimulus items have a low tendency to generalize with it.

This prediction is a special case covered by the argument under proposition IV. It has been stated separately, because the situation as put in the above prediction was the subject of an experiment by von Restorff (35). She presented to subjects series of paired associates which contained a high proportion of homogeneous items and a small proportion of items of other types. Items were always remembered better when they were "isolated" than when they were members of a homogeneous group within the list; the list was given the same number of repetitions in the two cases. The prediction was confirmed in an experiment of the writer's (7) exactly as it is stated in this proposition.

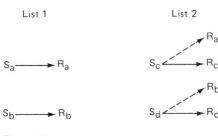

Figure 4.7

VII. *Inter-List Interference as a Function of Similarity*

More repetitions will be required to learn a second list, in proportion to the strength of the tendency for items of a first list to generalize with the items of the second list.

Suppose that generalization occurs from a first list to a second list, as provided for in postulate 3, and as illustrated in Fig. 4.7. As these lists are constituted, the right response to any stimulus will conflict with any generalized response, since the responses are all different. Now, as list 2 is being learned, responses from list 1 will tend to occur to stimulus items in list 2 by generalization. According to postulate 2, the right excitatory tendency will be weakened in proportion to the strength of the generalizing tendencies. Generalization can be decreased only through differential reinforcement (postulate 5) and the amount of reinforcement required to reduce any generalizing tendency to a given strength will increase with increasing strength of the generalizing tendency (postulate 6). Therefore, as strength of generalization from the first list to the second list increases, more repetitions will be required to learn list 2.

Internal generalization will also occur as list 2 is being learned, but the prediction as made above will not be affected, since this factor may remain constant as generalization from list 1 to list 2 is increased. The situation described is the one known variously as proactive inhibition, interference, or negative transfer. Naturally, errors of reversion to list 1 should be apparent during the learning of list 2. An experiment done by the writer (8) demonstrated that list 2 required more trials to learn as degree of generalization between the stimulus items of the two lists increased. Also, the expected type of error occurred.

VIII. *Interference Measured by Recall*

A second list will be more poorly recalled after a period of time, in proportion to the strength of the tendency for items of list 1 to generalize with it.

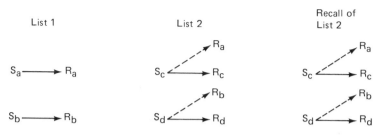

Figure 4.8

Suppose that generalization occurs from a first list to a second list as in the above case, but that list 2 has been learned to some criterion (Fig. 4.8). It has been demonstrated in the above argument that list 2 will require more trials to learn as generalization from list 1 to list 2 increases. As learning goes on, differentiation between the items is established. But if an interval of time is allowed to elapse after practice has been discontinued, spontaneous recovery of the generalization will occur (postulate 7), so that recall should be impaired in proportion to the strength of the generalization from list 1 to list 2.

This prediction amounts to saying that interference as a function of generalization can be measured equally as well by a recall test of list 2 as by a learning measure. Whitely and Blankenship (43) used this measure to demonstrate interference in recall of a second list when the material learned consisted of monosyllabic words preceded in the first list by other such words or by nonsense syllables. The method of complete presentation was employed. Probably an even higher degree of interference would have been obtained had greater inter-list generalization been present (e.g., had both lists been made up of nonsense syllables).

IX. *Retroactive Inhibition and Similarity*

A first list will be more poorly recalled as the strength of the tendency for items of a second list to generalize with it increases.

Suppose that a first list has been learned, and has been followed by a second list whose stimulus items potentially generalize with list 1. It is assumed that list 2 has been learned to some criterion. Now suppose that a recall of list 1 is asked for. When the stimulus items of list 1 are again presented responses from list 2 will tend to occur by generalization (see Fig. 4.2). According to postulate 2, the right excitatory tendencies will be weakened in proportion to the strength of the generalizing tendencies. Therefore, the recall of list 1 should suffer in proportion to the strength of the tendency for items of list 2 to generalize with it.[6]

The situation described is of course the one which results in "retroactive inhibition." It is an accepted fact that retroactive inhibition is a function of similarity of original and interpolated tasks (see Britt, 2, p. 389 ff.). However, degree of similarity has usually been estimated on an *a priori* basis. An experiment by the writer (8) has checked the prediction that a generalization gradient will correspond with a gradient of retroactive inhibition.

Degree of Learning

X. *Interference and Degree of Learning*

> *Difficulty of learning a second list will vary with the degree of learning of the preceding list, increasing to a peak and then decreasing as degree of learning of list 1 increases.*

Suppose that two lists, the items of which tend to generalize with one another, are to be learned in immediate succession. The tendency for items in the first list to generalize will *increase* to a maximum during the early stages of practice of the list, but from this point on, the tendency to generalize will *decrease* (postulate 4). Now a second list will be harder to learn as the strength of the tendency for items of list 1 to generalize with it increases (proposition VII), so that difficulty of learning list 2 should

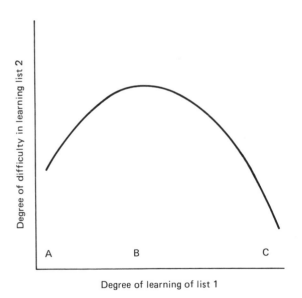

Degree of learning of list 1

Figure 4.9

increase with the practice of list 1 up to the point of maximum generalization. But as the stage of learning of list 1 passes this point, differentiation begins, and postulate 10 will apply—if differentiation has been set up in list 1, there will be less tendency for its members to generalize with list 2, the decrease in generalization being proportional to the amount of reinforcement given. Therefore, the difficulty of learning list 2 will *decrease* as differentiation in list 1 is carried further.

A theoretical curve of difficulty in learning list 2 as a function of degree of learning of list 1 is plotted in Fig. 4.9. The prediction assumes that learning of the second list is begun soon after cessation of practice on the first list. In the curve, the early increase in difficulty due to increasing generalization is represented by the rise from *A* to *B*, and the later decrease, due to increasing differentiation, is represented by the fall from *B* to *C*. The curve is drawn to show a sharp rise from *A* to *B* and a positively accelerated drop from *B* to *C*, since an experiment of the author's (7) demonstrated a curve of this sort for intra-list generalization during the progress of learning.

No check of this prediction is available, since the experiments in the field (18, 3) have used identical, rather than generalizing stimulus members in the two lists.

XI. *Retroaction as a Function of Degree of Interpolated Learning*

Retroactive inhibition for a list 1 will increase to a maximum and then decrease as degree of learning of an interpolated list 2 increases.

Suppose that two lists, having generalizing stimulus items, are to be learned in immediate succession, and that recall of list 1 is then to be tested. If degree of learning of list 1 is kept constant, and if degree of learning of list 2 is varied, retroactive inhibition in recalling and relearning list 1 should increase with practice of list 2 up to the point of maximum generalization, and then decrease as the degree of learning of list 2 increases. The argument is the same as that given in proposition X.

The point of maximum generalization in this situation will come earlier or later depending on how well list 1 has been learned, and on time-intervals, so that an accurate theoretical curve cannot be drawn. But in any case, the inflection predicted above should occur. McGeoch (23) has confirmed the first half of this prediction; and there is some indication that the second half might have been upheld had degree of interpolated learning been carried higher, since retroaction did not increase with degree of learning beyond the point at which the degree of learning of lists 1 and 2 was equal. Melton and McQueen-Irwin (29) definitely find the inflection.

XII. *Retroaction as a Function of Degree of Original Learning*

Retroactive inhibition for a list 1 will decrease as degree of original learning of the list is increased beyond the point of maximum generalization.

Suppose that two lists, having generalizing stimulus items, are to be learned in immediate succession and that recall of list 1 is then to be tested; degree of learning of list 2 is to be kept constant while degree of learning of list 1 is varied. Now, the initial *increase* in generalization as list 1 is given more practice will cause no corresponding increase in retroactive inhibition in this situation, because the *effective* generalization caused by this increase will be from list 1 to list 2 rather than from list 2 to list 1 (i.e., wrong responses will tend increasingly to occur in list 2, but list 1 will not become more susceptible to generalization of responses from list 2, because degree of learning in that list remains constant). On the other hand, differentiation in list 1 will increase with degree of learning after the peak of generalization has been reached (postulate 4); and if differentiation has been set up among a number of stimulus items (in list 1, here), there will be less tendency for new stimulus items (from list 2, here) to generalize with them, the decrease in generalization being proportional to the amount of reinforcement given (postulate 10). Since also retroactive inhibition is proportional to the strength of the tendency for members of list 2 to generalize with members of list 1 (proposition IX), it follows that retroactive inhibition will decrease as degree of learning of list 1 is carried beyond the peak of generalization.

McGeoch (22) has shown that degree of retroactive inhibition varies inversely with degree of learning of the first list, when the lists are made up of nonsense syllables and learned by the anticipation method.

Length of Interval

Many predictions can be made with reference to the effect of varying the length of the interval between learning and recall of a list, or between a first list and a second. Only a few of the predictions will be included here as examples.[7] These predictions depend principally on the notion of spontaneous recovery of generalization. But since the rate of spontaneous recovery will vary with the amount of differential reinforcement which has been applied, the predictions must always be stated in terms of two variables—length of the interval and amount of reinforcement or, roughly, degree of learning.

XIII. *Interference as a Function of Length of Interval Between Tasks*

The interval after which a list 2 must be introduced in order to obtain the maximum interference in learning it will vary with the degree of learning of list 1, being zero if degree of learning has been carried only as far as the peak of generalization or below, and thereafter occurring the later, the higher the degree of learning of list 1.

Suppose that two lists are to be learned, and that there is potential generalization of the items of the two lists. Now, if learning of list 1 is carried only to the point of maximum generalization, or below, maximum interference with list 2 will occur *immediately,* since there can in this case be no recovery of generalization in list 1, and since, according to proposition VII, interference will be proportional to the degree of generalization.

On the other hand, suppose that learning of list 1 is carried beyond the peak of generalization. Differentiation will increase as practice is continued beyond this point (postulate 4), and differentiation will protect the items from generalizing with a new list (postulate 10) in proportion to the amount of differential reinforcement given. But spontaneous recovery of the generalization will eventually occur (postulate 7). It will occur more slowly, the more differential reinforcement has been applied (postulate 8). So, the farther differential reinforcement has been carried, the later the maximum interference will occur.

Figure 4.10 shows the theoretical relationship. Maximum interference in learning list 2 will be obtained if it is introduced at once, when the first list has been learned only to the peak of generalization or below; the curve of interference would probably fall off, then, as the interval increases. But if

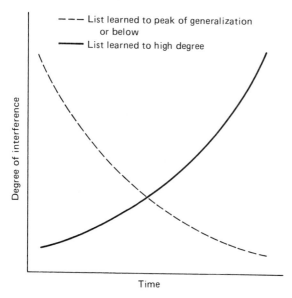

Figure 4.10

list 1 has been learned to a high degree, little interference would occur at once, but rather would be postponed until spontaneous recovery of the generalization occurred; it might then fall off again. The rate of rise and fall represented in the curves is perfectly arbitrary, since it depends on the rate at which spontaneous recovery occurs and the rate at which generalization tendencies are forgotten, and quantitative values for these factors can only be determined experimentally. No thorough test of these predictions exists, but an experiment of Lepley's (21) indicates that, with a high degree of learning, interference will increase to a maximum, and then decrease as the interval between list 1 and list 2 increases. This result is consistent with the second half of the above prediction. Under the conditions of Lepley's experiment, the peak of interference came at about 3 hours. In a more recent experiment by Bunch and McCraven (5), no tendency was found for the degree of transfer to change with varying length of interval, although syllable lists were learned to a high degree; but no tests were made between the zero interval and 48 hours, so that there is really no conflict with Lepley's results.[8]

XIV. *Retroaction as a Function of Interval between Tasks*

The interval after which maximum retroactive inhibition will occur for a list 1 will vary with the degree of learning of list 2, being zero if degree of learning of list 2 has been carried only as far as the peak of generalization or below, and thereafter occurring the later, the higher the degree of learning of list 2.

Suppose that two lists are to be learned in immediate succession, and that there is potential generalization between the two lists; and that retention of list 1 is to be tested after a variable interval. If the degree of learning of list 2 is low (reaching the peak of generalization or below) maximum retroactive inhibition should occur immediately, by the argument in proposition XIII above. But if the degree of learning of list 2 is high, maximum retroactive inhibition should occur later, again following the argument in proposition XIII.

A similar prediction can be made if the degree of learning of list 1 is varied, instead of list 2. No test of the temporal course of retroactive inhibition as a function of the degree of learning of the two lists has been made. But McGeoch (24, 25) and McGeoch and McKinney (26, 27) have investigated the course of inhibitory effects with time, and have not found a consistent tendency for retroaction to vary with time. Two of their experiments gave some indication of an increase of retroaction with lengthening of the interval, one showed no tendency for retroactive inhibition to vary uniformly in any direction, and a fourth showed a slight tendency for retroactive inhibition to decrease with time. Different materials, learning methods, and degrees of learning were employed in these experiments. The apparent inconsistency of the results points to the need for a further experiment in which temporal course of retroactive inhibition is studied in relation to degree of learning.

On the basis of this proposition, and assuming a constant interval between learning list 1 and recalling it, it is possible to make predictions for the well-known "point of interpolation" problem, with retroactive inhibition as a function of both interval and degree of learning (9). Results from a number of experiments on this problem are superficially conflicting (2, 399 ff.; 38). High degrees of retroactive inhibition have been obtained by one investigator or another with the second list interpolated at almost any point in the interval between learning and recall of list I. The discrepancy may be due, among other things, to the variable degrees of learning employed in different experiments on point of interpolation. The expectation will vary, depending on whether learning is carried to a low or a high degree.

Meaningful versus Nonsense Material

This group of predictions is related to the rest of the hypothesis through the definition of *meaning* which we have accepted. Meaning has been defined as one characteristic of a verbal or visual item which serves to *differentiate* it from other items—in other words, generalization is at a minimum for meaningful material, unless it occurs on a secondary basis, as in the case of synonyms (34). Proposition XV is included here because the pattern of the argument is similar to that in the predictions actually dealing with meaningful material.

XV. *Learning of Pre-differentiated Items*

If differentiation has been set up within a list, less generalization will occur in learning a new list which includes the same stimulus items paired with different responses; and the trials required to learn the new list will tend to be reduced by reduction of the internal generalization.

Suppose that a list 1 has been learned, and is followed by a list 2 whose stimulus items are the same as those in list 1, although the responses are different. Less total intra-list generalization should occur in learning list 2 than in list 1, because if differentiation has been set up among a number of stimulus items, it will be easier to differentiate them again later, even though they are paired with different responses (postulate 9). Furthermore, since the number of trials required to learn a list increases as the degree of

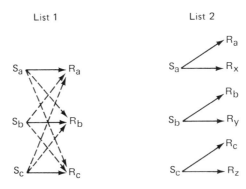

List 1   List 2

Figure 4.11

generalization within the list increases, the decrease of generalization in list 2 should tend to reduce the number of learning trials.

A clear case cannot be made for the second half of the above prediction, because a new factor, inter-list conflict of responses, is present in list 2 as well as reduced intra-list conflict. Figure 4.11 shows the original generalizing tendencies in list 1; these have been successfully inhibited before list 2 is undertaken. Therefore, no generalizing tendencies are represented in list 2; but tendencies for the stimuli to excite their first-learned responses as well as the new ones are represented in list 2. A control group which learned only list 2 would have the generalizing tendencies (as represented in list 1) to contend with, but inter-list conflict would be absent. It is impossible to say whether number of learning trials would be actually reduced in the case represented, without knowing quantitative weights of the two factors. The facilitating effect of reduction of generalization within the list would be pitted against "associative inhibition," to use the traditional name for conflict of learned responses to the same stimulus.

The first half of the prediction can be verified by comparing the number of cases of overt generalization (confusion errors) in the first and second lists. A reduction in such errors was found in an experiment of the writer's (8).

XVI. *Ease of Learning Meaningful Lists*

More trials will be required to learn a list in which the stimulus items are nonsense syllables, than one in which they are meaningful words.[9]

Suppose that two lists are to be learned which vary only in that the stimulus items of one list are meaningful words, while those of the other list are nonsense syllables, or relatively meaningless. According to definition 8, meaning is a characteristic of a verbal or visual item which serves to differentiate it from other items. Furthermore, if stimulus items have once been differentiated, it will be easier to differentiate them again later, even though they are paired with different responses than those learned when the original differentiation was set up (postulate 9). Therefore, more generalization will tend to occur in the list whose stimulus items are less meaningful; and since as the degree of generalization within a list is increased, more trials are required to learn the list (proposition IV), more trials will be required to learn the list whose stimulus items are less meaningful.

The fact that a list of meaningful words is easier to learn than one made up of nonsense syllables is notorious, and it seems certain that a check of the situation described above would yield positive results.

XVII. *Interference and Meaningfulness*

More trials will be required to learn a second list when the stimulus items of both first and second list are nonsense syllables, than when they are meaningful words.

Suppose that a second list is to be learned following a first list, and that ease of learning list 2 is to be compared when stimulus items of both lists are nonsense syllables, or relatively meaningless, with the case when stimulus items of both are meaningful words. In the former case, generalization from list 1 to list 2 should be greater than in the latter, since meaning serves to differentiate the items. And since more trials will be required to learn a second list in proportion to the strength of the tendency for items of a first list to generalize with it, more learning trials will be required when the stimulus items are relatively meaningless.

In a check of this prediction, it would be necessary to prevent such factors as overlearning in the nonsense syllable situation from cutting across the main variable (relative meaningfulness) and confusing the issue. If learning were carried to a criterion, many more trials would presumably be given the first list when stimulus items were meaningless, thus introducing a second variable, and incidentally tending to even up the two situations as regards degree of differentiation reached in the first list. This difficulty might be avoided by delaying presentation of list 2 for a length of time sufficient for spontaneous recovery to occur. Also, comparisons should in each case be made with control groups which have learned only list 2, but are otherwise identical with the experimental situations described, since list 2 would presumably be harder to learn when stimuli were nonsense syllables, even in the absence of list 1. Degree of relative negative transfer would be calculated separately for the two situations, and then compared.

XVIII. *Retroaction and Meaningfulness*

> *Retroactive inhibition will be greater for a first list when the stimulus items of both first and second list are nonsense syllables than when they are meaningful words.*

Suppose that retention of a first list is to be tested after interpolation of a second list in two cases: one, when stimulus items of both lists are nonsense syllables; and two, when stimulus items of both are meaningful words. More retroactive inhibition would be expected in the first case, by an argument similar to the one above.

Again, a number of variables other than the crucial one will tend to cut across the experimental situation, and it would be absolutely essential in a test of the prediction to provide control groups in which interpolated learning was omitted, so that actual percentages of retroactive inhibition could be calculated for the two cases. In an experiment by Sisson (37), retention was compared for list 1 when both lists were made of syllables of 100 percent associative value with a case in which both contained only syllables of 0 percent associative value. Presumably, a higher associative value is correlated with greater meaningfulness of the item. Sisson found slightly poorer retention in the first case; but percentages of retroactive inhibition could not be calculated, since no control groups were provided. More learning presentations were given 0 per cent lists, since a learning criterion was used. Time intervals between tasks were brief. This experiment should be repeated with adequate control groups, since it has certainly been generally assumed by investigators that the surest and highest percentages of retroaction are to be found with nonsense material.[10]

Possible Extensions of the Hypothesis

It has been possible to present only a sample of the predictions and implications of the hypothesis advanced. Many extensions may be made, especially if one or two new postulates are added. Among the potential extensions is a group of predictions involving various phenomena relating to overlearning. These predictions require a definition of overlearning, as well as the new assumption that the *variability* of trials needed to learn individual items will increase with aggregate generalization. Six or more predictions follow, among them these: increase of overlearning with greater generalization; later maximal loss as a result of high generalization; various length-of-list phenomena, such as decrease in retroaction with increasing length of list; decrease of retroaction as generalization *within* a first list increases.

If a postulate concerning "disinhibition" is added, a number of predictions regarding the effect of shock or distraction in learning and retroaction situations will follow. A further group of predictions ensue if an assumption regarding the effects of caffeine be included. These particular extensions have been mentioned, because they have been worked out in (9).

Evaluation

A hypothesis relating certain facts of verbal learning to the more general concepts of differentiation and generalization has been presented. Following this, a number of propositions dependent on the hypothesis were outlined in some detail. Since the potential number of deductions from a hypothesis may be almost infinite, it does not constitute a perfect evaluation of that hypothesis to calculate the percentage of verified propositions which have been shown to follow from it. Yet, it is certainly of interest to examine the evidence so far obtained, since negative results, at least, are a good indication that something is wrong. Where evidence relevant to the proposition was available, it has been referred to already. To summarize, conclusive positive evidence exists for eight of the propositions presented; some positive evidence exists for four others, though not conclusive; no evidence exists for four; and for the other two, the existing evidence is conflicting and not entirely relevant. In other words, none of these propositions has been shown to be false. Furthermore, of the propositions which have been worked out but not included here, none has been shown to be false.

A hypothesis may well be evaluated with reference to its scope, also —and in this connection, the types of learning phenomena which the hypothesis is not adapted to explain, as well as those which it can handle well, should be mentioned. Obviously, the hypothesis is framed to deal with that aspect of verbal learning in which development of discrimination between items is vital; and it is limited to a stimulus-response type of analysis. Facts relating to various types of transfer-effect, both intra-list and inter-list, constitute its principal applications. Many other facts of verbal learning are not predictable from the hypothesis as it stands. A number of these facts (serial position effects, reminiscence, etc.) can probably best be subsumed under a hypothesis which develops the implications of the *in-hibitory* aspects of mechanisms postulated as basic to learning, and the present hypothesis has left unexplored such possibilities.[11] Other facts of verbal learning not subsumed by the present hypothesis would be facts of recognition-memory, and memory "changes." Here a perceptual analysis, perhaps of the type made by the Gestalt psychologists (19, 20, 32) might be more profitable than a stimulus-response analysis. It may be that the problems of verbal learning must be approached from both these angles, at the present time at least. In spite of these limitations, the writer feels that the range of the present hypothesis is satisfactory, since no more comprehensive theory centered around those problems of learning which are broadly classifiable as "transfer" phenomena seems to have been proposed. The value of emphasizing discrimination as a factor in verbal learning seems unquestionable; and that generalization and differentiation are concepts suitable for its systematic development seems almost as likely.

Notes

1. This article is a part of a dissertation presented to the Faculty of Yale University in partial fulfillment of the requirements for the Ph.D. degree. The writer wishes to express thanks to Professor Clark Hull for his advice and assistance.

2. The term *differentiation* will be used in place of *differential inhibition*, since the term "inhibition" implies a theory of differentiation which the present hypothesis need not assume.

3. It will be noted that this definition makes no reference to nervous processes or to any physiological explanation. This usage is in accordance with that followed by Bass and Hull (1) and Hull (16). That generalization will occur with voluntary verbal responses in the form of a typical generalization gradient has been demonstrated by Gibson (6).

4. There is a possibility that a slight increase in specificity might be obtained by pure practice of a single connection. This possibility has not been included in the present system because the great overelaboration necessary would be out of proportion to the importance of the possibility.

5. From this point on, it will be assumed that the generalizing stimulus items have different responses, and the assumption will not be specifically mentioned.

6. There is a further possibility of explaining a decrement in recall of list 1. As list 2 is learned, items from list 1 tend to occur, and must be differentiated from the list 2 items. Suppose that this differentiation actually involves *inhibition* of the generalized responses. Then the more list 1 tends to generalize with list 2, the more items from list 1 will be inhibited. When list 1 is returned to, not only will list 2 items tend to occur by generalization, but also there will be spread of inhibition for the responses of list 1—in this case, the desired responses. Whether this possibility should be taken seriously depends partly on whether generalization of responses from list 2 is sufficient to account for the loss. A comparison of the loss in this situation with that in the situation described in proposition VIII should be relevant, for in that situation there could be no added inhibition with which to reckon. If recall of list 2 is not as poor as recall of list 1 after the same interval, then some further factor such as inhibition must be at work in the present situation.

7. For others, see dissertation on file in Yale University Library (9).

8. In Bunch and McCraven's experiment, the total transfer effect was positive; this would not, however, prevent relative degrees of interference from showing up.

9. An exception to this prediction should be a case in which the stimulus items are *mutually synonymous* meaningful words. This situation has actually been shown, in the Smith College Laboratory, to increase learning difficulty as compared with unrelated stimulus words.

10. If the material is really highly differentiated, being not only meaningful words, but, furthermore, words making up prose passages or poerty, rather small percentages of retroaction are apt to be obtained (26, 27).

11. The "Lepley hypothesis" (21, 14) covers some of these facts by exploitation of a postulated "inhibition of delay."

Bibliography

1. Bass, M. J., & Hull, C. L. The irradiation of a tactile conditioned reflex in man *J. comp. Psychol.*, 1934, 17, 47–65.
2. Britt, S. H. Retroactive inhibition: a review of the literature. *Psychol. Bull.*, 1935, 32, 381–440.
3. Bruce, R. W. Conditions of transfer of training. *J. exper. Psychol.*, 1933, 16, 343–361.
4. Bunch, M. E., & Winston, M. M. The relationship between the character of the transfer and retroactive inhibition. *Amer. J. Psychol.*, 1936, 48, 598–608.
5. ———, & McCraven, V. G. The temporal course of transfer in the learning of memory material. *J. comp. Psychol.*, 1938, 25, 481–496.
6. Gibson, E. J. Sensory generalization with voluntary reactions. *J. exper. Psychol.*, 1939, 24, 237–253.
7. ———. Intra-list generalization as a factor in verbal learning Manuscript in preparation.
8. ———. Retroactive inhibition as a function of degree of generalization. Manuscript in preparation.
9. ———. A systematic application of the concepts of generalization and differentiation to verbal learning. Doctor's Thesis, Yale University, 1938.
10. Gulliksen, H. Transfer of response in human subjects. *J. exper. Psychol.*, 1932, 15, 496–516.
11. Hovland, C. I. The generalization of conditioned responses: I. The sensory generalization of conditioned responses with varying frequencies of tone. *J. gen. Psychol.*, 1937, 17, 125–148.
12. ———. The generalization of conditioned responses: II. The sensory generalization of conditioned responses with varying intensities of tone. *J. genet. Psychol.*, 1937, 51, 279–291.
13. ———. The generalization of conditioned responses. III. Extinction, spontaneous recovery, and disinhibition of conditioned and of generalized responses. *J. exper. Psychol.*, 1937, 21, 47–62.
14. Hull, C. L. The conflicting psychologies of learning—a way out. Psychol. Rev., 1935, 42, 491–516.
15. ———. Mind, mechanism, and adaptive behavior. Psychol. Rev., 1937, 44, 1–32.
16. ———. The problem of stimulus equivalence in behavior theory. Psychol. Rev., 1939, 46, 9–30.
17. James, H. E. O. The problem of interference. *Brit. J. Psychol.*, 1931, 22, 31–42.
18. Kline, L. W. An experimental study of associative inhibition. *J. exper. Psychol.*, 1921, 4, 270–299.
19. Koffka, K. Principles of Gestalt psychology. New York: Harcourt, Brace and Co. 1935.
20. Köhler, W., & von Restorff, H. Analyse von Vorgängen im Spurenfeld. II. Zur Theorie der Reproduktion. *Psychol. Forsch.*, 1935, 21, 56–112.
21. Lepley, W. M. Serial reactions considered as conditioned reactions. *Psychol. Monogr.*, 1934, No. 205.
22. McGeoch, J. A. The influence of degree of learning upon retroactive inhibition. *Amer. J. Psychol.*, 1929, 41, 252–262.
23. ———. The influence of degree of interpolated learning upon retroactive inhibition. *Amer. J. Psychol.*, 1932, 44, 695–708.
24. ———. Studies in retroactive inhibition: I. The temporal course of the inhibitory effects of interpolated learning. *J. gen. Psychol.*, 1933, 9, 24–43.
25. ———. Studies in retroactive inhibition: II. Relationships between temporal point of interpolation, length of interval, and amount of retroactive inhibition. *J. gen. Psychol.*, 1933, 9, 44–57.

26. ———, & McKinney, F. Retroactive inhibition in the learning of poetry. *Amer. J. Psychol.*, 1934, 46, 1– 34.

27. ———. The susceptibility of prose to retroactive inhibition. *Amer. J. Psychol.*, 1934, 46, 429–437.

28. McGeoch, J. A., & McGeoch, G. O. Studies in retroactive inhibition: X. The influence of similarity of meaning between lists of paired associates. *J. exper. Psychol.*, 1937, 21, 320–329.

29. Melton, A. W., & McQueen-Irwin, J. Inter-serial competition of responses during the relearning of serial verbal material in the retroactive inhibition experiment. *Psychol. Bull.*, 1938, 35, 691–692.

30. Müller, G. E., & Pilzecker, A. Experimentelle Beiträge zur Lehre vom Gedächtniss. *Z. Psychol.*, Erg. 1, 1900.

31. Müller, I. Zur Analyse der Retentionsstörung durch Häufung. *Psychol. Forsch.*, 1937, 22, 180–210.

32. Ortner, A. Nachweis der Retentionsstörung beim Erkennen. *Psychol. Forsch.*, 1937, 22, 59–88.

33. Pavlov, I. P. Conditioned reflexes (trans. by G. V. Anrep). Oxford Univ. Press, 1927.

34. Razran, G. H. S. A quantitative study of meaning by a conditioned salivary technique (semantic conditioning). *Science*, 1939, 90, No. 2326, 89–90.

35. von Restorff, H. Analyse von Vorgängen im Spurenfeld. I. Über die Wirkung von Bereichsbildungen im Spurenfeld. *Psychol. Forsch.*, 1933, 18, 299–342.

36. Robinson, E. S. Association theory today. Century Psychology Series, 1932.

37. Sisson, E. D. Retroactive inhibition: the influence of degree of associative value of original and interpolated lists. *J. exper. Psychol.*, 1938, 22, 573–580.

38. ———. Retroactive inhibition: the temporal position of interpolated activity. *J. exper. Psychol.*, 1939, 25, 228–233.

39. Spence, K. W. The differential response in animals to stimuli varying within a single dimension. *Psychol. Rev.*, 1937, 44, 430–444.

40. Thorndike, E. L. Human learning. Century Psychology Series, 1931.

41. ———. A note on assimilation and interference. *Amer. J. Psychol.*, 1937, 49, 671–676.

42. Waters, R. H. The law of acquaintance. *J. exper. Psychol.*, 1939, 24, 180–191.

43. Whitely, P. L., & Blankenship, A. B. The influence of certain conditions prior to learning upon subsequent recall. *J. exper. Psychol.*, 1936, 19, 496–504.

44. Yum, K. S. An experimental test of the law of assimilation. *J. exper. Psychol.*, 1931, 14, 68–82.

5

Retroactive Inhibition as a Function of Degree of Generalization between Tasks

Eleanor J. Gibson

Looking back at this experiment, the novel aspect of it seems to me to be the preliminary experiment in which a measure of generalization among a set of items was secured, independent of the learning and recall called for in the main experiment on retroactive inhibition. Confusion between items was the measure of generalization, also a novelty. In choosing material to be sampled for degree of generalization among items of the set, I selected pictorial instead of verbal material. Similarity was to be judged, as well as the actual responses to an item confusing it with another. Nonsense forms were suggested as appropriate by an earlier experiment of my husband's (J. Gibson 1929; his thesis research, actually), in which he studied memory for forms and found that the memory of a form changed over time. I copied some of his forms in devising my set.

My first experiment, using this material as "cue" items for paired associates in a retroactive inhibition experiment, was performed as a group experiment, using students in five laboratory sections of the introductory course at Smith College. The results were in line with predictions and thus quite satisfactory, but Hull distrusted group experiments, and so it was repeated with individual subjects. The results of the first experiment were replicated, including a finding that strict analogy with conditioning would hardly have predicted: that a set of items, once differentiated, does not generalize again when new responses must be learned to them, and that differentiation obtains within the set as a whole, not as an acquisition of a particular item. Intralist generalization was greatly reduced in interpolated learning, even when the items were not the same ones presented for original learning. What occurs, it seemed to me, was a kind of perceptual learning, but not learning attributable to distinctiveness of particular responses learned to each individual item, as a burgeoning theory of "acquired distinctiveness of cues" assumed (Miller and Dollard 1941). Differentiation, once achieved, is not lost again, nor is it a specific result of attaching particular responses to individual

Journal of Experimental Psychology, 1941, 28, 93–115.

items. A set of confusable items is differentiated by means of discovering the features that are shared to varied extents by items within the set. This idea surfaced years later when I was groping for a theory of perceptual learning.

There were two more papers in this series, not reprinted here (one by one of my graduate students). A hiatus followed due to World War II and coping with a family along with teaching. But for me differentiation as a fundamental process in development and learning was firmly established, to be continued later.

A hypothesis relating verbal learning to two concepts from the literature of conditioning—generalization and differentiation—has recently been presented by the writer (4).[1,2] This hypothesis has advanced the general notion that *discrimination* is an essential process in verbal learning, and that the special difficulties referred to by such terms as *interference* and *retroactive inhibition* can be understood, at least in part, as cases of relatively low discriminability of learning material. When this notion is combined with the principle of establishment of differentiation between the previously undiscriminated items, many implications follow. These implications are stated as specifically as possible in the form of predictions in the article referred to. Figure 5.1 below may clarify the mechanism assumed to be at work. It represents a list of paired associates in which generalization is assumed to be taking place during learning. Generalization is defined as "the tendency for a response R_a learned to S_a to occur when S_b (with which it has not been previously associated) is presented" (4, p. 204). In other words, S_a, S_b and S_c possess low discriminability when they are presented separately. Generalization tendencies (represented by broken arrows) will tend to block the right responses (solid arrows) in proportion to the strength of the tendencies. Competitive blocking thus occurs, rendering learning difficult.

In a two-list situation also, generalization and competitive blocking may occur. Figure 5.2 represents the relationships. When the second list is learned, its stimulus members may generalize with those of the first list, and

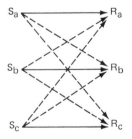

Figure 5.1

the responses of the first list tend to occur, or to block the right responses, during the new learning. Likewise, if List 1 is recalled after List 2, generalized responses from List 2 may interfere with recall, producing competitive blocking or overt generalization (reversion to the wrong list). The right excitatory tendencies will be weakened, it is assumed, in proportion to the degree of inter-list generalization. This argument leads to the prediction in the hypothesis (4, p. 215) that "a first list will be more poorly recalled as the strength of the tendency for items of a second list to generalize with it increases." The present experiment is designed to test this proposition; that retroactive inhibition is a function of degree of generalization between a primary and an interpolated list. The experimental situation will yield data relevant to the prediction of interference from List 1 to the learning of List 2 as well as retroactive inhibition. The hypothesis predicts that "more repetitions will be required to learn a second list, in proportion to the strength of the tendency for items of a first list to generalize with items of a second list."

Numerous experiments have demonstrated that retroactive inhibition varies with the degree of similarity between an original and an interpolated task (1, p. 389 ff.). The present hypothesis is obviously related to this work, but would maintain that *indistinguishability*, rather than *similarity* or *homogeneity* (14) is the important variable. Similarity implies a sophisticated phenomenal relationship involving both the likeness and the discriminability of the items in question. But it is the indistinguishability of the items, and the necessity for differentiating them which forms the basis of the present hypothesis. At the outset of learning, items usually have varying degrees of stimulus equivalence, particularly in the verbal learning situation where items are not presented side by side for perceptual comparison. It is reasonable to suppose that this equivalence or indistinguishability is essentially similar to the classical fact of generalization which appears in the early stages of conditioning.

Since the purpose of the present investigation was to discover the relationship between generalization and retroactive inhibition, a preliminary experiment was designed to standardize material in terms of degree of

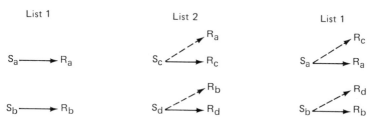

Figure 5.2

generalization. The method of standardization and the resulting data are presented in Experiment I. The standardized material is utilized in Experiment II, a retroactive inhibition experiment, to form series of primary and interpolated lists differing in degree of generalization. Experiment III is a repetition of Experiment II using individual subjects instead of the groups used in II.

Experiment I. Determination of Degree of Generalization of Stimulus Items

Procedure

For determining degree of generalization of items, a technique previously employed by Yum (15) was used. A series of *standard* forms was selected, to be used as cues in paired associates learning. A number of variations from each of these forms was then drawn. Twenty-four hours after a group of subjects had learned the list of paired associates, a recall series was given them, in which each cue form was either the original standard, or a *variation* substituted for the standard. The measure of generalization was taken as the extent to which the subjects responded to the variation *as if it were the standard*.[3] Yum was interested in relating the frequency of response to the variation with the degree of perceptual similarity between the variation and the standard. Perceptual similarity was determined by judges' ratings. To make the present experiment comparable, a number of groups of forms, each group consisting of a standard and several variations, were drawn on cards and presented to ten judges. They were asked to put each variation with the standard which it resembled most. When this was finished, they were asked to rank the variations according to degree of similarity to the standard. Thirteen groups of forms were treated in this way. Each finally consisted of a standard form and two variations from it. There were available then three classes of forms: standard, first degree similarity, and second degree similarity. Included also in the experiment was a fourth class of forms which bore no resemblance to any of the standards, as determined by the judges.

Relative degrees of generalization for the variation-forms were now determined. The 13 standard forms were used as the cue members of a list of paired associates. Each standard was paired with a monosyllabic word (again in accordance with Yum's procedure). The order of the pairs was varied with each presentation, so that no serial associations would be formed. Four *test* lists for determining degree of generalization were prepared, each composed of 13 forms, like the learning list, but forms of all 4 classes were included among them. In a typical test list there would be 3 of the standard forms, 3 forms highly similar to their standards, 3 forms less similar to their standards, and 3 forms which resembled none of the standards. (Actually, there had in any list to be 4 forms from one of the classes to make up 13.) There were necessarily 4 different test lists, to include the total of 54 forms. No variation ever appeared in the same list with its standard. Four groups of subjects took part in the experiment, varying in number from 19 to 29. Each group had the original learning list, but a different test list. The groups were four sections in an elementary psychology course.

A special serial exposure device was used to present the material to the subjects, consisting of a Jastrow memory apparatus placed behind a projector which threw a large image of each form-word pair on a translucent screen. The forms had been printed by mimeograph so that perfect copies were available for the different lists, and the response words were printed in black India ink. Exposure time for each pair was 2 seconds. Five learning trials of the original list were given; immediately following each presentation, recall was tested, the forms alone being presented in a different order each time. The subjects had to record the proper response words in a prepared booklet within 3 seconds. The subjects were then released but returned the next day at the same hour and were given one of the four test lists for determining degrees of generalization. This test was similar in procedure to one of the previous recall trials. Following this test series, an ordinary recall test was given using the original forms.

The following instructions were given the subjects at the beginning of the experiment:

You will be shown a group of forms, each one paired with a word. Study these pairs so that when a form is shown alone, you can write the appropriate word. You will be shown only one pair at a time. Do not try to learn these pairs in any particular order, because the order will be changed every time. The point is, to *associate* a particular word with the form with which it always appears.

After every presentation of the forms paired with words, you will be shown the forms by themselves in order to see whether you remember the appropriate word or not. If you do remember it, write it in the blank provided, being sure to put it in the proper space. Do not leave any blank spaces; if you do not remember the proper word, draw a line through the space. After we have finished one of these test trials, turn the page so that you always have a blank page before you during the learning.

On the second day, before the test series, these instructions were given:

Today I want you to look at some forms as they appear and put down the word for each one whenever you can. You will be shown forms by themselves; try to write the appropriate words, just as you did in the test series yesterday. You may not remember them all the first time, but you will be given another chance later.

The subjects could hardly fail to recognize at some point in the series that this was not the original list, since 3 or 4 of the forms were totally unfamiliar ones bearing no resemblance to the standards. This awareness probably had the effect (to judge from later questioning) of causing them to write responses only to those forms which they felt 'sure' of, so that in general when variations were responded to as if to the standards, the items were functioning as *equivalent* stimuli, not as merely recognizably similar stimuli.

Results

Degree of Original Learning   Since variations in the degree of learning attained are probably accompanied by variations in the degree of gen-

Table 5.1
Mean Number of Response Words Correctly Recalled after 5 Presentations

Group I	Group II	Group III	Group IV
12.5	12.0	11.9	11.9

eralization exhibited,[4] the mean number of response words correctly recalled after the fifth learning trial for each group of subjects is presented in Table 5.1. The degree of learning attained was high, being approximately 12 out of a possible 13 correct responses. This implies that many individuals were able to recall all 13 responses correctly. The differences between the averages of the 4 groups are satisfactorily small.

Degrees of Generalization for Individual Forms   The main purpose of the results was to establish four lists of forms varying in their tendency to call forth the same responses as did the original list of standard forms. To obtain such lists, the results were scored as follows. First, the number of subjects responding correctly to each standard form in the test list was obtained. Then, the number responding to each of the *variations* as if it were the standard was calculated. When these latter figures are expressed as percentages of the total number taking part in the group concerned, they constitute measures of the degree of generalization with the standard. Finally, it was determined whether any form rated dissimilar to the standards was responded to as if it were one of the standards; and whether any variation from a standard was responded to as if it were a different standard.

Figure 5.3 shows the forms grouped in classes according to their tendency to generalize with the standards. The standard forms themselves are Class I. The forms in Class II are those variations which produced the highest frequencies of responses belonging to their standards. Those grouped in Class III produced lower frequencies of the standard responses. In each case, the forms in Class II and Class III are listed next to their standards. The percentage of the group which responded appropriately is in each case given opposite the form. The means show a wide difference between Classes I, II, and III in terms of tendency to call forth the standard response. The forms grouped as Class IV are those which were judged dissimilar. Four of these forms were responded to by a few subjects, but with no consistency as regards the responses given. If the mean percent response is calculated regardless of the nature of the response, the figure is 2.8 percent. The order in which forms of this class are listed is necessarily arbitrary. None of the variations (Classes II and III) was responded to with any consistency as if it were a standard other than the one beside which it is listed in the chart. There were a total of 10 "wrong" responses each for

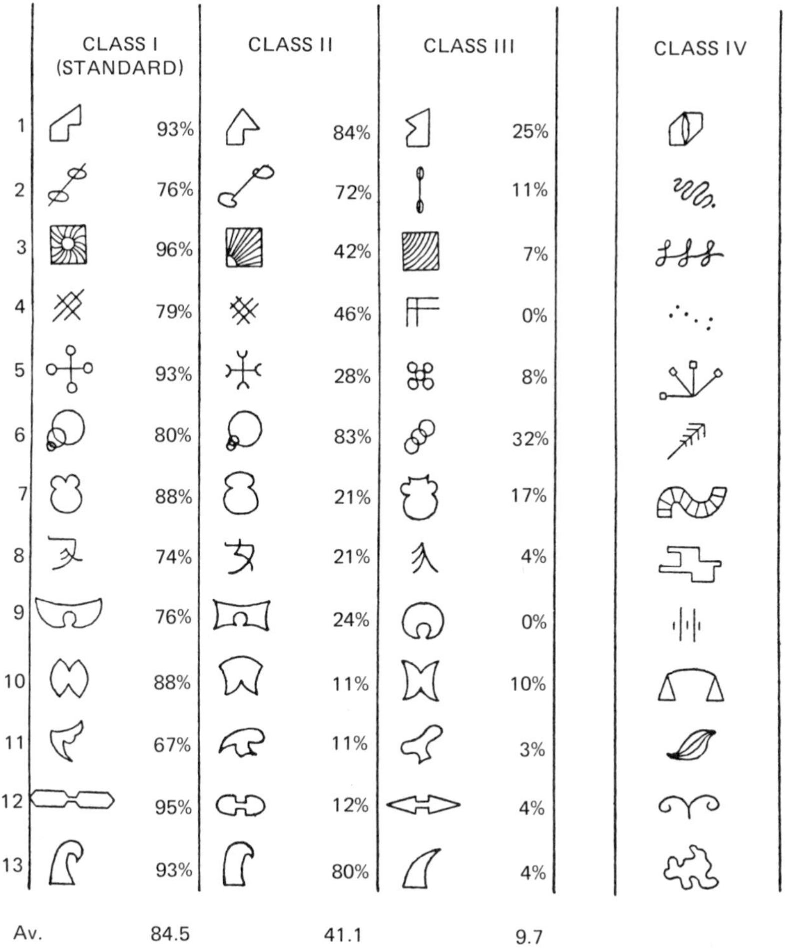

	CLASS I (STANDARD)		CLASS II		CLASS III		CLASS IV
1		93%		84%		25%	
2		76%		72%		11%	
3		96%		42%		7%	
4		79%		46%		0%	
5		93%		28%		8%	
6		80%		83%		32%	
7		88%		21%		17%	
8		74%		21%		4%	
9		76%		24%		0%	
10		88%		11%		10%	
11		67%		11%		3%	
12		95%		12%		4%	
13		93%		80%		4%	
Av.		84.5		41.1		9.7	

Figure 5.3
Stimulus forms grouped in classes according to the percentage of subjects giving the standard responses.

Class II and Class III—about 10 percent of the total possible responses in each case.

Two of the forms included in Class III were not responded to at all, although these two forms had been judged similar to the standards next which they are listed. Besides these two cases, there were only two discrepancies between similarity as rated by the judges and generalization as determined by quantitative score. These discrepancies caused a change from Class III to Class II in the case of forms 10 and 12. There was therefore a high correlation between judgments of similarity and objective tendency to generalize. To show this correlation, the results can also be scored according to a method used by Yum. He calculated for each test list the mean number of forms of each *similarity* group responded to "correctly," rather than scoring each form individually as has been done above. If this calculation is made in the present experiment, the data are consistent for the four test lists in showing the highest mean response to the standard forms, next highest to forms judged of first degree similarity, and least high to those judged of second degree similarity.[5]

Experiment II. Degree of Retroactive Inhibition and of Interference as Dependent on Degree of Generalization

Procedure
Since it was proposed to test the relationship between degree of inter-list generalization on the one hand, and degree of retroactive inhibition on the other, the conditions of the experiment were planned so as to include three different degrees of generalization between primary and interpolated lists (Conditions II, III and IV below). Another condition contained identical stimulus items in the two lists (Condition I), and a fifth served as a control for calculating retroactive inhibition (Condition V). In all conditions the primary learning list was made up of the standard (Class I) forms paired with nonsense syllables. The four classes of forms as they are grouped in Fig. 5.3 constituted the stimulus items for the four interpolated lists. The plan of the experiment was then as follows. The response

Condition	Learning of Primary List Stimulus Forms	Learning of Interpolated List Stimulus Forms	Retention of Primary List Stimulus Forms
I	Standard	Class I (Standard)	Standard
II	Standard	Class II	Standard
III	Standard	Class III	Standard
IV	Standard	Class IV	Standard
V	Standard	(No learning)	Standard

members of the interpolated lists were nonsense syllables different from those of the primary list, but identical in all four interpolated lists. Conditions I, II, III, and IV differed, therefore, only as to stimulus forms. The syllables for both primary and interpolated lists were chosen according to the usual rules from Hull's list (7). Only those of low association value were included. In condition V, the subjects were given copies of the *New Yorker* to read during the interpolated interval, with instructions to select the best and the worst cartoon.

The details of procedure were similar to those of Experiment I. Since the nature of the five conditions precluded using a subject more than once, five large, equivalent groups of subjects were secured. The sections of an elementary laboratory course offered the most available and suitable subjects. The same technique of exposure was employed, again allowing two seconds per pair for learning, and three seconds per item for the recall trial which followed. The order was varied with every learning trial and every test trial. Five learning and test trials were given.[6] The prepared booklets in which responses were recorded were collected immediately following the original learning, and new booklets passed out. Instructions for the interpolated learning followed and this task was begun at once. The interpolated list was also presented five times, with tests following each presentation. As soon as the interpolated learning was finished, books were collected, others distributed, further instructions given, and recall and relearning of the original list was begun. In all five conditions, the interpolated period between the end of the fifth test of original learning and the first recall test of it lasted fourteen minutes. Seven relearning repetitions of the first list were given. The number was limited to seven, owing to the termination of the class period; it did not allow learning to complete mastery in most cases.

The instructions were almost identical with those given in Experiment I and need not be repeated. After the 5 presentations of the first list, subjects were told: "We shall return to this list later on, and give enough more trials for everyone to finish learning." When the new record books had been handed out, they were told: "Now there will be a new list, of the same type, to be learned. The procedure will be exactly similar to that we have just followed. Please try again to work as hard as possible." The final instructions given before recall of the first list were these: "Now we shall go back to the first list and repeat it until everyone has learned all of the pairs. We shall start with a test trial to see how much you remember. Write every syllable which you can recall in the proper space when its form is shown, and draw a line in the others, as usual. Then we shall proceed with alternate learning and test trials as we did before."

Results

Degree of Original Learning   Since the validity of the results depends on the equivalence of the 5 groups of subjects as regards degree of original learning, the mean number of syllables correctly recalled on the final test for each condition is presented in Table 5.2. The means are fairly uniform, and the variation could not be responsible for the differences in recall which will appear later.

Table 5.2
Degree of Original Learning

Condition	I	II	III	IV	V
Mean No. Learned	8.21	7.86	8.05	7.92	7.91
No. of S's	24	22	22	39	23

Table 5.3
Degree of Learning and Mean Number of Reversion Errors in Interpolated Learning

Condition	I	II	III	IV
Mean No. Recalled at Trial 5	7.67	9.68	10.00	9.82
Mean Total No. Recalled	22.75	30.91	31.82	33.95
Mean No. Reversion Errors	.83	.45	.41	.41

Degree of Learning of Interpolated Lists   The degree of interpolated learning achieved in conditions I, II, III, and IV is interesting on two scores. First, the hypothesis predicts that higher degrees of generalization between a first and a second list should make the second list harder to learn. And second, variation in the degree of interpolated learning achieved may in itself affect the degree of retention of the primary list, since degree of retroactive inhibition has been shown to be a function of degree of interpolated learning (9, 12). Table 5.3 shows the mean number of syllables correctly recalled after the fifth trial of the interpolated list in each of the four conditions, as well as the mean total number recalled on all five tests of interpolated learning. Only the differences between Condition I and the other conditions approach statistical reliability,[7] but the totals show a definite tendency for more syllables to be correctly recalled as degree of generalization decreases from Condition I to Condition IV. The learning curves for each of the four conditions are presented in Fig. 5.4. Condition I is lower than the others throughout the five trials. In the early trials, Condition IV is noticeably higher than the other three, but in the later trials its curve is close to the curves for Conditions II and III. The chief fact shown is the much lower degree of learning achieved in Condition I, which is in keeping with the hypothesis under consideration. It might also affect the degree of retroactive inhibition for this condition by lowering it, since it has been shown that retroactive inhibition decreases with lower degrees of interpolated learning (within the range of partial learning).

When the responses given during interpolated learning are analyzed for reversion errors (cases of overt generalization with the preceding list) it should be expected, according to the hypothesis, that more such errors accompany the condition where learning is most difficult. The mean num-

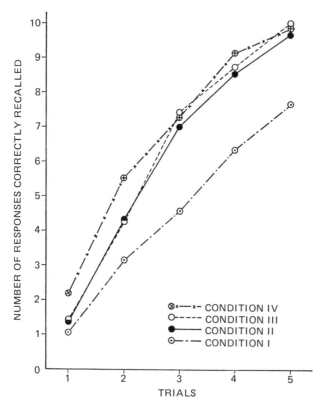

NUMBER OF RESPONSES CORRECTLY RECALLED

⊗ ⎯ ⨯ ⎯ CONDITION IV
○ ⎯ ⎯ ⎯ CONDITION III
● ⎯⎯⎯⎯ CONDITION II
⊙ ⎯ · ⎯ CONDITION I

TRIALS

Figure 5.4
Learning curves of the four interpolated lists. Degree of learning is plotted in terms of the number of responses correctly recalled after each trial.

ber of such errors for the four conditions are also given in Table 5.3. It is obvious that more such errors occur in Condition I, coinciding with the greater difficulty of learning in that series. The greatest difference between conditions according to both recall and reversion measures, comes between Condition I and Condition II. A striking feature of the reversion errors, however, is the low frequency with which such errors occur at all, overtly.

Degree of Retroactive Inhibition   The degree of retention of the first list may be calculated from several measures: from the first recall test immediately following interpolated learning (Recall 1), from the second recall test, which follows the first relearning trial (Recall 2), and from a relearning score. Table 5.4 gives the percent of retroactive inhibition based on the number of correct recalls at the first and second test.[8] All four experimental groups show a significant degree of retroactive inhibition in terms of both

Table 5.4
Recall Scores, Percent of Retroactive Inhibition Measured by Recall Scores, and Mean Number of Trials to Relearn 9 Items

Conditions	I	II	III	IV	V
Mean of Recall 1	3.04	3.00	4.18	5.79	7.57
Mean of Recall 2	5.92	6.55	7.00	8.36	9.78
Retroactive Inhibition, Recall 1	60.6%	59.9%	45.8%	23.5%	
Retroactive Inhibition, Recall 2	41.7%	32.6%	29.6%	14.6%	
Mean Trials to 'Relearn'	4.08	3.73	3.86	3.00	2.35

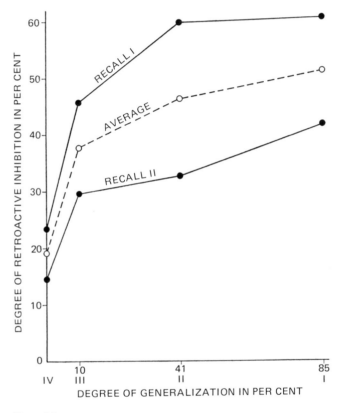

Figure 5.5
Degrees of retroactive inhibition plotted as a function of degree of generalization between stimulus forms of original and interpolated list. The Roman numerals under the percentages of generalization on the abscissa indicate the experimental condition previously described.

measures of recall. Furthermore, the degree of retention varies with the degree of generalization between the original and the interpolated learning.[9] Figure 5.5 shows degree of retroactive inhibition plotted against the degree of generalization as obtained in the standardization experiment. As the degree of generalization increases, so also does degree of retroactive inhibition, as the hypothesis predicts. When the two curves are averaged, the result is a smooth, negatively accelerated gradient.

It is noteworthy that Condition I (identical stimulus items) does not show a significant increase in retroactive inhibition over Condition II (Class II stimulus items), particularly in Recall I. A greater difference is apparent in Recall 2, but even here the critical ratio is only .74. This result may be due to the lower degree of interpolated learning for Condition I. In other words, had degree of interpolated learning in Condition I been as high as that in the other three series, a higher degree of retroactive inhibition might have been found.

Another feature of the curves is the sharp rise from Condition IV to Condition III—from o generalization to 10 percent generalization. Yet Condition IV itself shows 23.5 percent retroactive inhibition in the first recall. It may be questioned whether such a degree of retroaction for a condition of supposedly zero generalization is consistent with the theoretical prediction. Two explanations suggest themselves. The first is that syllable responses were learned in the interpolated list as well as in the primary list, and that something analogous to generalization may take place among *response members* as well as stimulus members. Doubt is cast on this possibility by the McGeochs' study (10), which showed that variation in degree of similarity of response members of interpolated paired associates to response members of a primary list was without effect in determining degree of retroactive inhibition. This fact is consistent with Thorndike's finding (13) that similar response members are not frequently substituted for one another in recall, but that similar stimulus members do frequently evoke one another's responses. The second possibility is that there was actually generalization between stimulus members of original and interpolated lists in Condition IV, in spite of the negligible tendency established in the standardization experiment. It will be remembered that a very high degree of original learning was achieved in the standardization experiment, while only 8 out of 13 responses, on the average, were learned in the present experiment. It is suggested that generalization, after reaching a maximum, decreases as learning increases; and that as generalization decreases, the stimuli most discriminable from the standard are the first to cease producing generalized responses. In this case, the forms belonging to Class IV were ineffective in producing generalization in the standardization experiment because the degree of learning was high and because they varied considerably from the standards. But in the present experiment, they were effective to some extent because the degree of learning was much lower. Evidence to support this explanation may be found in the fact that some cases of errors of reversion to the interpolated list actually did occur in Condition IV, though not as many as in the other conditions. But before this explanation can be accepted, it will be necessary to study the curve of generalization in relation to degree of learning under comparable conditions.[10]

The tendency for a greater decrement to accompany higher degrees of generalization is further supported by the number of trials required to relearn to a set criterion. This measure is of doubtful value, since learning was not carried to a criterion originally. But it should be of some significance, since the groups were equated as to number learned, on the average. Table IV gives the mean number of trials required in each condition to relearn to a criterion of 9 out of the 13 items. (A higher criterion could not be set, since some subjects learned no more than 9 in the seven relearning trials.) Condition I required more trials, on the average, to relearn 9 items, than did any of the others. There is not a perfect gradient here, since the average for Condition III is slightly higher than that for Condition II. It is interesting to note that the difference between Condition III and Condition IV is again the greatest, as was the case with the two other measures of retention.

Errors in Recall   In the light of the above results, it is interesting to examine the mean number per subject of errors of reversion to the interpolated list which occurred in recalling the first list in the four conditions. The figures for the four conditions are: Condition I, 1.00; Condition II, 1.09; Condition III, .91; Condition IV, .36. As was the case when retention was measured by first recall, there is little difference between Condition I and Condition II. What is especially interesting is the large difference between Condition III and Condition IV, which coincides with the great difference between these conditions in all three measures of retention.

It is obvious that actual reversions account for only a small percentage of the errors which occur in either interpolated learning or recall and relearning of the primary list. Superficially, this fact may appear to be out of line with the hypothesis under test. But when the nature of the other errors is studied, their occurrence seems compatible with the hypothesis. Omissions are the most frequent type of error. When the relearning trials in Condition I are examined, omissions account for 67.9 percent of the errors. Theoretically, omissions may occur because there is no strong excitatory tendency to respond, or because the tendency or tendencies are inhibited. The former explanation may account for a number of the omis-

sions, since the primary list was not learned to a very high degree originally. The second explanation is in line with the hypothesis, since it would
assume that when a correct response and a generalized response, or two
generalized responses both tend to occur at once, blocking may result. It is
also possible that a response, although learned, was extinguished during
the interpolated learning and is thereby inhibited. Such a possibility requires an extension of the hypothesis which will be considered later.

The errors other than omissions may be divided into three types—
reversions or cases of overt generalization *between* lists, cases of overt
generalization *within* the list, and misspellings. During the relearning of
Condition I, 3.2 percent of the errors were reversions; 5.6 percent were
cases of overt generalization within the list; and 23.4 percent were misspellings of the syllable responses. The question arises as to whether the errors
of misspelling are consistent with the hypothesis. When these errors are
examined carefully, a very interesting discovery emerges. Many of them
appear to be compromises resulting from conflicting excitatory tendencies.
For instance, two forms within a list have as their responses *ruv* and *tah*,
respectively; the subject, instead of responding correctly to either of them,
may respond with *tuv* to both. Or, a form in the interpolated list which has
been shown previously to generalize with a form in the primary list, may
have as its response *kiv*; the form in the primary list may be paired with *haj*.
But when the subject is asked to recall the primary list, he may write neither
of these responses, but instead *kij*. In such cases, the stimulus form seems
to have two excitatory tendencies, an associated one and a generalized one,
which result in a compromise response rather than blocking. Under what
conditions compromise will occur instead of blocking is an intriguing
question. It seems possible that the strength of both tendencies may be the
key to this problem—that two equal but weak tendencies may lead to
compromise, strong ones to blocking—but further study is required to
solve it. Probably not all the misspelling errors are of this type; an attempt
was made to estimate the percentage falling in this class, but it proved
impossible to classify many of the cases with certainty.

The errors of generalization *within the list* which occurred during the
learning of the primary and the interpolated lists show an interesting trend.
There is a mean decrease of 59 percent in such cases from primary learning
to interpolated learning. This decrease occurs consistently in all the four
conditions. The reduction in Condition I is consistent with a prediction
regarding the learning of pre-differentiated items—"If differentiation has
been set up within a list, less generalization will occur in learning a new list
which includes the same stimulus items paired with different responses" (4,
p. 222). The reduction in the other conditions is hard to understand unless
something like transfer of differentiation is postulated.

Experiment III. A Repetition of Experiment II Using Individual Subjects

Procedure

Since the third experiment was undertaken principally as a check on the reliability of the results obtained in Experiment II, conditions were kept as nearly the same as possible. In general, only those changes were made which were demanded by individual experimentation in place of a group procedure. The two major changes were omission of Condition V, and the use of a learning criterion rather than a set number of trials. Condition V (the control for retroactive inhibition in which the subjects read during the interpolated period) was omitted, because there could be no doubt of the fact that retroactive inhibition occurred and we wished only to verify the gradient observed from Condition I to Condition IV. The subjects always learned to a criterion in the primary learning, the interpolated learning, and the relearning so as to insure equal degrees of learning in the four conditions.

The lists learned by the subjects in Conditions I, II, III, and IV were identical with those of Experiment II, except that one pair was omitted, making them 12-unit instead of 13-unit lists. The forms were pasted on heavy paper, and the syllables were typed beside them. The learning material was presented on an electrically driven Chicago-type memory drum. Each pair was again exposed for 2 seconds. But when the forms were presented alone, in the test trials, they now appeared for 2 seconds each instead of 3 seconds, since the subjects had only to speak the right associates instead of to write them. Six random orders were prepared for each list, and the order was changed each time for both learning and test trials. All the subject's responses were recorded by the experimenter.

The procedure was as follows. As soon as the subject had received the instructions, which were the same as those of Experiment II, the first list was presented. When the list had been exposed, the forms alone were presented and the subject attempted to recall the appropriate responses. This same procedure was continued until the subject had recalled 8 of the 12 responses correctly in a single trial. Then the subject was given a four minute rest period while the list was changed. In order to prevent rehearsing, he was given a magazine to read. At the end of this period, the interpolated learning was begun. The procedure was exactly the same as during original learning, and was continued until the subject had learned 8 of the 12 responses. Another rest period ensued, and the subject read, as before, until the time interval was up. The total time allowed for the interpolated interval was 20 minutes. The subject then tried to recall the responses of the first list, and relearning followed. Relearning was carried to a criterion of one perfect recall trial. The experiment required about one hour.

Fourteen subjects were secured for each condition. Since it was important to equate the groups for number of trials spent in learning the first list, an attempt was made to secure similar distributions for the four conditions in this respect. That is, an attempt was made to distribute the fast learners and the slow learners equally over the four conditions. This could easily be done since it was possible to assign a subject to a condition after she had completed the original learning. The subjects were all students from elementary psychology courses, and comparable to the subjects in Experiment II.

Results

Trials to Learn Original List   The mean number of trials required to learn the original list to a criterion of 8 out of 12 right associates for each of the four conditions are as follows: Condition I, 6.86; Condition II, 7.00; Condition III, 7.07; Condition IV, 7.14. The means are very similar, and the slight differences which exist are in the opposite direction from the expected differences in retention. It is interesting that two more trials were required here, on the average, to learn 8 responses, than in Experiment II, where only five trials were given. The difference may possibly be due to the shorter recall time per syllable in this experiment, or to the influence of social facilitation in the earlier one.

Trials to Learn Interpolated List   The mean number of trials required to learn the interpolated list to a criterion of 8 out of 12 right responses is presented for each of the four conditions in Table 5.5. In general, the data corroborate those of Experiment II. There, fewer responses were learned in Condition I than in the other three conditions, which did not differ reliably from one another. Here, more trials are required to learn to the criterion in Condition I than in any other condition. But Condition IV also differs widely from the other three, requiring fewer trials. The difference between Conditions II and III is wholly unreliable.[11] These results tend to confirm the prediction that learning of a second list will be harder as the degree of generalization between the first and the second list increases.

Retention of Original List   The retention of the original list in the four conditions may be measured in four different ways—by a first recall score, a second recall score, and by two different relearning criteria. In Table 5.6 are presented the results for Recall 1 and 2. The trends in the results of Experiment II are confirmed beyond a doubt, since a gradient in recall from Condition I to Condition IV is again apparent in both Recall 1 and 2.[12] When the reciprocals of these figures are plotted, the curves are remarkably similar to the ones obtained in Experiment II. In spite of equivalence in degree of interpolated learning, Condition I again shows only slightly worse retention than Condition II. The difference between the two aver-

Table 5.5
Number of Trials Required to Learn the Interpolated List to a Criterion of 8 Correct Responses

Condition	I	II	III	IV
Mean Trials to Learn	7.43	5.43	5.71	3.93
σ av.	±1.07	±.65	±.77	±.28

Table 5.6
Retention of the Original List as Measured by Recall 1 and Recall 2

Condition	I	II	III	IV
Mean No. Retained, Recall 1	2.93	3.00	3.71	6.21
σ av. Recall 1	$\pm.45$	$\pm.46$	$\pm.64$	$\pm.34$
Mean No. Retained, Recall 2	5.00	5.71	7.29	8.36
σ av. Recall 2	$\pm.56$	$\pm.62$	$\pm.67$	$\pm.43$

11. The critical ratios (D/σ_{diff}) of the differences are: I and II, 1.60; I and III, 1.31; I and IV, 3.18; II and III, 2.8; II and IV, 2.12; III and IV, 2.18.

Table 5.7
Retention of the Original List as Measured by Relearning

Condition	I	II	III	IV
Mean Trials to Relearn 8 out of 12	3.79	2.79	2.00	1.36
σ av., 8 out of 12	$\pm.80$	$\pm.48$	$\pm.41$	$\pm.21$
Mean Trials to Relearn 12 out of 12	8.29	6.43	5.43	4.79
σ av., 12 out of 12	±1.30	±1.10	$\pm.69$	$\pm.53$

ages is unreliable.[13] The differences between the other conditions are all fairly reliable by one measure or the other. The recall scores thus bear out in every respect the results of the previous experiment and the expectation of the hypothesis that retention should be poorer as degree of generalization between the two lists increases.

Relearning scores in terms of the number of trials required to relearn to one perfect repetition, and the number required to relearn 8 out of the 12 responses may be calculated. Only the latter is correctly called relearning, since the first list was learned originally to this criterion. The results obtained by these two measures are shown in Table 5.7 and Fig. 5.6. Both relearning measures are consistent with the recall measures in revealing a gradient in retention from Condition I to Condition IV. The difference between Condition I and Condition II is relatively larger as measured by relearning than when it is measured by recall, though it is still not statistically reliable.[14] The slopes of the curves based on relearning are more gradual and nearly linear than those based on recall, but the trend of the results could hardly be more consistently supported.

Analysis of Errors   Table 5.8 shows the frequency of occurrence of errors of reversion to the previous list in interpolated learning and relearning. Totals, not averages, are presented, since the absolute numbers are very small. The figures are inconsistent, and show no general trend, except that the failure of any such errors to occur in Condition IV is probably sig-

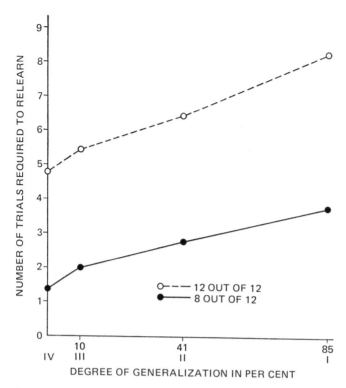

Figure 5.6
Trials to relearn List I as a function of degree of generalization between the primary and the interpolated lists. The two curves represent number of trials required to relearn to two different criteria.

Table 5.8
Frequency of Reversion Errors in Interpolated Learning and Relearning

Condition	I	II	III	IV
Interpolated Learning	2	4	7	0
Relearning	14	23	4	0

nificant. The most interesting aspect of these results is the tendency for a larger total number of reversions to the previous list to occur in relearning than in interpolated learning. McKinney and McGeoch (11), in a retro-active inhibition experiment, also noticed less "overt" transfer from the original to the interpolated list than from the interpolated list to recall of the original one. The reason for the increase in reversion errors in the latter case is probably not the mere difference in number of repetitions given in the two cases, for in the present experiment they are just about equal, and in McKinney and McGeoch's experiment, only a single recall test was in question. The increase may be related to the fact that a longer time intervened between interpolated learning and recall of List I than between original learning and interpolated learning,[15] thereby permitting greater spontaneous recovery of generalization. This explanation requires the as-sumption that differentiation accomplished *within* a list would have a cer-tain protective function against inter-list generalization. The hypothesis does make such an assumption (4, p. 207).

A fairly high percentage of the errors, as in Experiment II, can be classified as cases of generalization of stimulus members within the list. A total of 51 such errors occurred in each condition on the average during original learning, and 15 during interpolated learning. As in Experiment II, the frequency of intra-list generalization during interpolated learning is consistently less than during original learning in all the conditions, although the original and interpolated lists were learned to the same criterion.

Verbal Reports of Subjects   Most of the subjects reported that they had not thought of the lists during rest periods. Those who had done so reported that it was impossible really to rehearse, since they had learned to respond in a particular way to visual form cues, and could not think of the responses easily without the cues. In any case, these subjects were distributed among the four conditions, and could not have influenced the trend of the results. Almost all the subjects reported that two responses sometimes occurred to them simultaneously; that there was in such a case a strong tendency to make some response, but that none was made, ordinarily, because the interval was too short for decision. Therefore, some at least of the errors of omission must be due to blocking caused by active competition of responses.

Discussion

The consistency of the results and the complete corroboration of Experi-ment II when repeated with individual subjects leaves no room for doubt that retroactive inhibition is a function of the degree of generalization between primary and interpolated list. But a consideration of the dynamics of the process is again in order, since this fact does not tell us the actual role of generalization; nor does proof of this role necessarily exhaust the possibilities of explaining decrements in retention.

The process assumed to occur by the present hypothesis is briefly as follows. Generalization may occur from list to list—there will be a tendency for wrong responses to occur in learning a new list or in recalling an old one after interpolation. Active intrusion of wrong responses will thus be a factor leading to decrement. But since these intrusions are infrequent, importance falls on the notion of competition of responses, which may obviously lead to omissions or compromises. Generalized and right responses will tend to block one another. As far as our own data go, active generalization and competitive blocking seem to be sufficient explanations.

A recent article by Melton and Irwin (12) furnishes evidence, however, that some process besides the one described above occurs in the typical retroactive inhibition situation. This evidence is in the nature of a curve showing the relationship between the amount of retroactive inhibition and the degree of learning of the interpolated material. When a separate curve was plotted to show the decrement directly attributable to intrusions, the curve increased to a maximum and then decreased as the degree of interpolated learning was increased. This is the relationship predicted for generalization by the present hypothesis (4, p. 217). Competitive blocking, according to the hypothesis, should follow the same curve as overt generalization, since strength of the generalized tendency is the crucial factor in both. As differentiation is increased, blocking as well as overt generalization should decrease. But the residual retroactive inhibition, after the curve yielded by intrusions had been subtracted from the total, did not follow the same relationship. Some factor or factors other than generalization and competitive blocking must therefore have contributed to the total inhibitory effect.

The present experiment throws no light on other contributing causes of retroactive inhibition. The writer would like, however, to examine the possibility of extinction or unlearning of the type found in the conditioned response situation as a factor, since such an hypothesis has been attributed to her (12). The conditions for extinction are present during interpolated learning, in so far as differential reinforcement takes place. If the subject gives a generalized response, it will not be reinforced and another response will be indicated as the correct one. In this situation, therefore, the generalized response may be extinguished through differential inhibition. But this response itself is not generally inhibited, of course. When a salivary response to a bell is extinguished, there is not inhibition of salivation in general, but only of salivation in that situation or similar ones. If a parallel is drawn in the present situation, the generalized response has been extinguished as far as the stimulus in the interpolated list is concerned; another response has been learned as the positive one for that stimulus. But has the extinguished response been inhibited for its own stimulus of the first list— its positive stimulus? Generalization of inhibition is a well-known phenomenon (6, p. 178 ff.), but to the writer's knowledge it has not been demonstrated in a discrimination situation. There is not even an analogue, then, to support the required assumption that the inhibition of generalized responses during interpolated learning will itself generalize to the positive stimulus items of the first list. Suppose such an assumption is made, however. It is still a fact that very few generalized responses actually occurred overtly during interpolated learning, so that the opportunities for inhibition of generalized responses were few. It might be argued that non-reinforcement of *any* wrong response will produce inhibitory effects, or that *implicit* generalized responses might be extinguished. As for the effects of extinguishing *any* wrong response, it seems clear that such extinction could not contribute to retroactive inhibition, because unless the punished errors were due to generalization, they would not be at all relevant to recall of List 1. It would be necessary to assume a concept of "free-floating" inhibition to find a way for such non-reinforcement to affect recall of List 1. As for the possibility that inhibition may result from the non-reinforcement of implicit generalized responses, the following arguments present themselves. If a subject thinks of a generalized response, but does not speak it, one of two things is probably happening. If it is the only response he thinks of, he does not speak it because he already knows it to be wrong, in which case he *has differentiated* it. In the writer's opinion, the essential condition for retroactive inhibition is thereby removed. If it occurs along with another possible response, the situation which has been referred to as competitive blocking results. In so far as the competing generalized response is non-reinforced, it may be extinguished in that situation. The possibilities of extinction are therefore limited to overt generalized responses and competing generalized tendencies. Since in both these cases it is necessary to assume generalization of differential inhibition to the *positive* stimulus, the theoretical structure required is elaborate and not too plausible.

Other theoretical possibilities for retroactive inhibition must be kept in mind at the present time, especially because it has been shown to occur in certain situations which are difficult to analyze in the present terminology. Retention of forms in primary memory, especially, may be mentioned. Here Gibson and Raffel (5) have shown retroactive inhibitory effects for the reproducing of a given visual form when it has been succeeded by other forms. The retroactive inhibitory effect increases progressively with an increase in the number of different interpolated forms. Subjects reported a "blotting-out" of the memory image as new forms made their appearance. In this situation it seems likely, therefore, that the principal locus of the decrement occurred while the interpolated impressions were taking place, and that interference at the time of recall played a small part. Nor could inhibition resulting from differential reinforcement be involved. It is possible that when "content" retention is primarily involved, as in this situation (and presumably to some degree in any learning situation), a weakening of the original impression during interpolation is an important factor. The weakening effect does not necessarily depend upon the interruption of perseveration, as has often been assumed; it might take the form of distortion or deletion of the original "trace."

In conclusion, the writer feels that a determination of the role and weight of the various factors suggested can only be made after careful consideration has led to prediction of the effects which they should produce when the usual dimensions (similarity, degree of learning, etc.) are varied in the retroactive inhibition situation.

Conclusions

1. When syllable responses have been learned to a list of stimulus forms, variations from these forms may be shown to generalize with the original forms, since the variations are responded to in a test series as if they were the originals. Gradients of generalization in terms of frequency of response to the variations may be demonstrated, and such gradients correspond with gradients of perceptual similarity.

2. As the degree of generalization between corresponding stimulus members of a first and a second list is increased, when responses in the two lists are different, there is a tendency for the second list to be harder to learn. The second list is hardest to learn when the stimulus members of the two lists are identical.

3. The degree of retroactive inhibition of a first list varies directly with the strength of the tendency for stimulus members of an interpolated list to generalize with those of an original list.

4. Errors of overt generalization, or reversion to the previous list occur during both interpolated learning and relearning of the primary list. There is some tendency for frequency of such errors to vary with the degree of generalization between the two lists.

5. Errors of intra-list generalization occur during the learning of both the primary and the interpolated list, but such errors decrease considerably from primary to interpolated learning.

Notes

1. This experiment is one of a series of studies presented to the Faculty of the Graduate School of Yale University in partial fulfillment of the requirements for the degree of

Doctor of Philosophy. The writer wishes to acknowledge the valuable advice and assistance of Professor Clark L. Hull during the progress of this work.

2. This experiment was reported at the 1938 meeting of the American Psychological Association (3).

3. This criterion is appropriate to our definition of generalization—"the tendency for a response R_a learned to S_a to occur when S_b (with which it has not been previously associated) is presented" (4, p. 204).

4. Hilgard and Marquis (6, p. 182) present evidence to show that with conditioned responses the curve of generalized responses differs with different stages of practice.

5. The means for the four lists combined are: Standard forms, 2.47; first degree similarity, 1.12; second degree similarity, .33. The maximum response would be 3, since each test list contained forms from each of the four groups. The data are presented in detail in (2).

6. Five repetitions were chosen on the basis of a preliminary experiment. It allowed only partial learning of the lists (about 8 out of 13 items) which was desirable in order to secure a high degree of retroactive inhibition (8).

7. The critical ratio ($D/\sigma_{diff.}$) of the difference between Conditions I and IV is 2.84 when degree of learning is measured by the number recalled at trial 5, and 3.75 when measured by the total number recalled.

8. The retroactive inhibition scores have been calculated by the usual formula from the percent retained, rather than directly from the number recalled.

9. Critical ratios ($D/\sigma_{diff.}$) based on Recall 1 are: I and III, 1.69; I and IV, 3.83; I and V, 5.56 II and III, 1.56; II and IV, 3.5I; II and V, 5.17; III and IV, 2.1I; III and V, 3.96. These statistical reliabilities are in general satisfactory, considering that a gradient is involved. Critical ratios for Recall 2 range from 1.18 to 3.07 when alternate conditions are compared.

10. This problem has been taken up in an investigation to be published.

11. The critical ratios ($D/\sigma_{diff.}$) of the differences are: I and II, 1.60; I and III, 1.31, I and IV, 3.18; II and III, .28; II and IV, 2.12; III and IV, 2.18.

12. Critical ratios ($D/\sigma_{diff.}$) between alternate conditions are: I and III, .99 first recall, 2.61 second recall; II and IV, 5.61 first recall, 3.54 second recall.

13. Since interpolated learning was carried to a criterion, and the total interval of interpolation held constant, less time intervened between *cessation* of interpolated learning and *recall* of the original list in Condition I than in the other conditions, giving less opportunity for spontaneous recovery of generalization in this condition. If spontaneous recovery is an important variable, it would then tend to lower the recall scores of the other three conditions as compared with Condition I, thus bringing them all closer to Condition I, where differentiation was most recently achieved.

14. The critical ratio ($D/\sigma_{diff.}$) is 1.07 for 8 out of 12, and 1.09 for 12 out of 12.

References

1. Britt, S. H., Retroactive inhibition: a review of the literature, *Psychol. Bull.*, 1935, 32, 381—440.

2. Gibson, E. J., *A systematic application of the concepts of generalization and differentiation to verbal learning*, Dissertation on file in Yale University Library.

3. Gibson, E. J., Retroactive inhibition as a function of degree of generalization, *Psychol. Bull.*, 1938, 35, 626.

4. Gibson, E. J., A systematic application of the concepts of generalization and differentiation to verbal learning, *Psychol. Rev.*, 1940, 47, 196—229.

5. Gibson, J. J., and Raffel, G., A technique for investigating retroactive and other inhibitory effects in immediate memory, *J. gen. Psychol.*, 1936, 15, 107–116.

6. Hilgard, E. R., and Marquis, D. G., *Conditioning and Learning*, Appleton-Century Co., New York, 1940, pp. 429.

7. Hull, C. L., The meaningfulness of 320 selected nonsense syllables, *Amer. J. Psychol.*, 1933, 45, 730–734.

8. McGeoch, J. A., The influence of degree of learning upon retroactive inhibition, *Amer. J. Psychol.*, 1929, 41, 252–262.

9. McGeoch, J. A., The influence of degree of interpolated learning upon retroactive inhibition, *Amer. J. Psychol.*, 1932, 44, 695–708.

10. McGeoch, J. A., and McGeoch, G. O., Studies in retroactive inhibition: X. The influence of similarity of meaning between lists of paired associates, *J. exper. Psychol.*, 1937, 21, 320–329.

11. McKinney, F., and McGeoch, J. A., The character and extent of transfer in retroactive inhibition: disparate serial lists, *Amer. J. Psychol.*, 1935, 47, 409–423.

12. Melton, A. W., and Irwin, J. M., The influence of degree of interpolated learning on retroactive inhibition and the overt transfer of specific responses, *Amer. J. Psychol.*, 1940, 53, 173–203.

13. Thorndike, E. L., A note on assimilation and interference, *Amer. J. Psychol.*, 1937, 49, 671–676.

14. von Restorff, H., Analyse von Vorgängen im Spurenfeld. I. Über die Wirkung von Bereichsbildungen im Spurenfeld, *Psychol. Forsch.*, 1933, 18, 299–342.

15. Yum, K. S., An experimental test of the law of assimilation, *J. exper. Psychol.*, 1931, 14, 68–82.

Retrospect and Prospect: Are Theories Recycled?

Some of the concerns that were motivating psychologists in the thirties are in one way or another alive and well today. If we moved away from them, we have moved back again with some revision. *Functionalism*, for example, is one of them. It was discovered, during the fifties, that conditioning does not happen fortuitously and inevitably according to some simple formula for attaching a response to a stimulus with frequent repetition. Some situations are definitely favored for conditioning to certain responses depending on the species of animal and its way of life. Garcia, investigating learning of taste aversion in rats, emphasized the evolutionary basis of favored kinds of learning for a species (Garcia, McGowan and Green 1972). An animal learns what is functional and adaptive for its species. Present-day ecologically oriented views of animal learning abound (Bolles and Beecher 1988, Johnston and Pietrewicz 1985).

On the other hand, *connectionism* is also with us again, in an even sterner form than Thorndike or Hull could have imagined. Neural nets are thought to be shaped by repeated exercise of pathways in the network, without (as I understand it) any recourse to ultimate function or adaptive necessity (Rumelhart and McClelland 1986). This new form of connectionism emphasizes microstructure and mechanism, and contrasts sharply with the functional, evolutionary approach of the ecological biologists.

The preoccupation of the thirties and forties with learning theory gave way as the "cognitive revolution" came in in the late fifties and the sixties and information processing took over. The boxes in the flowcharts were labelled with terms like attention and memory (indeed, a proliferation of memories), but never learning. The cognitive psychologists to this day have neglected learning, leaving it to the biologists, neuropsychologists, and Skinnerians.

Cognitive psychology seems to derive more from a structuralist legacy than a functional one. As the ecological view strengthens today and spreads to humans, concern with learning can be expected to strengthen too I believe. This time, perhaps, perceptual learning will be in the forefront.

II
Comparative Research on Learning and Development (1952–1970)

Introduction to Part II

In the introduction to part I, I pointed out the significance of a comparative approach for functional psychology in America and the prevalence of research on animals as psychology became accepted as a science. It was this domain, in fact, that first attracted me to psychology as an undergraduate at Smith College. It was a severe disappointment to arrive at Yale as a graduate student and find that its primate laboratory, under the direction of Yerkes, was out of bounds for women. There were two younger professors in Yerkes's laboratory, Henry W. Nissen and Carlyle Jacobsen, who were sympathetic with my second-class status and found me minor ways to maintain a concern with comparative psychology.

I watched and eventually assisted a bit in brain surgery focused on the motor system in cats (extirpation was the style of the day) with a Dr. Marshall in the medical school. I also conducted experiments on maternal behavior in mice for a Dr. LeBlond, a postdoctoral researcher from France who was visiting at the medical school. The project involved the role of prolactin in instigation of maternal behavior. The idea was to inject prolactin in mature virgin female animals and test their behavior daily for evidence of ensuing maternal behavior. The test involved presenting them with pups of various ages (borrowed from other cages) and observing retrieval to the nest. The older the pups retrieved and the larger the number retrieved, the stronger the maternal drive was presumed to be. But the adult mice were necessarily exposed more and more to the presence of infant animals as the experiment continued, so I introduced a control group of adult females that received no prolactin but was tested daily in the same manner. *All* the animals, controls and experimentals, exhibited increasingly strong maternal behavior. LeBlond published the data, but without my name, perhaps because of a contretemps that may or may not have been my fault. The mice belonged to a colony bred for some other project, I think involving cancer, and it was important to return the litters to their proper home cages after using them for testing. Some months after I began working in the lab, a litter of mice with brown coats grew up in a cage with white parents. Although I had never cleaned the cages and had been very careful (I thought) in restoring litters to their home cages, I was accused of negligence. I was pretty sure the negligence was on the part of service people who cleaned the cages, and who had a high turnover. I finished the experiment but received no thanks and retired from the scene.

Although I taught a course in comparative psychology for a year or two after returning to Smith, there were inadequate facilities for animal research there. I had to wait until after World War II, when we moved to Cornell in 1949, for my chance to do research with animals again. I accompanied my husband, although not as a faculty member (Cornell had nepotism rules in those days). Since I had no laboratory to work in, I was glad to accept an invitation to work as research associate in the laboratory of Howard Liddell, at a sort of farm known as the Behavior Farm. The animals available were farm animals, sheep and goats. Liddell's research was supported lavishly by the Rockefeller Foundation and it was supposed to focus on the so-called experimental neurosis. That was not what I was interested in, but I was happy to have the opportunity to work with animals again, even if I could only do so at someone else's invitation.

The method employed for producing experimental neuroses in the sheep and goats was devised by Liddell from the classical conditioning paradigm—the animal was given a signal such as a buzzer, followed by shock (inescapable) to a forepaw. A daily routine of this procedure supposedly resulted in a neurosis, diagnosed by rapid heart rate and irregular breathing. Records were accordingly taken daily of heart rate and breathing, and these were indeed disturbed, but the animals would also struggle to get away when they saw an experimenter coming, which seemed to me a mark of quite reasonable dislike of a very uncomfortable procedure. I managed to perform a study of conditioning with avoidable and unavoidable shock (reprinted below), which fit nicely into a controversy current in learning theory at the time and so reinstated my earlier interest in learning.

My main interest during the two years I spent at the farm was in a project I began in the second year on maternal bonding of newborn kids to their mothers. Goats have the convenient habit of producing young in pairs, so the twins could be split up in experimental and control groups and given different rearing treatments. I attended the births (often on cold February nights) of eight pairs of twins, destined to be reared with their own mothers, or foster mothers, or a peer group, or alone (the latter two groups fed artificially from a nipple pail). A series of observations were made from birth at frequent intervals to observe evidence of imprinting and maternal-kid interactions of various kinds. A couple of interesting observations came out of the research before it came to a distressing (for me) end.

I was particularly interested in chemical information as a factor in bonding, and so at some births I removed the newborn kid from the mother before she could touch it and before the appearance of the after birth. The kid was then bathed in a detergent. On one such occasion, I had just completed the first kid's bath when its twin began to make an appearance. What to do with the freshly bathed one in a hurry? The farm manager, who was watching from a half-door, said "put it on the stand." The stand was a very high camera stand with a pedestal surface about a foot square. I said, "But won't it fall off?" He assured me that it would not. I stood the damp little animal on the stand, and it remained there, upright, looking around the room, until I could carry it off to its assigned place. Goats are prepared from birth to survive on a precipice, and this lesson was a good preparation for the visual cliff research later on.

It was also quite clear from a number of observations that the maternal goat, if deprived of its offspring for even a few hours after birth, did not welcome it and in fact would butt it rudely away if it approached and attempted to nurse. Licking the newborn kid and other chemical interchanges are important (as any sheep farmer could probably have told me). The kid, on the other hand, would approach any adult female for several days after birth. Imprinting did not occur very early, but it would eventually—to its peer group or a human caretaker, if its own or a foster mother was not provided.

This research ceased in the spring of my second year at the Behavior Farm when I discovered after the Easter weekend that some of my carefully reared subjects had been given away as Easter presents by the farm manager. It was never completed and so not written up, although I have a demonstration movie to show for it. That disappointment turned me to a more traditional kind of research that I describe in part III. My next period of comparative research began four years later after Richard Walk came to Cornell. We embarked together on a series of rearing experiments, this time with rats. At least, no one wanted them for Easter presents.

In the late 1940s a strong interest had grown in the role of environmental conditions during early rearing for development of sensory processes and perception. Hebb's work with dark-reared rats (1937) was a precursor of this concern; in 1947, Riesen's report on two chimpanzees reared in darkness from birth to six months was published and produced a real stir. If impoverishment of rearing conditions could have damaging effects on perception, might not "enriched" conditions have beneficial ones? How might environmental conditions function to constrain perceptual development? Walk and I, with two superb research assistants, planned and carried out a series of rearing experiments with hooded rats, providing quite specifically "enriched" environments for them to view as they grew to maturity, and after three months testing their perceptual competence with a very specifically related discrimination task. More of this later, when I comment on these experiments. They struck me after completion as the not too productive result of jumping on a bandwagon, but now in retrospect I think they provide a useful moral. Development is enormously flexible. The environmental milieu does indeed constrain development, but perception is not constructed over time from elementary pieces. Two of the five papers stemming from this research—the first and the last—are presented with a backwards glance and reconsideration of what they mean. Late in the program of rearing experiments, Walk and I decided to raise a group of rats in the dark so as to provide a major contrast with our "enrichment" groups. Dark rearing animals is a great deal of trouble. It is no joke to clean the cages and feed and water animals in total darkness. We decided that we should make all this trouble pay off by testing the dark-reared rats in more than one situation. What should that be, in addition to the usual discrimination learning? Walk suggested depth discrimination, and he reminded me of a story I had told him about driving east from California with our two children and worrying that the younger, only two years old, would fall over a cliff as we picnicked on the edge of canyons. Thus was conceived the idea of a cliff test for our dark-reared rats: would they walk over the edge of a cliff, for lack of seeing edges during their early development? This experiment was the most fun of any I have ever had a hand in. We went on to perform a truly comparative experiment, with as many animal species as we could collect.

We began with hooded rats because that was the animal we had been rearing in the dark. We moved on to albino rats to compare animals with a similar lifestyle but poorer vision, and then branched out to observe baby chicks, ungulates (lambs and kids), puppies, and kittens. The baby chicks and the kids were particularly interesting, because they were precocial animals, capable of locomotion at birth or minutes thereafter. They could be observed on the cliff before they had an opportunity to learn, without being deprived of a normal environment while they were attaining independent locomotion. Both the chicks and the kids shunned the deep side of the cliff, but moved onto and freely around the shallow side. Obviously, there are species that avoid a drop-off without learning from postnatal experience of any kind. For them, one can presumably claim that perceptually controlled avoidance of a drop-off is innate.

Naturally, we went on to observe human infants on a visual cliff. We advertised in the local newspaper for "crawling babies," providing a telephone number for parents who wished their offspring to take part in an experiment. Several colleagues (including my husband) predicted that we would get no answers, that parents would fear their babies would receive shocks or unpleasant tests. But the telephone rang furiously and after the experiment was explained to them, most parents brought the babies in. We observed only crawling infants in those experiments, though onset and length of crawling experience varied. Only three out of a total of thirty-six infants crawled off on the deep side, although all parents beseeched their babies to come over it. While we could not claim that the tendency to avoid the deep side was innate, since the infants had enjoyed six to ten months of growing up in a lighted, social environment, it seemed extremely unlikely that they had learned to avoid the deep side through falls or punishment of any kind. Parents, when questioned, seldom reported opportunities for such learning.

If learning is implicated in avoiding a "cliff" in human infants, it seems likely to me that it happens when an infant first attempts locomotion, in the course of exploring a surface (before moving onto it) to discover what kind of support it affords. The visible and palpable qualities of the surface are sampled and propulsion of the entire body onto a surface occurs only when there is a surface perceived as affording support. My later research (discussed in part VI) is related to this earlier research with the cliff which showed, perhaps for the first time, the close tie between perception and action in the human infant. This was an experiment on perceived affordances for action, although we did not conceive it primarily that way at the time. Perception doesn't have to *become* meaningful through associative learning, nor does it guide action by being associated via S-R bonds.

It is worth mentioning that throughout all this research we were never struck by an animal's apparent fear of the deep side of the cliff. All the nonhuman animals, to the extent that they could see it, simply avoided it. Human infants occasionally cried, but that was attributable to a frustrated urge to get to their mothers, who were calling to them across the invisible surface. Later work by Campos (Campos, Langer, and Krowitz 1970), supported the observation that fear of drop-offs was learned, probably after self-initiated locomotion is well under way. But by that time, it could easily be learned from anxious parents.

During these years I had no laboratory of my own and had to collaborate with a colleague on the faculty, I wrote grant proposals and had graduate research assistants, but could not sign the forms as principal investigator or adviser. I had a tiny office on the fourth floor of Morrill Hall, where the graduate students and the animals were housed. I enjoyed the company of both these groups. It was a good atmosphere for research to flourish, even without an empire of one's own.

6

The Role of Shock in Reinforcement
Eleanor J. Gibson

Traditionally, a classical conditioned reflex is supposed to consist of the original unconditioned reflex becoming instigated by some previously neutral stimulus (the "conditioned stimulus") after being paired many times with the unconditioned stimulus and its ensuing unconditioned response. My earlier experience with finger withdrawal to shock (paper 1) had taught me that the form of the response was not invariably the same and that it was even transferable to another appendage or muscle group. Watching the behavior of animals persistently shocked on a forelimb was nevertheless a revelation. The animals that we subjected to conditioning exhibited a number of patterns of behavior, sometimes going through a gamut of responses that appeared almost ritualistic. The behavior was not mechanical, but the animals could not get away. What was going on when shock was delivered inescapably, over and over? The conditioned stimulus was a warning, but how could it be useful and thus lead to adaptive behavior?

The essential contradiction in conditioning with shock that can not be avoided —occurrence of leg flexion to the conditioned stimulus that is immediately punished by ensuing shock—had already been the subject of considerable debate and was responsible for a two-factor or two-phase theory of conditioning (Mowrer 1947). The idea was that there takes place, first, classical conditioning of internal "emotional" responses (autonomic responses such as quickened heart rate, respiration, etc.) and that motor responses (e.g., leg flexion) are induced by this state. The motor response—behavior—would presumably be defense reactions characteristic of the species, such as freezing or running away. If this behavior were successful in avoiding the shock, it would recur, become habitual. If not, the animal should run through whatever repertory of defense reactions its nature and the situation permitted. The situation I had available was ideal for observing the response repertory and the animals' behavior as the conditioning procedure was administered and continued daily, because the animals were not restrained in a frame

Journal of Comparative and Physological Psychology, 1952, 45, 18–30.

and could move about within the fair-sized room where the experiment took place.

The animals did indeed exhibit an extensive repertory of actions, such as backward locomotion (retreat), rearing and head-lowering, crouching, freezing (inhibition of movement), and other postures that could be understood as manifestations of defense or avoidance. I would reword my description of what took place now, using a terminology taken from my husband's theory of affordances—these animals were learning what the conditioned stimulus (and indeed, the whole situation) afforded. Their behavior was highly complex and variable as they responded with defense and avoidance actions, gradually settling down to greater economy of action as they learned that attempts at gross locomotion were ineffective. The behavior was a far cry from a simple conditioned reflex.

One might ask whether the animals were learning to "be afraid" of the situation. We seem to this day to understand rather little about fears (maybe about emotions in general). This experiment certainly convinced me that fears can be learned. Later research with the visual cliff and with a "looming" situation gradually inclined me to the view that most fears are learned, although I doubt that conditioning (as in the presumed learning of "little Albert") is the answer.

Building a theory of learning on a concatenation of conditioned reflexes is clearly insupportable if a so-called conditioned reflex is itself a complex learned action that can shift its form in an animal's effort to achieve adaptation to circumstances that it cannot control. A good theory of how perception of affordances is learned and guides behavior is still badly needed.

Does electric shock act as a reinforcing agent to strengthen a conditioned response?[1,2] This purely experimental question has far-reaching implications. Shock may be regarded as punishment. The effects of punishment are of intense interest to social and child psychologists; but there are as yet no commonly accepted, well-founded principles of the operation or effects of punishment. The writer became interested in this problem in the course of training animals in one of the routines used at the Cornell Behavior Farm for developing "neuroses" in animals. The routine involves a classical (5) Pavlovian conditioning technique, with shock to a foreleg as the inevitable unconditioned stimulus. As the observer watches the relentless succession of metronome-beats followed by shock, the question presents itself more and more insistently, *Why* should the animal flex its foreleg to the sound of the metronome? The reaction yields it nothing, apparently, but another shock. Yet this routine has been a traditional method of establishing conditioned responses. From a Pavlovian standpoint, a conditioned response (leg flexion) is predicted. The shock regularly produces the flexion; hence, in terms of a contiguity-substitution theory, the metronome should do so after a number of paired stimulations. But such an expectation is wholly contradictory to effect theory. From the standpoint of the traditional law of effect, shock is unpleasant and is therefore a negative reinforcement; it should tend to suppress any action preceding it. If the animal begins to lift its leg to the metronome, and the shock follows, the action should be discontinued.

This paradox has been the subject of several experiments designed to compare the effectiveness of conditioning when shock occurs inevitably with conditioning when the CR avoids the shock. Schlosberg (17, 18, 8) performed experiments with white rats comparing inevitable shock with avoidance and found little difference in the efficiency with which the procedures produced a conditioned motor response (e.g., tail or foot withdrawal). In fact, the CR developed very slowly and remained unstable under both conditions. But evidence of emotional conditioning (sharp inspiration and squealing) was clearly present in both cases.

Two years later, Brogden, Lipman, and Culler (2) found shock avoidance much more effective than inevitable shock for producing conditioned running (wheel-turning) in the guinea pig. An avoidance group learned very quickly to a criterion of 100 percent; but the nonavoidance group never rose above 50 percent and showed, furthermore, an erratic learning curve. In 1918, Sheffield (20) suggested that the pig's actual response to shock might often have been stopping (freezing) rather than running. In such an event, a substitution theory would not predict that running should constantly prevail as a CR. Sheffield applied Guthrie's "postremity" theory to the situation and attempted to test the prediction that a CR on a given trial should repeat the UR of the just previous trial (running or other behavior). He found that whether the animal ran or stopped to shock increased or decreased, respectively, the probability of a conditioned run to the CS on the following trial. But conditioned running rose only to 52 percent when cases following other types of UR were omitted. In Brogden, Lipman, and Culler's study (2) it rose to 50 percent without such selection of cases. Also, conditioned running deteriorated in the later stages of training with unavoidable shock. Since other factors are required to explain these results, contiguity seems unpromising as a single explanatory principle.

These two theoretical positions (contiguity-substitution and effect) do not exhaust the possibilities. It can be assumed that cessation of shock is equivalent to drive reduction (6) and is thereby reinforcing. A recent experiment reported by Mowrer (16, pp. 278 ff.) renders this position less attractive, however. There is, finally, the possibility of a two-phase or two-factor theory (19, 3, 21, 13, 15).

The writer proposes to develop the implications of a two-phase theory for the unavoidable shock situation. (a) It is assumed, first, that an emotional response, involving the typical internal "emergency" reactions, is quickly conditioned to the CS. To support such an assumption, there is evidence from this laboratory, as well as others, for the occurrence of increased heart rate, irregular respiration, and psychogalvanic reaction to the CS, anticipating the US (10, pp. 510 ff.). (b) It is assumed, second, that this emotional state induces action, in all probability an escape or defense reaction characteristic of the species. It is likely that a repertory of such reactions exists for any given species, perhaps in a hierarchical relationship.[3] In an avoidance experiment, the shock plays a single role. It reinforces the conditioned emotional reaction to the signal, which, in turn, instigates one of the responses in the animal's "escape-defense repertory," as we shall tentatively name it. If the response is successful in avoiding the shock, it will presumably recur. Its recurrence may be due either to lack of interference by a competing reaction, inasmuch as no punishment results, or to positive reinforcement by fear reduction (14). On the other hand, with inevitable shock, the shock plays a dual role. It functions to promote one of the repertory of emergency reactions, but, also, it tends to suppress or inhibit this very reaction as soon as it has occurred. After a number of such inhibitory effects, a particular reaction may be eliminated entirely, and another member of the emergency repertory takes over. The result would be an appearance of trial and error. If our assumptions are correct, a number of predictions can be made for the situation where shock occurs inevitably 100 percent of the time. (a) There should be a rotation or shift of responses through the animal's escape-defense repertory (a kind of trial and error of his total repertory); (b) there should be a number of cases of total inhibition of response, after a motor response to CS has first appeared; (c) inhibitions of this type should terminate in a short time because the primarily conditioned emotional state is constantly strengthened by the same shock that tends to suppress the motor response; and (d) there should be great fluctuation or variability of response in the unavoidable shock group, contrasted with increasing uniformity in an avoidance group. A qualitative study of the responses as they develop in the two situations should provide a check of these predictions.

Method

Fourteen young goats (between 1 and 2 months old at the beginning of the experiment) were conditioned in a relatively free situation. They were not restrained in a Pavlov frame, but could move normally to any part of the experimental room, which was 10 ft. square and bare except for the observer's chair.[4] The CS was a darkening of the room for 10 sec. preceding the US, a mild shock delivered to the kid's right foreleg. Eight of the animals were given practice with inevitable shock, following the classical Pavlovian procedure (group Inev), while four were allowed to avoid the shock by sustained lifting of the right foreleg (group Av). Two animals were trained with 25 percent random shock. Here, the shock was unrelated to a critical avoidance response, making it inevitable, although it occurred only 25 percent of the time. Our principal data consist of detailed, qualitative, written observations and photographs of the development of behavior through many stages of training.

The shock was delivered by way of two electrode bracelets of saline-soaked cloth, placed one above the other on the right fore-ankle. Metal clips attached the bracelets to wires which coiled around the right foreleg and passed through a buckle on the animal's back. The wires coiled upward, forming a spring attachment to a 4-ft. long stick suspended from the center of the ceiling, allowing completely free locomotion to any part of the room and making the necessary electrical connections through a swivel joint so that no amount of turning would lead to tangled wires. The equipment was not uncomfortable, and the animal could walk normally. Intensity of the shock was regulated by a variable resistance and ranged from 10 to 20 v.; duration was 0.2 sec. The shock was adjusted so as to be strong enough to produce a reliable foreleg flexion, but not excited running and vocalization. The intensity did, nevertheless, vary slightly with factors such as the condition of the animal's coat, and sometimes it was strong enough to produce a jumping movement (both forefeet off the floor) in the animal.

The overhead suspension served a second purpose. The 4-ft. stick which, owing to its spring attachment to the animal, always points toward it as it moves about the room, is made to move two self-synchronous motors, one for each of the two dimensions of the plane of the floor. Each of these is paired with a similar motor in a recording instrument and moves a pencil to conform with the movements of the stick. A graphic recording was thus secured of the animal's total locomotion about the room—a kind of miniature map of its route and movements throughout the experimental hour.

The signal (CS) was a dimming of the room's illumination. During intervals between trials, the room was illuminated by a 300-w. bulb; at the beginning of the signal, this light went off, and a dim light, barely enough to allow the experimenter to perceive the animal's movement, remained on. The duration of this signal was 10 sec., followed immediately by the shock, but not overlapping it. Signals and shocks were timed and delivered by an automatic clocking device at regular 2-min. intervals. The shock for the avoidance subjects was controlled by means of an experimenter's key. The experimenter watched the animal closely, raising the key whenever the animal raised its leg, so that the circuit was broken if the animal had its foot off the floor at the end of the signal. The animal was not allowed to avoid the shock if the foreleg was returned to the floor again before the light came on. The key was also used for animals receiving 25 percent shock, though in this case the shock was given according to a random arrangement without regard to the animal's behavior.

At the beginning of the experiment, the kids were brought to the experimental room and the wires attached for two adaptation periods without signals or shocks. The animals very quickly became adjusted to the room and the harness and ceased to struggle during harnessing. When training began, they were given 20 signals per day, the experimental period lasting 40 min. As a rule they were run two to three times a week, though this timing varied slightly with the season, for training went on into the summer. All animals received 25 days of training (500 trials). Some were carried to 1,000 trials, but only the first 500 will be analyzed here. The animals lived a normal life with the rest of the herd, in pasture or barn, except during experimental sessions.

Results

Varieties of Reaction to the CS
Our first question is, What kinds of response were made to the CS? Did a family or repertory of defense reactions emerge, or was there merely foreleg flexion? The results definitely indicate a varied repertory. A classification of the different patterns of response to the CS through 25 days of training has been made from protocols of the Inev group. The first day of training has been disregarded in the data presented, because it was hard to judge at what moment during the first 20 trials the animal's behavior began to be affected by the CS. The observer, of course, always had to make a judgment as to whether the animal was affected at all by the CS, but this was very easy after the first day, for spontaneous activity rapidly decreased. A catalogue of the responses observed follows:

1. *Walking or running backward*, i.e., retreating from the apparent locus of the shock
2. *Walking or running forward.*
3. *Wheeling* (circling) to right or left.
4. *Side-stepping.*
5. *Independent leg-movements without locomotion*, e.g., pawing the floor, tapping, marking time, stepping in place.
6. *Flexion of* either foreleg. Flexion varied as to pattern, but we defined it as lifting a single leg off the floor with bent knee, whether the leg was lifted forward or retracted backward (see Fig. 6.1).
7. *Extension.* Extension also varied in direction. We defined it as stiff or rigid lifting of the leg from the shoulder (Fig 6.1).
8. *Humping* with head lowered to ground. A slightly bowed head was characteristic of many reactions, but an exaggerated lowering of the head usually accompanied a humped back. This peculiar posture is occasionally observed in the pasture in a frightened or angry animal.
9. *Rearing.* Rearing is also characteristic of a curious, excited, or frightened goat. One animal (see Figure 6.1) reared and walked backward on its hind legs. Rearing sustained by leaning with forefeet against the wall was more frequently observed.

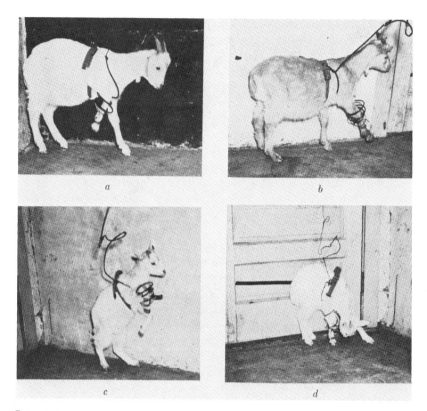

Figure 6.1
Four of the varieties of reaction to the CS: a, backward flexion; b, forward extension; c, rearing with backward locomotion; d, humping with lowered head.

Crouching, lying down, and butting were infrequently observed. Combinations among the nine responses above did occur, for instance, wheeling alternately from right to left, or walking backward followed by flexion. It is clear that many forms of action appear in response to the signal when the animal is not restrained in its movements.

Inhibition of Response
It was predicted that cases of total inhibition of motor response should sometimes occur during training in the Inev group. Such inhibition did, in fact, appear in 24 percent of the trials. Included in this count were cases where the animal made slight head or ear movements but no leg movement or gross postural adjustment. This absence of response did not look like lack of any reaction, for even when the animal stood completely still, it was frequently noted to look rigid, tense, or "as if it were pressing hard on the

floor." Inhibition seldom occurred on more than four successive trials, and it was generally followed after one or two trials by action again.

Frequency of Reaction Patterns

There was in the repertory of reactions some suggestion of a hierarchy of dominance. A comparison of the four most frequent types of reaction in the Inev group is provided in Figure 6.2. It may be seen that walking backward is dominant over all other reactions in early training, being the most frequent response to CS on the second, third, and fifth day of training. On day 2, it was the dominant response for seven of the eight animals. Walking or running forward appeared early in the course of training, being second most frequent on day 2, but its curve falls steadily thereafter. Inhibition was actually the most frequent response on day 4. Not until day 6 did flexion of the shocked leg gain top frequency. Its curve rises as the curves for running fall, but it never became the exclusive reaction, occurring only on 52.5 percent of the trials over-all.

In general, locomotion was reduced as training went on, both to signals and during intervals between them. Figure 6.3 shows locomotor maps for one animal made on the third day and the tenth day of training. By day 10, the animal has cut down both its range and amount of movement. Still later, the animal, unless disturbed, usually stood still at the wall without moving for the entire 40 min. and made single limb movements to the CS.

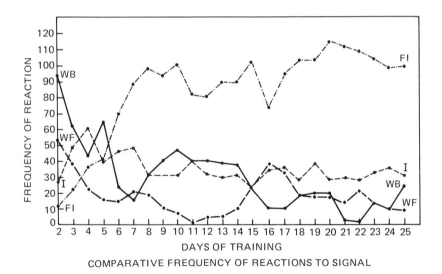

Figure 6.2
Comparative frequency of four types of reaction to a conditioned signal with unavoidable shock.

On the second day of training, animals in the Inev group made gross locomotor responses to CS on 93 per cent of the trials. But on training day 25, only 30 per cent of the signals produced locomotion; 70 percent of the overt responses recorded were single-limb movements. Locomotion was also reduced in the Av group, but here it was related to the experimenter's criterion for avoidance. Two of these animals were permitted to avoid the shock only when the right foreleg was lifted individually. On day 2, 75 percent of their responses were locomotor. On day 8, 100 percent of their responses were individual limb movements. These single-limb movements appear to have individuated from locomotion, as has been suggested before (12, 19). A backward flexion, for instance, is part of a backing movement. In many cases, the observer wrote, "kid started to back, but lifted only one leg, and stopped without setting it down." Yet, suppression of locomotion in the Inev group did not by any means result in stereotypy, although the repertory was gradually reduced.

Variability with Avoidance and with Inevitable Shock
It was predicted that frequent shifts from one reaction to another should occur in group Inev, whereas group Av should show a trend toward uniformity of reaction to the signal. Such was, indeed, the case, as Figure 6.4 demonstrates. Shifts from one reaction pattern to another were very frequent; both groups averaged 13 a day on the second day of training. By day 25, group Inev still averaged 12 shifts, but group Av now had a mean of 1. A shift was counted as any change in the reaction to the CS between one presentation of the CS and the next. Repetition of the previous response with a new response added was counted as a shift. Table 6.1 presents sample protocols, summarized and codified, for two animals from group Inev. Shifting from one reaction to another is evident in both.

DAY 3 (TRIALS 40-60)   DAY 10 (TRIALS 180-200)

Figure 6.3
Locomotor maps showing range and extent of movement of one animal on the third and the tenth day of training.

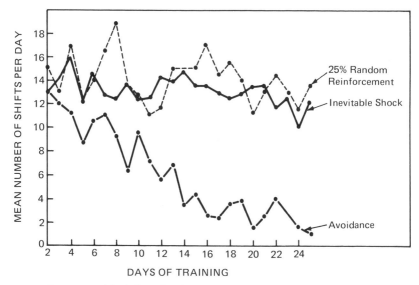

Frequency of Shift from One Reaction Pattern to Another

Figure 6.4
Frequency of shifts from one reaction pattern to another under three conditions of shock.

Animal 40 shows rather consistent reduction in locomotion and some stereotypy on day 25, although there is one regression to walking backward. Animal 7 exhibits no tendency at all to uniformity and shows a variety of reactions and frequent shifting on all four days. Avoidance animals, long before day 25, fixated one response and repeated it consistently. It may be concluded that the data show clearly the extreme variability of reaction under inevitable shock as contrasted with increasing uniformity under avoidance.

Change of Reaction with Avoidance
There have been several discussions of the form of conditioned reaction shown in shock avoidance when the shock was presented to the foreleg (3, 9, 22). According to our present assumptions, the reaction learned might be any response included in the animal's escape-defense repertory. To produce fixation of a given response, the experimenter need only wait till the animal makes that response and then consistently omit the shock whenever it occurs.

As a test of this prediction, we allowed one of our avoidance animals to escape shock by rearing; when the rearing to CS became absolutely regular, the animal was given inevitable shock. After variability of reaction had reasserted

Table 6.1
Sample Daily Protocols*

	Animal 40				Animal 7			
	Day 3	Day 13	Day 20	Day 25	Day 3	Day 13	Day 20	Day 25
1	Fl	Fl, R	Fl	H	I	WB	WF	WF
2	Fl, WB	R	Fl	H	WF	WF, Fl	Fl	WF, Wh
3	WF, WB	WB, Fl	Fl	H	H	Fl	WF, Fl	WF, Fl
4	WF	WB	WB, Fl	Fl	H	I	I	Wh
5	I	WB, Fl	I	Fl	LM	H	Fl	Ex
6	I	WB, Fl, R	Fl	H	H	Fl, Ex	H	WL
7	I	WB, Fl(L)	Fl	Fl	I	H	H	I
8	Fl	WB, R	WB, Fl	Fl	WB	LM	WF	H
9	WB	WB	Fl	Fl	WB	Fl	Ex(L)	Wh, WB
10	WB	WB	WB, Fl	Fl	I	Fl	Fl	Wh, WB
11	WB, Fl	WB, Wh	WB, Fl	WB	I	WF	Ex	Wh, WB
12	WB	WB, Fl	Fl	Fl	I	Fl	H	I
13	Fl, WL	WB, Fl	Fl	Fl	I	WF	Ex	Wh, WF
14	WB	WB, Wh	Fl	Fl	I	Fl	I	Wh
15	WB, Wh	WB	Fl	Fl	I	Fl	I	I
16	WB, WF	WB, Fl	Fl	Fl	WB	I	I	WF
17	WB	WB, Fl	Fl	Fl	H	Fl	Fl	WF
18	WL	WB, Fl	I	H	H	I	Fl	WF
19	WB, Fl	WB, WF, Fl	Fl	Fl	I	H	I	I
20	WB, Wh	I	Fl	Fl	I	I	H	I

*Key to abbreviations:

Fl	—flexes	I	—inhibition
Fl(L)	—flexes left leg	H	—head movements only
WB	—walks backward	Wh	—wheels
WF	—walks forward	Ex	—extends leg
WL, WR	—sidesteps to left or right	R	—rears
LM	—independent leg movement (other than flexion or extension)		

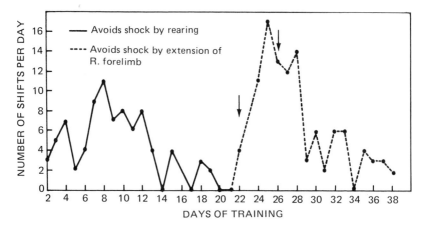

Figure 6.5
Frequency of shifts from one reaction pattern to another for one animal during two phases of avoidance training.

itself, the animal was again given avoidance training, but this time it could escape the shock only by a sustained lift of the right foreleg alone. Figure 6.5 portrays the number of shifts of reaction for each day's training for this single animal. Through day 21, the shock could be avoided by rearing, which the animal began performing on its first day of training. Shifts of response increased in the early stages (through day 8) because rearing was part of a complex pattern involving lying down between trials. When the CS occurred, it rose to a stance and then reared, placing the forefeet on the wall. As it began to avoid shock, it tended at first to eliminate rearing and to retain the rising from lying position only. After the eighth day, however, the animal gave up lying down, and rearing became gradually stereotyped. On days 22, 23, and 24, it received inevitable shock, with an accompanying rise in the number of shifts, as we should expect from our original assumptions. After day 24, it was allowed to avoid the shock by sustained lifting of the right foreleg and the number of shifts again diminished until a stereotyped reaction was achieved. The leg was extended forward and waved, usually rhythmically, until the light came on. Three days of inevitable shock cut out the rearing reaction completely, and it did not occur again. But a number of other responses did, and presumably it would have been possible to fixate any one of them.

Random Shock
One effect of 100 percent shock is to produce variability of reaction. If the number of shocks were to be decreased from 100 per cent, but in a random fashion so that no one reaction consistently led to avoidance, would variability decrease? In order to answer this question, an experiment was set up with 25 per cent shock, using two animals. This proportion was chosen in order to approximate, at least roughly, the number of shocks received by

the avoidance animals, and it seemed, as an early guess, about right. A new random distribution of the five shocks in each group of 20 trials was used for every training day. In these animals the reduction of locomotion and the development of individual limb movement proceeded very slowly. The animals made a large number of "conflictful" responses, jerking the head from side to side, circling alternately from right to left, or hitching backward and forward during the signal. But the most interesting result concerns variability. The reduced proportion of shocks was *not* accompanied by reduction in variability of reaction to the CS, as Figure 6.4 makes clear. Shifting from one reaction to another was very frequent. It is as if trial and error were at a maximum for an insoluble problem, which, indeed, it was. In a sense, the problem is even more baffling than inevitable 100 percent shock, for avoidance occurs without consistent relation to action. Absence of shock as such, consequently, cannot be the reason for increasing uniformity in avoidance training. Uniformity is created by the situation. Consistent avoidance of the shock functions as positive reinforcement. The present experiment does not permit determination of the nature of this reinforcement, but it might be, for instance, either fear reduction or confirmation of an expectancy.

Discussion

In general, the theoretical predictions made are clearly borne out by the results. But several questions arise concerning additional results which were not predicted. The theory demands that actions following the CS be part of the animal's escape-defense repertory. Some of those observed are clearly such: locomotion, which begins as running away; rearing and head-lowering, which are associated with startle or fright in the animal's life history; wheeling, which is a circling type of withdrawal; crouching and butting, which are defensive and offensive reactions, respectively. But what of the individual limb movements, the segmental reactions, such as single-leg flexion or extension, or stepping in place? The significance of these movements can be understood if it is recognized that they are actually segments of the original locomotor response. To quote Liddell: "May it not be that the conditioned limb movements graphically recorded in our experiments are stepping movements, and that these precise reactions represent an experimentally curtailed, or "symbolic" manifestation of running? ... The sheep, repeatedly flexing the foreleg in response to the conditioned stimulus, is really trying to run away from a situation about to become dangerous" (12, pp. 57 ff.).

This view is supported by the late appearance of single-limb movements in our results. Locomotion clearly dominated the repertory in the early stages of training. Schlosberg (17, 18, 8) and Wolf and Kellogg (22) also found that precise flexion came late, if at all. The real puzzle to be solved, then, is why locomotion is curtailed. When the animal is restrained in a stock or frame, as were the animals in all previous experiments of this sort, the problem is not so evident. But even in the present free situation locomotion was reduced. Liddell, in discussing development of neurotic manifestations, described this curtailment as "self-imposed restraint" (11). But what does this phrase mean in terms of learning theory? Differentiation and individuation of response are generally observed in studies of motor learning or development. Perhaps development of motor response will tend to go in the direction of elimination of gross movements even when the segmental responses are not specifically adaptive—particularly when the gross movements are not themselves adaptive. This is not generally true of the rodents, as has been pointed out; in their case, freezing or a tense quiescence seems to follow reduction of running or struggling. But in animals with, presumably, a somewhat more differentiated cortex, locomotion will break up into segmental responses if locomotion is inadequate; if a given segmental response does not answer, trial and error persists, yielding either a variety of segmental responses or a combination of these with regression to locomotion.

Such, in general, was the picture when the animals received inevitable shock. Even as late as the twenty-fifth day of training, variability persisted in these animals; segmental responses occurred but were not consistently repeated. Because uniformity did develop in animals permitted to avoid the shock, we conclude that the hypothesis of a dual role for unavoidable shock is supported. If it follows a motor response, this response tends eventually to be suppressed and supplanted by another. The result can be described as an interminable process of trial and error, by which the problem is never solved. This conclusion is in general agreement with Estes' (4) contention that shock causes suppression of preceding responses, although it does not accomplish complete extinction. In the course of the long trial and error with unavoidable shock observed here, the animals often regressed briefly to responses previously tried and dropped.

The other role of shock—strengthening of a conditioned emotional reaction to the signal—we find consistent with the behavior of both avoidance and nonavoidance animals, for, as we have tried to show, the resulting action is appropriate to a state of internal "emergency." There is, thus, support for Schlosberg (19) and, later, Mowrer (15) in assuming two processes of modification. One depends solely on paired stimulation with CS and US (the conditioned fear), whereas a second process follows the law of effect (fixation or suppression of the motor reaction to fear). The results tend to support Mowrer's contention that motor reactions (at least other than very diffuse emotional ones) are modified in accordance with the second process. It is impossible to agree with Culler that "the CR begins as a copy of UR and then grows into something different. In the first stages, it may be indistinguishable from UR; indeed with decorticate preparations it remains indistinguishable throughout. Normally, however, CR differentiates into a specific preparation for the oncoming US" (3, p. 142). It appears, rather, that the greatest resemblance between the CR and the UR comes in the late stages of training when single-limb flexion develops. The early reactions to the signal take the form of rapid backing or running and are not copies of the UR.

It will be asked by the supporters of Guthrie whether the reactions to the shock itself did not show equally wide variation, with the possibility that each reaction to the signal might vary in accordance with the reaction to the last shock. The data as here summarized do not offer proof to the contrary, but it was the experience of all the observers in the experiment that no such correlation existed. Variation of response to the signal was enormously greater than that to shock, not only in number of shifts but in variety of patterns. In other words, anticipation of noxious stimulation seems to have more ways of displaying itself than reaction to the noxious stimulation itself.

Summary and Conclusions

1. In line with recent two-factor learning theories it is suggested that conditioned responses developed with inevitable shock will exhibit characteristics derived from two functions of the shock; the shock reinforces a conditioned emotional state which instigates a motor response of a defensive character, and it also suppresses the motor response, causing it eventually to be supplanted by another action belonging to the animal's natural escape-defense repertory. Kids were trained in a situation permitting free locomotion under three arrangements of shock: (a) shock inevitable, (b) shock avoidable by a given consistent action, and (c) random shock.
2. At least ten different reactions to the CS were observed. The dominant reaction in early training was locomotion backward. All forms of locomotion became less frequent than segmental movements, such as flexion, in later stages of training.
3. Inhibition of response (standing still) occurred on 24 percent of the trials in the animals given inevitable shock.
4. With animals given inevitable shock, there were frequent shifts from one reaction to another, even on the twenty-fifth day of training; but when shock could be avoided, there was a definite trend toward uniformity of reaction.
5. After an animal had achieved a uniform response which avoided the shock, introduction of inevitable shock brought renewed vari-

ability of reaction. A different avoidance reaction could then be fixated.

6. Random delivery of shock in 25 percent of the trials did not reduce variability as compared with 100 percent shock.

7. Inevitable shock gave a general picture of continuous trial and error. There was no support for the Pavlovian view that shock acts to reinforce a withdrawal movement, in the sense of increasing the probability of recurrence of the same motor reaction; it had, instead, a tendency to suppress a preceding action, with the result that another took its place.

Notes

1. This investigation was supported (in part) by a research grant from the National Institute of Mental Health, U.S. Public Health Service.

2. Grateful appreciation is expressed to Dr. Howard Liddell, Dr. A. Ulric Moore, Mr. James Block, and Mrs. Miriam Salpeter, colleagues who shared in the observations to be reported. Dr. Moore was responsible for design and construction of apparatus.

3. It may be noted that James (7) found it impossible to condition leg flexion in the opossum, although it could be conditioned to attack or to "play possum"; Liddell and his co-workers (12) found it impossible to develop a precise flexion in the rabbit, which continued to react with struggling movements even after prolonged training; Brogden (1) noted that the guinea pig "sits tight" or freezes before delivery of inevitable shock; in this laboratory a young ram recently exhibited, instead of leg flexion, pawing and butting responses to the CS.

4. Four of the animals were accompanied in the experimental room by their mothers. This feature was irrelevant for the present purpose.

References

1. Brogden, W. J. The effect of frequency of reinforcement upon the level of conditioning. *J. exp. Psychol.*, 1939, 24, 419–431.

2. Brogden, W. J., Lipman, E. A., and Culler, E. The role of incentive in conditioning and extinction. *Amer. J. Psychol.*, 1938, 51, 109–117.

3. Culler, E. A. Recent advances in some concepts of conditioning. *Psychol. Rev.*, 1938, 45, 134–153.

4. Estes, W. K. An experimental study of punishment. *Psychol. Monogr.*, 1944, 57, No. 263.

5. Hilgard, E. R., and Marquis, D. G. *Conditioning and learning.* New York: Appleton-Century, 1940.

6. Hull, C. L. *Principles of behavior.* New York: Appleton-Century, 1943.

7. James, W. T. An experimental study of the defense mechanism in the opossum, with emphasis on natural behavior and its relation to mode of life. *J. genet. Psychol.*, 1937, 51, 95–100.

8. Kappauf, W. E., and Schlosberg, H. Conditioned responses in the white rat: III. Conditioning as a function of the length of the period of delay. *J. genet. Psychol.*, 1937, 50, 27–45

9. Kellogg, W. N. Evidence for both stimulus-substitution and original anticipatory responses in the conditioning of dogs. *J. exp. Psychol.*, 1938, 22, 186–192.

10. Liddell, H. S. The nervous system as a whole: the conditioned reflex. In J. F. Fulton, *Physiology of the nervous system* (2nd Ed.). New York: Oxford Univ. Press, 1943. Pp. 491–522.
11. Liddell, H. S. Conditioned reflex method and experimental neurosis. Ch. 12 in J. McV. Hunt (Ed.), *Personality and the behavior disorders*. New York: Ronald Press, 1944. Pp. 389–412.
12. Liddell, H. S., James, W. T., and Anderson, O. D. The comparative physiology of the conditioned motor reflex. *Comp. Psychol. Monogr.*, 1934, 11, No. 51.
13. Maier, N. R. F., and Schneirla, T. C. Mechanisms in conditioning. *Psychol. Rev.*, 1942, 49, 117–134.
14. Miller, N. E. Studies of fear as an acquirable drive: I. Fear as motivation and fear-reduction as reinforcement in the learning of new responses. *J. exp. Psychol.*, 1948, 38, 89–101.
15. Mowrer, O. H. On the dual nature of learning: A reinterpretation of "conditioning" and "problem-solving." *Harv. educ. Rev.*, 1947, 17, 107–148.
16. Mowrer, O. H. *Learning theory and personality dynamics.* New York: Ronald Press, 1950.
17. Schlosberg, H. Conditioned responses in the white rat. *J. genet. Psychol.*, 1934, 45, 303–335.
18. Schlosberg, H. Conditioned responses in the white rat: II. Conditioned responses based upon shock to the foreleg. *J. genet. Psychol.*, 1936, 49, 107–138.
19. Schlosberg, H. The relationship between success and the laws of conditioning. *Psychol. Rev.*, 1937, 44, 379–394.
20. Sheffleid, F. D. Avoidance training and the contiguity principle. *J. comp. physiol. Psychol.*, 1948, 41, 165–177.
21. Skinner, B. F. *The behavior of organisms: An experimental analysis.* New York: Appleton-Century, 1938.
22. Wolf, I. S., and Kellogg, W. N. Changes in general behavior during flexion conditioning and their importance for the learning process. *Amer. J. Psychol.*, 1940, 53, 384–396.

7

The Effect of Prolonged Exposure to Visually Presented Patterns on Learning to Discriminate Them

Eleanor J. Gibson, Richard D. Walk

Introduction to Chapters 7 and 8

Rearing experiments with either impoverished or enriched environments were very fashionable in the fifties. Interest began with histories of individuals deprived of normal environmental rearing conditions, the most extreme cases being persons born blind, who had later had sight restored by cataract removal (von Senden 1932, 1960), and persons thought to be reared in the wild, like the "wild boy of Aveyron" (Itard 1894, 1962). These cases had always stirred the imagination of philosophers, of course. But Donald Hebb's book (Hebb 1949), as well as the dark-rearing experiments of Lashley, (Lashley and Russell 1934), Hebb (1937) and Riesen (1947), brought questions of whether and how the environment exercised a role in development to the forefront of laboratory investigation. Hebb thought that "schemas" were developed from quite specific experiences that accounted for perceptual organization, with groups of cortical neurons exciting and reexciting one another. Hebb had been influenced by Senden's and Riesen's publications, remarking that "Both Senden's data and Riesen's said that there is no pattern perception without experience" (Hebb 1980, p. 295). (This despite the contrary results of his own experiments.)

Hebb's book and contemporary research on the neural development and organization of the visual system (Hubel and Wiesel 1959) inspired a spate of rearing experiments, involving deprivation of light, or patterned light (see E. Gibson 1969, ch. 12, for a summary). Hebb's own earlier experiments were designed to study the effect of light deprivation on visual discrimination in adult rats. But later on he designed an "early environment" program in which younger members of his department at McGill participated (Hymovitch 1952, Thompson and Heron 1954, Melzack and Scott 1957). This program emphasized positive contributions of the environment. Hebb said in his autobiography, "This program was less dramatic than sensory-deprivation work, but perhaps more important. It was a

Journal of Comparative and Physiological Psychology, 1956, 49, 239–242.

major influence in persuading psychologists that the IQ is not built-in at birth, and so a factor in such things as the Head Start program" (Hebb 1980, 300).

This work, interesting and valuable as it was, seemed to have rather little bearing on Hebb's theory of visual cortical development, with its emphasis on cell assemblies created in the beginning by eye movements following lines and angles in quite specific presentations. As a theory of perceptual learning, it was of real concern to me, and I proposed to Richard Walk that we rear infant rats in a controlled rat environment with the addition of triangles and circles on the cage walls. Though these were hardly typical of a rat's normal environment, the opportunity to view them daily throughout early development might result in appropriate cell assemblies developing, and thus facilitate later learning of a discrimination cued by them. The circles and triangles were cut out of metal, painted black, and hung on the wire mesh of the cages. When the animals were tested later in a discrimination box with the same black figures painted on the doors, they learned significantly faster than their litter-mates reared without similar exposure.

We might have left it there, with a triumphant "Well, well!" But we didn't. We pushed on to further experiments (nine in all), varying such factors as time of exposure (was there a "critical period" early on?), variations in the patterns at testing, the effects of differential reinforcement, and, finally, a comparison with dark-reared rats (Walk, Gibson, Pick, and Tighe 1958; Gibson, Walk, Pick, and Tighe 1958; Gibson, Walk, and Tighe 1959). Results in these replications, alas, were seldom as clear-cut as they had been in the original experiment. In fact, rats deprived of all light during their first ninety days of rearing learned the triangle-circle discrimination as readily as rats reared with an opportunity to view these patterns for the equivalent time. We had to conclude that we had no firm evidence that "perceptual discrimination of a form is an achievement resulting from an integration process of the neural elements involved" (Gibson, Walk, and Tighe 1959).

What might account for the positive results of the first experiment, and one or two later ones? Examination of all the experiments revealed one factor that appeared to favor a facilitation of later discrimination learning—that was whether the patterns hung on the cage wall were cut out, to provide depth at an edge, or were painted on a surface, with no edge depth, like pictures. Our last experiment, consequently, was a test of cutouts vs. painted patterns. The results of this experiment were positive, in the sense that the cutouts provided the only evidence for facilitation by prior experience with the patterns. But the effect was very weak. Location of an object as something separate and unitary in the layout is without doubt important in organizing perception and giving it meaning. But the notion that perceived form of an object depends on constructing a schema from repeated exposure to elementary pieces like lines and angles that fall upon the retina and are assembled in a phase sequence was unsupported. From my present approach— that perception does not start with something pictorial like a retinal image, but is rather a search for information about things in the world—that is not surprising.

We got the results we should have, and they make good sense, I think. Passive exposure to two-dimensional displays does not result in perceptual learning, even when reinforced, and deprivation of such exposure has no ill effects at all on later pattern discrimination learning. Exposure of similar patterns is quite as effective as exposure of the same ones, when any kind of effect occurs, as it did with cutouts. Perceiving an object segregated from its surrounding layout may have attentional value that carries over to another situation, but the object need not be the identical one. We needed a theory of perceptual learning, but not the one that led us to perform these rearing experiments.

Recent literature on the development of discrimination has shown an increasing trend toward acceptance of empiricistic explanations (2, 9). That ability to discriminate visually presented patterns develops with the experience and environmental reinforcement of the growing animal may be the case, but the evidence for this view is still inconclusive. Early studies by Lashley and Russell (11) and by Hebb (8) on the rat favored a nativistic interpretation of the differentiation of visual qualities, but later comparable studies with the chimpanzee and pigeon (13, 14) apparently favored an empiricistic explanation. Recent experiments by students of Hebb (5, 6, 10) have employed an "enrichment" technique, with results which appear to favor a learning hypothesis. These studies attempted to provide a generally "rich" environment and used as criteria tests of a rather general type. If opportunity to view a varied and patterned environment is important in the differentiation of visual qualities, we do not know how general or how specific the relevant experience must be.

The experiment to be reported proposed to investigate the dependence of visual form discrimination in adult rats on a specific variation in visual stimulation during growth. To this end, an experimental group of animals was raised from birth in cages which exhibited on the walls circles and triangles identical in form with ones later to be discriminated. The control group was raised under the same standard conditions but without opportunity to see these forms before the discrimination learning began. If the opportunity to view specific forms favors development of the ability to differentiate them in a later discrimination learning problem, the experimental animals should learn faster and show a higher proportion of Ss reaching the criterion than the control group.

Method

Rearing

The Ss were albino rats reared from birth in identical $\frac{1}{2}$-in. wire-mesh cages measuring 15 by 13 by 9 in. The cages were placed next to each other in a small, softly lighted empty room. Each cage was surrounded by white cardboard walls on three sides, several inches from the wire mesh and a blank wall of the room on the fourth side, 4 ft. from the mesh. At the top 7 ft. from the mesh was the ceiling of the room. Visible within the cage were only the cage mates, a water bottle on one wall, and food.

On the walls of the cages of the experimental animals were fastened four black metal forms, two equilateral triangles and two circles. The circles were 3 in. in diameter and the triangles were $3\frac{1}{2}$ in. on a side. These patterns were changed in position occasionally to assure a random relationship to food and water. All during the experiment stimulus patterns were left on the sides of the cages of experimental group animals.

A total of four groups was used, two experimental and two control. These will be numbered as follows: E_1 (experimental, litter 1), E_2 (experimental, litter 2), C_1 (control, litter 1), and C_2 (control, litter 2). Litters E_1 ($n = 8$) and C_1 ($n = 2$) were the first born. These litters were born five days apart and, because of the long interval between litters, not split. E_2 ($n = 10$) and C_2 ($n = 9$) were born within a day of each other, and litters were split when the pups were one or two days old. The young were weaned at four weeks of age, and at eight weeks sexes were divided so that males and females were in separate cages. The experiment was begun when the animals were approximately 90 days old.

Apparatus

The apparatus was a modification of one described by Grice (7). Two V-shaped discrimination compartments were joined together and a false floor constructed, as described in Baker and Lawrence (1). The two stimulus patterns were side by side at the 10-in.-wide end of both choice chambers. The $4\frac{3}{8}$-in. by $4\frac{3}{8}$-in. metal stimulus holders slid into grooves between the $1\frac{1}{4}$-in. center partition and the side of the apparatus. Masonite doors fitted into grooves $\frac{1}{4}$ in. in front of the stimulus holders. The apparatus was painted a flat black, and each section was covered by glass. A 25-w. bulb mounted 25 in. above the floor furnished the only illumination. The stimulus holders were first painted a flat white, and a black circle and triangle were painted on the white background. The circle was $2\frac{3}{4}$ in. in diameter and the equilateral triangle 3 in. on a side. The stimulus holders had $1\frac{1}{8}$-in. square doors in them, and the animal obtained food by pushing open the door in the center. There were four separate stimulus holders, one with the circle and one with the triangle, for each discrimination box.

Training Procedure

Pretraining.   Animals were placed on a 24-hr. feeding cycle for approximately one week prior to the start of experimentation. They were given three to four days' training in obtaining a small quantity of wet mash from the stimulus holders by pushing open the door in the center. The stimulus holders were painted flat black for this pretraining. The door on only one side of the discrimination box was raised at a time. As soon as the animal obtained the food from the food cup, E lowered the door in front of the stimulus holder. The door between the two discrimination boxes was then opened for the next trial, and the animal secured food by pushing its nose against the black stimulus holder at the opposite end. The animal ate ten times from the cup in the holder in the following order: RLLRRLLRRL.

Discrimination training.   During discrimination training both Masonite doors on the choice side of the apparatus were raised, exposing the two stimulus patterns side by side. Both stimulus holders were baited. As soon as the animal pushed against one stimulus door, the Masonite door in front of the opposite stimulus was closed. If the choice was correct, the animal was allowed to eat the wet mash in the food cup. After 60 sec., the door between the two compartments was opened and the animal proceeded to the opposite end, where the next choice was made. If it was incorrect, a modified correction procedure was followed. Both doors in front of the stimulus holders were closed. After 60 sec. the animal was allowed to make a choice in the opposite discrimination box. Animals were allowed up to three errors per trial. Following the third error the door in front of the correct stimulus figure remained open, and the animal was allowed to eat from it. This procedure meant that the animal ate equally often on each side of the apparatus. Ten trials were given each day with a maximum of three errors per trial.

The positive stimulus was presented in the following order: RLRRLLRLLR; LRLLRRLRRL; RRLLRRLRLL; LLRRLLRLRR. The order was repeated every four days. For half the animals in each group the circle was the positive stimulus, and for half the triangle. Animals were run until they attained a criterion of 18 out of 20 correct responses, with the last ten consecutive responses correct (one day's run), or until they were run in the experiment for 15 days (150 trials). After the experimental session animals were allowed to eat food pellets for 1 hr. The hunger drive was a function of approximately $22\frac{1}{2}$ hr. deprivation. Each of the two *E*s ran one-half of the experimental and one-half of the control animals.

Results

The number of days of discrimination training and the errors (initial and repetitive) are presented in Table 7.1 for both groups of animals. In the table are indicated the sex and litter of each animal. The second litters (LE_2 and LC_2), it will be remembered, were split at birth and thus provide a somewhat better controlled population. It is obvious from the table that there is a difference between experimental and control groups. Out of the control group, only 1 animal reached the criterion during 15 days of training. But 15 of the 18 experimental group animals did. By the chi-square test, this difference is significant at better than the .001 level of confidence. If we calculate the chi square for animals of the split-litter groups only, using Fisher's exact test (4), the significance of the difference is between .002 and .001. The errors, both initial and repetitive, reflect the same trend.

A further check on differences in the population studied is possible by testing males against females. When this comparison is made, the chances are exactly 50 in 100 that there is any difference between sex groups.

Table 7.1
Number of Days Trained and Errors for the Experimental and Control Groups

	Experimental Group			Control Group			
Animal	No. Days Run	Initial Errors	Repetitive Errors	Animal	No. Days Run	Initial Errors	Repetitive Errors
LE$_1$ 30 ♂	12*	39	44	LC$_1$ 2 ♂	14*	25	11
LE$_1$ 31 ♂	7*	22	34	LC$_1$ 20 ♀	15	68	52
LE$_1$ 32 ♂	11*	28	19	LC$_2$ 4 ♀	15	50	44
LE$_1$ 33 ♂	5*	11	9	LC$_2$ 6 ♀	15	59	30
LE$_1$ 35 ♀	15	32	21	LC$_2$ 7 ♀	15	67	18
LE$_1$ 37 ♂	14*	40	41	LC$_2$ 12 ♀	15	60	28
LE$_1$ 40 ♂	7*	24	29	LC$_2$ 15 ♀	15	80	80
LE$_1$ 41 ♂	8*	24	24	LC$_2$ 11 ♂	15	66	72
LE$_2$ 44 ♀	7*	23	28	LC$_2$ 5 ♂	15	68	80
LE$_2$ 47 ♀	10*	25	16	LC$_2$ 13 ♂	15	74	117
LE$_2$ 62 ♀	15	70	73	LC$_2$ 14 ♂	15	84	92
LE$_2$ 63 ♀	9*	23	16				
LE$_2$ 64 ♀	12*	39	50				
LE$_2$ 43 ♂	15	57	51				
LE$_2$ 45 ♂	13*	28	12				
LE$_2$ 46 ♂	10*	25	16				
LE$_2$ 60 ♂	9*	30	23				
LE$_2$ 61 ♂	10*	37	34				
Mean	10.50	32.06	30.00		14.91	63.73	56.73

*Indicates that animal reached criterion; the criterion day's trials are included in number of days run.

Figure 7.1 shows the learning curve for experimental and control groups. Percentage of correct responses is plotted against days of training. The animals that reached the criterion are included in the percentages on the assumption that they would continue at their final level of performance. The curves show that the groups begin to diverge by the third or fourth day of training and diverge increasingly thereafter until the tenth day, when a majority of the experimental group had learned.

Discussion

The results presented show conclusively a difference in ease of learning a circle-triangle discrimination between the group reared with these forms exhibited on the cage walls and the control group. Since the control group had the same conditions of training (and pretraining), the same living

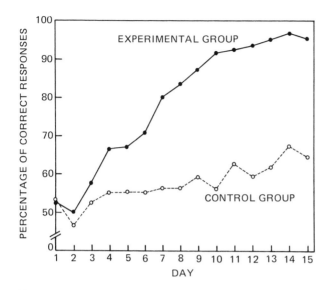

Figure 7.1
Learning curves, in percentage of correct responses per day, for the experimental and control groups.

conditions, and, in our second litters, the same heredity, the difference must be attributed to some advantage arising from the opportunity to look at the forms. This advantage could be something specific which happens early in the animals' development, analogous with "imprinting" (12) or with Hebb's postulated development of reverberating neural circuits (9). On the other hand, a learning theorist who favors "hypotheses" as a factor in learning a discrimination might suggest that seeing the forms on the cage walls favors formation of the correct hypothesis. Since the forms were left on the walls during the learning period, it is not possible to conclude that early experience in viewing the forms is the basis of the effect. Suitable controls are at present being run to clarify this point.

Since research in discrimination learning has centered round the continuity hypothesis in recent years, it might be asked whether the present results tend to confirm or deny this hypothesis. The animals in the experimental group profited, in the discrimination task, from an opportunity to view the two forms without any differential reinforcement of them. Nondifferential reinforcement in viewing these could have occurred, since the animals ate and drank in their presence. Spence's 1936 article (15) suggests that some degree of positive excitatory potential, irrespective of differential reinforcement, would be consistent with faster learning when differential reinforcement is introduced. On the other hand, the values selected for his analysis are purely arbitrary, so it cannot be concluded that effective nondifferential reinforcement either confirms or refutes his statement of the hypothesis. Bitterman and Elam (3) concluded that perceptual differentiation occurs in the course of sheer experience with test stimuli, despite lack of differential reinforcement. But this conclusion is beclouded by their further finding that there is a general retarding effect of nondifferential reinforcement. The present results seem to demonstrate clearly the positive transfer from experience in viewing the test stimuli, without the complications introduced by specific application of reinforcement.

Further research on the problem described will investigate whether there is an optimal or critical time for the visual experience, and the relative specificity of the resulting facilitation of discrimination learning.

Summary

This experiment sought to determine the effect of early and continued exposure to certain forms, presented visually, on the ease with which an adult animal learns to discriminate them. Two groups of animals were raised from birth in well-illuminated cages surrounded by white cardboard. Animals of the experimental group also had mounted on the walls of their cages black circles and triangles, from birth throughout the duration of the experiment. When the animals were approximately 90 days old, both experimental and control groups learned a circle-triangle discrimination. Animals of the experimental group reached the criterion significantly faster and made fewer errors than the control group. It was concluded that visual experience with the forms to be discriminated, even in the absence of differential reinforcement, facilitated the discrimination learning.

References

1. Baker, R. A., & Lawrence, D. H. The differential effects of simultaneous and successive stimuli presentation on transposition. *J. comp. physiol. Psychol.*, 1951, 44, 378–382.
2. Beach, F. A., & Jaynes, J. Effects of early experience upon the behavior of animals. *Psychol. Bull.*, 1954, 51, 239–263.
3. Bitterman, M. E., & Elam, C. B. Discrimination following varying amounts of non-differential reinforcement. *Amer. J. Psychol.*, 1954, 67, 133–137.
4. Fisher, R. A. *Statistical methods for research workers.* (11th Ed.) New York: Hafner, 1950.
5. Forgays, D. G., & Forgays, Janet W. The nature of the effect of free-environment experience in the rat. *J. comp. physiol.* Psychol., 1952, 45, 322–328.
6. Forgus, R. H. The effect of early perceptual learning on the behavioral organization of adult rats. *J. comp. physiol. Psychol.*, 1954, 47, 331–336.
7. Grice, G. R. The acquisition of a visual discrimination habit following response to a single stimulus. *J. exp. Psychol.*, 1948, 38, 633–642.
8. Hebb, D. O. The innate organization of visual activity. I. Perception of figures by rats reared in total darkness. *J. genet. Psychol.*, 1937, 51, 101–126.

9. Hebb, D. O. *The organization of behavior*. New York: Wiley, 1949.
10. Hymovitch, B. The effects of experimental variations on problem solving in the rat. *J. comp. physiol. Psychol.*, 1952, 45, 313–321.
11. Lashley, K. S., & Russell, J. T. The mechanism of vision. XI. A preliminary test of innate organization. *J. genet. Psychol.*, 1934, 45, 136–144.
12. Lorenz, K. Der Kumpan in der Umwelt des Vogels. *J. Orn. Lpz.*, 1935, 83, 137–213.
13. Riesen, A. H. The development of visual perception in man and chimpanzees. *Science*, 1947, 106, 107–108.
14. Siegel, A. I. Deprivation of visual form definition in the ring dove. I. Discriminatory learning. *J. comp. physiol. Psychol.*, 1953, 46, 115–119.
15. Spence, K. W. The nature of discrimination learning in animals. *Psychol. Rev.*, 1936, 43, 427–449.

8

The Effectiveness of Prolonged Exposure to Cutouts vs. Painted Patterns for Facilitation of Discrimination

Richard D. Walk, Eleanor J. Gibson,
Herbert L. Pick, Jr., Thomas J. Tighe

Experiments by the authors (Gibson & Walk, 1956; Gibson, Walk, Pick, & Tighe, 1958; Gibson, Walk, & Tighe, 1959; Walk, Gibson, Pick, & Tighe, 1958) have shown that prolonged exposure to visually presented patterns may, under certain conditions, facilitate discrimination of these patterns in a learning situation[1] An auxiliary finding was that in experiments where the patterns exposed in the cage were *cutouts*, facilitation always occurred, though in other experiments where the same patterns were painted on a plain rectangular background, there was no facilitation. This effect has been previously commented on (Gibson et al., 1959; Walk et al., 1958), but no single experiment has directly compared the effectiveness of cutouts with painted patterns. The present experiment was designed to do so.

The experiment included four groups of albino rats, treated as follows: Group I was reared with cutout patterns (triangle and circle) on the walls of the living cages; Group II was reared with the same patterns painted on metal rectangles on the cage walls; Group III was reared with plain-color rectangles, like Group II, but without the painted pattern; Group IV was reared with nothing mounted on the mesh walls of the living cages. From the results of the previous experiments, the following relationships among the four groups should hold.

1. The cutout-pattern group (I) should be superior to the control group (IV). This is a replication of our first experiment (Gibson & Walk, 1956).

2. The painted-pattern group (II) should not be significantly different from the plain-rectangle group (III) (Gibson et al., 1959; Walk et al., 1958).

3. The cutout-pattern group (I) should be superior to the painted-pattern group (II) and the plain-rectangle group (III). This difference

Journal of Comparative and Physiological Psychology, 1959, 52, 519–521.

has not been tested directly, but was hypothesized in two papers (Gibson et al., 1959; Walk et al., 1958).

4. The position of the painted-pattern group (II) and the plain-rectangle group (III) in relation to the control group (IV) cannot be predicted from previous research. If only the identical pattern, as a cutout, will produce facilitation, Groups II and III will be indistinguishable from Group IV. If the rectangles function as cutout figures and are sufficiently *similar* to the test figures to yield transfer (Gibson et al., 1958), then Groups II and III should learn the discrimination faster than Group IV.

Method

Subjects and Rearing Procedure

The Ss, 84 albino rats, were reared in identical $\frac{1}{2}$-in. wire-mesh cages painted white and measuring 16 by 13 by 9 in. The cages were placed in the center of compartments (27 by 23 by 22 in.) whose floors and walls were covered with masonite painted flat white. Illumination was supplied by fluorescent light 7 ft. above the cages.

Twelve pregnant rats from Rockland County Farm littered within a span of ten days. Litters were split among the four groups so that each group included offspring of all 12 mothers. The rectangles or cutouts were mounted on the cage walls of the appropriate groups before the pups' eyes opened and remained on the walls throughout the experiment. The patterns used for Group I were two sheet-metal circles (3 in. in diameter) and two sheet-metal triangles (3$\frac{1}{3}$ in. on each side). painted black. One form was mounted on each wall. For Group II, these patterns were painted on white rectangles, 4$\frac{1}{2}$ in. by 5 in. Group III's cage walls held four 4$\frac{1}{2}$-in. by 5-in. rectangles painted white.

Discrimination Training

Training began when the animals were 90 days old. They were placed on a 24-hr. feeding schedule and then habituated to the apparatus and pretrained. The modified Grice-type discrimination box already described (Gibson & Walk, 1956) was used. It contained two V-shaped compartments joined together so that the animal alternated from one to the other without handling. Stimulus holders painted black were used for pretraining. Animals learned to take food from holders with doors opened wide, and the doors were gradually closed. Pretraining continued until the animal pushed open closed doors, alternating from one compartment to the other, at least eight times in 10 min. Pretraining required a mean of 6.8 days.

For discrimination training the black stimulus holders were replaced by white holders on which was painted either a black triangle (3 in. on each side) or a black circle (2$\frac{3}{4}$ in. in diameter). When the door separating the two compartments was raised, an animal faced the two stimulus holders side by side. If the animal chose correctly by pushing the door of the positive stimulus, it was permitted to eat and a black door was lowered in front of the other holder, but if the animal moved the door of the negative stimulus (which was locked with $\frac{1}{8}$ in. of play), the doors were lowered in front of both stimuli and the animal made a second choice in the other compartment. Three errors (one initial and two repetitive) were allowed on each trial. When an animal made a second repetitive error, the door was lowered in front of the negative stimulus, and it was allowed to eat from the positive one. The right-left position of the positive stimulus was randomized. Ten trials were given a day, each trial followed by reinforcement, until S attained 18 correct choices in 20 trials with the last 10 correct. One animal in Group IV that had not learned in 300 trials was stopped. To control extraneous cues, eight stimulus holders were used. Four of these were used for Trials 1 to 5, the other four on Trials 6 to 10. Half the Ss had the circle as a positive stimulus, half had the triangle. Each of the four Es ran animals from each group.

Results

The mean trials and mean initial errors for each of the four groups are shown in Table 8.1. The test for replication is that between Group I (cutouts) and Group IV (control). The difference is in the predicted direction, but the *t*'s of 1.42 for trials and 1.54 for errors are only significant at the .10 level (one-tailed). Actually, the mean difference of 26 trials and of 12 initial errors (15% facilitation for trials and 20% for errors) was as large as that found in other experiments yielding significant differences (Gibson et al., 1958), but the variance is larger. The predicted no-difference between Group II (painted patterns) and Group III (white rectangles) was upheld with *t*'s of .39 for trials and .67 for errors ($p > .50$). The comparison between the cutout group (I) and the rectangle groups (II and III combined) was as predicted with *t*'s of 1.79 for trials and 1.73 for errors ($p < .05$, one-tailed). The question whether the stimuli for Groups II and III might yield some facilitation can apparently be answered negatively since the *t*'s of .10 for trials and .40 for errors ($p > .50$) that compared these groups with the controls were not significant.

This experiment, then, seems to uphold the hypothesis from previous research by the authors that only the cutouts yield facilitation in the

Table 8.1
Mean Trials to Criterion and Mean Initial Errors for the Four Groups

Group	Trials			Initial Errors	
	N	Mean	SD	Mean	SD
I (cutouts)	22	144.7	62.9	49.0	24.2
II (painted patterns)	21	175.2	54.9	57.0	17.6
III (white rectangles)	18	168.4	49.2	61.4	21.4
IV (control)	23	170.5	56.4	61.5	28.2

discrimination learning task, but the statistical level of the differences between the cutout group and the other groups is not very satisfactory.

Discussion

Including the experiment reported here, we have performed a series of nine separate experiments in which a total of 422 rodents were taught a triangle-circle discrimination, the experimental variable being always some type of exposure to visually presented patterns. In all experiments where cutouts were used as exposure stimuli, facilitation was observed (Gibson & Walk, 1956; Gibson et al., 1958, Experiments I and II; Gibson et al., l959, Experiment I; Walk et al., 1958, Experiment I; this experiment), but the amount of facilitation varied greatly from one experiment to the other. Painted patterns as exposure stimuli never yielded facilitation (Gibson et al., 1959, Experiments II and III; Walk et al., 1958, Experiment II; this experiment).

The reason suggested for the facilitation obtained by the cutouts is that the cutouts are "attention-getting." These solid pattern outlines stand out in contrast to the background as objects in depth. When later confronted by two painted patterns in the discrimination box, the animal is presumably more apt to differentiate the patterns from the total surroundings and to connect them as cues with the differential reinforcement. This hypothesis may be related to the superiority of "stereometric" over "planometric" stimuli in discrimination tasks with monkeys and children (Harlow & Warren, 1952; Stevenson & McBee, 1958; Weinstein, 1941).

Summary

An experiment was designed to test the effectiveness of metal cutouts compared with painted patterns as exposure stimuli during rearing. Four groups were used. Group I had black metal triangles and circles mounted on the cage walls during rearing. Group II had black painted triangles and circles on white rectangles. Group III had white rectangles in the living cages. Group IV had nothing mounted on the cage walls. Only Group I learned a triangle-circle discrimination faster than the other groups, which were indistinguishable from each other. While the experiment tentatively confirmed hypotheses derived from previous experimentation about the effectiveness of the cutouts as exposure stimuli to facilitate discrimination learning, the firmness of this conclusion is attenuated by the level of significance obtained in this experiment.

Notes

1. This experiment was supported, in part, by a grant from the National Science Foundation.

References

Gibson, E. J., & Walk, R. D. The effect of prolonged exposure to visually presented patterns on learning to discriminate them. *J. comp. physiol. Psychol.*, 1956, 49, 239–242.

Gibson, E. J., Walk, R. D., Pick, H. L., & Tighe, T. J. The effect of prolonged exposure to visual patterns on learning to discriminate similar and different patterns. *J. comp. physiol. Psychol.*, 1958, 51, 584–587.

Gibson, E. J., Walk, R. D., & Tighe, T. J. Enhancement and deprivation of visual stimulation during rearing as factors in visual discrimination learning. *J. comp. physiol. Psychol.*, 1959, 52, 74–81.

Harlow, H. F., & Warren, J. M. Formation and transfer of discrimination learning sets. *J. comp. physiol. Psychol.*, 1952, 45, 482–489.

Stevenson, H. W., & McBee, G. The learning of object and pattern discriminations by children. *J. comp. physiol. Psychol.*, 1958, 51, 752–754.

Walk, R. D., Gibson, E. J., Pick, H. L., & Tighe T. J. Further experiments on prolonged exposure to visual forms: The effect of single stimuli and prior reinforcement. *J. comp. physiol. Psychol.*, 1958, 51, 483–487.

Weinstein, B. Matching-from-sample by rhesus monkeys and by children. *J. comp. physiol. Psychol.*, 1941, 31, 195–213.

9

Behavior of Light- and Dark-Reared Rats on a Visual Cliff

Richard D. Walk, Eleanor J. Gibson, Thomas J. Tighe

It was truly serendipitous that the trouble required to rear a large group of rats in the dark inspired us to observe the rats in a second kind of test, a sort of artificial cliff. The idea was that the rats would walk out on it (glass over a void) if they had failed to develop depth discrimination during dark-rearing. T. J. Tighe, at that time our research assistant, and I hastily put together a simulated cliff with bits of wallpaper, glass, and rods and clamps that happened to be around the laboratory. Then we (Walk, Gibson, and Tighe, in a party) put the light-reared rats on a slightly raised center board, chosen as a starting place, and watched them as, one by one, they got down on the "shallow" side and crept around, but uniformly avoided the "deep" side. Then we took the dark-reared animals out of their seclusion and tried them, one by one. Their behavior was indistinguishable from their light-reared peers.

As we watched them, we began to be concerned that it might be just that side of the contraption that they didn't like—drafts or odors, who knows. We quickly fetched more of the wallpaper we had used on the shallow side, and put it directly under the glass of the deep side. Every rat was now given a second chance, and they all crossed back and forth from side to side, dark- and light-reared alike. As we returned the last rat to its cage, Tighe said, "I wouldn't have believed it if I hadn't seen it." It was a memorable day.

In the many experiments with the visual cliff that followed this one, our first, we concentrated on comparative studies with precocial and less precocial animals (Gibson and Walk 1960; Walk and Gibson 1961). It was several years later when we performed another dark-rearing study, with kittens as subjects. The results were an interesting contrast to the study with rats. When the kittens were brought out of the dark and placed on the cliff, they wandered about everywhere, not favoring one side or the other. But it could not be argued from their behavior that experiences with dropoffs was required for avoidance of them to appear. They

© AAAS. *Science,* 1957, 126, 80–81.

were put on the cliff daily following their introduction to a lighted environment. After two days in the light, eighty percent of the kittens avoided the deep side and after six days all did. Experience should have taught them that it was as safe as the other, if it taught them anything.

Dark rearing has problems as a method, but taking the results with those of other experiments one is struck with the species differences, first of all, in readiness to act at birth and, equally, with the amazing degree of preparedness to engage in perceptually guided behavior when an action system, such as locomotion, has matured to readiness in a normal environment. A light-reared kitten avoids a cliff when it is ready to walk, and detects the affordance of a supporting surface when it is visually specified. Normally maturing vision is essential for the proper outcome, but no learning of specific S-R bonds is involved.

From the 18th century to the present, the empiricist and the nativist theories of depth perception have been vigorously debated. One experiment aimed at resolving the dispute is Lashley and Russell's (1), in which rats reared in darkness jumped to a platform from a stand placed at a variable distance from it. The force of the jump was found to be graded in accordance with the distance of the platform. This is evidence for nativism. But, since the tests with graduated distances were not given until the rats' third day in the light, and after pretraining, the conclusion was not indubitable. Confirmation by another technique is desirable and has been provided in the experiment described in this report (2).

A technique of testing for visual depth perception which involves no pretraining at all—the "visual cliff"—was developed. It is based on the assumption that, given a choice, an animal will avoid descending over a vertical edge to a surface which appears to be far away (3). The apparatus (Fig 9.1) was constructed of two thicknesses of glass (24 in. by 32 in.), parallel to the floor and held by metal supports 53 in. above it. A board (4 in. wide, 24 in. long, and 3 in. high) extended across the glass, dividing it into two equal fields. On one side (the "near" side), patterned wallpaper was inserted between the two sheets of glass. Through the clear glass of the other side (the "far" side) the same pattern was visible on the floor and also on the walls below the glass surface.

Optically speaking, the edge on one side of the board dropped away for a distance of 53 in. (making the simulated cliff), while on the other side the edge dropped away for only 3 in. Thus, two visual fields existed, both filled with patterned wallpaper, but the pattern of the "far" field was optically much smaller and denser than that of the other and elicited more motion parallax. (More binocular parallax was also possible at one edge than at the other, but the rat is probably insensitive to this cue.) The fields were matched for reflected luminous intensity. The physical space, as distin-

Figure 9.1
(left) Apparatus for the experimental condition. The larger-checked field is the "near" side, optically; the clear glass field is the "far" or "cliff" side. Fig 9.2 (right) Apparatus for the control condition.

guished from the optical space, was identical on both sides, since a glass surface was present at a distance of 3 in. The only difference between the two fields, therefore, was a difference in optical stimulation. Other possible cues for safe descent (tactual, olfactory, auditory echolocation, air currents, or temperature differentials) were equalized by the glass.

In addition to the experimental condition described here, a control condition was included, in order to check on the presence of any unknown factors that would make for a preference for one side. A piece of wallpaper was inserted between the glass on both sides (Fig 9.2); otherwise, the apparatus was identical to that for the experimental condition. If controls are adequate, animals should show no preference for either side in this case.

Subjects for the experimental condition were 19 dark-reared, hooded rats, 90 days old, and 29 light-reared litter mates. Twenty minutes after coming into the light, the dark-reared rats were placed on the apparatus. An animal was placed on the center board in a box, to avoid any handling bias. It was then observed for 5 minutes. Results are summarized in Table 9.1. The percentage of animals that descended on the near side was not significantly different for light- and dark-reared rats. Of the light-reared rats, 23 descended on the near side, three descended on the far side, and three remained on the board for all 5 minutes. Of the dark-reared rats, 14 descended on the near side, three descended on the far side, and two remained on the board.

But a comparison of descent behavior of the experimental animals with the controls, for whom the visual surface was near on both sides, showed a difference. The control group, all light-reared litter mates of the experi-

Table 9.1

Comparison of Light- and Dark-Reared Animals on Visual Cliff (Experimental Group) and Comparsion of Both with a No-Cliff Control Group.

	Experimental group		Control group
	Light-reared ($N = 29$)	Dark-reared ($N = 19$)	Light-reared ($N = 10$)
Percentage descending on "near" side	88.5	82.4	50.0
Mean No. crossings	0.00	0.06	1.70
Percentage of time			
On "near"	76.0	57.9	24.1
On "far"*	10.0	16.9	61.5
On board	14.0	25.2	14.4

*The control group had no optically "far" side. Reference is to the same physical side that was "far" for the experimental group.

mental group, showed no preference in descending from the board; five went to each side. This group differs significantly from the experimental group ($p < 0.02$).

Even more interesting is a comparison of the exploratory behavior of the animals. The light-reared and dark-reared rats of the experimental group again behaved similarly; most of them stayed on the side of the center board that they had first chosen. Of the 43 experimental animals that descended from the board, only one crossed to the other side. But the control animals explored back and forth, often crossing the board to the other side several times. The difference in crossing behavior between experimental and control groups is highly significant ($p < 0.001$). The percentage of time spent on the two sides confirms the other measurements. Both experimental groups spent more than twice as much time on the side with the near optical pattern as on the side with the far optical pattern, while the control animals reversed this trend.

These results suggest two conclusions. First, hooded rats, 90 days of age, do discriminate visual depth or distance. They avoid a visual cliff as compared with a short visual drop-off, and this preference is eliminated when the visual cliff is eliminated. Second, such discrimination seems to be independent of previous visual experience, since dark-reared adult animals behaved like their light-reared litter mates only 20 minutes after being exposed to the light.

References and Notes

1. K. S Lashley and J. T. Russell, *J. Genet. Psychol.* 45, 136 (1934).
2. This research was supported, in part, by a grant from the National Science Foundation.

We wish to thank J. J. Gibson, for suggestions about apparatus and stimulus conditions.

3. The work of K. T. Waugh [*J. comp. Neurol.* 20, 549 (1910)] and J. T. Russell [*J. Genet. Psychol.* 40, 136 (1932)] makes this assumption seem plausible. Latency of jumping or "disinclination to jump" apparently increased as distance increased.

10

Development of Perception: Discrimination of Depth Compared with Discrimination of Graphic Symbols

Eleanor J. Gibson

The rearing studies and the research with infants on the visual cliff rekindled an interest in development that had begun (and been frustrated) with the work on kids at the Behavior Farm. How perception develops became a focal problem for me, as it still is. I wrote chapters for several books, one on methods of studying perceptual development (E. Gibson and Olum 1960) and one on perceptual development for a volume on child psychology published by the National Society for the Study of Education (E. Gibson 1963). The latter was an opportunity to think about a framework for studying perceptual development. The organization of the typical textbook chapter on perception, with sections on color vision, form perception, cues for depth, illusions, etc., was totally unsuitable. American psychology offered no framework for development except learning and conditioning theory, which made no reference at all to perception. Piaget was only beginning to exert an influence in the United States, and in any case he considered perception primitive, figurative, and merely preliminary to the construction of intelligence. I came up with an outline organized around what the environment offers the perceiver—places with surfaces and edges, objects, pictures, and graphic displays since these latter figured in most of the existing experimental literature. But the Yearbook the chapter appeared in was obscure, and a new impetus for getting perceptual development into the fore as a topic for research was needed.

The impetus came with a committee created by the Social Science Research Council in 1959, the Committee on Intellective Processes Research, specifically focused on the field of cognitive development. This committee planned six research conferences, to take place over a five-year period, and then a final summer institute. The time was ripe for the committee's efforts. They bore fruit in the conferences themselves, and finally in a totally revitalized discipline of developmental psychology. The proceedings of all the conferences were later gathered in

Reprinted from J. C. Wright and J. Kagan (eds.), Basic Cognitive Processes in Children, *Monographs of the Society for Research in Child Development*, 1963, 28, No. 2 (Serial No. 86).

one volume, a veritable classic (Cognitive Development in Children, published by the Society for Research in Child Development in 1970).

I was fortunate in being invited to prepare a paper for the second of these conferences, one called "Basic Cognitive Processes in Children." My partnership with Richard Walk had broken up in 1961 when he moved away from Cornell, and I shifted my research in other directions, including research on older children as they were introduced to coded symbols. This meeting gave me a chance to consider the way two quite distinct lines of research fit into the larger framework of perceptual development. I opened the paper with a comparison of the kind of information available in the two domains I was studying, perception of depth and perception of graphic symbols. The term "information" is not used—that came later—but choosing information as the logical place to start is a portent of how a present-day theory of perception came about.

Another forerunner of a growing theoretical view was the lesson suggested in this paper from the rat-rearing experiments: not only do solid objects, occupying their own place in the layout, take precedence in a viewer's attention over pictures or graphic presentations, but features of those objects can also be differentiated and may transfer later to the perceptual differentiation of pictorial copies or graphic compositions. Here stirs the embryo of a theory of pictorial perception. It is notable, too, that theorizing about graphic items harks back to the theory of paired associate learning in my dissertation: that items in a code have to be learned in two steps, first differentiated from others in their set and only thereafter associated (if that is what happens) with something called meaning.

This paper points ahead to work on reading, which I come to in part V. It seems instructive to put it here, however, to show how a theory of perceptual development was begun, and how research from ostensibly quite different domains was already converging on it.

The invitation to speak to this conference on my work in the field of perceptual development came at a most welcome moment for me. For the past six years I have worked, with several colleagues, on developmental aspects of two radically different kinds of perception—the perception of *depth* and the perception of outline forms inscribed on a piece of paper— that is, *letters* and *words*. Here was the opportunity to compare the two and, hopefully, to synthesize them.

Interest in the development of perception (especially space perception) goes back as far as the philosophical beginnings of psychology. The empiricism of the British philosophers and the nativism of the Germans have always formed the core of courses in the history of psychology. Everyone takes a position in the controversy, usually on the side of empiricism in this country. Textbooks of child psychology reflect this fact; here is a typical quotation from a well-known one, Goodenough's *Developmental Psychology:*

"Very early in life and without being aware that we are doing so, we learn to interpret this (binocular) difference in visual sensations in terms of tactual and muscular sensations we get from handling objects.... When we say the tree trunk *looks* rounded we mean only that the visual sensation has the qualities that from infancy on we have learned to associate with objects that *feel rounded*" (1934, p. 138). The current enthusiasm for experiments on "early experience" confirms the continued presence of the empiricist's bias.

On the other hand, we can find statements exhibiting the opposite bias, such as Pastore's that "All the significant aspects of perceiving are unlearned. These include pattern and depth perceptions, the so-called laws of organization, figure-ground relationship, solidity, the illusions, the constancies, the phi phenomenon, figural after-effects, and the perception of the world as upright" (1960, p. 93).

A recent criticism has been that the division of behavior into "innate" and "acquired" is an artificial dichotomy. Hebb, for instance, has said "I urge that there are two kinds of control of behavior and that the term "instinct" implying a mechanism or neural process independent of environmental factors, and distinct from the processes into which learning enters, is a misleading term and should be abandoned" (1953, P. 46).

The dismissal of the problem as false is not very satisfying. It is too easy to find cases of behavior which seem primarily learned or primarily unlearned. There may even be mechanisms "different from the processes into which learning enters." A more appealing approach is to study the ontogenetic process, asking how learned and unlearned processes develop and interact.

We have at present many methods available for the study of perceptual development. The developmental testing program that characterized the early stages of child psychology in this country can be supplemented by comparative studies with different animal species and by controlled experiments. Experimental methods include control of early environment (the deprivation experiment and the enrichment technique); perceptual learning experiments such as Kohler's with distorting lenses; or others providing controlled practice under more normal conditions (our own scribble experiment). Besides these, there is the procedure of logical analysis with inference of what "must have" happened, and experimental test of the inference. This latter procedure may seem roundabout, but some very impressive work of this kind can be cited (for instance, that at the Haskins laboratory on "acquired distinctiveness" of phoneme features [Liberman et al., 1957]).

My two cases have been or can be attacked by all these methods. But first they must be described in some detail. The potential information available in the stimuli for the two situations is the logical starting place.

Comparison of Stimuli

A standard situation for the study of depth discrimination was devised by Dr. Richard Walk and myself. We called this situation the "visual cliff." The important element of this situation is a drop-off downward, or depth-at-an-edge. The device consists essentially of a raised center runway with a sheet of strong glass extending outward on either side. Directly under the glass on one side is placed a textured pattern; farther below the glass on the other side, at any desired depth, is the same pattern. The simplest version of the stimulus situation might be conceived of as a platform with a drop-off to a floor below. Figure 10.1 shows the pattern of light rays projected to the subject's eye from the floor and from the platform on which he stands.

If the elements of the textured pattern are identical above and below, the light rays reaching the eye will differ in *density*, a finer density characterizing the surface farther below the eye. There is thus potential information in the light itself for the detection of the drop-off.

The same situation provides a second kind of differential stimulation if the animal moves. *Motion parallax* (differential velocity of elements in the stimulus array) will increase as the drop increases. There will be a velocity difference, therefore, between the projection of the floor under the animal's feet and that of the sunken surface below, which will characterize the amount of the drop-off.

Finally, the situation provides a third kind of differential stimulation, *binocular parallax*, if the animal has two eyes with overlapping fields and eye movements of convergence.

It could be said then that this stimulation literally specifies a drop-off. The proximal stimulus is unique and unequivocal. The information needed is present in the stimulation itself. If it is registered, the animal can make an appropriate response. Depending on the kind of organism it is, terrestrial, aquatic, or flying, it may avoid the deep side consistently, or not. A terrestrial animal would be expected to avoid it; an animal whose way of life includes diving into water from a height might approach it.

If the animal does not behave consistently and differentially, it may mean either that he does not "pick up" the stimulus difference, or else that the appropriate response has to be learned. But if he does respond differentially and consistently, it means that the difference is discriminated and that a response appropriate to his species can be made.

Now consider the kind of stimulation presented by graphic symbols. In the first place, the sources of the stimuli are marks on a piece of paper, not three-dimensional natural objects found in all men's environments. They are, in fact, man-made artifacts. The stimuli do not specify or refer to real objects or situations in space.

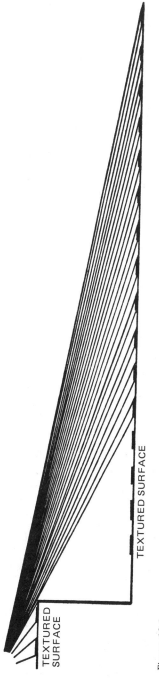

TEXTURED SURFACE

TEXTURED
SURFACE

Figure 10.1
Schematic representation of the visual cliff.

What they *do* specify is the sounds of speech. But notice that there is a *relayed* sequence involved. The light to the eyes specifies letters; the letters in turn specify speech sounds; the sounds in turn have morphic specificity relationships. Thus the graphic symbols have a *mediated* relationship with morphemes (referential meanings).

It is true that printed letters are unique, in the sense that one is discriminable from any other. But their meaning is not unequivocal, like that of a drop-off. The information for unequivocal specification of the appropriate speech sounds is *not* in the stimuli emanating from the letters; it is in a code characteristic of a given culture's writing system. Which mark or marks specify which sounds is arbitrary. A new code could be made up which would do as well or better (this, in fact, is often suggested by proponents of spelling reforms, speed writing, etc.).

It follows that at least two stages of development must be considered in the perception of graphic symbols: (1) the discrimination of the graphic symbols as unique items and (2) the mastery of the unequivocal specificity relations in the code.

Experiments on Discrimination of Depth

Our experiments with the visual cliff included comparative studies (both phylogenetic and ontogenetic) and experimental studies manipulating the environment during growth and some of the potentially available cues.

We built a small cliff first, tailored for rats, the most convenient and plentiful subjects. We provided a choice situation, a very shallow drop on one side of the runway and a deep drop on the other. The glass was at the same depth below the center runway on either side, as Figure 10.2 shows diagrammatically.

Pigmented adult rats, in a number of experiments, always descended from the center runway to the shallow side significantly more often than to the deep side. First choices, in all the experiments, ranged from 85 percent to 100 per cent to the shallow side. The choice was significant with a wide variety of patterns. A 10-inch drop on the deep side was sufficient to demonstrate the preference. Control experiments with equal depths, graduated depths, and absence of texture are described in a forthcoming monograph. Rats as young as 30 days were as discriminating as adults.

Comparative Studies

Experiments with cliffs constructed on the same plan, but adjusted to the size of the subject, were carried out on other animals as well: albino rats, baby chicks and adult chickens, lambs, kids, pigs, turtles, puppies, kittens, monkeys, and finally human infants (Figures 10.3 and 10.4). Many

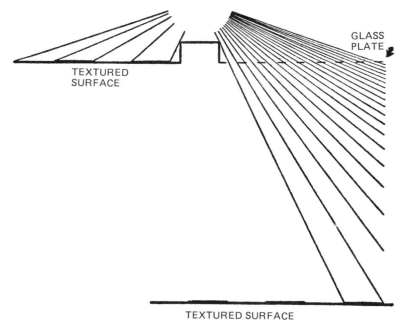

Figure 10.2
The visual cliff modified as a choice situation.

interesting species differences appear in these studies, but one generalization applies to all: all the animals that could locomote in any way at all avoided the deep side and descended to the shallow side in a significant majority of the trials. If aquatic animals had been included among the subjects, we might have found exceptions. The turtles (a semiaquatic species) showed the smallest preference for the shallow side.

There was a wide variety of ages in our subjects, for some of them could locomote immediately after birth; others could not do so until 8 months. Chicks and goats were tested before they were 24 hours old and showed as clear evidence of discrimination (100 per cent choice, in fact) as any adult animal.

The human infants could not be tested until they could crawl, so our subjects in this group ranged from $6\frac{1}{2}$ to 12 months old. The great majority of them avoided the deep side, despite the entreaties of their mothers and tempting toys. We are ready to assert, therefore, that perception of depth has developed as soon as locomotion is possible in this young organism. The same assertion applies to other slow-maturing organisms, such as kittens. Development of this discrimination, therefore, is not dependent on stepping down, climbing up, or walking into things.

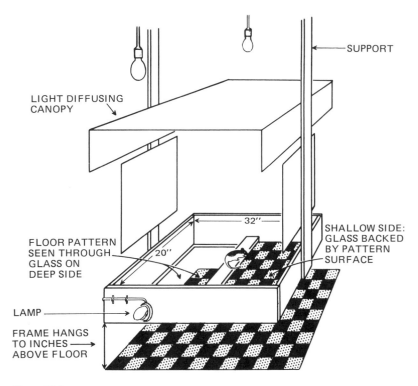

Figure 10.3
The visual cliff for small animals.

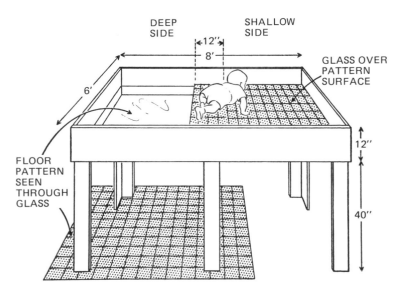

Figure 10.4
The visual cliff for human infants.

Dark-Rearing Experiments

The deprivation experiment is a technique which allows us to control some aspect of the animal's experience or practice during what is, normally, a developmental stage. Many groups of rats were reared in the dark, from birth to 90 days, or to 30 days, and compared with their litter-mates reared in the usual cages in the light. The dark-reared rats were tested on the cliff shortly after emergence from the dark-room, and they behaved as did their light-reared litter-mates, uniformly choosing the shallow side. Rats, therefore, although requiring maturation time after birth before locomotion is possible, discriminate depth *without any* previous visual experience.

Kittens were reared in the dark until 24 days of age, when their normal controls were walking and had good visual placing responses. When they were first put on the cliff, they presented the greatest contrast to their own controls and to the dark-reared rats. They crawled on their bellies, fell off the runway, and bumped into walls. Discrimination of drop-offs and even locomotion in the light were impaired. After some days in the light, the kittens had caught up and behaved normally. It seems clear that development in a lighted environment is required for this species. But learning the difference between visually deep and shallow drops through external re-

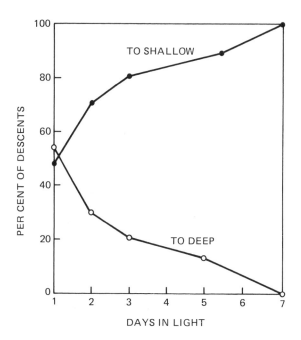

Figure 10.5
Performance of kittens, reared in darkness for 24 days, on the visual cliff.

inforcement (punishment from falling) was not the crucial factor, for the kittens in the beginning fell equally either way to a glass surface at the same depth below the center board on either side. Yet gradually, as Figure 10.5 shows, they began to avoid one side and choose the other, without reinforcement. Choices rose to 100 per cent by the seventh day.

Our conclusion is that discrimination of depth matures, when normal conditions of development are provided, without benefit of reward or punishment or associative learning. Progress may indeed continue after birth, through normal growth of organs. But early failure of discrimination is no reason to adopt the empiricist's bias. Differentiation of perception by developmental stages is characteristic of phylogenetic differences, and in the case we have just considered, of ontogenetic ones.

Enhancement Experiments

An interesting question arises at this point. Can we apply our generalization with respect to depth at an edge to discrimination of three-dimensional *objects* in the environment? If an object can be "seen around," conditions for parallax are present. It has, potentially, the attribute of depth and the possibility of being easily differentiated from the background.

We have a little evidence, from other experiments, that discrimination of objects having depth-at-an-edge occurs relatively early and is responsible for some *transfer* to two-dimensional pictured shapes.

Dr. Walk and I carried out a number of experiments of the "early experience" type, in which we hung cut-out triangles and circles on the walls of living cages of hooded rats from birth to 90 days. At 90 days these animals, as well as control litter-mates, learned a triangle-circle discrimination. For the discriminative learning, the figures were *painted* on flat surfaces (doors through which food was reached). In our first experiment, learning was significantly facilitated among the experimental animals.

In some further experiments, we painted the wall figures on a flat background, rather than cutting them out. To our chagrin, the transfer effect was no longer obtained. Our variables in these experiments were presence or absence of reinforcement, time of exposing the patterns, and so on. None of these seemed to make any difference; our original effect sometimes appeared and sometimes did not. We had decided that we were pursuing a will-o'-the-wisp until we noticed one factor which divided the results. Transfer occurred when the cage-hangings were cut-outs; it did not occur when they were painted on the flat surface that surrounded them.

Our interpretation of these facts is speculative, but rich in hypotheses. Objects having depth-at-an-edge are easily differentiated from their surroundings. They are therefore "noticed" by the animal. This noticeability, we guess, will transfer to similar pictured objects, thereby helping the animal to differentiate them from their surroundings when they must be isolated as cues for response.[1]

What transfers, exactly, is another question. For the rats, not dominantly "visual" animals, it may have been only differentiation of figure from background. It might also be features which serve to distinguish one object from another, such as curves opposed to corners, or openings (indentations) opposed to closure (smooth continuity). I should like to return to this possibility later, in the discussion of graphic symbols.

It should be apparent how different this view is from the traditional one that perception begins with something like a two-dimensional projection and progresses to appreciation of depth by associational meanings gained from experiences that are dependent on locomotion. The evidence suggests instead that discrimination of depth-at-an-edge is primitive, both phylogenetically and ontogenetically, and that development progresses toward discrimination of form in two-dimensional projections.

Experiments with Graphic Forms

The jump from discrimination of depth-at-an-edge to discrimination of graphic symbols is a big one. The fact that only human subjects are appropriate for studying this case is an indication in itself. Furthermore, analysis of the situation made it clear that the stimuli provided by words and letters do not contain in themselves information that specifies unequivocally anything about the world. What they do specify can only be found in a code which varies from one language to another and therefore must be learned.

We have said that at least two stages of development need to be considered in this process. The first stage is the discrimination of the graphic symbols themselves as unique items. Our first question, therefore, was whether there is a developmental process involved in accomplishing the differentiation.

An old experiment performed by my husband and myself (Gibson and Gibson, 1955) suggested that there was. We presented subjects divided into three age groups (6 to 8, $8\frac{1}{2}$ to 11, and adults) with drawn figures somewhat comparable to those of cursive writing. They were called "scribbles." The task was to recognize a presented figure when it was presented later in a series of similar figures. The standard to be recognized varied from the others along three dimensions (number of coils, horizontal compression, and right-left reversal). The subject looked at the standard and then went through a pack of cards on which the variants, some copies of the standard, and other quite different figures appeared (Figure, 10.6). On the first run through the pack, the adults were already very accurate in their recognitions (a mean of only three errors), but the children confused many

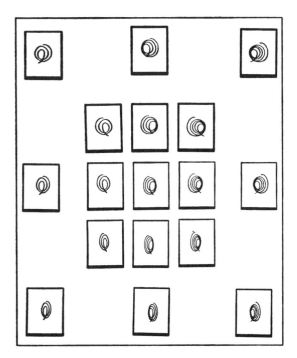

Figure 10.6
"Scribbles" used in the Gibson and Gibson experiment (1955).

variants with the standard. The youngest group had a mean of more than 13 errors, and some of them did not achieve perfect recognition even after 10 repetitions of the whole procedure.

We have recently completed a large-scale comparison of the ability to discriminate graphic items in preschool and early grade-school children.[2] Our object this time was to study qualitative as well as quantitative differences. A set of letter-like forms, comparable to printed capitals, was constructed by the following method. The letters themselves were analyzed, to yield a set of rules governing their formation. From these rules a population of new forms was generated, none of which violated the rules but none of which were actual letters. From among these stimuli 12 were chosen to serve as standards. Twelve variants were constructed from each standard to yield transformations of the following kinds: three degrees of transformation of line to curve or curve to line; five transformations of rotation or reversal; two perspective transformations (slant left and tilt back); and two topological changes, a break and a close (Figure 10.7).

The master drawings were copied photographically on small cards, and these were covered with plastic so that they could be handled without marking. The task given the children was to *match* the standard with all its variants and to select and hand to the experimenter only exact copies of it. The cards were presented in a matrix board, with a standard centered in the top row (Figure 10.8). All transformations of a particular standard were assembled randomly in one row, accompanied by at least one identical copy. When a child had finished matching for a given standard, it was removed and another inserted in its place. Demonstration with corrected practice was given before beginning, and then the child matched for all 12 forms.

An error score (choosing as "same" an item that did not match the standard) was obtained for each child, and the errors classified according to type of transformation. The subjects were 165 children aged 4 to 8 years.

Errors decrease rapidly from ages 4 to 8. Furthermore, it is very clear that some transformations are harder to discriminate from the standard than others and that improvement occurs at different rates for different transformations.

Error curves for changes of break and close start low and drop almost to zero by 8 years. Error curves for perspective transformations start very high and errors are still numerous at 8 years. Error curves for rotations and reversals start high, but the curves drop to nearly zero by 8 years. Error curves for changes from line to curve start relatively high (depending on the number of changes) and show a rapid drop. The curves for two and three changes have dropped to the same low point as the curves for break and close by 8 years.

In Figure 10.9 the data have been combined for the four transformation groups. Our justification for doing so was twofold: one, the resemblances of the curves within transformation groups, but differences between groups (statistically significant, in fact); and two, the high correlations within transformation groups.

The experiment was replicated for the 5-year-old group with actual letters and the same transformational variants. Again, the correlations within transformation groups were very high.

Interpretation of Error Curves

The interpretation of the error curves for these transformation groups leads us to some interesting hypotheses about the development of discrimination of letter forms. The concept of "distinctive features" is central to the argument. This term is borrowed from Roman Jakobson (Jakobson and Halle, 1956), who originated the concept of distinctive features of phonemes. Distinctive features are characteristics which a phoneme may or may not have; they are invariant; and they are critical for distinguishing

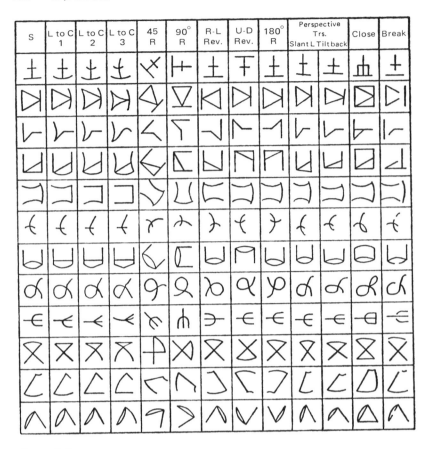

Figure 10.7
Artificial graphic forms and twelve variants.

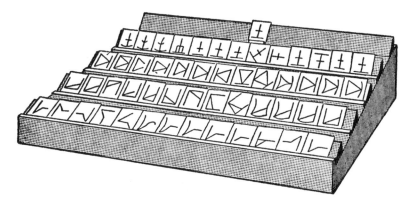

Figure 10.8
Matching board for studies of discrimination of graphic forms.

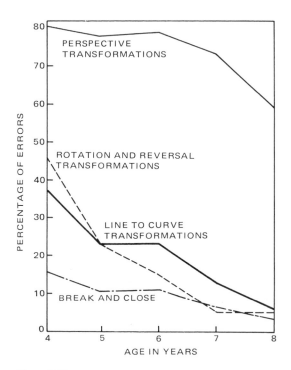

Figure 10.9
Errors in matching variants with standard graphic forms by type of variant and age of S.

one phoneme from another. "Bundles" of such features characterize any given phoneme. A child, presumably, learns to hear the distinctive features and can thereafter recognize phonemic patterns over a wide range of pitch and intensity variations (sung, whispered, shouted, and so on).[3] Taking some license with Jakobson's term, we have assumed that the solid objects of the world, and also the set of graphemes, possess "distinctive features"—characteristics which are invariant and critical for distinguishability within the set.

An attempt to analyze all the objects of the world into a classification of distinctive features is not our purpose, but some progress has been made with letters. Suffice it to say here that breaks and closes (O vs. C), transformations from line to curve (U vs. V), rotations (M vs. W), and reversals (d vs. b) are all distinctive features with respect to which letters may differ. They often occur in some combination as bundles of distinctive features. For instance, A vs. V includes both rotation and closure as critical differences.[4] Perspective transformations are *not* distinctive features of letters. Changes of compression (such as would result from tilt or slant) often occur in handwriting but are never critical for differentiating letters. "Constancy" of the grapheme requires tolerance of such variance.

We assumed further (see p. 14) that there will be transfer from discriminating ordinary solid objects of the world to two-dimentional line drawings of the letter-like variety. *Positive* transfer should occur when the variable dimension distinguishing two line drawings is one which has been critical for discriminating one object from another in the past. *No* transfer should occur when the variable dimension has not been critical for object identification. Sometimes a variable aspect has not only been irrelevant, but has even been assimilated to a "concept" allowing free variation along this dimension. For instance, shape constancy occurs despite variation in orientation.

When transfer is possible from earlier object identification, errors should be few. When it is not, they will be numerous to begin with, but they will decrease with age if the dimension varied is a critical one (distinctive feature) for differentiating letters. The four transformation types should therefore show the following error trends with age.

1. Errors for differences of the break and close type should be few initially and show only a small drop (discrimination already being nearly perfect). These changes are critical for object differentiation. There is no transition from break to close. Piaget (1956) has shown that such differences are discriminated very early with solid objects.

2. Initial errors for line to curve transformations will be higher than those for break and close but should drop rapidly. Line to curve differences are critical for distinguishing rigid objects, but not for live

or plastic ones (e.g., the nonrigid transformations of facial expression). Since they *may* indicate different states of the same object, perfect transfer cannot be expected. Nevertheless, the error curve should drop rapidly because such differences are critical for letter discrimination.

3. Initial errors for reversals and rotations should be very high because transformations of this type are not critical for object identification. (Rotation is used in fact to study transposability of form;[5] it gives information of position of an object, such as leaning or fallen down.) But rotation is critical for letter discrimination, so the error curve should drop rapidly after school has begun.

4. Initial errors for perspective transformation should also be very high. They are not critical for object identification, indicating instead a change in orientation in the third dimension (slant or tilt). There is little reason to expect a drop in errors, for slant and tilt are not critical for letter identification.

The curves obtained do actually follow those expectations. There is, therefore, support for the view that there is perceptual learning of the distinctive features of letters in the stage of development before decoding to phonemes begins. The kind of learning is not associative; it is instead a process of isolating and focusing on those features of letters that are both invariant and critical for rendering each one unique.

Teaching is provided the child in this stage of learning, but it is not of the paired associates type. It is rather helping the child to "pay attention to" those features that are invariant and distinctive. Learning a name for each letter, on the other hand, is a case of association, but necessarily a secondary stage.

Grapheme-Phoneme Correspondence

We have suggested that the development of discrimination of graphic symbols begins with the differentiation of letters, whose distinctive features must be learned, assisted by transfer from the earlier stage of object identification. Meanwhile the child has learned to recognize phonemes and to speak his language. But the final stage remains to be accomplished: the decoding of graphemic to phonemic units.

It is not enough to describe this stage as merely associating grapheme with phoneme patterns. What are the units to be associated? In the English language, no single letter has an invariant phonemic equivalent. Words do, and this fact has led to teaching by the "whole word" method. This method, however, is both uneconomical and insufficient to generate the reading of new words.

An alternative to these two possibilities exists. Dr. Charles Hockett and his collaborators at Cornell have shown that rules for predicting pronunciation from spelling can be formulated, if the rules are stated in terms of vowel and consonant "clusters" and what comes before and after. Higher order invariant spelling patterns exist which can be mapped into correspondence with phonemic patterns. It is the grapheme-phoneme invariant correspondences that the skilled reader has learned. Letter-groups having such correspondence in the language come to have a high perceptibility, since they form units as stimuli; those lacking such correspondence are not equally perceptible because they are not effective units for pronunciation.

We have conducted several experiments with tachistoscopic viewing of pseudo words, some following the rules of correspondence (invariant spelling to sound correlation), some not.[6] Skilled adult readers are consistently more successful in perceiving correctly the letter groups which are "pronounceable," even though they have no referential meaning. These letter groups have a higher "visibility." Here we have a final case, at the top of the developmental ladder, of perceptual learning. What the reader has learned here (albeit unconsciously) is to perceive the higher order stimuli as units in reading. These stimuli are letter groups (ways of spelling) that exist in the language as invariants in the sense that they have a corresponding consistent pronunciation. The reader acquiring skill comes to perceive these as units by experiencing the heard and seen patterns together. He may or may not be taught them.

The letter or spelling units are constituted, formally and objectively, by the rules of correspondence in the language. They are a psychological reality as well, as we have demonstrated. The problem for perceptual learning is to determine *how* the unit is constituted. Whether the process of unit formation is an associative one or one of "discovery" of the invariant relationships is yet to be determined.

Summary

From our comparison of the development of perception of depth and that of graphic symbols, several generalizations can be drawn. The first, stated below, is a conclusion. The others have the status of promising, partly substantiated hypotheses.

1. Perception of depth at an edge is primitive, both phylogenetically and ontogenetically. Some animals are fully mature in this accomplishment at birth. Animals which have a longer maturation time after birth (e.g., cats, human infants) discriminate depth at an edge as soon as locomotion is possible.

2. Solid objects, which possess depth at their edges, are discriminated earlier than two-dimentional pictures or line drawings. If perceptual

learning occurs in the earlier phase, it involves a discovery of invariant properties of the object which the stimulation itself specifies and which are critical for distinguishing one object from another. What is learned is isolation from background or differentiation rather than an associative meaning for depth.

3. Ability to discriminate those features of objects which are critical for identification may transfer to outline drawings such as letters, but some critical features of letters remain to be discriminated after four years of age. This process is again one of differentiation rather than association.

4. Unequivocal referential meaning of letters must be learned; it is *not* given in the stimulation emanating from them. At this stage (following differentiation) an associative process may be involved.

5. Mere association of letter with phoneme, however, is an inadequate description of the process of learning meaning. Letter clusters from "higher order units" which are invariant for pronunciation and reading pass through a learning phase of integration so that they are actually perceived as wholes.

This paper raises more problems than it solves. It is my hope that stirring up these problems will create interest in a field which I have found fascinating and productive.

Notes

1. Harlow's discovery that stereometric (solid) objects, as contrasted with planometric (flat) patterns, are discriminated more easily by young monkeys is one confirmation of this hypothesis.
2. Anne Danielson and Harry Osser collaborated in this experiment.
3. See also Brown (1958, pp. 202 ff.).
4. Note the comment of Deutsch's infant son (Deutsch [1960, p. 149]) when shown a "V": "Why isn't the A crossed?"
5. The 2-year-old children tested by Gellerman (1933) responded to a form as equivalent after rotation. *See also* Deutsch (1960, p. 149).
6. Collaborators in this experiment were Anne Danielson, Harry Osser, and Marcia Hammond.

References

Brown, R. *Words and things.* Free Press, 1958.
Deutsch, J. A. *The structural basis of behavior.* Univer. of Chicago Press, 1960.
Gellermann, L. W. Form discrimination in chimpanzees and two-year-old children: I. Form (triangularity) *per se. J. genet. Psychol.,* 1933, 42, 3–29.
Gibson, E. J., & Walk, R. D. The effect of prolonged exposure to visually presented patterns on learning to discriminate them. *J. comp. physiol. Psychol.,* 1956, 49, 239–241.
Gibson, E. J., & Walk, R. D. The "visual cliff." *Sci. Amer.,* 1960, 202, 2–9.

Gibson, E. J., Walk, R. D., & Tighe, T. J. Enhancement and deprivation of visual stimulation during rearing as factors in visual discrimination learning. *J. comp. physiol. Psychol.*, 1959, 52, 74–81.

Gibson, J. J., & Gibson, E. J. Perceptual learning: differentiation or enrichment? *Psychol. Rev.*, 1955, 62, 32–41.

Goodenough, F. *Developmental psychology.* Appleton-Century, 1934.

Harlow, H. F. & Warren, J. M. Formation and transfer of discrimination learning sets. *J. comp. physiol Psychol.*, 1952, 45, 483–489.

Hebb, D. O. Heredity and environment in mammalian behavior. *Brit. J. Anim. Behav.*, 1953, 1, 43–47.

Jakobson, R., & Halle, M. *Fundamentals of language.* The Hague: Morton, 1956.

Liberman, A. M., Harris, K. S., Horrman, S. H., & Griffith, B. C. The discrimination of speech sounds within and across phoneme boundaries. *J. exp. Psychol.*, 1957, 54, 358–368.

Pastore, N. Perceiving as innately determined. *J. genet. Psychol.*, 1960, 96, 93–99.

Piaget, J., & Inhelder, B. *The child's conception of space.* London: Humanities Press, 1956.

Walk, R. D., & Gibson, E. J. A comparative and analytic study of depth perception. *Psychol. Monogr.*, in press.

Walk, R. D., Gibson, E. J., Pick, H. L., Jr., & Tighe, T. J. The effectiveness of prolonged exposure to cutouts vs. painted patterns for facilitation of discrimination. *J. comp. physiol. Psychol.*, 1959, 52, 519–521.

Discussion

Herman A. Witkin

Gibson has approached, in a fresh way, problems that have been with us for a very long time; and the ingenious experiments she has done have provided new insights into these old problems. Gibson's careful, persistent working through of a variety of particular perceptual functions contributes much to our understanding of the role of learning in perceptual development. In her consideration of perception in children at different ages, and in animal forms of different kinds, Gibson has employed a truly comparative approach. It is gratifying to find such flexibility of research strategy in this era of specialization. The comparative approach has many advantages. A major one is that observation of a given perceptual function in different species, or in organisms of the same species at different stages of ontogenetic development, is likely to point up differences, which inevitably provide useful leads for further investigation and deeper understanding of the function. An example in Gibson's material is the finding that turtles, the most aquatic form studied, showed the least preference for the shallow side in the cliff experiment. Another interesting example is the difference observed in this same situation between kittens and some of the other forms studied.

The strategy of considering two quite different perceptual functions, rather than limiting herself to one, has the advantage that special features of each are pointed up through contrast with the other.

It is a reflection on the value of Gibson's approach and investigations that so many promising leads for further research have emerged and that her work has implications for the fields of perceptual and language development, and ultimately for such practical issues as how best to teach children to read.

There are several interesting issues raised by Gibson's material, which may perhaps be clarified in the subsequent discussion or in further work.

One concerns the mechanism underlying performance in the cliff situation—the discrimination between the shallow and deep alternatives and the expression of a preference for the shallow one. The process involved in each of these requires study in its own right for, as observed in the rat, discrimination may be possible even when a preference is not expressed. Thus far more attention has been given to possible bases of the discrimination than to causes of the preference. Although some animals are capable at birth of perception of depth at an edge, what is the precise nature of the process that occurs on first encounter with the cliff situation that results in the discrimination and preference observed? What difference is there in the process between such animals and others, like the cat, where things go differently? Is the achievement of locomotion important only in making possible the movement necessary to show the preference, or do events occur in the development of locomotion itself that contribute to the processes of discrimination and preference formation? Better knowledge of the mechanism involved would help in the search for determinants of its smooth operation. A search guided by such knowledge might perhaps reveal that experience plays more of a role than is now believed. The work of Schneirla and his students and of Lehrman provide examples of the complex and subtle ways in which experience, even in activities not directly involved in the pattern itself, may affect the emergence of an apparently "unlearned" behavior pattern. The need to identify underlying processes and their determinants exists apart from the question of whether experience is a factor or not.

As Gibson described her studies, I wondered at several points about the fate of individual subjects in the group results she reported. For example, in the study of graphic forms some transformations were harder to discriminate from the standard than others. There is a parallel here with the findings from studies of Gottschaldt figures. Depending on the structure of the complex figure, it may be easy or difficult to find the simple figure within it. Continuing the parallel, I wonder whether, just as some people find the Gottschaldt-figures task more difficult than do other people, there may be differences among children in ease of discriminating transformations from standards in Gibson's material. I recall here too that three of 36 children tested in the cliff situation seemed to prefer the deep side. Who were these exceptional children? Though their number is small, one wonders what made them violate the clear group trend. I hope that in time Gibson may be able to consider issues of individuality, as we may perhaps call them, raised by questions such as these. It is worth noting here that Werner has recently commented on the need, in both research and theory, for greater attention to the problem of individuality in development. The kind of careful working through of situations in which Gibson has been engaged is a necessary prelude to the study of differences among people in their behavior in these situations; Some of the work in the perception-personality field, for example, reflects the consequences of failure to respect such a sequence.

I should like to comment further on the concept of individuality, since it represents a different, though by no means contradictory, emphasis from that in Gibson's work.

In the area of perceptual development an interest in individual functioning, implied by the concept of individuality, involves concern with several issues. One is individual differences in pace and direction of development in various perceptual areas. Another is individual self-consistency in mode of perceptual functioning at any given stage of development, as judged from performance across a series of situations. A related issue concerns stability of characteristics of individual perceptual functioning over time. Still another issue is the relation between the course of a particular child's perceptual growth and events going on elsewhere in his psychological development, in the area of personality, if you will. Finally, there is the issue of the sources of individual differences in perceptual growth, which means, in effect, the nature of the forces, constitutional and experiential, which, in interaction, direct a child's perceptual development along the particular course it follows.

I would like to describe very briefly a few of our recent studies, carried out in collaboration with Ruth Dyk, Hanna Faterson, Donald Goodenough, and Stephen Karp (Witkin et al [1962]) that illustrate the possibilities and difficulties of studies directed at the issue mentioned. Because of our concern with analytical aspects of perception, some of these studies bear upon Gibson's interest in differentiation of object from background.

For some time now we have been conducting cross-sectional and longitudinal studies of development, guided by concepts which grew out of our earlier investigations of perception-personality relationships The particular studies I want to mention were based on the view, very briefly stated, that in early experience the body-field matrix is a more or less fused "perceptual mass." Segregation of self from field and the further crystallization of experience within each of these "segments" proceed in such a way during development that progress toward articulation in one area is dependent upon and fosters achievement of articulation in the other. This view implies that a tendency for experience to be articulated—that is, analyzed and structured—is apt to be manifested whether the experience has its primary source in one's own actions, attributes, and feelings or in objects and events outside. These notions led us to examine children's mode of experiencing, viewed from the standpoint of articulateness, in a variety of circumstances. Our earlier work had been concerned particularly with differences among people in the extent to which perception tends to be analytical. As one extension of that work we have explored the analytical quality in intellectual functioning. Results of these studies, and similar studies in other laboratories, have shown that a tendency to experience in more analytical or less analytical fashion characterizes a person's intellectual activity as much as his perception. There is now considerable evidence that children and adults with a relatively more analytical way of perceiving do significantly better at intellectual tasks in which essential elements must be isolated from the context in which they are presented and recombined into new relationships. For example, Harris[1] has shown that people whose perception tends to be analytical, or field independent, as we have called it, find it relatively easy, in Duncker's insight problems, to extract a "part" from a familiar functional context and use it in another context. As a second example, Goodenough and Karp (1961) found that tests of perceptual field dependence were loaded on the same factor as the block design, picture completion, and object assembly subtests of the Wechsler Intelligence Scale for Children, subtests which are similar to the perceptual tests in that they require the overcoming of an embedding context. The perceptual tests did not appear on verbal-comprehension or attention-concentration factors, defined by other WISC subtests.

Other studies also suggest that children who passively accept the prevailing organization of the field, rather than experiencing it analytically, tend to leave "as is" stimulus material that is unorganized and therefore experience it as poorly structured and vague. This was shown, for example, in a study of the extent to which children's Rorschach percepts reflected an attempt to impose structure on the amorphous ink-blot stimuli.

Considering "analysis" and "structuring" as complementary aspects of "articulation," it is suggested that there are identifiable differences among children in the extent to which their experience tends to be articulated, or, in contrast, "global."

Whereas the studies mentioned were concerned mainly with the nature of children's experience of situations external to themselves, other studies focused more on the nature of children's experience of themselves. One approach used in exploring experience of the self was to study children's conceptions of their bodies. These studies were carried out with the expectation that children who show a relatively articulated way of experiencing in various perceptual and intellectual tasks would tend to have a relatively articulated concept of the body. Such a relation was demonstrated in one study, for example, which evaluated children's figure drawings from the standpoint of such articulation criteria as form level, integration of parts, sex differentiation, and representation of role. This relation has been confirmed in other studies using more experimental procedures to infer a person's view of his body.

Another approach to the nature of experience of the self was based on the concept that progress toward self-differentiation during development entails the child's growing awareness of needs, feelings, and attributes which he recognizes as his own and their identification as distinct from those of others. We have used the term "sense of separate identity" to refer to the outcome of this trend in development. A sense of separate identity implies an experience of the self as segregated and structured. Ready and continuing use of external frames of reference for definition of one's needs, feelings, and attributes would be suggestive of a limited development of sense of separate identity.

A study of adults by Rudin and Stagner (1958) is illustrative of many studies showing that persons with a relatively articulated way of experiencing tend to have a relatively developed sense of separate identity.

The subject was asked to imagine himself in four situations and, using special rating scales, to describe himself in each. The scores derived reflected extent of similarity among a subject's self-descriptions for the four situations. As expected, relatively field-independent persons showed significantly less fluctuation in their views of themselves in the imaginary context, suggesting that their experience of themselves was relatively stable.

The evidence to date indicates consistency in way of experiencing the external field, the body, and the self. Degree of articulation appears to be a common quality running through much of an individual's experience. These findings are at least consistent with the concept that there is a linkage, during development, among achievement of a developed concept of the body, a segregated, structured self, and an articulated way of experiencing the world.

The evidence thus far bears upon one of the problems of individuality mentioned earlier—individual self-consistency. Some of the first results of our longitudinal studies deal with another of the problems: the relative stability of individual functioning during development. Though we have only begun to analyze the results of these studies, it is already clear that, within the general group changes that occur with growth, children show marked relative stability in the analytical aspect of perceiving and in articulateness of body concept, even over a seven-year period.

Our evidence at one point suggested differences among children in pace of development of the interrelated cluster of characteristics we were studying. We became involved in still another of the problems of individuality when we undertook to determine some of the possible sources of these differences. In one series of studies we have been investigating children's early relations to their families, particularly their mothers. From the conceptual framework we use in viewing the contrasting ways of experiencing, it must be evident why we consider early mother-child interactions as potentially important in the development of these ways of experiencing. The studies have been in progress for some time, but, because of the methodological complexities involved, they must be considered first steps. We have thus far investigated mother-child interrelations through interviews with mothers and, to a lesser extent, through interviews with children and through children's TAT stories. We have also done some studies of the mother "as a person." The results of these studies, and a confirmatory study by Seder, suggest that mothers of children whose experience of field, body, and self tends to be relatively articulated have interacted with their children in such a way as to foster separation from mother and to provide standards both for dealing with the environment and for handling impulses. The processes underlying these very general relations require more precise definition, and the important question of cause and effect remains unanswered.

We hope some progress may be made with these problems through studies of relations between characteristics of children in infancy and the kinds of differences we have been finding later in development. Through the cooperation of Sibylle Escalona and Lois Murphy we were recently able to see 72 of the children observed in infancy by Escalona and her collaborators. The children were 6 to 8 years old when we restudied them and their mothers. The data-collection stage of the investigation is completed, but the analysis of data has not yet begun.

I hope that in time the approach to perceptual development represented by Gibson's work and the approach represented by the studies just described will find a congenial meeting ground.

Note

1. Harris, Frances. Personal communication.

References

Goodenough, D. R.. & Karp, S. A. Field dependence and intellectual functioning. Unpublished study, 1961.

Rudin, S. A., & Stagner, R. Figure-ground phenomena in the perception of physical and social stimuli. *J. Psychol.*, 1958, 45, 213–225.

Witkin, H. A., Dyk, R. B., Faterson, H. F., Goodenough, D. R., & Karp, S. A. *Psychological differentiation: studies of development*. Wiley, 1962.

Group Discussion

The discussion of Gibson's paper centered around her two experimental situations. With respect to the perception of depth at an edge, Gibson made the following additional points:

1. There were so few exceptions in the preference of human infants for the shallow side of the visual cliff that consistent individual differences were hard to obtain. The only three infants in the original experiment who could be coaxed onto the deep side of the cliff were boys.

2. The apparent importance of visual experience for some species (e.g., dark- vs. light-reared kittens) may not mean that learning, as we usually think of it, is required for the development of perception of depth at an edge. Hess has shown that the response of certain birds to shadows, a response that matures during a critical period, does not develop in dark-reared animals, simply because shadows are not available during the critical period. Maturation after birth necessarily involves all interactions with environmental stimulation.

Levin, Berlyne, and Jeffrey raised questions about the mechanisms of depth perception in relation to the enhancement experiments reported by Gibson. Levin proposed that stereometric objects on the walls of the home cages offered tactile as well as visual cues for generating distinctiveness of the stimuli and enhancement of subsequent discrimination learning. Gibson agreed that this was possible, and consistent with Harlow's findings, but noted also that the most important depth cue in visual cliff performance appeared to be motion parallax. Berlyne proposed that the cut-out shapes on the home cages had the unique property of eliciting attentive or orienting responses because of the motion parallax taking place at their edges whenever the animal moved. He proposed that the inherently interesting perceptual events of disappearance and reappearance of more distant objects, when temporarily masked by the cut-outs, elicited orienting responses to the contours of the forms, which in turn enhanced their familiarity and distinctiveness as cues. Gibson agreed that attention would accompany movement, but noted that other depth cues are also relevant to differentiation of the stimuli. With respect to movement of the animal, she noted much cliff behavior resembling VTE movements in all species. Berlyne pointed out that, even if one could demonstrate that perception of depth at an edge is more a matter of maturation than of learning, there remains the response differentiation of animals on the visual cliff. Although they may perceive which side is deeper without much experience, learning must be involved in the appropriate responses and preferences which they display.

Kagan suggested that the responses might be explained on the basis of a generally nearsighted visual accommodation on the part of the organism and a corresponding level of adaptation for rate of change of visual patterns at an edge. When the relative rate of change of visual pattern accompanying head movements and locomotion is either too fast, too slow, or unexpected, an avoidance response may be elicited. In other words, the organism avoids discrepancies from the "usual" experiences in his visual field. Gibson replied that the level-of-adaptation argument would fail to explain the fully developed preferences in dark-reared rats, who could not have established adaptation levels for movement at an edge. The dark-reared rats, furthermore, showed the preference without "learning an appropriate response."

Sigel proposed that accessibility and the potentiality for exploration of the shallow side might make it more attractive, and Gibson replied that the failure of extinction of preference in many trials for rats would make such a hypothesis unlikely.

Discussion of the research on perception of graphic symbols centered on two problems. One was the degree to which the transformations selected by Gibson do in fact represent critical features of graphemes. Brown pointed out that, while a distinctive features analysis of graphic symbols is needed and can be carried out in the same way as the analysis of distinctive features of phonemes, some of the features proposed by Gibson are economical and others are not. Analogous transformations for phonemes can be either economical or not. For example, voicing is an economical distinctive feature because it is always relevant. In fact, it divides the population of phonemes into two groups: voiced and unvoiced. Features such as labial, dental, or plosive are not economical features, however. In many cases they are irrelevant. Similarly with respect to graphemes, the transformations, open vs. closed and straight vs. curved, are economical features. They are distinctions which divide the population into important subgroups. Reversal and rotation, however, are operations linking two graphemes, describing not their features, but their relation to one another. Hence, as features they are less economical and less distinctive. Baldwin suggested that, using some arbitrary specification, one could define all letters as being right-handed or left-handed, thus making reversal an absolute rather than a relative feature; but it was generally conceded that some of the features proposed for graphemes were more distinctive, while others were useful transformations in generating letter forms, but lacked independent distinctiveness for the perception of graphemes.

The second problem relating to the perception of graphemes that evoked considerable discussion was that of grapheme-phoneme correspondence. Some letter clusters are clearly more readily perceived than others, but there was some question as to whether the difference is due to the degree of invariant grapheme-phoneme correspondence, as Gibson suggested, or to the fluency and commonality of certain grapheme sequences in written language. Put another way, do certain letter clusters have lower tachistoscopic thresholds because they are more pronounceable, or because they are letter chains containing higher sequential probabilities in written language? Wallach reported that the finding of Miller and Bruner, that thresholds are lower when the nonsense words presented contain higher orders of statistical approximation to English, can be demonstrated in children. Moreover, when children are matched for their ability to perceive random aggregations of letters (zero order), then the amount of improvement they show at the fourth order of approximation predicts their reading and spelling achievement, but not their nonverbal achievements. That is, only children high in verbal and spelling skills could profit perceptually from increased correspondence of sequential probabilities to those encountered in ordinary English words. Jeffrey suggested that pronunciability was being used as an index of sequential dependency or frequency of occurrence, and Baldwin noted that the two variables could and should be separated. Gibson proposed that nonsense trigrams of high and low frequency and of high and low pronunciability could be developed in order independently to test the effects of the two variables on perception. However, Gibson pointed out that sequential probability, as such, does not operate to constitute units, and there is evidence now to show that higher order units are formed by invariant relationships of letter patterns to pronunciation.

Ervin stated that the use of trigrams ignores the position of the letter clusters in the word, a variable that is critical for recognition of whole words. One must consider not only the sequential probabilities of letters, but of clusters, phonemes, and syllables as well. Gibson provided an example of the three-cluster nonsense word GLURCK, which is pronounceable and can be perceived at relatively low thresholds. Reversing the two consonant clusters, however, gives CKURGL. Although this word is composed of three clusters in the order, consonant, vowel, consonant, it is virtually unpronounceable, and is perceived only at high thresholds. She went on to note that, although the first part of the word is most prominent and critical for recognition, perceptual differences were obtained on the basis of the pronunciability of the last part as well.

Baldwin proposed that the rules for generating grapheme clusters dictate that within the clusters the frequencies of letter sequence match those in English. In order to separate frequency from pronunciability, it would be necessary to consider the relations between clusters as well. Levin proposed that low commonality trigrams could be presented with controlled frequencies, thus making position in the word irrelevant.

Pick suggested the use of deaf mutes as controls for pronunciability. It was noted by Kessen that pronunciability is also a problem in response organization. If one could pretrain a differentiation of response sounds and independently vary the subject's experience with isolated graphemes, then one could predict differential performances when the stimulus is a novel combination of graphemes and the response is a novel combination of phonemes. Gibson replied that response organization is largely a problem of differentiating phonemes.

Brown proposed that three different sets of rules need to be considered: (1) the sequential and combinatorial rules for phonemes, (2) the sequential and combinatorial rules for graphemes, and (3) the rules of correspondence between grapheme and phoneme. The consensus appeared to be that these three types of rules need to be studied both separately and developmentally, in terms of distinctive features, as has been done by Jakobson, Gibson, and Hockett.

11

The Development of Perception as an Adaptive Process

Eleanor J. Gibson

This paper was prepared as a lecture in response to an invitation by Sigma Chi to travel to ten institutions in the Middle West as the Sigma Chi National Lecturer in the spring of 1969. The lecture often coincided with the annual banquet of the local chapter, and the audience was a varied group of scientists and graduate students. I decided that I should relate perceptual development to evolution as much as I could, in deference to the character of the audience, and give as many colorful examples as possible. One of my illustrations was a slide of Romanes's comparison of phylogenetic and ontogenetic development over species and in an individual human. It was a great chance to be comparative and to follow my, by now, strong feeling that a functional, evolutionary approach to perception was the right one. I went from large universities (University of Michigan at Ann Arbor) to small colleges (Alma College, a small Presbyterian college in Alma, Michigan) and even to a National Laboratory (the Argonne, in Illinois). I became acquainted with many scientists in other disciplines and talked to eight undergraduate psychology clubs. It cured me of the desire to undertake more one-night stands, but it was a good experience. I found that my approach, though neither clinical nor the "establishment" position, made sense to other scientists. This was a functional, comparative approach emphasizing an animal's ecology in relation to its dynamic and structural capacities.

Perception of events in space develops early, while perception of objects shows evolution and greater dependence on learning.

Since the time of Darwin and the acceptance of the doctrine of evolution of species, psychologists have contemplated the phylogenetic development of behavior as a mark of adaptation to an animal's environment. In

American Scientist, 1970, 58, 98–107.

the late nineteenth century, the comparative psychologist's eagerness to fit behavior into the evolutionary scheme took some amusing, and by hindsight, naive trends. G. J. Romanes, one of the best of the so-called "anecdotalists," spoke for them when he said, "I hold that if the doctrine of Organic Evolution is accepted, it carries with it, as a necessary corollary, the doctrine of Mental Evolution, at all events as far as the brute creation is concerned" (1895, p. 8). In two volumes called *Mental Evolution in Animals and Mental Evolution in Man* he prepared a tree and a chart which served, he thought, to represent the "leading features of psychogenesis throughout the animal kingdom" and also the "principal stages of Mental Evolution in Man."

The chart lists, under "products of intellectual development," a number of faculties which are ranked from lowest to highest—from protoplasmic movements to morality. Then, in a column titled the "psychological scale," there is listed in correlation with the faculties the animal order where each faculty presumably first makes its appearance. "Memory" comes in with the echinoderms, "association by contiguity" with molluscs, "association by similarity" with fish, "recognition of persons" with reptiles and cephalopods, "recognition of pictures, understanding of words, and dreaming" with birds, and "morality" with anthropoid apes and the dog. Along with this, in a third column, is "psychogenesis in man," and we find the order of appearance of the faculties recapitulated; association by contiguity at 7 weeks, association by similarity at 10 weeks, recognition of persons at 4 months, recognition of pictures and words at 8 months, and so on.

Evidence for this order was based almost entirely on anecdote and informal observation. As comparative psychology developed an experimental method, the work of Romanes and his generation was derided and banished as a shameful page in the history of a new science. Yet the adaptiveness of behavior and evolutionary continuity were never quite forgotten. One no longer looked for faculties but for "laws" of behavior. Hull's theory of learning, which converted half the psychological world, stressed the biological adaptiveness of the conditioned reflex and the principle of reinforcement which operated by reducing biological drives or need conditions, thereby strengthening behaviors useful to the organism (Hull 1943). The continuity was there too, because it was presumed that one could investigate these mechanisms in the rat and apply the findings to man.

Seeking to understand man's behavior by experimenting with the rat has fallen off in fashion, in its turn, but the ethologists have revived the biological tradition begun by Darwin and furthered by Romanes in a new and more sophisticated spirit of naturalism. Behavior that is specific to the species has become of interest and is studied in relation to the ecology of the species, thus revealing its adaptiveness.

In this abbreviated sketch of the influence of evolutionary concepts on psychology, where does perception come in? Do only executive behaviors like spinning webs, building nests, running through mazes, or pressing bars have adaptive value? Or is there a phylogenesis of perception and a parallel development in the individual? Is there perceptual learning which is adaptive? Or must learning be only on the response side, as behaviorists believed?

Karl Lashley was one of the first to raise these questions and to point out the role of perception in species-specific behavior and in evolution. In the "Experimental Analysis of Instinctive Behavior" (Lashley 1938) he stressed the importance of studying the innate components of "sensory organization," as well as the motor aspects of behavior. The essential first step, he said, was "analysis of the properties of the stimulus situation which are really effective in arousing the behavior." Understanding of the motor activities "hinges on these perceptual problems." Much of his work, from the early naturalistic studies of terns to later studies of stimulus equivalence in the rat, was directed at this problem. He never forgot the importance of evolution for understanding an animal's behavior. In "Persistent Problems in the Evolution of Mind" (1949), he told us that "the limits of capacity of each order of animals are set by the kinds of relations among objects that it can perceive. The development of the individual is a slow maturation of such capacities" (p. 460). "It is not the fact of learning but what is learned that differentiates animals in the evolutionary scale. The learning of higher animals involves a perception of relations which is beyond the capacity of the lower" (p. 458).

The latter statement he illustrated by comparing the behavior of a spider monkey and a chimpanzee in a matching problem. The monkey was required to choose a red or a green square, according as a red or a green square was given as a model. When the squares were placed as in row *a* in Figure 11.1 , the monkey never improved above chance in 1000 trials. But when there was *contact* between the model and the test square, as in rows *b, d, e,* and *g,* he quickly achieved errorless choice. He saw the model, Lashley thought, as a pointer or a signal but did not perceive the relation of similarity. The chimpanzee, on the other hand, grasped it quickly.

Background of the Theory

To tell you how I see perceptual development as a mark of adaptiveness, I must explain first what I think perception is and what perceptual learning is. Then I will distinguish two modes of perceiving and illustrate with experiments what we know about their development in phylogeny and in the individual.

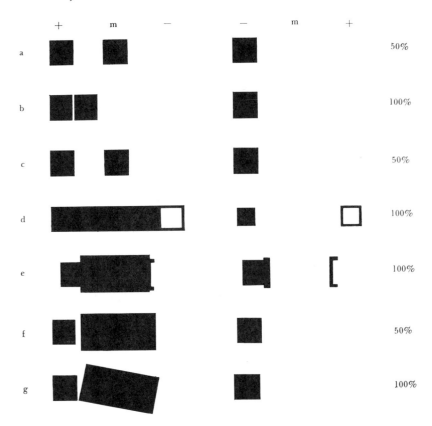

Figure 11.1
Arrangements of red and green squares presented to a spider monkey and a chimpanzee in a matching task. The percentages at the right represent the final level of accuracy attained in each situation (from Lashley 1949; reproduced by permission of the *Quarterly Review of Biology*).

Perception is extracting information from stimulation (Gibson 1966). Stimulation emanates from the objects and surfaces and events in the world around us and it *carries information about* them; though different from them, it *specifies* them. If we were to consider stimulation only as individual rays of light or vibrations in the air, this specification would not be intelligible, because information about objects and layout of the world around us lies in relations, like edges between things; it is not punctate, but structured over space and time. Not only is there information about things in stimulation; there is rich information, far more, potentially, than we utilize.

Let me give an example. Some animals, especially bats and dolphins, locate food and find their way around by means of echolocation. The dolphin emits clicking sounds at varying rates from one per second to bursts of 500 or more. These clicks are thought to be used for food-finding and navigation. To quote a dolphin expert, "The click trains, or sonar, search the seascape in front of a dolphin in much the same way that the cone of light from a miner's headlamp shows his way through a mine. In the presence of reflected light, we see where we look. In the presence of reflected sound, or the echoes of their own clicks, dolphins hear where they point their beam of sound. The click-echoes returned from the environment before the moving dolphin are information-bearing. The echoes contain information about the size, shape, location, movement if any, and texture of the living and non-living things in the water" (McVay 1967, p. 8). It has in fact been demonstrated that dolphins can differentiate in this way objects of different sizes and shape and even different metallic substances, and can swim an obstacle course without collision. Three points emerge from this: one, that potential stimulus information about features of the environment is vast; second, that the information accurately specifies the layout of the world and the objects in it; and third, that perception is an active process, a search for the relevant information that specifies the path an animal needs to travel, the obstacles to be avoided, the mate or the food to be approached.

So perception, functionally speaking, is extracting information about the world from stimulation, a highly adaptive process since the animal must somehow discover where to go, what to seize, and what to avoid. What kind of world is there to perceive? We can describe it in several ways. I choose a classification that refers to properties of the environment. These include properties of the *spatial layout* (surfaces, edges, drop-offs); properties of *events* (motion, occlusion, appearance, disappearance, and reappearance); and properties of *objects* that make them distinguishable and identifiable. For man at least we can include another class; man-made symbols—*coded items* that stand for objects and events, such as speech and writing.

Animals perceive the surfaces and objects and events in their surroundings by way of stimulation which specifies them. But they seldom do this perfectly, and the potential information in stimulation is vastly greater than that which becomes effective. To understand how potential information becomes effective we need the concepts of *perceptual development* and *perceptual learning*. As the higher-order invariants and structure that uniquely specify objects and events are progressively extracted from the total stimulus flux, so does perception become more differentiated and more specific to those things. This is a process which goes on in the evolution of species and also, I think, in the development of the individual.

How do animals *learn* to perceive the permanent distinguishable properties of the world in the changing flux of stimulation? Not, I believe, by association, but by a process of extracting the invariant information from the variable flux. I think several processes are involved, all attentional ones. (See Gibson 1969 for a detailed statement of the theory of perceptual learning) One is perceptual abstraction, akin to what James called "dissociation by varying concomitants" (note the dissociation as opposed to association; something is being pulled *out* from context, instead of being added *on*). Another is filtering of the irrelevant, an attenuation in the perceiving of random, varying, noninformative aspects of stimulation. A third is active, exploratory search. The dolphin beaming his clicking sounds is an example of the latter.

Another example is active touch (Gibson 1962) . When a blindfolded subject is handed an unfamiliar object and asked to learn to identify it so as to be able to match it visually to one of a larger set of similar objects, what does he do? He runs his fingers round its contours searching for distinguishing features, and presses it with different finger combinations to determine its proportions. The stimulation to which he exposes himself is constantly varying and, from the point of view of individual receptors, never the same. Yet he picks up from this variable flux of tactual-kinaesthetic stimulation constant structural properties like curves, edges, and indentations which are translatable into visual properties.

With respect to the search process in perceptual learning, a very important question is what terminates the search and thus selects what is learned. For many years no one questioned the proposition that external reinforcement (e.g. food or shock) is the selective principle for learning things like bar-pressing or choosing one arm of a maze rather than another. But is a distinctive feature selected as relevant because it wins a reward or avoids punishment? Is this the way that higher-order structural relations are detected? Although this might happen in a teaching situation, I do not think it is the true principle of perceptual learning. So much of it goes on very early in life and is necessarily self-regulated. No experimenter is on hand to deliver reinforcement; probably not even a parent could provide it deliberately, since he seldom has any way of knowing just what the child is perceiving.

I think the reinforcement is internal—the *reduction of uncertainty*. Stimulation is not only full of potential information; there is too much of it. There is a limit to what can be processed, and variable, random, irrelevant stimulation leads only to perception of confusion—what someone has referred to as cognitive clutter as opposed to cognitive order. But distinctive features, invariants, and higher-order structure serve the function of reducing uncertainty, taking order and continuity out of chaos and flux. The search for invariants, both low-level contrastive features and high-level order, is the task of perception, while detection of them at once reduces uncertainty and is reinforcing.

Perceptual Development Species and Individuals

With this brief background of theory, I propose to return to my first question. Is there perceptual development, in the animal series and in the individual, and is it adaptive? Are there trends in what is responded to, as Lashley suggested? In order to give some specific answers, I shall compare two modes of perceiving and give evidence, in both cases, of species differences and of development within the life span.

The two modes are perception of *space and events in space* and the perception of *objects and permanent items*, like written letters, that can be approached and examined closely. I have chosen to contrast these because there is reason to think that in their phylogenetic development there is a considerable difference between them. Localizing one-self in the spatial layout or monitoring events going on in the space around one seem to develop earlier and to be neurologically more primitive than fine-grain identification of objects and outline figures such as letters.

This difference is akin to a distinction within visual perception drawn in a recent paper by Trevarthen (1968), who speaks of "two mechanisms of vision." One of these he calls "ambient vision." It has to do with orientations of the head, postural adjustments, and locomotion in relationship to spatial configurations of contours, surfaces, events, and objects. The other he calls "focal vision." It is applied to one space and a specific kind of object; it serves to examine and identify.

"Ambient vision in primates," says Trevarthen, "resembles the vision of primitive active vertebrates.... At any instant, an extensive portion of the behavioral space around the body is mapped by this ambient visual mode; in primates, somewhat more than a frontal hemisphere is apprehended. With large rotations of the head or whole body, an animal may quickly scan all of the space close to his body and thus obtain a visual impression of the large features in it. The visual mechanism is strongly stimulated by parallax changes caused by translation of the eye, and the receptor mechanism is particularly sensitive to the velocities of displacement of continuities in the light pattern on the retina" (p. 328).

"In contrast with this vision of ambient space, focal vision, enormously developed in diurnal primates, is applied to obtain detailed vision." Its scope at any given instant is restricted, but it is extended over time by sampling movements of the eyes. An area of interest may thus be brought to full attention and "analyzed as if carried close in by a zoom lens" (p. 329).

Focal vision in primates appears to be primarily a function of the cortex. Even in rodents a comparable, though less pronounced, distinction may exist. Schneider (1967) working with hamsters found that ablation of the visual cortex left the animal with only a minimal ability to tell *what* he was seeing, but left nearly intact his ability to find *where* it was. He was unable to discriminate and identify objects, but could localize them in space. Ablation of the superior colliculus produced the opposite effect; the hamster knew what he was seeing but behaved as if he didn't know where it was.

I shall say no more about this neurological distinction, since I have made no contribution to it, but it supports the point I intend to make; that discrimination of events in space is primitive, both phylogenetically and ontogenetically, while development progresses toward differentiation of form in objects and two-dimensional projections. In other words, fine-grain identification of objects or patterns is the later achievement; its development continues over a long time; learning plays a prominent role in it as compared with perceiving the spatial layout and events; and we can expect to find more striking phylogenetic differences.

Perception of Space

Consider, first, development of the perception of space and of events in space. Is there phylogenetic continuity here within the vertebrate phylum? Indeed there is. The similarities between species are far greater than their differences in this respect. We can adduce evidence for this in three important cases—perception of imminent collision (called "looming"); perception of depth-downward; and perceived constancy of the sizes of things.

Looming can be defined as accelerated magnification of the form of an approaching object. It is an optical event over time. It specifies a future collision (Schiff, Caviness, and Gibson 1962) . If a vehicle or even a small object such as a baseball is perceived as coming directly toward him by a human adult, he ducks or dodges out of the way. Is the perception of imminent collision together with its avoidance instinctive? If so, in what species, and how early? Schiff (1965) constructed an artificial looming situation in which nothing actually approached the animal observer but there was abstract optical information for something approaching.

In Schiff's experiments, a shadow was projected by a shadow-casting device on a large translucent screen in front of the animal. The screen was large enough to fill a wide visual angle. The projected shadow could be made to undergo continuously accelerated magnification until it filled the screen or, on the other hand, continuously decelerating minification. Magnification resulted in a visual impression of an object approaching at a uniform speed. Minification gave a visual impression of an object receding into the distance. The projected silhouette could be varied in form, so as to compare, for instance, jagged contours with smooth ones, or silhouettes of meaningful objects with meaningless ones. Subjects studied included fiddler crabs, frogs, chicks, kittens, monkeys, and humans.

The crabs responded to magnification (but not to minification) by running backwards, flinching, or flattening out. Frogs jumped away from the ghostly approaching object. Chicks responded more often to magnification than minification by running, crouching, and hopping. Kittens (28 days old) tended to respond to magnification with struggle and head movements, but the kittens were restrained in holders and well-differentiated avoidance behavior did not show up clearly. Rhesus monkeys (including infants five to eight months of age) were observed in the situation under four conditions (magnification, minification, lightening of the screen, and darkening of the screen). Both young and adult animals withdrew rapidly in response to the approach display, leaping to the rear of the cage. Alarm cries frequently accompanied retreat in the younger animals. The receding display brought responses which might be described as curiosity, but never retreat. The lightening and darkening of the screen had no effect, and this served as a control, that is, a change of mere stimulation as compared with change of magnification.

The adaptiveness of the responses to optical magnification is illustrated by the turtle. Hayes and Saiff (1967) investigated what they termed the "visual alarm reaction" in the turtle. A looming shadow on a screen was used, as in Schiff's experiments. The turtles responded to magnification by withdrawing the head into the shell.

What about a human subject? Schiff measured the galvanic skin reflex in adult human subjects in the looming situation. There was decrease of skin resistance in the majority of subjects for magnification but not for minification. Human infants, Burton White found (1969), begin to blink at a rapidly approaching object (with air currents controlled) at about three weeks of age. The reliability of the response increased for another 10 or 12 weeks. Perhaps sensitivity to visual approach of a missile takes this long to mature or be learned in the human infant; but perhaps another indicator response would show that it is picked up even earlier. Some observers claim that attempted head withdrawal to visual looming occurs as early as two weeks in human infants.

Does it matter what shape or object characteristics the expanding silhouette has? Schiff tried objects of different shapes as shadow-casters, but he did not find that silhouettes of these objects had a differential influence on avoidance behavior. It was the event of looming as such, not an identifiable object, that controlled the avoidant behavior. The functional usefulness of this lack of specificity is obvious; quick avoidance of a fast approaching object is often necessary for avoidance of collision, while fine-grain identification of the object hardly matters.

Now let me give you some phylogenetic comparisons for avoidance of a falling-off place, that is, a drop-off of the ground. Depth downwards is specified in the light to the animal's eye. Does this information by itself cause the animal to avoid it? Some years ago, Dr. Richard Walk and I

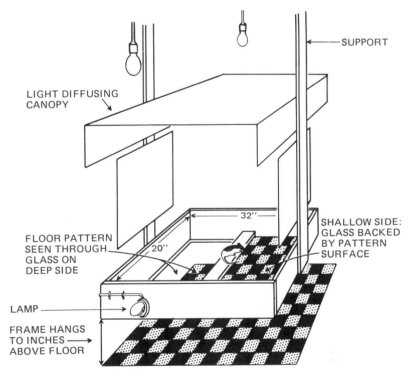

Figure 11.2
Drawing of a visual cliff (from Walk and Gibson 1961; copyright by American Psychological Assoc. and reproduced by permission).

constructed an apparatus for answering this question (Gibson and Walk 1960) . We called it a "visual cliff." "Cliff," because there was a simulated drop-off downward, and "visual" because we attempted to eliminate all other information for the drop-off. Figure 11.2 shows an apparatus constructed for testing small animals, such as a rat or a chick. The animal is placed on a center board. A checker-board floor extends out from the center board on one side, an inch or two below it. A similar floor is 10 inches or more below on the other side. A sheet of glass extends from the center board, above the floor, an inch or two below the board, so that tactual information for the cliff is eliminated, and air currents and echoes are equated.

What is the visual information? Figure 11.3 shows the difference in the density of optical texture from the two checkered surfaces in the light projected to the animal's eye. For some animals binocular parallax might yield differential information about the two sides. The best information, our experiments suggested, was the motion perspective produced by the animal's own movement—especially head movements—as the cliff edge is observed in comparison to the shallow edge. Differences in texture

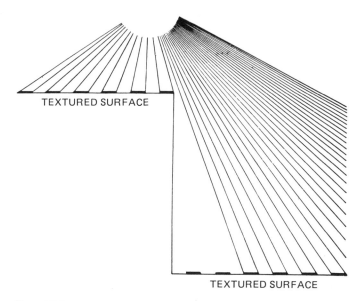

TEXTURED SURFACE

TEXTURED SURFACE

Figure 11.3
Cross section of a visual cliff. The diagram shows the pattern of light projected to the subject's eye from a textured surface at a shallow depth below his station point on a center runway and from an identical surface farther below (from Walk and Gibson 1961; copyright by American Psychological Assoc. and reproduced by permission).

density were eliminated and a monocular animal was used to make this observation.

Many animal species have been tested on the visual cliff: rodents, birds, turtles, cats (including lions, tigers, and snow leopards), sheep and goats, dogs, and of course primates (Walk and Gibson 1961; Routtenberg and Glickman 1964) . All these species, save flying ones or swimming ones, avoided the cliff edge of the apparatus and chose the safe, shallow edge on the basis of visual information alone. Texture must be present on the ground under the animal, however, for a safe surface of support to be perceived. The animal will not walk out upon a homogeneous, untextured surface—he demands "optical support" as well as felt support. This surely has value for survival.

Avoidance of a drop-off and dependence upon optical support must be developmentally primitive. This conclusion is suggested not only by the continuity of the behavior within the vertebrate phylum, but also by ablation experiments and ontogenetic data. When the striate cortex of the cat is removed (Meyer 1963) pattern vision in the sense of identification goes, but a cat will still avoid a cliff, if he can move freely.

Ontogenetically, Walk and I found that cliff avoidance develops very early and, in some species, without any opportunity for learning. Precocial animals such as chicks and goats avoid a cliff a few hours after birth, as soon as they can be tested. Rats reared in the dark avoid a cliff as soon as they are brought out, with no opportunity for preliminary visual experience. Primates cannot be tested at birth, but human infants avoid a cliff as early as they can crawl. Monkeys, like human infants, are carried by their mothers in early infancy. But monkeys placed on the untextured glass without optical support at three days of age (Rosenblum and Cross 1963) showed indications of emotional disturbance (crouching, vocalization, self-clasping, and rocking), whereas there was no disturbance when they were placed on the glass with a texture just below it. We may conclude that perception of a safe surface in contrast to a drop-off appears early in evolution and early in life, and that little learning may be required for its appearance. It is modified by biased circumstances, such as prolonged dark rearing, but terrestrial animals do not generally have to be taught this useful adaptation.

Now consider my third case: perceived constancy of the sizes of things. Information for size constancy is given normally by motion; motion of the object toward or away from a stationary observer, or movement of the observer toward the object. Since information for constant size—the rule relating size and distance—is given in motion, it should belong with my "primitive" mode of perceiving. Let us see if it does, if there is continuity over species and early development without any marked dependence on learning with external reinforcement.

As for continuity among animal species, size constancy has been demonstrated in the chimpanzee, by Köhler (1915); in the monkey by Klüver (1933) and by Locke (1937); in the cat by Gunter (1951) and by Freeman (1968); in the weanling rat (Heller 1968); in the duckling (Pastore 1958); and in fish (Herter 1953). It is no surprise to the thoughtful biologist that animals other than man exhibit size constancy. How indeed could they locomote or seize things accurately if the apparent sizes of things around them were constantly shrinking or expanding as distance changed with the target's movement or the observer's position?

Is learning involved in perceiving things as constant in size? It might well be, since the conditions for extracting the invariant depend on motion of an object or of the observer in relation to it. The mother's face approaches the baby as she bends to pick it up; the baby moves his hand toward and away from his eyes and moves them together and apart, for hours at a time. These are guaranteed opportunities for presenting him with appropriately structured stimulation. But such learning would have to take place very early, for Bower (1966) has found evidence of size constancy as young as two months in the human infant. He used the method of operant conditioning, the response being a leftward turning of the head. The infant was trained to respond thus to a 30-cm. white cube placed one meter from his eyes. The reinforcement for the head-turning response was an experimenter popping up and "peek-a-booing" at the infant and then disappearing again (an ingenious and, it turns out, remarkably effective reinforcement. The infant learns to do something to *get a perception*). After training, three new stimuli were introduced for generalization tests. These were the 30-cm. cube placed 3 meters away; a 90-cm. cube placed I meter away; and the 90-cm. cube placed 3 meters away (see Figure 11.4). These and the original training situation were presented in a counter-balanced order.

The conditioned stimulus situation would be expected to elicit the most head-turnings, and the one appearing to the infant most like it, the next most. If the infant has size constancy, one would expect the cube identical with the training one to evoke the next most responses, even when it is farther away (test stimulus 1) . If size constancy hasn't been attained, one might expect the cube projecting the same-sized retinal image (test stimulus 3) to elicit most response. The infants, in practice, responded to test stimulus 1 next most often after the training situation, evidence that they perceived the cube in its true, objective size. Next most often came the larger cube placed at the same distance as the training cube; and last of all, the large cube placed at 3 meters where it projected the identical-sized retinal image.

Does this result mean that *no* learning is involved in the development of size constancy? Definitely not, since even eight weeks gives a lot of

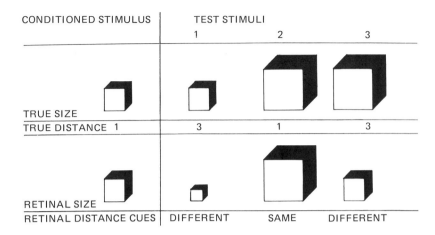

| CONDITIONED STIMULUS | TEST STIMULI |
| | 1   2   3 |

Figure 11.4
Schematic representation of cubes of different sizes placed at different distances in Bower's investigation of size constancy in infants (from "The Visual World of Infants," by T. G. R. Bower, December 1966. Copyright © 1966 by Scientific American, Inc. All rights reserved).

opportunity for visual experience. But it means that any learning could not have involved association with specific motor acts, such as reaching a certain distance or walking so many paces. But perceived motion of an object could provide an opportunity for discovery of the rule relating projective size of object to nearness of the object. Dark-reared rats (Heller 1968) did not exhibit size constancy when first brought into the light, despite normal performance on the visual cliff. Some visual experiences with objects moving in space may be necessary, therefore, for size constancy to develop, but it does so very early. Later changes, appearing when judgmental methods are used (Piaget 1961), probably indicate development of a more analytical attitude toward perceiving objects rather than the mere localizing of things in their true sizes .

Perception of Objects

Now, let me turn to my other class of perceptions—the fine-grain identification of objects, and the use of coded stimuli to substitute for them. Is there continuity over species and early appearance as there is with the spatial perceptions?

There is continuity, yes, but in this instance there is a good case for a striking evolutionary change, and also for a long course of perceptual learning in the individual. The human child must learn the distinctive features of the objects, representations, and symbolic items that human life requires him to differentiate.

What about the *phylogeny* of object identification? Certainly animals identify some objects at quite an early age. The herring gull chick identifies by a spot of red the beak of its parent hovering over it. This information is referred to by the ethologists as an "innate releaser." Releasers seem in many cases to be very simple unlearned signals for the discharging of a fixed unlearned pattern of responses, like the chemical signal that releases attack behavior in some species of snake. A mere trace of the chemical in a box will bring the attack. Sometimes the effective stimulus pattern is more complex, as is the visual pattern that constitutes "owlness" and releases mobbing behavior in the chaffinch, or the quite complex and informative song patterns of many birds, but the role of learning is still minimal in these cases.

Do we have studies of learned object identification in any animals but primates? Of course, the studies of imprinting in precocial animals come to mind. Certain properties of an object like high brightness contrast and motion release in the newborn animal a following response, and following the moving object serves, presumably, to "impress" its features on the "mind" of the subject so that he will later discriminate it from other objects and approach it rather than others. Here, in a manner insuring that the precocial animal will take to his parent or at least to his species, is a very immediate kind of learning that seems to contain the rudiments of perceptual learning. It is not a matter of association of stimulus and response; the response is ready to go at once and, besides, recognition can be measured by other responses than following. There is no external reinforcement; the mother can butt an infant goat away and he will follow her just the same. What is learned is typical of perceptual learning: an increased specificity of response to visual and auditory stimulation characteristic of the releasing object. To what extent there is increased differentiation we really don't know, for early imprinting is quickly followed by opportunities for learning to discriminate feature-contrasts that insure more precise differentiation.

We can study this latter process most easily in the young human animal, so I shall trace some of the steps in his learning to differentiate complex objects in his environment. Does he begin, like the precocial animal, with innate attention to high-contrast visual stimulation and to motion? Some people think so and like to compare the turning of the eyes or head toward a voice or a shiny moving thing to imprinting. One of the first and most prominent objects in an infant's world is the face of his caretaker. Studies of development of recognition of a human face tell us much (Gibson 1969, Ch. 16) . At first, it appears to be motion of the head (like a nod) that is compelling, but very shortly the eyes emerge as a prominent feature—the dominant feature for a discriminative response. They are bright, and they move. After a time, the facial contour, the contours of brow and nose around the eyes, and later the mouth (especially in motion) differentiate as critical features. But not until nearly four months must these features be present in an invariant and "face-like" relation for the recognition response to occur. At four months, a "realistic" face is smiled at more. Not until six months are individual faces differentiated, and not until much later still are facial expressions. We know little as yet about how this learning goes on, but it is perceptual learning; there is increasing differentiation of more and more specific stimulus information. Motor responses play little or no role, nor does reinforcement.

"Learning-to-learn" about objects was demonstrated in a long-term experiment with infants 6 to 12 months old by Ling (1941). She presented infants with a pair of solid wooden objects, differently shaped. Both were colored bright yellow and were of a graspable size. They were presented to the infant on a board within reaching distance. One was fastened tightly to the board. The other was removable and was furthermore sweet to taste, having been dipped in a saccharine solution. The infant learned over a period of days to reach at once for the shape that was sweetened. Then five series of problems were presented to him. The first series had four problems: circle vs. cross, circle vs. triangle, circle vs. square, and circle vs. oval. After successive mastery of these, the child progressed to a series in which one of the forms was rotated; then a series in which sizes were transformed; a fourth, in which the number of "wrong" blocks was increased; and a fifth, in which the positive and negative shapes were reversed. There was evidence of more and more rapid learning as the series continued, as well as transfer of discriminations with rotation and change of size. What were the babies learning that transferred? Distinctive features of the shapes they were comparing, to be sure, but something more general too, Ling thought. They learned search strategies of systematic observation and comparison, "attention to form differences, rather than improvement in form discrimination *per se*." Compared with control babies of the same age, they made a more immediate and minute examination of the stimulus patterns and inhibited extraneous bodily movement.

Now I want to finish with the top-level achievement of fine-grain identification—the identification of written symbols. Only man does this and only a well-grown, well-tutored man at that. Monkeys can indeed learn to discriminate a pair of fairly small line drawings from one another, but they are much slower at this task and make many more errors than human children of four or five (Hicks and Hunton 1964; Hunton and Hicks 1965). Both phylogenetically and ontogenetically, this is the peak of perceptual achievement. Here we find that education is most essential. How is one letter discriminated from another? I think by learning the distinctive features for the set of letters. There is evidence to show that this is the way letters really are discriminated, that there is a set of distinctive features, not idiosyncratic to an individual perceiver or to a given graphic character but characterizing the set and permitting each letter to be distinguished by its unique pattern of features within the set.

The set of letters, in this case, must be differentiated as a set from other outline drawings or similar things. Linda Lavine, at Cornell, found that this is done quite early. Children from three to five were shown a systematically chosen sample of graphic items: handwritten Roman letters, numerals, lower-case letters, cursive handwriting, artificial letters, scribbles, and simple line drawings of objects—a flower, a stick man, a child's attempt at drawing a house or a face, and so on. The children were asked to "tell me which of these are writing." Most children of three and four could separate the drawings of objects from the rest, but not the scribbling. Most children of five could differentiate the numbers and letters, whatever type or case, from both scribbling and pictures although they could seldom identify individual numbers or letters. Habits of observing differences between small objects, like those shown by Ling's babies, probably carry over from object perception to the perception of line drawings, and the set of graphic symbols is somehow differentiated from other marks on paper before individual items can be identified.

To discover what features are actually noted in comparing letters and identifying them, we performed a number of discrimination experiments using both children and adults (Gibson, Schapiro, and Yonas 1968). These experiments, which simply required the subject to decide whether a pair of letters was the same or different, allowed us to construct a "confusion matrix" for a set of letters. The time taken to judge same or different and the errors were entered in matrices to show which pairs were most often confused and which least. Then the matrices were analyzed to find what proximities or clusters underlie the structure of the matrix. This tells us what features are being used by the observer when he must decide whether a given pair is the same or different.

The method of analysis was a hierarchical cluster analysis (Johnson 1967). It looks progressively (in steps) for the most compact and isolable clusters, then for the next most compact, and so on till one winds up with loose clusters and finally the whole set. The results can be turned upside down and diagrammed in a tree structure. Figure 11.5 shows on the left the tree resulting from an analysis of 48 adult subjects' latency data for 9 letters. The first split separates the "sharp" letters with diagonality from all the others. On the left branch, the "round" letters, C and G, next split off from the others. At the next branch, the square right-angular letters E and F split off from letters differentiated from them by curvature. The error data for these letters with the same subjects reveal an identical structure.

On the right of Figure 11.5 is the hierarchical structure for 60 seven-year-old children, with the same letters. It is similar to the adults' but not quite the same. The first split is a simple curve-straight one. On the second

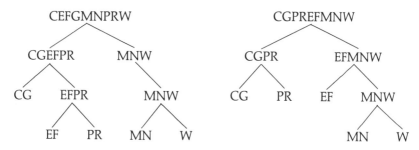

Figure 11.5
Tree structure yielded by confusions in making same-different judgments. The structure on the left was obtained with adult subjects; that on the right with seven-year-old children.

branch, the round letters are split off from the P and R. The square letters are now split off from those with diagonality. This is very neat, and it suggests to me that children at this stage are doing straightforward sequential processing of features, while adults have progressed to a more Gestalt-like processing, picking up higher orders of structure given by redundancy and tied relations. This is speculative, but it would be a highly adaptive kind of development, achieving the highest level of differentiation with the greatest economy of processing.

Conclusion

Is the development of perception an adaptive process? It is as much so as the development of locomotion. Nature seems to have insured first the means of detecting the information needed for getting around and avoiding such dangers as obstacles, pitfalls, and missiles. Discrimination of objects by simple signs based on single physical characteristics of high vividness is primitive too. But fine-grain differentiation of multidimensional complex sets of objects is high in the evolutionary scheme and in development, a process where adaptation is achieved only through education.

References

Bower, T. G. R. 1966. The visual world of infants. *Scient. Amer.* 215: 80–92.

Freeman, R. B. 1968. Perspective determinants of visual size-constancy in binocular and monocular cats. *Amer. J. Psychol.* 81: 67–73.

Gibson, E. J., and R. D. Walk. 1960. The "visual cliff." *Scient. Amer.* 202: 64–71.

Gibson, E. J., F. Schapiro, and A. Yonas. 1968. Confusion matrices for graphic patterns obtained with a latency measure. Pp. 76–96 in Final report, Project No. 5-1213, Contract No. OE6-10-156, Cornell University and the U. S. Office of Education.

Gibson, J. J. 1962. Observations on active touch. *Psychol. Rev.* 69: 477–91.

Gibson, J. J. 1966. *The senses considered as perceptual systems.* Boston: Houghton-Mifflin.

Gunter, R. 1951. Visual size constancy in the cat. *Brit. J. Psychol.* 42: 288–93.

Hayes, W. N., and E. I. Saiff. 1967. Visual alarm reactions in turtles. *Anim. Behav.* 15: 102–06.

Heller, D. P. 1968. Absence of size constancy in visually deprived rats. *J. Comp. Physiol. Psychol.* 65: 336–39.

Herter, K. 1953. *Die Fischdressuere und ihre sinnes physiologischen Grundlagen.* Berlin: Akademie-Verlag.

Hicks, L. H., and V. D. Hunton. 1964. The relative dominance of form and orientation in discrimination learning by monkeys and children. *Psychon. Sci.* 1: 411–12.

Hull, C. L. 1943. *Principles of behavior.* New York: Appleton.

Hunton, V. D., and L. H. Hicks. 1965. Discrimination of figural orientation by monkeys and children. *Percept. Mot. Skills* 21: 55–59.

Johnson, S. C. 1967. Hierarchical clustering schemes. *Psychometrika* 32: 241–54.

Klüver, H. 1933. *Behavior mechanisms in monkeys.* Chicago: Univ. Chicago Press.

Köhler, W. 1915. Untersuchungen am Schimpansen und am Haushuhn. *Abh. preuss. Akad. Wiss.* (phys.-math.) No. 3, 1–70.

Lashley, K. S. 1938. Experimental analysis of instinctive behavior. *Psychol. Rev.* 45 :445–71.

Lashley, K. S. 1949. Persistent problems in the evolution of mind. *Quart. Rev. Biol.* 24: 28–42.

Ling, B. C. 1941. Form discrimination as a learning cue in infants. *Comp. Psychol. Monogr.* 17, Whole No.86.

McVay, S. 1967. How hears the dolphin? *Princeton Alumni Weekly*, October, pp. 6–9.

Meyer, P. M. 1963. Analysis of visual behavior in cats with extensive neocortical ablations. *J. Comp. Physiol. Psychol.* 56: 397–401.

Pastore, N. 1958. Form perception and size constancy in the duckling. *J. Psychol.* 45: 259–61.

Piaget, J. 1961. *Les mécanismes perceptifs.* Paris: Presses Universitaires de France.

Romanes, G. J. 1893. *Mental evolution in man.* New York: D. Appleton.

Romanes, G. J. 1895. *Mental evolution in animals.* New York: D. Appleton.

Rosenblum, L. A., and H. A. Cross. 1963. Performance of neonatal monkeys on the visual cliff situation. *Amer. J. Psychol.* 76: 318–20.

Routtenberg, A., and S. E. Glickman. 1964. Visual cliff behavior in undomesticated rodents, land and aquatic turtles, and cats (panthera). *J. comp. physiol. Psychol.* 58: 143–46.

Schiff, W. 1965. The perception of impending collision: A study of visually directed avoidant behavior. *Psychol. Monogr. 79*, Whole No. 604.

Schiff, W., J. A. Caviness, and J. J. Gibson. 1962. Persistent fear responses in rhesus monkeys to the optical stimulus of "looming." *Science* 136: 982–83.

Schneider, G. E. 1967. Contrasting visuomotor functions of tectum and cortex in the Golden Hamster. *Psychol. Forsch.* 31: 52–62.

Trevarthen, C. B. 1968. Two mechanisms of vision in primates. *Psychol. Forsch.* 31: 299–337.

Walk, R. D., and E. J. Gibson. 1961. A comparative and analytical study of visual depth perception. *Psychol. Monogr.* 75, No. 15.

White, B. L. In press, 1969. Child development research: An edifice without a foundation. *Merrill-Palmer Quarterly.*

Retrospect and Prospect: Comparative Psychology and Animal Cognition

Although comparative psychology as envisaged by the early functional psychologists received a certain impetus from the ethologists, one of the effects was the severing of the tie between study of animal behavior and concern with learning theory. The ethologists, unlike the animal psychologists in the earlier days of the century, were not only uninterested in how a maze was learned, they were chiefly interested in so-called species-specific behavior and had strong biases toward nativism, inventing concepts such as "innate releasers." The old field of comparative psychology all but disappeared for a while. The emphasis on the animal in its niche, and on ecological and structural constraints, seems to have been a healthy one, however, and ecologically inclined psychologists are again interested in learning, now with an eye toward what an animal has to learn to survive in its natural environment. I think my own comparative research fits well with this emphasis, especially the research with the visual cliff since it has to do with perceptually guided action that contributes to an animal's survival. The concern with learning is shifting to exploratory activity and its contribution to perceptually guided behavior in activities such as safe locomotion, foraging, and interactions with other animals, especially maternal-infant interactions.

In contrast to this trend, there has emerged in recent years an interest in so-called "animal cognition." This concern has its forerunners too, in Hobhouse and Romanes and later Margaret Washburn's *Animal Mind* (1908). These ancestors are seldom referred to, however. In a recent review of animal cognition (Gallistel 1989), animal cognition is described as a "computational-representational approach." Gallistel is firmly opposed to any form of empiricism, quoting Leibnitz to the effect that "there is nothing in the mind that was not first in the senses, except the mind itself." This "cognitive revival in animal behavior" (Dewsbury 1989) stems partly from the very fashionable studies of language learning in primates other than man, but also covers processes related to ideas of space, time, and number (Gallistel 1989), intentionality, and self-recognition. Romanes' chart of the phylogenetic evolution of mind (Romanes 1989), fits in nicely—many of his terms, in fact, have been borrowed.

The old dichotomies—nativism vs. empiricism and mind vs. behavior—do not go away!

III

Perception: Pyschophysics to Transformations
(1954–1959)

Introduction to Part III

Although I had performed no research on problems of adult human perception in my own right, I was pretty closely in touch with the field because of my husband's work. During World War II, especially, I did some thinking about perception. I was a camp follower for four years, devoting my time to moving, running a household under trying conditions in Texas and Southern California, and being a mother. In California, where my husband spent two and a half years at the Santa Ana Army Air Base doing research for the Army Air Force, I had opportunities to discuss problems like the best way to train people in aircraft recognition (a nice problem in perceptual learning) and how distance might be perceived over long stretches, and targets located while both observer and target were moving. These were not the classic laboratory problems, and there was lively argument in James Gibson's unit on the best way to conceive of them and how to work on them. His unit included some young officers, most importantly Robert Gagné who had been a student of his briefly as an undergraduate at Yale, and some noncommissioned officers who were inducted part way through their graduate training in psychology. We had gatherings on weekends fairly often (baked beans and beer for supper) that were not unlike graduate student gatherings in normal times. Those gatherings were a heaven-sent opportunity for me to listen to and take a turn in some psychological shop talk, after my rather tiresome week of coping with wartime domestic problems and intellectual aridity. We had a lot of discussions of perceptual learning that interested me particularly and paid off a few years later.

In part II, I related the disappointing ending of my rearing research with kids at the Cornell Behavior Farm. Luckily, a promising research opportunity came up soon afterward. Two wartime friends, Arthur Melton and Robert Gagné, had once again left academia and gone to work for the military at Lackland Air Force Base in San Antonio, Texas. Melton was Technical Director of the Human Resources Research Center and Gagné was Director of Research at the Perceptual and Motor Skills Laboratory. This group had funds to support external research in addition to their internal research program. We were invited to apply for research funds, and I was glad to do so. My husband's research was being supported by the Office of Naval Research (and continued to be for many years), but the Perceptual and Motor Skills Laboratory actually wanted research on perceptual learning, and I wanted to do it.

Gagné suggested that I begin by putting together all the available research on perceptual learning to date, since it had never been collected. It was clear from a few older studies and from the World War II projects (see J. J. Gibson 1947) that perception was educable, but it had seldom (if ever) been thought of as an area for research. Psychophysical experiments sometimes found evidence of it (it was a nuisance to them) and industrial graders and tasters occasionally referred to it. Except for William James (James 1891) it was not mentioned in textbooks. It was a far cry from all the learning research and theory of the thirties and forties, inviting a fresh approach.

I spent a year or more delving through obscure sources and produced a lengthy report, with 206 references, for the Perceptual and Motor Skills Laboratory. I also prepared an article for the *Psychological Bulletin* (E. Gibson 1953) and managed to improve the organization of the material greatly in the course of revisions. I have always been grateful to the editor (Wayne Dennis, at that time).

The actual research to be performed was contracted for. The topic was to be the effect of training on judgments of distance, and the location was to be a real outdoor one, not a table top or a corridor, as in most traditional studies. Since I had no laboratory of my own, working out-of-doors was a piece of good luck. Fortunately, the Cornell campus was very large and was not yet crammed with buildings. There was a good-sized athletic field near the stadium, with a clear 550 yard stretch of grass. We somehow persuaded the administration to let us use this area exclusively (literally keep it clear of everything but our own equipment) throughout the summer vacation. We were also able to commandeer the big quandrangle of the arts campus. We used these areas for three summers, doing "open-air psychophysics," as we called it. Two excellent graduate research assistants, Richard Bergman and Jean Purdy, helped. Bergman had started out in engineering, and knew how to do surveying, which was useful. Purdy, as an undergraduate at Mt. Holyoke College, had had rigorous training in psychophysical methods, also useful. The three experiments that follow were modeled on traditional psychophysical research methods but were performed in a "real-world" setting that made them very unusual at the time. It was also unusual to introduce training deliberately within a psychophysical paradigm as the major variable of the experiment.

The biggest bonus of doing research for the Air Force was the subjects. When we were ready to go, a bus arrived every morning from Sampson Air Force Base, about thirty miles away on Seneca Lake, full of new recruits (Sampson was an induction center) and a sergeant to steer them around. Having submitted to several arduous days of physical and mental tests, these young men were happy to spend a day on the Cornell campus. We were sad when Sampson was closed down a couple of years later.

These three experiments, in many ways conforming strictly to traditional psychophysics, are in strong contrast to the two that follow, although the latter were performed only a few years afterward. There is a dramatic change in the way of viewing the perception of depth and distance, a new emphasis on the role of motion and the information contributed by events as opposed to static features of stimulation. James Gibson had begun thinking about motion perspective and how events enter into perception of the layout during the war years in the Army Air Force, as he considered the kind of information available to a pilot or a gunner in a moving airplane. By the 1950s he was well on the way to formulating a new theory about how we perceive where and how far away things are and the information provided by invariants dependent on changing points of view. Perspective transformations became part of our essential vocabulary for understanding depth perception. I should say that James Gibson was my tutor as regards perception, but although we often argued about experiments—how to do them and what they meant—we never really disagreed, as we did sometimes about learning.

The experiment on information in perspective transformations as information for shape and form utilized psychophysical procedures, to be sure, but the questions posed had to do with invariance over transformation, a novelty in the experimental literature at that time. The paper on motion parallax inquires into the role of change as information for perceived separation in depth. It led, eventually, to quite revolutionary ideas about the importance of occlusion and disocclusion as information for one thing in front of or behind another. This experiment also provided an opportunity for testing a classic theory of perceptual learning, welcome because I had begun searching for ways of putting the two fields, perception and learning, together.

Involvement in these experiments gave me a grasp of psychophysical methods, some insight into the important questions to ask about perception, and training in how to set up a perception experiment—not to mention gradual understanding of a new way of viewing perception. This background paved the way for later research on perceptual development in infants and children.

12

The Effect of Training on Absolute Estimation of Distance over the Ground

Eleanor J. Gibson, Richard Bergman

There had been several studies of training judgments of distance during World War II, sometimes simply when aiming at a target through empty air and sometimes on a firing range, but there was good reason to think that these studies had little generalizability and that the subjects had simply made specific associations between local "cues," like "familiar size," and a verbal response. This suspicion was particularly convincing because of an experiment performed at the very beginning of our project by Joann Smith (later Kinney) and myself. It occurred to us that training that could be conducted with photographic material would be extremely convenient and timesaving in a practical situation. A fine series of photographs existed, made by J. J. Gibson's unit at the Santa Ana Army Air Base, of variable stretches of distance over ground, with a set of distant stakes of different heights as targets for comparison with a standard stake close by. Size constancy judgments over different stretches of distance were thought to be dependent on accurate estimations of the distance from the observer to the target (sometimes expressed as "allowing for the distance").

The experiment we conducted presented a number of photographs to the subject for matching judgments, gave correction for errors to one group of subjects but not to a group without training, and then looked for transfer to another set of photographs. No transfer at all was found. Evidently, if the corrected group had learned anything, it was not better differentiation of distance. There was evidence of deliberate association of details in a photograph with particular verbal judgments. Any training that resulted in true perceptual learning, therefore, would have to be conducted so as to prevent rote memorizing of verbal responses to particular targets and avoid idiosyncratically marked paths from the subject to a target. It should be set up so that neither stimulus layouts nor responses were repeated.

Our final plan gave us 108 stretches of distance, all different numbers of yards. We contrived this by using multiple station points for the subjects' judgments as

Journal of Experimental Psychology, 1954, 48, 473–482.

well as multiple targets. The field was carefully surveyed and laid out, so that every stretch of ground used for a judgment was different. The subjects made egocentric judgments in yards (from themselves to a target) and were corrected during training. Learning unmistakably occurred, as the data in the paper show. The interesting question was (and still is) what exactly did the subjects learn? As the experiment was conducted, they could not have memorized specific paired associates. Constant errors in the use of a yard scale were corrected rather quickly during training. Was that all they learned, a correction of a conceptual scale of some kind? It was disappointing to think so.

There is information in a gradient of density over the ground from a subject's feet to a target's base. We thought that judgments might have improved in precision (as witnessed by reduction in intrasubject variability) due to more finely differentiated perception of these gradients. I now wonder if there was another source of information that subjects learned to detect and use—target height in relation to eye height. Targets were of three heights and any one of the three would cut the horizon in the same ratio to the subject's eye height at any distance from him. Relating this ratio to a scale would give a kind of invariant that could be used in increasing precision of any given judgment. This extremely subtle and certainly unremarked-on potential information did not occur to us at the time, but if the invariant were, unaware to the subject, detected and used, it would be a true case of perceptual learning. It is more than likely that we use this information unwittingly in our daily business of getting around in the world.

Does the judgment of distance depend on learning? This question has been of theoretical interest to psychologists for many years, but its practical importance is equally evident.[1,2] Even with advances in instrumental control of ranging and aiming, the necessity of human judgments of distance in many military operations has not been eliminated. Previous studies have shown that training can improve absolute estimations of the distance of a target from the observer (4, 5, 6, 7, 8, 9). The conditions under which greatest improvement will occur and the relative specificity of the resulting skill are questions in need of further investigation.

The training methods and situations used, to date, may have resulted in rather specific cue-response associations. In two studies (4, 8) Ss were given training in making absolute estimations, in yards, of the distance to aerial targets. Since distance cues for an object seen through the air are nonexistent, except for those in the object itself, judgment was probably based primarily on the apparent size of a familiar target (airplane). The Ss probably associated a certain perceived size of the airplane with the number of yards called out by E during training trials. Such training might have limited transfer value to unfamiliar targets or new field conditions.

On the other hand, when the target is located on the ground, the surface stretching between S and target would provide perspective and texture gradients in correspondence with varying distance stretches.[3] Training under these conditions might yield more generalizable improvement, since cues independent of any particular target would be available. One study with targets on the ground (5) has been performed, but since the targets were familiar existing landmarks, such as telephone poles, it is conceivable that improvement again was linked to the specific targets.

That Ss are likely to hit upon rather specific cues during practice and achieve improvement by associating them with those responses which are reinforced was suggested by an experiment by Gibson and Smith (1). It was proposed to measure transfer of training of distance estimations to size constancy judgments (which would presumably be an alternative measure of distance judgment). The experimental group was given training in estimating distance (in yards) to pictured targets (stakes) in photographs. Size judgments were then obtained for the stakes, following the matching procedure used in a previous study (2). A control group made the size judgments without any pre-training. No significant transfer was found by measures of constant or average error, though group variability was reduced by the training. The Ss showed a strong tendency to form highly specific associations between particular identifying clues in the photographs and a verbal response of so many yards. This accomplishment, which the correction procedure of the training encouraged, was apparently irrelevant for the judgment of the size of an object at a given distance.

These considerations suggested that the crucial question to be explored is whether it is possible to train Ss in judging distances in such a way that generalizable improvement is obtained. If there are changes from training to test in the target objects, stimulus values, or type of judgment required, can any transfer of improvement be expected? The experiment to be described was planned to determine whether training can improve the absolute estimation of distance over the ground when a different stretch of distance from S to the target is to be judged on every trial. If no opportunity is given to memorize the distance in yards to any target, will training by corrective reinforcement still result in improvement of estimation of other distance stretches? In other words, the distance stretches presented as stimuli for judgment during the training series were not repeated in the test series, so that it could be determined whether any skill had been achieved which would transfer to the judgment of different distance stretches.

The intention was to limit the potential cues to those provided by the ground surface, insofar as possible, rather than to permit the target itself to provide the cues for judgment. Consequently, the target could not be unique for each judgment, and the kind of terrain chosen for the judging ground was most important. We used a level athletic field, 132 × 488 yd., with a surface of mown grass. It was free of all objects except the targets, which were metal rectangles mounted on stakes. The field was bounded at the lower end, where Ss were stationed, by a terrace and a group of buildings. They looked toward the upper end, bounded by trees and a gymnasium. The 21 targets were arrayed permanently on the field, but none stood in line with another.

As S looked toward a target to make his judgment, he viewed a stretch of grass of a given distance bounded by a target with no particular contextual or associative value. There was no interposition, no shadows, and no linear perspective. Size perspective, in the sense of gradients of texture density on the ground surface, was present, and might have been enhanced by binocular disparity and motion parallax. Some of the other targets were visible in the periphery and might also have provided gradients of size perspective. The targets varied in up and down location in the field, since a horizon was clearly visible. The question is, could S improve his skill in making absolute estimates by responding to variables of texture density and size provided by the gound and target array, plus vertical location of the target, without memorizing specific cue-yard associations?

Method

Arrangement of targets   The principal problem in planning the experiment was to arrange the targets on the available ground so as to provide different distance stretches for every training trial, and for the test series. Six observer station points were located in the lower right hand corner of the field (indicated on the map, Fig. 12.1, as 1, 2, 3, 4, 5, and 6). The 21 targets (A to U on Fig. 12.1) were arrayed over the field in such a way that a large number of different distance stretches would be provided when they were combined variously with the six station points. One-hundred and eight stretches were chosen from the total possible number so that no target ever stood in a line between S and the one designated for judgment, and so that there was a fairly even distribution over the total range. True distances to the targets which S was asked to judge averaged approximately the same at all station points. Station points and target loci were staked out by a surveyor and were accurate to a few inches.

Targets   It would have been desirable to use a single target, which could be moved to the various target loci. This was impossible, due to the large size of the field, the necessity of accurate location, and the fact that two Ss were sometimes run at once. The targets had to be permanent and stationary, and they had to differ so that they could be indicated to S. Labels by number or letter were not possible, since even very large ones could not be read 400 yards away. Furthermore, some

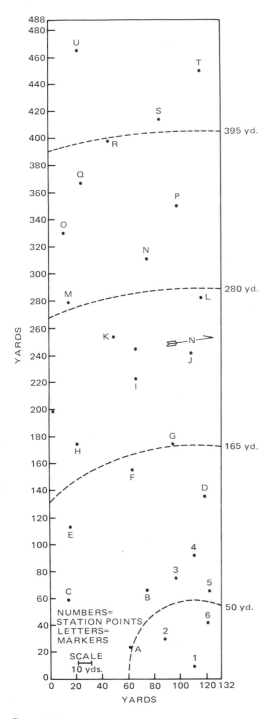

Figure 12.1
Map of field, showing station points (1 through 6) and target locations (A through U).

colors were difficult to identify at a distance. A 3-plate, 3-color system of target marking was therefore chosen. One to three metal plates, 18 × 24 in., were attached to a wooden stake. These plates were painted white, yellow, or black. A plate was always fastened at the bottom of the stake, close to the ground, since a raised target tends to "ground" itself and may, by appearing higher in the field, be increased in apparent distance. All the targets were readily identifiable from the station points.

Plan of experiment   Two groups of Ss, an experimental group and a control group, were given a pretest at Station Point 1 (18 judgments of distance, in yards, to targets ranging from 52 to 395 yd.) and a posttest with the same distance stretches. All these judgments were uncorrected. The experimental group received training between the two tests, consisting of 90 differing judgments of the distance of targets ranging from 39 to 435 yd. (targets viewed from Station Points 2, 3, 4, 5, and 6). After S had made his estimate, it was corrected by E. The control group received no training, but spent the interval between tests taking a paper and pencil test of mechanical aptitude.

Since the pretest and posttest utilized the same 18 depth stretches and targets, two random orders were made. Half of the Ss judged in order A for the pretest and B for the posttest; and half the reverse arrangement. The control group and experimental group were divided in the same way. The experimental group was also divided into two subgroups which differed in the order of station points during the training series. This alternative sequence of station points was not thought necessary as a control, but was adopted because it permitted two Ss to be run at the same time without one S and his E ever obstructing the view of the other S. The group of 18 judgments made at a station during the training will be referred to as a training trial. Since five station points were employed during training, there were five training trials.

Procedure   The S was first asked to read a Snellen chart, and then given his instructions. These included practice in identifying pictured targets using the same 3-plate, 3-color system as those on the field. He was told that he was to estimate how far away from him a target was, in yards, but no demonstration of a yard was given. He was told that he would judge the same target more than once, but never from the same station point. The Ss in Group E, who were given correction, were further told that there was no point in memorizing any one figure because no distance stretch would be exactly repeated.

Records were kept of all of S's estimates, in yards, as well as his age, civilian occupation, and potentially relevant experience (such as track and football). The time of day and the weather were also recorded. Two check lists for weather were utilized, a descriptive one (sunny, sunny hazy, cloudy scattered, cloudy broken, cloudy overcast) and a visibility rating. Subjects were not run when it rained.

Subjects   A group of 30 Ss drawn from the Cornell population was run first. These people varied in age, sex, and academic background. A second group of 92 Ss was drawn from the group of airmen in basic training at Sampson Air Force Base. They were highly motivated and obeyed instructions to the letter.

Results

Analysis by Target Distance
The Ss' estimates of distance to the 18 targets on the pretest and posttest were transformed to four-place logarithms, since previous studies (4, 5, 6) have shown the desirability of such a conversion. Frequency distributions of estimates in yards were skewed, since the yard scale used by S was "open-ended" at the top. The logarithmic transformation yielded reasonably normal distributions and also permitted use of geometric means of the estimates.

When the estimates are plotted as a function of true range, the relationship is seen to be linear. The geometric mean estimates plotted in Fig. 12.2 are taken from the pretest and posttest of Group E, airmen. The plots for Group C, airmen, and for the Cornell group are very similar. The means for the pretest show a slight tendency to underestimation, while the means for the posttest are generally higher. These plots (and those for the other groups as well) level off at the last target. The Ss are not discriminating between the last two targets—perhaps as a result of "end-anchoring"— that is, S's estimate of the end of the series may influence a target or targets close to it. It is clear from the other estimates, however, that apparent distance of an object increases as its real distance increases, in a predictable relationship.

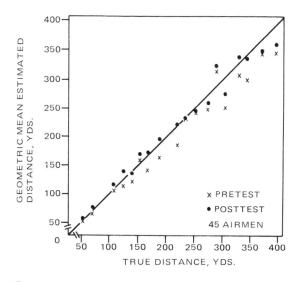

Figure 12.2
Function relating estimated distance to true distance (data from Group E, airmen).

Table 12.1
Percentage of Error of Ss' Estimates for Targets at Varying Distances (Airmen)*

Target Distance	Control Group		Experimental Group	
	Pretest	Posttest	Pretest	Posttest
52	− 7	0	+ 3	+ 9
68	− 14	− 17	− 2	+ 12
107	− 15	− 18	− 1	+ 8
126	− 11	− 11	− 9	+ 12
139	− 19	− 19	− 14	− 1
154	− 9	− 9	+ 3	+ 11
166	− 18	− 11	− 14	+ 4
188	− 11	− 10	− 13	+ 4
219	− 10	− 8	− 14	+ 1
232	− 10	− 5	+ 3	0
252	− 7	− 8	− 3	− 2
274	− 15	− 5	− 9	− 5
287	+ 5	+ 3	+ 9	+ 12
304	− 18	− 12	− 17	− 9
328	+ 1	+ 1	− 6	+ 2
342	− 10	− 8	− 12	− 2
369	− 12	− 9	− 7	− 6
395	− 13	− 13	− 13	− 9

*The error of the geometric mean of the estimates (in log scores) from the true range has been used to obtain the percentage of error; the antilogarithm of the error (the ratio of the geometric mean estimate of range to the true range) × 100 yields the percentage of error. The statistical method followed is essentially that described in reference 6.

Error in relation to distance   The percentage error at each target for the control and experimental groups, pre- and posttest, is given in Table 12.1. These errors are calculated from Ss' geometric mean estimates. Signs were kept, so these are constant errors. The errors are predominantly of underestimation, with the exception of the posttest for Group E, which followed the training series. All but one target in this group's posttest shows a shift in error away from minus and toward plus. No such trend appears for the control group, which had no interpolated correction. A notable feature of these results is the absence of any tendency for the direction or magnitude of the percentage error to vary with the distance. Similar calculations for the Cornell sample showed the same trends—a shift away from underestimation as a result of training, and independence of distance and magnitude of percentage error.

Variability in relation to distance   Table 12.2 gives percentage of SD's of estimates of the various targets. The most notable feature of these SD's

Table 12.2
Percentage of *SD*'s of *Ss*' Estimates for Targets at Varying Distances (Airmen)*

Target Distance	Control Group		Experimetnal Group	
	Pretest	Posttest	Pretest	Posttest
52	69	55	58	29
68	77	58	72	29
107	77	60	112	25
126	85	62	81	27
139	74	66	97	25
154	85	60	124	20
166	75	73	85	21
188	72	65	64	20
219	76	76	67	20
232	85	71	135	15
252	86	80	139	21
274	89	72	86	19
287	88	69	135	20
304	90	76	36	22
328	85	69	99	17
342	77	80	85	17
369	87	71	111	22
395	82	76	112	19

*The *SD*, in logarithms, is converted into a ratio by finding its antilogrithm; this, times the geometric mean, gives a score one *SD* above the mean; and, divided into it, one below. For instance, the antilog of the *SD* for the control group at 52 yd. is 1.69. The geometric mean is 49; the score one *SD* above is 83 yd., whereas the score one *SD* below is 29 yd. Values in the table have been converted to percentages by subtracting 1 and multiplying by 100.

is their size; the variability of the *Ss*, before training, was enormous. They were, actually, very different; one airman, an 18-year-old Puerto Rican, said that he had never seen a yard-stick. The effect of the training is to reduce the *SD*, as the figures for the posttest of the experimental group clearly show. Variability drops slightly for the control group, probably as a result of somewhat greater consistency of individual judgments, as will be shown later. The pretest figures and the posttest for the control group show no consistent tendency for percentage of *SD* to vary with distance. But there is some tendency for the *SD* to decrease as distance increases, after training. This tendency is confirmed by the data for Group E of the Cornell sample. Since it is most evident for the last few targets, it may again be a function of end-anchoring; i.e., the farthest point on the scale becomes a well-defined reference point and causes *Ss*' judgments near the end of the field to center closely around an estimate associated with the end of the distance scale.

Analysis by Subject

Accuracy   Since the principal object of the experiment was to determine whether training brought about improvement, a comparison of individual error and variability before and after training is of primary interest. Of the 45 Ss in Group E, 41 improved; that is, the mean constant error is reduced, whatever its direction. Of the 47 Ss in Group C, 26 improved. The percentage of Ss improving in Group E is 95.6; in Group C, 55.3. The figure for Group C is not significantly different from chance. The two percentages are significantly different from each other ($p < .0001$). If the mean net gain is determined by subtracting the amount of decrement from the amount of improvement and dividing by N, the resultant figure is nearly 16 times as great for Group E as for Group C (mean net gain $= .1625$, in logs, for Group E and .0128 for Group C).

It is interesting to compare the types of change, also, for the two groups. In Group E, 43 of the 45 Ss shift *away* from the previous constant error; for instance, an underestimator may shift to overestimation, but he is very unlikely to enhance his error of underestimation. In the control group, however, the original constant error was actually enhanced in 17 out of 47 cases. If the frequency of shift *away* from the previous CE is compared in the two groups by the chi-square test the difference is significant at the .001 level.

Variable error   A question of major theoretical interest was whether or not training caused Ss to become more consistent in their judgments, whatever the tendency to over- or underestimate. Does the variability of the estimates of the individual Ss decrease with corrected practice; or, for that matter, with uncorrected practice? To determine variability for individuals a formula[4] which corrected for man and target mean was employed since distance stretches were not repeated. It is clear that variability was reduced in the experimental group; the mean percentage of SD was 34.6 before training and 18.3 after it. There was a small reduction for the control group also; the mean dropped from 29.4% on the pretest to 25.5% on the posttest. The significance of these differences was tested by Wilcoxon's (10) non-parametric test for paired replicates. The difference between pretest and posttest for Group E is significant at the .001 level; that for Group C at the .04 level (using a one-tailed test). The training which Group E received was therefore very effective in reducing individual variability. The practice which Group C obtained on the pretest alone, without any special training or correction, seems also to have produced a small reduction in variability of judgment. Since constant errors did not shift toward any common norm in this group, it seems likely that this reduction in individual variability, even though small, accounted for the similar small reduction in group variability.

Analysis of variance   In order to check some of these trends, an analysis of variance was performed on the data yielded by the Cornell sample, Group E. Table 12.3 presents the results of these analyses for pretest and posttest. The estimates have been converted into log scores, as in the other sample. Our principal interest, again, was in a comparison of the pretest and posttest, between which training was given. The group variability (variance due to men) was reduced, as in the airman population. And the individual variability (variance due to man × target)[5] was reduced, likewise, from .0157 to .0056. This difference is significant at better than the .01 level, confirming the finding that within-S consistency is increased by training.

The analysis of variance permits, also, an examination of the effect of order of presentation of target. Order as such does not produce significant variance, and on the pretest, order-target interaction is barely significant at the .05 level. But after training, the variance due to this source is clearly apparent, perhaps because other sources of variance which masked it before have been reduced. It may be that S, in judging, always decided first whether the distance being judged at present was longer or shorter than the just previous one, and perhaps even what fraction or multiple it was. The size of the distance stretch or stretches preceding a given judgment, therefore, would have an effect on any given judgment; in fact, a different effect depending on the relative farness or nearness of the particular target currently to be judged.

Course of Learning
Having established the effectiveness of training for absolute judgments of distance, the question of the course of the learning arises. What kind of

Table 12.3
Analysis of Variance of Distance Estimates (in Logs) Made by Cornell Ss, Group E

Source	df	Pretest Mean Square	F	Posttest Mean Square	F
Order	1	.0306	.0207	.1186	1.1455
Between Ss in same group	18	1.4778		.0983	
Targets	17	.0216	1.3758	.0204	4.0000
Order × Target	17	.0260	1.6561*	.0143	2.5536**
S × Target	306	.0157		.0056	
Total	359				

*p = .05
**p < .01.

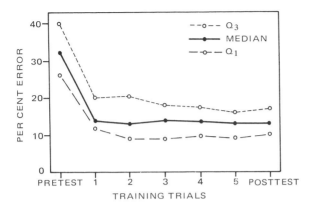

Figure 12.3
Course of learning as measured by crude median error (data from Group E, airmen).

learning curve is exhibited by these changes? Since the calculation of geometric means was too laborious to be carried out for all the training trials, medians were employed for studying the trend. These medians were calculated without regard to sign, since plus and minus errors might otherwise balance each other out and give the appearance of no error. Figure 12.3 shows a plot of the median error expressed as a percentage of true distance for the targets of the pretest combined, for each of the training trials consecutively arranged, and for the posttest. A training "trial," in this case, means all 18 judgments made at a given station point. The first and third quartiles are included in the plot also. The median error before training is high (33%), but on the first training trial it is reduced by more than half (to 14%). No further reduction occurs, except that the quartiles tend to approach the median more closely in later training trials. The most interesting aspect of these curves is the percentage of error for the posttest. Since no further correction was given on the posttest and since none of the judgments duplicated any made during training, it might have been supposed that the error would rise again. No such tendency occurred, however. The effects of training persisted undiminished, in spite of nonidentity of the stimuli in the test series with any of the training ones. Our original question is thus answered positively: improvement in absolute judgment is possible, when distances are judged over ground, even though identical judgments are not repeated and no opportunity for memorization occurs.

Learning trends for over- and under-estimators   What happens to persistent constant errors of individuals, when their judgments are corrected? To answer this question the airmen, Group E, were divided into over- and underestimators on the basis of their geometric mean errors on the pretest

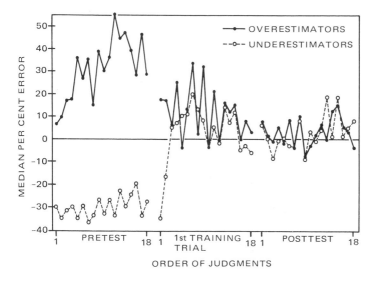

Figure 12.4
Changes in constant error as a function of training.

(these were constant errors). For each subgroup the median error was calculated as a percentage of true distance, retaining the signs. These errors are plotted in Fig. 12.4 for each judgment of the pretest, each judgment of the first training sequence, and the posttest judgments. The judgments are consecutively arranged in the order in which S was asked for them. The line drawn through the center represents zero constant error. During the pretest the overestimators show a consistent plus error for every judgment. The underestimators, on the other hand, stay consistently minus below the zero line. But on the second judgment of the first training sequence (after *one* correction), the curve for the underestimators rises, and that for the overestimators drops. There are, of course, fluctuations, but by the ninth training judgment the fluctuations begin to parallel one another for the two groups. The curves, hereafter, even in the posttest, are remarkably similar. The training does, therefore, cause a change in constant error. This change occurs very rapidly.

Discussion

The principal question of the experiment has been answered in the affirmative: absolute judgment of distance can be improved by training, even when no opportunity is given for memorizing the distance to particular targets. Under the conditions of the experiment there is transfer of training to the judgment of "new" stretches of distance. These are new in the sense that the distance from S to the target is not the same as that given as a stimulus for judgment in any training trial. (The target marking the end of the stretch has appeared before, during training, but is irrelevant as a cue, since it marked different lengths of ground during training.) The ground surface itself provided a basis for consistently varying cues (texture perspective, retinal disparity, motion parallax, vertical placement) and these *dimensions* of variation were present for every judgment. What S learned was to evaluate points along the relevant stimulus dimensions in accordance with a yard scale so that he was able to *identify* a given distance stretch by naming a quantity of yards.

The hypothesis will be advanced that what is learned here can best be described as a *conceptual scale* of yards in a psychophysical relationship with stimulation provided primarily by a receding stretch of ground. This scale might be characterized by having:

1. a unit (a yard, or more likely some convenient and rounded multiple of yards);
2. boundaries or anchors at both ends (the near anchor, zero, is given by S's own position, and the far anchor is acquired during the training; perhaps it is defined for S as the longest distance ever mentioned by the experimenter during training);
3. differentiated areas within the scale, which are fractions of the total and multiples of the basic unit (the S fractionates within his scale, we assume, when making an estimate in yards for a target at some intermediate point along the scale).

Does this hypothesis of a conceptual and perceptual scale explain the measurable changes brought about by learning? It certainly explains the correction of constant errors, for either a far anchor or the yard unit would provide a basis for shifting from any bias caused by an inaccurate scale unit. But what of the reduction in variable error found in comparing individual SD's on the pre- and posttest? It would appear that S became more discriminating in his assignment of categories within the scale. This might occur because he acquired a consistent unit and end anchor during the training to use in identifying or labeling the distance stretches presented for judgment. His concept of yard might have fluctuated before the training sessions presented him with an external anchor. However, it is also conceivable that he learned not only to *identify* consistently (by naming yard quantities), but also improved in the *ordering* of points along the stimulus dimension, whatever the categories used. This implies an improvement in discrimination—a better differentiated *perceptual* scale. Whether the ordering of stimuli, as well as categorizing, was affected by the training is a problem for further investigation.

Summary

Previous experiments have shown that absolute estimations of distance, in yards, can be improved, but there is reason to believe that these training situations resulted in improvement which was specific to the targets and other conditions of the training. The present experiment was designed to see whether training would result in improvement when the targets themselves provided no cues and when memorization of specific cues and yard numbers was not possible.

Targets were viewed over a mowed grass surface from six station points. Twenty-one targets were so placed that 108 judgments, all of different distances, could be made by rotating station point and target combinations. The experimental group judged the distance, in yards, to 18 targets (pretest), then made 90 corrected judgments (training series), and finally repeated the pretest. The control group performed the two test series without intervening practice.

Results suggested the following conclusions:

1. Improvement in absolute judgment of distance occurred as a result of training, even though none of the distances presented for judgment were repeated.

2. Training tended to correct constant errors of both over- and under-estimation in the experimental group. Learning curves showed that this shift occurred very quickly.

3. Variable error was reduced from pre- to posttest in both the experimental and the control group, but the reduction was greater for the experimental group.

4. The function relating true distance to estimated distance was shown to be linear.

5. The development of a conceptual scale of distance in a psychophysical relationship with stimulation provided by a receding stretch of ground was hypothesized.

Notes

1. This research was supported in part by the United States Air Force under Contract No. 33(038)-22373 monitored by the Perceptual and Motor Skills Research Laboratory, Human resources Research Center, Lackland Air Force Base. Permission is granted for reproduction, translation, publication, use, and disposal in whole and in part by or for the United States Government. A more detailed report will be available in a Research Bulletin of the AF Personnel and Training Research Center series.
2. Mrs. Noel Naisbitt, Mr. Alfred Steinschneider, and Mrs. Naomi Wolin assisted with the statistical analysis at various stages of the project. Miss Jean Graham drew the charts. Thanks are due Dr. T. A. Ryan for advice on the choice of statistical procedures.
3. See Gibson (3) for a discussion of the role of surface in space perception.
4. For each S, variability was determined by computing $(X - \bar{X}_M - \bar{X} + \bar{X}_T)^2$ in which $X = S$'s estimate on a given target, $\bar{X}_M =$ the mean of all S's estimates, $\bar{X}_T =$ the mean for the given target, and $\bar{X}$ the grand mean.
5. This is the error term. It is assumed that this term reflects degree of individual variability since variance due to individual differences and to targets has been removed. Experi-

mental error should remain constant from pretest to posttest, so that a difference between the error terms in the two tests would indicate a change in the factors producing within-S variance.

References

1. Gibson, E. J., Smith, J. A. The effect of training in distance estimation on the judgment of size-at-a-distance. *USAF, Hum. Resour. Res. Cent., Res. Bull.*, 1952, No. 52-39.
2. Gibson, J. J. (Ed.) Motion picture testing and research. Washington: U.S. Government Printing Office, 1947. (*AAF, Aviat. Psychol. Program Res. Rep.* No. 7.)
3. Gibson, J. J. *Perception of the visual world.* Boston: Houghton Mifflin, 1950.
4. Horowitz, M. W., Kappauf, W. E. *Aerial target range estimation.* (OSRD, 1945; Publ. Bd., No. 15812.) Washington: U.S. Dep. Commerce, 1946.
5. Princeton Branch, Fire Control Division, Frankford Arsenal. Analysis of range estimation data. Branch Memorandum No. 20, 1943.
6. Princeton Branch, Fire Control Division, Frankford Arsenal. Visual range estimation, direct and differential. Branch Memorandum No. 34, 1943.
7. Rogers, M. H., Sprol, S. J., Vitereles, M. S., Voss, H. A., & Wickens, D. D. *Evaluation of methods of training in estimating a fixed opening range.* (OSRD, 1945; Publ. Bd., No. 4021.) Washington; U.S. Dep. Commerce, 1946.
8. Viteles, M. S., Gorsuch, J. H., Bayroff, A. C., Rogers, M. D., & Wickens, D. D. *Learning range estimation on the firing line.* (OSRD, 1945; Publ. Bd., No. 4023.) Washington: U.S. Dep. Commerce, 1946.
9. Viteles, M. S., Gorsuch, J. H., Bayroff, A. C., Rogers, M.D. & Wickens, D. D. *History and final report of project N-105.* (OSRD, 1945; Publ. Bd., No. 4018.) Washington: U.S. Dep. Commerce, 1946.
10. Wilcoxon, F. *Some rapid approximate statistical procedures.* Stamford, Conn.: American Cyanamid Co., 1949.

13

The Effect of Prior Training with a Scale of Distance on Absolute and Relative Judgments of Distance over Ground

Eleanor J. Gibson, Richard Bergman, Jean Purdy

The previous experiment left us still in doubt as to whether precision in differentiating stretches of distance could really be improved. The subjects had achieved a better correspondence between a yard scale of distance and stimulation provided by ground stretches in one location, without duplicating particular stretches. But might the subjects only be gaining adroitness in using the scale with a particular kind of target and place? It seemed desirable to test for generalizability by conducting training in a different setting and with different targets than the test situation employed. It also seemed desirable to make a more direct test of the effect of training on relative judgments, not just on specific identifications. The result was two rather grandiose experiments that not only kept a team of experimenters busy but also provided entertainment at times for summer school spectators as they watched a bicycle cruise the quadrangle and stop at the blast of a police whistle.

The quadrangle was used in these experiments for training, and the tests were conducted again on the athletic field six blocks away. Subjects were literally taught a scale, as decribed in the paper that follows. The method required subjects to divide up the total space, which was marked as training proceeded with large posters giving distances in yards. Absolute judgments in yards were again collected during testing in the athletic field. The group given training did indeed improve relative to a control group, so there was some generalization of the training. Information provided by gradients along the ground must have played a role, since judgments of distant landmarks not located at the end of uncluttered ground stretches were no better than those of a control group.

The second experiment required a radically different kind of judgment in the test series, following the same kind of training as the first. The subject looked at a fixed target at one of three distances along a radius at an angle to one side. He then watched a variable comparison target that moved along a different radius on the other side. The angle of separation was sufficiently great (120) that the subjects

Journal of Experimental Psychology, 1955, 50, 97–105.

had to look back and forth. The judgments were not made in yards, but were "equal," "farther," or "nearer." The group that was given training did not show greater precision (lower differential limens) than the control group. The control group, in fact, was quite good at these judgments, which involved rather small magnitudes of distance change. There is information in gradients of textured ground surface, and young men, eighteen years old with good vision, are quite sensitive to it, as the DLs show. But this situation, looking back, was far from being the ideal one for studying perceptual learning. Perceptual learning is not merely a matter of increasing the correspondence between two scales, a physical one and a "mental" one, as this work tacitly assumed. That is much too narrow a way to conceive this kind of learning as I was gradually to discover.

The present experiments are part of a program of research concerned with the effect of training on judgments of distance viewed over a ground surface out-of-doors. A previous experiment (3) demonstrated that training by a correction method improved absolute estimation of distance in yards, even when none of the stretches of distance presented for training or test were duplicated. Since association of a particular stretch of ground with a particular yard value was prevented, it was hypothesized that S had achieved a better correspondence between a conceptual scale of yards and stimulation provided by the ground as it receded to the target. The conceptual scale would be in correspondence with gradients of stimulation provided by a ground surface but not with those of any *particular* ground surface.

In the experiments to be described, each S of the experimental group was "taught" a scale of distance (cf. 3, p. 481) on one judging ground and then was required to judge distances on a different field. The first experiment sought to determine the effect of this training on the absolute estimation of distance, in yards, to unfamiliar targets at varying distances. Would the preliminary training transfer, by comparison with a control group, to absolute judgments on a new field with new targets?

The second experiment was concerned with the effect of this training on relative judgments of distance. If the experimental group were to show reduced DL's (greater precision) than the control group, it could be concluded that perceptions of relative distance become better differentiated with practice.

Experiment I

Method

Training procedure   The training was carried out in a large grassy quadrangle approximately 350 yd. long. Trees and buildings were visible at the sides, and several walks cut across the terrain, but S had an uninterrupted view of its entire length. A 300-yd. flat stretch was chosen for the scale, and a large marker labeled 300 was set up. The boundaries or ends of the scale were thus provided by S's own station point and the 300-yd. marker. The only raised object along this stretch was a fire hydrant which stood exactly 10 yd. in front of S's station point and was used to mark off a *unit* for his scale. The unit and the end were thus defined for S at beginning of training.

The learning of the *intervals* within this scale was accomplished by having S divide the 300-yd. stretch into progressively smaller fractions. A moving marker (a bicycle equipped with white metal flaps on the front axle) was started at one end of the 300-yd. stretch and kept moving until S thought it had reached the appropriate division point. The E, who stood beside S, then signaled the bicycle rider to stop by blowing a policeman's whistle. The rider dismounted at this point and walked to the correct division point, where he set up a marker, painted white and labeled with the number of yards distant from S. This procedure enabled S to see the direction and approximate extent of his error. The rider then remounted the bicycle and began the procedure of the next fractionation judgment.

The total stretch was first bisected, and then further subdivided into halves or thirds until markers had been placed at 25-yd. intervals along the scale. (An exception was made at 275 yd. since the interval was very difficult to detect at this distance.) Thus practice consisted of 10 *corrected* fractionation judgments, ending with a scale marked at 25, 50, 75, 100, 125, 150, 175, 200, 225, 250, and 300 yd. For any given S the bicycle always approached, or always withdrew, for all the judgments, but the direction of movement was varied for different Ss. The entire procedure required about 20 min.

Testing procedure   The Ss who took part in the training just described constituted the experimental group. At the end of training, each S was conveyed by automobile to a large athletic field (488 × 132 yd.). Here he was asked to make absolute judgments in yards of the distance of targets spaced from 52 to 395 yd. away from his station point. The procedure for obtaining these judgments, the targets, and their layout on the field was exactly as described by Gibson and Bergman (3). Eighteen judgments, each of a different distance, were made. No anchor point was defined for S on this field. He was not told how long it was, or the distance to any point on it. The field resembled the training area in having a flat mowed grass surface, but there was no resemblance in other scenery or in the targets. The targets were constructed of metal plates mounted on stakes. The plates were painted white, yellow, or black so that each target was unique and could be identified. No target intercepted another as S viewed them. The judgments asked for were identical with the pre- and posttest of the earlier experiment (3), and were made from the same station point.

In addition to these 18 judgments, S was asked to estimate the distance to four "landmarks" visible from his station point. The landmarks were a tall chimney of the University heating plant, a tower of another University building, a low athletic building, and a house on a low hill adjacent to the campus. Trees and other objects intervened beyond the limits of the field, so there was not a continuous stretch of ground between S and these structures.

Procedure for the control group was identical with that for the experimental group, except that there was no preliminary training. There were 35 Ss in each group, all airmen in basic training from Sampson Air Force Base.

Results

Analysis by subjects   Before statistical treatment, all the estimates were converted into three-place logarithms. The individual error scores for the experimental group and the control group were compared by obtaining a constant error of estimation for each S. These errors were then ranked, regardless of sign, and the two groups compared by Wilcoxon's nonparametric test for paired replicates (9). The control group's error exceeded that of the experimental group at the .0002 level of confidence, indicating that the training effectively carried over. This finding verifies the expectation that training with the distance scale effects an improvement in absolute estimations of the distance to unfamiliar targets on an unfamiliar field.

Analysis by target distance   Table 13.1 gives the geometric mean estimate in yards and the percentage *SD* for each of the 18 target distances. The mean estimates of the experimental group are more accurate than those of the control group for 15 of the 18 target distances. By a sign test, this difference is significant at better than the .01 level, indicating again that training influenced favorably the yard estimates made on the new field. The *SD* also is decreased markedly as a result of training. The percentage *SD*'s are very large for the control group, and show no tendency to vary with distance. Not only are they reduced for the experimental group, they also show a tendency to grow smaller as distance increases.

The function relating true distance to estimated distance is plotted in Fig. 13.1. The relationship is linear, as previous studies have shown (6, 3); perceived distance increases as real distance does. But it will be noted that the control group tended to underestimate; 14 of the 18 targets yielded negative CE's. The experimental group, on the other hand, underestimated for 9 of the 18 targets and overestimated for the other 9. The five most distant targets are underestimated. They are all beyond 300 yd., the point at which the practice scale ended.

An analysis of variance (Table 13.2) was performed on the errors of estimation for each group. The component variances are all lower for the experimental group. Between-S variance was especially reduced by the pretraining ($p < .001$ when the variances are compared by an F test). The residual variances are interpreted as an estimate of individual variable error (7). When no judgment is repeated by the individual, the residual variance ("error" term) is the best measure of intraindividual variability,

Table 13.1

Geometric Mean Estimates in Yards and Percentage SD* for Targets at Varying Distances

True Distance of Target	Group E (N = 35)		Group C (N = 35)	
	Estimated Distance (Yards)	SD (%)	Estimated Distance (Yards)	SD (%)
52	63.6	52	47.3	113
68	71.4	53	60.5	87
107	107.7	42	86.8	92
126	115.4	45	102.2	82
139	148.7	46	105.6	77
154	181.4	42	124.6	100
166	163.0	43	131.0	82
188	188.6	31	151.2	101
219	190.7	38	171.9	75
232	238.5	31	234.8	139
252	255.0	27	218.5	90
274	267.2	29	240.3	105
287	315.4	23	348.4	125
304	280.0	30	274.2	113
328	311.3	36	356.5	114
242	309.2	25	288.3	101
369	360.9	22	400.0	102
395	333.8	24	353.5	105

*The SD, in logs, is converted into a ratio by finding its antilogrithm; this, times the geometric mean, gives a score 1 SD above the mean; and divided into it, 1 below. Values in the table have been converted to percentages by subtracting 1 and multiplying by 100.

since component variances due to target and individual differences have been removed. Furthermore, any variance caused by experimental error should be equal for the two groups. If, therefore, the control exceeded the experimental group in the residual variance, it can be inferred that intraindividual variability was reduced by training. An F test reveals a difference in the expected direction at a little better than the .05 level of confidence.

Estimation of distance of landmarks   For the distance estimates so far considered, there was an uninterrupted grass surface extending from S's station point to the base of the target. Whether the preliminary training effects any improvement when an uninterrupted flat surface is not present can be found in the estimates of the landmarks. The CE'S were not consistently smaller for the experimental group (they were greater for this group in two of the

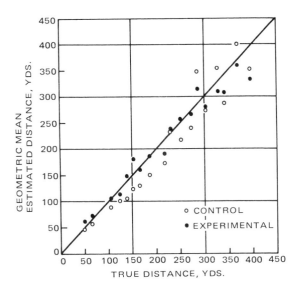

Figure 13.1
Geometric mean estimated distance as a function of true distance for the experimental and control group.

Table 13.2
Analysis of Variance of Errors of Distance Estimation (in Log Units)

Source	df	Mean Square Group E	Group C	F: C/E*	p
Targets	17	.0625	.1091	1.74	>.05
Men	34	.1558	1.4029	9.00	<.001
Residual	578	.0107	.0169	1.579	<.05
Total	629				

*These comparisons by the F test are presented as a matter of interest, although the variances for the two groups are clearly unequal. The principal conclusion is supported by nonparametric tests.

four cases). Variance was greater for the control group in three of the four cases, but not significantly. The mean error, regardless of sign, was smaller for the experimental group in all four cases, significantly so ($p < .02$) in three. The evidence for transfer of training to these judgments is therefore equivocal. The absence of a continuous ground stretch is probably responsible for the lack of a clear difference between the two groups.

Comparison with training by correction   In the previous experiment (3) in which Ss were trained by a correction procedure, training and test judgments were made on the *same* field. In this experiment Ss had preliminary training by a scaling method, on a *different* field. Improvement in the two experiments can be compared by calculating the percentage transfer in each case.[2] For the previous experiment, there was 79% transfer based on constant errors; for the present one, 62%. It seems, then, that training with a scale of distance is nearly as effective as correction of judgments on the very same ground where estimation is tested.

Experiment II

Method

The Ss were again divided into two groups, experimental and control, and the experimental group was given preliminary training identical with that given the experimental group in Exp. I. Both the control and experimental groups were then required to make relative judgments for pairs of distances over a ground surface. A single distance was thought of as an imaginary line extending radially away from S. The question was, how accurately could S compare a given stretch of ground along one radius with another along a different radius.

The Ss were taken to the same athletic field used in Exp. I for relative judgments. The ground was mowed grass, and the field was empty except for the two targets. These were at the ends of two distance stretches making an angle of 120° with S's station point, so that he had to turn his head to compare the distance to each of them. The wide angle was used so that S would actually compare the distance stretches, not merely the up and down location of two targets located on the same radius. The targets were of different shapes. The standard target was a white triangle (altitude 94 cm. and base 90 cm.). The variable taget was a rectangle (91 cm. wide and 183 cm. high). The variable target was moved toward or away from S by a man concealed behind it. It ran smoothly on bicycle wheels and always made contact with the ground.

The paths of the two targets formed a V, with S at the junction point and the standard and variable located at some point along the arms. There were three distances for the standard target, 50, 100, and 200 yd. (The maximum distance of the path along each arm of the V to the corners of the field was 275 yd.) The field had been surveyed by an engineer and stakes were laid at 1-yd. intervals along these lines. They were driven flush with the ground, so that they were invisible to

Ss. Thin wire was stretched along each line so that the target man could follow a straight course. The wire also was invisible to S.

The method of judgment was a combination of a method of limits and a constant method. The variable target starting at a distance either much greater than or much less than that of the standard, made a run which took it up to the equal point and then a considerable distance beyond it. During the run, it stopped 10 times at assigned positions to enable S to make a judgment of "farther," "equal," or "nearer." The total path traversed on one run by the variable stimulus was 12 yd. for the 50-yd. standard, 24 for the 100-yd. standard, and 48 for the 200-yd. standard. For a typical run where the standard target was 50 yd., the variable target was started at 57 yd. and stopped for judgments at 55, 53, 52, 51, 50, 49, 48, 47, and 45. A typical run for the 200-yd. standard began at 228 yd. with stops at 220, 212, 208, 204, 200, 196, 192, 188, and 180. Approach and withdrawal runs were alternated, and the starting point was always varied. For each standard distance the variable made three approach and three withdrawal runs, so that S made 60 judgments for each standard distance. The target man kept in constant touch with E by radio,[3] so that judgments and stops were co-ordinated.

For half the Ss, the standard stimulus was on the left, and for half on the right. Since the illumination of the targets changed from morning to afternoon, these right-left positions were rotated so as to be equally divided between morning and afternoon. Half of the Ss began their judgments with the 50-yd. standard distance and half with the 200-yd. standard distance. All 60 judgments for a given standard were completed before going on to the next standard. One practice run (10 judgments) was given to make sure S understood the task. A rest period of about 10 min. was given after completing judgments for each standard. The judgments for all three standards required about $2\frac{1}{2}$ hr.

Four Ss took part in the experiment at one time. Each man recorded his own judgments. Two Es were always present and watched constantly to insure that S was recording in the right blank. The Ss faced straight ahead after each judgment, while the variable target was moved. The E said "Judge" when the target was in place. The S was informed when a new run began, and was told that for each run the direction of movement of the variable target would be the same. He was also told that the starting point would vary for each run, and was asked to be sure to compare the stretch of ground between himself and the two targets before making his judgment.

The four Ss at each session included two members of the experimental group and two of the control group. They stood behind one another, and positions from front to rear were rotated for the two groups so that any advantage of station point would be equalized. All four men could see the targets easily, however. There were 32 Ss in each group, all airmen in basic training at Sampson Air Force Base.

Results

The effect of training on differential sensitivity to distance   Two measures of sensitivity were obtained, group psychometric functions and individual

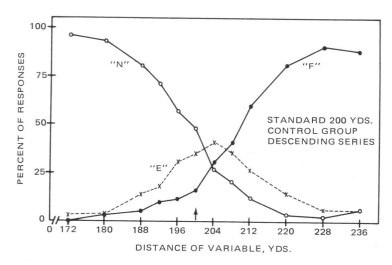

Figure 13.2

Group psychometric function of the control group, with the standard set at 200 yd. and variable approaching. The percentage of responses of nearer, equal, and farther is plotted as a function of the variable distance.

DL's. To obtain the group psychometric functions, the percentage of responses of *nearer, equal,* and *farther* was plotted as a function of the variable distance. Figure 13.2 shows the function for the control group at 200 yd., with the variable approaching. This plot is fairly typical of all the conditions, showing the expected distribution of responses. The point of subjective equality in this case was displaced outward from the standard distance, at 204 yd. The approach, or descending series, all gave positive constant errors (variable set farther than standard), while the ascending series gave negative ones (variable nearer).

The DL's obtained by this method were very similar to those obtained by averaging the DL's of individuals. Individual DL's and the points of subjective equality (PSE) were obtained from each S's responses on the six runs for each standard, according to the method described by Woodworth (10, p. 420). Table 3 presents the mean DL's, mean PSE's, and their respective SD's for both control and experimental groups. The limens for the experimental group are slightly lower than those for the control group at all three standard distances, but in no case is the difference significant. A t test by paired observations (2, p. 105) was made, since this test does not require the assumption of equal variances. None of the t's reaches the .05 level of confidence. It must therefore be concluded that training with a scale of distance did not lower differential sensitivity to distance. Limens obtained from the group psychometric functions likewise showed no significant change as a result of the training.

The effect of illumination of the standard and the effect of order (beginning with the 200-yd. standard vs. beginning with the 50-yd. standard) on the DL were calculated separately for experimental and control groups. For illumination, no significant difference in DL was found for either group. That is, it made no difference in the limen whether the standard target was illuminated by direct sunlight or not. Order had no significant effect on the DL for the experimental group, but the control group had significantly lower DL's for two of the three standards (50 yd. and 100 yd.) when S began his judgments with the standard at 50 yd., rather than at 200.

Constant error as a function of training and luminance of standard   The PSE did not differ significantly between experimental and control groups. However, there was a small constant error for both groups when ascending and descending trials were averaged (see Table 13.3). The CE, small as it is, tends to be positive—that is, the variable looked the same distance away as the standard when it was slightly farther.

It might be asked whether bright sunlight shining directly on the standard target would make it appear nearer than when it is not directly illuminated. Many Ss commented on the apparent difference in brightness depending on the sun's location with respect to the targets. The PSE's were therefore compared for the three standard distances when the standard target was in a position to be directly illuminated and when it was not (when it "looked brighter" or "looked shaded"). None of these differed significantly from the standard distance. In other words, no CE was produced by direct or indirect illumination of the standard target.

DL as a function of distance   As Table 13.3 shows, the DL in yards increases with distance. The SD likewise increases, and is notably large. There was considerable variability in DL's for different individuals. The increment

Table 13.3
Mean Individual DL's (in Yards) and PSE's (in Yards) at Three Standard Distances

| | Difference Limens | | | | Point of Subjective Equality | | | |
| | Control | | Experimental | | Control | | Experimental | |
Distance	Mean	SD	Mean	SD	Mean	SD	Mean	SD
50 yd.	1.31	.59	1.24	.52	50.65*	1.40	50.29	1.74
100 yd.	2.70	1.32	2.63	1.89	100.38	3.03	101.40*	3.00
200 yd.	5.27	2.46	4.57	2.16	200.94	4.35	201.76	5.76

*These two values differed significantly from the standard distance, showing a small positive CE.

required to produce a change in judgment can be expressed as a percentage of the standard

$$\left(\frac{\Delta D}{D} \times 100\right).$$

For the three standard distances, the mean DL is constant at about 2.5%. Over the range of distances used, Weber's Law appears to hold.

Effect of target separation on SD   The judgments of distance obtained in this study required that S compare two stretches of ground receding radially from him, the two radii separated by an angle of 120°. By comparing the present results with those of Teichner, Kobrick, and Wehrkamp (8), the effect of increasing angular separation of the standard and variable target can be roughly determined, since their targets were separated by only 3 min. of arc. They used as estimates of linear threshold the SD of S's settings around the CE. Comparable measures were computed for our data. For each S for each run, we obtained the first variable distance judged "equal" to the standard distance. The SD of this distribution is given below for each standard distance (in feet, rather than yards, to conform with the other study):

Distance	SD
150 ft.	10.83 ft.
300 ft.	21.48 ft.
600 ft.	40.80 ft.

These SD's are all higher than those obtained by Teichner et al. for the same distances. Here they are about 7% of the standard distance, compared to about $2\frac{1}{2}$% in the other study. Thus judgment of comparative distances over ground gives higher threshold values than does judgment of the coincidence or alignment of two targets at a distance. But reasonably sensitive judgments can clearly be made for comparative distances of two ground stretches.

Discussion

The results of Exp. I showed clearly that preliminary training with a scale of distance improves absolute estimation of the distance to an unfamiliar target in a new location. The ground surface itself provides a stimulus basis for S's judgment in both training and test fields. The S observes along an imaginary line stretching from his feet to the target. Certain optical properties of *any* such line on any level terrain would remain constant in the stimulus array: farther stretches (relative to nearer) are characterized by decreased size and increased density of texture particles, by increased uncrossed disparity, and by increased uncrossed parallactic motion (4). Vertical position of a target in the field of view also moves upward with increasing distance. The other classical "cues" for distance are probably irrelevant for the present situation. Familiar size and interposition have been eliminated in the experiment, and the kinesthetic cues are probably of little value for the distances employed.

These variables, we believe, are in a psychophysical correspondence with *impressions of distance along the ground*. The conceptual scale of yards would have to be related to the concomitant gradients of stimulation by means of learning. The relationship, in fact, was vastly improved by the training provided in Exp. I. The S can bring with him a scale relationship which will have a beneficial effect on estimations in a new location; even the absence of any objectively confirmed reference point on the new field seemed to be no handicap. And if the yard scale was related, in the training process, to stimulation provided by a continuous stretch of ground, it is not surprising that transfer should be partial or absent when the intervening surface is interrupted by objects or hills or gulleys, as was the case with the "landmark" targets .

The present experiment does not permit us to evaluate the three components included in the scale training. The "unit" of 10 yd., for instance, may have played little role. That the fractionation into 25-yd. intervals had an effect is revealed by a comparison of the categories used for estimation by control and experimental groups. Both tended to use response categories which are multiples of 25, but the experimental group used many more—564 to Group C's 459. The difference is significant ($p < .01$). The far boundary of the training scale (300 yd.) appeared to exert an effect on the judgments of distances greater than this value. Further experiment with the componenets given singly might throw more light on what S learns.

Experiment II was designed to discover whether the training received by members of the experimental group increased their sensitivity to small differences in distance magnitudes. Since the DL's for the experimental group were not significantly lower than the control group's, it must be concluded that differentiation within the distance dimension was not increased. It should not be concluded that the relative judgment of distance cannot be improved, however; the amount of practice may have been too little, for Ss' performance was already quite good and was perhaps at an asymptote. Also, the judgment made in the training situation was not very similar to that made in the test of relative judgment. The training actually was concerned with judgment of grosser distance magnitudes than was the test.

The results of Exp. II do, however, strengthen our assumption that a psychophysical scale exists in which stimulation deriving from a ground surface is correlated with perceptual judgments of greater or lesser distance.

Highly typical psychophysical functions were found (see Fig. 13.2). Since the targets as such provided little basis for a judgment of their distance and a judgment of alignment was impossible, it follows that for any object in contact with the ground the perception of distance of the object may be determined by the impression of distance of the background surface at the point of contact.

For an object *not* in contact with the ground, the perception of distance must depend largely on stimulation deriving from the object itself yielding impressions of edges, depth, etc. The classical list of cues, as well as factors of knowledge and inference, would be relevant. An experiment by Bourdon 1; and 10, p. 670) obtained DL's for judgments of relative nearness and farness of two luminous circles, placed at right angles to one another at distances averaging around 20 meters. The surroundings were dark. The DL's for this judgment were about 22% of the standard distance, compared to $2\frac{1}{2}$% in our study (DL defined as one-half the interval of uncertainty). The absence of stimulation from a ground surface in Bourdon's experiment is probably the principal reason for the difference in results. Convergence, retinal disparity, and motion parallax were all operative to some extent in Bourdon's situation, since when he modified it by restricting the conditions to monocular vision and a motionless head, he obtained completely equivocal judgments.

For a pair of objects in contact with a surface, but located so that the stretch of distance to one coincides or nearly coincides with that to the other, the perception of distance as such will be accompanied or even supplanted by a different type of tridimensional perception, the impression of *in front of* or *behind*. For this judgment, there is a different basis in stimulation. The object behind will be optically above the one in front and vice versa. We cannot agree with Teichner, Kobrick, and Wehrkamp (8) as to the prevailing importance of this type of stimulation for impressions of distance. When the two target objects are not optically adjacent, the observer *must* discriminate the respective stretches of distance in order to decide which object is farther or nearer. This is a frequent type of judgment in daily life, and it is probably associated with locomotion of all kinds.

Summary

The purpose of the two experiments described was to determine the effect of training on (a) absolute judgments of distance, in yards, and (b) relative (nearer-farther) judgments of distance to variable targets. Training with a scale of distance was given the experimental group in both experiments. A 300-yd. stretch along a grass surface was bounded for S, and a 10-yd. unit designated for his scale. Then S made corrected fractionation judgments until the ground was divided into 25-yd. intervals. Following training, Ss of Exp. I were taken to a different field where they made *absolute* estimations of the distance, in yards, to unfamiliar targets at varying distances (52 to 395 yd. away). A control group made the absolute estimations without previous training. In Exp. II, *S*s were taken to a large field and asked to make *relative* judgments of the distance from *S* to two targets separated by 120°. The standard was set at 50, 100, or 200 yd. from *S*. The method of judgment was a combination of a method of limits and a constant method. A control group made the same judgments without pretraining.

Results of Exp. I indicated that *S*s who received the pretraining were superior to control *S*s in both constant and variable error. Absolute estimation was improved even though *S*s were not tested in the same field where they were trained, the targets were unfamiliar, and the distances varied. It was proposed that *S* learned a scale relating responses, in yards, to gradients of stimulation deriving from the ground surface.

Pretraining with a scale of distance did not, however, lower DL's for distance in Exp. II. Sensitivity of the psychophysical relationship is apparently not increased by this training, although the yard-responses become more accurately tied to it. The DL for distance was about $2\frac{1}{2}$% of the standard distance and was constant for the three standard distances employed. The fact that consistent psychophysical functions of the expected kind were found with wide angular separation of the standard and comparison target strengthens the hypothesis that gradients of stimulation made available by the ground surface itself are in correspondence with impressions of distance of varying magnitudes.

Notes

1. This research was supported in part by the United States Air Force under Contract No. 33(038) 22373 monitored by the Perceptual and Motor Skills Laboratory, Human Resources Research Center, Lackland Air Force Base. Permission is granted for reproduction, translation, publication, use, and disposal in whole and in part by or for the United States Government. The research was assisted by Dr. Leigh Minturn, who acted as experimenter for the scale training, and Dorothy Serrie, who rode the bicycle.

2. Percentage transfer was calulated by the formula

$$\frac{\text{Group C} - \text{Group E}}{\text{Group C}} \times 100.$$

A transfer comparison was made rather than direct comparison of the two experimental groups because of the desirability of comparing each Group E with its own control group.

3. Portable radio equipment was kindly loaned by the Cornell Department of Military Training.

References

1. Bourdon, B. *La perception visuelle de l'espace.* Paris: Schleicher Frères, 1902.
2. Dixon, W. J., & Massey, F. J. *Introduction to statistical analysis.* New York: McGraw-Hill, 1951.
3. Gibson, E. J. & Bergman, R. The effect of training on absolute estimation of distance over the ground. *J. exp. Psychol.,* 1943, 48, 473–482.
4. Gisbon, J. J. *The perception of the visual world.* Boston: Houghton Mifflin, 1950.

5. Holway, A. H., Jameson, D.A., Zigler, M. J., Hurvich, L. M., Warren, A. B., & Cook, E. B. *Factors influencing the magnitude of range-errors in free-space and telescopic vision.* Division of Research, Graduate School of Business Administration, Harvard Univ., Cambridge, 1945.

6. Horowitz, M. W., & Kappauf, W. E. *Aerial target range estimation.* (O.S.R.D., 1945; Publ. Bd., No. 15812.) Washington: U. S. Dep. Commerce, 1946.

7. Princeton Branch, Fire Control Division, Frankford Arsenal. *Analysis of range estimation data.* Branch Memorandum No. 20, 1943.

8. Teichner, W. H., Kobrick, J. L., & Wehrkamp, R. F. *Effects of terrain and observation distance on depth discrimination.* Quartermaster Research and Development Command, Environmental Protection Division, Report No. 228, Natick, Mass., 1954.

9. Wilcoxon, R. *Some rapid approximate statistical procedures.* Stamford, Conn.: American Cyanimid Co., 1949.

10. Woodworth, R. S. *Experimental psychology.* New York: Holt, 1938.

14

Distance Judgment by the Method of Fractionation
Jean Purdy, Eleanor J. Gibson

As this project progressed, we became more and more interested in how accurate people really are in judging distances to be traversed and how they do it. They are seldom asked to estimate verbally distance stretches in yards or in any absolute scale. But they make their way around (in cars, for example) with no problem. Cars at any distance are perceived as constant in size. Is size constancy perceived peculiarly for objects, perhaps derived from knowledge of familiar size? J. J. Gibson had suggested (1950) that constancy was not a characteristic of object perception but rather was a characteristic of perception of the total layout within which objects were situated. It should be discoverable in perception of stretches of ground surface, not only objects located on these surfaces. It seems now that a scale for such layout constancy should also be relative in some way to the perceiver. It may be given in the perceiver's eyeheight in relation to the horizon, which is a constant peculiar to every individual and provides automatically a neat unit of measurement. We did not think of that in 1955, but the desirability of studying the consistency (or nonconsistency) of people's scaling of the layout and objects contained in it had become evident. Still in a psychophysical tradition, we turned to the method of fractionation. If there were consistency of perceived scale of layout, it should show up with this method. The subjects made fractionation judgments as they had in the previous experiment, but this time we were not so much concerned with learning as with the consistency and unity of the dimensions of their perceived world.

The results were very illuminating for our question. The subjects were, on the whole, surprisingly accurate. More important, errors were not related to visual angle subtended on the retina; the subjects did not make "retinal matches" but showed good constancy for stretches over ground. As Gibson said (1950, p. 181), "Scale, not size is actually what remains constant in perception." But what gave the scale? Not correction, certainly, as it was presented in this experiment. A large group of subjects that received correction was not superior in fractionation to a group of naive subjects. We had no answer at that time. What is the information

J. Purdy & E. J. Gibson

for the remarkable consistency of perceived dimensions of the spatial layout? If learning is involved, what kind of learning? Certainly not simple reinforcement of responses.

Two questions begged for an answer. What information is available for perceiving consistent, accurate dimensions of the ground and its furnishings in our environment? What kind of a theory of perceptual learning can we look to if simple correction or reinforcement is not the answer?

The literature of space perception abounds in both experiments and theoretical discussions of the perceived size and distance of objects.[1] The continuum of distance itself, however, has seldom been specifically studied as a psychological dimension. That distance must be perceived accurately for objects to remain constant in their dimensions is a generally accepted proposition. Errors of constancy, indeed, have been attributed to errors in the estimation of distance (3; 5, p. 151). It is time to inquire, therefore, what kind of psychological scale for a dimension of continuing distance exists. Can an observer tell when far and near stretches of distance are equal, or when one is half or twice the other? Gibson predicted that constancy would hold for the distances between objects (2, p. 165) on the hypothesis that constancy is a property not merely of perceived objects but of perceived tridimensional space itself. Little evidence is available on this question. Gilinsky (3, p. 473 ff.) had two Os bisect distances from 8 to 200 ft. long, starting from O. She predicted that physically equal units of distance would appear shorter as their distance from O increased. This result apparently was found in her data, but the small number of O's used make further experiments desirable, especially since the results of recent size constancy experiments indicate that constancy or even "over-constancy" (4) holds for objects at very long distances. It would appear reasonable in the light of such a result, that "constancy," or better, objective accuracy, should characterize the judgments of *all* the physical dimensions of a surface like the ground.

In the present experiment the nature of a psychological scale for distance was investigated by a method of fractionation. The O was asked to bisect or trisect distances along an imaginary line stretching over the ground from O to an indicated marker. A further group of Os was available whose judgments were corrected as they were made. These fractionation judgments had served as a training procedure in another experiment (1).

Method

The experiment took place in a quadrangle 350 yd. long. The ground was mowed grass, intersected by three walks. Trees and buildings lined the sides, but the view

Table 14.1
Plan of Fractionation Judgments

Serial No. of Judgment	Bicycle Approaching		Bicycle Withdrawing	
	Stretches Bisected (yd.)	Stretches Trisected (yd.)	Stretches Bisected (yd.)	Stretches Trisected (yd.)
1	300 (300 to 0)		300 (0 to 300)	
2	150 (150 to 0)		150 (150 to 300)	
3	150 (300 to 150)		150 (0 to 150)	
4		75 (300 to 225)		75 (0 to 75)
5		75 (225 to 150)	50 (25 to 75)	
6	50 (200 to 150)			75 (75 to 150)
7		75 (150 to 75)	50 (100 to 150)	
8	50 (125 to 75)			75 (150 to 225)
9		75 (75 to 0)	50 (175 to 225)	
10	50 (50 to 0)			75 (225 to 300)

to the end of the quadrangle was unobstructed. A 300-yd. stretch was chosen for O's scaling operations. The O stood at one end of the quadrangle, accompanied by E. A bicycle and rider moved up or down the quadrangle, as needed, as an indicator of the division point which O was asked to find. The bicycle rider had a prearranged schedule of movements to follow and could be signalled by a whistle when O wanted him to stop. The area had been surveyed and had marks at 25-yd. intervals to guide the rider, but these marks were invisible to O.

Each O made 10 fractionation judgments. Six of these were bisections and four were trisections. A "bisection" is the act of stopping the bicycle at half the distance covered by the stretch; a "trisection" is the act of stopping the bicycle at one-third the distance covered, the judgment in the latter case being the first third or the nearest third of the stretch covered. Table 14.1 shows the actual stretches divided, and the order in which the fractionations were made. The plan was such that the true division points for the 10 judgments made up a series at 25-yd. intervals from 25 through 250 yd. as indicated in the left-hand column of Table 2. The Os were divided into two equal subgroups depending on whether the bicycle rode away from O or toward him. The order of judging, and whether O halved or trisected, varied between the two subgroups so as to keep within bounds the mileage required of the bicycle rider. The first three bisections, however, were comparable for withdrawal and approach trials.

Before O was asked to make a given judgment, markers were set up to indicate the two ends of the stretch that he was to divide. The markers were plain white rectangles, unlabeled. In some trials, O's own station point was the origin of the distance stretch indicated, so that only one marker was required.

The O was brought to his station point, given his instructions, and asked to turn his back while the markers were set up. When these were in place and the bicycle at the starting point of the stretch to be divided, E asked O to turn and judge when the moving target had reached the division point of the specified fraction. The E signalled the rider when O said "Stop." If O was not satisfied with his first setting, one further adjustment was permitted. He then faced the other way during the interval between judgments. The error was measured by the bicycle rider with the aid of a fixed confered point that was invisible to O. There were 40 Os, half with the bicycle approaching and half with the bicycle withdrawing.

The separate group of Os who were corrected made the same judgments, except that O was permitted to see the direction and extent of his error, and permanent yard markers labeled with the number of yards distant were set up at the appropriate division points as the judgments were completed. There were 67 Os in this group, of whom 53 watched the bicycle approach and 14 watched it withdraw. All Os were Airmen in basic training at Sampson Air Force Base.

Results

The data obtained from the bisections and trisections are presented in Table 14.2. Group mean constant errors (CE) in yards and SD's are given for each of the 10 true division points of the stretches divided. A positive error means that O divided the stretch so that the segment nearer him was too large; a negative error indicates that O divided the stretch so that the segment nearer him was too small. (It may be noted that if the subject divided the stretch into optical extents of equal visual angle, the nearer segment, by optical geometry, would be much too small.) The length of the interval fractionated and its terminal points can be found by consulting Table 14.1.

Accuracy of fractionation   The first question concerns the relation of the judged half-way or third-of-the-way point to the actual division point. Figure 14.1 presents these data for the main group of Os who were not given knowledge of their errors. The most striking feature of these results is the small amount of error for many of the judgments. Only for one act of fractionation out of 20 does the mean CE go above $6\frac{1}{2}$ yd. When O indicates one-half or one-third of a distance stretch, the fraction corresponds very well with the measured half or third. Nine of the 20 CE's are significantly different from zero (see Table 2, uncorrected group), but even the largest is only 7.2% of the total distance fractionated. On the average, the CE is 3.1% of the total distance fractionated. There is a tendency for the CE to be large when large distance stretches are fractionated. The average error (without regard to sign) is directly related to the total distance fractionated, increasing as the length of the stretch to be fractionated increases. It ranges from 3.2 for a 50-yd. bisection to 21.2 for the 300-yd. bisection.

The size and direction of the error appear to be affected by the direction of movement of the "target." When the two uncorrected subgroups are compared in the first three judgments, the means differ significantly at 150

Table 14.2
Group Mean CE and SD of Fractionation Judgments

Distance of True Division Point, Yd.	Without Correction						With Correction					
	Target Approaching			Target Withdrawing			Target Approaching			Target Withdrawing		
	Serial No. of Judgment	Mean CE yd.	SD yd.	Serial No. of Judgment	Mean CE yd.	SD yd.	Serial No. of Judgment	Mean CE yd.	SD yd.	Serial No. of Judgment	Mean CE yd.	SD yd.
25	10	−1.2*	2.0	4	−2.8*	2.3	10	+2.3*	3.7	4	+4.1*	3.6
50	9	−1.1	3.7	5	−0.7	2.6	9	−0.5	4.6	5	−1.7	3.3
75	2	+5.9*	11.1	3	+0.4	13.7	2	+2.1	8.7	3	+0.1	3.1
100	8	+0.5	3.8	6	+1.6	3.9	8	+1.5*	3.4	6	+3.1*	4.1
125	7	−0.3	3.7	7	+1.8*	3.4	7	−1.1	4.8	7	+5.7*	7.8
150	1	+21.6*	19.0	1	−2.8	23.9	1	+17.5*	19.4	1	+7.6	16.9
175	6	−2.0*	4.3	8	−0.4	6.1	6	−0.1	4.6	8	+2.4*	2.7
200	5	−1.0	8.1	9	−2.9*	4.5	5	−7.4*	11.8	9	−12.4*	6.4
225	3	+6.6*	12.6	2	−5.8	16.2	3	+6.4*	15.1	2	−12.4*	17.0
250	4	+1.6	9.8	10	−4.7*	7.4	4	+6.2*	10.4	10	−0.9	11.9

*CE significantly different from 0 ($p < .05$).

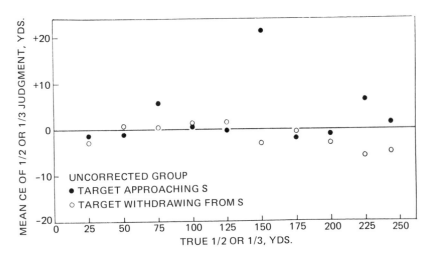

Figure 14.1
Plot of the group mean constant error of the judged fraction (in yd. from the true point)
relative to the true point of division, arranged in a continuum of distance.

and 225 yd. The means for approach and withdrawal also differ on fractionations represented by points at 250 yd. and 25 yd. However, these
last two differences are not necessarily due to the direction of movement of
the target alone. Other differences confounded with direction of movement
for all judgments after the third were: (a) the judgments were made in
different orders, (b) Os were not always making the same kinds of fractionation of the same distance stretch (see Table 14.1). Thus the difference
between approach and withdrawal CE's for fractionations at 25 and 250 yd.
could have been due to any of these variations in procedure. In general, the
error appears to be positive on approach trials but much less positive or
negative on withdrawal trials. At the 150-yd. division point, for instance,
88% of the approach group but only 53% of the withdrawal group made
positive errors.

No difference in the variability of fractionation was produced by the
direction of target movement and the kind of accompanying fractionation
except at 200 yd. where the SD for the approach condition was higher.

A comparison of the accuracy of bisections and trisections can be made
by comparing the mean CE's of halving 50-yd. stretches with the mean
CE's of taking one-third of 75-yd. stretches. By such a comparison, the
size of the CE is no larger for division into thirds than for division into
halves, though group variability is larger for the one-third judgments.

Variability was also influenced by the distance from O of the stretch
to be fractionated. Trisections of 75 yd. can be compared for four stretches

which begin at 0, 75, 150, and 225 yds. from *O*. As the distance of the stretch from *O* increases, the *SD* also increases.

Indications of distance "constancy" It might be supposed that perceptual judgments of distance magnitudes are based wholly or in part on the visual angles subtended at the retina by the stretches of distance. If two physically equal stretches, one near and one far, were compared on this basis, the resulting relative subjective magnitudes would not be equal; the farther stretch would subtend a smaller visual angle and would appear less. In order to make it *appear* equal, the further stretch would have to be actually greater (a negative error in our experiment). Thus if *O* made fractionation judgments wholly or partly on the basis of such information, a negative CE would be the result. Gilinsky (3) may have assumed something like this in stating that "Perceived distances are foreshortened. The perceived distance *d* increases with the true distance *D* but at a reduced and diminishing rate" (p. 462). The present data, however, do not substantiate such a hypothesis. The errors in general are positive—that is, *O* made the nearer segment too large in comparison with the farther. And the high degree of accuracy in general indicates that distance judgment exhibits a kind of constancy analo-

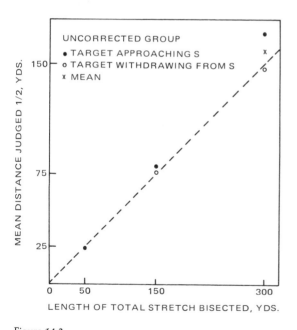

Figure 14.2
The relationship between the point judged halfway between O and a marker, and the distance of the marker in yd. The line at 45° on the graph represents accurate fractionation.

gous to size judgments. The term *length or depth constancy*, as distinguished from *width or height constancy*, might be applied to O's judgments. The fact is that a distance stretch beginning at his own feet can be matched fairly accurately with another stretch beginning at a distance from his feet along the same axis.

In Fig. 14.2 the mean distance judged one-half has been plotted for the three distance stretches which began at O's feet: 50, 150, and 300 yd. Judgments for approach and withdrawal trials are presented separately, as well as the means for the two combined. The 45° line describes correct half judgments. Though points for the approach condition diverge from accuracy, the mean values lie extremely close to that line. There is a slight indication that as the distance to be halved increases, O's subjective halfway point may move farther away from him so that the nearer segment is physically larger than the farther segment.

Figure 14.3 shows the error that resulted from the fractionation of distance stretches as the distance of those stretches from O increased. The points connected by solid lines represent bisections of 50-yd. stretches.

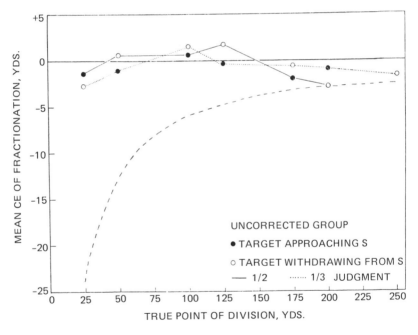

Figure 14.3
The group mean CE of (a) halving a 50-yd. stretch (solid line) and (b) dividing a 75-yd. stretch into one-third and two-thirds (dotted line) as a function of the true division point in yd. The dashed curve represents the expected error if O were to divide the stretches so that the resulting fraction subtended appropriate fractions of visual angle.

The error for each bisection is plotted at the true half-way point of the stretch bisected. For instance, the point at 125 yd. represents a bisection of a stretch extending from 100 yd. to 150 yd. The dotted lines connect error values that resulted from dividing a 75-yd. stretch into intervals subjectively equal to one-third and two-thirds.

The horizontal line drawn at zero error indicates the expected judgments if "constancy" for distance stretches were perfect. The dashed curve, on the other hand, describes the judgments expected from a hypothetical O (6 ft. tall) who fractionated the stretches by making the two fractions subtend (a) equal visual angles in the case of halving 50 yd., or (b) visual angles equal to one-third and two-thirds of the total angle subtended by 75 yd. The obtained judgments are close to the line of objective accuracy and do not follow the hypothetical visual angle judgment curve. The judgments at the far stretches show some tendency to be negative. Since the error is small and since the two hypothetical curves are close together at the far stretches, it is not possible to conclude that the plotted points follow either one or the other curve at 175, 200, and 250 yd. The points plotted at 25, 50, 100, and 125 yd. follow the "constancy" line.

This demonstration suggests the interdependence of all spatial constancies. All the dimensions of a surface, both frontal dimensions (termed size) and the third dimension (termed depth or distance) show constancy of magnitude. Gibson's more general statement may thus be applicable—that "Scale, not size, is actually what remains constant in perception" (2, p. 181).

The effect of correction on fractionation   So far, only the results of uncorrected Os have been considered. Another large group of Os whose errors were corrected as the judgments proceeded can be compared with them. Table 14.2 gives mean CE's and SD's for both groups. The corrected group had 12 of 20 CE's significantly greater than zero, while only 9 of the uncorrected group's were significantly greater. A *t* test comparing the magnitude of the CE's of the corrected and uncorrected groups shows that five of the CE's are significantly larger ($p < .05$) in the corrected group (at 125 and 200 yd. with bicycle withdrawing, and at 25, 200, and 250 yd. with bicycle approaching). The mean CE is in no case significantly larger in the uncorrected group. Correction, therefore, does not appear to increase the accuracy of fractionation, which is, indeed, very good already. The fractionation with correction did, however, serve as an effective training procedure for later absolute estimates of distance (1).

Summary

The present study is an application of a psychological scaling operation (fractionation) to perceived distance. A 300-yd. stretch of grasscovered flat ground was used for O's judgments. A bicycle moved up or down this stretch, and O indicated his judgment by stopping the rider at what he considered the correct division point. Six bisections and four trisections were made, with different intervals and ground stretches so chosen that one of the true division points would lie every 25 yd. from zero (O's station point) through the 250-yd. point.

The results suggest the following conclusions:

1. Observers can divide stretches of distance (up to 300 yd.) into halves or thirds with very good accuracy. Perceived magnitudes of distance appear to correspond well with physical magnitudes of distance.

2. There is no tendency for the judgments to follow a hypothetical curve which would result from their being based on the magnitude of the visual angle subtended by different distance stretches.

3. Error is related to the direction of motion of the target, the CE tends to be positive as the bicycle approaches, and either less positive or negative when the bicycle withdraws.

4. Fractionation of distances was not improved by correcting O's errors, nor was variability reduced.

Note

1. This research was supported in part by the United States Air Force under Contract No. 33(038)-22373 monitored by the Perceptual and Motor Skills Laboratory, Human Resources Research Center, Lackland Air Force Base. Permission is granted for reproduction, translation, publication, use, and disposal in whole and in part by or for the United States Government.

References

1. Gibson, E. J. Bergman, R., & Purdy, J. The effect of prior training with a scale of distance on absolute and relative estimation of distance over ground. *J. exp. Psychol.*, 1955, 50, 97–105.
2. Gibson, J. J. *Perception of the visual world*. Boston: Houghton Mifflin, 1950.
3. Gilinsky, A. S. Perceived size and distance in visual space. *Psychol. Rev.*, 1951, 58, 460–482.
4. Gilinsky, A. S. Perception of size of objects at various distances. *USAF Personnel Training Res. Cent. Bull.*, 1954, No. TR-54-92 .
5. Smith, W. M. A methodological study of size-distance perception, *J. Psychol.*, 1953, 35, 143–153.

15

Continuous Perspective Transformations and the Perception of Rigid Motion

James J. Gibson, Eleanor J. Gibson

Constancy of perceived dimensions of things and the ground surface was discussed in connection with the previous paper, and it was suggested that constancy characterizes the scale of the entire surrounding layout, not just objects here and there. There is also constancy of perceived shapes of things and pathways as we move around in the environment, and constancy of perceived substance—things don't appear to shrink as we move away or grow as we approach them; if they are rigid they maintain rigidity. How do we understand these constancies? What is the information for them?

It was questions like these that led to a theory of the role of motion in the perception of shapes and substance expounded by J. J. Gibson (1957). Wertheimer had suggested the law of common fate in 1923, Johansson's monograph on "Configurations in Event Perception" appeared in 1950, and the kinetic depth effect had recently been discovered by Wallach and O'Connell (1953), so there was a concern with the role of motion in perception. But the theory of invariance under transformation—that is, the effectiveness of change for exposing underlying persisting properties of things, such as shape, location, and rigidity—is here brought forward for the first time. Johansson's work on perception of events was more closely related to Wertheimer's principles at that time, although he later emphasized the importance of projective geometry for perception of rigidity and form. Wallach sought to explain the kinetic depth effect by past experience and memory, rather than looking for information in transformations of stimulation over time. The experiment reprinted here was designed to investigate the role of perspective transformations as information for shape and rigidity.

The shadow caster used for stimulus displays in the experiment was also innovative. It was absolutely convincing to the most skeptical witness watching these displays that information for depth did not need to have depth itself or resemble the static setup; the screen was perfectly flat, but the transformations

Journal of Experimental Psychology, 1957, 54, 120–138.

were inevitably seen as an object moving in depth, rather like a gate swinging. We made movies of this experiment, for that reason, and took them along to San Francisco, where my husband showed them in connection with his presidential address to Division 3 of the American Psychological Association, and then on to Oxford where we were about to spend a sabbatical year. The film travelled around Europe, in fact, to a number of colloquia that year. I still show it to a seminar occasionally, although it is a little embarrassing to hear the sudents wondering if that could really be me (thirty or more years ago) demonstrating the experiment. The final display in the film of four layers of surface (made of transparent wire net), all moving at once in different arcs, separated, and the paths of movement beautifully visible, was our chef d'oeuvre. We made the film ourselves and our two children helped, each moving (off screen) a wire surface in a practised path of rotation.

One of the discoveries of this experiment that was to impress us more and more as time went on was the ability of the visual system to perceive both change and nonchange at the same time, and even to perceive two or more types of change simultaneously. The experiment demonstrates that the observer detects, although he or she never sees it presented completely or statically or straightforward, the rectangular shape of the object behind the screen that is casting the shadow. The observer also detects the angle of the arc through which the object is swinging— that is, both the constant form and its path of rotation. Constancy of shape, rigidity, and a particular event of moving through space are all detected in an act of simultaneous perception. Furthermore, no memory of a familiar object need be involved, since the subject never saw the object that cast the shadow, and irregular "blobs" fared as well as geometrical "ideal" forms. This phenomenon was later referred to as perceptual duality, and the concept was of great use in arriving at a theory of visual perception during locomotion. An observer, when in motion, obtains information not only about objects and movement of objects in the world, but also about his own movement (see J. J. Gibson 1979, pp. 182 ff.), another case of perceptual duality.

An exploratory survey of the varieties of optical motion which could serve as stimuli for the perception of motions in the world (6, 7) suggested the hypothesis that one kind of geometrical motion in a plane yields an impression of a rigid motion in space but that any other kind of geometrical motion in a plane does not.[1] The stimulus pattern was always a "texture," that is, a grouping of dark shapes on a light background. If, on a motion picture screen, it underwent a *continuous sequence of perspective transformations* in any of six ways, it gave a perception of a rigid surface moving in one of six ways—the three transpositions and three rotations which, in combination, exhaust the possibilities of mechanical movement. If it underwent continuous transformations *not* of this geometrical kind (but only a few examples were presented) it aroused perceptions of non-rigid or elastic surface motions, of the kind exemplified in the movements of organisms.

Of the six rigid phenomenal motions, three (rotation around the line of sight, transposition up or down, and transposition right or left) are induced by a stimulus which common sense would call motion; one (transposition along the line of sight) by a stimulus which common sense would call expansion or contraction; and only the other two (rotation around a horizontal or a vertical axis) by a stimulus which common sense would call a *transformation*. Optics, however, demands geometrical terms. All six projected motions are different parameters of continuous perspective transformation, and they are mathematically akin. Common sense tells us that the first three optical motions *should* give the perceptions they do (a motion yields a motion) and that the last three should not (how can a change of size or shape yield a motion?). The assumption is that a visual experience has to resemble visually the optical stimulus that produced it. But a better assumption is that experiences need only correlate with their stimuli, not replicate them, and the present hypothesis says that any continuous sequence of perspective transformations is the correlate of perceptually rigid motion.

There was in the film some evidence to suggest that this hypothesis must be qualified if the perspective transformations are those obtained with parallel projection instead of polar projection, that is, with the special case of transformations when the focus of projection is at infinity. The two apparent rotations around a horizontal or a vertical axis then seemed to become somewhat ambiguous as to rigidity or elasticity, and apparent reversals of direction of rotation appeared. The apparent approach or recession also fails of necessity in this case because the change of size of the stimulus disappears with parallel projection. If the above observations are verified, the hypothesis should specify perspective transformations with polar projection. Previous experimental work on the kinetic depth effect (14, 15) or on other appearances of depth in moving fields (3, 12) does not supply evidence for or against the amended hypothesis since in general the changes of shape studied in them were not polar projective. These experiments, moreover, are mainly concerned with what can be called the appearance of *internal depth* of an object, whereas what we are here talking about is the appearance of *slant depth* of the face of an object. The distinction is made clear in the film. The *apparent motion in depth* previously studied by Smith (13), however, is relevant to our hypothesis. One or two of Wallach's many experiments on the kinetic depth effect (14, p. 212 ff.) are relevant indirectly if the changes of such impoverished stimuli as line segments or angles are restated in terms of perspective transformations.

This hypothesis is comparable to, but different from, the principle involved in Wertheimer's "law of common fate" (16) in several respects.

Both refer to some kind of motion in or of a grouping of spots or forms, but Wertheimer's law predicts the organization of a figure in the visual field, whereas this predicts the quality of rigidity of a surface or surface-like experience in space. Wertheimer's law seems to imply that the various parts of the complex are united by sharing a common motion (such as moving in the same direction with the same velocity) but this hypothesis asserts that any perspective transformation is a single motion mathematically, including the size and slant transformations where, analytically considered, every part moves in relation to every other. Wertheimer's law leads to experiments, on "configurations of motions" (9, 12) in which each part of the complex undergoes components of translation or rotation but the part is not itself transformed; a geometrical transformation, however, is something that permeates every part as well as the whole of a texture, and the apparatus used in the present experiment satisfies this condition.

It might be noted that the problem of how we discriminate the rigidity of rotating solid objects and of approaching or receding solid objects in the environment is closely connected with the traditional problems of shape constancy and size constancy. Langdon has recently shown that the shape constancy of an object is considerably increased under conditions highly unfavorable for it when the object is made to rotate (10). Likewise the question of why we see a rigid environment when we move among the solid surfaces around us is closely connected with the traditional problem of space perception (8).

Aim of the experiment   The experiment to be reported sought to answer four questions. First, does the appropriate parameter of continuous perspective transformations with polar projection always give the perception of the changing slant of a constant shape? Second, are the judgments of amount of change of slant away from the picture-plane in good psychophysical correspondence with the "extent" or "length" of the transformation sequence? Also, how variable are these judgments? Third, is the outcome dependent on or independent of the *kind* of shape or texture on which the transformation is imposed? Fourth, how accurate, if at all, is the judgment of slant away from the picture-plane when only the static end product of the transformation sequence is presented to O but not the motion leading to it?

Method

Apparatus and Stimuli
The optical geometry of the apparatus used is shown in Fig. 15.1. The device can be termed a "shadow transformer." Essentially, it presents to an eye an optic array

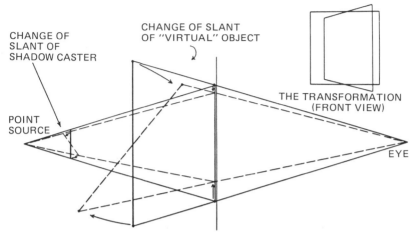

Figure 15.1
The shadow transformer.

of limited scope within the boundaries of which either static patterns or continuous perspective transformations can occur. In this optic array, unlike those of everyday vision, the differential light intensities and their structure are under E's control; the pattern is the same for either eye, and the need for differential convergence and accommodation is eliminated. All the "cues for depth," in short, tend to determine a flat plane except those of form and motion, which are thus isolated for study. The source of this converging array is a window in a translucent screen.

This optical stimulus is artificially produced by the diverging ray sheaf from a point source of light, into which shadows are introduced by opacities of one sort or another attached to a transparent plane mount. Rotations or translations of the mount (on bearings or tracks outside the ray sheaf) yield corresponding transformation sequences of the shadow. This experiment utilized rotation on a vertical axis. The stimuli were the mirror reversals of these moving shadows, visible on the other side of the translucent screen. If an apparent rotation of a "virtual object" is induced by such a stimulus it should always be opposite to the rotation of the shadow caster, without ambiguity.

The seated O, in a dimly illuminated room facing a large white surface, saw a luminous square window 36 cm. on a side at a distance of 180 cm., made of translucent plastic $\frac{1}{8}$ in. thick. The light source was fixed at the same distance behind the window as the eye was in front. It was a 300-w. Sylvania point source carbon arc lamp, but any lamp with a single filament of small diameter (up to 1 mm. or more) will serve the purpose. The window was visibly flat. Binocular vision was permitted O after preliminary work failed to show any difference between the use of one or two eyes. The mounts were transparent rectangular sheets of $\frac{1}{8}$-in. plastic, of such size (30 × 100 cm.) that when they were centered and rotated on a turntable placed midway between the point source and the window they could be turned 70° from the parallel plane without the edges being projected within the window. The turntable could be rotated back and forth through an arc of variable length by an adjustable eccentric linkage, geared to a motor with a variable speed drive. A speed which gave 2-sec. cycles of semirotation was chosen, after exploration indicated that an optimum might be in this neighborhood, although the rate was not critical for the experiment. The quantitative variable of this experiment, then, was the "length" of the transformation sequence, as expressed in degrees of angular excursion of the turntable. We shall return to this point later. Five degrees of semirotation were presented: 15°, 30°, 45°, 60°, and 70°. Each cycle began with and returned to the parallel plane.

The forms transformed The variety of forms, patterns, and textures that can be projected with this device has been suggested elsewhere (7). Four were used in the experiment: an amoeboid group of amoeboid dark shapes or spots (the irregular texture), a solid amoeboid contour form (the irregular form), a square group of dark squares (the regular texture), and a solid square (the regular form). Each was cut out of gummed paper and attached to the central area of a transparent mount so that its shadow was projected to the center of the square translucent window. With the mount parallel, the regular shadows extended 20 cm. each way in the 36 cm. square window, and the irregular shadows about the same. It may be noted that the "regular" stimuli are constituted of rectilinear contours and alignments and the "irregular" stimuli of randomly curved contours and alignments. There are also differences in symmetry, and perhaps other geometrical properties. The "forms" are bounded by a single closed contour and the "textures" by many closed contours; the total contour length is much greater in the latter stimuli. A texture might be described as a "form of forms," as distinguished from a form as such. These textures were, however, very "coarse"; there were 36 squares in the "platoon" and 36 "amoebas" in the "colony."

The variable protractor For recording judgments of change of slant, O had before him a sort of protractor with its baseline parallel to the plane of the screen. It bore an adjustable pointer which could be moved to indicate an angle of semirotation. The top side was blank but the bottom side carried another pointer and a scale which could be read accurately by E after each trial.

Instructions and Procedure

The experimental group Before receiving any formal instructions for the experiment, each O was seated and told: "You see in front of you a screen with a window in it which will be illuminated during the experiment. I will first show you a moving pattern of dark lines filling the window. If what you see is a movement of some kind of object, describe it."

A network (woven wire fencing of a common type) was then placed on the turntable and turned through various excursions. Although the question was intended to suggest neither a deformation in the plane nor a rigid rotation out of the plane, all *O*s reported seeing the latter, and spontaneously reported different amounts of rotation. The suggestions in the following instructions were hence considered permissible:

"During the experiment proper, a dark form or pattern will appear in the middle of the window. It will seem to rotate back and forth on a vertical axis—to turn away from the plane of the screen and return. Your task is to judge how far it rotates, or the maximum angle it makes with the screen. Use the circular model in front of you to make this judgment."

One of the four patterns was then presented at one of the five degrees of transformation for 20 sec., which permitted 10 cycles of stimulation. The *O* had no difficulty in making his judgment during that interval. Twenty such trials (five for each pattern) in an order counterbalanced for the group were made, and then another 20 trials in reverse order to determine whether a practice effect would appear. The *O* was not told his errors. There were 20 *O*s in the group.

The control group   A separate group of 30 *O*s was treated as similarly as possible except that the four stimulus patterns were motionless. Only the end product of each transformation sequence was presented, and only one degree of transformation was used—that with the mount at 60°. For the preliminary exposure, *O* was shown a motionless pattern filling the window, half the group seeing the network of lines and the other half a less objective cloud-like pattern (this making no difference in the outcome) and he was asked if he saw an object of some sort. Then *O* was told that he would see a form or pattern in the middle of the window. It might be parallel or slanted away from the screen. If he saw it slanted away from the plane he was asked to judge the angle it made using the model in front of him. Four trials ,were given (one for each pattern) in an order counterbalanced for the group.

Results

The experimental group   The first question is whether all *O*s saw the changing slant of a rigid shape. As stated above, all did at the outset. During the 40 trials which followed, each of considerable duration, many spontaneous descriptions were offered, and 8 of the 20 *O*s observed at some stage that the display could be seen as a compression of a two-dimensional pattern. They were all psychologists. Twelve did not so report, and stated at the end that they had never observed it. The two-dimensional impressions did not persist long enough to prevent the requested judgments of changing slant. There was no difference in this respect between the regular or irregular forms or textures.

The second question is whether the judgments of change of slant are a function of the amount of change of form. The "length" of the transformation sequence is expressed as the inverse angular excursion of the shadow caster, and this variable is plotted on the horizontal axis of Fig. 15.2. The

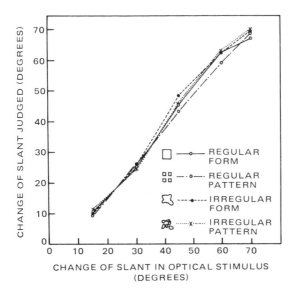

Figure 15.2
Judgments of change of slant as a function of the length of the transformation sequence.

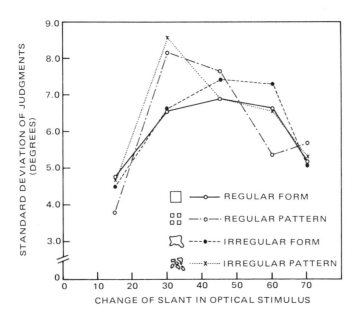

Figure 15.3
Variability of judgments as a function of the length of the transformation sequence.

judgments are plotted on the vertical axis, each point representing a mean of 40 reproductions. The function is linear, except for a small tendency to underestimate (about 4 to 5°) the 15° and 30° angles. Even more striking, however, is the similarity of the functions for the regular and irregular and also for the single and multiple stimuli. This suggests that a transformation can be responded to as such, independently of what gets transformed.

A related question is how variable the judgments are within the group. Figure 15.3 shows the SD's of the judgments as a function of the change of slant "in" the stimulus. The variable errors range between about 4° and 8°. They rise, but fall again as the maximum slant begins to approach 90°, at which limit a phenomenal surface becomes an edge.

The graph does not show any obvious differences between the errors obtained with the four kinds of pattern used. An analysis of variance (Table 15.1), however, is necessary to discover whether either multiplicity or regularity of the patterns is significantly related to errors of judgment. Multiplicity or "texturedness" is not. The effect of regularity is significant at only the 5% level.[2] The tendency is in the expected direction but is weak, considering predictions that might be made from Gestalt theory about "good form." It is strengthened, perhaps, by the significant interac-

Table 15.1
Analysis of Variance of Errors of Judgments of Change of Slant

Source	df	MS	F
Degree of excursion of turntable (A)	4	1437.07	13.12**
Regular or irregular (R)	1	320.68	5.56*
Form or texture (T)	1	72.90	
Subjects (S)	19	453.93	
Practice (P)	1	.53	
A × S	76	109.47	
R × S	19	57.69	
T × S	19	52.63	
P × S	19	23.07	
A × R	4	60.54	4.77**
A × T	4	67.09	2.66*
T × R	1	13.15	
A × S × R	76	12.69	
A × T × S	76	25.24	
T × R × S	19	299.13	

Note: Only those interactions which appeared to be of some interest or were used for the F tests (11, p. 330 and 338) are included in the Table.
*P = .05.
**P = .01.

tion between angle and regularity which seems to reflect the tendency, barely noticeable in the graphs, for the irregular forms to depart slightly more from linearity at the larger angles. All the forms in this experiment were apparently good enough to carry the transformation, and it was this which mainly determined the judgments. This answers the third question. The form of the *change* seems to be what is important, not the form itself. A conception of the various forms that optical change may take is, however unfamiliar, probably necessary for an understanding of the perceptual process.

It may be noted from Table 15.1 that no significant practice effect appeared between the first and second blocks of 20 trials. They have been pooled in Fig. 15.2 and 15.3. The two halves of the data independently warrant the same conclusions, when the curve of Fig. 15.2 is plotted separately for them.

The control group   The outcome of the control experiment was radically different inasmuch as the judgments of slant depended on the regularity of the form or texture presented. The irregular stimuli, in fact, generally appeared in the plane of the screen (85% of 60 judgments) while the regular stimuli generally appeared at a slant from the screen (97% of 60 judgments). Even for the regular stimuli, however, the mean degree of slant perceived was only 24° (SD about 12°) whereas for the moving regular stimuli the mean had been 61° (SD about 6°). This is gross underestimation for the motionless and great accuracy for the moving stimuli. The underestimation of slant is consistent with previous research on static optical forms and optical textures under similar conditions. A trapezoidal form can sometimes arouse an impression of slant, but an exact linkage between the apparent shape and the apparent slant (a "psychological invariant") is not obtained (2). A static optical texture with a compression of texture on one meridian relative to the other induces a perception of surface slant, but even when the texture is regular the slant is underestimated, and when the texture is less regular the slant is more underestimated (4, p. 380).

The irregular form and the irregular texture displayed in this experiment were evidently not of such a kind as to appear slanted when altered by a slant transformation, since they generally still looked frontal. The Os, of course, had never seen them *before* transformation.[3] A truer statement of the matter is that the family of perspective transformations of the amoeboid stimuli has no unique member with immediately identifiable properties. The family of perspective transformations of the quadrilateral stimuli *does* have such a member—the square. At the outset there is one in this family which the other members can be transformations *of*, but none in the former family. Hence, rectilinear contour and alignment—a rectilinear structure—provide a primary basis for presumptions of slant which nonrectilinear structure does not.

One of the writers has argued that there exists a better basis than contour for presumptions or even perceptions of surface slant, namely, internal texture and its density variables (4).[4] It might be expected, therefore, that the texture of amoeboid spots would induce slant more often than the amoeboid form, and the texture of squares more slant than the square. Neither expectation was fulfilled. The explanation may be that the textures used (36 elements, or only about 6 each way) were too coarse to make the density variables determinate.

Evidently a configuration with only the feeblest stimulating power for depth perception, or none at all, can nevertheless carry a transformation sequence which yields accurate depth perception. This answers the fourth question.

Individual results   Time did not permit more than two judgments for each condition per O in the experiment just reported. It was thought desirable to run a more exhaustive series in order to determine the extent of the variable error of the slant judgments for single individuals. Accordingly, two O's were run for five days each, so that 10 judgments per condition were available.[5] Table 15.2 shows the means and SD's of these judgments. The means are strikingly like those for the group, especially for O_1, who underestimates the smaller angles and is more accurate or overestimates on the larger. The second O tends to underestimate throughout. All the curves, when plotted, are close to linearity, and the particular pattern makes little difference. The SD's are of the same order as for the group.

Discussion

Kinetic depth effect and memory   Wallach believes that the kinetic depth effect of what we call a transformation sequence must be due to some effect of past experience on present momentary experience (15, p. 364). He argues that since any single member of the sequence looks flat in isolation, the present member has depth only because the memory traces of past members enter into the present perception. He assumes that only the present member of the sequence can be a stimulus for the eye. This is a perfectly logical extension of the classical theory which strictly separates "traces" and "stimuli" as determiners of perception (or behavior). But does it not reduce the theory to an absurdity? Does a stimulus last for a second, a millisecond, or a microsecond? And what about the doctrine that "a stimulus is always a change"? Is it not theoretically preferable to suppose that a transformation is a stimulus in its own right, just as a nontransforma-

Table 15.2
Means and SD's of Judgments of Change of Slant for Two O's

Angular Excursion of Truntable	Solid Square				Square of Squares				Soild Amoeba				Groups of Amoebas			
	O_1		O_2		O_1		O_2		O_1		O_2		O_1		O_2	
	M	SD	M	SD	M	SD	M	SD	M	SD	M	SD	M	SD	M	SD
15°	8.4	3.0	9.4	3.3	9.1	2.4	7.9	2.2	9.7	4.6	9.2	1.7	8.7	2.6	9.3	4.1
30°	20.7	4.9	25.0	7.1	21.3	6.2	26.2	4.4	21.3	4.8	27.9	9.0	22.0	4.6	26.3	6.2
45°	47.3	8.0	43.2	7.1	39.8	7.6	44.1	4.1	45.5	5.4	44.4	5.2	41.8	9.5	43.2	5.9
60°	66.2	5.4	59.5	6.1	64.2	4.8	63.6	4.9	66.6	5.0	58.0	5.6	66.1	7.7	58.4	5.2
70°	69.2	5.6	60.8	4.6	72.2	3.7	67.5	9.1	76.6	3.4	65.2	6.0	78.2	2.6	68.2	6.7

Note: Each cell in the table represents 10 judgments.

tion is a stimulus? Or, still better, that sequence, as well as pattern, is a variable of stimulation? Is it not better to take the risk that traces might vanish from psychological theory than the risk that the stimulus might vanish? Perhaps the addiction of Gestalt theorists to the concept of traces is what has prevented some of them from studying temporal forms as effectively as they have spatial forms.

Wallach has convincingly demonstrated (and the present observations confirm it) that a motionless nonsense pattern of a certain sort on a shadow screen which at the outset usually looks flat will usually look deep after *O* has seen it in transformation. This result may well be considered a genuine effect of memory, or at least of recognition. But it is far from proving that memory traces are necessary for the perception of rigid motion. It might prove not an effect of memory on depth perception but an effect of memory on the depth interpretation of an ambiguous static picture. It is possible that the role of *learning* in space perception is quite a different affair, consisting not of the enriching of bare stimuli but the discriminating of rich stimuli.

The anchoring of a transformation sequence and the identifying of the object   A motionless pattern of sufficient irregularity appears in the plane of the screen even when its shadow-making pattern is slanted to the screen. What, then, would happen to the judgment of *change* of slant if the shadow caster were rotated between, say, 30° and 60° instead of between 0° and 60°? Would *O* then see the pattern as departing from and returning to the frontal parallel plane? Is the neat correspondence between length of transformation sequence and change of slant shown in Fig. 15.2 destroyed in these circumstances? These questions lead into fundamental problems of psychophysical scaling and shape constancy; complete answers cannot be given, but enough evidence has been obtained to be worth reporting here.

If the 30° to 60° cycle is presented to a naive *O* with a rectilinear or regular pattern, judgments are made with some accuracy. The apparent surface does not begin and end in the parallel plane. If the cycle is presented with an irregular pattern, however, the naive *O* reports a large change of slant which seems difficult to estimate, and the object *does* seem to return to the parallel plane. The crucial experience seems to be his first view of the motionless pattern. He sees an object *but his first impression of it is an object thinner than the shadow-casting pattern.* All observations so far suggest that if he is thus led to identify at the outset an object of the "wrong" shape, the judgments of change of slant will persistently be out of scale. His scale of slant will be stretched and displaced, as it were, until he is given the opportunity of anchoring it at 0° and 90° which, at the same time, enables him to identify the rigid shape of the object.

The size and distance of the virtual object are *never* determined by the optical stimulus in our experiment. Similarly, the slant and shape of the virtual object may be misdetermined at the outset by showing it, even briefly, as a continuous nontransformation—a static frontal pattern. This establishes a false shape constancy for the phenomenal object. When it rotates, anomalies of space perception will occur of the sort demonstrated strikingly by Ames with the "rotating trapezoidal window" (1). If care is taken by E, however, to avoid the procedure above, the evidence indicates that an intermediate transformation cycle can be correctly judged from the outset, whenever the length of the transformation sequence is sufficient. If a naive O is first shown an anchored transformation sequence from 0° to 90°, or even if he is first shown the motionless pattern at 45° but is told not to assume that the object is necessarily in the plane of the picture, then a 30° to 60° cycle is judged approximately as such. The tentative conclusion is that a motion consisting of a perspective transformation sequence can determine both a definite rigid shape and a definite change of slant in perception, for a wholly unfamiliar object, without the need of any presumption whatever about the probable shape of the object based on memory (2).

It sounds very paradoxical to assert that a change of form of the stimulus can yield a constant form with change of slant in the percept. The paradox probably arises because two different meanings of the word "form" are employed (5), the first being geometrical and the second substantial. In any event, the assertion is inaccurate since the evidence now suggests that the *form* of the change of form of the stimulus is what determines the perception of rigid motion.

If the impression of surface rigidity in visual perception can be accounted for, the constancy of shape of objects is explained at the same time. The face of a unique solid object is ordinarily given not as a form but as a unique family of transformations to the eye. The difference between one solid object and another, in contrast, is *not* given as a relation of perspective transformation, nor is the difference between an earlier and a later state of a physically *changing* object. The perceptual problem of the recognizing or identifying of unchanging objects by their shape has to be approached in the light of these facts.

Summary

Continuous perspective transformations of varying length were presented in 2-sec. cycles to each O on the visibly flat surface of a translucent screen. Judgments of the amount of change of slant of the apparently rigid object were in good correspondence with the length of the transformation sequence, without depending on the kind of pattern which carried the transformation. The patterns differed with respect to regularity vs. irregularity and form vs. texture. Regularity may have had a small effect on the variability of judgments but texturedness did not.

As a control, the same patterns were presented motionless at the end of a transformation sequence. In general the irregular patterns appeared to be in the frontal plane but altered in shape; the regular pattern appeared at some degree of slant, but the judgments were not accurate. Evidently impressions of changing slant are precise whereas corresponding impressions of unchanging slant are ambiguous or weak. Rectilinear contours and alignments seem to provide some basis for impressions of unchanging slant. A sequence of perspective transformations, on the other hand, seems to yield an impression of changing slant whether or not such regularity is present.

For irregular unfamiliar patterns there was evidence to suggest that the perceiving of the rigid shape of the virtual object is intimately connected with the perceiving of change of slant of the object. Misidentification of the shape at the outset was accompanied by anomalies in the perception of slant.

The eye appears to be very sensitive to a continuous perspective transformation in the optic array. Psychophysical experiments are possible if the parameters of this stimulus are isolated and controlled.

Notes

1. This experiment was reported by the first author as part of an address entitled *Stimulation and Perception* delivered as retiring President of the Division of Experimental Psychology, APA, in September, 1955. The work was supported in part by the Office of Naval Research under Contract NONR 401(14) with Cornell University. An early form of the apparatus to be described was constructed, and preliminary experiments were performed by H. R. Cort. The writers are also obligated to Dr. O. W. Smith for ideas and assistance.

2. The 5% level is probably not acceptable here, since some inhomogeneity of variance is evident in the data.

3. An *O* who had become familiar with the frontal aspect of the irregular form or texture (such as either *E*) could see another aspect as slanted. So also could an *O* who had persistently observed these patterns undergoing continuous transformations. Presumably these *O*'s had learned to *identify the surface*, i.e., to recognize a previously unfamiliar object in nonfrontal aspects. This, we believe, is Wallach's "memory effect" in the perception of tridimensional forms (15).

4. In the study referred to, the correlate of slant was said loosely to be a "gradient" of texture density. The correlate might as well be expressed as an unequal density along two meridians, or the ratio of these densities, or a special sort of compression of texture. These are all comprehended in the geometrical notion of a perspective transformation.

5. Mr. John Hay kindly obtained these data.

References

1. Ames, A., Jr. Visual perception and the rotating trapezoidal window. *Psychol. Monogr.*, 1951, 65, No. 7 (Whole No. 324).

2. Beck, J., & Gibson, J. J. The relation of apparent shape to apparent slant in the perception of objects. *J. exp. Psychol.*, 1955, 50, 125–133.

3. Fisichelli, V. R. Effect of rotational axis and dimensional variations on the reversals of apparent movement in Lissajous figures. *Amer. J. Psychol.*, 1946, 59, 669–675.

4. Gibson, J. J. The perception of visual surfaces. *Amer. J. Psychol.*, 1950, 63, 367–384.

5. Gibson, J. J. What is a form? *Psychol. Rev.*, 1951, 58, 403–412.

6. Gibson, J. J. *Optical motions and transformations as stimuli for visual perception.* (Motion picture film). State College, Pa.: Psychol. Cinema Register, 1955.

7. Gibson, J. J. Optical motions and transformations as stimuli for visual perception. *Psychol. Rev.*, in press.

8. Gibson, J. J., Olum, P., & Rosenblatt, F. Parallax and perspective during aircraft landings. *Amer. J. Psychol.*, 1955, 68, 372–385.

9. Johannson, G. *Configurations in event perception.* Uppsala: Almqvist and Wiksell, 1950.

10. Langdon, J. The perception of a changing shape. *Quart. J. exp. Psychol.*, 1951, 3, 157–165.

11. McNemar, Q. *Psychological statistics.* (2nd ed.) New York: Wiley, 1955.

12. Metzger, W. Tiefenerscheinungen in optischen Bewegungsfeldern. *Psychol. Forsch.*, 1935, 20, 195–260.

13. Smith, W. A. Sensitivity to apparent movement in depth as a function of "property of movement." *J. exp. Psychol.*, 1951, 42, 143–152.

14. Wallach, H., & O'Connell, D. N. The kinetic depth effect. *J. exp. Psychol.*, 1953, 45, 205–217.

15. Wallach, H., O'Connell, D. N., & Neisser, U. The memory effect of visual perception of three-dimensional form. *J. exp. Psychol.*, 1953, 45, 360–368.

16. Wertheimer, M. Untersuchungen zur Lehre von der Gestalt. II. *Psychol. Forsch.*, 1923, 4, 301–350.

16

Motion Parallax as a Determinant of Perceived Depth

Eleanor J. Gibson, James J. Gibson, O. W. Smith, H. Flock

The following paper was a further investigation of the role of motion as information for layout features, this time for one surface in front of another. The demonstration of this phenomenon in the film made from the previous experiment convinced us (if we needed to be convinced) that differential movement does indeed serve to separate surfaces. The extent to which this occurs, the conditions to be met, and whether any metric correspondences exist were some of the questions to be explored. But the problem that awaited solution was really the deeper problem of what kind of information the eye can pick up and how exactly the information can specify arrangements of things in the real world. Note the following paragraph from the introduction:

> *The trouble with positions and angular velocities of elements in a field is the difficulty of understanding how an eye can register them. As the Gestalt theorists have emphasized, what the eye seems to pick up is the mutual separation of elements, their pattern, rather than their positions or directions. And, accordingly, it is easier to suppose that the eye responds to changes of separation or change of pattern, rather than to absolute displacements or velocities. Helmholtz might better have asserted that a difference between the angular velocities of two elements in the field will be directly related to the difference in distance between the corresponding objects in space. Such relative velocities involve a transformation of pattern, and this may be what the eye is primarily sensitive to. It is not immediately evident what the best method is for specifying the information about objects in an array of light projected to the eye (p. 43).*

This statement sounds rather like Marr's much later pronouncements about computation (Marr 1982). But the question here was whether differential veloci-

Journal of Experimental Psychology, 1959, 58, 40–51.

ties *carry information for separation in depth and whether they can specify absolute, as well as relative, amounts of separation.*

The shadow caster setup was used again, this time with translucent surfaces in front of the subject. The actual surfaces were plexiglass and they were randomly textured by sprinkling them with a cleaning powder. When they were motionless, the appearance was of one surface. As soon as any motion was introduced, the surfaces sprang apart, but extent of separation was ambiguous. Note the suggestion in the discussion that the information for separation might be disruption of adjacent order between the two sets of texture. The suggestion foreshadows J. J. Gibson's later working out of accretion and deletion at an edge as information for specification of separation. What was emphasized in both cases is change in optical structure, a discovery that has been made by others several times since then (Ullman 1979).

The second experiment presented a gradient of velocity differences rather than just two separated surfaces, attempting to create a continuous flow field of velocity change, on the hypothesis that the metric ambiguity of a difference in just two surfaces could be overcome by a smooth flow of changing velocity ratios. There was good indication of a correspondence between differential velocity ratios and perceived slant in this case. These results are interesting in the light of recent research findings on the same question (Anderson 1989) that under some circumstances positive results (metric correspondence without smooth continuity of change) are obtained. It is possible that continuity of change becomes a factor only when no information is available for an opaque surface. I found a comment written in the margin of J. J. Gibson's reprint of this paper, "The transparencies should have been emphasized." The setup was too much like empty space, perhaps.

I conducted most of this research during a couple of summer months when I was the only senior investigator in the laboratory, my husband and others having departed for Brussels where an international congress was going on. During a recent move, I found two letters written to my husband giving details about the early progress of the experiments:

> *I was very discouraged about the experiment yesterday. I ran Howard Flock and he couldn't discriminate anything except the smallest separation (1/2 in.) from all the rest. When I plotted his judgments they were scattered anywhere at all. Then I tried him with rating (1, 2, 3, 4, 5). Still worse. But today I have been giving him training, demonstrating with an arbitrary scale and correcting him. After 25 corrected judgments he was nearly perfect (did not confuse 10 different settings). But he had deliberately attended to the ratios of the two motion speeds of the patterns and attached the scale to the ratios. I am going to keep running him and see if this sticks, and whether it ever gets converted to a depth experience. If it did, it would be a real case of learning to discriminate a complex stimulus variable and getting a phenomenological change along with it (July 24, 1957).*

Later reports were more cheerful:

The experiment is going fine, really. I have 3 kinds of subjects. The summer school people aren't too eager, so I only ask them to "Describe what you see." They all say "two layers" or "levels." Then I ask "how far apart?" One said 5 ft today, and one said 4 in. This is with the largest separation. Then I show the smallest. Some can't see the separation—then I increase it till they do. The second class of S's are asked to make 20 judgments, random order (takes about 40 min.). The third class of S's are Flock and Hay, who are practising daily with correction, for 10 trials and then next day without (July 30, 1957).

The last mentioned subjects, senior graduate students Howard Flock and John Hay, were incorporated into experiment III of the paper, a study of the effect of giving varied amounts of information about the actual setup to the subjects. If some sort of Helmholtzian inference principle were to explain how velocity differences functioned as a "cue" to depth, we might have found an effect of conversion of bidimensional impressions into experiences of depth—referred to sometimes as percept-percept coupling (Epstein 1982). But this did not happen. The two most practiced subjects made inferences about depth, to be sure, on the basis of perceived velocity ratios. But they never reported a perceptual change in the depth perceived. This experiment discouraged any tendency I had to go along with a Helmholtzian or a Brunswikian theory of perceptual learning. However, it did not discourage my interest in perceptual learning, and my pursuit of a viable, adequate theory of perceptual learning took off in new directions, as continued in part IV.

Motion parallax is the optical change of the visual field of an observer which results from a change of his viewing position.[1] It is often defined as the set of "apparent motions" of stationary objects which arise during locomotion. Psychologists assert that it is a "cue" for perceiving the depth of the objects, but the optical fact of motion parallax must be distinguished from its capacity to induce perceptions. It has not been experimentally demonstrated that motions in the field of view will actually yield corresponding judgments of depth. This is a purely psychological problem. The optics of motion parallax, on the other hand, is a problem for geometry and ecology.

Recently, the suggestion has been made that a continuous gradient of motions in the field of view will induce the perception of slant-depth (J. J. Gibson, Olum, & Rosenblatt, 1955) inasmuch as the perception of depth is intimately connected with the perception of surfaces (J. J. Gibson, 1950). This statement also needs experimental test. The purpose of the present study is to investigate what kinds of motion in the light entering an eye do in fact consistently arouse certain judgments of depth, and what do not.

The experiments must be carried out with artificial motions in a field of view rather than those obtained in a natural environment if we wish to study the effect of motion parallax in isolation from other cues or stimuli for depth. The variables of size, density, linear perspective, differential blur, and binocular parallax should be eliminated or so reduced as to be ineffective in the array of light entering O's eye. A method of achieving this result has been devised, and a suitable control employed.

The experimental method should also preclude actual movement or locomotion of O. If the cue of motion parallax is so defined as to require *active* head movement or locomotion, proprioceptive and vestibular stimulation is also present. This definition is unjustified, since passive locomotion in trains and airplanes should be admitted as circumstances when motion parallax occurs. Certain patterns of motion in the field of view of O do induce impressions of being moved through space if we accept as evidence the illusions of locomotion obtained in viewing a panoramic motion picture, or in a training device for simulating aerial flight.

Perception of absolute distance and of relative depth   The apparent displacements of the sensations of objects are said to be cues for perceptions of their depth. What kind of depth? The question arises whether their distances from the perceiver can be judged or whether they will only appear to be separated in the third dimension. Helmholtz, in his description of motion parallax, asserted both hypotheses. On one page he described the appearance of objects "gliding past us" as we walk through the countryside, and asserted that "evidently under these circumstances the apparent angular velocities of objects in the field of view will be inversely proportional to their real distances away; and consequently safe conclusions can be drawn as to the real distance of the body from its apparent angular velocity" (Helmholtz, 1925, p. 295). On the next page he described the appearance of an indistinguishable tangle of foliage and branches in a thick woods as a man stands motionless, but noted that "the moment he begins to move forward everything disentangles itself and immediately he gets an apperception of the material contents of the woods and their relations to each other in space, just as if he were looking at a good stereoscopic view of it" (Helmholtz, 1925 p. 296).

In the first quotation Helmholtz says that angular velocity is a cue for the perception of absolute distance. In the second, he suggests that a difference in angular velocity is a cue for the perception of separation in depth, or of relative distance only. These two hypotheses are by no means the same, and they should be considered separately and tested separately. We will be concerned here primarily with the second.

Two-velocity motion parallax and flow-velocity motion parallax   Although motion parallax has been said to apply to the whole array of objects in an environment and a large array of apparent motions in the field, the experiments performed have in the past been confined to two objects and two velocities in a restricted field of view.

Bourdon (1902) reported experiments in which O looked with one eye at a pair of luminous spots in a dark corridor. The sources were at different distances but the spots were of the same angular size. When the head was fixed with a biting-board, O "could not judge at all accurately" which light was the nearer, but with the slightest movement of the head from side to side "it was easy to judge" the relative depth of the two. But the absolute distance of neither light was detectable.

Tschermak-Seysenegg (1939) improved on this arrangement with what he called a "parallactoscope," by analogy with the stereoscope. He defined motion parallax as arising from movement either of a group of visible objects on the one hand, or the position of O's eye on the other, emphasizing the relativity of the situation. But, he studied only the detection of depth of two objects with voluntary head movement. His apparatus was a modification of the familiar two-pins setup used to obtain the threshold for binocular depth perception. It permitted O to move one eye from side to side, with a sliding headrest, so as to obtain *successive* impressions equivalent to the *simultaneous* impressions obtained with both eyes open. The average error of equating the distance of the vertical wires was small under these conditions, although not as small as the error with both eyes open. When only one eye with a fixed head was used, the error was very large.

Graham, Baker, Hecht, and Lloyd (1948; see also Graham, 1951) obtained the threshold for separation in depth of two needles pointing toward one another, as seen on a uniform field through a window. The needles moved from side to side on a common carriage. They appeared to be aligned at the center of their motion cycle and offset at the extremes of the cycle unless the adjustable needle had been set into the same frontal plane as the fixed needle. Graham thus eliminated for the first time in this type of experiment the additional sensory information produced by voluntary head movement.

More exactly, what Graham obtained was the just noticeable difference between two angular velocities in a field of view, under probably optimal conditions. The threshold was extremely low—about 30 sec. of arc per second of time. It is notable that the reports of what Os perceived, however, were not unanimous. Some saw the separation in depth as such; others perceived either the difference in velocity of the two needles or noticed the change of alignment or offset of the needles. Although the latter impressions may be cues for the former, the experiment was not concerned with the effectiveness of such cues for producing depth impressions.

Somewhat later, a case of motion parallax different from the two-velocity case was defined mathematically by Gibson, Olum, and Rosenblatt (1955). This is the array of angular velocities of the optical elements projected from a surface to a moving station point. There is a flow of velocities rather than a pair of velocities in such an array, and the phenomenon was named motion perspective to distinguish it from motion parallax as it had been studied up to that time.

For the study of the perceptions induced by flow-velocity in a field of view, including gradients of velocity, skew motions, and transformations, a different sort of apparatus is required from that previously employed. The two-velocity experimenters used a pair of real objects at real distances to produce the optical motions. More freedom is achieved by using a projection screen or some other optical means to produce them. The experiments to be described used shadows on a translucent screen. Accommodation is thereby controlled.

Several exploratory experiments have been published on flowing motion. They are of various types, and they have been produced in various ways. J. J. Gibson and Carel (1952) attempted to induce the perception of a receding surface in a darkroom with a bank of luminous points which carried a gradient of velocities. This stimulus failed to arouse the perception of a surface, however, and the depth judgments were ambiguous. O. W. Smith and P. C. Smith (1957) investigated the perception of convexity or curvature of a textured surface with various combinations of depth cues, including the flow-velocity type of motion parallax. Although motion in the field contributed to the judgment of convexity, in no case did motion cause a surface otherwise judged as flat to be judged as curved. Hochberg and O. W. Smith (1955) studied the perception of depth induced by the centrifugal flow of luminous pattern elements in the dark, the expansion phenomenon. J. J. Gibson and E. J. Gibson (1957) investigated the perception of the rigid rotation of an apparent surface elicited by the continuous perspective transformation of regular and irregular patterns or forms.

These experiments differed in the structure of the optic array used to "carry" the motion in question, and they also differed in the degree to which perceptions of space were aroused. They led to the choice of the kind of random texture employed in the present experiments, which is intended to yield the experience of a plane surface.

What is now needed is an experimental comparison of the judgments obtained with *two* velocities in a field of view and those obtained with *many* velocities in a field of view. Although no clear line can be drawn between them, the two-velocity type of motion parallax applies to the problem of perceiving a group of objects in otherwise empty space, while the flow-velocity type of motion parallax applies to the perceiving of a background surface such as a wall (or substratum). These are not the same problem for perception even though it may be difficult to distinguish sharply between their respective kinds of stimulation.

Optical geometry of motion parallax   The environmental situation which leads to an array of different motions in a visual field should be defined more carefully. This is the optical geometry of motion parallax, as distinguished from the visual appearance of motion parallax. Graham (1951, pp. 878 ff.) has given the geometry of certain special cases of this situation. J. J. Gibson et al. (1955) have analysed the case of an extended surface such as the ground. What will be discussed here is the case of an environment of discrete objects.

When light rays from permanent objects of an environment converge to a point, they constitute what may be called an optic array, and the elements of this array constitute a pattern. An eye or a camera at the station point can register this pattern of luminous elements. If the point moves, the pattern is altered in a way which depends on both the displacement of the point and the layout of the objects. How the eye responds to this alteration of pattern is our problem.

The first question is how to specify mathematically the change of pattern in a way that is relevant for vision. By choosing a coordinate system for the array, one can specify the absolute position of each element and the displacement of each element per unit of time, that is, its absolute angular velocity. It would then be true in a certain sense, as Helmholtz (1925, p. 295) said, that "the apparent angular velocities of objects in the field of view will be inversely proportional to their real distances away." But more exactly, it would be true only if the linear velocity of the station point were constant (J. J. Gibson et al., 1955). A given angular velocity is a cue for distance, or permits a "safe conclusion" about distance, only if the speed and direction of one's locomotion is known.

The trouble with positions and angular velocities of elements in a field is the difficulty of understanding how an eye can register them. As the Gestalt theorists have emphasized, what the eye seems to pick up is the mutual separation of elements, their pattern, rather than their position or directions. And, accordingly, it is easier to suppose that the eye responds to changes of separation, or change of pattern, rather than to absolute displacements or velocities. Helmholtz might better have asserted that a difference between the angular velocities of two elements in the field will be directly related to the difference in distance between the corresponding objects in space. Such relative velocities involve a transformation of pattern, and this may be what the eye is primarily sensitive to. It is not immediately evident what the best method is for specifying the information about objects in an array of light projected to an eye.

But one fact should be clear. Only if there is an eye at the point of projection and only if it is sensitive to the motions in the optic array, relative or absolute, does a psychological question arise. Will the possessor of the eye see merely the change of pattern of the array? Or will he see moving objects in the field of view? Or will he see stationary objects at different distances? In order to show that motion parallax is effective for the perception of depth it must be demonstrated experimentally that differential motions in an array of light to an eye will yield differential judgments of depth. And the array should be such that when the motion is eliminated the judgments of depth will cease, for only then will motion parallax have been isolated from other cues for depth.

Experiment I: Motion Parallax with Two Velocities

Problem and Method
The two-velocity experiments were repeated with (*a*) two spots in a field to carry the motions, and (*b*) two superimposed textures filling the field to carry them. In both cases the velocity *difference* was taken to be the essential cue for possible judgments of depth, not the absolute velocities. In this experiment, reports were obtained for a large velocity difference, a small velocity difference, and no velocity difference, that is, a motionless field. The last was a control.

Apparatus and stimuli   The light entering *O*'s eye came from the translucent screen of a point source shadow-projector (J. J. Gibson, 1951; J. J. Gibson & E. J. Gibson, 1957). He saw only a luminous rectangular field in which dark circles or textures could be made to appear and to move. These were actually the shadows of opaque substances attached to a transparent mount behind the screen. This was a large sheet of glass or plastic whose edges were never visible. Differential translatory velocity of the shadows was produced with two mounts, one behind the other, which could be made to move parallel to the screen on a common carriage. The array of light to the eye was simply the reverse of the array projected to the screen, since the eye and the point source were symmetrically located equidistant from the screen (Fig. 16.1). The window was 32.2 × 36 cm. at a distance of 126 cm. from the eye, subtending an array 14.5° high and 16.2° wide. The window was viewed through an aperture by a seated *O*.

The carriage which bore the two mounts rolled silently on tracks and could be pulled from side to side through an excursion of 45 cm. It was operated by hand to produce a motion cycle in about 8 sec. A small shutter close to the point source enabled *E* to eliminate the shadow between trials, leaving the screen illuminated by diffuse light.

The two adjacent spots in the field were produced by attaching small paper circles to each mount, at different elevations so that their shadows did not pass through one another as they moved across the field. The faster spot was above the slower spot. The diameter of both was 5.2°, one paper circle being compensated in size to match the shadow of the other.

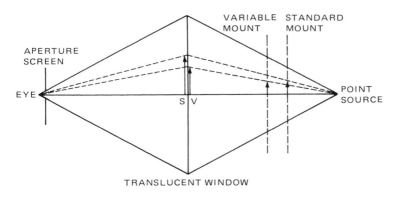

Figure 16.1
The shadow projector viewed from above. In a unit of time, the shadow of a spot at the center of the standard mount sweeps through a certain angle and that of a corresponding spot on the variable mount sweeps through a lesser angle, as shown. The two mounts roll on the same carriage. If they are close together, there is no difference in angular velocity, but as the variable mount is positioned farther from the point source and closer to the screen, the angular velocity of its shadow decreases. With this apparatus, it can decrease to about one half of the angular velocity of the standard. By trigonometry, the ratio of the lesser (V) to the greater (S) angular velocity is equal to the inverse of the ratio of the distances of their respective mounts from the point source. In the diagram above, it is about 0.7.

The superimposed random textures were produced by a technique of sprinkling talcum powder over the surfaces of the two transparent mounts. This yields an optical texture with indefinite contours and indefinite elements. When the two were superimposed but motionless, they constituted a single texture with no cue for superposition, and gave the appearance of a single surface, something like that of a cloud. This apparent surface filled the whole window and appeared at an indefinite distance from O.

As noted, the two angular velocities as such were not uniform, decreasing to zero at either end of a motion cycle, and changing direction alternately. Minor variations in velocity also occurred as a consequence of moving the carriage by hand. The independent variable of this experiment was the difference in velocity between the two shadows. It was expressed as the ratio of the slower (the variable) velocity to that of the faster (the standard) velocity, or V/S.

Procedure   Each O was seated at the apparatus, asked to apply his preferred eye to the aperture, and instructed simply to "describe what he saw in the window." He was first presented with a motionless field for as long as he needed to make a report, which was recorded. He was then presented with continuous cycles of motion at the maximum velocity difference (V/S = .51) until his report was completed. Finally he was given the minimum velocity-difference (V/S = .97). The E made no comment at any time, since wholly spontaneous reports were desired.

The order of presentation was intended to minimize the effect of suggestion on the perceiving of depth.

A group of 26 Os went through this procedure with the spot field and another group of 46 with the textured field. Formal judgments and answers to questions were obtained afterwards from some Os, which will be described when relevant. They were requested in the terms used spontaneously by the O.

Results
The words used by the Os to describe what they saw varied widely, and the effort to identify things was reminiscent of descriptions of cognitive inference (Vernon, 1957). But the reports could later be classified easily with respect to depth or distance. The motionless textured field was unanimously reported to be a single surface without any difference in depth. The motionless spots, however, were reported at different distances by 4 of the 26 Os. The spots, therefore, did not wholly satisfy the requirement that impressions of depth be absent in the absence of motion, although the combined textures did.

A large velocity difference (.51) for the textured field always gave a perception of two surfaces separated in depth, as evidenced by the reports of all 46 Os. For the spot field, the reports were not unanimous, but 22 out of 26 Os did describe a difference in depth of the two objects.

The small velocity difference (.97) was evidently close to the threshold. None of the Os reported two separated surfaces for the textured field, and only 7 out of 26 reported different distances for the spots.

The direction of the difference in depth reported was not unanimous for either the spots or the textures. Insofar as two-velocity parallax is a reliable and effective indicator of relative depth, the faster velocity should correspond to the nearer object or surface. But 7 out of 26 Os saw the slower spot as the nearer object instead of the reverse, and 10 out of 46 Os saw the slower texture as the nearer surface. Some degree of ambiguity as to the depth-difference is also indicated by the fact that 7 Os reported spontaneous reversals of the front-back relationship between the two surfaces at one time or another.

The amount of separation in depth between the two objects or the two surfaces was estimated on formal request by a sample of these Os, after the main procedure. The estimates were highly variable. For the spots they ranged from zero to 5 ft. For the textures they ranged from 2 in. to 3 ft. Some Os were unwilling to judge, saying, "It depends on what it is," or "It could be infinity." Evidently the impression of how far apart these entities were was indefinite, as also was the impression of how far away they were.

Figure 16.2 represents an ideal theoretical possibility of what the Os might have seen in this experiment, but it cannot be asserted that this,

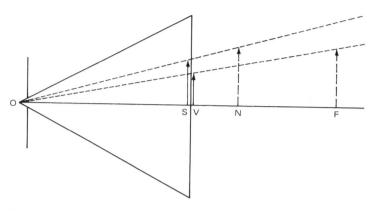

Figure 16.2
The two angular velocities of Figure 16.1 with a pair of virtual objects at different distances moving in apparent space. The two apparent objects (or surfaces) are shown as if seen behind the translucent window. The nearer (N) is shown close to the window; the farther (F) is shown at the distance it would have to be if the two were taken to be in rigid translation (if the two vectors were equal). In the diagram ON/OF = V/S, by trigonometry. That is, the distances are such that the optical velocities are inversely proportional to them. (Note that N corresponds to S, and F to V.) But this relation depends entirely on the assumption of rigidity. The absolute distances of N and F may vary, but the ratio of ON/OF will remain constant on that assumption. If rigidity is *not* assumed, however, there is no rationale for predicting any relation of distance or depth or even which object will be seen in front of the other.

is what they did see. The reports indicated that they perceived two things of some kind in some kind of space behind the screen, but neither the direction nor the amount of their separation in the third dimension was definite.

Discussion

The significant result of this two-velocity experiment is not so much the effect of motion on depth perception as its effect in separating one surface into two. With the textures, all Os saw a single frontal surface when there was no differential motion, and all Os saw two frontal surfaces when there was a sufficient degree of differential motion. This separation is not what is ordinarily meant by depth, since it was not always clear which surface appeared in front and which behind.

The phenomenon is similar to the "disentanglement" of foliage and branches which Helmholtz noted when he began to move in the thick woods. But this is not the same as his "apperception of depth." The separation is probably related to Wertheimer's (1923) demonstration that a group of spots interspersed among others will be unified by what he called their "common fate" if they moved together. Other conditions for the seeing of one thing in front of another, for transparency and superposition, have been discussed by Koffka (1935). Although the phenomenon may not seem relevant for some kinds of space perception it is certainly relevant for object perception.

How can this result be explained? Instead of appealing to a process of organization, or a law of "common fate," one might look for its basis in the geometry of the optical stimulus. Geometry distinguishes between (a) perspective transformation of forms, (b) topological transformations of forms, and (c) *disruptions*. These correspond roughly with the distinctions in physics between rigid motions of bodies, elastic motions of bodies, and the motions of breaking, tearing, or splitting. In this experiment, the motion of one set of textural elements relative to the other was a disruption, geometrically speaking. When sufficiently different velocities were imposed on them, the *adjacent order of elements* in the textures was destroyed. More exactly, there was a permutation of this order. It was a particular sort of permutation, to be sure, for each of two sets of elements retained an adjacent order, but the disruption of order as between these sets broke the original continuity. And this produced the perception of different surfaces with separation between. The detection by the eye of continuity or solidity as compared with discontinuity, disruption, or separation, is probably a fundamental kind of perception. The continuity of a single surface in two dimensions may be given by a static optical texture. But the continuity of a solid object in three dimensions probably depends on the kind of optical motion presented to the eye. Perhaps it was this lack of solid continuity or rigid connectedness between the nearer and farther surface in our experiment which prevented the ideal possibility represented in Fig. 16. 2 from having been realized.

The earlier investigators of motion parallax were willing to assume that an eye was sensitive to the stimulus of motion, but they did not seem to realize that differential motion necessarily entails a *change of pattern*. In our experiment there were motions of the elements relative to the window but there were also motions of one set of elements relative to the other. For example, when both sets of elements were moving to the left, relative to the window. and one moved faster than the other. the slower was moving to the right, relative to the faster. Spontaneous reports of this appearance were given by several Os. Why should not a differential velocity be perceived just as directly as the two component velocities? When two moving elements are far apart in the field, one might suppose the slower and the faster velocity might have to be compared in order to detect a difference between them. But when the elements are adjacent in the field the difference is given by the change of pattern. Permutation of order is one type of change of pattern. In order to study the sensitivity of the eye to *form*, to *change* of form, and to the *forms* of change of form, a taxonomy of these variables is desirable.

Experiment II: Motion Parallax with a Flow of Velocities

Problem and Method

If a two-velocity field does not arouse consistent perceptions of depth, will a flow-velocity field do so? In order to make this comparison, the apparatus already described was modified so as to present to the eye a texture in which the horizontal velocities of the elements varied from slow to fast from the top to the bottom of the field, that is, a gradient. As before, the field could also be motionless.

Apparatus   The shadows on the screen were produced by spattering paint on a transparent sheet interposed between the point source and the screen. This mount was slanted toward the screen at an angle of 45° (Fig. 16.3). By the principle of mirror reversal, the gradient at the eye should yield an apparent slant *away* from the screen.

If this texture had been composed of elements regularly spaced in a grid or pattern, then the gradients of size and spacing would have been effective in producing the impression of a slanted surface even when the texture was motionless, as previous research has demonstrated (J. J. Gibson, 1955). But as it was, the brightness-transitions which composed the texture were not sharp, the

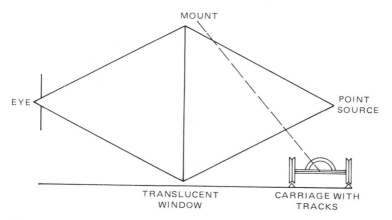

Figure 16.3
The shadow projector giving a gradient of angular velocities, viewed from the side. The carriage and mount move back and forth parallel to the translucent window. The angular velocity is greatest at the bottom of the window, where the mount is closest to the point source, and least at the top, where the mount is farthest from the point source. At an inclination of 45°, this yielded a ratio of the minimum to the maximum velocity of 3 to 1. The apparent surface should appear to slant backward at the top.

elements had indefinite sizes and shapes, and the static gradients, if present, were not effective in producing a perception of slant. This texture was nevertheless sufficient to produce the perception of a continuous surface.

As before, O looked through an aperture which prevented his seeing either the edges of the window or any other part of the apparatus. The field was 82° wide by 52° high. The eye and the point source were each 75 cm. from the window.

Procedure   All Os were naive. Each was told that when he applied his eye to the aperture he would see a gray field of view, and was asked to report what he saw. They were divided into two groups, one of which was presented with the moving texture without ever seeing it static (Group I), and the other with the moving texture after having seen it static (Group II). Their spontaneous descriptions were recorded and later classified. Questions were asked only after these reports, and in the same terminology used by O.

Results
Nineteen out of 21 Os (Group I) reported a rigid moving plane surface of some kind slanting away from them at the top of the field. The inclination of the surface was estimated without difficulty, and they judged it to be receding upward. Of the 2 remaining Os, one's report was uninterpretable, and the other's was of a surface perpendicular to his line of sight.

With the static texture, 25 Os out of 28 (Group II) reported something which could be classed as surface-like, but which was in no case slanted backward into space. Of the remaining 3 Os, 2 saw a surface whose lower part was perpendicular but whose upper part was slanted back, and one saw the surface slanting back into space. When these 28 Os were later presented with the moving field, 26 saw it unambiguously to be a receding rigid surface at a fixed inclination. Of the remaining two, one saw it perpendicular to the line of sight; the other's report was uninterpretable.

Estimates of the slant of the apparent moving surface were obtained from each O in terms of degrees of inclination backward from the frontal plane. For Group I, the 19 judgments varied from 20° to 60° with a median of 40°. For Group II, the 26 judgments varied from $12\frac{1}{2}°$ to 55° with a median at $37\frac{1}{2}°$. The theoretical value based on the gradient of velocities alone would be 45°. The medians show a constant error of underestimation. The surface never appeared to be at 90°, that is, it never looked like a ground on which O might be standing.

Estimates were requested of *how far away* the apparent moving surface seemed to be from O, but these judgments, in contrast to those of slant, could not as easily be made. For the total of 49 Os, they varied from 3 in. to 5 miles. Some of these Os reported that it was possible to see themselves moving with respect to the surface instead of the surface moving with respect to them.

Discussion

These results indicate that motion parallax with a continuous gradient of velocities does induce consistent judgments of slant. This is the property of receding in depth in a certain direction. It is combined with the experience of a continuous rigid surface. The second experiment was like the first in most respects except that continuity of differential motion was introduced. To put it another way, permutation of textural elements was absent, but a skew of the pattern of elements was present. Judgments of distance in this experiment were highly variable and were made with reluctance, as they were in the first experiment.

There is evidently more than one kind of "depth" and more than one kind of motion parallax. The two experimental situations so far described were sufficient for judgments by naive *O*s of two kinds of spatial perception, (*a*) the phenomenon of separation in the third dimension and (*b*) the phenomenon of recession in the third dimension . Neither situation, however, was sufficient for absolute judgments of distance. This may be connected with the fact that no perception of a level ground was induced.

Experiment III: Correspondence Between Velocity-Pairs and Judgments of Depth Under Various Instructions

Problem and Method

In Exp. I, a difference in optical velocity did not induce the perception of a difference in visual distance with any great consistency. An explanation of this result has been suggested in terms of the absence of continuity between the two velocities. Another possible explanation however, in the spirit of Helmholtz, would be that the expected perception did not occur because *O* did not interpret the two motions as a difference in distance, or had not learned to perceive differential velocity as a difference in distance. On this theory, the suggestion that there was always an element of depth between the objects, with instructions about the limits of this separation, would be expected to alter the perceptions and lead to consistent judgments of depth. This prediction was tested in Exp. III, using the textures and spots of Exp. I.

Naive *O*s were given one of three degrees of suggestion or verbal information about depth, and were asked to reproduce on an adjustable but unmarked scale 1 m. in length the separation between the nearer and the farther apparent surface. The degree of velocity difference, the V/S ratio, was systematically varied so that judgments could be correlated with it.

Procedure All *O*s, as previously described, initially made spontaneous observations to the request "Describe what you see," in response to the motionless stimulus, the greatest velocity difference (V/S = .51), and the least velocity difference (V/S = .97). The apparatus was that of Exp. I. Each *O* then made 20 judgments of amount of separation for both the textures and the spots. The variable transparent mount was so set as to produce 10 velocity ratios of .51, .54, .57, .61, .65, .70, .76, .83, .90, and .97. Each ratio was presented twice, in random order, in the texture series and the spot series. Half the Os began with one series and half with the other. An O was assigned to one of three groups, and then instructed as follows:

Group I (Least information): The O was shown the sliding scale beside his chair and was told that it could be used to indicate the distance between the nearer and farther of the two (surfaces, spots). If O had used other terms instead of "nearer" and "farther," these terms were employed. He was then told that he would be shown a number of different settings of the apparatus, and that each time he would be asked to make a judgment (degree of separation, distance between, etc.). No other information was given. The O was encouraged to report as he went along but no comments were made on his performance. There were 16 Os.

Group II (Maximum and minimum): After the adjustable scale had been demonstrated, these Os were given another demonstration of the greatest and the least velocity-difference and were told which one was the maximum and which the minimum. The procedure thereafter was the same as for Group I. There were 17 Os.

Group III (Most information): After the preliminaries described, these Os were told: "These are shadows of two (surfaces, objects) which are actually at different distances from you. One is farther away from you than the other. This is what they look like at their maximum separation, which is 18 in. (The O was shown 18 in. on the adjustable scale.) This is what they look like at their minimum separation, which is $\frac{1}{2}$ in. (The O was shown $\frac{1}{2}$ in. on the scale.) Each time I will ask you to estimate how far apart the (surfaces, objects) making the shadows are." The procedure was thereafter the same as for the other groups. There were 20 Os.

When each O had finished his judgments he was questioned by E as to how he had made them unless he had already made this clear. The questions were: How did you make your judgments 7 Did you go by appearance of depth, or did you try to use some other cue? If some other cue, what was it? Did you ever see the front and back (surfaces, spots) change places or fluctuate? Did the two (surfaces, spots) ever appear to be connected, like parts of a rigid object?

Results

For each O a rank order correlation was run between his 20 judgments of separation and the corresponding velocity-ratios. Table 16.1 summarizes the median coefficients for the three kinds of instruction and for the two kinds of apparent objects, surfaces and spots. They range from .51 to .84. Eighty-seven of the 106 correlations were significant at the 5% level ($r > .44$). The data thus demonstrate some correlation between amount of differential velocity and degree of depth judged. The spread of the individual correlations was very great, however, ranging from $-.52$ to $+.99$.

Group III, which was given the most information, had higher correlations (medians of .83 and .84) than the other two groups. If individual correlations are considered, 19 out of 20 were significant for both the

Table 16.1
Medians and Ranges of Correlations Between Velocity Ratios and Judgments of Depth

Measure	Stimuli	Group I (N = 16)	Group II (N = 17)	Group III (N = 20)
Median r	Surfaces	+.72	+.67	+.83
	Spots	+.57	+.51	+.84
Range	Surfaces	−.23 to +.95	+.34 to +.85	−.18 to +.96
	Spots	−.52 to +.94	−.14 to +.85	−.45 to +.99
Number r's significant at <.05	Surfaces	12/16	15/17	19/20
	Spots	14/16	8/17	19/20

surfaces and the spots. The correlations of Groups I and II do not differ from one another. The demonstrating of the maximum and minimum stimulus presentations at the ends of the scale did not, therefore, improve the ordering of the estimates. But telling O that he was seeing shadows of two things separated by a given amount of space did so.

When the instructions were given, they seemed to make O begin searching at once, and quite deliberately, for cues which he could put into some order. Only a minority of the Os reported that they had depended on any "appearance of depth" in making their estimates. Considering all Os, 70% reported that they had used the "relative motion," or the "difference in speed," or "how far one passes the other" as the basis for judgment. Evidently, most of them saw motions of some kind of entities but did not clearly see the amount of space separating them.

The appearance of a connection between the two surfaces or spots "like parts of a rigid object" was almost never reported in answer to the question. The appearance of exchanging place or fluctuating in depth was reported by 17 out of 53 Os.

Because the more specific instructions raised the correlations, two Os (both psychologists and familiar with the apparatus and the problem) were run on consecutive days with reinforcement, to see how high the correlations might go and how stable they might become. The spots were not used in this experiment. The first 20 trials on each day were run without comment. But on the next 10 trials O was corrected after each judgment. The E did so by marking off on the scale the actual distance which separated the standard and variable mounts behind the translucent screen. This procedure of 20 uncorrected and 10 corrected trials was repeated for 9 days with one O and 7 days with the other.

The correlations improved rapidly from coefficients of .20 and .30 to ones of .90 or more. The introduction of new and unfamiliar textures had little effect on the correlation. Neither did the requiring of one O to use a verbal rating scale of 1 to 10 instead of the adjustable sliding scale.

These Os definitely took a problem-solving approach to the task and checked their methods of judging against the corrections given by E. One estimated the ratio of the two velocities and tried to express this numerically each time. The other said, after a few days, that the task had become similar to memorizing paried associates; he was trying to link up ordered "cues" with particular scale positions. The training did not have the effect of producing or enhancing an immediate appearance of depth.

Discussion

After verbal suggestion, information, or training concerning separation in depth, a correlation was present between the degree of velocity-difference and the degree of separation judged. It was raised by information and corrected training. But the reports indicated that the Os generally saw motions rather than depths, and that the appearance of depth was not induced by information or training. They were led to look for and use cues for the required judgments of depth, but not to report that they perceived it. They could interpret a velocity-difference as a depth-difference if given instructions, and they could improve the consistency of their estimates if given reinforcement. They could learn to perceive in one sense of the term, but they did not learn to see a differential velocity as a difference in depth.

This result does not support the theory of "unconscious inference" or point to any process for the conversion of bidimensional impressions into perceptions. It should be remembered, of course, that in these experiments motion has been isolated from other determinants of perception. This does not occur in everyday life. Motion usually comes in conjunction with size, shape, density, and disparity. But it might be supposed that the fact of this conjunction over years of past experience would have given an associative cue value to the motions in our experiment. In that case the velocity-pairs should have produced spontaneous judgments at once. Since they did not, this particular theory of cue learning is not supported by our results.

Summary

The common assertion that motion parallax is a cue for depth perception is vague. The optics of differential velocities of the elements in a field of view were examined and two cases were distinguished: that of *two* velocities in the field and that of a *gradient* of velocities in the field. The two-velocity case yielded consistent perceptions of the separation of one surface into two. The flow-gradient case (motion perspective) yielded consistent perceptions of slant, or rate of recession in depth. In neither case were there consistent judgments of distance from O. Still another case, that of two different velocities of two different spots in an otherwise empty field, did not yield consistent space perceptions of any kind. Evidently Helmholtz was wrong about an "immediate apperception" of the distances of bodies or the depth between them solely from an impression of the velocities of spots in the field of view. The only consistent or "immediate" impressions obtained were those of separation in depth (in response to a permutation of adjacent order of texture), and recession in depth (in response to a transformation of the texture).

These were spontaneous perceptions in the sense that no other information was given O than that carried in the optical stimulation. When he was given verbal information about depth in the two-velocity situation he was able to correlate a judgment of depth with an impression of motion. But the correlations were not perfect, and a minority of Os "saw" the depth. One might conclude from these facts that there are two kinds of optical stimulation for experiences of space: a kind which requires additional information to yield consistent judgments, and another kind which does not require it—which is compelling or coercive. The facts also suggest that there are two kinds of experience of space: "empty" depth, as exemplified by one surface in front of another, and "filled" depth, as exemplified by the slant or recession of a surface. The depth of a surface is perceived more consistently than is the depth of the space between surfaces, in our situation.

As regards the perception of absolute distances, this probably depends on the perception of a terrain or ground surface, the conditions for which were not reproduced in the present experiments. For the investigation of this problem, a very large field of view is required.

Note

1. This work was supported by the Office of Naval Research under Contract NONR 401 (14) with Cornell University. Reproduction in whole or in part is permitted for any purpose of the U. S. Government.

References

Bourdon, B. La perception visuelle de l'espace. Paris: Schleicher, 1906.

Gibson, J. J. The perception of visual surfaces. Amer. J. Psychol., 1950, 63, 367–384.

Gibson, J. J. Optical motions and transformations as stimuli for visual perception. Psychol. Rev., 1957, 64, 288–295.

Gibson, J. J., & Carel, W. Does motion perspective independently produce the impression of a receding surface? J. exp. Psychol., 1952, 44, 16–18.

Gibson, J. J., & Gibson, E. J. Continuous perspective transformations and the perception of rigid motion. J. exp. Psychol., 1957, 54, 129–138.

Gibson, J. J., Olum, P., & Rosenblatt, F. Parallax and perspective during aircraft landings. Amer. J. Psychol., 1955, 68, 372–385.

Graham, C. H. Visual perception. In S. S. Stevens (Ed.), Handbook of experimental psychology. New York: Wiley, 1951, 868–920.

Graham, C. H., Baker, K. E., Hecht, M., & Lloyd, V. V. Factors influencing thresholds for monocular movement parallax. J. exp. Psychol., 1948, 38, 205–223.

Helmholtz, H. Physiological optics. Vol. III. J. P. Southall, Ed., Optical Soc. America, 1925.

Hochberg, J., & Smith, O. W. Landing strip markings and the "expansion pattern": I. Program, preliminary analysis, and apparatus. Percpt. mot. Skills, 1955, 2, 81–92.

Koffka, K. Principles of Gestalt psychology. New York: Harcourt, Brace, 1935.

Smith, O. W., & Smith, P. C. Interaction of the effects of cues involved in judgments of curvature. Amer. J. Psychol., 1957, 70, 361–375.

Tschermak-Seysenegg, A. Über Parallaktoskopie. *Pflüg. Arch. ges. Physiol.*, 1939, 241, 454–469.

Vernon, M. D. Cognitive inference in perceptual activity. *Brit. J. Psychol.*, 1957, 48, 35–47.

Wertheimer, M. Untersuchungen zur Lehre von der Gestalt. II. *Psychol. Forsch.*, 1923, 4, 301–350.

Retrospect and Prospect: Psychophysics to Computation

These experiments, performed during the 1950s, paved the way for future developments in research and theory on perception. They underlie James Gibson's later works, of course—*The Senses Considered as Perceptual Systems* (1966) and *The Ecological Approach to Visual Perception* (1979). But they also, especially the last two papers, point toward Marr's computational theory of perception (Marr 1982). Marr tried, as did Gibson, to analyze the information available for detecting layout in the world. His approach is more like Gibson's earlier theorizing than the later, since Marr never gave up the fixed retinal image as the fundamental datum for knowing about the world. Whether he would eventually have discovered the optic array and the necessity of treating information as a flow to be explored, as Gibson did, we'll never know.

Psychophysics, as a method and even as instigator of problems for research, has never died out and is today holding sway over a big field of research, mislabeled by some as perception. The most recent edition of *Stevens' Handbook of Experimental Psychology* (1988) demonstrates the pervasive influence of psychophysics as both a method and a way of thinking about psychology up to the present moment. A recent meeting of the Psychonomic Society devoted many hours of its program to psychophysical research. Is this bad? In one sense, not at all, because the research is likely to be technically elegant. But it can be stultifying too. Very often, psychophysical research seems to be set by the paradigm, rather than by a true psychological question. The backing of the Establishment does not make up for failure to ask the right questions. The situation is a little like the role of the Establishment in art in England in the nineteenth and early twentieth centuries. What was hung in the annual exhibitions of the Royal Academy was determined by established convention and taste, not by new ways of viewing the world.

In one sense, psychophysics is more than a method. To Boring, when he wrote *The Physical Dimensions of Consciousness* (1933), it was a kind of statement of the task of psychology. One lays out the physical dimension, an intensive one, for example, or frequency, like pitch, or distance from one point to another measured in some physical scale, and then looks for the psychological scale that corresponds. The question of correspondence between two domains is as old as science itself, absolutely basic. Theoretical disagreements or the possibility of a futile search for correspondences that matter are likely to come in the choice of domains and scales. Are the physicists' measurements that are so often used appropriately scaled for relevance to human perception? We can measure distances in the universe in light years, or wave lengths in millimicrons, but these scales will not be appropriate for enlightening us about human perception in a human-sized environment.

IV

Perceptual Learning (1955–1969)

Introduction to Part IV

The two previous sections included several experiments designed to enhance perceptual learning by introducing correction or reinforcement, none of which worked very well. The field experiments worked in a way, since constant errors were all reduced and there was some evidence of an increase in precision. But the shift in constant error could have been simply judgmental, a deliberate correction of a scale of verbal responses rather than a change in what was perceived. In one of the rat rearing experiments (Walk, Gibson, Pick, and Tighe 1958), we introduced during rearing reinforcement of one of the forms to be discriminated in later learning. The rats obtained food by pushing their noses through a small door in a food holder that displayed one of the forms to be discriminated, whereas animals in a control group obtained their food through an unadorned door. There was a small advantage in later discrimination learning for the reinforced animals, but it turned out that it made no difference whether or not the form reinforced during discrimination learning was the same one that had been displayed during rearing. In a second experiment, reinforcement (differential or otherwise) had no effect whatever and so had to be ruled out as a facilitator. In a different context, the two-layer depth experiment with prolonged training of human subjects (reprinted in part III) resulted in no phenomenal change in the depth experienced by the subjects.

Despite these failures, there was ample reason to think that perceptual learning occurs. I reported an experiment in which it did with children and adults at the meeting of the American Psychological Association in 1950 (Gibson and Gibson 1950). The trouble was that the old learning theories were inadequate to handle it. We needed a new approach. Neither rewarding responses differentially nor providing correlated information as a basis for making inferences accounted for perceptual learning. Perceptual learning became the important problem for me by the 1950s, and I gradually expanded it to include perceptual development. Infancy is the time when perceptual learning should be most prominent, since language is not yet available and the response repertory is at a minimum.

For a period of about fifteen years, I performed experiments in the general area of perceptual learning and development and gradually evolved a theory, culminating with my book, *Principles of Perceptual Learning and Development*, published in 1969. James Gibson and I spent the year of 1959–60 as fellows at the Institute for Advanced Study in Princeton. My plan was to spend that year writing a book about perceptual learning. I did make a start, but it was not long before I felt that I was not ready for a book yet and needed more time for thinking. I put away the few chapters I had completed and worked instead on chapters I had been invited to contribute to other books, good preparation for the one I intended to write on my own. I found I had a lot of work to do if I wanted to include (or rather create) the whole field of perceptual learning, criticize alternative theories, and propose my own theory.

During the years before the book finally appeared, many things happened to further my education and broaden my knowledge base—acquaintance with some prominent European thinkers (notably Piaget and several Russian psychologists), a trip to Geneva and to Russia, a memorable summer conference hosted by Held and Hein at MIT on the effects of visual adaptation to prisms and what they meant, and a brief attraction to information processing, among other things. Most important was a year at the Institute for Advanced Study in the Behavioral Sciences in 1964–65 when I got back to the book seriously once more, threw away what I had written earlier, plotted it all out, and began to write again. I made great progress that year, but the book turned out to be a much bigger project than I had first envisioned—twenty chapters in all—and covered history of the subject, animals and children, as well as my own theoretical views. It has four introductory and historical chapters, four chapters on my own theory, four factual chapters on different research areas, two chapters on animals, five on human perceptual development in children, and a final theoretical chapter that focusses on general trends in perceptual development and some classic developmental issues like priority of perceiving wholes or parts.

Since the book can't be reprinted here, I include some milestones along the way and excerpts from the book's final chapter. But first I present a brief statement of the central ideas that I espoused. The basic concept is the emphasis on differentiation as opposed to association or any form of add-on. The problem of perception was taken to be how we keep in touch with the world around us. How we can know the world has been the age-old problem for theories of perception; the problem for a theory of perceptual learning must be how we improve our knowledge of the world and make better use of the information about it. A differentiation theory assumes, necessarily, that the information about the world is abundant, rather than minimal and impoverished. Perception is the process of obtaining this information. Perceptual learning goes on because in the beginning only gross imprecise information is obtained. Development proceeds via differentiation of information that specifies things and events in the world, by discovery of invariants as changes in stimulation are produced by movements of things and of the observer, and by encounters with novel and broader environments.

The theory divides into three parts: what is learned, the processes involved, and factors that select what is learned. What is learned concerned me more than anything else, because perceptual learning—an effect of learning on perception, not response learning or memory of verbal material —had been so neglected by modern psychology. What was learned was taken to be differentiation of the distinctive features of things, invariants of events, and higher order structure of both. I was much impressed by the notion of distinctive features, which I had read a good deal about when we were at the Princeton Institute. Noam Chomsky was there at the same time, and I picked up a bit about linguistics, hitherto unknown to me, through him. I used what was learned, especially the emphasis on differentiation, as the basis for several principles that might have applications.

The processes I thought were involved in achieving differentiation were abstraction, filtering, and peripheral mechanisms of attention used to tune the perceiver for optimal search (important because I thought of the process as a search, and an active one). This part of the theory has borne the heaviest brunt of criticism by people who are impressed with mechanism rather than function. I think they really wanted association or inference, which I had ruled out. I found more promising the notion of stripping away the noise and unwanted garbage so as to sculpt a clean outline of the information that specified the persisting structure of things and events in the world. This process could involve both extraction and filtering (inhibition). I am glad to see that this idea has found some favor lately in neuroembryology (e.g., Changeux, Heidmann, and Patte 1984). My husband thought of and referred to perceptual learning as the "education of attention,"—a good phrase, but I thought it too general to carry me very far.

It was important to tie motivation in with the theory, since in the last anaysis both perception and learning are selective processes. What does motivate perception and perceptual learning? Not metabolic needs, like Hull's old drive stimulus. Perception is a search for information, an intrinsic motive that is exhibited especially strongly in young animals, including human infants. It underlies perceptual learning as well. But what selects what is learned if not reduction of a drive stimulus? I maintained that it is the discovery of economical structure such as the distinctive feature, the invariant that underlies all the transformations, the higher order structure that is superordinate over all embedded structures. I called this principle the *reduction of uncertainty*. It is a kind of economy principle, by no means unfamiliar in the history of science (Hatfield and Epstein 1985).

In a nutshell, I thought of my theory (and referred to it) as a *specificity* theory of perceptual learning, meaning the kind of achievement reflected by the perceptual changes as they come to correspond uniquely to what is going on in the world. Paul Weiss considered specificity a major question for science, defining it as "a sort of resonance between two systems attuned to each other by corresponding properties" (Weiss 1970, 162). In the case of perceptual learning, three systems are implicated: the world of events and objects in an environmental layout, the information in ambient arrays of energy that specifies the happenings and layout of the environment, and the changing perceptions of the observer. Achievement of specificity of perception to the information specifying the world is the function and the result of perceptual learning.

The description of these correspondences was not far advanced, and their relations were not so clear to me when this book was written as they became later. The papers that follow reveal stages on the way to a more sophisticated definition of the true questions. This quest continued through publication of my husband's last two books (J. Gibson 1966 and 1979) and still requires our attention in pursuing an adequate theory of perceptual learning. It was clear from the start, however, that fortuitous association is an unlikely conceptual mechanism for a theory focussed on the description and matching of correspondences.

17

Perceptual Learning: Differentiation or Enrichment?
James J. Gibson, Eleanor J. Gibson

This is a series of three papers, all published in 1955, but the first was long in the making and has some stories attached. More than ten years before, I had written a dissertation about the importance of differentiation in learning. I classified the research as verbal learning at that time, but the material to be differentiated in my research consisted of a set of drawn nonsense forms. I had said very little about how the differentiation was accomplished or what kind of learning was really entailed, and I had wanted for a long time to get back to those questions. My husband was interested because of his research with Robert Gagné on identification of aircraft during World War II, so we often discussed how to do an experiment of a more systematic kind on what we had come to call identification learning. *The move to Cornell left me with no teaching responsibilities (except as a pinch hitter for the learning course when a faculty member defected at midyear), so we set about designing an experiment for me to run. We used (as a matter of course) a set of drawn nonsense forms, which had built-in dimensional variables of three kinds. We called them "systematic scribbles." The idea was to show them to subjects in random order requiring the subjects to identify, accurately, just one scribble, the chosen standard. The subject was shown the entire set over and over until he or she achieved an errorless run. No correction was given as the experiment proceeded.*

I was ready for subjects in the spring of 1950, and I included children of two age groups as well as adults. The children performed the experiment during the spring, since I had access to two ages of scout groups (my children's groups). That was fine. I got rather a shock when two of my adult subjects (one of them Richard Solomon who had come to Ithaca for a summer conference) performed flawlessly on the first run and thus gave me no learning data! But the others did, and the experiment was finished in time for me to present it at A.P.A. in September (Gibson and Gibson 1950). The experiment lay fallow for a while until

Psychological Review, 1955, 62, 32–41.

my husband was invited to give a paper on military training at a panel meeting on Training Devices in Washington. We got out the experiment and gave more thought, then, to what the results meant for learning theory and training. That paper seems not to be in existence any longer—perhaps it was just delivered from notes. But I remember the discussions at the meeting and the interest aroused in the question of whether we can learn something by perceiving alone, or only by performing something. This was the era of the so-called "new look" in perception (Blake and Ramsay 1951), so views on perception were shifting away from psychophysics per se. But the "new look" was not at all the new view that we had in mind. The preface to Blake and Ramsay's book (1951) says, for example: "Perceptual activity supplies the materials from which the individual constructs his own personally meaningful environment" (p. iii). Bruner, one of the contributors to the book, presented a theory of perception as a constructive process, with hypotheses, sets, and check of hypotheses as the working concepts. Stimulation was thought to be impoverished and unreliable, leaving the door open for autistic factors to determine what is perceived.

Our view was radically opposed to these notions. An opportunity to say so to a psychological audience came up when James Gibson was invited, as Chairperson of Section I, to organize up a program for the Christmas meeting of The American Association for Advancement of Science in Berkeley, 1954. We were spending the fall term at the University of California at Berkeley, on leave from Cornell, so we had planned to attend. Leo Postman, our good friend on the faculty at Berkeley, agreed to prepare an opposing view, to ensure a lively debate. Postman had coauthored some papers with Bruner in the "new look" tradition, but he was more interested in a traditional learning view, as his paper that follows makes clear. He spoke eloquently for association and learning theory, and for perceptual learning as a matter of behavior change, presenting the best arguments that could have (or still have) been made against our proposals. We replied with arguments about what is learned (not connections with responses, but changes in what is responded to). It was a lively and friendly argument, the kind I would like to see more often in psychology.

The views in our paper emphasize differentiation of available information, rather than an add-on of anything, whether it be response, ideas, affective states, etc., as the basis of perceptual learning. This was the major hypothesis of my book on perceptual learning and I am still committed to it—more than ever as the ecological approach to perception has progressed in sophistication in recent years.

The term "perceptual learning" means different things to different psychologists.[1] To some it implies that human perception is, in large part, learned —that we learn to see depth, for instance, or form, or meaningful objects. In that case the theoretical issue involved is *how much* of perception is learned, and the corresponding controversy is that of nativism or empiricism. To others the term implies that human learning is in whole or part a matter of perception—that learning depends on comprehension, expectation, or insight, and that the learning process is to be found in a central process of cognition rather than in a motor process of performance. In this second case, the theoretical issue involved is whether or not one has to study a man's perceptions before one can understand his behavior, and the controversy is one of long standing which began with old-fashioned behaviorism.

These two sets of implications are by no means the same, and the two problems should be separated. The problem of the role of learning in perception has to do with perception and the effect of past experience or practice on it. The problem of the role of perception in learning has to do with behavior and the question of whether we can learn to do something by perceiving, or whether we can only learn by doing it. The questions, then, are these: (*a*) In what sense do we learn to perceive? (*b*) In what sense can we learn by perceiving? Both questions are important for the practical problems of education and training, but this paper will be concerned with the former.

In What Sense Do We Learn to Perceive?

This question has roots in philosophy and was debated long before experimental psychology came of age. Does all knowledge (information is the contemporary term) come through the sense organs or is some knowledge contributed by the mind itself? Inasmuch as sensory psychology has been unable to explain how as much information about the world as we manifestly do obtain is transmitted by the receptors, some theory is required for this unexplained surplus. There has been a variety of such theories ever since the days of John Locke. An early notion was that the surplus is contributed by the rational faculty (rationalism). Another was that it comes from innate ideas (nativism). In modern times there have been few adherents to these positions. The most popular theory over the years has been that this supplement to the sensations is the result of learning and that it comes from past experience. A contemporary formula for this explanation is that the brain stores information—possibly in the form of traces or memory images, but conceivably as attitudes, or mental sets, or general ideas, or concepts. This approach has been called empiricism. It preserves the dictum that all knowledge comes from experience by assuming that past experience somehow gets *mixed with* present experience. It assumes, in other words, that experience *accumulates*, that traces of the past somehow exist in our perception of the present. One of its high-water marks was Helmholtz's theory of unconscious inference, which supposes that we learn to see depth by interpreting the clues furnished by the depthless sensations of color. Another was Titchener's context theory of meaning, which asserts that we learn to perceive objects when a core of sensations acquires by association a context of memory images.

Over a generation ago this whole line of thought was challenged by what seemed to be a different explanation for the discrepancy between the sensory input and the finished percept—the theory of sensory organization. The gestalt theorists made destructive criticisms of the notion of *acquired* linkages among sensory elements and their traces. Instead they asserted that the linkages were *intrinsic*, or that they arose *spontaneously*, taking visual forms as their best example. Perception and knowledge, they said, were or came to be *structured*.

The theory of sensory organization or cognitive structure, although it generated a quantity of experimentation along new lines, has not after 30 years overthrown the theory of association. In this country the old line of empiricist thinking has begun to recover from the critical attack, and there are signs of a revival. Brunswik (2, pp. 23 ff.) has followed from the start the line laid down by Helmholtz. Ames and Cantril and their followers have announced what might be called a neoempiricist revelation (3, 11, 14). Other psychologists are striving for a theoretical synthesis which will include the lessons of gestalt theory but retain the notion that perception is learned. Tolman, Bartlett, and Woodworth began the trend. Leeper took a hand in it at an early date (15). The effort to reconcile the principle of sensory organization with the principle of determination by past experience has recently been strenuously pursued by Bruner (1) and by Postman (16). Hilgard seems to accept both a process of organization governed by relational structure and a process of association governed by the classical laws (10). Hebb has recently made a systematic full-scale attempt to combine the best of gestalt theory and of learning theory at the physiological level (9). What all these theorists seem to us to be saying is that the organization process and the learning process are not inconsistent after all, that both explanations are valid in their way, and that there is no value in continuing the old argument over whether learning is really organization or organization is really learning. The experiments on this issue (beginning with the Gottschaldt experiment) were inconclusive, and the controversy itself was inconclusive. Hence, they argue, the best solution is to agree with both sides.

It seems to us that all extant theories of the perceptual process, including those based on association, those based on organization, and those based on a mixture of the two (including attitudes, habits, assumptions, hypotheses, expectation, images, contexts, or inferences) have at least this feature in common: they take for granted a discrepancy between the sensory input and the finished percept and they aim to explain the difference. They assume that somehow we get more information about the environment than can be transmitted through the receptor system. In other words, they accept the distinction between sensation and perception. The development of perception must then necessarily be one of supplementing or interpreting or organizing.

Let us consider the possibility of rejecting this assumption altogether. Let us assume tentatively that the stimulus input contains within it everything that the percept has. What if the flux of stimulation at receptors *does* yield all the information anyone needs about the environment? Perhaps all knowledge comes through the senses in an even simpler way than John Locke was able to conceive—by way of variations, shadings, and subtleties of energy which are properly to be called stimuli.

The Enrichment Theory versus the Specificity Theory

The entertaining of this hypothesis faces us with two theories of perceptual learning which are clear rather than vague alternatives. It cuts across the schools and theories, and presents us with an issue. Is perception a creative process or is it a discriminative process? Is learning a matter of enriching previously meagre sensations or is it a matter of differentiating previously vague impressions? On the first alternative we might learn to perceive in this sense: that percepts change over time by acquiring progressively more memory images, and that a context of memories accrues by association to a sensory core. The theorist can substitute attitudes or inferences or assumptions for images in the above Titchenerian proposition, but perhaps all this does is to make the theory less neat while making the terminology more fashionable. In any case perception is progressively in *decreasing correspondence with stimulation*. The latter point is notable. Perceptual learning, thus conceived, necessarily consists of experience becoming more imaginary, more assumptive, or more inferential. The dependence of perception on learning seems to be contradictory to the principle of the dependence of perception on stimulation.

On the second alternative we learn to perceive in this sense: that percepts change over time by progressive elaboration of qualities, features, and dimensions of variation; that perceptual experience even at the outset consists of a world, not of sensation, and that the world gets more and more properties as the objects in it get more distinctive; finally, that the phenomenal properties and the phenomenal objects correspond to physical properties and physical objects in the environment *whenever learning is successful*. In this theory perception gets richer in differential responses, not in images. It is progressively in *greater* correspondence with stimulation, not in less. Instead of becoming more imaginary it becomes more discriminating. Perceptual learning, then, consists of responding to variables of physical stimulation not previously responded to. The notable point about this theory is that learning is always supposed to be a matter of improvement—of getting in closer touch with the environment. It consequently does not account for hallucination or delusions or, in fact, for any kind of maladjustment.

The latter kind of theory is certainly worth exploring. It is not novel, of course, to suggest that perceptual development is a matter of differentiation. As phenomenal description this was asserted by some of the gestalt psychologists, notably Koffka and Lewin. (Just how differentiation was related to organization, however, was not clear.) What *is* novel is to suggest that perceptual development is always a matter of the correspondence between stimulation and perception—that it is strictly governed by the relationships of the perceiver to his environment. The rule would be that, as the number of distinct percepts a man can have increases, so also the number of different physical objects to which they are specific increases. An example may clarify this rule. One man, let us say, can identify sherry, champagne, white wine, and red wine. He has four percepts in response to the total possible range of stimulation. Another man can identify a dozen types of sherry, each with many varieties, and numerous blends, and so on for the others. He has four thousand percepts in response to the range of stimulation. The crucial question to ask about this example of differentiated perception is its relation to stimulation.

Stimulus is a slippery term in psychology. Properly speaking stimulation is always energy at receptors, that is, proximal stimulation. An individual is surrounded by an array of energy and immersed in a flow of it. This sea of stimulation consists of variation and invariants, patterns and transformations, some of which we know how to isolate and control and others of which we do not. An experimenter chooses or constructs a sample of this energy when he performs a psychological experiment. But it is easy for him to forget this fact and to assume that a glass of wine is a stimulus when actually it is a complex of radiant and chemical energies which is the stimulus. When the psychologist refers to stimuli as cues, or clues, or carriers of information he is skipping lightly over the problem of how stimuli come to *function* as cues. Energies do not have cue properties unless and until the differences in energy have correspondingly different effects in perception. The total range of physical stimulation is very rich in complex variables and these are theoretically capable of becoming cues and constituting information. This is just where learning comes in.

All responses to stimulation, including perceptual responses, manifest some degree of specificity, and, inversely, some degree of nonspecificity.

The gentleman who is discriminating about his wine shows a high specificity of perception, whereas the crude fellow who is not shows a low specificity. A whole class of chemically different fluids is equivalent for the latter individual; he can't tell the difference between claret, burgundy, and chianti; his perceptions are relatively undifferentiated. What has the first man learned that the second man has not? Associations? Memories? Attitudes? Inferences? Has he learned to have perceptions instead of merely sensations? Perhaps, but a simpler statement might be made. The statement is that he has learned to taste and smell more of the qualities of wine, that is, he discriminates more of the variables of chemical stimulation. If he is a genuine connoisseur and not a fake, one combination of such variables can evoke a specific response of naming or identifying and another combination can evoke a different specific response. He can consistently apply nouns to the different fluids of a class and he can apply adjectives to the differences between the fluids.

The classical theory of perceptual learning, with its emphasis on subjective determination of perception in contrast to stimulus determination, gets its plausibility from experiments on errors in form perception, from the study of illusions and systematic distortions, and from the fact of individual differences in and social influences on perception. The learning process is assumed to have occurred in the past life of the experimental subject; it is seldom controlled by the experimenter. These are *not* learning experiments insofar as they do not control practice or take measures before and after training. True perceptual learning experiments are limited to those concerned with discrimination.

One source of evidence about discriminative learning comes from the study of the cues for verbal learning. The analysis of these cues made by one of the authors in terms of stimulus generalization and differentiation (4) suggests the present line of thought. It has also led to a series of experiments concerned with what we call *identifying responses*. Motor reactions. verbal reactions, or percepts, we assume, are identifying responses if they are in specific correspondence with a set of objects or events. Code learning (13), aircraft recognition (7), and learning to name the faces of one's friends are all examples of an increasingly specific correspondence between the items of stimulation presented and the items of response recorded. As a given response gains univocality, the percept is reported to gain in the feeling of familiarity or recognition and to acquire meaning.

An Illustrative Experiment[2]

In order to provide a clear example of such learning, we studied the development of a single identifying response. The S was presented with a visual item consisting of a nonsense "scribble"; his recognition of it was tested when it was interspersed

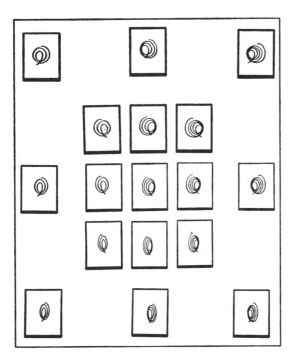

Figure 17.1
Nonsense items differing in three dimensions of variation.

in a series of similar scribbles, and then the single showing and the multiple presentation were repeated until the item could be identified. We devised a set of 17 scribbles intended to be indistinguishable from the critical item on the first trial, and another set of 12 items intended to be distinguishable from the critical item on the first trial.

The items which had to be differentiated are shown in Fig 17.1. The critical item, a four-coil scribble, is in the center and 16 other items are arranged outward from it. The eighteenth item (a reversal of the critical item) is not shown. It may be noted that there are three dimensions of variation from the critical item: (a) number of coils—three, four, or five, (b) horizontal compression or stretching, and (c) orientation or right-left reversal. The latter two kinds of variation were produced by photographic transformation. There are three degrees of coil frequency, three degrees of compression, and two types of orientation, which yields 18 items. Since one of these is the critical item, 17 remain for use in the experiment. The reader may observe that when these differences are verbally specified and the figures are displayed for immediate comparison, as in Fig. 1, they are clearly distinguishable. The Ss of the experiment, however, saw the items only in succession.

The 12 additional items presented on each recognition trial are shown in Fig. 17.2. Each differs from every other and from all of the set of 18. The differences

Figure 17.2
Nonsense items differing in many dimensions of variation.

from the scribbles were intended to be sufficient to make them appear different at the outset to Ss with a normal amount of experience with drawn forms. The 30 items (12 plus 18) were printed photographically on stiff 2 in. × 4 in. cards with black borders, and made into a pack. The material available for any one learning trial consisted of the critical item plus a shuffled pack of cards among which were interspersed four replicas of the critical item.

The S was shown the critical item for about 5 sec. and told that some of the items in the pack would be exactly like the one shown. The series of 34 was then presented each with a 3-sec. exposure and S was asked to report which of them were the same figure. The identifying response recorded was any report such as "that's it" or "this is the one I saw before." The S was never told whether an identification was correct or incorrect. A record was kept not only of the identifying responses, but also of any spontaneous *descriptions* offered by S, which were later classified as *naming* responses and *qualifying* responses.

At the end of the first trial the critical figure was presented a second time and another shuffled pack was run through. The procedure of examining a figure and then trying to identify it when mixed with a series including figures of both great and little similarity was continued until S made only the four correct identifications in one trial. Three groups took part in the experiment: 12 adults, 10 older children ($8\frac{1}{2}$ to 11 years), and 10 younger children (6 to 8 years).

Results

In this experiment, learning is taken to be an increase in the specificity of an identifying response or, in other words, a decrease in the size of the class of items that will elicit the response. The data therefore consist of the

Table 17.1
Increase in Specificity of an Identifying Response for Three Age Groups

Variable	Adults (N = 12)	Older children (N = 10)	Younger Children (N = 10)
Mean number of undifferentiated items on first trial	3.0	7.9	13.4
Mean number of trials required for completely specific response	3.1	4.7	6.7*
Percentage of erroneous recognitions for items differing in *one* quality	17	27	53
Percentage of erroneous recognitions for items differing in *two* qualities	2	7	35
Percentage of erroneous recognitions for items differing in *three* qualities	0.7	2	28

*Only two of the younger children achieved a completely specific identification. The mean number of undifferentiated items on the last trial was still 3.9.

number of items (out of a probable maximum of 17) reacted to as if they were the critical figure. As will be evident, this class of undifferentiated items was reduced as a result of repetition. The three groups of Ss, however, began to learn at very different levels and learned at very different rates. The results are given in Table 17.1. For adults, the class of undifferentiated items at the outset was small (Mean = 3.0), and only a few trials were needed before this class was reduced to the critical item alone (Mean = 3.1). Two of these adults were able to make no other than correct identifying responses on the first trial. Both were psychologists who could have had previous acquaintance with nonsense figures. The learning task was so easy for this group that not much information about the learning process could be obtained. At the other extreme, however, the younger children "recognized" nearly all of the scribbles on the first trial (Mean = 13.4), which is to say, that the class of undifferentiated items was large. The number of trials needed to reduce this class to the correct item was so great that most of the Ss could not be required to complete the experiment. Two out of 10 reached the criterion, but for the remainder the trials had to be stopped for reasons of fatigue. After an average of 6.7 trials the mean number of undifferentiated items was still 3.9. One child had so much difficulty with the task that E finally gave differential reinforcement by saying "right" or "wrong" after each presentation of a card. Although this procedure helped, wholly specific identifications were never achieved. The failures of the younger children to discriminate did not seem to be due merely to "inattention"; they understood that they were to select only the figures which were *exactly* the same as the critical figure.

For the older children (between $8\frac{1}{2}$ and 11 years of age) the results were intermediate between these extremes. For them the particular task and the particular items were neither too hard nor too easy. The average number of undifferentiated items on the first trial was 7.9, and all children succeeded in reducing this to a single item after a mean of 4.7 trials.

Table 17.1 also indicates for each group an important fact about the unspecific responses: they tend to occur more often as the differences between the test item and the critical item become fewer. As Fig. 17.1 shows, a given scribble may differ in *one* quality or dimension (thickness, coil frequency, or orientation), or in *two* of these qualities, or in all *three* of them. Five of the scribbles differ in one feature, eight differ in two features, and four differ in three features. It will be recalled that the 12 additional forms shown in Fig. 17.2 differed from the critical item with respect to *more* than three features. Amount of difference can be usefully stated as number of differing qualities or, conversely, amount of sameness as the fewness of differing qualities.[3] The lower half of Table 17.1 gives the percentage of occurrence of false recognitions in the case of scribbles with one quality different, with two qualities different, and with three qualities different. These percentages are based on the number of times the items in question were presented during the whole series of trials. The "dissimilar" figures, which had many qualities different, yielded a zero percentage of false recognitions except for a few scattered instances among the younger children.

Discussion

The results show clearly that the kind of perceptual learning hypothesized has occurred in this experiment. A stimulus item starts out by being indistinguishable from a whole class of items in the stimulus universe tested, and ends by being distinguishable from all of them. The evidence for this assertion is that the specificity of *S*'s identifying response has increased. What has happened to produce this result?

The *S*s were encouraged to describe all the items of each series as they were presented, and a special effort was made to obtain and record these spontaneous verbal responses for seven of the older children. In general they tended to fall into two types, either naming responses or qualifying responses. Considering only the responses to the 17 scribbles, the record showed that the frequency of the latter type increased during the progress of learning. Examples of the former are nouns like *figure 6, curl, spiral, scroll*. Examples of the latter are adjectival phrases like *too thin, rounder, reversed*. It is notable that the latter are responses not to the item as such but to the relation between it and the critical item. They are analogous to differential judgments in a psychophysical experiment. An adjective, in general, is a response which is specific not to an object but to a property of two or more objects. It is likely, then, that the development of a specific response to an item is correlated with the development of specific responses to the qualities, dimensions, or variables that relate it to other items. The implication is that, for a child to identify an object, he must be able to identify the differences between it and other objects, or at least that *when* he can identify an object he *also* can identify its properties.

The verbal reactions of the children to the 17 scribbles, both naming and qualifying, could be categorized by E as specific or nonspecific to the item in question. These judgments were necessarily subjective, but they were carried out with the usual precautions. Although a single adjective cannot be specific to a single item, a combination of adjectives can be. An example of a nonspecific reaction is "another curlicue," and of a specific reaction is "this one is thinner and rounder." The latter sort may be considered a spontaneously developing, identifying reaction, not of the "that's it" type, it is true, but nevertheless fulfilling our definition. The mean number of such verbal reactions on the first trial was 7.7 out of 17, or 45 percent. The mean number of such reactions on the last trial was 16.5. or 97 percent. This suggests that, as a single identifying response becomes increasingly specific to one member of a group of similar items, verbal identifying responses also tend to become specific to the other members of the group. As the class of indistinguishable items which will elicit one response is diminished, the number of responses which can be made to the class increases.

Other evidence

Another source of experimental evidence about perceptual learning comes from psychophysics. Contrary to what might be expected, psychophysical experimenters over the years have shown a lively interest in perceptual learning, or at least in the bettering of perceptual judgments with practice. One of the authors has recently surveyed this neglected literature insofar as it concerns improvement of perception or increase in perceptual skills (5). There is a great quantity of evidence about progressive change in acuity, variability, and accuracy of perception, including both relative judgments and absolute judgments. It proves beyond a shadow of doubt that the notion of fixed thresholds for a certain set of innate sensory dimensions is oversimplified. Discrimination gets better with practice, both with and without knowledge of results. An example may be taken from the two-point threshold on the skin.

As long ago as 1858 it was discovered that there is a certain distance at which two points are felt double by a blindfolded subject that is characteristic of the area of the skin tested. At the same time, it was found that only a few hours of practice in this discrimination had the effect of reducing the distance to half of what it had been (17). Later experiments showed that the lowering of the threshold continued slowly for thousands of trials; for instance, it might go from 30 mm. to 5 mm. during four weeks of training. Moreover, the improved discrimination transferred to other untrained areas of the skin, transfers being nearly complete for the bilaterally symmetrical area. It was found that blind subjects had very much lower thresholds than seeing subjects even at the beginning of testing (12, 18). The experimental improvement was largely lost after a period of disuse. It seemed to depend on confirmation or correction of the judgment, or, in the absence of that, on the development of a sort of scale from "close together" to "far apart" (5). It is clear that any theory of supposedly distinct sensations of oneness and twoness never had any support from these data. As one writer put it, the observer adopts different and finer *criteria* of doubleness. What might these criteria be? We suggest that the stimulation is complex, not simple, and that the observer continues to discover higher-order variables of stimulation in it. The percept becomes differentiated.

Conclusion

There is no evidence in all of this literature on perceptual learning, nor is there evidence in the experiment reported in the last section, to *require* the theory that an accurate percept is one which is enriched by past experience, whereas a less accurate percept is one *not* enriched by past experience. Repetition or practice is necessary for the development of the improved percept, but there is no proof that it incorporates memories. The notion that learned perception is less and less determined by external stimulation as learning progresses finds no support in these experiments. The observer sees and hears more, but this may be not because he imagines more, or infers more, or assumes more, but because he discriminates more. He is more sensitive to the variables of the stimulus array. Perhaps the ability to summon up memories is merely incidental to perceptual learning and the ability to differentiate stimuli is basic. Perhaps the dependence of perception on learning and the dependence of perception on stimulation are not contradictory principles after all.

This theoretical approach to perceptual learning, it must be admitted, has points of weakness as well as points of strength. It accounts for veridical perception, but it does not account for misperception. It says nothing about imagination or fantasy, or wishful thinking. It is not an obviously useful approach for the study of abnormal behavior or personality, if one is convinced that a man's perceptions are the clues to his motives. But if one is concerned instead with the practical question of whether training can affect favorably a man's perception of the world around him, a very productive field for theory and experiment is opened up.

Notes

1. This paper is a revision, with added experimental material, of one given in May 1953 at a symposium on the psychology of learning basic to problems of military training (8) conducted by the Panel on Training and Training Devices of the Research and Development Board, Washington, D.C.
2. This experiment was first reported at the meeting of the American Psychological Association in September 1950 in a paper read by Eleanor J. Gibson, and an abstract has been published (6).
3. Experiments on primary stimulus generalization have usually varied the magnitude of a *single* difference, not the number of differences, between the critical stimulus and the undifferentiated stimulus. However, our method of quantifying "amount of difference" has much to recommend it.

References

1. Bruner, J. S. Personality dynamics and the process of perceiving. In R. R. Blake & G. V. Ramsey (Eds.), *Perception: an approach to personality*. New York: Ronald, 1951. Pp. 121−147.
2. Brunswik, E. The conceptual framework of psychology. *Int. Encycl. unif. Sci.*, 1952, 1, No. 10.
3. Cantril, H., Ames, A., Jr., Hastorf, A. H., & Ittelson, W. H. Psychology and scientific research. *Science*, 1949, 110, 461−464, 491−197, 517−522.
4. Gibson, Eleanor J. A systematic application of the concepts of generalization and differentiation to verbal learning. *Psychol. Rev.*, 1940, 47, 196−229.
5. Gibson, Eleanor, J. Improvement in perceptual judgments as a function of controlled practice or training. *Psychol. Bull.*, 1953, 50, 401−431.
6. Gibson, Eleanor J., & Gibson, J. J. The identifying response: a study of a neglected form of learning. *Amer. Psychologist*, 1950, 7, 276. (Abstract)
7 Gibson, J. J. (Ed.) *Motion picture testing and research*. Washington, D.C.: Government Printing Office, 1947. (*AAF Aviat. Psychol. Program Res. Rep.*, No. 7.)
8. Gibson, J. J., & Gibson, Eleanor J. Perceptual learning in relation to training In *Symposium on psychology of learning basic to military training problems*. Dept. of Defense, HR-HTD-201-1, 1953, 151−159.
9. Hebb, D. O. *The organization of behavior*. New York: Wiley, 1949.
10. Hilgard, E. R. The role of learning in perception. In R. R. Blake & G. V. Ramsey (Eds.), *Perception: an approach to personality*. New York: Ronald, 1951. Pp. 95−120.
11. Ittelson, W. H. The constancies in perceptual theory. *Psychol. Rev.* 1951, 58, 285−294.
12. Jastrow, J. Psychological notes on Helen Keller. *Psychol. Rev.*, 1894, 1, 356−362.
13. Keller, F. S. Studies in International Morse Code. I. A new method of teaching code reception. *J. appl. Psychol.*, 1943, 27, 407−415.
14. Kilpatrick, F. P. *Human behavior from the transactional point of view*. Hanover, N. H.: Institute for Associated Research, 1952.
15. Leeper, R. A study of a neglected portion of the field of learning—the development of sensory organization. *J. genet. Psychol.*, 1935, 46, 41−75.
16. Postman, L. Toward a general theory of cognition. In J. H. Rohrer & M. Sherif (Eds.), *Social psychology at the crossroads*. New York: Harper, 1951. Pp. 242−272.
17. Volkmann, A. Ueber den Einfluss der Uebung auf das Erkennen raumlicher Distanzen. *Ber. d. Sachs. Ges. d. Wiss., math. phys. Abth.*, 1858, 10, 38−69.
18. Whipple, G. M. *Manual of mental and physical tests*. Part I. *Simpler processes*. Baltimore: Warwick and York, 1924.

Association Theory and Perceptual Learning

Leo Postman

The theoretical discussion of perceptual learning has received a welcome impetus from a recent critical analysis by Gibson and Gibson (6).[1] These writers focus on two opposing interpretations of perceptual learning which they designate as the *enrichment theory* and the *specificity theory*. Enrichment theory is presented as the embodiment of associationistic thinking about perceptual learning, whereas specificity theory represents the hypothesis of psychophysical correspondence. The Gibsons' argument is directed at a refutation of the associationistic position in general and the enrichment theory in particular. At the same time, a strong plea is made the hypothesis of psychophysical correspondence, as represented by the specificity theory. This paper will attempt to state the case for the associationistic position.

"Is perception a creative process or is it a discriminative process? Is learning a matter of enriching previously meagre sensations or is it a matter of differentiating previously vague impressions?" (6, p. 34). These are the questions to which the enrichment theory and the specificity theory are said to provide diametrically opposed answers. According to enrichment theory, perceptual learning results from the association of sensory elements with memories of past experiences. These memories may be conceived as images or as physiological traces. The essential point is that sensory elements produced by stimulation are assumed to be "enriched" by the arousal of such memories. As the fringe of associated memories grows, a constant sensory input gives rise to progressively more complex and more diversified experiences. This is Titchener's context theory or its modern equivalent. Such a view faces two major difficulties: (*a*) it perpetuates the distinction between sensation and perception, and hence inherits the thankless task of specifying the bare sensations to which memorial associations accrue; and (*b*) it implies that perception comes to be in "*decreasing correspondence with stimulation*" (6, p. 34). The richer the context which accrues to the sensory core, the further removed the percept is from the sensory data transmitted through the receptor system.

By contrast, the specificity theory holds that perceptual learning consists of the "progressive elaboration of qualities, features, and dimensions of variation" (6, p. 34). Such elaboration becomes possible because the organism responds to more and more variables of physical stimulation. Percep-

Psychological Review, 1955, 62, 438–446.

tual discrimination becomes more subtle and more refined because the stimulus variables with which it stands in psychophysical correspondence become more subtle and more refined. This view is said to avoid both of the difficulties upon which associationistic theory has foundered. It is (a) no longer necessary to distinguish between sensation and perception, for perception is from the beginning and is always a matter of psychophysical discrimination; and (b) whenever perceptual learning occurs, it means increasing rather than decreasing correspondence with the variables of stimulation. Note, however, that no mechanism is proposed to account for the progressive changes in psychophysical relationships which constitute perceptual learning. At this point, the specificity theory is essentially the statement of an assumption or expectation, viz., that all perception follows a strict law of psychophysical correspondence. If perceptions change, there *must* be changes in the effective stimulus variables.

In developing our own discussion of the theory of perceptual learning, we shall find it useful to reaffirm the historical distinction between two facets of the associationistic position: the psychological and the physiological. Psychological associationism refers to the language in which the facts of learning are stated and the experimental problems are formulated. The conception of learning as consisting of linkages between ideas, or between stimuli and responses, exemplifies psychological associationism. Experimentally, the study of learning becomes the investigation of the conditions under which such linkages are established. Physiological associationism, on the other hand, refers to a class of hypotheses concerning the mechanisms which mediate the observed changes in experience or behavior. Thus, the hypotheses that learning depends on lowered synaptic resistances or on the formation of cell assemblies are examples of physiological associationism. We would expect to find the two kinds of associationism to be highly correlated in the thinking of psychological theorists. Physiological hypotheses which are associationistic in nature will necessarily be reflected in coordinate descriptions of behavior. It is possible, however, to argue for a psychological associationism without committing one-self to a specific physiological hypothesis. Such is precisely the position in which we shall find ourselves with respect to the problem of perceptual learning.

In their critique of the associationistic point of view, Gibson and Gibson have bracketed both its psychological and physiological implications. While stressing this distinction, we shall state our disagreement with the Gibsons' thesis on three counts: (a) The enrichment hypothesis discussed by them represents merely one historical stage in the associationistic approach to perceptual learning, and in some of its major aspects has long since been superseded by the formulations of behavior theory. Associationistic theory need not stand or fall with the historical version of the enrichment hypothesis. (b) Experimental methodology favors a formulation of the facts and problems of perceptual learning in the language of psychological associationism. (c) The specificity theory fails to generate testable hypotheses concerning the conditions and mechanisms of perceptual learning. We shall conclude that the specificity hypothesis has failed to challenge the associationistic position on either logical or empirical grounds.

Associationism and the Enrichment Hypothesis

The enrichment hypothesis, as exemplified by Titchener's context theory, represents the associationism of the structuralists and the introspectionists. The hypothesis had both a psychological and physiological component, and Titchener was careful to distinguish between them. Psychologically, a perception was regarded as a complex mental event which resolves into a number of sensations supplemented by images. Perceptual learning has occurred when an imaginal fringe has accrued to the sensory core, so that the complement of images "puts more in the perception than the sensory stimuli can account for" (12, p. 115). Both the nucleus and the fringe can be discovered by introspection. But, adds Titchener, "we perceive more than is furnished us by sensations and images .... every perception is shaped and moulded by the action of nerve-forces which show themselves neither in sensation nor in image" (12, p. 115). The sensations and the images are the descriptive psychological data; the causative physiological factors behind them are dispositions in the central nervous system. In fact, in the case of well-practiced perceptions, the imaginal fringe may all but disappear and the meaning of a percept be carried by the neural dispositions alone. Thus, Titchener draws a sharp distinction between the givens of consciousness and the neural processes underlying them, between the "law of nervous action" and the "law of mental connection." He quotes with approval James's dictum: "Association, so far as the word stands for an *effect*, is between things *thought of* .... And so far as association stands for a cause, it is between *processes in the brain*—it is these which, by being associated in certain ways, determine what successive objects shall be thought" (9, p. 554). And Titchener sums up succinctly, "*The brain associates and meanings are associated*" (12, p. 149).

Thus, the structuralist position encompassed both a psychological and a physiological associationism. The arguments of Gibson and Gibson are directed against both these historical views. However, contemporary associationists have lost interest in Titchener's "law of mental connection" and have substituted for it a new psychological associationism. At the same time, many of them have continued the search for a "law of nervous action." We must evaluate the validity of the Gibsons' arguments not against the historical position of structuralism but against the psychological and physiological associationism of present behavior theory.

Psychological Associationism and the Criteria of Perceptual Learning

Associationists have long since left behind the introspective pursuit of bare sensations and accruing imaginal contexts. The timeworn arguments of the behaviorists and operationists which led to rejection of the introspective method need not be repeated here. The contemporary associationist deals neither with sensory cores nor with images. On the contrary, he would naturally begin by formulating the problem of perceptual learning in terms of stimuli and responses. The behavioral criterion of perceptual learning is a change in the nature of the responses evoked by a particular configuration or sequence of stimuli, where stimuli are defined in terms of physical operations. The two major classes of such responses with which we are concerned in experiments on perceptual learning with human Ss are (a) identifying responses, such as naming or labeling; and (b) discriminative responses such as *same* or *different*, *larger* or *smaller*, *higher* or *lower*—in short, the types of responses which we obtain in conventional psychophysical experiments.[2] We assert that perceptual learning has taken place when the relative frequencies of such responses undergo significant changes under controlled conditions of practice.

Experimentally, then, perceptual learning is defined by changes in stimulus-response relationships under controlled conditions of practice. We see no alternative formulation, short of recourse to introspection or the vague language of phenomenology. Once the problem has been so formulated, the relevance of the variables governing stimulus-response association to perceptual learning becomes clear. Examination of the literature shows that such principles as frequency, recency, effect, and associative interference are relevant to perceptual learning just as they are to verbal and motor learning (5, 10). The psychological associationism of a stimulus-response formulation serves to emphasize the continuity between perceptual learning, and other types of learning, with respect to both experimental operations and functional relationships. Descriptively, perceptual learning *is* the attachment of new responses, or a change in the frequency of responses, to particular configurations or sequence of stimuli.

There are undoubtedly those who will say that insistence on a stimulus-response formulation robs the study of perception of its very core and, indeed, its fascination, for it looks away from the richness and subtlety of perceptual experience. We do not share this anxiety. There is no reason why all the valid facts of perception cannot eventually be translated into the language of stimulus-response relationships. In the meantime, the unpopular pedantry of insisting on stimulus-response formulations may serve a healthy purpose. In arguing for a stimulus-response formulation of perceptual experiments, Graham writes: "... it may be argued that it does not provide a description of perception. Certainly it does not describe *perception* if by that term is meant any area of knowledge that exists between the limits of sensory nerve impulses on the one hand and the language responses ('private experience') of the patient on the other. Such a usage, of course, deprives the term of any significance or specificity" (7, p. 69). We agree with Graham that a stimulus-response formulation helps to make perception an integral part of the study of behavior. By the same token, the problem of perceptual learning, formulated in terms of changing stimulus-response relationships, becomes part of the broader problem of associative learning.

The psychological associationism of stimulus and response avoids the two major difficulties which were raised in criticism of the psychological associationism of Titchener. (*a*) As Graham has pointed out, in terms of a stimulus-response formulation, "any presumed differences between 'sensory' and 'perceptual' research evaporate. Both types of research give rise to the same sort of stimulus-behavior function" (7, p. 69). (*b*) As for the question of whether learning results in increasing or decreasing psychophysical correspondence, the present formulation does not require us to give an a priori answer. We may adopt one of two positions. We can, as a matter of definition, restrict the term *learning* to those cases in which controlled practice results in improved discrimination. Preferably, however, we can leave the question open, and let the facts decide whether and under what conditions changes produced by training do or do not result in improved discrimination. The question of psychophysical correspondence cannot be decided by fiat except at the peril of begging the question.

The Problem of Associative Mechanisms

One may well object at this point that we have defended the associationistic position by means of a restatement in operational terms which avoids the problem on which the analysis of Gibson and Gibson has focused, viz., the problem of enrichment vs. differentiation. However, our insistence on a reformulation of the problem of perceptual learning in stimulus-response terms is an essential step in the development of the argument for two major reasons. (*a*) It was necessary to divorce once and for all the associationistic position from the concepts and methods of introspectionism, modern or old-fashioned. (*b*) It was equally essential to emphasize the fact that a theory of perceptual learning, of whatever persuasion, cannot sidestep the fact that discriminative *responses*—words, movements, autonomic responses, etc.—change as a result of training. Gibson and Gibson appear to take it for granted that appropriate responses will be somehow attached to the differentiated perceptions developed in the course of learning. We wish to stress the fact that the changes in response are part and parcel of the problem of perceptual learning. The need to account for changes in response inevitably endows the problem of perceptual learning with an associative component.

The problem of mediating mechanisms, however, remains. One may, to be sure, rest content with the psychological associationism of stimulus and response, and pursue the specifications of the conditions of perceptual learning within this framework. I take it that this is essentially the position advocated by Graham. For those who have, like the present writer, failed to be convinced by the explanatory powers of current theories of mediation, the position has much to recommend for itself. It is true, nevertheless, that there is an old and continuing tradition of physiological associationism, and we must examine its logical status in the light of the criticisms advanced by Gibson and Gibson. Historically, the enrichment hypothesis does, indeed, represent a major strand in the tradition of physiological associationism. In evaluating the physiological facet of the enrichment hypothesis, we must stress again that a "law of nervous action" can stand as an independent hypothesis, divorced from assumed correlations with introspective content. There are modern formulations of the enrichment hypothesis which confirm its independence of introspective data. A good example is provided by Spence's schematic analysis of perception into a series of events, beginning with sense reception and followed by the redintegration of past sensory events, which in turn leads to anticipatory responses, manipulations, or verbal responses (11). In Spence's analysis, however, the associations aroused by the sensory events have the status of hypothetical constructs anchored to stimulus variables and observable responses, and do not depend for their validity on introspective or phenomenological evidence. It is possible to hold to a physiological enrichment hypothesis without implying an introspective distinction between sensation and perception. Nor does such a physiological associationism prejudge the question of increasing or decreasing psychophysical correspondence.

Physiological associationism does not necessarily take the form of an enrichment hypothesis. Consider Hebb's neurophysiological theory of perceptual learning. The fundamental assumptions of the theory are associationistic, but the process of perceptual learning is not described as the enrichment of invariant sensory events but rather in terms of progressive modifications of the central activities produced by stimulation. "According to the schema, the perception is constituted by a temporal sequence of activity in supra-sensory (or association-area) structures which owe their organization to change at the synapse" (8, p. 102). The changes at the synapse which constitute the physiological mechanism of learning govern the central transformations of sensory input.

The main point to be stressed concerning such physiological hypotheses is that one may assume an associative mechanism of perceptual learning without insisting that the events which are associated retain their identity or remain recoverable in perceptual analysis. This point is by no means new in the history of associationism. In contrasting the mental chemistry of John Stuart Mill with the mental compounding of James Mill, Boring writes: "... we never know about any element that *all* which we think ideally would enable us to predict the laws of the compound. We have always to study the compound directly, independently of its known or supposed elemental composition ... even when we know the generative process, we cannot deduce the law of the resultant: those laws must be found in every case from direct experiment" (1, p. 230 f.). While Boring's remarks are directed specifically at the difference between two versions of psychological associationism, they apply to hypotheses about mediating mechanisms as well. Associationistic hypotheses about the mechanism of perceptual learning may be formulated without affirming that the associated elements must retain their identity in the resultant. What they must do is entail testable predictions about the resultant. Hebb and his associates have, indeed, been able to make specific predictions concerning the development of perceptual acuity which lend support to their assumptions concerning the generative process (8, p. 49 f.).

It must be recognized, however, that the body of facts supporting associationistic theories of the *mechanism* of perceptual learning remains small. For example, the perceptual constancies which are a mainstay of Helmholtzian empiricism continue to present a puzzle to physiological associationism or, for that matter, to any physiological theory of perception. It is true that the organism acts as though it had learned to make inferences about sizes, colors, and forms, but what the associative processes might be which underlie such inferential learning is far from clear. We can specify the cues which the organism appears to use in the attainment of the distal properties of objects (3), but we know little about how the organism comes to use certain stimuli as cues or about the mechanisms which make the utilization of these cues possible. It is easy to agree with Brunswik (4) that hypotheses about specific mediating mechanisms of perception may be premature at the present stage of development.

Much of the experimental work on perceptual learning has been done under conditions of impoverished stimulation. In such cases it is particularly plausible to conceive of a neural redintegrative process initiated by a fragmentary sensory input. However, the components of the redintegrative chain have never been sufficiently specified to constitute a testable theory of mediating mechanisms. This essential vagueness and invulnerability is shared by other physiological and neurological theories of perceptual learning, such as, for example, the gestalt theory of traces. The experimental facts have been all too ineffective in checking the elaboration of physiological fancies. However, to recognize that physiological associationism is as yet in a highly undeveloped state is very different from denying its possibility on a priori or logical grounds. We see no compelling reasons for such rejection.

Differentiation vs. Association

From the defense of associationism—psychological associationism now and physiological associationism as a possibility for the future—we turn to a re-examination of the specificity hypothesis. The critical difference between associationism and the specificity point of view appears to concern the degree of psychophysical correspondence assumed by the two positions. According to the specificity hypothesis, perceptual learning consists of "responding to variables of stimulation not previously responded to," and hence, "perceptual development is always a matter of correspondence between stimulation and perception" (6, p. 34). By contrast, association theory is said to stress the enrichment of constant stimulus effects by the organism. It is our contention that the specificity position can be maintained only at the expense of avoiding or begging the question of learning.

What are the exact implications of the statement that perceptual learning consists of *responding* to variables of stimulation not previously responded to? If we take this statement at its face value, it would seem to assert that as a result of practice with certain stimuli new responses are associated with these stimuli. These responses, whatever their specific nature, have the function of mediating the differentiation of new qualities. We might, for example, conceive of such responses as receptor adjustments ensuring optimal exposure to the stimuli, such as focusing, scanning, etc. It is clear, however, that such an interpretation is not intended by the specificity theory, for perceptual learning is said to consist not of the attachment of responses to stimuli but of the elaboration of new qualities. Thus, contrasting the connoisseur of wines with a man whose untutored palate cannot tell the difference between Chianti and claret, Gibson and Gibson write: "What has the first man learned that the second man has not? . . . he has learned to taste and smell more of the qualities of wine, that is, he discriminates more of the variables of chemical stimulation" (6, p. 35). But if his learning is mediated neither by new receptor adjustments nor by centrally aroused associations, how are we to account for the acquisition of new differential responses? Surely we cannot assume that the stimuli have changed, for the stimuli are whatever they are. The fact that the organism has learned to discriminate more qualities is *the very fact that we need to explain*. The end result—the improvement in discrimination—cannot be accepted as a description of the learning process. It appears that the specificity hypothesis achieves its overriding emphasis on psychophysical correspondence by avoiding the critical problem of perceptual learning, viz., the nature of the processes which mediate the increased differentiation of the stimuli. Improvement in discrimination cannot be invoked to explain improvement in discrimination.

Inherent Limitations of the Specificity Hypothesis

Even though the specificity hypothesis may not qualify as a theory of perceptual *learning*, one may wish to uphold it as a descriptive generalization to the effect that after practice as well as before practice "the stimulus input contains within it everything that the percept has" (6, p. 34). Quite apart from the problem of mediating mechanisms, this generalization would assert that all the *results* of perceptual learning can be described adequately —and, indeed, exhaustively—as changes in psychophysical correspondence. Although such a generalization is logically tenable, its empirical adequacy is doubtful. The inherent limitations of the doctrine of psychophysical correspondence are brought out most clearly with reference to the perception of signs and symbols.

The perception of sign properties
Environmental events do not occur in complete independence of each other, the occurrence of one event implies, with some degree of probability, the occurrence of others. The existence of these sequential linkages makes it possible for the organism to learn means-end relationships, to respond to objects as signs of absent significates (13, p. 135 f.). Tolman and Brunswik speak of the causal texture of the environment in which the organism is immersed and which is reflected in his perceptions and cognitions (14). A general theory of perceptual learning must account for the development of sign perception. But the discrimination of sign properties necessarily depends on commerce with environmental sequences. Hence, sign perception would appear to be, almost by definition, an associative phenomenon: an object can be perceived as a sign only by virtue of the fact that the organism has associated the sign object with the object signified. The fact of sign perception makes it difficult to accept the impassable barrier between perception and memory erected by the specificity theorists. It is, indeed, the analysis of sign perception which led Tolman to conclude that "the differences between perceptions and mnemonizations, are probably, in actuality, always differences in degree only ... there are probably no actual cases of pure perceptions i.e., perceptions unaided by

any memory—save in new-born organisms" (13, p. 139). The only alternative open to the specificity theorist is to assert that the facts of environmental linkage somehow become part of the *physical* stimulus pattern which constitutes the sign object! This would be tantamount to saying that the organism's past experiences somehow become translated into physical properties of stimuli, or at least that the organism comes to discover stimulus variables which carry the sign properties of the stimulus object in all their specific details. Every possible stimulus would have to have physical properties adequate for signifiying every possible significate.

The perception of symbols

Consideration of the perception of symbols similarly points to a breakdown of the specificity hypothesis. An important segment of the man-made perceptual world consists of symbols, of which words and numbers are the most familiar and frequent. Here are marks and sounds which the individual learns to perceive so that they carry meaning and significance. This is a case of perceptual learning par excellence, the environmental determination of which cannot be questioned. Little as we may know about the development of symbol perception, the very facts seem to demand an associationistic interpretation. Marks and sounds which are initially meaningless and undifferentiated come to be discriminated and identified, by virtue of their appearance and usage in specific sequences and contexts. Again the specificity theory would have to maintain that all that is encompassed in the recognition or identification of a letter, a word, or a series of numbers or mathematical symbols is somehow carried by high-order stimulus variables. And, indeed, since any arbitrary mark or sound can be made into a symbol, all possible marks and sounds would have to have physical properties that can carry all possible connotations!

Thus the historical problem of meaning in perception raises serious difficulties for the specificity position. It is precisely here that stimulus-response analysis comes into its own. As Boring pointed out in discussing the behavioristic analysis of meaning, "Response is the context which gives the stimulus its meaning for the responding organism. One sees, therefore, that a theory of perception lies implicit in modern psychological positivism" (2, p. 18 f.). A theory of perceptual learning is equally implied. The organism has learned to perceive the meaning of a stimulus when it has learned to make the appropriate response.

Summary

We have examined two contrasting approaches to the problem of perceptual learning—traditional associationism and the specificity hypothesis of

Gibson and Gibson, which ascribes all perceptual learning to the increasing effectiveness of stimulus variables. The case for the associationistic position has been reaffirmed, and the adequacy of the specificity formulation has been questioned. The argument stresses three major points. (*a*) Perceptual learning is a problem of behavior change, and experimentally reduces to the study of stimulus-response associations. (*b*) Associationistic hypotheses about the mechanism of perceptual learning can be entertained without reference to introspective evidence, without commitment to a particular epistomological position and without prejudice to the problem of psychophysical correspondence. (*c*) The specificity hypothesis assumes, but does not account for, improvement in discrimination, and does not entail a testable theory of perceptual learning.

Notes

1. Paper read before a joint session of Section I of the AAAS and the Western Psychological Association, Berkeley, December, 1954.
2. As I have suggested elsewhere (10), our conclusions concerning the parameters of perceptual discrimination gain in generality if they are based on observations using more than one class of discriminatory responses.

References

1. Boring, E. G. *A history of experimental psychology.* (2nd Ed.) New York: Appleton-Century-Crofts, 1950.
2. Boring, E. G. *Sensation and perception in the history of experimental psychology.* New York: Appleton-Century, 1942.
3. Brunswik, E. Systematic and representative design of psychological experiments. *Univer. of Calif. Syllabus Ser.,* No. 304, 1947.
4. Brunswik, E. *The conceptual framework of psychology.* Chicago: Univer. of Chicago Press, 1952.
5. Gibson, E. J. Improvement in perceptual judgments as a function of controlled practice or training. *Psychol. Bull.,* 1953, 50, 401–431.
6. Gibson, J. J., & Gibson, E. J. Perceptual learning—differentiation or enrichment? *Psychol. Rev.,* 1955, 62, 32–41.
7. Graham, C. H. Behavior and the psychophysical methods: an analysis of some recent experiments. *Psychol. Rev.,* 1952, 59, 62–70.
8. Hebb, D. O. *Organization of behavior.* New York: Wiley, 1949.
9. James, W. *Principles of psychology, Vol. I.* New York: Dover, 1950.
10. Postman, L. Experimental analysis of motivational factors in perception. In *Current theory and research in motivation.* Lincoln: Univer. of Nebraska Press, 1952.
11. Spence, K. W. Cognitive versus stimulus-response theories of learning. *Psychol. Rev.,* 1950, 57, 159–172.
12. Titchener, E. B. *A beginner's psychology.* New York: Macmillan, 1915.
13. Tolman, E. C. *Purposive behavior in animals and men.* New York: Appleton-Century, 1932.
14. Tolman, E. C., & Brunswik, E. The organism and the causal texture of the environment. *Psychol. Rev.,* 1935, 42, 43–77.

What Is Learned in Perceptual Learning?
A Reply to Professor Postman

James J. Gibson, Eleanor J. Gibson

Contemporary association theory, says Professor Postman, formulates the problem of perceptual learning in terms of associations between stimuli and responses instead of associations between sensations and memory images. He seems to admit the theoretical difficulties in the way of an enrichment theory when the associations refer to phenomenal experience, but he implies that they are avoided when the associations refer to S-R connections. Here lies our main disagreement, for we do not believe that the difficulties can be so easily avoided. By reformulating the problem, can the associationist escape a reformulated difficulty? Professor Postman may not have to face the issue of whether perceptual learning is the enriching or the differentiating of experience, but he has to face another issue—whether such learning is a change in the attachment of responses to stimuli or an increase in the specificity of responses to stimuli.

Our critic should not suggest that the differentiation hypothesis we proposed is limited to conscious perception, or that it cannot be given a stimulus-response formulation. We believe it can be stated either in the language of phenomenology or in the language of behavior theory. The useful portions of both are intertranslatable. In the fable of the two wine-bibbers (perhaps from California and New York, respectively) we were at some pains to put the abstruse contrast between a tutored and an untutored palate in strict stimulus response terms. And in the sample experiment we offered, concerning the development of an isolated identifying response, the procedure and the outcome were stated in these terms—namely, that there resulted an increased specificity of response to stimulation accompanied by an increase in the ability to respond differentially to the dimensional variables of the stimuli. An interesting thing about this outcome, however, was, that it is also formulable in terms of what the subjects were aware of.

Professor Postman objects to the differentiation hypothesis for perceptual learning, presumably even in S-R terms, because no mechanism is proposed to account for the progressive change. It "begs the question" of learning; it does not explain *how* learning occurs. He must imply that the association hypothesis can account for the change and does explain how. But he himself, when discussing the difference between psychological and physiological associationism betrays a certain lack of confidence in the explanatory power of the concept. It is true that the history of psychology is full of "laws of association" having empirical validity, and that there are as yet no accepted "laws of differentiation" or "laws of stimulus-response specificity." But the age and respectability of the term "association" should not give it more explanatory power than it has. Our alternative hypothesis is not a theory but only the promise of a theory, and its explanatory value remains to be seen. It points to facts the explanation of which must be sought. It is concerned with the question of what is learned in perceptual learning, not how it occurs, or at least not as yet. "What is learned?" is the first question to ask, we think; the question of the mechanism is secondary.

Even learning theorists who limit their research to animal behavior have been arguing the fundamental question of what learning is instead of how it occurs. Considering the performance of an animal before, during, and after practice, what *kind* of change in performance exists? Only if this is understood does the psychologist know what to try to explain. The "what is learned?" debate has so-far been concerned with the response side of the stimulus-response formula. If a psychology of perceptual learning is to develop along with a psychology of motor learning the question must be faced on the stimulus side. This was the question explicitly formulated in our original paper. In what sense do we learn to perceive?

Professor Postman has his own idea of what perceptual learning is. He believes that it is "a change in the nature of responses evoked by ... stimuli". It is also described on the same page as "changes in stimulus-response relationships under controlled conditions of practice" or, a little later) as "the attachment of new responses, or a change in the frequency of responses, to particular configurations or sequences of stimuli." The emphasis is wholly on the change in the responses. We argue that, where perceptual learning is concerned, it ought to be on the change in what the organism responds *to*. We suggested that perceptual learning consists of responding to variables of stimulation not previously responded to. We believe that the emphasis on change in the effective stimuli for responses will greatly increase the explanatory power of S-R theory. The stimulus can no longer be thought of as a bit of energy at a single receptor, true, but it never should have been so conceived in the first place. The organism is surrounded by energies of every sort and description. How they function as cues—that is, how certain variables and variations of this energy come to be specifically responded to—is the basic problem for perceptual learning. Just here is where psychophysics can help. Classical psychophysics has always been concerned with the correspondence between variables of energy and variables of response, although it was a serious mistake to suppose that the correspondence was innate or immutable.

The above quoted descriptions of perceptual learning, if taken as definitions, are not consistent with one another. It is said to be a *change*, either in the nature of responses, or in the frequency of responses, or in the stimulus-response relationships. But it is also said to be an *attachment* of responses to stimuli. This term reveals the strain of associationist thinking which we criticized and called the enrichment hypothesis. The changes in S-R relationships are not adequately described by speaking of the attaching, or connecting, or the forming of bonds between stimuli and responses The inadequacy is evident if we inquire what is *new* in learning—new responses or new stimuli? Or is it merely the connections that are new? The change in S-R relationships that occurs with learning, we suggest, is one of progressive specification and abstraction. The organism discriminates and conceptualizes at the same time that he elaborates his repertory of responses. If both stimuli and responses are to be conceived as "molar" rather than "molecular," as Postman should be willing to admit, the change cannot be conceived as one of attachment between entities.

The main difficulty in the way of the traditional enrichment theory is its implication that learning involves a decreasing psychophysical correspondence between perception and stimulation. But the associationism of stimulus and response, Postman says, avoids this difficulty. Does it? We suggest that it only refuses to face the difficulty. Postman himself pleads that he does not wish to prejudge the question of increasing or decreasing correspondence between perception and stimulation. He suggests that we let the facts decide whether practice does or does not result in improved discrimination. He will assert that perceptual learning has taken place when the *relative frequencies* of judgments of *same* or *different, larger* or *smaller, higher* or *lower* have changed. He seems not to care whether the judgments are correct or incorrect. The student of perception, however, has to face the problem of veridical judgments. He has to count or compute *errors*. The experimental methods for studying discrimination require it. Let us try to push Postman to the wall. Does he really wish to assert that a progressive decrease in discriminative accuracy (increase in variable error or constant error) should be considered learning?

We come finally to the problem of signs and symbols, and the perception of meaning. Our specificity hypothesis cannot account for such facts, it is said, and yet this is required of a theory of perceptual learning. "... sign-perception would appear to be, almost by definition, an associative phenomenon: an object can be perceived as a sign only by virtue of the fact that the organism has associated the sign object with the object specified". This sounds very convincing. It is true that the theory of association comes into its own when treating signs, signals, symbols, indicators, cues, clues, surrogates, or substitute stimuli. The relation between a word and its referent has fascinated thinkers for centuries. Perhaps this is why the theory of association has lasted for centuries. It should be noted, however, that in the quotation above Postman falls back on the kind of association he has rejected—that between objects of experience. To have made the same point in terms of association between stimulus and response would have been much more difficult. The plausibility lent to classical association theory by its success with signs and symbols is not inherited intact by an S-R association theory.

The relation between a word and its referent is the best example of an association. It is arbitrary; it seems wholly unlike the relation between a pitch and a tone, or a wave length and a hue. Is it then the relation which should be postulated to exist between a stimulus and a response, as Postman does? In the case of perceptual responses, this seems to violate some of the facts.

A stimulus-response theory with emphasis not on association but on specificity of responses and discriminative behavior could be extended to explain meaning, signs, and symbols even though it has not yet been formally attempted. We do not agree that the specificity hypothesis breaks down when it comes to the problem of human reactions to man-made sources of stimulation. Just because they are man-made, the problem of perception is one stage more complicated with such objects than it is with objects of the natural environment, and the problem of perceptual learning is equally more complicated. Nevertheless the basic tenet of the specificity approach still holds: men learn to perceive symbols by a process which involves an increase in the specificity of their responses to physically different symbols. Symbols, like natural objects, must be differentiated or identified in order to be carriers of meaning. They come in sets, not singly. And it is quite possible that the meaning of a symbol, in the mathematico-logical sense, is given by its univocality within the set. This seems to be the assumption which has proved so fruitful in information theory. The meaning of a symbol in the psychological sense may be given by the univocality of the response to the stimulus. Note the difference between this formula and Postman's. He says the organism has perceived the meaning of a stimulus "when it has learned to make the appropriate response". We would say *when it has learned to identify the stimulus relative to all possible stimuli.*

A theory of perceptual learning which takes the line suggested would unquestionably throw a great burden on the stimulus. The specificity hypothesis for perceptual learning depends on the validity of a psychophysical approach to perception itself. The organism must be ultimately capable of response to extremely high-order variables of stimulation, including those of temporal succession, if meaning is to be explained in this way. Professor Postman has pointed out what seem to be implausible complexities of such stimulation. Others could be cited which seem equally absurd on first consideration. The only possible answer to this argument is to ask for time to test the absurdities experimentally. Meanwhile the possibility of a new empiricism based on discrimination at least should be considered along with the old empiricism based on association.

18
Perceptual Learning
Eleanor J. Gibson

The choice of a review paper for reprinting may seem dubious, since reviews are often merely annotated bibliographies, inevitably out of date. This paper is not the usual review, however, since it was an attempt to provide structure for a new field. It also points out some timely events that are now memorable as having a certain historical significance, such as a book on perceptual development by a French psychologist (Frances, 1962) and a symposium at an International Congress that brought an interesting and diverse group of people together. Of more general interest is the striking influence of artificial intelligence people and programs already apparent in the theories of perceptual learning that were just beginning to surface. More than a quarter century ago, the contrast between models that emphasized feature lists and models that emphasized matching to prototypes was clearly established. The long-term effects are still with us, for example feature lists in a recent model of visual identification of Kosslyn's (Kosslyn 1989), and matching to prototypes in a book about categories in perception (Harnad 1987).

Sources of my own theory were also in the literature—Jakobson and Halle on distinctive features, and information theory. The four areas that I singled out for reviews of research in my book were all represented and gave me the basis for the classification that I adopted for the book: improvement of perceptual skills with practice, perceptual learning with imposed transformation of the stimulus array, intermodal transfer of perceptual learning, and the study of perceptual development by means of controlled rearing.

There was quite a lot of work on predifferentiation, relating to my doctoral dissertation and sometimes taking off from it, and research on "acquired distinctiveness" (a counter theory) that was grist for the mill as I put my book together and weighed theories. Especially useful in this respect was a quantity of research purporting to be on effects of reinforcement on perceptual learning—I

Reproduced, with permission, from the *Annual Review of Psychology*, Vol. 14, 29–56. © 1963 by Annual Reviews Inc.

summed it up in the conclusion that "extrinsic reinforcement was not a necessary condition of perceptual learning"—an understatement.

It is fun to look back on some other conclusions—that "attention has made a comeback," and the importance of the learning-performance distinction that Tolman had emphasized earlier. It was relevant then, and it still is. I wound up pointing out the need for a theory and the prediction that "more specific cognitive theories of perceptual learning are on the way." I was wrong there—the cognitive psychologists have seldom concerned themselves with perceptual learning.

It is only a matter of three years since perceptual learning acquired the status of an area worthy of separate review.[1] In 1960 this field was reviewed by Drever (24), who proposed a classification of theories and some "landmarks" for summarizing research. The present review will make a further effort to clarify and expose the issues which are specifically relevant to the problems and definition of perceptual learning. The definition of the area, still a new one for present-day psychology, is not easy and required the reviewer to exercise her own discretion in the selection of material which is truly relevant, and better included here than under some other aegis. A systematic discussion of what perceptual learning is does not belong in a survey of literature, but some boundaries must be set.

The obvious requirement for theories and experiments which should be considered is that the process studied be perception (not imagination or hallucination or guessing) and that the kind of modification called learning be involved. Any relatively permanent and consistent change in the perception of a stimulus array, following practice or experience with this array, will be considered perceptual learning. It could be argued that only changes which are biologically adaptive which result in increased correspondence or fidelity of perception to dimensions of stimulation—are relevant. Since this point is arguable (whether only improvement in the sense of increased accuracy or "veridicality" is learning) it will not be a criterion for the present review.

The definition chosen does exclude certain phenomena which are conceivably related. Anchoring effects and sensory adaptation are excluded since they are not permanent modifications. Perceptual negative aftereffects and figural aftereffects [Prentice (109)] are excluded on similar grounds. Sensory deprivation, in the opinion of some writers [Freedman (39); Held (60); Riesen (111); Teuber (124)], is a phenomenon related to perceptual learning. But the changes produced by temporary deprivation of stimulation in the adult ("sensory isolation") seem to be random and bizarre, are in the nature of the case not consistently related to present stimulation, and do not appear to be indicative of permanent modification. Hebb (58), in commenting on the distinction, says, "So it seems to me that we may be dealing with two kinds of process here, both of which perhaps can be called learning, but one of which is more fundamental and long-lasting, the other being a more superficial and transient effect super-imposed on it" (p. 42).

Another phenomenon more clearly related to perceptual learning is imprinting. However, the experiments on imprinting have attained such numbers in the last three years that this topic will be excluded on the grounds that it is better reviewed separately. Animal studies of discrimination learning are also excluded, except when they bear specifically on one of the issues critical for theories of perceptual learning. Illusions will be arbitrarily excluded, on the grounds that their status with respect to learning is so inconsistent as to make them uninstructive as a class, and on the somewhat better grounds that a comprehensive study of illusions and development is available [Piaget (108)]. Perceptual development (growth or ontogeny of perception in the individual) might surely be justified for inclusion, but it will be omitted as a topic because some recent, extensive surveys are available [Gibson & Olum (46); Wohlwill (134)]. Piaget's new book (108) summarizes all the work of the Geneva laboratory on perception, and the major emphasis, of course, is developmental. This very convenient summary includes the work on illusions, the effects of "centration," the constancies, perception of causality, and perception of movement, speed, and time. In three concluding theoretical chapters, Piaget compares perception and intelligence, the origins (perceptual or not) of intelligence, and discusses the epistemology of perception. The book is marred by the total absence of any subject or author index, but the information is there if one has the patience to find it.

In general, the material included here will be organized around theories of perceptual learning, and some more specific issues and controversies which have been the focus of research. Representative experimental paradigms ("reference experiments") are as yet so few in this area that parametric research is infrequent, although it could be exploited in the case of some perceptual skills.

General Treatments

For the first time, two books devoted entirely to problems of perceptual learning have appeared. The earlier of these, by Solley & Murphy (121), summarizes a considerable amount of literature, but it is oriented toward presenting the authors' theoretical point of view. They describe themselves, at one point, as eclectic; but the book, which began with discussions in a seminar at the Menninger Foundation, considers primarily the role of affect in perception. Detailed accounts of research performed at the Foundation are reported. The other book, by R. Francès (38), has a broader outlook and wide coverage (there are 408 references, from French, English,

Italian, German, and Russian sources). The book is less closely tied to a theoretical bias than the first-mentioned, but the author makes some useful distinctions. For instance, he makes a sharp division between identification and discrimination. For discrimination learning, biological adaptiveness increases with fidelity to the objective situation; but for recognition, or identification, he says this is not the case; particulars are neglected for the sake of categorizing, classifying into a type. Topics covered in the book include improvement of thresholds and sensory capacities with practice, "impoverishment" experiments, frequency and the mechanisms by which it may influence perception, perceptual modifications in objective characteristics of content (constancies, etc)., the effects of context, and the effects of motivation and individual habits and attitudes.

Bevan (11) has summarized a number of experiments in perceptual learning and presented his own view—that perceptual development depends on the evolution of a system of perceptual scales, through a process of differentiation. Dember's (22) textbook on perception includes a chapter on perceptual learning in which Dember acknowledges particularly the influence of Hebb. Koch's Volume 4 includes a chapter by Attneave called "Perception and Related Areas" (5), but the portion devoted to learning and perception is disappointingly brief. A recent book by Hunt (71) includes a chapter on the effects of early experience on perception of form and objects.

Perceptual learning was one of the "themes" of the 16th International Congress of Psychology held at Bonn in 1960. Besides a number of contributed papers in the area a symposium was organized by J. J. Gibson (49). The speakers were G. De Montpelier, J. Piaget, E. J. Gibson, and A. V. Zhaporozets; discussants were J. Drever, M. D. Vernon, and I. Kohler.

Theories

Drever (24) classified theories of perceptual learning into four types— judgmental, stimulation, association, and adaptation theories. Rigid classification will be eschewed here. But, in considering possibilities of classifying, some other strongly divisive principles emerge. One can think of perception as actively "structuring" the environment. One author (39), for instance, speaks of "imposing constancies and stabilities on the perceived world." Or one may consider perceptual learning as mainly a task of discovering structure, order, and stability in the environment. There are many ways of handling the problem, whichever line is chosen. An example of the second is an article by Bruner, Wallach & Galanter (16) on the identification of recurrent regularity. They consider that theories of reinforcement are not useful for this type of learning; rather, "the answer probably lies in how the organism learns to use techniques of weighing the relevancy of different features of input for regularity-to-be-discovered" (p. 208). Whether reinforcement is given a role or not, a discovery theory could be either a stimulation theory [e.g., E. J. Gibson in Bonn Symposium (49)] or an association theory (a Brunswikian probabilistic type, for instance), to use Drever's terms. A Brunswikian experiment by Fraisse (35) illustrates the probabilistic approach; proximity groupings of one type of material exposed to Ss during a sort of training series were weighted more heavily than another type, and the Ss eventually applied the grouping principle differentially to impoverished test stimuli.

Another distinction can be made between theories of perceptual learning built on a classification or categorizing principle, and those of a "feature detection" type. It seems to the reviewer extremely interesting that programs for pattern-recognition by machines [see Selfridge & Neisser (117), for a review of these] also divide into these two types. Rosenblatt (113) describes the "perceptron" as performing by "comparing new stimulus patterns with previously recorded prototypes and placing each stimulus in an appropriate class" (p. 12), and arriving spontaneously at "perceptual concepts." Minsky (93) has a clear statement of this approach and the contrasting one. "These pattern-recognition methods must extract the heuristically significant features of the objects in question. The simplest methods simply match the objects against standards or prototypes. More powerful 'property-list' methods subject each object to a series of tests, each detecting some *property* of heuristic importance. These properties have to be invariant under commonly encountered forms of distortion" (p. 10). The first method employs what Minsky refers to as "prototype-derived patterns." Identification may proceed by a *"normalization and template-matching* process." The template matching scheme is limited as compared with the "property-list system." A property is a binary function and must be invariant under equivalence transformations. Minsky discusses the problem of generating useful properties and also "articulation"—a process which seems roughly analogous to attention.

The "matching to prototype" model, analogous to a schema or categorizing theory of perceptual learning, has always been popular with psychologists. Vernon (129), long an advocate of the role of the schema in perception, has again presented her ideas, relating them now to aspects of information analysis. Bruner and his co-workers (15) have employed the "ambiguiter," a lens mechanism which impoverishes the stimulus by poor focusing, to study perceptual identification. They emphasize the judgmental nature of S's behavior—hypotheses, testing, categorizing, etc. The method of impoverishment is the typical experimental situation used by schema theorists for studying recognition. Experiments by Binder & Feldman (12) with recognition of ambiguous stimuli (brief presentation and reduction of cues) investigated the role of frequency, reward, and punishment. The S had to learn to respond with the relevant identification to test stimuli possessing only cues which had been common to a previously presented set. Recognition of test stimuli with the response made to the common cues was related to previous frequency of occurrence of those cues. The task required of S was a classification, actually, to a "prototype" which presumably emerged as the set of stimuli possessing the common features was presented. Uhr, Vossler & Uleman (125) had Ss learn to respond with the proper name for a pattern over a set of variant examples of the pattern. The Ss were, in fact, required to build up a "pattern class." Their performance was compared with that of a computer model for pattern recognition. The simulator out-performed the human Ss in recognizing members of a class despite distortion. Marx, Murphy & Brownstein (90) were likewise interested in the recognition of complex visual stimuli occurring in a variety of distorted forms. They trained their Ss with abstracted versions of the pattern and then presented them with test items which had been randomly impoverished or had random "noise" added. The S, in this situation, is presented with a prototype rather than having to abstract it himself. One type of abstraction (a simple geometric design) was markedly effective in the training procedure. Another, a line drawing, was not. The question of why one kind of abstraction was best is not answered. Perhaps this question leads to the other approach—detecting "heuristic properties" or distinctive features.

A "distinctive feature" theory is exemplified by Jakobson & Halle's (74) treatment of the distinctive features of phonemes. The emphasis in such a theory is not on the class. The class is defined by properties. What matters is the *differences* in feature patterns which permit uniqueness of one phoneme compared to the others. The authors propose 12 feature oppositions which are sufficient to give minimal distinctions between all phonemes. Distinctive features are invariant under certain transformations, and are relational properties. They may be ordered or stratified so as to suggest their development by a process of differentiation, or progressive splitting. Such an elegant system has not, as yet, been achieved by any psychologist, but an attempt to apply the notion of distinctive features to the development of letter-discrimination in the child has been made by Gibson (45). The discussion proposes that certain distinctive features which differentiate objects of the world are transferred to letter-discrimination and that other specified features, previously not critical but needed to differentiate letters, are detected after school age when graphic material is encountered.

It would be naive to suppose that the moment is at hand for making a decision between a prototype theory and a distinctive feature theory, since neither has as yet been spelled out in sufficient detail. An experiment by Vurpillot & Brault (130) provides an example. They showed children of different ages (five through nine) familiar objects on a turntable, which was rotated so that S saw the object from all angles. Then the child was shown eight photographs of the object in varying orientations and asked to choose the one most "like" it. Changes with age were toward choice of the most "informative" view. The authors concluded that the child develops a schema of an object. But the data support equally well the idea that the child detects better and better the features which distinguish an object uniquely from other objects. It would be unwise, however, to conclude that the two concepts, schema and distinctive features, are perfectly parallel.

Progress toward more adequate theories might depend on recognizing two separate problems to be accounted for. One, the recognition of a pattern under its transformations, has already received considerable attention. The other, how critical features emerge or how, to use Minsky's terms, a good "property-list" is generated, needs work. An experiment by Kossov (81) was designed to study methods of "bringing out essential features of perceived objects" in visual perception. He used two techniques of differentiation and concluded that transformation of a feature into a "dominant component" is better achieved by variation of the essential feature than by variation of the non-essential one. More work of this kind should be useful, even though critical experiments await progress in theoretical models.

There have been a number of other contributions to theories of perceptual learning in the past three years, not necessarily relevant to the issues just examined. Solley & Murphy's book (121) is one. The point of view is well characterized by Santos & Murphy (115): "We assume that this process (perception) has some properties which are similar to those of motor activity and, like motor activity, it can be modified by learning. Perception should therefore obey the principles relevant to response learning" (p. 7). Conditioning is obviously one of the latter. Reward value and punishment value may therefore be "conditioned to stimuli." Solley & Murphy divide perception into stages: expectancy, attending, reception, trial-and-check, and percept. There is a loop to autonomic and proprioceptive arousal at the trial and check stage. This is a judgmental theory, to use Drever's term. "Trial-and-check is the analyzing and synthesizing process by which tentative assumptions and sensory input are structured into percepts" (p. 221). It is also a "schema" theory: "As the sensory samples are memorically accumulated, cognitive frames of reference or schemata are developed and new sensory data are 'matched' with the stored samples" (p. 172). Of course, it is associationistic too, since attention is said to be conditioned. But it is most of all dynamic. For example, sets "determine which perceptual acts will be learned" (p. 169); "with young children a simple pleasure-pain principle predicts what will be organized as figure in a figure-ground learning experiment" (p. 142); and "it is only through the impact of society's negative reinforcement of autistic perceptions that veridical perception is ever achieved, even in part" (p. 78). Order is created: "Unless men were motivated to create an orderly universe in perception, there would be no functional utility in perceiving" (p. 222). The point of view of the book is rather similar to the transactionalists, whose work is quoted.

The transactional group also has produced several books in the past three years. There is Ittleson's book on visual space perception (72), his chapter in the fourth Koch volume (73), and a volume of essays edited by Kilpatrick (76). Most of the 21 papers in the last are reprints of previous journal publications by Ames, Cantril, Ittleson, and Kilpatrick. Ittleson again asserts the view that perception rests on the "chaotic and fragmentary data of present experience" (73, p. 701). Perception involves a constant checking and re-evaluating procedure, and "Perceiving is a creative process in which the individual constructs for himself his own world of experiences" (73, p. 697). There is not really a theory of perceptual learning here, but the transactional view puts great weight on past experience.

Trace theories of perceptual learning do not seem to be much in evidence these days. But Epstein & Rock (29) and Epstein & DeShazo (28) have treated perceptual learning in terms of a gestalt type of trace theory, asking how a recent trace influences the current perception. Under marginal perceiving conditions, they think, there is oscillation of the "perceptual alternatives" and when the alternative appears which is congruent with the recently implanted trace, arousal of the trace occurs on the basis of distinctive similarity. This hypothesis is contrasted with an expectancy type of theory.

Finally, some contributions of information theory to perceptual learning should be mentioned. Information theorists do not have a full-blown model of perceptual learning but they have concepts which are pertinent and can be, in the reviewer's opinion, a healthy influence. The emphasis on measurement of input-output relationships obviously fits a correspondence theory, rather than a creative process theory. Ways of accounting for increase or decrease in channel capacity, and information transmitted, may eventually help clarify the present vagueness in theories of perceptual learning. Garner's new book (41) considers a number of relevant problems, such as the effect of redundancy on pattern discrimination. The effect turns out to be a very complex one, involving specification of amount of redundancy, kind of redundancy, and the requirements of the task. Francès (38), as well, points out the importance of considering the perceptual task in using information analysis. He discusses the nature of "repertorys" and their formation, and has reported an experiment (37) in which perceptual learning of two kinds, (a) learning the set of alternatives and (b) adjustments of the receptor channel, had a greater effect on a recognition task than on a discrimination task. Broadbent (13) has applied his filter hypothesis to discrimination learning and makes the interesting suggestion that "the mechanism which attaches outputs to inputs, stimulus to response, acts only on filtered information" (p. 266). Barlow (9) suggests that reduction of redundancy, or "compression," is an essential mechanism in the coding of sensory messages. He says that the features of the sensory input which are discriminated from one another are the very ones which enable the sensory message to be compressed. "The idea of removing redundancy and so compressing the sensory message into the smallest possible channel was brought forward because it seemed that the subsequent step of learning to discriminate different sensory stimuli would be easier if the sensory information was presented in this compressed form" (p. 359). This idea seems to link up very nicely with a distinctive feature theory of perceptual learning.

Focal Issues for Research

Whatever their relation to theoretical positions, a limited number of issues are the focus of most research in perceptual learning. The questions asked are seldom capable of an immediate decisive answer, but the phrasing of them is becoming sharper.

Nativism-empiricism   The nature-nurture question is one of those often supposed to be unanswerable. Nevertheless, sorting out the relative contributions of genetic and environmental factors continues to be a fascinating pursuit. Whether the abilities to perceive the spatial aspects of our environment must be learned or are more or less built-in is of interest to psychologists as much today as ever. One finds eloquent backers of nativism [Pastore (103)] as well as of the more popular empiricist position. Hochberg (67) has written a full discussion of the historical background, the logic, and the present status of the question.

   The classic technique for investigation has always been study of the effects of *deprivation* of some normally present environmental contribution, such as stimulation by patterned light. The "born blind" patients corrected (or somewhat corrected) by surgery are the most dramatic cases. The cases summarized by von Senden have appeared in an English translation (118), but shed no more light than they ever did, since all the confounding effects of nystagmus, emotional upset, interference from old habits, and unreliable testing procedures are still inevitably present in the reports. London (86) has summarized a Russian report of six cases of "postoperatively newly seeing persons." (Choice of a proper label for such research is difficult, for these people were not born blind but developed cataracts at various fairly early ages after birth.) Progress to "fuller vision" seemed to be related to age when blindness occurred and to length of visual deprivation; but still one never knows how much of the slow progress is occasioned by reliance on habits of recognition by touch and auditory information necessarily utilized during the blind period. Gregory & Wallace (54) have reported a case which they themselves studied at some length. Visual discrimination and recognition seemed to be far more adequate in this case than in most of those reported. Whether the patient was more intelligent, the testing procedures were better, or something else is hard to say.

Axelrod (6) studied the effects of early blindness on perceptual performance in modalities other than vision by comparing blind and sighted children. Differences between the groups were not consistent in direction. The early-blind Ss had lower two-point limens than sighted Ss on the right index finger (presumably due to practice), but they were not superior in light-touch sensitivity. The early-blind Ss were inferior in tasks which required abstraction and in transfer of a principle of solution across modalities (haptic to aural, for instance). The tasks were said not to be spatial. The reason for this deficit is not clear, though it seems to indicate the important role of visual experience in cognitive development in general.

Deprivation of a less drastic type was exploited by Hudson (70) to study perception of pictorial cues to depth, in sub-cultural groups in Africa (groups often thought to be pictorially naive). He manipulated objectsize, superimposition, and perspective, in the conventional artistic manner, to create pictures in a series roughly increasing in redundancy of these pictorial cues. His results seem to indicate a difference between school-going and non school-going populations, the former more often reporting three-dimensionality. Hochberg & Brooks (68) reared their infant son in an environment pictorially impoverished until he was 19 months old. Though pictures were occasionally in his field of view, he was never given a name or specific response for one (i.e., his vocabulary was taught entirely with objects). Despite this, tests with pictures at 19 months revealed that they were recognized and labeled. Pictorial recognition, in other words, was not dependent on association between the picture and either the represented object or a naming response.

Although the problems of control and interpretation are formidable with natural cases of deprivation, experimental deprivation with animals is feasible and often undertaken. Much recent experimental work with rats makes clear the negligible effect of dark-rearing on visual discrimination in this animal. Gibson, Walk & Tighe (48) found that dark-reared rats learned a triangle-circle discrimination at about the same rate as ordinary laboratory reared animals. Dark-reared rats tested on a "visual cliff" [Gibson & Walk (47); Walk & Gibson (132)] performed like their light-reared litter mates, consistently choosing a shallow over a deep visual drop-off. Nealey & Edwards (97) confirmed this result, with added controls. Young rats (relatively inexperienced visually) avoided the drop-off as consistently as mature ones (132). Results of experiments involving cue isolation (132) suggested that some cues may be "built-in" whereas others are a function of previous visual experience (the texture cue in isolation was effective in light-reared but not in dark-reared animals). Walk & Gibson (132) also found that chicks less than a day old avoided the visual cliff with perfect consistency. This result has been confirmed by Tallarico (122) with newly hatched chicks. Very young goats have been shown to avoid the cliff (132). Early appearance of various perceptual achievements in ducklings has been reported by Pastore (102).

On the other hand, Riesen (111) has suggested that with encephalization of the visual system, patterned visual stimulation becomes essential for ontogenetic development. Dark-reared kittens did not develop a normal visual placing response. Riesen & Aarons (112) found that kittens reared without patterned-light stimulation or with patterned light for one hour, but with restraint of movement in either condition, failed to learn a visual movement discrimination in twice the time required by controls. Gibson & Walk (47, 132) found, likewise, that dark-reared kittens tested at 28 days had not developed a visual placing response and did not avoid the deep side of a visual cliff, unlike their normally reared controls. However, discriminative behavior on the cliff recovered after the kittens were brought into the light, without differential reinforcement, suggesting that maturation in the light is a sufficient condition for development of this behavior.

Rhesus monkeys tested on the cliff at 10 days (132) could be coaxed to the deep side, though locomotion differed on the two sides. At 18 days, they could not be coaxed to cross the deep side. Ganz & Riesen (40), comparing dark- and light-reared Macaques, found evidence for modified generalization gradients to hue in light-reared animals, which they interpreted as indicating the importance of sensory learning.

Human infants, as soon as they can be tested on a visual cliff, show adequate discrimination of visual depth (47, 131,132). But testing is not possible before locomotion is possible. Fantz (32) has used a preference method for testing shape and pattern discrimination in human infants, as well as other young animals, and found convincing evidence for differential response to pattern, suggesting that at least some degree of visual form perception is innate even in the human infant.

Enhancement or "enrichment" experiments have been done, in contrast to deprivation ones, to see if the enhanced experience facilitates later perceptual performance. Sometimes results are positive and sometimes not [Gibson, Walk & Tighe (48)]. Meier & McGee (91) obtained positive results with rats in an "enriched" rearing experiment and concluded that progressive differentiation of the objects in the environment had taken place during rearing, thus speeding up a later discrimination task. Positive results such as these do not bear precisely on the nature-nurture problem. They show that perceptual learning may occur, but not that all perception depends on learning, as a radical empiristic view would hold. Fowler (34), surveying cognitive learning in infancy and early childhood, summarized cases of early cognitive learning (language, reading, drawing, etc.) and emphasized the role of "enrichment" and learning, as opposed to genetic factors.

Cross-modal transfer   One of the questions most often asked about the "born blind" cases is whether or not acquaintance through one sensory modality will transfer without further practice to a different one. Could the patient with newly restored sight recognize visually something which he had previously known only tactually? Gregory's case (54) provided a remarkable example of such transfer with upper-case letters. The patient had learned to recognize by touch raised upper-case (but not lower-case) letters. After surgery, he could name the upper-case letters, but not the lower-case ones, when they were presented visually. This evidence is the more convincing, because the lower-case letters, never identified by touch, provide a control. A number of Russian experiments on transfer from haptic to visual recognition have been briefly summarized by Zinchenko & Lomov (137). Patterned figures were prepared for both tactual and visual presentation and crossmodal transfer was studied in both directions, with children as subjects. Acquaintance by one modality did transfer to some extent to recognition by the other. Zinchenko & Lomov emphasized the role of exploratory movements (both tactual and visual). "They construct an image of it, take a cast or a copy" (p. 16). There is not perfect isomorphism, however, for different fingers describe different paths, and eye movements vary with restriction of the field. These authors suggest that touch and vision are "parallel senses" and that there is a genetic connection between them.

Ettlinger (31), on the other hand, found no cross-modal transfer in monkeys in discriminating a sphere from a pyramid, either tactual to visual, or vice versa. Is this because cross-modal transfer is verbally mediated? An experiment by Hermelin & O'Connor (65), again on tactual and visual shape recognition, makes this unlikely. The Ss were normal and subnormal (imbecile) children. Five stimulus objects (Russian letters) were inspected or manipulated (but never named) and later selected from a group containing five new ones. Better than chance cross-modal recognition occurred for both groups.

Rudel (114) studied the decrement of the Muller-Lyer illusion in adult Ss with repeated exposure in both the visual and tactual modalities, and measured transfer from one to the other. There was cross-modal transfer of the decrement in both directions, slightly greater from haptic to visual. It seems unlikely in this case as well that there is verbal mediation of transfer. Caviness & Gibson (18) compared the effects of two kinds of training on cross-modal transfer in adult Ss. Solid, unfamiliar "nonsense" objects were presented haptically and matched visually. Training, both by visual-tactual association and by tactual comparison alone, resulted in transfer as compared to a control group without training. One experiment attempting auditory-visual transfer has been reported by Chorover, Cole & Ettlinger (20). Results were negative.

Why cross-modal transfer is found in some cases, but not others, and what "carries" the transfer when it occurs are clearly questions for further study.

Compensation for transformed stimulus-arrays   Experiments on optical distortion produced by spectacles or goggles comprised of mirrors, right-angle prisms, wedge prisms, or half-colored glasses have continued, following the earlier work of Kohler (78). The experiments have usually been performed with the view of discovering how perception of space is learned. It is assumed that the compensation or rehabituation which takes place while wearing the spectacles is analogous to the original development of perception in the child. This reasoning is dubious, but the experiments are instructive for other reasons. What to call the change in stimulus-array is important, since the wrong term can prejudice thinking. All the cases so far investigated are transformations, rather than permutations, of spatial order, so that the new stimulus order is still in systematic correspondence with the old one (right-left reversal, for instance, is still perfectly correlated with the normal order). The term "distortion" was criticized by Held (60), who suggested the terms "rearrangement" and "disarrangement." Rearrangement would apply to the transformations so far studied, like reversals. Disarrangement would apply to a random change no longer in correspondence with the normal order. Cohen & Held (21) attempted to create such a situation with rotary prisms of continually varying power, which produced a continually varying image of S's hand as he viewed and moved it. Dispersion of target markings (test for compensation) increased, rather than decreased, indicating "degraded"performance.

In Kohler's (80) recent summary of his goggle experiments, he comments on the complexity of the adjustment demanded by some of the transformations, such as that caused by two-color glasses when the eyes move from left to right. Adjustment to this change "involves a process more complex than all previously known processes of visual adaptation" (p. 67). Yet it occurs, as long as there is ordered correspondence. Kohler comments that "in all cases where adaptation occurs the eye is provided with systematic clues as to the nature of the distortion" (p. 72). The fact that adjustment or compensation takes place with ordered stimulus-change but seemingly not with random change (see also 60, 61, 124) fits well with the view that perceptual learning is essentially detection of order and regularity rather than creation of it. Kohler (79) has made this point in a theoretical article contrasting the classic gestalt organization theory (internal organization) with an ordered stimulus theory (external organization). Held and his co-workers (21, 62, 63) have performed a number of experiments in this field. These papers emphasize particularly the role of spontaneous or "self-produced" movements made by the subject and the feed-back stimuli dependent on these movements for the occurrence or nonoccurrence of compensation for errors produced by prisms. Order in the stimulation coming from the environment, plus self-produced movements and the resultant feedback are held to be essential for normal sensory development as well as for adaptation to "rearrangement" (59, 62). "Reafferent stimulation is the source of ordered contact with the environment which is responsible for the stability, under typical conditions, and the adaptability, to certain atypical conditions, of visual-spatial performance" (62, p. 37). In the Cohen & Held experiment (21) mentioned above, the authors proposed that self-produced movement was necessary for degrading performance under a varying transformation as well as for compensation for invariant transformations.

Differentiation and acquired distinctiveness   That originally confusable objects of stimulation may become discriminable with practice, or that the original level of discriminability may be enhanced, is generally accepted as a fact of perceptual learning. But under what conditions discriminability is increased, and by what mechanism or process, are far from settled. Two opposing views have been the bases of hypotheses for most of the research to be reported. These were called by Gibson & Gibson (50) the "differentiation" view and the "enrichment" view. The differentiation view holds that practice serves to reduce generalization among the stimuli, to increase precision of discrimination of variables actually present in stimulation, and to detect relevant variables or distinctive features not previously detected. The position holds that the effective stimuli for perception are changed by learning, and it requires a new concept of stimulation. The enrichment view, on the other hand, emphasizes addition to the stimulus impressions by an associative process. An older form of this view, Titchener's context theory, would assume that stimulus-impressions become more distinctive by the addition of meaningful associations. A related view more in keeping with behavior theory was originally proposed by William James and later developed by Miller & Dollard (92). The process is generally referred to as "acquired distinctiveness." It holds that responses learned to the stimuli add response-produced cues to the original stimuli. The more distinctive the responses learned, the more effective the response-produced stimulation will be in increasing distinctiveness of the original cues. Language responses (labels) are often employed in research. The theory also demands "acquired equivalence" (greater confusability of cues) with the attachment of the same label to different stimuli.

The difficulty of deciding between these two hypotheses may be illustrated by an elegant experiment by Liberman et al. (85). They measured discriminability of acoustic differences within and between phoneme boundaries, and compared the data with comparable acoustic differences in sounds not perceived as speech. Discrimination was considerably better across a phoneme boundary than in the middle of a phoneme category. Discrimination data with the control stimuli revealed no increase in discriminability in the region corresponding to the phoneme boundary. The authors conclude that sharpening of discrimination at the phoneme boundary is an effect of learning, and more specifically is an "acquired distinctiveness" due to long practice in attaching phoneme labels. That the sharpened discrimination is an effect of learning seems clear, but the role of labeling is not so clear, since "acquired equivalence" (higher thresholds) did not occur *within* the phoneme category, relative to the controls. The heightened discrimination could, moreover, equally well have been due to finer differentiation of the complex variable.

An experiment by Chistovitch, Klass & Alekin (19) corroborates the difference in discriminability of speech and nonspeech sounds. They taped sound sequences of three Russian vowels or three pure tones and asked Ss either to identify the sequences by naming or to make a same-different discrimination. Sequences of vowels (named by vowel labels) were both better identified and better discriminated as same-or-different than were sequences of tones (labeled high, medium, or low). But when high tones similar to certain vowel sounds were identified by vowel labels, as opposed to the words "high, medium, or low," more information was transmitted. This result suggests that the label used for identification may play a role in the identification task itself, but not in acquisition of distinctiveness.

Lane & Moore (83) trained an aphasic patient to discriminate two phonemic patterns previously indiscriminable by conditioning with labels. The aphasic pressed one or the other of two suitably labeled buttons, and a flash of light followed if the correct one was pressed. Differential responses were quickly acquired, and accuracy transferred to an ABX discrimination task. This was a dramatic case of "acquired distinctiveness." But the dramatic change occurred so rapidly (after a few minutes) that one wonders again what the role of the label, as such, was.

An experiment by Phaup & Caldwell (107) was aimed against the differentiation hypothesis, rather than toward testing acquired distinctiveness. They repeated an earlier experiment by Gibson & Gibson (50) but added familiarizing training (looking three times at all the items which were later to be discriminated from the standard). Because familiarization facilitated the later achievement of discrimination, they concluded that enrichment, as well as differentiation, must be involved. But the familiarization could, of course, simply have provided an opportunity for differentiation of those features which made the items distinct. E. J. Gibson [in (49)] discussed whether one could "have it both ways" and proposed that differentiation must precede association, even with stimuli such as written symbols.

The means of investigating these opposed processes experimentally is the so-called "predifferentiation" experiment. In this paradigm, a set of stimuli are first tested for discriminability or identifiability. Training of some type is then given, and finally discriminability or identifiability is retested. Ideally, a control group or, at least, control stimuli are included. The effectiveness of the training is measured by transfer to the final discriminability test. There are obviously a large number of possible variables in this type of experiment. The critical one for the two opposed theories is the type of training introduced in stage two. It might be a matter of learning different labels or other specific responses; or it might be equivalent exposure to the stimulus material with a nonassociative task such as comparing one item with another. But other parameters may be important in determining whether, or how much, transfer occurs. Two of these are the kind of stimulus material and the nature of the criterion task.

Several recent experiments have compared types of training in the predifferentiation experiment. DeRivera (23) had Ss learn letters as responses to fingerprint-patterns (training), and afterward learn numbers as responses to them (transfer stage). One group learned a specific letter for each print. Two other groups learned only two letters, half the prints having one letter and half the other as a common response. One of these two groups was told to learn the response to each print individually; the other was told to look for something common to the prints having the same letter-response. Transfer to the second task (numbers) was significantly poorer for the group told to look for common characteristics, but was equivalent for the other two groups. It was concluded that the labels themselves were irrelevant and merely forced S to search for discriminable aspects of the stimuli.

An experiment by Pfafflin (106) was run with three conditions of pretraining: (a) relevant labels learned to visual forms (of three levels of meaningfulness), (b) irrelevant labels learned to the same forms, (c) observation of forms. A discrimination task followed (S pressed one of two buttons for each form). All kinds of pretraining resulted in a decrease in errors, over all, compared to a control group. Observation, over all, resulted in the greatest error decrease and was the only condition which produced facilitation with all levels of meaningfulness. With highly meaningful forms, learning relevant labels produced interference. With very low meaningfulness, relevant labels were facilitating, probably, Pfafflin suggests, because they helped S to select distinctive features of these items.

An experiment by Ellis et al. (26) tested the hypothesis of acquired distinctiveness and acquired equivalence, employing a recognition task with tactual shapes. The three pretraining conditions were: (a) learning relevant labels, one to each "prototype" shape; (b) learning one label to half the shapes and another to the other half, both relevant; (c) observation by tactual inspection. Group a was not superior to Group c in the criterion (recognition) task. Group b was poorer, probably because the Ss disregarded all distinctive features save the one suggested by the label. The addition of response-produced cues here did not facilitate later recognition, beyond the instruction to inspect and differentiate shapes.

A little further evidence is provided indirectly in an experiment by Rasmussen & Archer (110), who tested the effect of language pretraining (learning relevant labels to nonsense shapes) on a concept identification task. It was hypothesized that pretraining with labels would enhance discrimination and thereby facilitate concept identification. It did not, but another group which judged the shapes for aesthetic qualities instead of learning responses did perform better on the criterion task, presumably because they had attended to and discriminated among the several dimensions of the stimulus figures. To summarize, none of these four experiments yields decisive supporting evidence for acquired distinctiveness in the form of cues generated by specific labels or responses learned to the stimulus items. But pretraining of any kind that allows detection of distinctive features appears to be facilitating.

Another parameter of the predifferentiation experiment is the nature of the stimulus items, i.e., their complexity, meaningfulness, and the original degree of confusability with other items of the set. Obviously, there is no point in this kind of experiment if the items are already easily discriminated or identified. Neither is there if they are so nearly identical as to be beyond the basic limits of the discriminatory capacity of the sensory system. Albert (1) had Ss repeat labels (given by E) while hefting weights previously shown to be indiscriminable, on the theory that learned cue-producing responses would facilitate later discrimination. It did not. The author suggested that it did not because the weights were literally below the physiological limit of discriminability. Vanderplas & Garvin (127) studied the role of complexity and association value in shape recognition following labeling practice, testing the hypothesis that the initial difficulty of the material determines in part the effect of practice on recognition. Complexity turned out to be the only main variable of significance, and there was a significant complexity by practice interaction. Labeling practice as such was not significantly related to either correct recognition or correct rejection, as might have been expected from an unelaborated acquired distinctiveness (response-produced cue) hypothesis.

The third parameter of importance in determining whether transfer has resulted from predifferentiation training is the criterion selected for measurement. Yarczower (135) showed that predifferentiation training was effective in lowering generalization (conditioned galvanic skin response) even though similar training in another experiment did not appear to facilitate recognition. Lenneberg's (84) study of the effect of color-naming habits on discrimination gives further evidence that the criterion task must be specified. He found that hue discrimination (differential limens for simultaneously presented stimuli) was not affected by naming habits but that color recognition was, to the degree that memory was taxed and that S was forced to search for anchoring points. He commented that "semantic habits provide no absolute, invariable means of distinguishing stimuli, but serve as a device for classification or articulation of a continuum and thus help us in many situations to find points of reference, 'anchorage,' for judgments, whatever they may be" (p. 382). Hayes, Robinson & Brown (57), in a replication of an earlier experiment by Henle (64), found that normally oriented letters were identified better than disoriented ones, due presumably to past experience. But when a sameness-difference test procedure was employed, there was no significant difference in thresholds for the two types of orientation.

Vanderplas (126) has suggested that five kinds of perceptual tasks be distinguished (detection, discrimination, recognition, identification, and judgment), since transfer may depend on similarity of operations in the training and the transfer task. Vanderplas, Sanderson & Vanderplas (128) reported an experiment in which transfer was determined for several kinds of training (observing and discriminating, or labeling random shapes) to several kinds of criterion task (discriminating, recognizing, labeling, or differential switch-pressing). Transfer of training (relative to a control group), by both a discrimination and a recognition test, was equal for the several kinds of pretraining. By an identification measure (learning labels), observing and discriminating yielded some transfer, but not as much as previous labeling practice. With the motor task (differential switch-pressing) as criterion, transfer occurred for all groups but slightly more for one group which learned labels (girl's names were better than nonsense syllables). There was, thus, over-all transfer from all three kinds of training to all four criterion tasks, but the amount depended to some extent upon the relation of the two tasks.

Future progress with regard to this issue will depend, in the reviewer's opinion, on more creative handling of the hypotheses, and on careful selection of experimental design with regard to the parameters just discussed.

Education of attention   In considering how cues become distinctive, or to put it the other way, how distinctive features are selected and differentiated from the potential stimulus input, it is useful to talk about attention and its education. The word attention, for years suspect, has made a come-back, though some behavior theorists prefer to speak of observing responses [Atkinson (4) for instance, uses "observing responses" as criteria for what might well be selective attention]. Broadbent's filter theory (13) is another way of dealing with attention. Solley & Murphy (121) speak of the "conditioning of attention," which puts them in head-on conflict with Broadbent, who hypothesizes that only already filtered stimuli can be conditioned. Broadbent's hypothesis is similar to one proposed by Zeaman & House (136), who developed an attention theory of discrimination learning in retarded children. Their theory is a two-stage one which assumes that attention to the relevant dimension must take place before any differential cue-learning can occur. That is, acquisition of two responses is required: (*a*) attending to the relevant stimulus dimension and (*b*) approaching the correct cue of that dimension. The retardates' difficulty is with (*a*) not (*b*), since "reverse" learning curves all looked alike at the end. There is transfer within stage (*a*); an intradimensional shift was very fast, but an extradimensional shift was difficult. Furthermore, if an easy discrimination within a dimension is run first, it will transfer to a hard one. A discrimination problem is hard for retarded children when stimuli are patterns painted on a background, whereas the same patterns as cut-out three-dimensional objects are easily discriminated. House & Zeaman (69) found that the difficult pattern discrimination could be accomplished if it were preceded by the cut-out discrimination (68 percent of such a group learned in 10 days compared to only 10 percent of a group without transfer from cut-outs). Walk et al. (133) explained in a similar way the facilitating effect of prolonged exposure to metal cut-out patterns on later discrimination learning in rats, as opposed to no facilitation from similar exposure to painted patterns.

Karn & Gregg (75) reported an experiment which seems to the reviewer to be concerned with the education of attention. The Ss were shown three circles simultaneously on a screen, tachistoscopically, and asked to report presence or absence of a dot within the circles. The circles were so "loaded" with the dots that there were always two stable conditions and one unstable. If S detected these conditions, attention could be directed to the unstable condition and accuracy improved. With repetition it was found that accuracy did improve, without reinforcement of any kind. Improvement was not over all a sudden shift, but was very rapid for targets which were consistently positively loaded. It seems impossible to describe this type of learning as conditioning, but it is certainly perceptual. Kossov's experiment (81) is also relevant here.

Learning to disregard "noisy" stimulus-input may be another aspect of education of attention. An experiment by Gollin (53) required Ss to make a tactual discrimination (same-different) of patterns made by raised tacks on a board. The task was also presented with "interfering" tacks scattered about, which S was told to disregard. Pretraining with the noninterference task brought about improvement with Ss of two age groups, but pretraining with the interference task was effective only with an older age group (9–10 years), not a younger one (7–8 years). There seems, therefore, to be a developmental difference in the kind of learning going on here. Education of attention to the relevant dimension or features under difficult conditions may be slower with younger children, as Zeaman found it to be with retardates.

Response bias   There is no occasion to review all the literature on tachistoscopic recognition of verbal material, since it was reviewed recently under "Psycholinguistics" (113a). But the issue of so-called "response bias" is a special plague for the psychologist interested in perceptual learning. The contention of many psychologists is that what appear to be effects of learning on the perception of words (for instance, that recognition is a function of word frequency) are really only manifestations of a high operant level of verbal responses. Response availability is sometimes held to influence the report so much as to make the role of the stimulus negligible, if any. It is true that the tachistoscopic situation encourages guessing, especially when thresholds are obtained by a method of limits. Does it matter what is on the stimulus card at all? It must if we are going to consider the experiment a perceptual one.

Results of a number of experiments leave the issue still in the realm of theory. That response bias can affect results in a frequency of usage experiment was shown by Goldstein & Ratliff (52) with a forced-choice method. It was shown by Newbigging (98) and by Smock & Kanfer (119) in "pseudoperceptual" experiments in which no stimulus was presented to S [the method of Goldiamond & Hawkins (51)]. Moscovici & Humbert (96) reported that emitted frequency was a better predictor than a word count. But on the other hand, Smock & Kanfer found that a perceptual set reduced response bias; Newbigging (99) in another experiment found that sensory information was a determinant of word-recognition as well as response bias. Brown & Rubenstein (14), using auditory stimuli, concluded that stimulus words have at least some role in producing the word-frequency effect; and Schiff (116), comparing a control group shown blank slides with an experimental group shown a set of forms at a presumably subliminal level, found that the experimental group guessed correctly significantly more often. It seems, then, that response bias is a factor to be considered in interpreting results of tachistoscopic experiments; but that the instructions given S (to guess, or to try for accuracy of perception) and the stimuli presented are also effective. That the number of response alternatives affects recognition threshold was recently demonstrated by Fraisse & Blancheteau (36). It is clear that the size of the set would influence guessing.

That this question of response bias is not simply a red herring becomes clear in the interpretation of many experiments. Newbigging & Hay (100) made predictions for recognition thresholds on the basis of the differentiation-enrichment issue in perceptual learning. The differentiation hypothesis should predict, they contended, that as trials progress, "more" of the stimulus word will be discriminated at a given exposure (responses should show increasing similarity to the actual word). They then test this hypothesis by examining S's successive responses to a particular stimulus item as he works up to threshold and conclude that the prediction is not confirmed. But to what extent perception is involved is a serious question since S was instructed to "make a guess" after each presentation as to what the word was. There is no good reason to suppose that the laws of guessing are the same as the laws of perception. The problem of response bias is also a vexing one for interpretation of experiments with ambiguous figures, some of which are described below.

Reinforcement in perceptual learning   To what extent is reinforcement, either the effects of reward and punishment or knowledge of results, necessary for perceptual learning? Solley & Murphy (121) emphasized the role of reward and punishment in perceptual learning, as noted earlier, and quoted a number of pertinent experiments as evidence. Three questions for defining their roles may be asked: (*a*) Is the observed effect of reward or punishment a function of the criterion test? (*b*) Is the effect of reward and punishment differential? (*c*) Is their role more than informational?

As for the first question, there seems to be evidence that rewarding a categorical response to ambiguous material, such as inkblots, increases the frequency of the response [Essman (30)]. But here the response bias rears its ugly head. Is this effect merely verbal conditioning? Solley & Engel (120) attempted to eliminate this possibility by training an S (with reward or punishment) to name one or another profile in an ambiguous figure and later testing the effect of the training by having S merely point to indicate which face he saw (i.e., make a response which had not been specifically reinforced). Since the rewarded profile was more often pointed to under these conditions, they concluded that a genuine perceptual shift had occurred.

The differential effect of reward and punishment was also observed in Solley & Engel's experiment (120). Money reward and withdrawal served as reward and punishment. They concluded that differential effects occurred, but changed developmentally, the younger children revealing an "autistic" effect of punishment, whereas the older children revealed its effects as "attention- getting." This finding seems to shed more light on the role of punishment (and its interaction with development) in the motivation of action than in learning. In another experimental with profiles using money reward and withdrawal, Beatty, Dameron & Greene (10) found both ineffective as reinforcing agents. No differential effect was observed between rewarded and punished stimulus alternatives. A different criterion, the threshold for correct identification, was used. McNamara (87) found that reward and punishment were effective in producing constant errors of over- or underestimation of lines, direction of error being differential in the predicted directions (e.g., reward for overestimation produced errors of overestimation; punishment of overestimation led to underestimation). The effect transferred to different figure. The shift in constant error here is comparable to that produced by knowledge of results.

Figure-ground shifts produced by punishment with electric shock have been studied by Mangan (88, 89) with three degrees of shock intensity. The principal effect with weak or medium shock was a vigilance reaction rather than a defense reaction; that is, response changes emphasized the shocked material. With strong shock, the effect was the opposite. The vigilance effect was retained for some time. The role of the shock does not seem to be informational here, but the interpretation of the differential effects of different intensities need not be in terms of learning.

A survey of knowledge of results, including its role in perceptual learning, was prepared by Annett (3). A helpful distinction is made between intrinsic and extrinsic knowledge of results. The point is emphasized that the information, rather than the motivation, content of knowledge of results is important to learning; whereas motivation is an important variable in performance. An earlier study by Annett (2) demonstrated the value of intrinsic information for learning and retention. The task was reproducing a precise amount of pressure. Extrinsic feedback from a supplementary cue made Ss more accurate at the time, but immediately less accurate on withdrawal of it. Annett's results underline the importance of the perceptual aspect of a task and intrinsic feedback in learning; merely repeating a precise response was insufficient for learning even if S were informed at once that it was correct. Baker & Young (8) considered effect of knowledge of results (and withdrawal of knowledge) on constant and variable error in a Thorndike-type line-drawing experiment. The sign of the constant error was learned early in training, whereas subsequent learning increased improvement by gradual reduction of variable error.

One cannot conclude from these studies that reinforcement or knowledge of results is a necessary condition for perceptual learning. Experiments by Pearson & Hauty (104, 105) provide evidence that extrinsic knowledge, at least, is not necessary. Their Ss set themselves to the vertical from an offset position in a lateral tilt-chair. Error was compared under conditions of visual knowledge of results (a visual error scale on a disc opposite to S), postural anchoring (E returned S to correct setting), and no extrinsic knowledge. The Ss improved in all conditions. When no knowledge of results or anchoring was given by E, alternation through the vertical favored progressive error reduction. A control experiment ruled out adaptation as a factor and strengthened the interpretation that passing through the vertical gave S unique proprioceptive cues. This seems to be a kind of intrinsic knowledge of results, allowing S to check his last setting against the unique feeling of the vertical as he passes through it.

Action and feedback   All feedback from action is in a sense potential information. The question can be raised then whether action and the feedback from it is essential to all perceptual development and learning. There are in fact psychologists who strongly hold this view. Drever made an eloquent plea for it, referring particularly to Piaget's view that "awareness of space is based upon action in space" (25, p. 4). The role of exploratory movements of both the hand and the eye in perception has been studied by Russian psychologists (137). There are, they proposed, two types, (*a*) searching and directing, and (*b*) pursuit or "gnostic." The latter movements have a constructive function; that is, there is a correspondence between the form of the tracing movements and the contour of the object perceived. With maturity and familiarity with objects the movements are presumably reduced. Ghent (42) and Ghent & Bernstein (43), in explaining some results on recognition of figures in different orientations by young children, proposed (à la Hebb) that in the early stages of development the child scans a form, looking first at one portion and then another, and that this sequential process proceeds in a top-to-bottom direction. On the other hand, Mooney (94, 95) reasoned that if eye movements are essential in learning to see visually presented configurations, then recognition of meaningless novel configurations should be markedly more effective when initially observed by visual inspection than by single brief fixations. His experiments indicated that such was not the case.

The role of gross postural movements, as well as exploratory and tracking movements of the sense organs has been held to be important (60, 61, 111, 112). Held and his colleagues, mentioned earlier, consider cues from self-produced movement critical not only for compensation for transformed stimulus orders, but also for perceptual development. Hein & Held (59) reared kittens either with self-produced or passive movements. The "active" animals developed effective response to visual spatial situations, but the "passive" animals did not. Many questions remain to be answered. Did the passive kittens, pulled round and round, get dizzy, for instance? Research in this area will undoubtedly multiply.

Perceptual Skills

Heightened sensitivity   Very little applied research on perceptual skills is to be found in psychological journals, though one supposes it must exist in trade journals. The delicate palates of wine and tea tasters, so often assumed, are worth experimental study if only for the importance of grading in industry. Both methods of testing skill and methods of scaling or categorizing stimuli are probably important. Engen (27) measured olfactory thresholds with a forced-choice method of limits for relatively pure odorants in weak solution. Thresholds were appreciably lowered by practice and, especially, by changes in S's criterion of discrimination. Absolute identification does not, typically, show a large improvement with practice by information measures. However, one subject [Hanes & Rhoades (55)] practicing with Munsell color chips for five months increased the number of absolutely identifiable colors from 15 to 50. Errors increased markedly after a three-month period of no practice. It seems likely that the more complex stimuli emanating from real objects of the world yield more discriminable categories, for absolute identification, and that perception is highly educable with respect to them.

Code learning   A factor study, of successive stages of learning Morse code, by Fleishman & Fruchter (33) revealed that factor loadings changed with stage of training, indicating (to the reviewer) a two-stage learning process. In the early stages, Auditory Rhythm Discrimination and Auditory Perceptual Speed were the only factors with high loadings. But at a later stage, they played a smaller role with Speed of Closure highest. Does this not suggest that S first has to learn to differentiate the items, and that later, stimuli are organized into higher-order units for perception? These stages are characteristic of reading, as well.

Reading   Most of the voluminous literature on reading skill is not pertinent to perceptual learning. But perceptual learning is a part of the skill of reading. One aspect of reading is the acquiring of the directional scanning habit. That this habit involves some perceptual learning, as well as motor, is suggested by a number of tachistoscopic experiments in which letters are exposed simultaneously on both sides of a fixation point. Following Heron's experiment (66), recognition has been found to be better for material to the left than to the right [Kimura (77); L'Abate (82)]. Sometimes nonalphabetical material has not yielded the same differential effect as letters [Terrace (123); Bryden (17)], but in other experiments the results were similar to those with verbal material [Ayres & Harcum (7); Harcum & Dyer (56); Kimura (77)]. A number of factors, such as succession or simultaneity of presentation, spacing, and order of reporting, have been found to affect results in these experiments. Interpretation of the results is not self-evident, but it is generally agreed that habits acquired through reading experience develop a kind of perceptual primacy phenomenon.

That perceptual learning is involved in letter differentiation is the conclusion of a developmental study of the discrimination of letter-like forms [Gibson (45); Osser & Gibson (101)]. Standard forms were constructed according to rules which describe letters and 12 specified transformations of each of those prepared. The task was to match a standard with a form from a set containing the standard and 12 transformations of it. Developmental curves of progressive accuracy varied with transformation type, suggesting an explanation based on learning of distinctive features of letters.

As with the learning of Morse code, there is a second stage of perceptual learning in reading, wherein the letter units, now discriminable, are organized into higher-order units, so that more is perceived at a glance. Familiarity and meaning have always been assumed to be the organizing factors at this stage, but reason has been found [Gibson (44)] to believe that grapheme-phoneme correspondence rules, complex as they may be for the English language, generate higher-order units for skilled readers. Pseudowords (meaningless and unfamiliar) were perceived more accurately with tachistoscopic presentation when they followed these rules.

In Conclusion

The picture which emerges of the area of perceptual learning is that of a healthily growing one, in terms of interest and amount of research being produced. This growth makes especially apparent the looseness of theoretical development. Any tightly worked theories that might be considered at all relevant tend to be couched in response terms and therefore fail to take into account some of the most interesting problems. Response bias is still a bias of many experimenters. But more attention is being paid to attention. People who work on computer models for pattern recognition are not afraid to use cognitive terms. Their example should shake up some of the response-biased theory makers. It is predicted that more specific cognitive theories of perceptual learning are on the way, and that the parameters of the paradigmatic experiments will get more careful consideration and control.

Notes

1. The survey of the literature pertaining to this review was concluded April 1, 1962.

References

1. Albert, R. S. The function of verbal labels in the discrimination of subtle stimulus differences. *J. Genet. Psychol.*, 94, 287–96 (1959)
2. Annett, J. Learning a pressure under conditions of immediate and delayed knowledge of results. *Quart. J. Psychol.*, 11, 3–15 (1959)
3. Annett, J. *The Role of Knowledge of Results in Learning: A Survey* (Tech. Rept: NAVTRA DEVCEN 342–3, Port Washington, N.Y., 53 pp., 1961)
4. Atkinson, R. C. The observing response in discrimination learning. *J. Exptl. Psychol.*, 62, 253–62 (1961)
5. Attneave, F. Perception and related areas. In *Psychology: A Study of a Science*. Vol. 4: *Biologically Oriented Fields: Their Place in Psychology and in Biological Science*, 619–59 (Koch, S., Ed., McGraw-Hill Book Co., New York, N.Y., 731 pp., 1962)
6. Axelrod, S. *Effects of Early Blindness: Performance of Blind and Sighted Children on Tactile and Auditory Tasks* (American Foundation for the Blind, New York, N.Y., 83 pp., 1959)
7. Ayres, J. J., and Harcum, E. R. Directional response-bias in reproducing brief visual patterns. *Perceptual Motor Skills*, 14, 155–65 (1962)
8. Baker, C. H., and Young, P. Feedback during training and retention of motor skills. *Can. J. Psychol.*, 14, 257–64 (1960)
9. Barlow, H. B. The coding of sensory messages. In *Current Problems in Animal Behavior*, 331–60 (Thorpe, W. H., and Zangwill, O. L., Eds., Cambridge Univ. Press, London, England, 424 pp., 1961)
10. Beatty, F. S., Dameron, L. E., and Greene, J. E. An investigation of the effects of reward and punishment on visual perception. *J. Psychol.*, 47, 267–76 (1959)
11. Bevan, W. Perceptual learning: an overview. *J. Gen. Psychol.*, 64, 69–99 (1961)
12. Binder, A., and Feldman, S. E. The effects of experimentally controlled experience upon recognition responses. *Psychol. Monographs*, 74 (9), 43 pp. (1960)
13. Broadbent, D. E. Human perception and animal learning. In *Current Problems in Animal Behavior*, 248–272 (Thorpe, W. H., and Zangwill, O. L., Eds., Cambridge Univ. Press, London, England, 424 pp., 1961)
14. Brown, C. R., and Rubenstein, H. Test of response bias explanation of word-frequency effect. *Science*, 133, 280–81 (1961)
15. Bruner, J. S. (Chairman). Special session on *Processes of Cognitive Growth* (Eastern Psychol. Assoc., 33rd meeting, Atlantic City, N.J., April 26–28, 1962)
16. Bruner, J. S., Wallach, M . A., and Galanter, E. H. The identification of recurrent regularity. *Am. J. Psychol.*, 72, 200–9 (1959)
17. Bryden, M. P. Tachistoscopic recognition of non-alphabetical material. *Can. J. Psychol.*, 14, 78–86 (1960)
18. Caviness, J. A., and Gibson, J. J. *The Equivalence of Visual and Tactual Stimulation for the Perception of Solid Forms* (Presented at Eastern Psychol. Assoc., 33rd meeting, Atlantic City, N.J., April 26–28, 1962)
19. Chistovitch, L. A., Klass, Yu. A., and Alekin, R. O. O Znachenii imitatsii dlya raspoznavaniya zvukovykh posledovatel' nostei (On the significance of imitation for the discrimination of sound sequences.) *Voprosy Psikhologii*, 7 (5), 173–82 (1961)*
20. Chorover, S. L., Cole, M., and Ettlinger, G. *Apparent Lack of Positive Cross-modal Transfer*

*English translation was announced in *Technical Translations*, issued by the Office of Technical Services, U. S. Department of Commerce, and was made available by the Photoduplication Service, Library of Congress, and by the SLA Translation Center at the John Crerar Library, Chicago, Illinois.

of Training with Auditory and Visual Rhythms in Man (Presented at Eastern Psychol. Assoc., 33rd meeting, Atlantic City, N.J., April 26–28, 1962)

21. Cohen, M., and Held, R. *Degrading Eye-hand Coordination by Exposure to Disordered Re-afferent Stimulation* (Presented at Eastern Psychol. Assoc., 31st meeting, New York, N.Y., April 15–16, 1960)

22. Dember, W. N. *The Psychology of Perception* (Henry Holt and Co., New York, N.Y., 402 pp., 1960)

23. DeRivera, J. Some conditions governing the use of the cue-producing response as an explanatory device. *J. Exptl. Psychol.*, 57, 299–304 (1959)

24. Drever, J. D. Perceptual learning. *Ann. Rev. Psychol.*, 11, 131–60 (1960)

25. Drever, J. D. Perception and action. *Bull. Brit. Psychol. Soc.*, 45, 1–9 (1961)

26. Ellis, H. C., Bessemer, D. W., Devine, J. V., and Trafton, C. L. Recognition of random tactual shapes following predifferentiation training. Perceptual Motor Skills, 10, 99–102 (1962)

27. Engen, T. Effect of practice and instruction on olfactory thresholds. *Perceptual Motor Skills*, 10, 195–98 (1960)

28. Epstein, W., and DeShazo, D. Recency as a function of perceptual oscillation. *Am. J. Psychol.*, 74, 215–23 (1961)

29. Epstein, W., and Rock, I. Perceptual set as an artifact of recency. *Am. J. Psychol.*, 73, 214–28 (1960)

30. Essman, W. B. "Learning without awareness" of responses to perceptual and verbal stimuli as a function of reinforcement schedule. *Perceptual Motor Skills*, 9, 15–25 (1959)

31. Ettlinger, E. Cross-modal transfer of training in monkeys. *Behavior*, 16, 56–65 (1960)

32. Fantz, R. L. The origin of form perception. *Sci. Am.*, 204, 66–72 (1961)

33. Fleishman, E. A., and Fruchter, B. Factor structure and predictability of successive stages of learning Morse code. *J. Appl. Psychol.*, 44, 97–101 (1960)

34. Fowler, W. Cognitive learning in infancy and early childhood. *Psychol. Bull.*, 59, 116–52 (1962)

35. Fraisse, P. Mise en évidence d'un apprentissage perceptif des groupements par proximité. *Année psychol.*, 59, 374–80 (1959)

36. Fraisse, P., and Blancheteau, M. The influence of number of alternatives on the perceptual recognition threshold. *Quart. J. Psychol.*, 14, 52–55 (1962)

37. Francès, R. Information et ajustment dans l'apprentissage perceptif. In *Proceedings 16th Intern. Congr. of Psychol.* Bonn, Germany, July 31–Aug. 6, 1960, 331–2 (North Holland Publishing Co., Amsterdam, 944 pp., 1962)

38. Francès, R. Le *Développement Perceptif* (Presses Universitaires de France, Paris, France, 275 pp., 1962)

39. Freedman, S. J. Perceptual changes in sensory deprivation: suggestions for a conative theory. *J. Nervous Mental Disease*, 132, 17–21 (1961)

40. Ganz, L., and Riesen, A. H. Stimulus generalization to hue in the dark-reared Macaque. *J. Comp. Physiol. Psychol.*, 55, 92–99 (1962)

41. Garner, W. R. *Uncertainty and Structure as Psychological Concepts* (John Wiley & Sons, Inc., New York, N.Y., 369 pp., 1962)

42. Ghent, L. Recognition by children of realistic figures presented in various orientations. *Can. J. Psychol.*, 14, 249–56 (1960)

43. Ghent, L., and Bernstein, L. Influence of the orientation of geometric forms on their recognition by children. *Perceptual Motor Skills*, 12, 95–101 (1961)

44. Gibson, E. J. *The Role of Grapheme-phoneme Correspondence in Word Recognition* (Presented at Eastern Psychol. Assoc., 33rd meeting, Atlantic City, N.J., April 26–28, 1962)

45. Gibson, E. J. *The Development of Perception: Discrimination of Depth Compared with the Discrimination of Graphic Symbols* (Presented at Conference on *Basic Cognitive Processes*

in Children, Minneapolis, Minn. April, 1961) *Monographs Soc. Research Child Develop.* (In press)

46. Gibson, E. J., and Olum, V. Experimental methods of studying perception in children. In *Handbook of Research Methods in Child Development*, 311–373 (Mussen, P. H., Ed., John Wiley & Sons, Inc., New York, N.Y., 1061 pp., 1960).

47. Gibson, E. J., and Walk, R. D. The "Visual cliff." *Sci. Am.*, 202, 64–71 (1960)

48. Gibson, E. J., Walk, R. D., and Tighe, T. J. Enhancement and deprivation of visual stimulation during rearing as factors in visual discrimination learning. *J. Comp. Physiol. Psychol.*, 52, 74–81 (1959)

49. Gibson, J. J., *et al.* Symposium on perceptual learning. In *Proceedings 16th Intern. Congr. of Psychol.*, Bonn, Germany, July 31–Aug. 6, 1960, 317–330 (North Holland Publishing Co., Amsterdam, 944 pp., 1962)

50. Gibson, J. J., and Gibson, E. J. Perceptual learning: differentiation or enrichment? *Psychol. Rev.*, 62, 32–41 (1955)

51. Goldiamond, I., and Hawkins, W. F. Vexierversuch: the log relationship between word-frequency and recognition obtained in the absence of stimulus words. *J. Exptl. Psychol.*, 56, 457–63 (1958)

52. Goldstein, M. J., and Ratliff, J. Relationship between frequency of usage and ease of recognition with response bias controlled. *Perceptual Motor Skills*, 13, 171–77 (1961)

53. Gollin, E. S. Tactual form discrimination: developmental differences in the effect of training under conditions of spacial interference. *J. Psychol.*, 51, 131–40 (1961)

54. Gregory, R. L., and Wallace, J. G. Recovery from early blindness—a case study, *Quart. J. Exptl. Psychol., Monograph Suppl.* 2 (1962) (In press)

55. Hanes, R. M., and Rhoades, M. V. Color identification as a function of extended practice. *J. Opt. Soc. Am.*, 49, 1060–64 (1959)

56. Harcum, E. R., and Dyer, D. W. Monocular and binocular reproduction of binary stimuli appearing right and left of fixation. *Am. J. Psychol.*, 75, 56–65 (1962)

57. Hayes, W. N., Robinson, J. S., and Brown, L. T. *An Effect of Past Experience on Perception: An Artifact* (Presented at American Psychol. Assoc., 69th meeting, New York, N.Y., Aug. 31-Sept. 6, 1961) (Abstr. in *Am. Psychol.*, 16, 420, 1961)

58. Hebb, D. O. Discussion (Symposium on sensory deprivation: facts in search of a theory). *J. Nervous Mental Disease*, 132, 40–43 (1961).

59. Hein, A. V., and Held, R. *Movement-produced Stimulation in the Development of Visually-guided Behavior* (Presented at Eastern Psychol. Assoc., 33rd meeting, Atlantic City, N.J., April 26–28, 1962)

60. Held, R. Exposure-history as a factor in maintaining stability of perception and coordination. *J. Nervous Mental Disease*, 132, 26–32 (1961)

61. Held, R. Adaptation to rearrangement and visual-spatial aftereffects. *Psychol. Beit.*, 6, 439–50 (1962)

62. Held, R., and Bossom, J. Neonatal deprivation and adult rearrangement: complementary techniques for analyzing plastic sensory-motor coordinations. *J. Comp. Physiol. Psychol.*, 54, 33–37 (1961)

63. Held, R., and Schlank, M. Adaptation to dissarranged eye-hand coordination in the distance-dimension. *Am. J. Psychol.*, 72, 603–5 (1959)

64. Henle, M. An experimental investigation of past experience as a determinant of visual form perception. *J. Exptl. Psychol.*, 30, 1–22 (1942)

65. Hermelin, B., and O'Connor, N. Recognition of shapes by normal and subnormal children. *Brit. J. Psychol.*, 52, 281–84 (1961)

66. Heron, W. Perception as a function of retinal locus and attention. *Am. J. Psychol.*, 70, 38–48 (1957)

67. Hochberg, J. Nature and nurture in perception. In *Psychology in the Making* (Postman, L., Ed., Knopf, New York, N.Y., in press)
68. Hochberg, J., and Brooks, V. Pictorial recognition as an unlearned ability: a study of one child's performance. *Am. J. Psychol.* (In press)
69. House, B. J., and Zeaman, D. Transfer of a discrimination from objects to patterns. *J. Exptl. Psychol.*, 59, 298–302 (1960)
70. Hudson, W. Pictorial depth perception in sub-cultural groups in Africa. *J. Social Psychol.*, 52, 183–208 (1960)
71. Hunt, J. McV. *Intelligence and Experience* (The Ronald Press Co., New York, N.Y., 416 pp., 1961)
72. Ittleson, W. H. *Visual Space Perception* (Springer Publishing Co., New York, N.Y., 212 pp., 1960)
73. Ittleson, W. H. Perception and transactional psychology. In *Psychology: A Study of a Science*. Vol . 4: *Biologically Oriented Fields: Their Place in Psychology and in Biological Science*, 660–704 (Koch, S., Ed., McGraw-Hill Book Co., New York, N.Y., 837 pp., 1962)
74. Jakobson, R., and Halle, M. *Fundamentals of Language* (Mouton & Co., The Hague, Netherlands, 87 pp., 1956)
75. Karn, H. W., and Gregg, L. W. Acquisition of perceptual responses as a function of loading, location, and repetition. *J. Exptl. Psychol.*, 62, 62–69 (1961)
76. Kilpatrick, F. P. *Explorations in Transactional Psychology* (New York Univ. Press, New York, N.Y., 405 pp., 1961)
77. Kimura, D. The effect of letter position on recognition. *Can. J. Psychol.*, 13, 1–10 (1959)
78. Kohler, I. *Über Aufbau und Wandlungen der Wahrnemungswelt* (Rohrer, Vienna, Austria, 118 pp., 1951)
79. Kohler, I. Interne und externe organization in der Warnehmung. *Psychol. Beit.*, 6, 426–38 (1962)
80. Kohler, I. Experiments with goggles. *Sci. Am.*, 206, 62–72 (1962)
81. Kossov, B. B. Some methods for bringing out essential features in perceived objects. *Problems of Psychol.*, 1, 71–81 (1960)
82. L'Abate, L. Recognition of paired trigrams as a function of associative value and associative strength. *Science*, 131, 984–85 (1960)
83. Lane, H. L., and Moore, D. J. Operant reconditioning of a consonant discrimination in an aphasic. *Progr. Rept. No. 1 Exptl. Analysis of Control of Speech Production and Perception* (Contract No. SAE-9265, U.S. Office of Education, Washington, D.C., 1961)
84. Lenneberg, E. Color naming, color recognition, color discrimination: a reappraisal. *Perceptual Motor Skills*, 12, 375–82 (1961)
85. Liberman, A. M., Harris, K. S., Kinney, J., and Lane, H. The discrimination of relative onset-time of the components of certain speech and nonspeech patterns. *J. Exptl. Psychol.*, 61, 379–88 (1961)
86. London, I. D. A Russian report on the postoperative newly seeing. *Am. J. Psychol.*, 73, 478–82 (1960)
87. McNamara, H. J. Nonveridical perception as a function of rewards and punishments. *Perceptual Motor Skills*, 9, 67–80 (1959)
88. Mangan, G. L. The role of punishment in figure-ground reorganization. *J. Exptl. Psychol.*, 58, 369–75 (1959)
89. Mangan, G. L. Retention of figure-ground reorganization occurring under electric-shock punishment. *Perceptual Motor Skills*, 12, 151–54 (1961)
90. Marx, M. H., Murphy, W. W., and Brownstein, A. J. Recognition of complex visual stimuli as a function of training with abstracted patterns. *J. Exptl. Psychol.*, 62, 456–60 (1961)

91. Meier, G. W., and McGee, R. K. A re-evaluation of the effect of early perceptual experience on discrimination performance during adulthood *J. Comp. Physiol. Psychol.*, 52, 390–95 (1959)

92. Miller, N. E., and Dollard, J. *Social Learning and Imitation* (Yale Univ. Press, New Haven, Conn. 341 pp., 1941)

93. Minsky, M. Steps toward artificial intelligence. *Proc. Inst. Radio Engrs.*, 49, 8–30 (1961)

94. Mooney, C. M. Recognition of symmetrical and non-symmetrical inkblots with and without eye movements. *Can. J. Psychol.*, 13, 11–19 (1959).

95. Mooney, C. M. Recognition of ambiguous and unambiguous visual configurations with short and longer exposures. *Brit. J. Psychol.*, 51, 119–25 (1960)

96. Moscovici, S., and Humbert, C. Usage et disponibilité comme facteurs déterminant la durée de stimuli verbaux. *Bull. Psychol.*, 13, 406–12 (1960)

97. Nealey, S. M., and Edwards, B. J. "Depth perception" in rats without pattern-vision experience. *J. Comp. Physiol. Psychol.*, 53, 468–69 (1960)

98. Newbigging, P. L. Personal values and response strength of value-related words as measured in a pseudoperceptual task. *Can. J. Psychol.* 14, 38–44 (1960)

99. Newbigging, P. L. The perceptual redintegration of frequent and infrequent words. *Can. J. Psychol.* 15, 123–32 (1961)

100. Newbigging, P. L., and Hay, J. M. *The Practice Effect in Recognition Threshold Determinations as a Function of Word Frequency and Length* (Presented at Eastern Psychol. Assoc., 33rd meeting, Atlantic City, N.J., April 26–28, 1962)

101. Osser, H., and Gibson, E. J. *A Developmental Study of the Discrimination of Letter-like Forms* (Presented at Eastern Psychol. Assoc., 32nd meeting, Philadelphia, Pa., April 7–8, 1961)

102. Pastore, N. Perceptual functioning in the ducking. *J. Genet. Psychol.*, 95, 157–69 (1959)

103. Pastore, N. Perceiving as innately determined. *J. Genet. Psychol.*, 96, 93–99 (1960)

104. Pearson, R. G., and Hauty, G. T. Adaptive processes determining proprioceptive perception of verticality. *J. Exptl. Psychol.*, 57, 367–71 (1959)

105. Pearson, R. G., and Hauty, G. T. Role of postural experiences in proprioceptive perception of verticality. *J. Exptl. Psychol.*, 59, 425–28 (1960)

106. Pfafflin, S. M. Stimulus meaning in stimulus predifferentiation. *J. Exptl. Psychol.*, 59, 269–74 (1960)

107. Phaup, M. R., and Caldwell, W. E. Perceptual learning: differentiation and enrichment of past experience. *J. Gen. Psychol.*, 60, 137–47 (1959)

108. Piaget, J. *Les Mécanismes Perceptifs* (Presses Universitaires de France, Paris, France, 457 pp., 1961)

109. Prentice, W. C. H. Aftereffects in perception. *Sci. Am.*, 206, 44–49 (1962)

110. Rasmussen, E. A., and Archer, E. J. Concept identification as a function of language pretraining and task complexity. *J. Exptl. Psychol.*, 61, 437–41 (1961)

111. Riesen, A. H. Studying perceptual development using the technique of sensory deprivation. *J. Nervous Mental Disease*, 132, 21–25 (1961)

112. Riesen, A. H., and Aarons, L. Visual movement and intensity discrimination in cats after early deprivation of pattern vision. *J. Comp. Physiol. Psychol.*, 52, 142–49 (1959)

113. Rosenblatt, F. The design of an intelligent automaton. *Research Reviews* (ONR), 5–13, (October, 1958)

113a. Rubenstein, H., and Aborn, M. Psycholinguistics. *Ann. Rev. Psychol.*, 11, 291–322 (1960)

114. Rudel, R. *Decrement of the Müller-Lyer Illusion: A Study of Intermodal Transfer* (Presented at Eastern Psychol. Assoc., 31st meeting, New York, N.Y., April 15–16, 1960)

115. Santos, J. F., and Murphy, G. An Odyssey in perceptual learning. *Bull. Menninger Clin.*, 24, 6–17 (1960)

116. Schiff, W. The effect of subliminal stimuli on guessing-accuracy. *Am. J. Psychol.*, 74, 54–60 (1961)

117. Selfridge, O. G., and Neisser, U. Pattern recognition by machine. *Sci. Am.*, 203, 60–68 (1960)

118. Senden, M. von. *Space and Sight* (Free Press, Glencoe, Ill., 348 pp., 1960)

119. Smock, C. D., and Kanfer, F. H. Response bias and perception. *J. Exptl. Psychol.*, 62, 158–63 (1961)

120. Solley, C. M., and Engel, M. Perceptual autism in children: the effects of reward, punishment, and neutral conditions upon perceptual learning. *J. Genet. Psychol.*, 97, 77–91 (1960)

121. Solley, C. M., and Murphy, G. *Development of the Perceptual World* (Basic Books, Inc., New York, N.Y., 353 pp., 1960)

122. Tallarico, R. B. Studies of visual depth perception: III. Choice behavior of newly hatched chicks on a visual cliff. *Perceptual Motor Skills*, 12, 259–62 (1961)

123. Terrace, H. S. The effects of retinal locus and attention on the perception of words. *J. Exptl. Psychol.*, 58, 382–85 (1959)

124. Teuber, H. L. Sensory deprivation, sensory suppression and agnosia: notes for a neurologic theory. *J. Nervous Mental Disease*, 132, 32–40 (1961)

125. Uhr, L., Vossler, C., and Uleman, J. Pattern recognition over distortions, by human subjects and by a computer simulation of a model for human form perception. *J. Exptl. Psychol.*, 63, 227–34 (1962)

126. Vanderplas, J. M. *Some Relations of Learning to Form Perception* (Presented at meeting of the Southern Soc. for Phil. and Psychol., Biloxi, Miss., April, 14–16, 1960)

127. Vanderplas, J. M., and Garvin, E. A. Complexity, association value, and practice as factors in shape recognition following paired-associates training. *J. Exptl. Psychol.*, 57, 155–63 (1959)

128. Vanderplas, J. M., Sanderson, W. A., and Vanderplas, J. N. *Some Task-related Determinants of Transfer in Perceptual Learning* (Presented at meeting of Southern Soc. for Phil. and Psychol., Memphis, Tenn., April, 19–21, 1962)

129. Vernon, M. D. Perception, attention and consciousnesss. *Advanc. Sci.*, 62, 111–23 (1959)

130. Vurpillot, E., and Brault, H. Étude experimentale sur la formation des schèmes empiriques. *Année psychol.*, 59, 381–94 (1959)

131. Walk, R. D. *A Study of Some Factors Influencing the Depth Perception of Human Infants* (Presented at Eastern Psychol. Assoc., 32nd meeting, Philadelphia, Pa., April, 7–8, 1961.)

132. Walk, R. D., and Gibson, E. J. A comparative and analytical study of visual depth perception. *Psychol. Monographs*, 75 (15), 44 pp. (1961)

133. Walk, R. D., Gibson, E. J., Pick, H. L., Jr., and Tighe, T. J. The effectiveness of prolonged exposure to cutouts vs. painted patterns for facilitation of discrimination. *J. Comp. Physiol. Psychol.*, 52, 519–21 (1959)

134. Wohlwill, J. F. Developmental studies of perception. *Psychol. Bull.*, 57, 249–88 (1960)

135. Yarczower, M. Conditioning test of stimulus-predifferentiation. *Am. J. Psychol.*, 72, 572–76 (1959)

136. Zeaman, D., and House, B. J. An attention theory of retardate discrimination learning. *Prog. Rept. No. 3* (Research Grant M-1099, Natl. Inst. Mental Health, Bethesda, Md., November, 1962).

137. Zinchenko, V. P., and Lomov, B. F. The functions of hand and eye movements in the process of perception. *Problems Psychol.*, 1, 12–26 (1960)

19

Perceptual Development and the Reduction of Uncertainty

Eleanor J. Gibson

The reader will find this paper dated, to be sure, but I think in a rather instructive fashion. The 1960s was a time for a revolution of ideas in the colleges of the country, not only among the undergraduates but also among the leaders of the disciplines they were taught. Psychology was no exception, and ideas from outside—from neuroscience, computer science, and even engineering—were eagerly received. Single fiber recording, information theory, artificial intelligence, and cybernetics all had a hearing and were enthusiastically incorporated into psychology, frequently rather uncritically. I was no exception, as this paper makes clear.

The paper was written for an International Congress of Psychology in Moscow of which I have mixed memories, some very pleasant such as a dinner given by A.V. Zaporozhets in his three-room apartment for American psychologists who had been invited to prepare papers for his symposium. The title of the symposium was "The Development of Perception and Activity." Psychologists included were myself, Julian Hochberg, Richard Held, A. V. Zaporozhets, V. P. Zinchenko, M. I. Lissina, R. D. Walk, Herbert Pick, John Hay, O. W. and P. C. Smith, J. B. Gippenreiter, Elaine Vurpillot, L. A. Venger, Allen Hein and a number of Soviet psychologists whom I cannot remember. The Soviet psychologists were all students or followers of Vigotsky and Leontiev, a second generation of clever theorists and researchers. Unfortunately, concern with perception in Russian psychology has declined since then, although a translation of J. J. Gibson's Ecological Approach to Visual Perception *has recently appeared (Logvinenko 1988).*

A Soviet psychologist I remember particularly well from this symposium is Zinchenko, whose talk impressed me greatly. His point of view was (to some extent) a Soviet "party line" view and involved constructing an internal model through action, but at the same time he incorporated ideas that were rather similar to my own. Here is a sample:

In *Proceedings of the 18th International Congress of Psychology*, Symposium 30, Perception and Action, 7–17, Moscow, 1966.

During the first stages the process of recognition is substantially like that of acquaintance. Here we also see such actions as discovering and selecting the informative content, adequate to the task. When it is selected, the subject begins to collate and identify the object with the etalon, recorded in the memory. When there are a great number of essential features in the object, the process of collating is divided into elements. It lasts the longer, the more we have such features in the object and its model created in the course of acquaintance. This includes a detailed and repeated observation of the object, accompanied by numerous movements of the hand and eye. But the character of the identification process changes with learning the given alphabet of the objects. The process of collating is radically reduced at the expense of eliminating excessive and redundant information, selecting critical and basic features, and transforming groups of separate features into structural "unit" ones. The identification of objects by such consolidated "unit" features is very rational, as the process of collating several features is replaced by collating one feature. (Zinchenko 1966, 70)

The last two sentences were very compatible with the theme of my own paper, the reduction of uncertainty. So was his definition of perception: "A perceptual action is a self-regulating process of search for and processing of information," although I would reword it to read "search for information to guide action."

An experiment performed by Albert Yonas as part of his Ph.D. dissertation at Cornell (Yonas and Gibson 1967) is an excellent illustration of the principle of reduction of information in perceptual learning. The design utilized the disjunctive reaction time experiment, much in vogue at the time owing to experiments of Sternberg (1967). The subject was given a set of nine letters, some of which were designated as the positive set and some the negative set. Any letter might be displayed, but the subject was to press the reaction key a certain way only for a member of the positive set. The membership of the positive set differed in three experimental conditions. In one, only one letter was designated positive. Both the other conditions had three letters assigned to the positive set. In one of these conditions they were not selected according to any useful rule, but in the other, the three positive numbers shared a distinctive feature that could be used to distinguish each one from every member of the negative set. Subjects needed only to search for that feature to reduce their reaction time to the level of the condition with only one positive member. Given practice, subjects did indeed reduce latencies in that condition relative to the one with a randomly selected positive set of three. Few subjects noticed the common feature. This seemed to us a neat case of an economy principle operating in a self-regulatory and highly adaptive fashion.

Reduction of uncertainty may sound a bit like Hull's reduction of a drive stimulus, but it involves no drive in his sense. Cognitive economy makes sense, and discovery of invariance is the essence of economy, finding order in change.

Introduction

In the 1940s, psychologists were very secure and very smug. They had a choice of two brands of S-R reinforcement theory, and if they didn't like it, there was S-S association theory. Almost no one bothered defining the S's and the R's.

But in the fifties a great blow fell. Information theory had its impact on psychology. It was suddenly obvious that you can't talk about *an* S or *an* R. You have to talk about a *set* of them. You have to know *what* the set of alternatives is and how big it is. Not only that, you have to know *how* members of the set differ from one another. And still worse, you have to know what the task is in relation to these differences (is it discrimination? recognition? free recall?) because potential distinctive features within a set, it begins to be clear, are determined by their task utility.

As if this were not enough, the sixties have brought the most shattering stroke of all. It has become obvious that the old concept of a stimulus as a *point* in space or an *instant* of energy cannot possibly be right. To be a stimulus, the energy *must contain information* and that means, at the very least, inhomogeneity and change. A few psychologists, among them Kurt Koffka, my husband, and Wendell Garner, have been pointing this out for a long time. They were, I fear, voices crying in the wilderness until some very respectable neurophysiologists (Maturana et al. 1960; Hubel and Wiesel 1962, 1963) came along and showed that even single nerve fibers in the optic system are fired by invariant patterned stimulation—by edges, convexities, lines at different orientations, and terminal endings of lines— in other words, by structural features of stimulation, however simple. These facts hold for newborn anesthetized cats. So God only knows what complexities of stimulus information can be picked up by a mature, unanesthetized, educated man.

On the other hand, we know that there is a limit to the capacities of information pickup of even this God-like creature. There is too much information, as a rule, in the total stimulus flux. He cannot handle it all. He must, therefore, develop some strategies of information processing— for example, selection, adaptation, and inhibition.

And so now, at this point in history, the question of perceptual development comes into its own. Nature does not turn out an infant with knowledge and operations ready-made in all these respects. We are faced with the following questions (and more). How are the sets of S's and R's sorted out and assembled? How does the person learn how members of a set differ? How does he learn to utilize distinctive features of the set in relation to the task? Are higher orders of stimulus information picked up increasingly with development? What strategies of information processing are correlated with development?

The perception psychologist is not responsible for the answers to *all* these questions, but he must face his share of them. So let me try.

A Twentieth-Century Theory of Perceptual Learning

Theories of perceptual learning have existed since the day of Bishop Berkeley. Perhaps, though, I should say *a* theory, for one theory persisted with a stranglehold even into the thirties and in fact gained new strength with Titchener and even with the functionalists of Carr's laboratories. That was, in essence, the notion that sensory elements are welded together by association to form perceptions, and that sensations are enriched, or added to through associative processes, by memory images or by experiences in another modality (e.g., vision was thought to gain meaning from association with touch).

The naive simplicity of this notion was rejected by the Behaviorists but was supplanted with something equally indefensible, again an "enrichment" or additive theory, but with the difference that *responses* were thought to be added, rather than mental contexts. My husband and I debated this view with Leo Postman in the *Psychological Review* in 1955 (Gibson and Gibson 1955; Postman 1955). I think all three of us have changed our minds a bit in the meantime (see Gibson 1959, and Postman 1963), but there are still current several versions of an additive mediation theory of perceptual learning.

They can be classified in various ways. The main division of *additive mediation* theories, as I shall call them, is into cognitively oriented and response-oriented theories. Theories which assume unconscious inference (or a kind of submerged problem-solving process) are of the cognitively oriented type. They can be traced back to Helmholtz, but they have their modern advocates as well: notably, Brunswik, Bruner, and the transactionalists. Another form of cognitively oriented theory assumes that the underlying mediational process is not inference, but rather accruing of a representation or schema to which input can be matched. M. D. Vernon seems sometimes to advocate this position, as often does Piaget (though in his case there is more emphasis on activity than passive accrual). A number of computer-based models of perceptual learning and recognition are perhaps the purest examples of accounting for one aspect of perceptual learning by storage of a representation and matching it, template fashion.

The response-oriented theories also can be divided into two groups. I call one the "motor copy" theory. This theory holds that objects in the world are reflected in perception by action—that is, by responses which trace them or embody them in such a way as to recreate their form or structure. The process is analogous to schema formation, but the "representation" is motor rather than some kind of cognitive mediation. Soviet theories of perception especially have favored this theory (cf. Leontiev 1957). Typical examples of its application are experiments that study hand-tracing of objects, and the eye movements made in scanning pictured forms, relating them to perceptual development (cf. Pick 1963). In America, Hebb's theory of development of form perception is somewhat similar.

But the perceptual learning model favored by most American response-oriented psychologists does not stress copy or reflection of objects in the world, but rather emphasizes discrimination learning based on additive mediation of individual responses, and goes by the name of acquired distinctiveness of cues. William James was the originator of the essential idea that improvement in discrimination takes place by learning distinctive associates to originally barely discriminable pairs of stimuli. "First, the *terms* whose differences come to be felt contract disparate associates and these help to drag them apart.... The effect of practice in increasing discrimination must then, in part, be due to the reinforcing effect, upon an original slight difference between the terms, of *additional* differences between the diverse associates which they severally affect" (James 1890, 510–511).

Miller and Dollard (1941) cast this idea into its modern S-R form, the associates of course being responses. Distinctiveness is added by learning a distinctive response; equivalence is added, on the other hand, by learning a response already associated with something else.

To me, all these additive theories seem wrong. They do not square with the points I made about the nature of stimuli and responses—that information, the degree of uncertainty in both, must be considered, and furthermore that stimulation always has some structure. I could quote experimental evidence against them, as well, but I think the strongest argument is their failure to take account of twentieth century developments in our knowledge of how perception works.

Let me, therefore, present another point of view, which I shall refer to as the *specificity* view. This view holds that stimulation is very rich in potential variables and information which may or may not be responded to. Discrimination learning proceeds not by adding images or distinctive responses, nor by building motor copies or cognitive representations, but rather by discovering distinctive features of objects and invariants of events in stimulation. The features (distinguishing is perhaps a better term than distinctive) and the invariants over time are there to be discovered, not added on by attaching responses or images or anything. The criterion of perceptual learning is thus increased differentiation of the stimulus array, greater specificity and correlation between stimulation and discriminative response. The operations by which relevant distinguishing features are discovered do indeed include responses—exploratory responses such as scanning, feeling, fixating, and searching. But it is not the addition of these responses which explains differentiation, for they are not themselves specific to the differences to be discovered. Objects are discriminated by their dimensions of difference. There are sets or classes of objects which share certain features. But insofar as they are discriminable, each has a pattern of features which is unique. This unique pattern is not created by the mind, but is discovered by the individual as he develops, or when he is exposed to a new class of objects. When I first arrived at Cornell, I was invited to work at the Behavior Farm where Professor Liddell had a large experimental population of goats—a herd of one hundred or more. I was assigned some goats as subjects and had the daily problem of extracting my subjects from the herd. I had never seen a goat up close before, and for a few weeks I spent most of my working day just finding my goat. But with daily exposure and plenty of searching, I eventually learned to recognize individual goats and to identify new ones almost immediately. I had learned the distinctive features of goats. Though I could not tell you what they were, members of the set came to possess, for me, unique patterns of these features.

The most elegant example I know of is the system of distinctive features worked out for phonemes by Roman Jakobson. Jakobson and Halle (1956) enumerated a set of twelve distinctive features for phonemes such that any phoneme is distinguishable from any other by its bundle of attributes. All of the features have a plus and a minus value—that is, form a binary opposition. The opposition may require a choice between polar qualities of the same dimension, or presence or absence of a given attribute.

The choice of these features is both intuitive and empirical. Objective criteria for choosing a feature table are the requirements that the table must provide a *unique* bundle for each member of the set, and that the properties chosen must be *invariant* over certain transformations (for instance, different speakers, shouting, and whispering). To quote Jakobson and Halle, "A distinctive feature is a *relational* property so that the 'minimum same' of a feature in its combination with various other concurrent or successive features lies in the essentially identical *relation* between the two opposite alternatives" (p. 14).

This feature description of phonemes constitutes, presumably, a set of rules which the speaker must obey, even though he is unaware of them (as he surely is). The psychologist will wonder, at this point, whether we have any convincing experimental evidence that these rules actually operate, that they have psychological as well as logical validity. I am afraid there is very little. For this reason, I have been interested in working out a feature table for a set of material that I could, myself, manipulate experimentally.

Research with Distinctive Features of Letters

I chose as my set of items printed letters—a set of simplified Roman capitals. Developmental research on the discrimination of letterlike forms had convinced me that there is progressive learning of contrastive relational features which permits the forms to be distinguished. The problem was, first, to specify these features in a table so as to provide a unique pattern for each letter. The features, furthermore, must be invariant under various transformations—specifiable transformations such as size, perspective and brightness changes, and others such as the personal idiosyncracies of different writers. Having chosen a list on a rational basis, the next problem was to check it by any experimental means I could devise.

A list of features that I selected for the test is arranged in a chart comparable to a phoneme feature chart. Each letter has a unique pattern of features. For some letter pairs the distinction is minimal (one feature), for some great. Because of this variance, a good test of the validity of the list could be obtained in a confusion matrix. For if discrimination of letters depends on the detection of certain critical differences between them, then the rate of confusion errors made between letter pairs should depend on the number of feature contrasts between them.

Accordingly, an experiment was run to obtain the confusion matrix for every letter paired with every other. A discrimination task required the subject to match a standard letter with a list of six letters, randomly selected but always containing a correct match. Every letter had an equal chance to be confused with every other, over a large number of subjects and trials. The subjects were four-year-old children.

Correlations were obtained between percent feature differences and number of confusions, one for every letter. Of the twenty-six correlations, twelve were positive, only a fair batting average.

Another experiment was run comparing two conditions of discrimination—one a set of letter matching trials with "high,confusion" context, another with a "low-confusion" context. The high- and low-confusion values were predicted from the feature table. Errors and reaction times were recorded, and results for the two experimental conditions differed as predicted.

The feature list so far tested requires revision. Hints for revising it can be obtained, I believe, from the kind of multidimensional analysis that Dr. Warren Torgerson works with. Dr. Torgerson has, in fact, analyzed my confusion matrix with results both gratifying and puzzling. Two dimensions came out which accord beautifully with the feature list—curve-straight, and diagonality. Beyond that, it was not clear what we had. Our next step will be collection of data for a better error matrix, using adult subjects, and a further attempt at analysis. The feature list can then be amended and a new experimental test run.

Besides asking whether a list of distinctive features of letters exists which is really utilized in letter discrimination, it is interesting to ask how discrimination takes place—how the features are processed in the act of discrimination, and how the list is learned and its processing strategy developed. These questions lead me back to my original thesis, how perceptual learning and development actually occur.

The Role of Activity

I have said that what is learned in perceptual learning and development is the distinctive features of objects and the invariant features of events over time. What can be said about the processes involved? The topic of this symposium is the role of activity in perceptual development. And here I can begin. Perception is active. It is not registration, or assimilation, or composite photography, or automatic hitching of responses to stimuli, but rather active exploration and search for critical features and invariants. Search, it will be noted, takes place over time and this is important, implying again that perception is never correlated with an isolated momentary stimulus.

The idea that perception crucially involves exploratory activity has been sressed by my husband, who distinguishes between exploratory and performatory activity. Perception does not incorporate performatory activity of the kind that does things to the environment and its furnishings; rather it explores and searches out information from the environment and the stimulation it provides. The total potential stimulation reaching his receptors is never perceived by any man. He samples from this vast pool; only part of the potential stimulation becomes effective. To perceive most selectively, strategies of active exploration must be developed.

The exploratory and active role of perception has been stressed by other psychologists, Pavlov for one. Pavlov spoke of the "investigatory reflex," which he contrasted with the conditioned reflex. I believe he meant by this term what I should prefer to call attention, the active exploratory, selective aspect of perception.

I have said that some stimulus information is selected from the total stimulation, and that the strategy of perceptual search and selection can be good or bad. This implies, to me, the necessity of perceptual learning. Optimal strategies differ for different tasks and different sets of potential stimuli, so learning takes place in the exploratory activity itself.

At once, the question arises, how is it determined what gets selected when learning occurs in a given situation between one occasion and the next? Do we want to invoke reinforcement? I think not in the traditional sense of an external reward or confirmation, but instead in the sense of task utility. The ultimate goal of perception, I think, is differentiation, the reducing of uncertainty; or to put it another way, the extraction of distinguishing features and invariants from a stimulus flux where information is very great. Where it isn't great, no learning is needed. Babies almost certainly distinguish contrasts of lines and edges presented on homogeneous backgrounds without any learning at all. But faces, with their variety of features and expressions, present too much information and take time and practice to differentiate.

Reduction of Uncertainty

The principle of reinforcement in perceptual learning is *utility for the reduction of uncertainty*. That is just exactly what distinguishing features and invariants of events have; they serve to reduce uncertainty in a world otherwise too full of information. Features that are not distinguishing and variables that do not serve to cut down uncertainty must be ignored. The constancies are examples of invariance in perception, cases of reduction of uncertainty by attending to the right features of the stimulus. When a car drives toward me, its projected size, proximal-stimulus-wise, keeps increasing. But I do not see an infinite number of different cars of larger and larger size. There is an invariant aspect of the stimulation, over time, which can be and is attended to.

Now it will be clear why I am against additive theories of perceptual learning. It is because I think the secret of it is just the opposite, reduction. Perceptual learning is taking out, not adding on. The effective stimulus which active and educated perception picks out is a reduced stimulus. It is extracted, filtered out, whereas other stimulus information which has no utility for differentiation is ignored by the educated attention.

Someone may ask what motivates this kind of learning. I am content with the notion that there is a built-in need for differentiation, for the reduction of uncertainty. Others (Berlyne 1957) have spoken of "perceptual curiosity." This construct has been related, by Berlyne, to "arousal" and also to stimulus conditions characterized by novelty, complexity, surprisingness, incongruity, and uncertainty. These properties are said to increase exploratory activity. Measurements of "perceptual curiosity," in Berlyne's sense of the term, do tend to show less such curiosity in retardates than in equal M. A. and C. A. normal male subjects (Hoats, Miller, and Spitz 1963). But whatever one calls the motive, more active exploration would be expected to effect greater perceptual learning and thus cognitive growth.

I would like to bring in a little support from information theory, specifically from the work of Garner and Clement (1963). Garner and Clement showed that "goodness" of pattern is correlated with its uncertainty, the size of the set to which it belongs. To quote them, "A good pattern ... is one which is perceived as stable, as not easily changed, and as having few alternatives.... the best possible pattern is that perceived as unique." (p. 452) This statement delights me—the "good" pattern is invariant and unique. These attributes, I believe, are the ends of perceptual development; thus follows the reduction of the set and the trend toward specificity. I doubt that the correlation between perceived size of set and goodness is a causal one. They are both, I think, results of discrimination of stimulus attributes of the set and patterns of attributes of members of the set. Some attributes, such as linearity and symmetry, evidently are easily picked up, even by young children and retardates. Other nonlinear ones are not so obvious, and this is where development comes in.

Let me cite one more example of a developmental trend toward perception of higher-dependency constraints. Perception of language provides many examples of "chunking," to use George Miller's term; that is, processing big units instead of little ones. Long ago, Cattell (1885) showed that only four unconnected letters could be perceived in a very brief exposure, but twelve or more could when the letters formed a word, and still more if subunits of words formed a sentence. Bryan and Harter (1899), also long ago, showed that reception of Morse code shifts during learning toward decoding by larger units, syllables, words and so on, rather than decoding the symbols for single letters. Obviously, the internal dependencies which structure the superordinate units are learned in both these cases.

I myself have studied the development of perception of spelling patterns in reading. Children in learning to read move rather quickly from single letter discrimination to discrimination of longer strings of letters which have predictable correspondences with speech sounds. These spelling-to-sound correspondences form units and, as the child develops skill he progressively handles units of increased length and dependency order. He perceives these units, ordered by internal regularities, although he could not verbalize the rules for you.

Conclusion

A poet once remarked that "the world is so full of a number of things." It is, but that does not make us happy as kings, it is only bewildering. Being happy as a king, cognitively speaking, is being able to select out of the massive stimulus flux information that is relevant and that is invariant over time, and thus to reduce uncertainty. The rest is thrown away, ignored, by a smart adult. He handles as much as he can, learning as he grows up to pick the attributes which have greatest utility for reducing uncertainty.

References

Berlyne, D. E. Conflict and information-theory variables as determinants of human perceptual curiosity. *J. Exp. Psychol.*, 1957, 53, 399–404.

Cattell, J. McK. Ueber die Zeit der Erkennung und Benennung von Schiftzeichen Bildern und Farken. *Phil. Stud.*, 1885, 2, 635–650.

Bryan, W. L., and Harter, N. Studies on the telegraphic language. *Psychol. Rev.*, 1899, 6, 345–375.

Garner, W. R. To perceive is to know. *Amer. Psychol.*, 1965, 20, 569 (Address given as recipient of Distinguished Scientific Contribution Award).

Garner, W. R., and Clement, D. E. Goodness of pattern and pattern uncertainty. *J. verb. learn. verb. behav.*, 1963, 2, 446–452.

Gibson, J. J. Perception as a function of stimulation. Pp. 456–501 in S. Koch (Ed.), *Psychology: A Study of a Science*, Vol. I. New York: McGraw-Hill, 1959.

Gibson, J. J. and Gibson, E. J. Perceptual learning: differentiation or enrichment? *Psychol. Rev.*, 1955, 62, 32–44.

Hoats, D. L., Miller, M. B., and Spitz, H. H. Experiments on perceptual curiosity in mental retardates and normals. *Amer. J. Ment. Defic.*, 1963, 68, 386–395.

Hubel, D. H., and Wiesel, T. N. Receptive fields, binocular interaction and functional architecture in the cat's visual cortex. *J. Physiol.*, 1962, 160, 106–154.

Hubel, D. H., and Wiesel, T. N. Receptive fields of cells in striate cortex of very young, visually inexperienced kittens. *J. Neurophysiol.*, 1963, 26, 994–1002.

Jakobson, R., and Halle, M. *Fundamentals of Language*. The Hague: Mouton and Company, 1956.

James, W. *The Principles of Psychology*, Vol. I. New York: Henry Holt and Co., 1890.

Leontiev, A. N. The nature and formation of human psychic properties. Pp. 226-232 in B. Simon (Ed.), *Psychology in the Soviet Union*. Stanford: Stanford Univ. Press, 1957.

Maturana, H. R., Lettvin, J. Y., McCulloch, W. S., & Pitts, W. H. Anatomy and physiology of vision in the frog (Rana pipiens). *J. gen. Physiol.*, 1960, 43, 129–175.

Postman, L. (1955). Association theory and perceptual learning. *Psychol. Rev.*, 62, 438–446.

Postman, L. (1963). Perception and learning. In S. Koch (Ed.), *Psychology: A study of a science*. Vol. 5. New York: McGraw-Hill, 1963, Pp. 30–113.

Pick, H. (1963). Some Soviet research on learning and perception in children. In J. C. Wright & J. Kagan (Eds.), *Basic cognitive processes in children. Monogr. Soc. Res. Child Develpm.*, 1963, 28, No. 86. 185–190.

Miller, N. E. & Dollard, J. (1941). *Social learning and imitation*. New Haven: Yale Univ. Press.

20

Trends in Perceptual Development
Eleanor J. Gibson

I have chosen to reprint parts of this last chapter from my book on perceptual learning for several reasons. It stands alone fairly well as a kind of last word or summing up. A version of it served as my presidential address to the Eastern Psychological Association in 1969. This was a memorable occasion for me—the book had just come out, it had won the Century Prize, I had been made a faculty member at Cornell at last, and there were all my friends in the Grand Ballroom of the Sheraton-Park Hotel in Washington. Not only that, there was a serious political confrontation at the business meeting, which just preceded the president's address. Adrenalin flowed, especially mine. Nonmembers occupied the platform and addressed the association in favor of a vote for some highly politicized issue of the day. I can't remember what the issue was, but I remember the turbulance of the audience. It all turned out happily, in the end, and we celebrated that night in a suite donated by the hotel—very grand and gaudy.

In the address I tried to deal with some age-old problems that had dominated work in perceptual development for decades and I believe still do to some extent— for example, which is prior, the whole or the part. That issue was a major one as late as 1981, when I was discussant at a conference held at Dartmouth College's Holderness Conference Center (Tighe and Shepp 1983). There was recurrent discussion for several days as to whether development progresses from "wholistic" to "analytic." I found myself arguing all over again that perception is always unified, however differentiated. The layout of the world and events, especially events, are typically embedded, units within units. We perceive wholes—the units can be of any size. A shift to perceiving larger units is as natural as the other way round, because order in the world is embedded and perceptual learning yields detection of both finer texture and more encompassing structure, another example of the duality of perception. It has been suggested, occasionally, that this is an example of the philosophical issue of "the one and the many." But I think the

Excerpts from Chapter 20 of *Principles of Perceptual Learning and Development*, © 1969, pp. 450–472. Reprinted by permission of Prentice-Hall, Inc., Englewood Cliffs, NJ.

world we perceive is always one, however deeply nested the information we can obtain.

The other issues persist among some developmental psychologists, but as they wane, new ones come to take their place. There is little talk of stages, nowadays, nor of development from raw perception to inference. Instead there is a new argument about inference—whether it already exists as a rather sophisticated form of logic in neonates (see, for example, Bower 1989). Some classic issues that persist despite changing fashions in theory are discussed in a recent paper of mine (E. Gibson 1987). Heredity vs. environment, continuity vs. discontinuity, mechanism vs. function are hardy perennials.

The three trends observed in perceptual development still seem valid—increase in specificity, optimization of attention, and increasing economy of information pickup—although they could do with some revision. One of the trends, optimization of attention, needs a lot of revision. I have come to doubt that perception becomes more active, or more exploratory, or more selective with development. We know much more about perception in infants than we did in 1969, and there is a wealth of evidence that perception is active, exploratory, and selective from the beginning. Mechanisms of exploration develop and efficiency increases as new action systems become available. By this time, one could write a much fuller story about discovery of structure—the role (or nonrole) of Gestalt principles in perceptual development for instance. The big gap, what was missing in all the evidence summarized for these trends (most of which I omit here), is the absence of any research on the role of dynamic factors in perceptual development. No research existed in 1969 on perception of events or the role of motion in pickup of structure in early development. Now there is a wealth of it to put to work in an up-to-date view of perceptual development.

The big new emphasis for many psychologists nowadays is the tight linkage of perception and action in a systems theory. Provocative, considering what was in the air in the sixties, is the hint that that was on the way. The idea was around in many forms, in the Russian dogmas, in Piagetian thinking, and in J. J. Gibson's perceptual systems, which emphasized active search and exploration. These ideas would be refashioned many times in the next twenty years and come to fruition in the ecological approach to perception (Gibson 1979).

Last Thoughts on Some Classic False Issues

Learning or Maturation?

This issue was examined in chapter 12, where we considered rearing experiments and the light they throw on perceptual development. It seems clear that as a dilemma it can be buried, for concurrent processes of both maturation and learning can be demonstrated. As for learning, children (and animals) learn to attend to distinctive features of things, to invariants that lead to perceptual constancy and permanence, and to higher order structures and rules. The latter may be best observed in human skills such as speech and reading, but perception of invariance over transformations, such as a ball being seen to roll behind a screen and out again, can be demonstrated to develop in a cat.

It was also demonstrated that all the progress witnessed in these accomplishments is not solely a matter of learning. Experiments on the visual cliff with animals of different ages, species, and rearing histories show that maturation has a role in depth perception. The effects of special rearing conditions also made it clear that maturation assumes an environment ecologically normal for the species, and that abilities already mature require it for their maintenance. The trends in perceptual development emerge as the product of both experience with an environment and the maturing powers of an individual. There is no either-or issue.

Perception and Production
The question of which comes first, perception or action, is like the question of which comes first, the hen or the egg. The currently fashionable predilection for motor theories of perception would seem to imply that action has priority, but we know, on the other hand, that production often follows after discriminatory achievements. We considered this fact in the chapter on perception of symbolic stimuli, for speech is a case in point where discrimination often precedes production. Another interesting case is the drawing of a diagonal line (see chapter 8). A child can draw an acceptable circle at age three, a square at four, a triangle at five, but a diamond only later still, at seven. This is an interesting progression in itself, but it becomes still more interesting when one learns that the diagonals of the triangle and the diamond can be discriminated considerably earlier than they can be drawn. It is not the motor performance as such that is wanting, for training in executing the movement does not facilitate accurate production, while training in discrimination does.

Leaving visible tracings on paper with a tool, trace making, is an interesting event to children, as J. J. Gibson and Patricia Yonas have shown, whereas the motor act without the tracings, as with a pencil that leaves no marks, is not interesting. Even watching the tracings being made, although the child himself is not the direct executor, is interesting. I observed children at an exhibition of kinetic sculpture by the artist Tingueley. One of the exhibits was a complicated machine which held a pencil. When activated the pencil made random marks on a piece of paper—scribbles. The machine was provided with pads of paper and colored marking pens which a child could put in place. Crowds of children were waiting for a turn at this machine. So there is a strong motivation merely to observe marks being made on paper, and it is not the motor act as such, the feel of it, that is responsible. There is no particular reason, therefore, why the ability to produce a given pattern and the ability to discriminate it should emerge at the same time. Motor schemata there may be, and response-produced stimulation as well. But perception is an activity in its own right—an exploratory activity, not a performatory activity. Performatory acts have a developmental history, but so do exploratory acts, and the histories are not the same.

Which comes first, perception or production? The question is a red herring that leads us off the scent. Perception and production serve different purposes. Adaptiveness of behavior is served by exploratory perceptual activity that provides information about the environment prior to performance. Exploratory activity begins early, yielding informative stimulation with the first eye movements. We would not call these eye movements production, but they are a kind of activity. Performatory action, like seizing a proffered rattle, or banging a spoon on a tin plate, appears later than looking at the object. But when it comes about, there is informative feedback from this action, too, which takes on a role in monitoring behavior.

The Part or the Whole?
Another "which comes first" question that has bewildered developmental psychologists is the part-whole controversy. It has been the contention of many child psychologists that children begin by perceiving globally, and progressively analyze or differentiate out the details. But just as many have taken the opposite view—that the young child begins by noticing only details in isolation and gradually, through a learning process, integrates them into a whole.

This issue was considered in chapter 16, on the perception of objects. It is another false issue. Children learn to perceive distinctive features of objects, and so one might be inclined to say that these are parts and that they are being differentiated from a whole. But what kind of whole? Not a whole with intricate structure, certainly. It is equally true that the pickup of structure characterizes development, in fact progressively higher order levels of structure, and this sounds like progress toward a whole. But the very notion of parts and wholes in perception is mistaken; objects are differentiated by distinctive features which must be discriminated, and objects are also characterized by structure. Higher order structure creates new units by grouping subordinate units, enabling more information to be handled while reducing uncertainty. Enlarging the chunks might be considered integration of parts into wholes, but we must not forget that there is also progress toward discovery of the most economical and critical set of distinctive features. Which of these two equally adaptive kinds of change characterizes behavior will depend upon the task and the stimulus information, and both may even occur at once.

From Perception to Inference

It is often asserted that the young child is stimulus bound, enslaved by the surrounding milieu, dependent on the present sensory information, and that perceptual development is a process of liberation from the constraints of stimulation. Another way of putting this has been to say that he is misled by perceptual factors and must make inferences. A related statement is that cognitive development consists in "going beyond the information given" (Bruner 1957).

One cannot doubt that the child's conceptual life expands as he matures and gains experience. Concepts and generalized rules can have a guiding and directing effect on perception, just as labels and verbal instructions can direct attention to distinctive parts of a display, and concepts, especially rulelike ones, can help to reveal structure not easily or automatically detected perceptually. But this is not to say that perception is left behind in favor of inference as we grow up, nor is it even to say that perception develops by making use of inference.

What is wrong with saying that the young child is stimulus bound, and that cognitive development is a liberation from these bonds by the operations of intelligence? This is Piaget's opinion. One must admit its popularity and its persuasiveness, for a neonate's attention does seem to be captured by a few kinds of events in its environment. But the developmental change is not one of doing without stimulus information; it is one of seeking stimulus information in a directed, systematic fashion. Does perception mislead us, whereas conception and generalization lead to truth and reality? Concepts and generalizations can sometimes themselves mislead us; we speak of biased observation. It is then not perception that is misleading. We are misled by the failure to grasp the invariants in the stimulus flux. When the invariants occur over a temporal sequence of transformations, as in an event like the pouring of water from one container to another, they may or may not be detected. A still shot of a filled container at one moment of stimulation can be misleading, like a single frame from a motion picture, for invariants occur that can be discovered only over variation and transformation.

Does the child need more information in stimulation, or more redundancy in stimulation, than adults do because his concepts are immature? One kind of evidence cited for this conclusion is drawn from experiments with incomplete figures. Children can fill in the figures and recognize them better as age increases. To quote Wohlwill, "Compared to the adult the young child requires more redundancy in a pattern to perceive it correctly; thus both incomplete and very complex patterns will be difficult for him"

(1960, p. 281). They may be more difficult but not, I suggest, because "the younger child requires a greater amount of surplus information." He cannot handle more information than an adult, and is far less adept at seeing and using redundancy in stimulation when it is present. Distinctive features of objects do have to be learned, however, and an increased knowledge of them would be expected to aid in recognizing incomplete pictures.

Bruner, also, has claimed that "less redundancy is needed as we grow older" (Bruner, et al. 1966, 23), using again the evidence from recognition of incomplete pictures. The reasoning is that perception is based on representations, on a constructed model of reality against which the input is tested. As this model grows richer, he suggests, the child uses it to fill in details that are not given in stimulation.

As the reader knows by now, I disagree with this interpretation of perception and perceptual development. Perception is not a process of matching to a representation in the head, but one of extracting the invariants in stimulus information. Constraints in stimulation can be useful, and adaptive development depends on more effective pickup of this information rather than less dependence upon it. Although our concepts increase in number, richness, and complexity as we grow older, it does not follow that our percepts become more and more reflections of our concepts. We do not perceive less because we conceptualize more. If we did, it would be maladaptive for getting information about what is going on in the world around us.

Stages or Transitions?
The manifestations of change over time are a fascinating problem for the dramatist, the archaeologist, and the biologist alike. Shakespeare celebrated the seven ages of man, wondering how the mewling infant could possibly be identified with the whining schoolboy, the lover, and the "lean and slippered pantaloon." Yet, dramatic as these contrasts are, there is some identity over the ages of man. Are these different stages arbitrarily chosen from a sequence that really proceeds in continuous fashion, or are there times in the sequence when the transition is abrupt and a quite new organization follows? Biologically, there is no clear-cut answer to this question. One can point to the insects where there is a metamorphosis in development, with a radical shift in structure and manner of adapting to the environment, but one can also point to cases of continuous growth where the transformation is spectacular only if it is speeded up, as if in a time-lapse motion picture that emphasizes the change.

This chapter is concerned with trends. But the identifying of psychological trends is difficult. Does a trend imply a gradual transition in a kind of behavior, maintaining identity while exhibiting progress toward some biological adaptation? If so, how do we describe the changed behavior and still recognize the identity? Or does a trend imply not gradual transitions but stages of behavior, with abrupt changes in organization comparable to metamorphosis in insects?

Human growth, after birth, does not display metamorphosis. The closest thing to it is the speeded-up change at adolescence, and perhaps the heightened responsiveness occurring at so-called critical periods during infancy. We are aware of the great docility of the human organism, and the extent to which its behavior can be shaped by programmed schedules of training. The contribution of the environment is so great that the appearance of stages might result from the program that the culture has provided for the child's education.

I want to look for trends in development, but I am very dubious about stages. Instead of the child study psychologists of fifty years ago, who thought of the child as almost a distinct species, or even the more recent experimental child psychologists, let us try to be developmental psychologists. Let us examine developmental studies of perceptual activity, hoping to discover generalizations that will reveal the laws of behavior and its adaptation to ongoing events. We look for a progressive sequence which spans the activity from birth to maturity.

It is a hazardous undertaking, but I am going to propose, and summarize evidence for, certain trends in perceptual development. To repeat, trends do not imply stages in each of which a radically new process emerges, nor do they imply maturation in which a new direction exclusive of learning is created.

Three Trends in Perceptual Development

Increasing Specificity of Discrimination

In earlier chapters, it was shown that perceptual learning is characterized by a progressive increase in the specificity of discrimination to stimulus information. In chapter 9, I described the effects of practice on acuity judgments, on differential limens, and on absolute estimations along a stimulus dimension; all showed this kind of change—a narrowing of the band of stimulus values eliciting any given response value within the continuum. The same trend, though complicated by species-specific methods of adaptation, appears in phylogenetic development. With evolution, specialized receptors proliferated, along with distinct modes of sensitivity to different types of energy change.

The evidence cited in preceding chapters showed that the human infant differentiates properties of things and events to some degree quite early. Nevertheless, a developmental trend toward specificity can be demonstrated in the ways described below.

Decrease in Stimulus Generalization   The experimental measurement of what is called stimulus generalization affords a method of comparing the size of the class of different stimulus events that will elicit the same response at various age levels. It is a method in the strict stimulus-response tradition of psychology. The generalization gradient around a stimulus to which a given response has been associated does in fact steepen between infancy and maturity; the amount of generalization decreases. One example is an experiment by Riess (1946), in which subjects of four age groups, ranging from seven years to eighteen and a half, had an electrodermal response conditioned to a word for which a homophone, an antonym, and a synonym existed, and then were tested for generalization to these. The youngest group generalized most to homophones. Generalization to synonyms increased with age, relative to the other words, if only the three older groups were compared. But the youngest group generalized more to all words, regardless of the particular relationship of the words. Properties that relate or distinguish words were not yet effectively differentiated and merely the appearance of a word elicited the conditioned response. (Other examples followed.)

Reduction of Variability   In chapter 9 many cases were cited showing reduction with practice of the variable error in a psychophysical experiment. Decrease in this kind of error is also characteristic of development with age. The experiments of Piaget and his collaborators on perception provide many demonstrations (Lambercier 1946). The change in size constancy with age shows a striking decrease in variability of size matches (for the height of a rod) from five years to an asymptote at about twelve years. This is a drop in the variability of judgments made by each child, not by different children, so it is a genuine increase in the precision and consistency of their discrimination. The constant error, plotted on the same graph, also changes with age but remarkably little as compared to the variable error. The youngest age group accepts as equivalent in height to a standard rod a group of rods varying over more than half the height of the standard. The width of the area of uncertainty—the variable error—is about six times as great as the mean constant error, and it narrows progressively with age. (Other examples followed.)

Reduction of Discrimination Time   Psychologists have known for many years that the reaction time required for making different responses to different objects that are suddenly presented increases with the similarity of the objects. The latency corresponds, in other words, with their discriminability. It is interesting, therefore, to find that the reaction time for discriminating between objects decreases with age.

The disjunctive reaction time experiment by Yonas and Gibson, described in chapter 7, is an example. The subject pushed a lever in one direction if a letter exposed on a small screen before him was a letter that had been designated by the experimenter; he pushed it in the other direction if it was any other letter. The class of letters used was limited. Children from second grade, from fourth grade, and college students took part in the experiment. There were huge differences between the age groups.

Could it be that the younger children simply do not understand the task, or are not always paying attention? The latter explanation is possible but it is not sufficient, for latencies of reaction reflect the influence of similarities and differences between stimulus displays much as do the adults'. In an experiment with same-different judgments, a confusion matrix for a set of letters was obtained (see chapter 5). The latencies for discrimination correspond to the tendency to confuse the letters very well; for example, discriminating E and F has an extremely long latency and the letters are frequently confused, while discriminating C and M has a very much shorter one and they are almost never confused. These differences appear in the data of both seven-year-old children and adults, although the children's reaction times for any given pair are up to twice as long as the adults'. There may be a shift with age in the set of distinctive features used in discrimination that accounts for the shorter time; either a reduction of the set to a more economical one, or a pickup of tied features (higher order structures) that reduces the number of comparisons required for discrimination as same or different.

The Optimization of Attention

The second trend in perceptual development I shall call the optimization of attention. We refer to the selective aspect of perception as attention, implying activity on the part of the perceiver. Now I want to point out that there are changes in the strategy of this exploratory activity, which are in fact correlated with other developmental changes in perception. They are, first, the tendency for attention to become more exploratory and less captive; second, the tendency for the exploratory search to become more systematic and less random; third, the tendency for attention to become more selective; and fourth, the inverse tendency for attention to become more exclusive.

From Capture to Activity   The aim of perception is to get information from the environment. But from the vast array of potential stimulation arriving at receptor surfaces at any instant, selection must occur. There seems to be some mechanism for selection very early in life. Precocial animals at birth will follow instinctively a moving, shining, clucking object; they will in fact become imprinted by it. A human infant is incapable of running bodily after a moving thing, but he will pursue it with his eyes, demonstrating his attention by prolonged fixation. As Ames and Silfen (1965) pointed out, the young infant is not so much himself selecting the bright corner or the dancing sunbeam to attend to, as it is capturing his attention. Others have referred to this kind of attention as "obligatory" or "involuntary." William James, who was not afraid to use the word "voluntary," said: "This reflex and passive character of the attention which, as a French writer says, makes the child seem to belong less to himself than to every object which happens to catch his notice, is the first thing which the teacher must overcome" (1890, p. 417).

Along the same lines, Piaget speaks of centration, meaning that the young child is caught by what he calls Gestalt-like structural features of the stimulus array, from which he is later able to release himself by letting his intelligence take over. I do not like to make this distinction between perception and intelligence, for I think there is intelligent perception. I cannot doubt, however, that perception becomes more active. Periods of fixation become shorter and visual exploration of the world increases.

How attention becomes voluntary, we cannot say, but we can describe some ways in which it changes from being captured to being exploratory; from being wandering and mobile to being sustained; and from being random and repetitive to being systematic; in short, toward optimizing the active search for information in the world of stimulation.

Strategies of Search   How is the search for information optimized? We have noted some characteristics of the early development of visual exploration in the chapter on object perception—how the infant reaches out to the world visually, with stationary fixations and pursuit fixations of his eyes, long before he can grasp objects with his hands. Zinchenko et al. (1963) studied the child's method of visually familiarizing himself with an object and the way the method changes from three years of age to six. They photographed the eye movements of a child while he was examining an unfamiliar design to be remembered. The three year olds kept their eyes fixed on a single spot longer than did the older children, did not seek out distinctive features, and stayed within the area of the figure rather than following the contour. The visual exploration of the six year old was quite different. Fixed gazes were of briefer duration, the number of movements was much greater, there were movements along contour, and there was orientation to distinctive features. This was not due to mere loosening up of the eye muscles, for Zinchenko showed that children of three could pursue a lighted moving target following the same contour very accurately. What was lacking at three years was locating the distinctive features and singling them out from the total display. Zinchenko also compared the eye movements during the later act of recognition of the picture previously given for familiarization. The three year olds who had not adequately searched were poor at recognition and now made many more eye movements than they had originally; but the six year olds showed a different strategy. There was a diminution of the number of movements, an economical eye-movement trajectory, examination of a few key features, and a passing over of the redundant information, such as much of the outline. (Other examples followed.)

Attention develops, then, from a relatively fixed or forced activity to an exploratory activity, which in turn progresses toward selective, systematic, and flexible patterns of search that are adapted to the task. This activity cannot be described in terms of a chain of stimuli and responses, or in terms of a sequence of sensations. In writing about active touch, Gibson (1962) pointed out the complexity of the stimulation to which the subject intentionally exposes himself when he moves his fingers over the object in a variety of ways; he does so in order to get the information from the flux of stimulation. He is actively selecting the information or maximizing it.

Selective Pickup of Information   Selective attention, focusing on the wanted information, seems to mature developmentally. People working with disadvantaged children who make little progress in school describe their lack of attentiveness as the outstanding quality marking them off from children who make satisfactory progress. But until recently we have had little other than anecdotal evidence to show that the ability to attend selectively in a sustained and directed manner grows with age. We now have some experimental evidence. Eleanor Maccoby has modified Broadbent's technique of "selective listening" to ask whether children's ability to attend to one kind of message and filter it out from the total auditory input increases with age (Maccoby 1967). The method involves presenting the subject with two messages concurrently, coming over a loudspeaker or through earphones. When children listened to a man's voice and a woman's voice speaking words at the same time, with instructions to report what only one of the voices was saying, the number of correct reports of the word spoken by the specified voice increased with age. Conversely, the number of intrusive erors, that is, reports of words spoken by the nonspecified voice, decreased progressively. There was improvement in the ability to select the wanted stimulus information.

Does the growing child really improve in his ability to filter the relevant from the irrelevant, to select what is wanted and discard what is unwanted before final perception occurs? Or does he, perhaps, sense both messages equally and only remember better the message that was designated as relevant? This is a debatable question at present. Experiments with a preparatory set (telling the child before the messages which voice to listen for, rather than after) indicated that perception is truly selective, for a prior set to listen to one voice improved the report as compared to an immediately subsequent instruction about which voice to report. The advantage was present, Maccoby found, to as great an extent in the younger subjects as the older. (Other examples followed.)

These experiments, especially the one investigating the role of preparatory set, demonstrate that six-year-old children do have the ability to select wanted information from a complex stimulus display, though they do so less efficiently than older children.

Ignoring Irrelevant Information   If a component is to be selected from a complex of ongoing stimulation, then the rest—all that is irrelevant—must be discarded. The opposite of attention to something is inattention to something else. Is it the ability to ignore what is unwanted that develops with age? Is it, perhaps, the ability not to attend that increases?

The so-called incidental learning experiment seems to be an appropriate paradigm for this question. Do both incidental learning and intentional learning become more effective as a child grows older or, on the other hand, does the task set progressively enable a child to shut out stimulation that does not aid him in achieving the assigned end? In an unpublished experiment on learning to identify letters, Sharon Shepela and I found that five-year-old preschool children noticed and remembered characteristics of the letters which did not distinguish them uniquely and were not needed for the identification. The task was simply to learn the names of nine roman capital letters of the alphabet. The letters presented were colored, three of them red, three blue, and three yellow. After a number of practice sessions, the children were asked to identify the same nine forms but uncolored; they were now black. As expected, if a child had learned to identify correctly (say) five or six of the colored letters, he could do about as well with the black letters. We then asked the child if he remembered what color each letter had been, showing him the black letters one at a time. To our surprise, these children remembered correctly as many or more colors as they did letter names, although the former were incidental and irrelevant. Correct responses of the two sorts did not necessarily coincide. Confusion errors during learning were influenced by sharing a color, further evidence that the colors had been noticed and remembered.

We now asked whether older subjects would do the same thing. We repeated the above experiment as nearly as possible with nine-year-old children, but used unfamiliar artificial graphemes instead of familiar letters. Arbitrary names of seven or eight of the colored graphemes were learned in about six trials, and the names transferred to the black copies. But the number of colors correctly remembered was at chance level. Some nine year olds did not even remember what colors had been present. In short, there was no incidental learning. (Other examples followed.)

It can be concluded that changes in ability to focus on wanted information and shut out the irrelevant do occur with age. As the child matures, he is better able to select out and use those properties that serve to distinguish things from one another and are adapted to his task, and to disregard nonessential properties. This improved filtering ability is itself evidence of increasing economy in information pickup, my third trend.

Increasing Economy of Information Pickup, and the Search for Invariance
The third trend in perceptual development that I identified at the outset of the chapter is progressive economy in the extraction of information from stimulation. I think of extraction as usually being a search for and discovery of invariants in the stimulus flux. Ways in which economy is achieved are by the detection of distinctive features of things, by the extraction of invariants over time, and by the processing of larger units of structure.

Distinctive Features   It is highly economical to discriminate the objects of the world by means of the minimal set of features that will serve to distinguish them. As my husband put it, "Those features of a thing are noticed which distinguish it from other things that it is not—but not *all* the features that distinguish it from *everything* that it is not" (Gibson 1966, 286). Many illustrations, both anecdotal and experimental, were given in the preceding chapters to show that children do learn such sets, and learn to assign priorities to critical features in the course of development. Caricature in art is a case of enhancing that which serves to distinguish and omitting that which does not. There is a minimal feature set that makes the caricatured object unique, and the good cartoonist has left out of his drawing that which is redundant or nondistinguishing. Children appreciate caricatures astonishingly early, as all publishers of comic books know. They can learn to perceive objects on the basis of sparse details, as long as they are essential details.

In chapter 7 I described an experiment by Albert Yonas and myself in which both children and adults learned to abstract a single feature in order to discriminate two subsets of stimulus figures. With practice there was increasing use of an optimal strategy. While the reaction times of the children were very much longer than the adults', the same trend was found. Discrimination time was faster with only one letter in the positive set. But when a single feature could be extracted from a positive set of three letters and used for differentiation, the curve fell faster with practice than in a control condition.

An interesting example of economical extraction of a single differentiating feature occurs in a developmental study by Vurpillot et al. (1966). The experiment is ostensibly a study of concept identification, since the aim was to compare two theories of how concepts are identified when common dimensions are perceptually present in the instances given. When positive instances presented to a child contain several common features, does the child learn a concept by abstracting all these features and representing them schematically, or does he simply learn to differentiate the positive from the negative instances on the basis of the fewest criteria that will suffice?

Vurpillot designed a transfer experiment to test this idea, using children aged six and a half to ten, and adults. The positive instances of the concept all contained four specified values of features of a cartoon drawing of a bird (a round tail, lined eye, two chevrons on the wing, and spots on the chest), while the negative instances contained different values of these features (e.g., square tail, three chevrons on the wing, etc.). They were assigned, however, so that a single feature difference would suffice to separate the two sets. After sorting the examples to learn which ones were positive instances and had the name designated for the concept, the subjects were given a number of new instances in a transfer series to see what was generalized as a positive instance.

The new instances presented in the transfer task were chosen so that the subject could generalize to only those instances carrying all four of the common features, or to all the instances carrying a single feature that sufficed to differentiate the sets in Task I. In the transfer task, no subject chose only the cards which contained all four of the common features of the concept. They chose, instead, all the cards which had just one feature that sufficed, the one they had selected as criterial for sorting.

The interesting thing here is that four features, all common to the positive instances, were uniformly reinforced, but what was learned and generalized was only a single distinctive feature that was sufficient for differentiation. This demonstrates remarkable economy in learning, and it is especially interesting to note that the children behaved in essentially the same way as the adults.

Invariants   The search for an invariant—the relation that remains constant over change—is the essence of object perception. The stimulus invariant that keeps its identity despite the transformations of stimulation caused by a motion of the object or a movement of the observer is the basis for perception of that object. Let me give an example from an experiment by Gibson and Gibson (1957). (The example given was the experiment described in paper 15 on perceiving an object via perspective transformations).

Does the child progress from experiencing a succession of ever-changing retinal images at birth toward the perceiving of a moving object of this sort as he grows older? Such has been the assumption of the empiricists in philosophy and psychology for centuries, but there is no evidence for it. What kind of progress might the child make in the perceiving of objects? I believe it is progress in the search for invariants under transformations. If this is true, some of the invariant properties in the stimulus flux are picked up by the infant, and other more complex invariants are only detected later, but at no time does the child, young or old, experience the stimulus flux as a flow of changing sensations. Observation of the stimulus flux, perception over time, is necessary for progress in detecting invariants because it permits the invariants to be extracted, not because it permits associating of separate sensations. The child seems to have built-in propensities for teaching himself about the permanent aspects of the world. One device is observing his own hands, bringing them together, rotating them, moving them toward or away from himself, and later grasping objects and manipulating them. The invariants over the resulting perspective transformations give him the information for shape and size constancy. Another propensity for self-teaching is dropping things, or throwing them from a crib or a high chair, or spilling milk. These are wonderful ways to learn about properties like rigidity, elasticity, and fluidity, and the child tries most of them. (Other examples followed.)

Higher Order Structure   Does the span of perception stretch with age? Does the ability to process a lot of things simultaneously increase? The length of a perceptual span does seem to distinguish the perception of adults from that of children, but I believe it is the ability to find the structure, the embedded relations constituting subordinate units or clusters, that makes the difference. It is not just a stretching out but a making of one unit out of many smaller units.

The visual grouping principles embodied in Wertheimer's laws of figural perception, the law of proximity, of similarity, of good continuation, and of common fate, are relations that structure units for perception. There is reason to believe that the law of similarity does not function as well to structure larger units early in development as it does later, or in backward children compared to bright ones. Honkavaara (1958) gave a sorting task to backward and bright children five to eight years old. In one task they were shown twenty-four cards of four different shapes scattered over a table and were asked to sort them into piles. The normal older children instantly sorted them into four piles, but the younger and retarded children put them in rows without matching, or left them in disorder. In another test, they were given cards on which were drawn dot patterns embedded among different shapes. When asked to find a pattern matching a model, the older children surpassed the younger and the bright surpassed the backward children of the same age. Rush (1937) made developmental comparisons of the effectiveness of several Gestalt principles on perceptual grouping within drawn patterns and found that the effectiveness of similarity increased with age. (Other examples of detecting order based on pattern regularities followed.)

The examples just quoted were chosen to illustrate the pickup of structure considered as a perceptual economy that develops with age and experience. The abstracting of common features or dimensions over time also increases developmentally. The literature of discrimination learning provides examples of the latter. One of these is the oddity problem. The requirement is as follows. Over a series of single problems with varying stimulus objects, or varying properties of similar objects, the subject must learn to choose the odd object from a set of three, whatever the nature of the variation. Then he must perform without error on a new problem. Instead of treating each problem as a new and independent one, in which a specific S-R connection must be learned, the subject must operate with a rule which covers all the problems, despite change in absolute properties of stimuli. A rule does not mean a verbalized rule, for a monkey can solve the general oddity problem (Meyer and Harlow 1949, Moon and Harlow 1955). Children may verbalize the rule, but they need not, as House (1964) has shown. In any case, learning of a three-position oddity problem by human children improves from kindergarten to third grade (Lipsitt and Serunian 1963). Perceptual enhancement of the odd item by increasing the number of identical items facilitates solution for kindergarten children, but does not help preschool children, who still fail to reach criterion (Gollin, Saravo, and Salten 1967).

These relationships are less complex than the order found in spelling patterns. In the last chapter, I discussed perception of higher order structure in letter strings, and presented evidence that patterns and clusters of letters within words are perceived as units by adults, and that there is developmental progress in detecting the kind of structure found in orthography and in spelling-to-sound correspondences. Rules come to be used as learning progresses, despite the fact that the user could not explain the rules and that the order in the constraints has only recently been penetrated by trained linguists.

Psychology has not gone far enough in investigating the growth of ability to detect regularity, order, and structure. This ability is basic for cognition. The detection of similarity, equality, symmetry, transitivity, and congruence is essential for learning mathematics, and the good teacher does his best to make them perceptible by clearing away the superfluous details and baring the skeleton. Here is a last example, taken from Wertheimer's book on *Productive Thinking* (1945). He taught a child of 5-1/2 how to find the area of a rectangle by drawing it for him, filling it with small squares, and counting them in various ways. Then he presented him with a parallelogram and asked if he could find its area. After some moments of puzzled staring at the new figure, the child asked, "Do we have a pair of scissors?" They were produced and he proceeded to snip a triangle off one end of the parallelogram and fit it neatly on the other, thus converting it into a rectangle. Then he said, "Now I can do it." He had literally perceived the solution. (It is notable that research in recent years has disclosed that Wertheimer's laws of organization, except for common fate, which involves motion, are not functional in infancy before about 7 months [Schmidt and Spelke 1984]. Order in static displays is not easily detected in early years, at least in artificial cases such as dot patterns. It may be that natural cases, where some affordance for action exists, would be more easily grasped.)

References

Ames, E. W. & Silfen, C. K. (1965). Methodological issues in the study of age differences in infants' attention to stimuli varying in movement and complexity. Paper presented at the meeting of the Society for Research in Child Development, Minneapolis, Minn., 1965.

Bruner, J. S. (1957). On perceptual readiness. *Psychol. Rev.*, 64, 123–152.

Bruner, J. S., Olver, R. R., and Greenfield, P. M., et al. (1966). *Studies in cognitive growth*. New York: Wiley.

Gollin, E. S., Saravo, A., and Salten, C. (1967). Perceptual distinctiveness and oddity-problem solving in children. *Journal of Experimental Child Psychology*, 5, 586–596.

Honkavaara, S. (1958). Organization processes in perception as a measure of intelligence. *Journal of Psychology*, 46, 3–12.

House, B. J. (1964). Oddity performance in retardates. I. Size discrimination functions from oddity and verbal methods. *Child development*, 35, 645–651.

Lambercier, M. (1946). Recherche sur le développement des perceptions: VI. La constance de grandeurs en comparaisons sériales. *Arch. Psychol. Genève*, 31, 79–282.

Lippsitt, L. P. and Serunian, S. A. (1963). Oddity-problem learning in young children. *Child Development*, 34, 201–206.

Maccoby, E. E. (1967). Selective auditory attention in children. In L. P. Lipsitt and C. C. Spiker (Eds.) *Recent advances in child development and behavior*. Vol. 3. New York: Academic Press, pp. 99–124.

Meyer, D. R. and Harlow, H. F. (1949). The development of transfer of response to patterning by monkeys. *Journal of comparative and physiological psychology*, 42, 454–462.

Moon, L. E., and Harlow, H. F. (1955). Analysis of oddity learning by rhesus monkeys. *Journal of comparative and physiological psychology*, 48, 188–195.

Riess, B. F. (1946). Genetic changes in semantic conditioning. *Journal of Experimental Psychology*, 36, 143–152.

Rush, G. P. (1937). Visual grouping in relation to age. *Archives of Psychology, N.Y.*, 31, Whole No. 217.

Vurpillot, E., Lacoursière, A., de Schonen, S., and Werck, C. (1966). Apprentissage de concepts et différenciacion. *Bulletin de Psychologie*, 252, XX, 1–7.

Wertheimer, M. (1945). *Productive thinking*. New York: Harper.

Zinchenko, V. P., van Chzhi-Tsin, and Tarakanov, V. V. (1963). The formation and development of perceptual activity. *Soviet psychology and psychiatry*, 2, 3–12.

Retrospect and Prospect: The Coming of Age of Perceptual Development

Ten years after the appearance of *Principles of Perceptual Learning and Development*, it was named as a "citation classic" (*Current Contents*, 1979), and I was asked to write a few paragraphs about why a number of people should be disposed to cite the book. I quote the paragraphs below. Their rather optimistic concluding suggestion about application doesn't seem too optimistic to me now.

Learning by perceiving the world around us, its permanent properties, its furnishings and ongoing events has always been of interest to philosophers, and deservedly so. Where else has an adult acquired the information about his environment that permits him to act adaptively in it and upon it? Yet modern experimental psychologists generally ignored the problem, although their interests for many years were dominated by learning. Motor learning, verbal learning, affective learning, and simple contingency learning were studied intensively, but comprehensive books on learning never mentioned perceptual learning. Developmental psychology, a younger branch of the science than experimental psychology, was almost equally negligent, but for better reasons—no one had devised feasible, reliable methods for studying early perceptual development.

It is gratifying, therefore, to see that the problems discussed in this book and the attempt to provide a framework for understanding them have had an impact. The book alone, however, was not responsible for the progress that has taken place since its publication in our knowledge of perceptual development. There is always an element of luck in the success of a book or a theory. There has to be an audience ready to listen and experimental progress depends on concomitant advances in technology. Fortunately, the theory and these factors appeared together at the right time. Psychologists were dissatisfied with S-R learning theory and were ready to pay attention to a theory of perceptual learning. At the same time, new methods of studying perception in infants were being worked out and a whole new field of research opened up.

A third factor explains why this book is widely cited. It has an important field of application. While I was writing the book, I was conducting research on processes involved in learning to read. Reading was making a comeback as an area for scientific study. Granting agencies were generous with funds, and my own work made the connection between a theory of perceptual learning and learning to read.

It is interesting to consider progress in the book's field since its publication. The theory of perceptual learning in adults has progressed scarcely at all. Work on reading has burgeoned. There has been a surge of research on perception in infants and very young children, accounting for many of the citations. I have recently directed my own research to this area, and I find that the theory generating my experiments is reflected more and more in work of others on similar problems. As we discover more about early development, it will be possible to refine the theory of perceptual development and to provide guidelines for applied work.

Now, twenty years later, it is striking to see how the trends noted in the last paragraph were borne out. There is still little or nothing new on the theory of perceptual learning. Research on reading is firmly ensconced in the information processing camp, prolific but going nowhere, in my opinion. But research on perceptual development in infants has proliferated vigorously and is leading us to new insights. How did it happen?

When I wrote the 1969 book, there was little research on perception in preverbal children, mainly because of inadequate methodology. But since that time we have had a kind of technological explosion. If you can't ask a preverbal child to tell you what she sees in a neat psychophysical paradigm, how do you find out what information she is picking up? The answer was right there, waiting for us. Babies are motivated to obtain information; they are active perceivers from the start. They are endowed with perceptual systems that include exploratory activity—looking, mouthing, listening. We have learned to use these exploratory activities as indicators of what is perceived.

Even newborns can look at and listen to events and explore substances put in their mouths. Looking preferentially at one of two displays can tell us whether or not the baby differentiates them, and on what basis, if the displays are designed and ordered strategically. A baby will look preferentially at new information, so habituation and familiarization have become the basis of an elaborate technology. And a baby will explore the consequences of any change that is contingent on its own activity, such as turning its head, sucking, kicking, or arm pulling. Exploring the world for information about what it affords underlies most of the methods put to use over the last twenty years, and the result has been a remarkable collection of data on infant perception, telling us that babies are far more competent perceivers than anyone had thought. They detect properties of the layout; they differentiate important parameters of the human voice; they pick up variables of motion and use it for detecting structure in the world; they discriminate their mothers' voices and faces from others, just as a starter.

We have accepted these wondrous accomplishments with awe and admiration as the research accumulated. Now we need to take stock, digest the new corpus, and look at development afresh. The questions abound. What changes between day 1 and day 365? What is moving development along? Is there a pattern or an order? The flood of facts given us by the burst of technology is subsiding now as research moves toward careful longitudinal studies and questions based on interaction of factors in a complex system. Of course, the question of what the baby knows to begin with (if anything) is still with us. Many researchers nowadays are so impressed with the infant's wisdom that they impute to it an inherited conceptual foundation for what the world is like, or even a system of logical inference (for example, Bower, 1989). I return to these questions in part VI, where I try to show that this new knowledge of infant perception can lead us to a revised and better view of perceptual learning.

V

Years of Significance: Research on Reading
(1965–1977)

Introduction to Part V

During the year at the Princeton Institute, when I was thinking about perceptual learning, I was approached by two Cornell colleagues, Harry Levin and Alfred Baldwin, and urged to join them in an about-to-be-formed interdisciplinary consortium devoted to basic research on the reading process. This incident occurred in the early sixties, when a kind of age of relevance was in vogue, so federal agencies offered encouragement and lavish support for the project. It was to embrace the talents of experimental and developmental psychologists and linguists as well. I was hesitant to start a brand new enterprise, since I was determined to devote my best energies to perceptual learning, but I was eventually persuaded that the two projects could be carried on simultaneously. So, I became a member of a group dubbed "Project Literacy" and began to think about how children learn to read. The project lasted for over a decade, culminating in a book, the *Psychology of Reading*, which Harry Levin and I coauthored.

My thinking about reading (as well as perceptual learning) went through many changes during that time. I wrote a number of general papers, the first appearing in 1965 in *Science* and the last in 1977 in a symposium on reading and cognition. The scene, as well as my ideas, had changed greatly in the course of those twelve years. When Project Literacy began, reading was a defunct topic in experimental psychology. The last time it was so much as mentioned in that context was in Woodworth's classic *Experimental Psychology*, published in 1938. The book had later editions, none of them of equal stature, and reading did not appear as a topic again. Like the other chapters in that book, the reading chapter was good, beginning with a short history of writing and getting into the still-persisting questions of the relationship between speech and reading and the role (or nonrole) of eye movements. Good experimental research performed before 1900 by such time-honored pioneer psychologists as Cattell and Dodge was reported. Alas, the topic had fallen into disrepute as psychology became a "respectable" science. But the effort to bring it back into the fold worked, because by 1975 the climate was right and there was plenty of research. The topic had become a popular one with information processers, as it still is.

A splendid book about reading was published by Edmund Burke Huey in 1908, the *Psychology and Pedagogy of Reading*. Except for Woodworth's classic chapter, this book, with an astute analysis of the reading process, was a kind of swan song. In psychology, stimulus-response theory appeared, and in education, where the topic might have been kept alive, curriculum research became the fashion. Classroom questions (shall we teach phonics or whole word?) preoccupied educators, and theory-based research, on the kind of learning process engaged in as reading skill is acquired, disappeared. The cognitive revolution has brought it back, but the information processing approach neglects learning and also generally neglects the fact that skilled reading varies with the kind of text and what sort of information the reader is seeking. Reading is an active process, like perception, and it has many affordances.

On the other hand, all readers share one very general purpose—getting information from printed text—and cross-language comparisons do not show as drastic differences as one might at first expect. One of the most intriguing questions having to do with learning to read concerns the influence of the writing system. Does an alphabetic system have an advantage over an ideographic system? Does a language that has a strict one-to-one phonetic correlation with its alphabet have an advantage? Answers to these questions have been eagerly pursued in recent years, but they seem to have yielded little knowledge about the way children learn. My last exercise relating to reading occurred during a sojourn of six weeks in China, in 1982, when I was invited to give a seminar for a group of Chinese psychologists who were catching up after ten years out of business during the cultural revolution. Some of the members of the group wanted to perform an experiment, one that could be completed quickly, during my stay there. I thought we might try a kind of Stroop experiment, with pictures and Chinese characters, similar to ones performed with children in this country using English spelling (Rosinski, Golinkoff, and Kukish 1975). The pictures were drawn, appropriately labeled with Chinese characters, and three groups of subjects were run through the experiment in five weeks. The result—that the Stroop effect is present even in very early readers (second grade, in fact) and does not increase in more skilled readers—was the same as the result found with readers of English (Rosinski 1977). Details of processing may vary with the task, but the cognitive process of reading appears to be similar from one language or writing system to another, even in rather early stages. Writing (and spelling) systems have different constraints, but they all have them. And whatever the rules, the search for meaning is universal.

Experiments examining the development of a Stroop effect were of particular interest for questions asked by information-processing theories of reading. One such theory asserted that beginning readers attended primarily to the decoding aspect of converting the graphic characters to sound and only secondarily, after determining the phonetic mapping, searched a phonetic representation for meaning. As skill in decoding increased, the decoding task should become automatic and meaning should be accessed quickly and thus become a strong competitor in any kind of interference test, such as a Stroop task. In that case, interference on a Stroop task should increase with reading skill. But many experimental results have shown that pickup of meaning from words is very direct, even in beginning readers (Gibson and Levin 1975, 279 ff.). Information-processing approaches sometimes interpret this result in terms of shared or nonshared "semantic stores" or semantic representations, which compete for attention at a response level. Such arguments about processing seem to me trivial. What is really impressive is the strong indication that reading affords pickup of information *about* something, as does direct perception of events and objects in the world, and that learning to read is, and should be, a search for meaning from the start.

Discrimination of written characters may present more problems in very early stages with some systems (Hebrew and Arabic, for example), but the process of finding meaning and discovering rules that reduce the information seems to be universal. The papers I have chosen to reprint show a pilgrim's progress from an early analysis of the process, through a phase of thinking close to information processing, to a developmental emphasis, and finally to a functional, ecological approach. The book on reading, especially the section on learning to read, has been translated into other languages and still gets some use, so the effort seems to have been worthwhile.

The reading project gave me the pleasure of a number of top-notch research assistants, such as Anne Pick, Harry Osser, Albert Yonas, Carol Bishop, and Richard Rosinski and several good graduate students who performed theses on related topics. Rather than reprint research papers that we produced, I have chosen primarily more general papers that attempt to analyze the reading process, summarize the research, and illustrate the progress in thinking along the way. These essays were originally prepared for oral presentation to some group, one way of spreading the word that reading was a good topic for serious research.

21

Learning to Read

Eleanor J. Gibson

This was my first general paper on reading, prepared for a conference supported by the Social Science Research Council (SSRC) and held at the Center for Advanced Study in the Behavioral Sciences in Palo Alto. I was a fellow there for the year 1964–1965, member of a "cutting-edge" group that also included Lee Cronbach, Richard Atkinson, and Jack Wohlwill. We were supposed to be plotting about educational research, dear to the heart of Ralph Tyler, then director of the center. This conference was one of our projects.

We were asked by SSRC to consider especially something called the Initial Teaching Alphabet (ITA), which was being pushed by John Downing, a British educator who wanted to sell the idea to planners of reading curricula. It was a kind of alphabet semireform, designed for teaching beginning reading as a one-to-one letter-sound code, later to be given up for conventional spelling. It seemed to us just another fad for restyling a curriculum and psychologically quite unsound. Why train students in something soon to be dropped? And, more important, is reading really a matter of deciphering a code? Or are there, perhaps, rules for reading text that transcend a decoding approach and, once internalized, provide a more economical way of extracting information from text? At that time, I thought of economical reading as decoding "higher order units," as this essay proposes. Over the years, I changed this view to one more akin to the ecological approach to perception. That view emerged only gradually: the notion that text contains information in the form of invariants (both syntactic and semantic) that we learn (via perceptual learning) to extract for the sake of economical pickup of what the text affords.

This first essay was a rather long way from that idea. I tried to analyze the reading process (not unlike what an information processor might do), and I came up with several stages. The first stage confronting children, I thought, was learning to discriminate the graphic symbols used by their native writing system.

© AAAS. *Science*, 1965, 148, 1066–1072.

The reader can imagine how easily that idea was come by, in a direct line from the theoretical notions proposed in my Ph.D. thesis. The first research I planned (with the help of Anne Pick and Harry Osser) was an experiment on differentiation of what we called "letterlike forms." The experiment, comparing children four through eight years of age, is summarized in the paper that follows. We thought that the children learned over this period to differentiate the characters by learning the dimensions by which they differed, discovering a set of distinctive features, rather than learning a kind of prototype for each one. Anne Pick's thesis (1965) later investigated this question, showing that dimensions of difference can be discovered in perceptual learning and will be generalized to a new group of items if they are distinguished by the same feature set.

These experiments had two results. One was theoretical, my (perhaps premature) conclusion that the principal thing learned in perceptual learning was distinctive features of objects and later of representations of them and of items such as graphic symbols. The other was a search for the distinctive features that characterize the letters in our written alphabet. There were several attempts to do this. The method was to obtain a confusion matrix and then analyze it searching for the features underlying confusions of one letter with another. The first attempt at this, based on errors made when matching letters by four-year-old children, is summarized in this paper. A more sophisticated one is presented in a later paper.

The second stage in learning to read proposed in this paper was decoding from graphic presentations to sound. This presumed process was typical of the way many people thought about reading at the time. Note Bloomfield's (1942) statement, "In order to read alphabetic writing one must have an ingrained habit of producing the sounds of one's language when one sees the written marks which conventionally represent the phonemes (p. 128)." This statement sounds as if the process of learning to read is like a simple S-R learning paradigm. Indeed, Bloomfield was a hard-core behaviorist. We did not think of the matter as being that simple and were looking for rules that would permit transfer and ways for them to be taught. Carol Bishop's master's thesis (1964) was an early effort to investigate simple rule transfer and is summarized here. The tricky part was, of course, that English does not have rules of one letter to one sound correspondence.

In an effort to supersede this apparent difficulty, we diverted much of our effort to a search for mapping rules that would involve larger, "higher-order" units. The solution we came up with at the time was a functional unit that we referred to as a "spelling pattern"—a set of letters constrained as to position in a word that had a consistent mapping to sound. We performed a number of experiments with what we dubbed pseudowords to show that these units were being used. A pseudoword like GLURCK was compared with its reversal CKURGL, which did not follow the mapping rules, by various methods, most often using tachistoscopic presentations. The pronounceable nonsense words were always easier to read. This method has been used in innumerable experiments since that time by information-processing psychologists. I still favor the notion that children must in some way internalize the constraints provided in the spelling system in order to become efficient readers, but we did not at that time appreciate sufficiently that the spelling of English is morphophonemic, not just letter-sound mapping of greater or less complexity. The main change that took place eventually, however, was the discarding of the notion that reading is essentially a decoding process.

Experimental psychologists examine the process by which a fundamental intellectual skill is acquired.

Educators and the public have exhibited a keen interest in the teaching of reading ever since free public education became a fact (1). Either because of or despite their interest, this most important subject has been remarkably susceptible to the influence of fads and fashions and curiously unaffected by disciplined experimental and theoretical psychology. The psychologists have traditionally pursued the study of verbal learning by means of experiments with nonsense syllables and the like—that is, materials carefully divested of useful information. And the educators, who found little in this work that seemed relevant to the classroom, have stayed with the classroom; when they performed experiments, the method was apt to be a gross comparison of classes privileged and unprivileged with respect to the latest fad. The result has been two cultures: the pure scientists in the laboratory, and the practical teachers ignorant of the progress that has been made in the theory of human learning and in methods of studying it.

That this split was unfortunate is clear enough. True, most children do learn to read. But some learn to read badly, so that school systems must provide remedial clinics; and a small proportion (but still a large number of future citizens) remain functional illiterates. The fashions which have led to classroom experiments, such as the "whole word" method, emphasis on context and pictures for "meaning," the "flash" method, "speed reading," revised alphabets, the "return" to "phonics," and so on, have done little to change the situation.

Yet a systematic approach to the understanding of reading skill is possible. The psychologist has only to treat reading as a learning problem, to apply ingenuity in theory construction and experimental design to this fundamental activity on which the rest of man's education depends. A beginning has recently been made in this direction, and it can be expected that a number of theoretical and experimental studies of reading will be forthcoming (2).

Analysis of the Reading Process

A prerequisite to good research on reading is a psychological analysis of the reading process. What is it that a skilled reader has learned? Knowing this (or having a pretty good idea of it), one may consider how the skill is learned, and next how it could best be taught. Hypotheses designed to answer all three of these questions can then be tested by experiment.

There are several ways of characterizing the behavior we call reading. It is receiving communication; it is making discriminative responses to graphic symbols; it is decoding graphic symbols to speech; and it is getting meaning from the printed page. A child in the early stages of acquiring reading skill may not be doing all these things, however. Some aspects of reading must be mastered before others and have an essential function in a sequence of development of the final skill. The average child, when he begins learning to read, has already mastered to a marvelous extent the art of communication. He can speak and understand his own language in a fairly complex way, employing units of language organized in a hierarchy and with a grammatical structure. Since a writing system must correspond to the spoken one, and since speech is prior to writing, the frame-work and unit structure of speech will determine more or less the structure of the writing system, though the rules of correspondence vary for different languages and writing systems. Some alphabetic writing systems have nearly perfect single-letter-to-sound correspondences, but some, like English, have far more complex correspondence between spelling patterns and speech patterns. Whatever the nature of the correspondences, it is vital to a proper analysis of the reading task that they be understood. And it is vital to remember, as well, that the first stage in the child's mastery of reading is learning to communicate by means of spoken language.

Once a child begins his progression from spoken language to written language, there are, I think, three phases of learning to be considered. They present three different kinds of learning tasks, and they are roughly sequential, though there must be considerable overlapping. These three phases are: learning to differentiate graphic symbols; learning to decode letters to sounds ("map" the letters into sounds); and using progressively higher-order units of structure. I shall consider these three stages in order and in some detail and describe experiments exploring each stage.

Differentiation of Written Symbols

Making any discriminative response to printed characters is considered by some a kind of reading. A very young child, or even a monkey, can be taught to point to a patch of yellow color, rather than a patch of blue, when the printed characters YELLOW are presented. Various people, in recent popular publications, have seriously suggested teaching infants to respond discriminatively in this way to letter patterns, implying that this is teaching them to "read." Such responses are not reading, however; reading entails decoding to speech. Letters are, essentially, an instruction to produce a given speech sound.

Nevertheless, differentiation of written characters from one another is a logically preliminary stage to decoding them to speech. The learning problem is one of discriminating and recognizing a set of line figures, all very similar in a number of ways (for example, all are tracings on paper) and each differing from all the others in one or more features (as straight versus curved). The differentiating features must remain invariant under certain transformations (size, brightness, and perspective transformations and less easily described ones produced by different type faces and handwriting). They must therefore be relational, so that these transformations will not destroy them.

It might be questioned whether learning is necessary for these figures to be discriminated from one another. This question has been investigated by Gibson, Gibson, Pick, and Osser (3). In order to trace the development of letter differentiation as it is related to those features of letters which are critical for the task, we designed specified transformations for each of a group of standard, artificial letter-like forms comparable to printed Roman capitals. Variants were constructed from each standard figure to yield the following 12 transformations for each one: three degrees of transformation from line to curve; five transformations of rotation or reversal; two perspective transformations; and two topological transformations (see Fig. 21.1 for examples). All of these except the perspective transformations we considered critical for discriminating letters. For example, contrast v and u; c and u; o and c.

The discrimination task required the subject to match a standard figure against all of its transformations and some copies of it and to select only identical copies. An error score (the number of times an item that was not an identical copy was selected) was obtained for each child, and the errors were classified according to the type of transformation. The subjects were children aged 4 through 8 years. As would be expected, the visual discrimination of these letter-like forms improved from age 4 to age 8, but the slopes of the error curves were different, depending on the transformation to be discriminated (Fig. 21. 2). In other words. some transformations are harder to discriminate than others, and improvement occurs at different rates for different transformations. Even the youngest subjects made relatively few errors involving changes of break or close, and among the 8-year-olds these errors dropped to zero. Errors for perspective transformations were very numerous among 4-year-olds and still numerous among 8-year-olds. Errors for rotations and reversals started high but dropped to

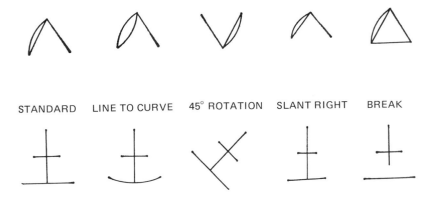

STANDARD   LINE TO CURVE   180° ROTATION   SLANT BACK   CLOSE

STANDARD   LINE TO CURVE   45° ROTATION   SLANT RIGHT   BREAK

Figure 21.1
Examples of letterlike figures illustrating different types of transformation .

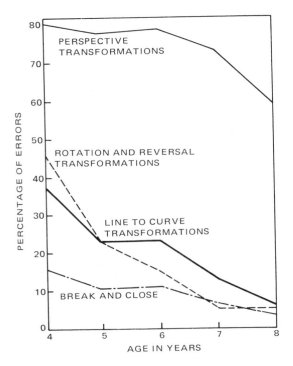

Figure 21.2
Error curves showing rate of improvement in discriminating four types of transformation.

nearly zero by 8 years. Errors for changes from line to curve were relatively numerous (depending on the number of changes) among the youngest children and showed a rapid drop among the older—almost to zero for the 8-year-olds.

The experiment was replicated with the same transformations of real letters on the 5-year-old group. The correlation between confusions of the same transformations for real letters and for the letter-like forms was very high ($r = +.87$), so the effect of a given transformation has generality (is not specific to a given form).

What happens, in the years from 4 to 8, to produce or hamper improvement in discrimination? Our results suggest that the children have learned the features or dimensions of difference which are critical for differentiating letters. Some differences are critical, such as break versus close, line versus curve, and rotations and reversals; but some, such as the perspective transformations, are not, and must in fact be tolerated. The child of 4 does not start "cold" upon this task, because some of his previous experience with distinctive features of objects and pictures will transfer to letter differentiation. But the set of letters has a unique feature pattern for each of its members, so learning of the distinctive features goes on during the period we investigated.

If this interpretation is correct, it would be useful to know just what the distinctive features of letters are. What dimensions of difference must a child learn to detect in order to perceive each letter as unique? Gibson, Osser, Schiff, and Smith (4) investigated this question. Our method was to draw up a chart of the features of a given set of letters (5), test to see which of these letters were most frequently confused by prereading children, and compare the errors in the resulting "confusion matrix" with those predicted by the feature chart.

A set of distinctive features for letters must be relational in the sense that each feature presents a contrast which is invariant under certain transformations, and it must yield a unique pattern for each letter. The set must also be reasonably economical. Two feature lists which satisfy these requirements for a specified type face were tried out against the results of a confusion matrix obtained with the same type (simplified Roman capitals available on a sign-typewriter).

Each of the features in the list in Fig. 21.3 is or is not a characteristic of each of the 26 letters. Regarding each letter one asks, for example, "Is there a curved segment?" and gets a yes or no answer. A filled-in feature chart gives a unique pattern for each letter. However, the number of potential features for letter-shapes is very large, and would vary from one alphabet and type font to another. Whether or not we have the right set can be tested with a confusion matrix. Children should confuse with greatest

Features	A	B	C	E	K	L	N	U	X	Z
Straight segment										
Horizontal	+			+		+				+
Vertical		+		+	+		+			
Oblique /	+				+				+	+
Oblique \	+				+		+		+	
Curve										
Closed		+								
Open vertically								+		
Open horizontally			+							
Intersection	+	+		+	+				+	
Redundancy										
Cyclic change		+		+						
Symmetry	+	+	+	+	+				+	+
Discontinuity										
Vertical	+						+		+	
Horizontal						+	+	+		+

Figure 21.3
Example of a "feature chart." Whether the features chosen are actually effective for discriminating letters must be determined by experiment.

frequency the letters having the smallest number of feature differences, if the features have been chosen correctly.

We obtained our confusion matrix from 4-year-old children, who made matching judgments of letters, programmed so that every letter had an equal opportunity to be mistaken for any other, without bias from order effects. The "percent feature difference" for any two letters was determined by dividing the total number of features possessed by either letter, but not both, by the total number possessed by both, whether shared or not. Correlations were then calculated between percent feature difference and number of confusions, one for each letter. The feature list of Fig. 21.3 yielded 12 out of 26 positive significant correlations. Prediction from this feature list is fairly good, in view of the fact that features were not weighted. A multi-dimensional analysis of the matrix corroborated the choice of the curve-straight and obliqueness variables, suggesting that these features may have priority in the discrimination process and perhaps developmentally. Refinement of the feature list will take these facts into account, and other methods of validation will be tried.

Detecting Distinctive Features

If we are correct in thinking that the child comes to discriminate graphemes by detecting their distinctive features, what is the learning process like?

Table 21.1
Number of Errors Made in Transfer Stage by Groups with Three Types of Training

Group	Type of training		Errors
	Standards	Transformations	
E1	Same	Different	69
E2	Different	Same	39
C	Different	Different	101

That it is perceptual learning and need not be verbalized is probable (though teachers do often call attention to contrasts between letter shapes.) An experiment by Anne D. Pick (6) was designed to compare two hypotheses about how this type of discrimination develops. One might be called a "schema" or "prototype" hypothesis, and is based on the supposition that the child builds up a kind of model or memory image of each letter by repeated experience of visual presentations of the letter; perceptual theories which propose that discrimination occurs by matching sensory experience to a previously stored concept or categorical model are of this kind. In the other hypothesis it is assumed that the child learns by discovering how the forms differ, and then easily transfers this knowledge to new letter-like figures.

Pick employed a transfer design in which subjects were presented in step 1 with initially confusable stimuli (letter-like forms) and trained to discriminate between them. For step 2 (the transfer stage) the subjects were divided into three groups. One experimental group was given sets of stimuli to discriminate which varied in new dimensions from the *same standards* discriminated in stage 1. A second experimental group was given sets of stimuli which deviated from *new standards*, but in the same dimensions of difference discriminated in stage 1. A control group was given both new standards and new dimensions of difference to discriminate in stage 2. Better performance by the first experimental group would suggest that discrimination learning proceeded by construction of a model or memory image of the standards against which the variants could be matched. Conversely, better performance by the second experimental group would suggest that dimensions of difference had been detected.

The subjects were kindergarten children. The stimuli were letter-like forms of the type described earlier. There were six standard forms and six transformations of each of them. The transformations consisted of two changes of line to curve, a right-left reversal, a 45-degree rotation, a perspective transformation, and a size transformation. Table 21.1 gives the errors of discrimination for all three groups in stage 2. Both experimental groups performed significantly better than the control group, but the group that had familiar transformations of new standards performed significantly better than the group given new transformations of old standards.

We infer from these results that, while children probably do learn prototypes of letter shapes, the prototypes themselves are not the original basis for differentiation. The most relevant kind of training for discrimination is practice which provides experience with the characteristic differences that distinguish the set of items. Features which are actually distinctive for letters could be emphasized by presenting letters in contrast pairs.

Decoding Letters to Sounds

When the graphemes are reasonably discriminable from one another, the decoding process becomes possible. This process, common sense and many psychologists would tell us, is simply a matter of associating a graphic stimulus with the appropriate spoken response—that is to say, it is the traditional stimulus-response paradigm, a kind of paired-associate learning.

Obvious as this description seems, problems arise when one takes a closer look. Here are just a few. The graphic code is related to the speech code by rules of correspondence. If these rules are known, decoding of new items is predictable. Do we want to build up, one by one, automatically cued responses, or do we want to teach with transfer in mind? If we want to teach for transfer, how do we do it? Should the child be aware that this is a code game with rules? Or will induction of the rules be automatic? What units of both codes should we start with? Should we start with single letters, in the hope that knowledge of single-letter-to-sound relationships will yield the most transfer? Or should we start with whole words, in the hope that component relationships will be induced?

Carol Bishop (7) investigated the question of the significance of knowledge of component letter-sound relationships in reading new words. In her experiment, the child's process of learning to read was simulated by teaching adult subjects to read some Arabic words. The purpose was to determine the transfer value of training with individual letters as opposed to whole words, and to investigate the role of component letter-sound associations in transfer to learning new words.

A three-stage transfer design was employed. The letters were 12 Arabic characters, each with a one-to-one letter-sound correspondence. There were eight consonants and four vowels, which were combined to form two sets of eight Arabic words. The 12 letters appeared at least once in both sets of words. A native speaker of the language recorded on tape the 12 letter-sounds and the two sets of words. The graphic form of each letter or word was printed on a card.

The subjects were divided into three groups—the letter training group (L), the whole-word training group (W), and a control group (C). Stage I of

the experiment was identical for all groups. The subjects learned to pro-
nounce the set of words (transfer set) which would appear in stage 3 by
listening to the recording and repeating the words. Stage 2 varied. Group L
listened to and repeated the 12 letter-sounds and then learned to associate
the individual graphic shapes with their correct sounds. Group W followed
the same procedure, except that eight words were given them to learn,
rather than letters. Learning time was equal for the two groups. Group C
spent the same time-interval on an unrelated task. Stage 3 was the same for
the three groups. All subjects learned to read the set of words they had
heard in stage 1, responding to the presentation of a word on a card by
pronouncing it. This was the transfer stage on which the three groups were
compared.

At the close of stage 3, all subjects were tested on their ability to give
the correct letter-sound following the presentation of each printed letter.
They were asked afterward to explain how they tried to learn the transfer
words.

Figure 21.4 shows that learning took place in fewest trials for the letter
group and next fewest for the word group. That is, letter training had more
transfer value than word training, but word training did produce some
transfer. The subjects of group L also knew, on the average, a greater
number of component letter-sound correspondences, but some subjects in
group W had learned all 12. Most of the subjects in group L reported that
they had tried to learn by using knowledge of component correspon-

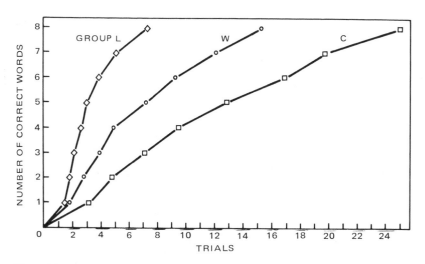

Figure 21.4
Learning curves on transfer task for group trained originally with whole words (W), group
trained with single letters (L), and control group (C).

dences. But so did 12 of the 20 subjects in group W, and the scores of these 12 subjects on the transfer task were similar to those of the letter-trained group. The subjects who had learned by whole words and had not used individual correspondences performed no better on the task than the control subjects.

It is possible, then, to learn to read words without learning the component letter-sound correspondences. But transfer to new words depends on use of them, whatever the method of original training. Word training was as good as letter training if the subject had analyzed for himself the component relationships.

Learning Variable and Constant Component Correspondences

In Bishop's experiment, the component letter-sound relationships were regular and consistent. It has often been pointed out, especially by advocates of spelling reform and revised alphabets (8), that in English this is not the case. Bloomfield (9) suggested that the beginning reader should, therefore, be presented with material carefully programmed for teaching those orthographic-phonic regularities which exist in English, and should be introduced later and only gradually to the complexities of English spelling and to the fact that single-letter-to-sound relationships are often variable. But actually, there has been no hard evidence to suggest that transfer, later, to reading spelling-patterns with more variable component correspondence will be facilitated by beginning with only constant ones. Although variable ones may be harder to learn in the beginning, the original difficulty may be compensated for by facilitating later learning.

A series of experiments directed by Harry Levin (10) dealt with the effect of learning variable as opposed to constant letter-sound relationships, on transfer to learning new letter-sound relationships. In one experiment, the learning material was short lists of paired-associates, with a word written in artificial characters as stimulus and a triphoneme familiar English word as response. Subjects (third-grade children) in one group were given a list which contained constant graph-to-sound relationships (one-to-one component correspondence) followed by a list in which this correspondence was variable with respect to the medial vowel sound. Another group started with a similarly constructed variable list and followed it with a second one. The group that learned lists with a variable component in both stages was superior to the other group in the second stage. The results suggest that initiating the task with a variable list created an expectation or learning set for variability of correspondence which was transferred to the second list and facilitated learning it.

In a second experiment, the constant or variable graph-sound relation occurred on the first letter. Again, the group with original variable training performed better on the second, variable list. In a third experiment adult native speakers of English and Spanish were compared. The artificial graphs were paired with nonsense words. Again there was more transfer from a variable first list to a variable second list than from a constant to a variable one. Variable lists were more difficult, on the whole, for the Spanish speakers, perhaps because their native language contains highly regular letter-sound relationships.

A "set for diversity" may, therefore, facilitate transfer to learning of new letter-sound correspondences which contain variable relationships. But many questions about how the code is learned remain to be solved, because the true units of the graphic code are not necessarily single letters. While single letter-sound relations in English are indeed variable, at other levels of structure regularity may be discovered.

Lower- and Higher-Order Units

For many years, linguists have been concerned with the question of units in language. That language has a hierarchical structure, with units of different kinds and levels, is generally accepted, though the definition of the units is not easily reached. One criterion of a unit is recodability—consistent mapping or translation to another code. If such a criterion be granted, graphic units must parallel linguistic units. The units of the writing system should be defined, in other words, by mapping rules which link them to the speech code, at all levels of structure.

What then are the true graphic units? What levels of units are there? Exactly how are they mapped to linguistic units? In what "chunks" are they perceived? We must first try to answer these questions by a logical analysis of properties of the writing and speech systems and the correspondences between them. Then we can look at the behavior of skilled readers and see how units are processed during reading. If the logical analysis of the correspondence rules is correct, we should be able to predict what kinds of units are actually processed and to check our predictions experimentally.

Common sense suggests that the unit for reading is the single grapheme, and that the reader proceeds sequentially from left to right, letter by letter, across the page. But we can assert at once and unequivocally that this picture is false. For the English language, the single graphemes map consistently into speech only as morphemes—that is, the names of the letters of the alphabet. It is possible, of course, to name letters sequentially across a line of print ("spell out" a word), but that is not the goal of a skilled reader, nor is it what he does. Dodge (11) showed, nearly 60 years ago, that perception occurs in reading only during fixations, and not at all during the saccadic jumps from one fixation to the next. With a fast tachistoscopic exposure, a skilled reader can perceive four unconnected letters, a very long word, and four or more words if they form a sentence (*12*). Even first graders can read three-letter words exposed for only 40 milliseconds, too short a time for sequential eye-movements to occur.

Broadbent (*13*) has pointed out that speech, although it consists of a temporal sequence of stimuli, is responded to at the end of a sequence. That is, it is normal for a whole sequence to be delivered before a response is made. For instance, the sentence "Would you give me your _____?" might end with any of a large number of words, such as "name" or "wallet" or "wife." The response depends on the total message. The fact that the component stimuli for speech and reading are spread over time does not mean that the phonemes or letters or words are processed one at a time, with each stimulus decoded to a separate response. The fact that o is pronounced differently in BOAT and BOMB is not a hideous peculiarity of English which must consequently be reformed. The o is read only in context and is never responded to in isolation. It is part of a sequence which contains constraints of two kinds, one morphological and the other the spelling patterns which are characteristic of English.

If any doubt remains as to the unlikelihood of sequential processing letter by letter, there is recent evidence of Newman (*14*) and of Kolers (*15*) on sequential exposure of letters. When letters forming a familiar word are exposed sequentially in the same place, it is almost impossible to read the word. With an exposure of 100 milliseconds per letter, words of six letters are read with only 20 percent probability of accuracy; and with an exposure of 375 milliseconds per letter, the probability is still well under 100 percent. But that is more than 2 seconds to perceive a short, well-known word! We can conclude that, however graphemes are processed perceptually in reading, it is not a letter-by-letter sequence of acts.

If the single grapheme does not map consistently to a phoneme, and furthermore, if perception normally takes in bigger "chunks" of graphic stimuli in a single fixation, what are the smallest graphic units consistently coded into phonemic patterns? Must they be whole words? Are there different levels of units? Are they achieved at different stages of development?

Spelling Patterns

It is my belief that the smallest component units in written English are spelling patterns (*16*). By a spelling pattern, I mean a cluster of graphemes in a given environment which has an invariant pronunciation according to the rules of English. These rules are the regularities which appear when, for instance, any vowel or consonant or cluster is shown to correspond with a given pronunciation in an initial, medial, or final position in the spelling of a word. This kind of regularity is not merely "frequency" (bigram frequency, trigram frequency, and so on), for it implies that frequency counts are relevant for establishing rules only if the right units and the right relationships are counted. The relevant graphic unit is a functional unit of one or more letters, in a given position within the word, which is in correspondence with a specified pronunciation (17).

If potential regularities exist within words—the spelling patterns that occur in regular correspondence with speech patterns—one may hypothesize that these correspondences have been assimilated by the skilled reader of English (whether or not he can verbalize the rules) and have the effect of organizing units for perception. It follows that strings of letters which are generated by the rules will be perceived more easily than ones which are not, even when they are unfamiliar words or not words at all.

Several experiments testing this prediction were performed by Gibson, Pick, Osser, and Hammond (18). The basic design was to compare the perceptibility (with a very short tachistoscopic exposure) of two sets of letterstrings, all nonsense or pseudo words, which differed in their spelling-to-sound correlation. One list, called the "pronounceable" list, contained words with a high spelling-to-sound correlation. Each of them had an initial consonant-spelling with a single, regular pronunciation; a final consonant-spelling having a single regular pronunciation; and a vowel-spelling, placed between them, having a single regular pronunciation when it follows and is followed by the given initial and final consonant spellings, respectively —for example, GL/UR/CK. The words in the second list, called the "unpronounceable" list, had a low spelling-to-sound correlation. They were constructed from the words in the first list by reversing the initial and final consonant spellings; The medial vowel spelling was not changed. For example, GLURCK became CKURGL. There were 25 such pseudo words in each list, varying in length from four to eight letters. The pronounceability of the resulting lists was validated in two ways, first by ratings, and second by obtaining the number of variations when the pseudo words were actually pronounced.

The words were projected on a screen in random order, in five successive presentations with an exposure time beginning at 50 milliseconds and progressing up to 250 milliseconds. The subjects (college students) were instructed to write each word as it was projected. The mean percentage of pronounceable words correctly perceived was consistently and significantly greater at all exposure times.

The experiment was later repeated with the same material but a different judgment. After the pseudo word was exposed, it was followed by a multiple-choice list of four items, one of the correct one and the other three the most common errors produced in the previous experiment. The subject chose the word he thought he had seen from the choice list and recorded a number (its order in the list). Again the mean of pronounceable pseudo words correctly perceived significantly exceeded that of their unpronounceable counter-parts. We conclude from these experiments that skilled readers more easily perceive as a unit pseudo words which follow the rules of English spelling-to-sound correspondence; that spelling patterns which have invariant relations to sound patterns function as a unit, thus facilitating the decoding process.

In another experiment, Gibson, Osser, and Pick (19) studied the development of perception of graphemephoneme correspondences. We wanted to know how early, in learning to read, children begin to respond to spelling-patterns as units. The experiment was designed to compare children at the end of the first grade and at the end of the third grade in ability to recognize familiar three-letter words, pronounceable trigrams, and unpronounceable trigrams. The three-letter words were taken from the first-grade reading list: each word chosen could be rearranged into a meaningless but pronounceable trigram and a meaningless and unpronounceable one (for example, RAN, NAR, RNA). Some longer pseudo words (four and five letters) taken from the previous experiments were included as well. The words and pseudo words were exposed tachistoscopically to individual children, who were required to spell them orally. The first-graders read (spelled out) most accurately the familiar three-letter words, but read the pronounceable trigrams significantly better than the unpronounceable ones. The longer pseudo words were seldom read accurately and were not differentiated by pronounceability. The third-grade girls read all three-letter combinations with high and about equal accuracy, but differentiated the longer pseudo words; that is, the pronounceable four- and five-letter pseudo words were more often perceived correctly than their unpronounceable counterparts.

These results suggest that a child in the first stages of reading skill typically reads in short units, but has already generalized certain regularities of spelling-to-sound correspondence, so that three-letter pseudo words which fit the rules are more easily read as units. As skill develops, span increases, and a similar difference can be observed for longer items. The longer items involve more complex conditional rules and longer clusters, so that the generalizations must increase in complexity. The fact that a child can begin very early to perceive regularities of correspondence between the printed and spoken patterns, and transfer them to the reading of unfamiliar items as units, suggests that the opportunities for discovering the correspondences between patterns might well be enhanced in programming reading materials.

I have referred several times to *levels* of units. The last experiment showed that the size and complexity of the spelling patterns which can be perceived as units increase with development of reading skill. That other levels of structure, both syntactic and semantic, contain units as large as and larger than the word, and that perception of skilled readers will be found, in suitable experiments, to be a function of these factors is almost axiomatic. As yet we have little direct evidence better than Cattell's original discovery (12) that when words are structured into a sentence, more letters can be accurately perceived "at a glance." Developmental studies of perceptual "chunking" in relation to structural complexity may be very instructive.

Where does meaning come in? Within the immediate span of visual perception, meaning is less effective in structuring written material than good spelling-to-sound correspondence, as Gibson, Bishop, Schiff, and Smith (20) have shown. Real words which are both meaningful and, as strings of letters, structured in accordance with English spelling patterns are more easily perceived than nonword pronounceable strings of letters; but the latter are more easily perceived than meaningful but unpronounceable letter-strings (for example, BIM is perceived accurately, with tachistoscopic exposure, faster than IBM). The role of meaning in the visual perception of words probably increases as longer strings of words (more than one) are dealt with. A sentence has two kinds of constraint, semantic and syntactic, which make it intelligible (easily heard) and memorable (21). It is important that the child develop reading habits which utilize all the types of constraint present in the stimulus, since they constitute structure and are, therefore, unit-formers. The skills which the child should acquire in reading are habits of utilizing the constraints in letter strings (the spelling and morphemic patterns) and in word strings (the syntactic and semantic patterns). We could go on to consider still superordinate ones, perhaps, but the problem of the unit, of levels of units, and mapping rules from writing to speech has just begun to be explored with experimental techniques. Further research on the definition and processing of units should lead to new insights about the nature of reading skill and its attainment.

Summary

Reading begins with the child's acquisition of spoken language. Later he learns to differentiate the graphic symbols from one another and to decode these to familiar speech sounds. As he learns the code, he must progressively utilize the structural constraints which are built into it in order to attain the skilled performance which is characterized by processing of higher-order units—the spelling and morphological patterns of the language.

Because of my firm conviction that good pedagogy is based on a deep understanding of the discipline to be taught and the nature of the learning process involved, I have tried to show that the psychology of reading can benefit from a program of theoretical analysis and experiment. An analysis of the reading task—its discriminatory and decoding aspects as well as the semantic and syntactical aspects—tells us *what* must be learned. An analysis of the learning process tells us *how*. The consideration of formal instruction comes only after these steps, and its precepts should follow from them.

References and Notes

1. See C. C. Fries, *Linguistics and Reading* (Holt, Rinehart, and Winston, New York, 1963), for an excellent chapter on past practice and theory in the teaching of reading.
2. In 1959, Cornell University was awarded a grant for a Basic Research Project on Reading by the Cooperative Research Program of the Office of Education, U.S. Department of Health, Education, and Welfare. Most of the work reported in this article was supported by this grant. The Office of Education has recently organized "Project Literacy," which will promote research on reading in a number of laboratories, as well as encourage mutual understanding between experimentalists and teachers of reading.
3. E. J. Gibson, J. J. Gibson, A. D. Pick, H. Osser, *J. Comp. Physiol. Psychol.* 55, 897 (1962).
4. E. J. Gibson, H. Osser, W. Schiff, J. Smith in *A Basic Research Program on Reading*, Final Report on Cooperative Research Project No. 639 to the Office of Education, Department of Health, Education, and Welfare.
5. The method was greatly influenced by the analysis of distinctive features of phonemes by Jakobsen and M. Halle, presented in *Fundamentals of Language* (Mouton, The Hague, 1956). A table of 12 features, each in binary opposition, yields a unique pattern for all phonemes, so that any one is distinguishable from any other by its pattern of attributes. A pair of phonemes may differ by any number of features, the minimal distinction being one feature opposition. The features must be invariant under certain transformations and essentially relational, so as to remain distinctive over a wide range of speakers, intonations, and so on.
6. A. D. Pick, *J. Exp. Psychol.*, in press.
7. C. H. Bishop, *J. Verbal Learning Verbal Behav.* 3, 215 (1964).
8. Current advocates of a revised alphabet who emphasize the low letter-sound correspondence in English are Sir James Pitman and John A. Downing. Pitman's revised alphabet, called the Initial Teaching Alphabet, consists of 43 characters, some traditional and some new. It is designed for instruction of the beginning reader, who later transfers to traditional English spelling. See I. J. Pitman, *J. Roy. Soc. Arts* 109, 149 (1961); J. A. Downing, *Brit. J. Educ. Psychol.* 32, 166 (1962); ———, "Experiments with Pitman's initial teaching alphabet in British schools," paper presented at the Eighth Annual Conference of International Reading Association, Miami, Fla., May 1963.
9. L. Bloomfield, *Elem. Engl. Rev.* 19, 125, 183 (1942).
10. See research reports of H. Levin and J. Watson, and H. Levin, E. Baum, and S. Bostwick, in *A Basic Research Program on Reading* (see 4).
11. R. Dodge, *Psychol. Bull.* 2, 193 (1905).
12. J. McK. Cattell, *Phil. Studies* 2, 635 (1885).
13. D. E. Broadbent, *Perception and Communication* (Pergamon, New York, 1958).
14. E. Newman, *Am. J. Psychol.*, in press.
15. P. A. Kolers and M. T. Katzman, paper presented before the Psychonomic Society, Aug. 1963, Bryn Mawr, Pa.
16. Spelling patterns in English have been discussed by C. C. Fries in *Linguistics and Reading* (Holt, Rinehart, and Winston, New York, 1963), p. 169 ff. C. F. Hockett, in *A Basic Research Program on Reading* (see 4), has made an analysis of English graphic monosyllables which presents regularities of spelling patterns in relation to pronunciation. This study was continued by R. Venezky (thesis, Cornell Univ., 1962), who wrote

a computer program for obtaining the regularities of English spelling-to-sound correspondence. The data obtained by means of the computer permit one to look up any vowel or consonant cluster of up to five letters and find its pronunciation in initial, medial, and final positions in a word. Letter environments as well have now been included in the analysis. See also R. H. Weir, *Formulation of Grapheme-Phoneme Correspondence Rules to Aid in the Teaching of Reading*, Report on Cooperative Research Project No. 5-039 to the Office of Education, Department of Health, Education and Welfare.

17. For example, the cluster GH may lawfully be pronounced as an F at the end of a word, but never at the beginning. The vowel cluster EIGH, pronounced /ā/ (/ej/), may occur in initial, medial, and final positions, and does so with nearly equal distribution. These cases account for all but two occurrences of the cluster in English orthography. A good example of regularity influenced by environment is [c] in a medial position before I plus a vowel. It is always pronounced /S/ (*social, ancient, judicious*).

18. E. J. Gibson, A. D. Pick, H. Osser, M. Hammond, *Am. J. Psychol.* 75, 554 (1962).

19. E. J. Gibson, H. Osser, A. D. Pick, *J. Verbal Learning Verbal Behav.* 2, 142 (1963).

20. E. J. Gibson, C. H. Bishop, W. Schiff, J. Smith, *J. Exp. Psychol.*, 67, 173 (1964).

21. G. A. Miller and S. Isard, *J. Verbal Learning Verbal Behav.* 2, 217 (1963); also L. E. Marks and G. A. Miller, *ibid.* 3, 1 (1964).

22

A Developmental Study of Visual Search Behavior
Eleanor J. Gibson, Albert Yonas

It seems only fair to acknowledge just how much I was attracted, at one time, to the information-processing approach to reading. To that end I include this paper, a developmental study of letter search that discussed "processing models" in relation to presumed feature lists somewhere in the head that served to distinguish letters. We even went on to a further question about processing models in an experiment that inquired whether reading alphabetic characters involved translation to a phonological mode of processing (Gibson and Yonas 1966). In that experiment (not reprinted here), children heard letter names being pronounced over earphones as they searched for letters in the same way they did in the task described in the paper reprinted here. Even when the letter names rhymed with the target letter's name, there was no interference with the rate or accuracy of the scan. Three (then) graduate students, Kaplan, Yonas, and Shurcliff (1966), performed another scanning experiment in which the target letter was placed in a context of high or low acoustic confusability. The acoustic confusability, unlike graphic confusability, did not slow the scanning rate at all.

This issue—the role of phonological "processing" in a scanning or reading task—was pursued in other experiments, most notably one performed with deaf students at Gallaudet College (Gibson, Shurcliff, and Yonas 1970), but we found no evidence for a phonetic decoding stage. The main conclusion to be drawn from this, I think, is that the question is not a very profitable one to consider for understanding reading. But children's performance in a letter-search task is essentially like that of adults, except for longer latencies. For better or worse, they approach set verbal tasks like little adults soon after they enter school. Why is it, then, that the secret of turning them all into skilled, mature readers still eludes us?

Reprinted by permission of Psychonomic Society, Inc. *Perception and Psychophysics,* 1966, 1, 169–171.

Children in second, fourth and sixth grades and college sophomores were compared on a visual search and scanning task under three experimental conditions.[1,2] In Condition I, a single target letter was sought in a list of letters of low visual confusability. In Condition II, two target letters were sought but only one appeared in a given list. In Condition III, a single target letter was sought in a list of letters of high confusability. Search time decreased with age in all three tasks. Searching for two targets was no harder than searching for one. A highly confusable visual context increased search time at all age levels.

It has long been assumed that there are both qualitative and quantitative differences, developmentally, in attentive behavior; that there is increasing skill in filtering incoming information from the environment, selecting what has utility for the task and ignoring what is irrelevant. Systematically searching for a designated target, while ignoring distracting and unwanted back-ground context, seemed to us to epitomize an activity in which strategies of selecting and processing information should vary with age. The present experiment investigated this question, employing a search and scanning task devised by Neisser (1964). The task requires searching for a specified target, such as a letter, embedded in a context of more or less similar items. If there are qualitative differences over age groups, these should show up as age and variable interactions when suitable parameters of the task are manipulated.

Two variables were manipulated in the present experiment, number of targets sought at one time, and contextual confusability. Neisser et al. (1963) have shown that adult Ss, after long practice, can search for as many as ten targets at once with little loss of speed. If parallel processing, or number of things that can be attended to at once, increases with age, we should expect an age interaction with increase in number of targets. On the other hand, if selective attention involves the learning of distinctive features of the set of items presented (i.e., those contrasting properties which make matching and differentiating possible), a highly confusable context might be relatively more difficult for children than for adults. Such a context would maximize the number of features shared by target and background items.

Method

Letters were chosen as stimuli. They were typed in lists of 30 four-letter strings, one string to a line. The typed list was 10 in. long, the letters 1/4 in. high. The list was fixed to a longer cardboard mounting which could be inserted in the display apparatus. The apparatus was a light-tight

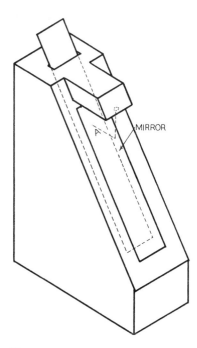

Figure 22.1
Three-quarter view of the scanning apparatus.

box with a slanting glass window (see Fig. 22.1). The glass was partially silvered so that the list was visible only when two lumiline lamps inside the box were turned on. Above the glass window, a small covered bulb was positioned so that a dot of light appeared on the mirror at the same point in space as the top line of the list when the lamps were on. This allowed S to accommodate properly and start his scan precisely at the top of the list. The S's eyes were approximately 14 in. from the mirror. The slope of the mirror (and list beneath it) were such as to keep this distance approximately constant as the scan progressed downward.

The S was instructed to start at the top of the list and scan downward until he found the designated target letter, proceeding as rapidly as possible. He was urged to scan downward in order, without skipping any lines. He held a push button in his hand. When he was ready to begin scanning, he pressed the button which caused the list to appear and also started a Hunter clock-counter (calibrated in .001 sec.). The S immediately started scanning down the list. On finding the target letter, he pressed the button again. This stopped the clock and turned off the lamps. He was asked to indicate the approximate spot on the mirror where the target had appeared in order to discourage guessing. The E then recorded the time and placed another list in the display box. If S had failed to find the target when he reached the bottom of the list, the list was set aside and rerun later. Five practice trials preceded the experiment proper.

The letters chosen were simplified capitals typed with an IBM sign-typewriter, because these are easy for a child to read and because this type had previously been analyzed for distinctive features and a confusion matrix was available (Gibson et al. 1964). The experimental design included three conditions.

Condition I   was a single target search, with low contextual confusability. The S was told to search for the letter G, which would appear only once on a list. The target letter remained the same for 20 trials. Its position in the 20 lists was randomized, with the restriction that it appeared equally often in four quadrants of the list (from top to bottom), never in the same line, and never in the first or the last line. In the practice trials, the target item did appear once in each of these lines to insure that a complete scan would be made. The six context letters in Condition I (L, K, V, M, X, A) were ones which had seldom or never been confused with G in the confusion matrix. They were randomly placed across and down the list, but appeared an equal number of times.

Condition II   was a two-target search. The context was low-confusion again, but S was told to look for either of two letters, G or R, only one of which would appear on any given list. He was not told which one. Each target appeared 10 times, randomly ordered through the 20 trials.

Condition III   was again a single target task, hut the context was highly confusable with the target letter G (the letters B, Q, C, J, S,; and R, which ranked highest in confusability with G in the confusion matrix). There were 20 lists, with target position ordered as before.

The Ss were 72 children, 24 from each of three grades (second, fourth, and sixth), and a group of 12 college sophomores who were fulfilling a requirement of the introductory course in psychology. There was an approximately equal number of each sex in each age group. Each S took part in two of the three conditions of the experiment, Condition I and either Condition II or Condition III. Condition I was always run first. Ss within a grade were paired by age, with one of the pair assigned to Condition II, the other to Condition III. Two rather than all three conditions were run because the children's time was limited to one-half hour. The experiment was run at a school[3], during school hours. The college Ss were run in the laboratory.

Results

In treating the results, the latency of detecting the target for each trial was transformed to take account of its position in the list. Theoretically, a linear relationship might be expected between target position and scanning rate. The expectation did not hold true for the first few list positions, however. Since a similar initial lag appeared for all three conditions, and for all age groups, all the transformed scores were included in the analysis. Means for the transformed scores are plotted by age group for the three conditions in Fig. 22.2. As expected, it is evident that speed of scan increased from second grade to college sophomores on all three conditions.

Three analyses of variance were performed on the transformed scores, one for the high- and low-confusion conditions, one for the one- and two-target conditions, and one for the two-target and high-confusion conditions. Grade differences were significant at the .05 level of significance or better in all conditions. The difference between the high- and low-confusion conditions was significant (p < .001), but the grade by conditions interaction was not. Context confusability was, it appears, equally damaging at all age levels. The difference between the one- and two-target conditions was not significant, nor was the interaction with grade. Two targets were searched for as efficiently as one, at all age levels. The high-confusion condition was significantly more difficult than the two-target condition (p < .001).

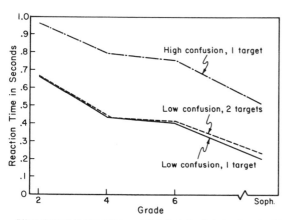

Effect of Target Number and Low and High-Confusion Context on Scanning Rate.

Figure 22.2
Mean latencies for the three conditions of the experiment plotted by age group.

Individual differences between Ss were marked, especially in the younger age groups. These differences interacted significantly with conditions, suggesting that strategies for different Ss vary with the task. This strategy difference was especially noticeable when younger Ss began the high-confusion task; some lowered the pace of scanning almost at once, while others were slower to do this and traded time for errors (missing the target). In general, however, the omissions reflected the same trends as the latencies.

Discussion

Our expectation that increasing the number of things sought for at one time would be relatively more difficult for the younger Ss was not confirmed. The fact that the double-target search was no harder than the single-target search confirms the finding of Neisser et al. (1963), though searching for two targets is surely not as difficult as searching for ten. The Ss had the benefit of practice on Condition I in the double target task, so performance might have looked poorer if practice had been balanced. But it seems clear that any difference, with two targets at least, would be negligible. One need not infer, however, that parallel processing is going on. Another explanation of the good performance in Condition II stems from analysis of distinctive features. The two target letters, G and R, had in common a curve, but none of the context letters did. Optimal strategy, by feature processing, would be searching for one feature, a curve, which would differentiate the target from context letters . This possibility is at present being explored further in another experiment.

The effect of context on search speed is impressive. When the target letter is embedded in a context of letters containing a high percentage of common distinctive features (as these did) the search task is rendered far more difficult. However the features may be processed, sequentially or in parallel, discovery of the target takes much longer. It is not clear exactly how a simultaneous processing model would handle this finding, although a sequential model of visual discrimination, when a matching or discriminating judgment is required, would predict it. If discrimination involves tests of a feature list (the distinctive features of letters), then moving down the list until a difference is found would take much longer when the number of features common to the target and the context items is increased. That younger children should take longer than older ones or adults might be expected, since the feature set might be less well assembled and a possible hierarchical ordering of tests for greatest efficiency not yet optimized. The lack of an age-condition interaction, however, fails to support the possibility of a qualitative process change during development.

Notes

1. This research was supported by NIH Grant MH-07226-02.
2. We wish to express gratitude to Mr. Arthur McCaffrey for valueable assistance in running subjects.
3. Thanks are due Mr. Pastre, principal of the Cayuga Heights School, the teachers, and the children.

References

Gibson, E. J ., Osser, H., Schiff, W., & Smith, J . An analysis of critical features of letters, tested by a confusion matrix. In Final Report, Cooperative Research Project No. 639 with the Office of Education, *A basic research program on reading.*

Neisser, U. Visual search. *Scient. American,* 1964, 210, 94–101.

Neisser, U., Novick, R., & Lazar, R. Searching for ten targets simultaneously. *Percept. mot. Skills,* 1963, 17, 955–961.

23

Confusion Matrices for Graphic Patterns Obtained with a Latency Measure

Eleanor J. Gibson, Frank Schapiro, Albert Yonas

This paper was never published and was in a sense a kind of termination of a line of thought. I remember Frank Schapiro saying to me one day as the very ambitious experiment was nearing completion, "This is terminal research, isn't it?" I was surprised and wondered for a while what he meant. But it was an astute comment. I was becoming less and less attracted by an information-processing approach, and this experiment was a prime example of it. It had begun to seem to me that it was either leading nowhere, or worse, to the wrong place. I had been thinking of distinctive features as bits of information lodged in static wedges of print, and that didn't capture what goes on when we really read at all.

Nevertheless, this was a kind of super-experiment. A vast number of subjects took part (72 adults and 84 children), each one giving us a large number of judgments, "same" and "different" responses, and reaction times in milliseconds. The only reason we could handle the mammoth amount of resulting data was that the experiment was "automated." The subject pressed a key for same or different and, when ready, operated a foot pedal to bring up the next presentation (a pair of letters or artificial graphemes). The judgment and its latency were automatically recorded on an IBM card. We had rented a keypunch and amassed files full of IBM cards that could be dealt with by the computer directly. Such technical wonders! We felt we were at the forefront of the art. But it was only a couple of years before the whole procedure was outmoded and cards were a thing of the past.

Other psychologists were interested in our results, however, and we had a great many requests for the data. The results were written up for circulation, and they are reprinted here as I sent them out. They are useful for a data bank and have been replicated in other laboratories (see Garner 1979), but I lost interest in them and the kind of "processing" talk that this approach led to.

Developmentally, the data do have a certain interest however. The remarkably straightforward partitioning of the children's judgments in the cluster analyses led me to think that, whether they could tell you so or not, the children were having no trouble differentiating letters and were not held up by tendencies to global, nonanalytic perception. Any difficulties children face in learning to read are not likely to be found at this level, I think.

One of the more difficult but essential tasks for a child in learning to read is the identification of the letters of the alphabet. This achievement involves not only the attaching of a unique name to each letter; there must be a one-to-one matching of the graphic pattern to the name, and that accomplishment requires visual differentiation of each of the graphic patterns as uniquely different from the others. How are these patterns differentiated? It has been suggested (Gibson et al. 1963, Gibson 1969) that this is accomplished not by a process of matching the total form of a letter to a stored representation that is independent of other letters, but rather by a more economical process of discriminating a smaller set of relational distinctive features that yields a unique pattern for each letter. The features are *distinguishing with respect to the set*, not components fitted together to build the letter.

What might these features be, and how can we investigate such a hypothesis? It is apparent that a set of distinctive features smaller than the total set of letters requires that some letters share certain features with others. Uniqueness for a given letter can be achieved only by a *pattern* of features that is distinct from the others. It follows from this that two letters that share a number of features and differ from one another minimally by only one or two should be harder to discriminate than two letters that differ from one another by many features. We can test this prediction by determining experimentally the actual confusability of the letters with one another.

This program was followed by Gibson et al. (1963), and a confusion matrix was obtained for the 26 Roman capitals, using errors in a matching task as the measure. Subjects were 87 preschool children. Since every letter had to be matched against every other with equal opportunities for error, a very large number of comparisons were required. Any one child could go through only a small block of the design before becoming fatigued. Since we did not want errors due to inattention or misunderstanding of the task, there was a very small yield of errors, despite a large investment of experimental time. The error matrix contained many "holes" where no errors occurred. Those that did occur, however, showed a low but significant relationship to an intuitively generated feature list. While the correlations between degree of feature-difference and confusion errors were not large, it seemed worthwhile to make a new attempt to collect more satisfactory data on confusability of letters.

It was decided to use a latency measure, rather than errors, since there would then be a yield of information on every trial and no empty spaces in the final matrix. The old literature on disjunctive reaction time (Cattell 1902; Lemmon 1927; Woodworth 1938) suggested that response latency is increased when highly similar items must be discriminated. Latency should, therefore, yield a good measure of confusability. It was possible to check this expectation by correlating latencies with such errors as occurred.

The judgment chosen was "same" or "different." A pair of items was presented simultaneously and the subject responded by pressing a button with one hand if they were the same and by pressing another button with the other hand if they were different. We were interested in this judgment because the comparison of mean latencies for "same" responses with mean latencies for "different" responses is pertinent to the question of what processes go on in discrimination, as well as is the distribution of latencies for "different" pairs (Egeth 1966).

Two sets of nine letters each were chosen for test. Each set was chosen to include a range from very different to very similar pairs, as predicted by feature differences. This would give us two 9 × 9 confusion matrices to check on our predictions. We did not attempt to obtain the 26 × 26 matrix of all the letters, since running only once through the simplest design for this would require 1,300 judgments. We also devised a set of nine artificial graphemes, constructed so that the features we thought might distinguish letters would also distinguish them. This would permit another check on the predictability of features, one with unfamiliar letterlike patterns. We were also interested in comparing mean "same" and "different" latencies for these unfamiliar patterns, which might lack codability or "Gestalt-like" properties characterizing real letters.

It was possible that our rather low correlations between feature differences and errors in the earlier experiment had to do with the age of our subjects (a mean around four years) who were as yet rather inexperienced in discriminating letters. We therefore ran subjects of two age groups: adults and seven-year-old children. Whether the same features are selected for discrimination at all developmental levels is an interesting question, and it is possible that adults, after long experience, achieve some higher-order more economical means of processing visual letter patterns. Since there are so many unknown possibilities for processing differences dependent on age and material, it was decided to analyze the data by a cluster method in order to compare it with our a priori feature analysis.

Method

Material Both the letters and artificial graphic stimuli were prepared photographically on slides. The first set of letters run was C, E, F, G, M, N, P, R, W. The second set was A, D, H, K, O, Q, S, T, X. The type was

Figure 23.1
Artificial graphemes.

simplified Roman capitals. The same "master" copies were photographed for all the slides. The artificial graphemes are sketched in Figure 23.1. A master copy was prepared for each one, black on white, with the same line-thickness as the letters. The artificial graphemes differed from one another in such features as curve, straight, diagonality, intersection, and others deemed characteristic of letters. We attempted to include items that were very similar and others that differed by many features, on an a priori basis.

Apparatus   The subject sat in a chair with his eyes approximately 5-1/2 feet from a display apparatus. His foot was on a starting pedal and the index finger of each hand on a response button. The slides were presented to him simultaneously, via a projector. They were projected in two small windows of a Foringer display apparatus. The windows were 2 × 2 in. and were separated by 1-1/8 in., one to the right of the other at the same height. They could be observed without shifting fixation. The slides were presented automatically, paced at a 3 to 4 second interval by a pro-gramming device. If the pace became fatiguing for the subject, he could remove his foot from a pedal and stop the displays. He could start them again when he was ready by pressing the pedal. A pair of slides presented for the same-different judgment was exposed until the subject made his decision, when he pressed one of the two buttons for a "same" or a "different" judgment.

When the subject pressed the button, a shutter closed, terminating the display, and the subject's response time from the beginning of the display was measured and recorded automatically by an IBM keypunch. A green light went on when the subject responded correctly. A red light came on if he made an error.

Procedure   The adult subjects made 360 judgments of same or different, following a brief practice period to become accustomed to the set-up. Half of the presentations were "same" pairs and half were "different" pairs, to control for response bias. Each of the 9 same pairs was presented 20 times. Each of 36 different pairs was presented 5 times. Order of presentation was randomized on replications within and between subjects. Only one arrangement for a given different pair was used (e.g., either AB or BA but not both), but a given letter, throughout, appeared equally often on left and right. Procedure was similar with the artificial characters.

It was essentially the same with the children, but the number of judgments was reduced to two replications for each "different" pair and eight for each "same" pair. The children were allowed to choose a toy when they came in and were presented with it at the close of the experiment. The experiment was conducted in the laboratory with adult subjects but in a mobile laboratory at the school with the children.

Instructions were as follows:

> Every three or four seconds two letters (or forms) will appear on the screen before you. You are to decide if these two are the same or different. If they are identical press the button marked *same* with your index finger. (Keep your finger on that button so that you can respond rapidly.) If they are different, press the button marked *different* with the index finger of your other hand.
>
> Focus between the two windows.
>
> So long as your foot is pressing the foot pedal, the experiment will continue. If you need to stop, lift your foot; this stops the projector until you are ready to continue.
>
> You are to respond as quickly as you can without making mistakes.
>
> We will have 3 practice trials. Try to learn which hand is same and which is different. The green light means you were correct; the red light indicates that you were in error.

A subject was asked which was his dominant hand. The dominant hand was assigned to the same key or the different key with alternate subjects.

Twenty-four adult subjects were run in the first experiment with the first set of letters. This experiment was then replicated with another 24 adult subjects, since we wanted a check on reliability of our measure. Sixty 7-year-old children were run on this set of letters. Twenty-four adult subjects were run on the artificial graphemes, and 24 more on the second set of letters. Twenty-four children were run on the artificial graphemes, but the time cost was so great that this phase was then discontinued.

Subjects The adult subjects were college students obtained from the subject pool of the introductory psychology course. The children were obtained from a summer day camp at a school.

Results

Latency Data for Letter Pairs

Adults The results for the two groups of 24 adult subjects run on the first set of letters were very similar; the correlation between the two was

Table 23.1
Mean Latencies (in msec.) for a Response of "Same" or "Different" to Pairs of Nine
Roman Capital Letters (48 Adult Subjects)

	C	E	F	G	M	N	P	R	W
C	467	500	495	552	481	465	496	483	467
E		475	560	479	502	495	504	490	485
F			488	464	488	491	495	495	482
G				496	463	470	501	481	458
M					497	545	477	481	538
N						500	463	486	510
P							466	571	461
R								487	489
W									488

+.82. The data were therefore combined and are presented in Table
23.1.

The latencies for responding to a pair of different letters by pressing the
appropriate key varied from 458 msec. (GW) to 571 msec. (PR), a range of
over 100 msec. The difference in latency of responding to these two pairs,
the extremes of the range, was very significant (P < .0001). In fact, differences as low as 30 msec. are significant at .05 or better. This method of
testing confusability thus gives a useful spread of responses and, judging
from the confirmatory results of the replication, is reliable. The correlation
is particularly satisfactory, since the replication was run by a different
experimenter in a different place.

There is also a range of latencies for judging "same" to identical pairs
(down the diagonal), from 466 msec. (PP) to 500 msec. (NN). The range is
by no means as great as for different pairs, but the extremes of the range
are nevertheless significantly different (P < .01). Deciding that NN or MM
is a "same" pair requires a longer time than does PP or CC. Something that
is peculiar to the letter is influential in even such a simple perception as
sameness. Letters containing diagonality seem to be associated with longer
latencies, but the observation may not hold up and the reason for it, in any
case, is not clear. It may be that speed of a "same" judgment depends on
the composition of the series to some extent, such as whether other letters
highly confusable with it are part of the set being tested.

The results for the second set of letters run on 24 adult subjects are
presented in Table 23.2. The range of latencies for "different" judgments
extends from 472 msec. (QT) to 593 msec. (OQ), a slightly longer range
than the first set. The mean for all the judgments is also a little higher for
this set, whether due to the sample of letters or to the sample of subjects is
not clear. In any case, there is a wide spread of latencies and the difference

Table 23.2
Latencies (in msec.) for a Response of "Same" or "Different" to Nine Pairs of Letters
(24 Adult Subjects)

	A	D	H	K	O	Q	S	T	X
A	476	509	534	521	505	489	535	484	520
D		494	497	510	548	521	507	511	491
H			514	580	505	484	499	540	542
K				526	504	493	496	492	588
O					491	593	512	490	490
Q						555	506	472	490
S							486	514	501
T								487	524
X									523

Table 23.3
Latencies (in msec.) for a Response of "Same" or "Different" to Nine Pairs of Letters
(60 Seven-year-old Subjects)

	C	E	F	G	M	N	P	R	W
C	1047	1097	1112	1252	1130	1093	1128	1107	1110
E		1033	1229	1107	1112	1124	1054	1114	1144
F			1072	1108	1139	1132	1092	1148	1106
G				1082	1127	1148	1099	1091	1042
M					1043	1279	1063	1057	1203
N						1075	1084	1112	1155
P							1030	1138	1070
R								1050	1036
W									1038

between extremes is highly significant ($P < .0001$). Differences over 30 msec. are significant at .05 or better.

There is again a variation in "same" judgments, from 476 msec. (AA) to 555 msec. (QQ). This is a considerably longer range of "same" latencies than for the first set. The difference between extremes is very significant ($P < .0001$). Letters containing diagonals do not generally take longer. The Q, which takes longest, has a very confusable letter, O, in the set, but the OO pair is judged "same" comparatively rapidly. There may be some structural feature of the "same" pair as a whole, like symmetry, that influences speed of processing. We shall return to this speculation in a later section.

Children   Latency data for the 60 seven-year-olds are presented in Table 23.3. Latencies are much longer than those of adult subjects, but again there is a range of latencies. The shortest latency was 1036 msec. (RW) and the longest 1279 msec. (MN), a range of 243 msec. The extreme differences are satisfactorily significant ($P < .001$), although the children are quite variable.

Artificial Graphemes

Adults   The latencies for judging pairs of artificial graphemes "same" or "different" are presented in Table 23.4. Judgments of "different" vary from 459 msec. (⌐ vs. ⊖) to 527 msec. (ᴗ vs. ᴖ), a range of 68 msec. This is not as long as the range of "different" latencies for either set of letters. Is this because the set of artificial graphemes is not as well differentiated as the very familiar letters? If that were the case one would expect the overall mean latencies for the artificial graphemes to be considerably longer than those for letters, but they are not. They are slightly shorter, in fact, than the overall means for the second set of letters. We conclude that although the artificial graphemes are not familiar in the sense of figures identified or codable as wholes, nevertheless their distinguishing features (curve-

Table 23.4
Latencies (in msec.) for a Response of "Same" or "Different" to Pairs of Nine Artificial Graphemes (24 Adult Subjects)

	Ψ	φ	ᴗ	⌐	±	⊖	ᴗ	⥾	/.
Ψ	479	472	488	473	493	497	477	507	496
φ		456	477	470	487	515	467	569	454
ᴗ			459	476	462	467	527	481	475
⌐				455	474	459	463	482	492
±					477	474	488	516	503
⊖						481	496	468	498
ᴗ							479	472	498
⥾								487	514
/.									484

straight, diagonality, etc.) are the same as those of letters and are thus readily detected. The shorter range may very likely be due to the fact that we simply didn't construct a pair as similar as, for instance, OQ. The difference between the shortest and the longest latencies for the artificial graphemes is nevertheless significant (<.001).

The judgments of "same" vary from 455 msec. (⌐⌐) to 487 (↘↘), a range of 32 msec. The extreme difference is significant at < .001. Again, detection of replication is easier for some pairs than for others. Why? We know very little about detection of regularities in general and our ignorance here is manifest. There are the same number of lines in the two figures. But are there more features to be processed in one than the other? Or is a judgment of "same" made on the basis of a higher-order feature characterizing the pair as a whole?

Children   Latency data for artificial graphemes for 24 children are presented in Table 23.5. The number of judgments for each pair is small (two per child) and the variability between subjects very great, so few of the

Table 23.5
Latencies (in msec.) for Discriminating Pairs of Artificial Graphemes as Different
($N = 24$ Children)

	ⴄ	♀	Ϭ	⌐	±	Ɵ	∨	↘	∠
ⴄ	1216	1295	1267	1305	1332	1244	1304	1253	1313
♀		1183	1275	1265	1105	1177	1086	1299	1223
Ϭ			1161	1285	1213	1383	1271	1269	1355
⌐				1177	1245	1277	1178	1137	1240
±					1139	1255	1252	1257	1239
Ɵ						1178	1385	1228	1231
∨							1175	1144	1220
↘								1234	1317
∠									1208

latency differences between pairs are reliable, and they do not correlate very well with those of the adults.

Latency of "Same" and "Different" Judgments

If the latency of judging "different" increases as the similarity of two items increases, should it not take longest of all to judge that two identical items are the same? If one conceives of a sequential feature-testing process that compares two items to find a match, the process might be expected to take longer if an exhaustive search of every single feature must be carried out, as a judgment of "same" would presumably require. A decision of "different" could be reached as soon as any difference was found and the search could stop. The range of latencies for judgments of "different" supports such a notion; the more two items differ, the sooner a difference should be found, and that is exactly how the latencies for "different" pairs look.

But when one looks at the mean latencies for "same" as compared with "different", this reasoning breaks down. The overall means for "same" judgments are *shorter* than the means for "different," as Table 23.6 shows. This trend is present in the adults' judgments of both sets of letters, in the children's judgments of letters, and in the judgments of artificial graphemes for both children and adults. The trend was particularly striking (and surprising) in the children. Of the 60 children run on letters, 53 had shorter mean latencies for "same" judgments. Of the 24 run on artificial graphemes, 21 had shorter mean latencies for "sames".

How is this to be interpreted? Does it mean that a feature-testing model of discrimination must be wrong? Would a template-matching model do any better? It might for successive discrimination, for, as Sorenson (1968) has suggested, a subject could be "set" with an appropriate template for a "same" judgment. If the second item matches the template that is "ready", the decision is made. If not, a further search of some sort must go on. But what sort? It it were a comparison with a set of templates, why should there be such a systematic range of latencies for "differents"? Indeed, why

Table 23.6
Mean Latencies of "Same" and "Different" Judgments in msec.

	Different	Same
Adults, first set of letters	493	485
Adults, second set of letters	514	505
Children, letters	1121	1052
Adults, artificial graphemes	507	496
Children, artificial graphemes	1270	1186

should there be a significant difference in latency between some of the "same" judgments?

One simple explanation that cannot be easily dismissed is that the "same" pairs are repeated more often. This procedure was necessary to control for response bias in our experiment, since there were 36 "different" pairs and only 9 "sames." It seems reasonable that repetition should reduce latency. The finding that "sames" are shorter, on the average, has been reported by others before us (Nickerson 1965, Egeth 1966), but so has the opposite finding (Bindra, Williams, and Wise 1965, Chananie and Tikofsky 1968). Bindra, Donderi, and Nishisato (1968) compared "same" with "different" latencies as a function of several variables (stimulus modality, simultaneous versus successive presentation, intertrial interval, etc.). All pairs of stimuli were presented equally often, which appears to dispose of repetition as the sole explanation of discrepancies. They concluded that the discrepant findings were due to codability (or lack of it) of the stimulus items. Letters, for instance, are readily codable (identifiable by name) and yielded shorter latencies for "sames." Pairs of tones differing in pitch or pairs of lines of different length are not easy to identify absolutely, and these items showed longer latencies for "sames." This observation, interesting as it is, seems unsatisfactory as an explanation, because it gives no inkling of *why* "sames" should be shorter or longer depending on their codability. It also does not explain the range within "same" distributions. Certainly one letter is just as codable as another, and yet decisions are made significantly faster on some pairs than on others (and not even on the most frequent ones). Finally, the artificial graphemes in our experiment were far less codable than the letters, but the same relationship held as with letters.

These rather baffling discrepancies suggest that the process of deciding that two things are the same is not like that of deciding that they are different; that a simple model that says check out all the features, either sequentially or in parallel, is just not appropriate for both. It seems more likely that under certain circumstances, a decision of "same" is a *direct perception of replication*; of a structural property of the pair as a whole that requires no further look at subordinate features. Replication would be more readily detectable under some circumstances than others—perhaps when simplicity and symmetry are present—but the conditions for it are certainly not well understood. In any case, perception of replication can be a fast shortcut to deciding that two things are the same, as contrasted with a feature-by-feature check. This interpretation is born out by an experiment of Sekuler and Abrams (1968). Recognition of *identity* of a pair in their experiment was very much faster than finding similarity, even though the similarity decision involved finding a "same" feature (*any* feature) in two pairs. It is thus not the judgment of "same" as such that is faster, but the opportunity for immediate apprehension of replication—"Gestalt processing" as Sekular and Abrams put it.

Cluster Analysis of "Different" Pairs

The question of greatest interest to us is what is linked with what in pairs of different items so as to make them confusable to different degrees. Can we pull out from our data some indication of what the basis for differentiation or confusion is? A hierarchical cluster analysis (Johnson) seemed to offer a promising method. This is, loosely speaking, a method of progressively clustering the set of letters. If we find systematic differentiation in our letter sets and artificial graphemes, perhaps we can identify the features that account for clustering. If the same ones turn up in replications of the same letter set and with different letter sets, we are in luck.

Tables 23.7a through 23.7c show the results of cluster analysis of latency matrices for both sets of letters. Consider Table 23.7a, based on latency data of 48 adult subjects for the first set of letters. Results of two methods, "connectedness" and "diameter" are presented. These are very similar, so we shall discuss only one, that by diameter. The analysis pulls out in the first row the most compact and isolable cluster, PR; in the next row, EF appears. Other pairs appear progressively, until longer and looser clusters are left, winding up with only two separated ones: CGEFPR on the one hand, and MNW on the other. One can think of the analysis the other way around, as a progression from the total undifferentiated set toward more and more specific clusters. A tree structure shows nicely the contrasts that emerge when the clusters appear. At the first branch, all the letters on

Table 23.7a
Cluster Analysis and Tree Structure Set 1 Letters, Latency (48 Adult Subjects)

Connectedness Method				Diameter Method			
PR				PR			
PR	EF			EF	PR		
CG	PR	EF		CG	EF	PR	
CG	PR	EF	MN	CG	EF	PR	MN
CG	PR	EF	MNW	CG	EF	PR	MNW
CG	PREF	MNW		CG	EFPR		MNW
CG	PREFMNW			CGEFPR	MNW		

the right contain diagonals (MNW) while those on the left have straight lines and/or curves. At the next branch, MNW splits into MN versus W (all diagonals); the big cluster CGEFPR splits into round letters, CG, versus letters with verticality, EFPR. At the next branch the cluster EFPR differentiates into a purely vertical-horizontal cluster, EF, versus one with curves and verticals, PR.

The children's latency data (Table 23.7b, 60 subjects) are very straightforward. The first branch is a curve-straight differentiation, all the letters with curves bunched together. Then the cluster with curves separates into the round cluster and the curve and straight cluster (PR). The right branch separates into a diagonality cluster and a vertical-horizontal cluster, etc., exactly as with both sets of adult data.

The other set of letters yields similar contrasts, as Table 23.7c shows. Latency data for 24 adults are presented. Again the first branch contrasts curved-straight, branching again on the left to round vs. curve and straight (OQ vs. D). On the right the last branch again yields a diagonality vs. vertical-horizontal split. The structure here is not as orderly as for the other set (the AS cluster looks strange), probably because there were only 24 subjects and a few confusions are accidental. There is a hint here of something that does not show up in other letter sets in the T vs. KXHAS split. One might call it intersection or "information in the middle." Since the data in each case are based on a sample of only nine letters, a new feature could easily turn up in the second set.

Since we do not have the complete matrix of all 26 letters, we cannot expect these analyses to generate all the features that would be necessary

Table 23.7b
Cluster Analysis and Tree Structure
Set 1 Letters, Latency (60 Seven-year-old Subjects)

Connectedness Method			Diameter Method			
MN			MN			
MN	EF	CG	CG	EF	MN	
MNW	CG	EF	CG	EF	MNW	
CGMNXW	EFR		CG	PR	EF	MNW
			CG	PR	EFMNW	
			CGPR		EFMNW	

Table 23.7c
Cluster Analysis and Tree Structure
Sets 2 Letters, Latency (24 Adult Subjects)

Connectedness Method			Diameter Method		
OQ			OQ		
OQ	KX		OQ	KX	
OQ	KXH		OQ	KXH	
DOQ	KXH		OQ	KXH	AS
DOQ	TKXH		DOQ	KXH	AS
DOQ	TKXH	AS	DOQ	KXHAS	
DOQ	TKXHAS		DOQ	TKXHAS	

to provide a unique pattern for all 26 letters. But one can easily see in the two sets of shapes certain features that are high in the tree structure: curve vs. straight; diagonality; vertical vs. horizontal; intersection; and relatively closed (round) vs. open. These are the first features chosen intuitively in our earlier attempt at a feature analysis. The replications within these experiments indicate to us that perception of difference in a pair of shapes does depend on detecting a set of distinguishing features; and that the set of features is not random or idiosyncratic for either a shape or a perceiver but is rather an orderly hierarchy of fairly abstract properties.

Conclusions

The latency for discriminating a pair of graphic characters gives a wide range of times, depending on the pair to be discriminated. Differences between pairs are significant for both adults and seven-year-old children. The latencies, furthermore, reflect the tendency to confuse the members of the pair. Two sets of nine letters and a set of artificial graphemes bore out these trends. The mean latency for deciding that a pair was the same was slightly but reliably shorter than deciding that it was different. This trend held for artificial graphemes as well as for the familiar letters, and for children as well as adults. Not all "same" pairs had equal latencies, some being significantly shorter than others. The reason for this, we think, is that a judgment of same may be in some cases a direct perception of replication, without further analysis of features.

There is reason to think, however, that a judgment of "different" for these graphic characters involves an analysis of distinguishing features. A pair that differs by many features is seldom confused and the decision is faster than for a pair sharing many features. Furthermore, hierarchical cluster analyses of the matrices yielded tree structures that showed an orderly progressive differentiation of features. Latency data for children and adults on the first set of letters yielded very similar structures. The latency data of the adults for the second set of letters, suggest that a very similar hierarchy of features is detected in the discrimination process for both sets of letters. We conclude that perceiving a difference between two letters is not a matter of matching to a Gestalt-like template, or decoding to a name, but involves detection of distinctive features.

References

Bindra, D., Donderi, D. C. & Nishisato, S. Decision latencies of "same" and "different" judgments. *Perception and Psychophysics*, 1968, 3, 121–130.

Bindra, D., Williams, J. & Wise, S. S. Judgments of sameness and difference: Experiments on reaction time. *Science*, 1965, 150, 1625–26.

Cattell, J. McK. The time of perception as a measure of differences in intensity. *Philosophical Studies*, 1902, 19, 63–68.

Chananie, J. D. & Tikofsky, R. S. Reaction time and distinctive features in speech discrimination. Report No. 49, in a Program on Development of Language Functions, University of Michigan, 1968.

Egeth, H. E. Parallel versus serial processes in multi-dimensional stimulus discrimination. *Perception and Psychophysics*, 1966, 1, 243–252.

Gibson, E. J. *Principles of Perceptual Learning and Development.* New York: Appleton-Century-Crofts, 1969.

Gibson, E. J., Osser, H., Schiff, W. and Smith, J. An analysis of critical features of letters, tested by a confusion matrix. In Final Report on *A Basic Research Program on Reading*, Cooperative Research Project No. 639, Cornell University and U.S. Office of Education, 1963.

Johnson, S. C. Hierarchical clustering schemes. Bell Telephone Labs., Murray Hill, NJ.

Lemmon, V. W. The relation of reaction time to measures of intelligence, memory, and learning. *Arch. Psychology*, 1927, 15, No. 94.

Nickerson, R. S. Response times for "same" "different" judgments. *Perceptual Motor Skills*, 1965, 20, 16–18.

Sekuler, R. W. and Abrams, M. Visual sameness: A choice time analysis of pattern recognition processes. *Journal of Experimental Psychology*, 1968, 77, 232–238.

Sorenson, R. T. Guidance of attention in character recognition: The effect of looking for specific letters. Ph.D. dissertation, Cornell University, 1968.

Woodworth, R. S. *Experimental Psychology.* New York: Holt, 1938.

24

The Ontogeny of Reading
Eleanor J. Gibson

By the time this paper was written, I had become very dissatisfied with an approach to reading that seemed to me artificial and to be leading into bypaths that were not going to take us further in discovering how people become skilled readers. It seemed a good idea to look at the way the skill began and progressed in as natural a way as possible, borrowing a lesson from ethology where we could. This paper describes our attempts to do that. The first two studies, the one on scribbling by J. J. Gibson and P. Yonas, and Linda Lavine's work on children's developing conceptualization of what constitutes writing (Lavine 1977) are good examples. Both studies showed that children growing up in a culture that provides appropriate material and opportunities discover a great deal about writing, how it is constituted, and what its uses are by themselves. The moral seemed to be the wisdom of providing young children with an environment supplied with plenty of literature of the kind one wants them to be curious about, and letting them explore a variety of reading material with adults who are ready to answer questions and provide role models by reading themselves and to the children. Head Start is in the right direction, but we seem nowadays to give children more opportunities to gaze at television than at books.

A method of naturalistic observation becomes more difficult to implement once children have embarked on the routines of school instruction. We tried to apply the method to finding what children know, at progressive levels through the grades, about spelling patterns. Some of those studies are described here. A further large-scale study was carried out for her Ph.D. dissertation by Carol Bishop (1976). She tested children in third and sixth grades for knowledge of spelling patterns and correlated those results with several tests of reading progress. She found that children who are progressing normally through school generally know something about spelling patterns by late third grade, but individual differences do

American Psychologist, 1970, 25, 136–143. Copyright 1970 by the American Psychological Association. Reprinted by permission of the publisher.

not carry a lot of predictive weight for overall reading ability. Something more is needed.

It began to seem to me that the crucial ingredient for learning to read is motivation that drives a search for the information in text. More study of the learning process and better analysis of the information to be extracted were indicated. An ethological approach is fine, so far as it goes, but it is not a substitute for a good developmental theory. One lesson seemed to stand out from the attempt to be ethological, however: that one doesn't teach reading to someone, rather that person learns to read. We can only learn to read by engaging in reading, and we have to do it for ourselves. Motivating a child to do it (read) is one place where we often fail.

Despite decades of concern on the part of educators, parents, and proponents of homespun wisdom, we seem to know little more about how to teach reading than our great grandparents did. In fact we do not even know why it has to be taught. Why doesn't it just grow, like language? No one teaches a child to speak. We do not know much about how a child acquires speech either, but in recent years studies of the developmental process have been very instructive. I think the reason for this is that we have begun to look at the process as a piece of natural history, somewhat as the ethologist looks at behavior. Observation followed by a careful analysis may be the essential preliminary to a good theory. Perhaps we have not really tried it with reading.

I would like to consider, as a start, the natural history of the origins of reading skill, before it is "taught" in a formal sense. Where does its developmental history begin?

I think we could agree that it has twin beginnings. One is its linguistic origin—it is a special form of speech; and one is its origin in writing—making marks on a piece of paper. The origin of reading in speech is obvious. Long before the child goes to school he has learned to segment a sequential stream of acoustic information; to divide it into valid units of structure; to discriminate these units by means of an economical set of distinctive features; to assign symbolic meanings to units of an appropriate size; to infer the rules that structure the units in permissible ways; and even to recombine units in these rulelike ways so as to produce original messages. Surely this massive achievement must transfer in some way to the perception of written speech, which is also processed sequentially. It, too, must be segmented, discriminated, assigned symbolic meaning, and its combination rules mastered. That there is a carry-over is clear from a comparison of hearing children with deaf children, who must do without this head start.

I am going to leave the early history of speech to people more expert than I and begin with the early history of writing behavior. It starts, in James Gibson's opinion, with what he calls the "fundamental graphic act." It consists of producing visible traces on a piece of paper or some other surface such as rock or sand. The traces left on rock surfaces by prehistoric men are the earliest known attempt at graphic communication; pictorial, to be sure, not symbolic, but the evolution of writing seems to have been a gradual transition from pictures to symbols. Pictures have a projective relationship to what they stand for, while symbols bear a coded relationship to their surrogates. In infants, the earliest graphic act is not even a picture, only a scribble, but the child's scribbling is remarkable for one thing—his intense interest in the visible marks that he is making. It seems to me comparable to babbling, in the early stages of speech acquisition, and the motivation for both may well be built-in and arise spontaneously when opportunity is afforded.

As early as 12 months, according to the Cattell Infant Intelligence Tests (Cattell, 1960), a child given a paper and pencil will make marks on the paper. At 14 months, he will make a definite scribble, that is, a progressive, continuous tracing. The tester simply says, "Tommy write." If necessary, after a few minutes he gives a demonstration. By 18 months, the average child needs no demonstration, but scribbles spontaneously. At 27 months, he can draw a line as distinct from a scribble. At 30 months, he can draw a line as distinct from a circular stroke.

It has often been held that scribbling yields satisfaction simply as a motor activity—as "arm gymnastics," a mere exercise of kinesthesis. Gibson and Yonas (1968) compared this with the alternative hypothesis that what motivates the child is the resulting new source of visual stimulation. They compared the scribbling behavior of children given a stylus that did not leave a trace with that when the stylus left marks on a surface. The children ranged in age from 15 to 38 months and were observed at home in a playlike situation. Each child had a session with both tools, which were identical except for the marking potential of one. Elimination of the trace significantly reduced scribbling activity. Mean time of voluntary scribbling was 72 seconds with the tracing tool as against 21 seconds with the nontracing tool. Some of the children stopped immediately on discovering that the nontracing tool "didn't work." One 16-month-old child had no previous experience with tracing tools. When given the marking stylus, she waved it and struck the paper until a fortuitous mark resulted, after which she began to scribble with great interest and increasing control. These children were not only interested in making scribbles, but the older subjects were also eager for the experimenter to look at them and demanded that she do so. What the child can see in practicing the graphic act are variable properties of lines, such as curve–straight, vertical–horizontal, long–short, and features of graphic structure, such as intersection, closure, symmetry, and continuation.

How does the child come to distinguish the important variables of graphic information? I have thought for some time that letters, like the phonemic information that they code to, are discriminable and convey information by virtue of their distinctive features; and that letters share a set of distinctive features that characterizes them as writing, contrasted with pictures and scribbling. How early does a child begin to recognize "writing" as such? Must he learn to identify and name the letters first? At Cornell University, Linda Lavine is studying preschool children's responses to simple line drawings, geometric figures, letters, numbers, words printed in upper and lower case, cursive writing, scribbling, artificial letters, and characters from strange scripts. The drawings, characters, and scribbles were inscribed on 4 × 6 inch cards, inked in lines of approximately equal thickness. A few characters (Roman capitals and some pseudoletters) were a little heavier. Size varied as it might in everyday printing or writing. Figure 24.1 shows samples of the material. The children were merely told, "I'm going to show you some things, and I want you to tell me what they are."

Children of three and four from the Cornell Nursery School served as the first subjects. All the three-year-old children showed that they could separate the pictures from the writing, the numbers, and the scribbles. The children of four could not only do this, they could separate the scribbles from the writing. However, in a cooperative nursery school, few of the four-year-olds could distinguish scribbling from writing. Children in seven different kindergartens were tested. They varied markedly; but in the school with the highest socioeconomic status, 75% distinguished scribbling from cursive writing, although they could not write yet. They identified all the printed characters correctly as letters, although in many cases none or only a few could be named. They also frequently called the artificial letters and the samples of other script (e.g., Hebrew script) writing. This is particularly interesting, because it substantiates the idea that there is something categorical in the structure of writing that distinguishes it from random marks on paper and from pictures even when none or only a few individual characters can be identified. We intend to find out, in future experiments, what the visual information (the graphic composition) is that permits this early classification of a set.

The distinctive features of *individual* letters—those features by which they differ from one another so that a unique pattern characterizes each one—have been investigated in a number of experiments by my students and myself. Gibson, Osser, Schiff, and Smith (1963) obtained a confusion matrix for the 26 Roman capitals based on the errors of 90 four-year-old children. We compared the errors with a list (intuitively derived) of 12

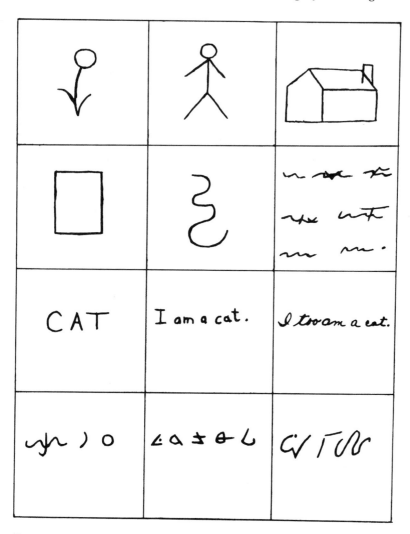

Figure 24.1
Redrawn samples of material presented to preschool children for differentiation as "writing."

features including verticality, horizontality, diagonality, curvature, openness or closure, intersection, etc. The straight–curve and diagonality distinctions also emerged from a multidimensional analysis performed for us by Warren Torgerson. More recently, Gibson, Schapiro, and Yonas (1968) have obtained confusion matrices for two sets of nine Roman capitals and for a set of nine artificial graphemes. In this experiment, the subjects made a same–different judgment. The data included both errors and latencies. Forty-eight adults and 60 seven-year-old children took part in the experiments.

The results seem to me to confirm the hypothesis that letters are distinguished from one another by way of distinctive features that are shared to greater and lesser degrees by different pairs of letters, but that yield a unique pattern for every member of the set. Mean latencies for pairs of *different* letters varied very significantly, by more than 100 milliseconds at extremes of the range. Latencies and errors were highly correlated, and the degree of confusability for given pairs ranked the same in a replication of the experiment. The artificial grapheme pairs also had a significant spread of latencies. The mean latency for discriminating artificial graphemes was nearly identical with that for letters. This may indicate that although the artificial graphemes were unfamiliar and had no names, we were successful in building into them the same set of distinctive features that characterizes letters as a set.

Each of the matrices was subjected to Johnson's (1967) hierarchical cluster analysis to find out what underlies the structure of the matrix. This should tell us what features are used by the observer when he must decide whether a given pair is the same or different. The analysis looks progressively (in steps) for the most compact and isolable clusters, then for the next most compact and so on until it winds up with loose clusters and finally the whole set. The results can be turned upside down and diagrammed in a tree structure. Figure 24.2 shows the tree resulting from an

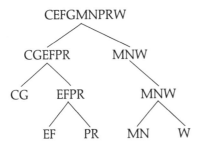

Figure 24.2
Tree structure resulting from a hierarchical cluster analysis of latency data for discriminating pairs of letters by adult subjects.

analysis of 48 adult subjects' latency data for nine characters paired in all combinations. The first split separates the letters with diagonality from all the others. On the left branch, the "round" letters, C and G, next split off from the others. At the third branch, the square right-angular letters, E and F, split off from letters differentiated from them by curvature. The error data for these letters with the same subjects reveal an identical structure.

Now consider the hierarchical structure for 60 seven-year-old children in Figure 24.3. It is similar, but not quite the same. The first split is a clean curve—straight one. On the second branch, the round letters are split off from the P and R. The square letters next split off from those with diagonality. This is very neat, and it suggests to me that children at this stage may be doing straightforward sequential processing of features, while adults have progressed to a more Gestalt-like processing picking up higher orders of structure given by redundancy and tied relations. This is speculative, but it would be a most adaptive kind of development, achieving the highest level of differentiation with the greatest economy.

Differentiating letters, however fundamental, is still a very low-order aspect of reading skill. The heart of the matter is surely the process of decoding the written symbols to speech. We should know a great deal about how the writing-to-speech code is learned. I am afraid that we do not, but we do know that it is not a simple matter of paired-associate learning, either of a letter to a sound, or of a written word to a spoken one. Since writing is alphabetic, why doesn't a child just pair each letter with a corresponding phoneme and decode the letters one at a time? For one thing he cannot, because the letter-to-sound correspondence in English orthography is not a one-to-one matching of each letter to a sound element. For another, as research at the Haskins Laboratory has shown us (Liberman, Cooper, Shankweiler, & Studdert-Kennedy, 1967), phonemes are not recognized by the hearer as invariant over a speech segment smaller than a syllable, so such a method would be impossible even with "regular" ortho-

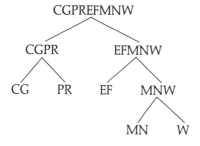

Figure 24.3
Tree structure resulting from a hierarchical cluster analysis of latency data for discriminating pairs of letters by seven-year-old children.

graphy. The presumed "elements" carry information about their context (and vice versa) as well as about themselves. This is true not only of speech but of written language as well.

Furthermore, a skilled reader does not read letter by letter. Cattell (1885) showed long ago that a word, if not too long or unfamiliar, can be read with as short an exposure time as a single letter. (For a five-letter word like START, for instance, one millisecond is enough if contrast is good.) This finding led many educators after Cattell to conclude that reading should be taught by the so-called "whole word" method. But difficulties arose here, too. Many children taught this way could not recognize new words. They did not analyze component relationships within words (Bowden, 1911). Research from our own laboratory (Bishop, 1964), and from others (Jeffrey & Samuels, 1967) has shown that knowledge of component relationships within the word is necessary for transfer.

I think the solution to this apparent dilemma is to aim our research at discovering the *unitforming principles* in reading activity. What are the rules, the constraints, the structure for creating units ? Only if we know this will we know how to teach so as to optimize perception of the most economical units for reading.

There are many possibilities. The white spaces between words might seem to afford an obvious basis for segmentation into words, at least. Carry-over from principles of unit formation in speech, as I mentioned earlier, is another possibility, and suggests at least three levels of rules: regular correspondence between clusters of graphemes and phonemes (often referred to as "pronounceability" of a string of letters); morphological rules; and grammatical syntax. There also may be *orthographic rules*, that is, spelling patterns that give structure without regard to the speech they decode to. We have begun investigating all these possibilities, and I would like to mention briefly some of the experiments.

Consider first the white spaces between words. We know that nearly all kindergarten children toward the end of their fifth year can recognize letters as letters even when they cannot identify individual ones. Can they recognize words as words before formal instruction has begun? At Cornell, Lorelei Brush and Nancy Tither asked children to point out words in various samples of print. The children were about six years old, just finishing kindergarten. Nearly half of these children could not point out words correctly, even after a demonstration. They sometimes ignored the spaces between words and sometimes chose letters as word units. It is not obvious, therefore, that the word is automatically a unit for a child. Even if it were, simple segmentation of this sort would not provide the rules for which we are looking.

I have been especially attracted to the idea that there is a carry-over to reading of unit-forming principles in speech. Clusters of phonemes do map with considerable regularity to clusters of letters. Certain combinations of sounds may begin a word, for instance, and also are spelled congruently in a consistent way in this position. These might be called pronounceable combinations, and it could be that pronounceability forms units for the skilled reader. There might be articulatory or acoustical encoding of what is read, so that the unit is formed on a kind of analysis-by-synthesis principle. Early in my research on reading, I investigated this possibility, that is, that pronounceability of letter strings facilitates reading them because of the correspondence of component clusters of letters with units of speech. Gibson, Pick, Osser, and Hammond (1962) did tachistoscopic experiments with two kinds of letter strings, one that we called pronounceable and one that we called unpronounceable. The pronounceable ones began and ended with consonant clusters permissible in English speech that also map regularly to spelling in those positions. The medial vowel clusters were also regular in their context. An example would be the nonsense word GLURCK. The unpronounceable control words were made by exchanging the initial and final consonant clusters so that the word was no longer a permissible sequence of sounds or letters in English, for example, CKURGL. The pronounceable combinations were read with far greater accuracy with short exposures than were the unpronounceable ones.

Although I replicated this finding many times, I came to have misgivings about its interpretation. Several people suggested to me that the pronounceable words merely had higher sequential probability of the letters, calculated by summed bigram or trigram frequency. Was the correspondence with heard speech really important? I decided to run the experiment with deaf subjects. If it were the pronounceability of the letter strings that facilitated their reading, we should find an interaction with ability to hear and speak them. With the cooperation of the students and faculty at Gallaudet College, this hypothesis was tested (Gibson, Shurcliff, & Yonas, 1970). There was no interaction. The deaf subjects profited just as much in reading so-called pronounceable combinations as hearing subjects did. The term "pronounceable" now seems misleading to me. I believe the difference between the two types of words can be accounted for by rules of orthography, that is, spelling patterns. I do not mean simply statistical structure, like transitional probability, but real rules such as what consonant combinations can begin a word.[1] There is a kind of grammar for letter sequences that generates permissible combinations. This grammar may be analogous to that devised artificially by Miller (1958) for his experiment on memory for redundant strings of letters, but it is natural to the writing system. At Cornell, Richard Rosinski and Kirk Wheeler have found that most children can differentiate permissible from nonpermissible combinations of letters during the third grade.

Morphological usage is another possible cause of units, either carried over from speech or found in orthography. Berko (1958) found that morphological transforms, such as the past tense, had been learned so as to transfer to new words or nonsense words spoken to a child of four years. Should not this be true for reading, too? If endings that mark tenses or verb forms carry over as units to reading, we might expect that a child could read a longer word, with a short exposure, when part of its letters are accounted for by such an ending. A four-letter word is about as long as a third grader can read with a brief exposure. But if we expand the word by adding an *ed* or *ing* does this vocally well-known transformation create a larger unit that is easily detected? Lynne Guinet and I have been trying such an experiment with third-and fifth-grade children.

Table 24.1 shows samples of the words we used. There were three kinds of stem words: real words, pronounceable pseudowords and unpronounceable ones, both anagrams of the real words. There were three kinds of verb transformations added to the words; an *s* to form the third person present, an *ed* to form a past tense, and an *ing* to form a progressive. We used stems of varied length (three to six letters). No child was shown more than one form of a stem word. The main findings are very clear. The third graders make many more errors than the fifth graders, for any kind of word. Real words are read with fewer errors than pseudowords, and pronounceable pseudowords with many fewer errors than unpronounceable ones. The longer the word, the more the errors. But would this be true if the length were increased by a regular ending? To our disappointment we found very little evidence that this method of increasing length increased span of perception. The evidence was in this direction for the pronounceable pseudowords, but not for the other two types. We cannot say that there was automatic carry-over of such a structural principle from speech.

There was evidence, however, that the ending itself gains status as a structural unit. Errors in responding to the transformed words did not occur very frequently in the endings, as compared with nontransformed words of equal length. But when there was an error in the ending, there was a significant tendency for it to be a substitution of another regular ending, for instance, *ing* for *ed*. This substitution of an ending happened more often for the transformed words than for the nontransformed ones, and the tendency was more marked for fifth than for third graders. It is as if the subject detected the ending first as a marker or feature added to the stem word, and only then identified it specifically.

Because I have become convinced that rulelike information in orthography structures units for reading, I want to know how these rules or spelling patterns are learned. Two hypotheses that seemed most reasonable to me were first that there is abstraction of an invariant pattern over many variable contexts; and second that a learning set develops for finding

Table 24.1
Words and Morphological Transformations Presented for Tachistoscopic Identification to Third- and Fifth-Grade Subjects

Item	Third person		Past tense		Progressive	
	Stem word	Transformed word	Stem word	Transformed word	Stem word	Transformed word
Real word	RAIN	RAINS	START	STARTED	LISTEN	LISTENING
Pseudoword (pronounceable)	NAIR	NAIRS	TRAST	TRASTED	TENSIL	TENSILING
Pseudoword (unpronounceable)	NRAI	NRAIS	TRSTA	RTSTAED	TSLENI	TSLENING

Table 24.2
Distinctive Clusters in Invariant Positions and Variable Contexts, All Varied Across Problems

SONG	TEAM	CHOP
RING	READ	CHIN
BANG	SEAL	CHAT
HUNG	LEAN	CHUM

regular patterns in orthography. A training procedure was designed therefore to provide opportunities of both sorts. Gibson, Farber, and Shepela (1967) constructed a large number of "problems" that required the subject to sort positive from negative instances, like a simple concept-learning experiment. All the problems had four positive instances, each of which contained a cluster of two letters in an invariant position—initial, medial or final. The other letters always varied. Table 24.2 shows sets of the positive instances from three of the problems. The negative instances for each problem were words containing various similarities to the positive ones in order to control for sorting on the basis of a single letter or some other superficial similarity.

The child was given one problem at a time. On the first trial, the experimenter laid two cards, one bearing a single positive instance and one a single negative instance, before him, and said, "This is mail for you, and this other [negative instance] is for someone else. You sort the mail and put all yours here [indicating positive card] and everyone else's here." The child then was given a randomly arranged deck of negative and positive instances to sort. The experimenter corrected him when he was wrong. He sorted for one problem four times, and then went on to another whether he had succeeded in a perfect sort or not, following a procedure much like that of a discrimination learning-set experiment.

We first tried this training procedure on kindergarten children and first graders, running them on six problems a day for five consecutive days. This task was extremely hard for the kindergarten children. Only 1 out of 12 developed an indubitable learning set. This child could sort all the new problems correctly on the first sort by the fifth day. The task was somewhat easier for first-grade children; about half of a first-grade sample showed evidence of developing a learning set to abstract common patterns of orthography.

We wondered whether these subjects had really attained a set to search for invariant structure over a series of items, or whether more specific habits already had been learned in first grade that helped on this task. My student, Arlene Amidon, and I therefore tried an experiment comparing success on the spelling pattern problems with success on analogous problems in which the elements were color chips instead of letters.

Subjects for this experiment were first-grade and third-grade children, some run first with colors and some run first with letters. For the first-grade children, color and letter patterns were equally (and very) difficult. If success occurred on the color problem, however, it transferred to the spelling patterns. For third graders, the letter patterns were picked up much more easily than the color patterns, and color problems were far more likely to be solved if they followed solution of letter problems than if they were given first.

We concluded from this that a set to look for structure can be developed and can transfer to new problems, and that the ability to detect structure in letter patterns improves with age and schooling. It seems that this is more than specific learning, since it transferred to color patterns. The third graders, I think, had learned mostly to search actively for invariant spelling patterns. Following a task in which a child found them, he could pursue an analogous search for color patterns. Finding structure, I think, is rewarding, and when these children had found it, they repeated their successful strategy.

How could we assist the first graders toward success in finding the structure, so as to facilitate transfer to new cases? Lowenstein (1969) compared three procedures in a new experiment with first graders. One group was given no special hints or help, as in the preceding experiments. One group was given specific help. When a problem was first presented, the experimenter said, "You will be able to find your own mail, because all the cards will have these two letters on them." The pair of common letters was pointed out. This was repeated for each problem. A third group was told, "You will be able to find your own mail because your cards will have the same two letters on them." But they were never told which letters. After two days of practice, all the subjects had a posttest set of problems without any further instructions.

The group given specific help made very few errors during training, even on the first day. The group given no help made many, although some improvement occurred. The group given the general hint made many more errors to begin with than the children given specific help (a mean of 6 errors), but they improved steadily and on the posttest had a median of 0 errors; whereas errors rose on the posttest to a median of 5.5 for the group that had received specific help. This was more than five times as many as they had made on Day 1. Although 70% of the subjects in the "specific" group made no errors on Day 2, only 20% made no errors on Day 3, the posttest. But in the group given the general instruction to look for an invariant letter pattern, 40% made no errors on Day 2, and 60% made none on Day 3.

Response latencies confirmed these results. The specific group showed no change from Day 1 to Day 3, whereas the group given the general hint showed a steady and significant decrease in latency over the three days.

We conclude then that first-grade children can easily sort words on the basis of presence or absence of two specific letters that have been pointed out to them. But it is not this ability as such that leads to detecting common spelling patterns across items. I think there must be a search for an invariant pattern and discovery of such structure for transfer of this kind of abstraction to new problems. Subjects given no special instructions or hints may eventually accomplish this on their own—20% of the subjects in the control group made no errors on Day 3 (the same percentage as the "specific" help group on Day 3). But it is clearly better to have attention directed to search for invariant features in the stimulus array, and finding them is reinforcing; it leads to repetition of the successful strategy and thus to consistently accelerated performance.

This is the point that I wish to emphasize in concluding. Motivation and reinforcement for cognitive learning such as speech and reading are internal. Reinforcement is not reduction of a drive, but reduction of uncertainty, specifically the discovery of structure that reduces the information processing and increases cognitive economy. This is perceptual learning, not just remembering something.

I realize that my evidence for this conclusion is as yet rather slender, and therefore I am aiming my research efforts at obtaining better evidence and further clarification of the process. A current experiment is aimed at promoting discovery of semantic structure and consequent transfer of the strategy to a new problem. But that is another story, since we have only begun the experiments. I feel confident enough to predict, however, that the search for invariants and the discovery of structure are basic forces in cognitive motivation. If this proves true, methods of teaching that would promote efficient strategies of perceptual search and detection of invariant order should be a first concern in instructional programs.

Note

1. The results of this study were subjected to a multiple regression analysis in which several summed frequency counts (all that we could find) were tested as predictors. All turned out to be remarkably unsuccessful.

References

Berko, J. The child's learning of English morphology. *Word*, 1958, 14, 150–177.

Bishop, C. H. Transfer effects of word and letter training in reading. *Journal of Verbal Learning and Verbal Behavior*, 1964, 3, 215–221.

Bowden, J. H. Learning to read. *Elementary School Teacher*, 1911, 12, 21–33.

Cattell, J. M. Ueber die Zeit der Erkennung und Benennung von Schriftzeichen Bildern und Farben. *Philosophische Studien*, 1885, 2, 635–650.

Cattell, P. *The measurement of intelligence of infants and young children.* (Rev. ed.) New York: Psychological Corporation, 1960.

Gibson, E. J., Farber, J., & Shepela, S. Test of a learning set procedure for the abstraction of spelling patterns. *Project Literacy Reports*, 1967, No. 8, Cornell University, Ithaca, New York.

Gibson, E. J., Osser, H., Schiff, W., & Smith, J. An analysis of critical features of letters, tested by a confusion matrix. In, *A basic research program on reading.* (Cornell University and United States Office of Education Cooperative Research Project No. 639) Ithaca, N.Y.: Cornell University, 1963.

Gibson, E. J., Pick, A., Osser, H., & Hammond, M. The role of grapheme-phoneme correspondence in the perception of words. *American Journal of Psychology*, 1962, 75, 554–570.

Gibson, E. J., Schapiro, F., & Yonas, A. Confusion matrices for graphic patterns obtained with a latency measure. In, *The analysis of reading skill: A program of basic and applied research.* (Cornell University and United States Office of Education, Final Report, Project No. 5-1213) Ithaca, N.Y.: Cornell University, 1968.

Gibson, E. J., Shurcliff A., & Yonas, A. Utilization of spelling patterns by deaf and hearing subjects. In H. Levin & J. P. Williams (Eds.). *Basic studies on reading.* New York: Harper & Row, 1970.

Gibson, J. J.. & Yonas, P. M. A new theory of scribbling and drawing in children. In, *The analysis of reading skill: A program of basic and applied research.* (Cornell University and United States Office of Education Final Report, Project No. 5-1213) Ithaca, N.Y.: Cornell University, 1968.

Jeffrey, W. E., & Samuels, S. J. Effect of reading training on initial learning and transfer. *Journal of Verbal learning and Verbal Behavior*, 1967, 6, 354–358.

Johnson, S. C. Hierarchical clustering schemes. *Psychometrika*, 1967, 32, 241–254.

Liberman, A. M., Cooper, F. S., Shankweiler, D. P., & Studdert-Kennedy, M. Perception of the speech code. *Psychological Review*, 1967, 74, 431–461.

Lowenstein, A. M. Effects of instructions on the abstraction of spelling patterns. Unpublished master's thesis, Cornell University, 1969.

Miller, G. A. Free recall of redundant strings of letters. *Journal of Experimental Psychology*, 1958, 56, 484–491.

25

Perceptual Learning and the Theory of Word Perception

Eleanor J. Gibson

While I was making attempts at a naturalistic, ethological approach to reading, I was at the same time trying to improve on a theory of learning appropriate for reading. What it is that must be learned is the key question, and it has to be answered before there is any point in asking how the information is processed or what the learning mechanisms are. What is the information? Oddly enough, information processors do not spend much time on that question.

At the same time, it is important to remember that reading has a function, more than one of course, but like perception itself reading is a tool for learning, for acquiring information. That both complicates the question and simplifies the answer. One can analyze text and ask what kinds of information it contains, but it is often the case that not all of it is wanted. Certainly it often happens that not all of it is obtained, just as we seldom pick up all the information available for perception of our surroundings. Reading, like perception, is selective. So, not only must we learn to extract whatever kinds of information are available, but we also must learn to select what the text offers that is useful in any given reading task.

This paper is an example of the way I tried to combine a theory of perceptual learning with investigations of the way we learn to read. I would not now argue very hard for the success of my attempt to combine the two with a concept of distinctive features, but looking for the kinds of information in text was the right tack. I think it was also the right tack to emphasize that the information in text has to be based on information in the world, in the final analysis, as in the relationship of semantic information to events occurring in the world, even a child's world. The structure of text is nested, like events in the world. This paper does not go as far as it might have in exploring the possible relationships, but there has been progress in doing so since then.

I think the main contribution of this paper is its analysis of the kinds of information in text. My preoccupation with distinctive features led me to dwell on

© Academic Press *Cognitive Psychology*, 1971, 2, 351–367.

features of words *rather than text in larger units, but things were moving in the right direction. Earlier we had focussed a lot of research on graphic and orthographic aspects of text, but now we were moving toward semantic and syntactic information and combinations of them. An experiment on perception of morphological features of words (Gibson and Guinet 1971) is an example of this trend.*

The influence of information processing is still evident in this paper, however. It is suggested, for example, that the classes of information are "processed independently and sequentially." This idea now seems to me patently wrong—not because "parallel processing" is in the air, but because information is obtained, as opposed to processed, and the search for it is directed by the reader's task. The hypothesis about developmental shifts is too rigid, also. Young readers do look for meaning, only less expertly and flexibly than they will as skill increases. The tasks that provided evidence for a developmental sequence of word "features" were not natural reading tasks. But I am content with the emphasis on search for the information that has utility for the task, and the evidence for it, even when the tasks are rather artificial ones.

I am especially content with the evidence presented that subjects, even children, learn in the course of a task what features have utility and shift toward the most economical extraction of information. The conclusion in the last paragraph still holds good—that word perception, like other kinds of perception, is a search for relevant information and that the search evolves toward the most economical strategy that has utility for the task. Showing that this principle holds for reading provides a bridge from everyday perception to a more "cognitive" process.

Perceptual learning involves the learning of distinctive features and higher-order invariants, learning progressing actively toward the most economical features and structure. Features of words are classified as phonological, graphic, semantic and syntactic. Features of these classes are processed independently and sequentially. Ordering of priorities changes with development, and shifts strategically with the demands of the task. Evidence is presented for priority differences for each class of feature depending on task differences.

This paper is the outcome of two long-time endeavors of the author—the development of a theory of perceptual learning, and a program of research on reading.[1] The aim is to try to show how the two are related. First, the theory of perceptual learning will be described, as briefly as possible. It attempts to answer three questions: First, what is learned? Second, how? What are the processes involved? Third, what is the motivation and reinforcement for perceptual learning?

What is Learned?

I believe that what is learned in perceptual learning are *distinctive features* of things, of representations of things, and of symbolic entities like words; also the *invariants* of events that occur over time; and finally the economical *structuring* of both. I think the information for learning these is potentially present in stimulation, to be picked up by the observer given the proper conditions for it.

Consider some examples. Sets of distinctive features characterize objects and entities both natural and artifactual—the furnishings of the world, such as people, dwelling places, things to eat; and, particularly relevant for the present topic, symbols written on pieces of paper, like letters and words. The set of letters of our alphabet is characterized by a set of distinctive features, which in different combinations permit a unique characterization of each one. My students and I have spent much time trying to describe the set of distinctive features that are shared by letters of the Roman alphabet. We have had some success, since confusion matrices obtained experimentally reveal, *via* cluster analysis, some contrasting features that can be diagrammed in a tree structure (Gibson, Schapiro, & Yonas, 1968).

What about invariants of events? These occur over time. The nicest examples of learning to detect them occur in perceptual development. The constancies can be understood as invariants under transformations that occur in an event like the approaching or receding of an object, or rotation of it. Perceived existence of an object despite temporary occlusion by a screen of some sort is another (the event of "going in front of" or "going behind"). What has this to do with words? Events like appearance, disappearance, and reappearance have *meaning*, and these very meanings are expressed spontaneously in the child's earliest two-word utterances (Hi Daddy; all-gone ball; more milk; ball again). These utterances appear to be invoked by the event, quite literally mapped to it (Bloom, 1970; Brown, 1970). Detection of invariance, in other words, is prior to symbolic referential meanings and is reflected in them. Semantic features of words generally indicate perceivable features of the world, both events and things. Verbs for instance can be classified as *action* or *state*, an important semantic distinction arising directly from differentiating invariants in the environment. Nouns can be classified as *count* or *mass*, a distinction that depends on differentiating things that have fixed borders or shapes from substances like fluid, sand or water.

Finally, what are some structures discovered by perceptual learning? Entities in the world, both natural and artifactual, have structure; that is, relations between features. These relations can be subordinate and superordinate. Both superordinate and subordinate structure are progressively discovered in development for both objects and events—the structure of events was referred to by Brunswik as the "causal texture of the environment." Examples of the subordinate and superordinate structure of words are obvious. Words come in sentences; sentences are parts of paragraphs; phrases are parts of sentences.

Processes of Perceptual Learning

How are these things learned? Not, I believe, by associating a response of any sort, or an image or a word, to a "stimulus." Distinctive features and invariants must be discovered—extracted from the multiplicity of information in the flowing array of stimulation. We have always accepted the notion of abstraction to explain the genesis of concepts. I think a process akin to abstraction—the dissociation of an invariant from transforming or variable context—happens also at a perceptual level. The phoneme is segregated from the flow of speech heard by the pre-verbal infant and its invariant distinctive features are abstracted from many varying samples and over many transformations produced by different speakers. The process has to be one of abstraction—there is no response to be associated, nor is there an identically repeated unvarying stimulus.

What happens to the variable, irrelevant components of stimulation? When something invariant is abstracted and selected out for attention, what happens to the rest? I think that the process of abstraction is accompanied by a filtering process that attenuates and suppresses the irrelevant— this is what happens to the words that aren't heard in the dichotic listening experiments, for instance.

Finally, a very important process in perceptual learning is the operation of mechanisms of external attention. The sensory systems are all active and exploratory. "Looking," "listening," and "feeling" are terms that describe the search for information in stimulation. They also underline the fact that perception and perceptual learning are active processes. There is improvement and flexibility in attentive strategies depending on age and on the business in hand.

Motivation and Reinforcement

What selects the good strategy, the economical feature, the structure that most effectively orders the information? This is the question of motivation and reinforcement in perceptual learning. I do not think the motivation is to be found in drives like tissue needs, nor the reinforcement in reduction of a metabolic drive, nor in cessation of punishment. I think there is a built-in need to get information about one's environment. One could call this, as a number of psychologists do, "intrinsic cognitive motivation." I can call it the "search for invariance." This motivation is always related to the task in hand, for different information is needed for different tasks. But active looking for information about the solid, permanent safe places of the world, and the invariant aspects of events (like the swift approach of an object) is essential for behaviors like locomotion and avoidance of predators. A desire to understand what others are saying seems equally basic for learning to comprehend language.

Reinforcement of perceptual learning (indeed of all cognitive learning) is, I would contend, the reduction of uncertainty. Discovery of structure, or discovery of the economical distinctive feature, or of the rule describing an invariant reduces the "information load," and leads to permanent perceptual reorganization for the viewer of the world so viewed. This kind of discovery also leads to repetition of the successful strategy when a similar occasion occurs. The evidence for this is slight at present, but I have been conducting experiments to see whether discovery of structure is indeed reinforcing. I think the experiments I am going to cite as illustrations of changing strategies in selection of word features will show the self-regulating, adaptive character of the process.

How Are Words Perceived?

Now we are ready for the question of how words are perceived. I shall concentrate on how they are perceived in reading, since that is where my research has been centered. The answer sounds simple, and is not new. *Words, like other entities in our environment, are perceived by detecting their distinctive features.*[2] But what are a word's distinctive features?

Features of Words

A word is part of a vast system of information. The way to identify this information is to refer to what is learned when we learn to hear and speak, and to read and write. The information dealt with in hearing-speaking is traditionally divided into three aspects or classes, phonological, semantic and syntactic information. There are three parallel aspects for reading–writing; graphological, semantic and syntactic information.

These classes of information tell us what kinds of features a word can have. When written, it can have *graphological* features of many kinds. For example, it has a characteristic shape and length (referred to as "word shape" by reading teachers). Within the word there are letter shapes, themselves differentiated by distinctive features. And then the word has *orthographic* structure; letters are combined into words according to a rule system so that given combinations or clusters are permissible only in certain locations and contexts. Q must be followed by U, for instance; Qu can begin a word or a syllable, but it cannot end them (Venezky, 1970).

How do we know whether a potential feature of a word is actually being detected as a feature? A useful method has been to set up tasks that produce some errors and then to study what is confused in the errors. We can infer some of the features of letter shapes that are being noticed when a child confuses E and F but not E and O. We infer that a larger graphic structure is perceived when the child confuses palindromes, like "saw" and "was." He is generalizing something relational. We can also study features by looking at accurate generalizations, like discovering a rule about spelling patterns and transferring it to new cases (Gibson, 1970).

A word has potential *phonological* features, even when it is perceived by reading instead of being perceived by hearing. When we read poetry, we are keenly aware of acoustic similarity in the rhymes, for instance. Homophones, albeit they are spelled differently, are sometimes confused. The fact that a string of letters presented visually is pronounceable vastly affects its readability. This was demonstrated by Gibson, Pick, Osser, and Hammond (1962). We made up pseudo-words that could be pronounced, though they were not "real" words. We constructed them so that they began with initial consonant clusters that could not end a word, and were terminated with clusters which could not begin one. Then unpronounceable strings were constructed from the pronounceable ones by exchanging the initial and final consonant clusters. An example is the construction of CKURGL from GLURCK.

When these letter-strings were presented tachistoscopically in a mixed order, subjects invariably read the pronounceable version more accurately than the unpronounceable version. The advantage might have been due to an easier pick-up of acoustic structure; or easier pick-up of articulatory structure. But it could also have been influenced by good orthographic structure, quite apart from phonological features, for we found later that profoundly deaf Ss showed the same relative advantage (Gibson, Schurcliff, and Yonas, 1970). These are all potential features of a word, but from different feature classes.

A word has many *semantic* features. It may have markers of various kinds indicating classes or properties, like "animate" nouns, "proper" nouns, "count" nouns, "mass" nouns. It may stand for objects belonging to taxonomic categories like edible things, or for events like looming or disappearance. It has similarity and contrast relations—that is, synonyms and antonyms. We know these features are picked up because one can show experimentally that they are confusible within classes,[3] and they tend to "cluster" in recall. Semantic features of a word include values, as well. Words can be rated for pleasantness-unpleasantness, or ranked on Osgood's semantic-differential scales.

A word's *syntactic* features are equally obvious. It is a part of speech, like noun or verb or adjective. It has a role in a sentence, like subject or object. And it may possess a morphological marker, like pluralization or tense. This last feature, morphological information, was investigated in an experiment by Gibson and Guinet (1971) . We wondered whether the length of a word correctly perceived tachistoscopically could be increased by adding a well-known inflected ending to a base word, as compared to an uninflected word of equal length. Are the endings themselves a unitary structure?

We added inflected verb endings to three types of base words; real familiar words, pronounceable pseudo-words that were anagrams of them, and unpronounceable pseudo-words, and provided comparisons of uninflected words of different lengths. These words were shown tachistoscopically to subjects from third grade, fifth grade, and the elementary psychology course. The results were not what we had anticipated, but they were very illuminating. Subjects were not able to perceive a longer word correctly when a base word was expanded by adding an inflected ending. But the endings gave evidence of unitariness, for there were significantly fewer errors in inflected endings than in endings of base words of equivalent length (especially when these were not meaningful or pronounceable). Furthermore, when there were errors in the inflected endings, the errors tended to be substitutions of other inflected endings. There was a confusion within a morphological feature-class. These latter two tendencies increased from third to fifth grade, showing progressive pick-up of syntactic features.

Why wasn't a longer word perceptible when the syntactic marker was added? Because the subject had to process an extra feature. It is features that must be processed, not elements like letters or syllables, and the process takes time. No matter how long the base word, its features must be recognized and so must the morphological tag.

Three Hypotheses

I would like to suggest three hypotheses about how these features are perceived in reading. First, I think the four general classes of features, phonological, graphological, semantic, and syntactic are processed independently and sequentially, in a kind of hierarchy. If presentation time is cut short, a feature low in the hierarchy may be missed. It may not be deleted, but just not fully detected, so a confusion within its feature-class may result (like substituting *ing* for *ed*). Proofreader's errors are a case of not fully processing an orthographic feature; but as a matter of fact, spelling is generally noticed in reading, when the time is not limited. Something looks odd and we go back after a sentence or two and verify the mistake.

A classic piece of evidence for ordered, independent processing of word features is so-called "semantic satiation" or "loss of meaning," where presentation time is exaggeratedly prolonged, instead of cut short. If I put a printed word in front of you and tell you to stare at it for five minutes, its "meaning" is said to slip away. What happens is that first the semantic features go, then the phonological features go, then one is left finally with the graphic features only, and even these will eventually fragment. There is a very interesting implication here. Meaning, for an adult reader, is embedded in the word. He doesn't begin by decoding it letter by letter; the concept symbolized by the word "hits him." It is specified for him in stimulus information.

The Stroop test is further evidence of this (Stroop, 1935). In this experiment, two features are put in opposition, meaning and a graphic feature, the color of the ink the word is printed in. The subject is shown an array of words and asked to name the color each word is printed in, going from left to right as in reading—green, red, blue, and so on. But the words themselves are the names of colors. When the name and the color of the ink conflict, the subject is in trouble. The word comes first to mind and his performance is badly slowed up compared to just giving the name of a color patch. There seems to be less interference in this task with the very young readers. The meaning isn't yet as firmly embedded in, or specified by, the word on the page.

The second hypothesis is that there is a developmental change with age and schooling in feature analysis and pick-up. At an early age, phonological features of a word seem to have more control, in the sense of yielding greater generalization, than semantic ones. Riess (1946), using a conditioned GSR technique, found greater generalization at eight years of age to homonyms than to synonyms, but by adolescence the situation was reversed and semantic similarity became more effective. Perhaps the younger Ss simply had less knowledge of similarity of meaning. Rice and DiVesta (1965) controlled for this in an experiment using a paired associates method, making sure that the homonyms, synonyms, and antonyms used were recognized as such by the subjects. In the younger children (third and fifth grades) generalization occurred as a result of phonetic but not semantic similarity. But semantic generalization became increasingly apparent in older age groups. Felzen and Anisfeld (1970) confirmed these findings using a continuous recognition method. Children in third and sixth grade listened to a list of words and judged for each word whether it had appeared before on the list. False recognition of phonetically related (rhyming) words was more frequent for third graders than false recognition of semantically related words, but semantic similarity was more effective in producing errors for sixth graders.

We can find further evidence for developmental shifts by examining reading errors at progressive levels of instruction. Errors in oral reading through the first grade were studied by Weber (1970) and Biemiller (1970). The earliest errors, at the beginning of first grade, can generally be attributed to meaningful context. When the child reaches a word he does not "know," he uses all the semantic information at his disposal (context of the words already decoded, pictures, and so on) and guesses. He produces a word that makes sense, both semantically and syntactically, but bears no resemblance otherwise to the one on the page. A little later the child stops when he reaches an unknown word and simply says nothing. This is a transition to a stage where errors become determined by graphic similarity. The child is engrossed by discriminating letters and by correspondence of letters and sounds. Semantic features of the word are temporarily lowered in priority as the child strives to "break the code." (This is the period when he may be chided by the teacher for "reading without expression," but the stage nevertheless marks progress.)

Semantic features return as the decoding process becomes easier and the orthographic features demand a lesser share of the child's attention. But the orthographic and syntactic rule systems probably do not operate fully as important structural constraints until later. The influence of orthographic structure begins to be quite apparent by third grade. Besides the evidence from tachistoscopic experiments (Gibson, Osser, & Pick, 1963), it has been shown by Rosinski and Wheeler (personal communication) that third graders can judge correctly over 80% of the time which of two pseudo-words is "more like a word." First graders, however, make this judgment at a chance level.

In the Gibson and Guinet experiment (1971), morphological inflections such as verb endings were found to operate as unitary features of a written word. This function was more apparent in the fifth graders than the third graders, and most apparent in college students.

Finally, syntactic constraints like phrase structure and grammatical conventions—the word's role in the sentence—have been shown in studies with the eye-voice span to operate in reading, and again this rule system increases in usefulness as reading skill progresses, being noticeably more functional in fifth than in third graders. The influence of phrase boundaries, for example, only shows up after grade 2 (Levin & Turner, 1968) The young reader does appear, then, to show a developmental sequence in the pick-up of word-features. This progression is no doubt not as fixed as I may have implied and probably begins before very long to be influenced by the reader's task, in accordance with my next hypothesis.

My third hypothesis holds that the order of pick-up of word-features changes with the task. To put it a little differently, priorities of pick-up are geared strategically to task utility. I repeat now my earlier argument that perception is an active search for information, that the perceptual strategy that develops will be as economical as possible and that ordering of priorities is adaptive and self-regulating. Common sense suggests that this is so—when we are looking for a weather report in the newspaper, we assign a very low priority to graphic features of the words we read. But in addition there exists a large number of experiments which go to prove my point, some of my own and many by others.[4]

We can influence priorities by instructions, of course. In a tachistoscopic experiment, if a subject is told to guess at words shown him, features like meaning and word frequency are evident. If he is told to report only what is literally seen graphic features are advanced in priority (Haber, 1965). But quite aside from instructions, different tasks seem to have acquired their own priorities in the cognitive economy either in the course of development or by learning during the task. All a word's features have their importance for one task or another.

Phonological features, we have learned in recent years, have a high priority for short-term memory. If I am trying to hang onto a telephone number and someone speaks to me before I have dialed it, it is lost. Conrad (1964) and others have shown in a number of experiments that acoustic similarity produces confusions in short-term memory even when the material is presented visually (Baddeley, 1968). Graphic and semantic confusions in short-term memory, on the other hand, are infrequent (Baddeley, 1966). Auditory presentation has an advantage over visual presentation in short-term memory (Murdock, 1967), even when memory is tested by recognition (Murdock, 1968). But as lists are made longer (e.g., 14 vs 7 items) acoustic confusability effects disappear entirely (Anderson, 1969); Ss no longer give the acoustic feature priority, but adopt some other strategy.[5] Articulatory similarity may play a role in short-term memory tasks, as well (Crowder & Morton, 1969). I shall class this with phonological information, but it undoubtedly plays its own role, distinct from acoustic similarity, in some tasks.

A word's pronounceability, I suggested earlier, is one of its phonological features, and it strongly facilitates pick-up with tachistoscopically-presented displays. Does it do so equally for another task, like later recall or recognition? Gibson, Bishop, Schiff, and Smith (1964) tried to separate pronounceability and semantic reference and to compare their effects in these two kinds of tasks. Trigrams were prepared which either rated high in pronounceability (like MIB), or in referential meaning (like the initials IBM), or in neither (like MBI). In one experiment, they were presented tachistoscopically and recognition thresholds were obtained. Pronounceability very effectively facilitated accurate perception of the trigram. Meaning helped little.[6] In another experiment, the same items were presented to subjects for 2 sec each and 24 hours later recall was tested. This time the effect of meaning and pronounceability was reversed. Meaning facilitated recall far more than pronounceability and there was evidence of categorizing, for some subjects made up sets of initials, like FDR, that had not been in the list.

While phonological features of words dominate pick-up in short-term memory, there is considerable evidence to show that they have low priority for long-term memory. Acoustic similarity has little or no interfering effect in a paired-associate retroactive-inhibition paradigm (Dale & Baddeley, 1969; Bruce & Murdock, 1968), whereas semantic similarity does. Wickens, Ory, and Graf (1970) found that acoustic similarity had some negative effects in a transfer paradigm, but the effect was slight compared to semantic similarity in the same paradigm. Sharing taxonomic category membership was a powerful influence on the subject's ability to recall items of a list, for either good or ill depending on task relations.

Concrete words are in general superior to those of abstract meaning in almost any long-term memory task, such as PA learning, free recall, serial recall, or recognition (Tulving & Madigan, 1970, p. 452), but this is not true for tachistoscopic recognition, where pronounceability has such a strong advantage (Paivio & O'Neill, 1970).

The utility (and utilization) of semantic features of a word for later recall has often been demonstrated by evidence of clustering in long-term recall. This was brought out cleverly in an experiment by Hyde and Jenkins (1969). In this experiment, the subjects were sometimes asked to do two tasks at once. They were presented with a list of words for later recall. In two conditions, Ss had to extract some graphic information about a word as it was presented—either estimate its length (number of letters), or detect the presence or absence of the letter E. Another group had to rate the word as it was presented for pleasantness or unpleasantness.

Compared to a control group with no second task, recall was greatly reduced for the first two groups and so was the amount of organization in recall as measured by clustering of words in categories. But the task of rating words as pleasant or unpleasant did not reduce recall nor organization in recall as compared with a control group that had no incidental task. When the subject was performing a second task that gave priority to *semantic* features of the word, neither recall nor its organization suffered. But when the second task required attention to a word's *graphic* features, like detecting E's or estimating word-length, the semantic pick-up which is apparently vital to later recall of words was blocked.

The Hyde and Jenkins experiment suggests that features of the same class, like semantic features of all kinds, are picked up together, while different feature-classes are processed sequentially (though probably overlapping one another). The value of the word—pleasant or unpleasant—could apparently be assessed at the same time as pick-up of semantic categories of the kind that operate in clustering. I will consider this again in connection with a different task, visual search.

Over the past five years, I have been particularly interested in visual search tasks, partly because I am interested in how perceptual search develops in children and also because they offer a good opportunity for studying what the subject learns incidentally. A lot of perceptual learning goes on during this task. Visual search also provides a fine opportunity for comparing pick-up of different types of word-features. I have made such comparisons in a number of experiments. The task is similar to one used repeatedly by Neisser (1963) and involves scanning systematically through a matrix of letters for a target letter or word.

When the subject is asked to search for a target letter embedded in a context of other letters by scanning down a column of letters arranged five or six to a row, he very quickly sets his priorities for graphic features. Even seven-year-old children do this. Gibson and Yonas (1966) compared the effect of high and low graphic similarity of context letters to the target letter. Graphic similarity slows the scanning rate enormously, both for adults and children. Given an opportunity for practice, the subject will learn to scan for a single very economical distinctive feature, as Yonas (1969) and Schapiro (1970) have shown in appropriate transfer experiments.

What about phonological features of the letters in this task? They seem to be virtually, if not entirely ignored. Gibson and Yonas (1966) tried to produce interference by exposing the subject to a voice pronouncing letters that sounded like the target letter while he scanned the list visually. There was no effect at all on scanning rate, even in children of seven years who might have been expected to subvocalize while reading. Kaplan, Yonas, and Shurcliff (1966) compared the effect of high and low acoustic similarity of context letters to the target. That is, the target was embedded in a context of letters that rhymed with it (B, V, D, and so on) or in a context of letters that sounded unlike it. Acoustic similarity did not slow scanning rate at all, in contrast to a powerful effect of graphic similarity.

An experiment by Krueger (1970) found some effect of acoustic confusability in visual search, but it is possible that acoustic was confounded with visual confusability (for instance, C and G, and M and N have both types of confusability and were used within the same target-list set). In the paper by Kaplan et al. (1966) this factor was controlled. Changing or maintaining target items from trial to trial (Krueger changed them, while Kaplan et al. did not) is also an important task variable, since practice with a target or target set to be discriminated visually from another set (Yonas, 1969) is very effective in reducing search to the most economical visual distinctive feature.

Subjects typically remember context letters in the scanning task very poorly, even when they are tested by recognition with the letters presented to them visually (Schapiro, 1970). I wondered whether introduction of some structure of a higher order in the context would not bring it to the fore perceptually. If subjects can learn to take advantage of the most economical possible single graphic feature that distinguishes the target, will they not also discover and use superordinate orthographic structure if it is present?

Gibson, Tenney, Barron, and Zaslow (1971) performed an experiment in which we compared scanning rate for a letter target, either embedded in letter-strings which, though not meaningful, were orthographically possible words and were pronounceable; or with the target embedded in strings of the same letters scrambled so as to be unpronounceable. I had thought that orthographic structure might be picked up along with graphic structure, which is so salient in this task. If so, it might facilitate search, because the subject could filter the irrelevant context in larger units—strip it off in bigger chunks, so to speak.

On the other hand, if the subject subvocally articulated the pronounceable context items, scanning rate ought to be slowed down. (I have been trying to find out for a long time whether redundant orthographic structure and pronounceability are necessarily functionally tied—my bête noire, in fact.) We ran 76 children in the fifth grade in this experiment. There was no difference in mean rate of scan between the two conditions. What was happening? It would appear that the children were not articulating the pronounceable items. Like lower-order phonological features, pronounceability of a letter-string in its literal sense of pronunciation seems not to influence the kind of verbal processing that goes on in this task. But what about the orthographic structure as such? Does it go unnoticed or can it not be used without an accompanying act of articulation that would be uneconomical? I think the latter may be the case here. When the children were questioned after the experiment they appeared, when context strings were pronounceable, to have been aware of it. Sometimes they commented on it spontaneously. But still it did not affect the mean scanning rate. The child could of course have processed the whole string as a unit, and then searched it for the target letter as a second step. This would contradict the suggestion I made earlier, that a given class of word features gets processed simultaneously. It is also contradicted by recent experiments of Reicher (1969), Wheeler (1970), and Krueger (1970).

On the other hand, the children may have found the orthographic structure early in the task (since they so often commented on it), but learned to disregard it, perhaps because they could not use it without articulation—a handicap in a scanning task where speed is emphasized. This would be a kind of perceptual learning involving an inhibitory or filtering process, one of the three processes for perceptual selectivity that I hypothesized earlier. We thought that adult readers might use the structure without articulation and would speed up their scanning rate even though the children did not. Further experiments did not confirm this possibility.

What would happen if *semantic* structure were introduced in the scanning task? Would it be picked up, when presented incidentally? Would it speed the search, and if so would it transfer as a strategy—that is, lead to a search for similar structure in a second task? These questions were investigated in another experiment (Gibson, Tenney, and Zaslow, 1971). We introduced semantic structure by building categorical meaning into the context to be searched through in looking for a target *word*.

Context words, in one condition, were all the same length and all belonged to the same semantic category—e.g., kinds of fruit. We used categorical material that had previously been shown to cluster well in recall experiments. The target word was the name of an animal, and it varied from trial to trial. The S was told to search for the name of an animal, rather than for a specified word, because we found in preliminary work that S searched for nothing but graphic features if he was given a specific target word. We wanted to facilitate pick-up of the categorical relation among context words, if it could be done. A control group had context words chosen at random as regards meaning, but equated with the other condition for frequency, length, and as many graphic attributes as possible.

The results of this experiment ruled out unequivocally the possibility that categorical meaning plays any role at all in a search task of this sort. Semantic structure of the kind we introduced is evidently *not* an economical feature for a search task when the words are presented in a list, as unconnected prose. It did not speed up scanning rate and was not used by the Ss. Many Ss did not even notice the categorical relation within the context although they were told to use category membership for locating the target. What they actually did, it turned out, was very economical indeed. They looked, after a few trials, not for a word of any particular meaning, but simply for any combination of letters that had not appeared before.

Subjects do learn in this task. They learn the strategy that is most economical for the task. The conclusion is inescapable that semantic features of words have little utility for a search task of this type and are ignored in favor of graphic features that do. It is not that structure is never utilized; graphic structure in the sense of a redundant graphic feature that helps differentiate the target from the background is picked up and used as Schapiro (1970) has shown. But perceptual strategy in this task sets the graphic features a high priority, and other features—semantic, acoustic, even orthographic, low.

What happens in a search task if words are presented in a passage of connected prose and the S asked to search for semantic, or graphic or phonemic targets? Cohen (1970) tried this with all three types of targets and with combinations of them. The semantic target was a word of a given category (e.g., an animal)—in fact, 10 different words belonging to the category were to be cancelled in a meaningful paragraph. In this situation, search for the semantic feature was faster than search for a graphic feature (a letter), and both were much faster than searching for a phonological feature. The semantic feature had the advantage over the other two of redundancy with syntactic and topical predictability, but for adults it is not surprising if meaning is detected early in reading a meaningful connected passage, especially when S is searching for a member of a concept group and not a specific word. The effect of even small changes in task variables in shifting feature priorities is impressive and is witness to the remarkable adaptiveness of human linguistic processing.

One may ask, finally, if there is any task where syntactic features of words have priority. In laboratory tasks as far as I know, this has not been the case, although they are certainly picked up (Gibson & Guinet, 1971). A feature like part-of-speech (noun vs verb or adjective) is not very effective for producing clustering in recall (Cofer & Bruce, 1965), generalization in verbal conditioning or interference in short term memory (Wickens, Clark, Hill, & Wittlinger, 1968). That may be, one could object, because syntactical information is generally spread over a string of words and is incomplete in one. But although a word always tells us more in context, it appears that its different features are picked up independently and differentially. I find that there is one real-life task in which I seem, willy-nilly, to give first priority to syntactic information. That is, reading students' papers, or a thesis. A split infinitive, or a singular verb following the word "data" distracts me so that I lose the meaning!

Conclusion

Does perceptual learning occur in word perception? I think it does—both during development and within a task, without instruction or even apparent intention. Words contain many kinds of information, and we learn to perceive them as a complex of features. Words should not be thought of as made up of elements of a given length, or as bits of sense-data to be "coded" into something, but rather as entities possessing information classifiable as phonological, graphic, semantic, and syntactic features. All these kinds of information are in words, I think, in the sense that a word *specifies* its information. It is not constructed by putting together letters or adding on associations, but must be found by discovering invariant features and relations. The perceiver *does* something, indeed, but he does not invent the information.

Word perception, like other kinds of perception, is active, searching for the relevant information in stimulation. Perceptual learning with words, like other examples of perceptual learning, develops toward the strategy that is most economical. This means that priorities for features shift adaptively, with practice in a task, toward those that have most utility for it.

Notes

1. Invited address for Division 3, American Psychological Association, 1970. This work was supported in part by a grant (USOE OEG-2-9-420446-1071-010) to the author from the Office of Education.
2. The notion that a word is essentially a complex of features has been suggested and explored previously by Anisfeld and Knapp (1968), Bower (1967), Fillenbaum (1969), Katz and Fodor (1963), and Wickens (1970). The present paper shares this notion with these authors, but differs from a number of them in conceiving the perception of words, like that of things and events, to be a process of selective detection of information rather than one of encoding from bits of sense-data.
3. See Wickens (1970) for a summary of many relevant experiments.
4. There is so much evidence for this third hypothesis that I can only give examples of it here, roughly one for each feature class. My apologies to the authors whose results are relevant but not included
5. Strategies which reduce the information will be adopted in short-term memory, when possible. Baddeley (1971) has shown that redundant strings of letters will be organized in groups (e.g., B-E-D as the word bed, rather than as three independent letters). Effects of acoustic confusability then drop out.
6. An experiment by Pynte and Noizet (1971) also found a strong effect of pronounceability on tachistoscopic recognition of trigrams while finding meaningful sets of initials also facilitating. But this type of meaning was effective principally when the trigram was unpronounceable and had little effect when it was.

References

Anderson, N. S. The influence of acoustic similarity on serial recall of letter sequences. *Quarterly Journal of Experimental Psychology*, 1969, 21, 248–255.

Anisfeld, M., & Knapp, M. Association, synonymity, and directionality in false recognition. *Journal of Experimental Psychology*, 1968, 77, 171–179.

Baddeley, A. D. Short term memory for word sequences as a function of acoustic, semantic, and formal similarity. *Quarterly Journal of Experimental Psychology*, 1966, 18, 362–365.

Baddeley, A. D. How does acoustic similarity influence short-term memory? *Quarterly Journal of Experimental Psychology*, 1968, 20, 249–264.

Baddeley, A. D. Language habits, acoustic confusability, and immediate memory for redundant letter sequences. *Psychonomic Science*, 1971, 22, 120–121.

Biemiller, A. The development of the use of graphic and contextual information as children learn to read. *Reading Research Quarterly*, 1970, 6, 75–96.

Bloom, L. *Language development: Form and function in emerging grammars.* Cambridge: MIT Press, 1970.

Bower, G. H. A multicomponent theory of the memory trace. In K. W. Spence & J. T. Spence (Eds.), *The psychology of learning and motivation.* Vol. 1. New York: Academic Press, 1967.

Bower, R. The first sentences of child and chimpanzee. In R. Brown, *Psycholinguistics.* New York: The Free Press, 1970.

Bruce, D., & Murdock, B. B. Acoustic similarity effects on memory for paired associates. *Journal of Verbal Learning and Verbal Behavior*, 1968, 7, 627–631.

Cofer, C. N., & Bruce, D. R. Form-class as the basis for clustering in the recall of non-associated words. *Journal of Verbal Learning and Verbal Behavior*, 1965, 4, 386–389.

Cohen, G. Search times for combinations of visual, phonemic, and semantic targets in reading prose. *Perception and Psychophysics*, 1970, 8, 370–372.

Conrad, R. Acoustic confusions in immediate memory. *British Journal of Psychology*, 1964, 55, 75–84.

Crowder, R. G., & Morton, J. Precategorical acoustic storage. *Perception and Psychophysics*, 1969, 5, 365–373.

Dale, H. C. A., & Baddeley, A. D. Acoustic similarity in long-term paired-associate learning. *Psychonomic Science*, 1969, 16, 209–211.

Felzen, E,, & Anisfeld, M. Semantic and phonetic relations in the false recognition of words by third- and sixth-grade children. *Developmental Psychology*, 1970, 3, 163–168.

Fillenbaum, S. Words as feature complexes: False recognition of antonyms and synonyms. *Journal of Experimental Psychology*, 1969, 82, 400–402.

Gibson, E. J. *Principles of perceptual learning and development*. New York: Appleton-Century-Crofts, 1969.

Gibson, E. J. The ontogeny of reading. *American Psychologist*, 1970, 25, 136–143.

Gibson, E. J., Bishop, C., Schiff, W., & Smith, J. Comparison of meaningfulness and pronunciability as grouping principles in the perception and retention of verbal material. *Journal of Experimental Psychology*, 1964, 67, 173–182.

Gibson, E. J., & Guinet, L. The perception of inflections in brief visual presentations of words. *Journal of Verbal Learning and Verbal Behavior*, 1971, 10, 182–189.

Gibson, E. J., Pick, A., Osser, H., & Hammond, M. The role of grapheme phoneme correspondence in the perception of words. *American Journal of Psychology*, 1962, 75, 554–570.

Gibson, E. J., Osser, H., & Pick, A. A study in the development of grapheme phoneme correspondences. *Journal of Verbal Learning and Verbal Behavior*, 1963, 2, 142–146.

Gibson, E. J., Schapiro, F., & Yonas, A. Confusion matrices for graphic patterns obtained with a latency measure. In *The analysis of reading skill: A program of basic and applied research*. Final report, Project No. 5-1213, Cornell University & U.S.O.E., 1968. Pp. 76–96.

Gibson, E. J., Shurcliff, A., & Yonas, A. Utilization of spelling patterns by deaf and hearing subjects. In H. Levin & J. P. Williams (Eds.), *Basic studies on reading*. New York: Basic Books, 1970.

Gibson, E. J., Tenney, Y. J., & Zaslow, M. The effect of categorizable context on scanning for verbal targets. Mss. Cornell Univ., 1971.

Gibson, E. J., Tenney, Y. J., Barron, R. W., & Zaslow, M. The effect of orthographic structure on letter search. Mss. Cornell Univ., 1971.

Gibson, E. J., & Yonas, A. A developmental study of the effects of visual and auditory interference on a visual scanning task. *Psychonomic Science*, 1966, 5, 163–164.

Haber, R. N. Effect of prior knowledge of the stimulus on word-recognition processes. *Journal of Experimental Psychology*, 1965, 69, 282–286.

Hyde, T. S., & Jenkins, J. J. Differential effects of incidental tasks on the organization of recall of a list of highly associated words. *Journal of Experimental Psychology*, 1969, 82, 472–481.

Kaplan, G., Yonas, A., & Shurcliff, A. Visual and acoustic confusability in a visual search task. *Perception and Psychophysics*, 1966, 1, 172–174.

Katz, J. J., & Fodor, J. A. The structure of semantic theory. *Language*, 1963, 39, 170-210.

Krueger, L. E. Search time in a redundant visual display. *Journal of Experimental Psychology*, 1970, 83, 391–399.

Krueger, L. E. The effect of acoustic confusability on visual search. *American Journal of Psychology*, 1970, 83, 389–400.

Levin, H., & Turner, E. A. Sentence structure and the eye voice span. In The analysis of reading skill: A program of basic and applied research. Final report, Project No. 5-1213, Cornell Univ. & U.S.O.E., 1968.

Murdock, B. B., Jr. Auditory and visual stores in short-term memory. *Acta Psychologica,* 1967, 27, 316–324.

Murdock, B. B., Jr. Modality effects in short-term memory: Storage or retrieval? *Journal of Experimental Psychology,* 1968, 77, 79–86.

Neisser, U. Decision-time without reaction-time: Experiments in visual scanning. *American Journal of Psychology,* 1963, 70, 376–385.

Paivio, A., & O'Neill, B. J. Visual recognition thresholds and dimensions of word meaning. *Perception and Psychophysics,* 1970, 8, 273–275.

Pynte, J., & Noizet, G. Trigrammes, syllables et sigles: Étude comparative de la facilité de leur perception. Mimeo, Lab. de Psych. Expérimentale, Aix-en-Provence, 1971.

Reicher, G. M. Perceptual recognition as a function of meaningfulness of stimulus material. *Journal of Experimental Psychology,* 1969, 81, 275–280.

Rice, U. M., & DiVesta, F. J. A developmental study of semantic and phonetic generalization in paired-associate learning. *Child Development,* 1965, 36, 721–730.

Riess, B. F. Genetic changes in semantic conditioning. *Journal of Experimental Psychology,* 1946, 36, 143–152.

Schapiro, F. Information extraction and filtering during perceptual learning in visual search. Unpublished Ph.D. dissertation, Cornell University, Ithaca, NY, 1970.

Stroop, J. R. Studies of interference in serial verbal reactions. *Journal of Experimental Psychology,* 1935, 18, 643–661.

Tulving, E., & Madigan, S. A. Memory and verbal learning. *Annual Review of Psychology,* 1970, 21, 437–484.

Venezky, R. L. *The structure of English orthography.* The Hague: Mouton, 1970.

Weber, R. M. First graders' use of grammatical context in reading. In H. Levin & J. Williams (Eds.), *Basic studies on reading.* New York: Basic Books, 1970.

Wheeler, D. D. Processes in word recognition. *Cognitive Psychology,* 1970, 1, 59–85.

Wickens, D. D. Encoding categories of words: An empirical approach to meaning. *Psychological Review,* 1970, 77, 1–15.

Wickens, D. D., Clark, S. E., Hill, F. A., & Wittlinger, R. P. Grammatical class as an encoding category in short-term memory. *Journal of Experimental Psychology,* 1968, 78, 559–604.

Wickens, D. D., Ory, N. E., & Graf, S. A. Encoding by taxonomic and acoustic categories in long-term memory. *Journal of Experimental Psychology,* 1970, 84, 462–469.

Yonas, A. The acquisition of information-processing strategies in a time-dependent task. Unpublished Ph.D. dissertation, Cornell University, Ithaca, NY, 1969.

26

How Perception Really Develops: A View from outside the Network

Eleanor J. Gibson

This paper was written for a summer institute held in 1975 at the Center for Research in Human Learning at the University of Minnesota. The psychologists invited to give presentations, except for myself, were zealots of information processing. The book that resulted foreshadows the present move toward "cognitive science" and includes chapters on neurophysiological "substrata" of perception and comprehension, and computer models of language acquisition. Perceptual models presented (e.g., Estes' "hierarchical filter model," and Johnson's "pattern-unit model") take a constructionist view of how units are built and how words, as a consequence, are perceived in reading. These views do not deal with perception (as I conceive it) at all but are more concerned with entities like "icons," "stores," and building of representations. The title I chose was intended to express this feeling.

I quoted some lines from Auden before beginning because I wanted to empha-size that there is a "world of lasting objects" and that the information for them is there to be obtained. We essay to obtain it—the truth—but one does not con-struct truth. I felt, and still feel, that the view expressed here applies to perceptual processes in reading as well as in the world of objects. The strong language in the opening paragraphs did not seem to offend anyone, I suppose because I was a lone voice crying in the wilderness.

Having railed against the elementarism and constructionism of the information processing approach, I tried to set forth my view that perception is extraction of information about the affordances of things in the world, like layout and events, and that perceiving text involves extraction of information about these things as well. It is a less direct process, to be sure, but the aim and function are the same. I tried to bring in the notion of affordance, a concept that has preoccupied me in planning a research program ever since.

D. Laberge and S. J. Samuels (eds.), *Basic Processes in Reading: Perception and Comprehension.* Hillsdale, N.J.: L. Erlbaum Assoc., 1977. Pp. 155–173.

I chose to organize my talk around the trends I identified earlier in learning and development (see chapter 20). At the heart of my conception of perceptual learning is the notion that its result is increasing specificity of correspondence between information in stimulation and what is perceived. Learning to read is replete with examples of this change. But increasing economy of information pickup is at the heart of progression toward skilled reading. There is a vast amount of evidence for this trend, some of which is presented here. I argued, of course, that this progression is not the result of gradually stringing together longer units via an associative process, but is instead the result of discovering order and rules that generate textual units. They exist at many levels (orthographic rules in words, syntax in bigger chunks of text, and nested semantic units that can be as great as the organization of a book and as small as a metaphor carried in a single word).

The ability to extract selectively these kinds of information exists to some extent in even the youngest readers, but it grows as a reader reads on over the years. An experiment by three of my graduate students (Condry, McMahon-Rideout, and Levy 1979) provided a neat, concrete example of this development. But it shows at the same time that second graders are already capable of seeking information from text and do so in much the same way as adult readers do, however inexpertly.

In the notes for the last colloquium I gave on reading I find this conclusion:

> *Mature reading is marked by discovery of structure; by use of structure and rules to achieve economy of performance; and by adapting information pickup to the reader's task.*
>
> *The difference between a reader who uses the redundancy given by all these kinds of structure efficiently and automatically, and a beginning scholar who is presumed to stumble along decoding letter by letter into speech sounds cannot be exaggerated. The accomplishment of reading and comprehending the text of* War and Peace *is as wonderful as reading the score of a symphony, which does not come through note by note any more than the former comes through letter by letter.*

Can a process so fundamental as perception be subject to the fads and fancies induced by a Zeitgeist in the minds of those who seek to understand it? Perception, the most solidly based of all cognitive processes, surely cannot be whipped about with the wind of the times, however processes like memory ("short" or "long"?), images ("reproductions" or "constructions"?), or intelligence ("normative" or "operational"?) may be conceived variously by fickle thinkers in one decade or another. And yet, signs and portents assure us (uneasy psychologists) that it is. Recall unconscious inference, dredged up from time to time ever since Helmholtz. What about the fact that it wasn't fashionable to mention perception at all during the heyday of S–R theorizing? What about the "new look" in the early Fifties? And now, what about the craze for information-processing models of perception?

The craze is with us; one has only to consider other chapters in this book. How did it come about? The answer lies, I think, in the transition from S–R theories to cognitive theories via computer simulation. How respectable it is! If a computer can "model" a cognitive process, there is something substantial to take hold of. I believe people who would not have dreamed of working on what they think of as perception in 1950 are happy to now because they can invent stages of "processing" that can be duplicated in computer software, if not hardware. But there is something else that makes it acceptable to these people. It is still elementaristic, just as much as S–R theory. One starts by assuming that "input" comes in pieces or bits. The assumption is seldom defended; it is just made. And then, of course, if the input is only bits and pieces, a construction process must be devised to assemble things in the head, to reconstruct reality, because it is obvious that we don't perceive bits and pieces, but a world. The goal is how to build "a world of lasting objects," when, in fact, they are already there in the world.

I am inclined to think that many present-day cognitive psychologists consider themselves redeemed because they have foresworn behaviorism but that they are really pursuing the same course because they conceive of the stuff of the world that is available to an organism as meaningless and atomistic. Such a conception requires them to invent "processing mechanisms" to put the world together. Sensations have traditionally been the bits and pieces—unstructured, although having a few dimensions like intensity by means of which they can be arranged in a scale. Now, however, we have a mysterious construct known as a "feature detector" that implies that (for vision at least) the pieces at some early stage have a wee semblance of form, such as tiny lines in varying orientations. These may, however, have to be "coded" from the sensations; and in any case, the orientation seems to be with respect to the retina, so it still doesn't help with construction of a world.

There must in fact, to judge from the models of perception and cognition, be a series of "coding" and "decoding" processes (world to stimulus; stimulus to ikon; ikon to features; features to parsed units of some kind; those units to short-term memory; short-term memory to another code where meaning is somehow incorporated, etc.). There is a "processor" at each of these stages of recoding, and in the end cognitive psychology becomes a branch of cryptology. The tendency to homunculize appears irresistible; there are cryptologists in the brain. But how to put Humpty Dumpty back together again? No answer to this has ever been proposed, except "integration with past experience," or "inference from past experience." But what was the past experience like? How was it obtained? How did it become complete and meaningful?

Information processors quite often conclude that there is no such thing as perception, that what we experience as perception is really memory. The conclusion is almost inevitable from this kind of analysis, for indeed there is no frozen instant of time in which a perception may be said to occur. Perceiving goes on continuously; temporal information is not only available but *must* be extracted. If it were not, we would not perceive a hurled object looming at us on a collision course, or even feel our own arms reaching out toward a target. So eliminating perception may be consistent, but it leaves us where we started. If what we are talking about is really memory, where did we get the meaningful information to remember? Of course, once something gets constructed, the information processor can make progress because he can start matching the bits and pieces to the construction, but the original structure of the information and the meaning have still escaped the processors.

Suppose one does not accept this view of the way the world comes to us in experience as atomic bits or even "pictures" frozen in time and without spatial organization?[1] I do not believe it is essential to invent mechanisms for assembling what we know we actually *do* perceive: things, a spatial layout, events that take place in it. There is structure in the array, relational information that does not have to be pieced together because, like truth, it is already there. This is the assumption I want to proceed with. I do not want a construction theory, with processors at every stage like an assembly line. What kind of theory do I want, then ?

I might call it a "seek and ye shall find" theory (find sometimes, at least). What do we seek? Living organisms search for information for invariant properties of the world: of the *spatial layout*, which must have a stable structure (in fact, an objective one in which not only I but other animals too can locate things); of *objects*, with constant dimensions (not shrinking, expanding, or losing and gaining substance as we move around) and reliable affordances that meet our requirements for survival; and of *events*, in which things happen with predictable relations (not randomly or chaotically).

This search is so much a part of man's nature, evolved over millions of years, that it is as ingrained, strong, and unconscious as the functions of digestion and breathing and much more elaborately provided for. We have many windows on the world: systems for listening, looking, touching, tasting, and accompanying patterns of exploration like scanning, palpating, and licking. I think we have been fooled by our own laboratory paradigms into believing that we have to bribe an animal or an infant into learning something with material rewards like food. For human infants, this procedure does not even work very well. It turns out that they learn best if they are allowed to discover an interesting source of information or a predictable contingency or a problem to be solved.

From this perspective, if I look for any mechanism at all, it will not be an associative process or a construction process, but an abstraction process. What is needed is abstraction (extraction?) of the relevant information from the flood of available information. Abstraction is supposed to be a very high level process. Can babies do it, on a perceptual level at least? It seems that they must, if only to abstract phonemes, for instance, from a continuous speech flow. That they do, indeed, abstract consonantal phonemes from vowel contexts has been demonstrated by Fodor, Garrett, and Brill (1975).

With this view that perception is not constructed from sensory particles go a few caveats. Does it carry the implication that all the information in stimulation, provided it is available to an organism, is picked up automatically, regardless of species, age, or earlier experience? Certainly not. The information has to be extracted (but it is information that is extracted, a relation, not an element). What does extraction depend on? For the sake of brevity, I note just three important points:

1. What is extracted depends on the species. Every living organism is equipped appropriately to extract the information needed for survival in its ecological niche. All get some kind of information for the spatial layout, the events, and the objects that are relevant for them, but the information differs. Recordings from single cells in the auditory system of monkeys, for instance, have shown that they are tuned so as to make it possible to hear the range of vocalizations characteristic of the species. Similar studies have shown appropriate tuning in bats and other species. Primates and birds are equipped to get excellent information for the spatial layout by visual means. Bats, on the other hand, have highly specialized systems for getting acoustic information for where they are going.

2. What is extracted depends on developmental maturity. Human infants appear to differentiate and identify stationary objects rather poorly before they are four or five months old. But they seem to locate things quite well very early. Their attention is greatly drawn to events; how soon these are differentiated in any fine-grained way we do not yet know, but highly contrasting ones like looming and zooming are probably distinguished by a month or so. Small events embedded in larger events seem to be differentiated considerably later.

3. What is extracted depends on learning. There is learning common to members of a species, who share an ecology and pickup systems, and there is also idiosyncratic learning by individuals. It is very

instructive to look at what is learned, because that will give us clues to how learning itself can or cannot be understood. One of the most impressive examples of idiosyncratic perceptual learning has been provided to us in the literature on chess masters (Chase & Simon, 1973). A chess master can look for as little as two seconds at a board as it stood in midgame (although he did not play that game) and reconstruct it almost perfectly. An amateur cannot. But when the same number of chessmen have been arranged randomly on the board, the master is no better than the amateur. What has he learned? He does not "remember" that particular arrangement. It is not an image of an arrangement on a board that he once saw that gives him the advantage. He picks up quickly an order in the arrangement that results from an abstract set of rules that someone else has followed. But they are rules that he knows. Rules are abstract, but cases are generated from them. We perceive the cases as ordered because they are derived from the rules that generated them. They are meaningful as well, because they "afford" something—in this case, what move to make next so as to win the game. The chess master is not matching to some specific stored image or schema in his brain. There is no "feature detector" for every arrangement of a chessboard. We perceive specific things, yes, but always with internal and contextual relations.

If I look for mechanisms, therefore, they are going to have to be ones that deal with relations and ones that abstract information, rather than add on or integrate pieces. I am not primarily interested in processing mechanisms. I am interested in what is learned in perceptual learning, and I am interested in trends in perceptual development, not over a fraction of a second, but in the growing individual. I have chosen to talk about the latter, but I will consider along with these trends whether I need to invoke a process of integration—of construction from elements.

Trends in Perceptual Development

Twice before, I have talked about "trends in perceptual development," once in my book on perceptual learning and development, and once at the University of Minnesota about two years ago. What I had to say on each occasion was quite different, five or six years having intervened, but the trends were the same. They still are, although I begin to think that two of them can be combined into one. They are descriptions that characterize perceptual development, its end points and how it moves toward them, to be authenticated and explained if one can. I have spent more time in describing them and in demonstrating their authenticity than in explaining them. I shall still do that, but I shall ask whether the concepts I have been using—differentiation; search for distinctive features, invariants, and order; a process of abstraction; and reduction of uncertainty by finding order —are sufficient for an adequate account of where perception is going developmentally.

Increasing Specificity of Correspondence between What Is Perceived and Information in Stimulation
A striking trend in perceptual development is the increasing specificity of correspondence between information in stimulation in the world and in what is perceived. I think objects and events and layout are perceived from the start, insofar as anything is, but with little differentiation. I am not persuaded by experiments that display line drawings of geometrical forms to neonates that perceiving begins with the pickup of a line, and then gradually more lines, welded together into cell assemblies by eye movements. What do babies normally look at? Not line drawings. They certainly look frequently at faces, and research has tended to focus, quite properly, on the development of perception of faces.

Unfortunately, even this research does not have all the ecological validity one might wish, because the displays used are often flat, motionless, silent, over-simplified cartoons. Real faces move and talk. But if we think of the displays used as varied degrees and types of simulation, attempting to isolate critical information, they can perhaps still tell us something. It seems pretty clear that during the first few months of life infants progressively differentiate the human face *as a face*; gross outer contour appears to compel attention very early, then internal details like the eyes; but gradually superordinate relations are noticed and right ones are differentiated from wrong ones. Only later are individual faces differentiated as unique, and properly identified. Work in our laboratory by Spelke with motion pictures of people doing things (chewing gum, nodding, yawning, and so on) shows that a person is recognized despite different activities by about $5\frac{1}{2}$ months. Invariant, enduring properties peculiar to the person are picked up despite varying actions. The truly unique features seem to be discovered over change. It is impossible for me to conceive of recognition that develops over varying activities as a process of associating elements or constructing from elements a schema to be matched. There certainly is no frozen image to be viewed or "processed" by a comparator.

Since the chapters that preceded mine all deal with the perception of words (single words or alphanumeric symbols of some sort), I shall try now to choose my examples from this realm. An early case of developing specificity of correspondence is the differentiation of graphic symbols. Research by Lavine (1977) showed that children in our society differentiate "writing" from pictures (simplified line drawings) at age 3. When tested with many samples of printing, cursive writing, and scribbles simulating writing, they unhesitatingly identified them as writing, although few could identify a single letter by name. Lavine's experiments showed that the youngest children tend to make use of some class features, such as linearity, repetition, and recombination of items, for distinguishing writing from pictures. But older children, at ages 5 to 6, were making greater use of distinctive features of individual letters. They differentiated one from another (still usually without naming) and discarded scribbles and artificial characters. Many, however, classified unfamiliar characters (e.g., Hebrew and Chinese) as writing, pointing out that it was not *their* kind of writing. Differentiation of global features for writing as a class evidently preceded differentiation of *kinds* of writing and of individual letters.

I have given a good deal of attention, in the past, to an analysis of distinctive features of letters. Does that not set me up as one who calls upon "feature detectors," one who assumes that features are the elements out of which letters are constructed? Our sins do seem to come home to roost, and I have certainly been thought to hold his notion. It was my own doing, I now see, since I suggested a table of features that others interpreted in this way. But it is not too late to protest. I have always thought of distinctive features as relational, as Roman Jakobson defined them for phonemes. They are contrasting properties useful to distinguish one thing from another, not bricks. They are discovered in a "differencing process" and are abstract.

Most children seem to have little trouble learning to distinguish letters —even rather confusable ones (cf. Gibson & Levin, 1975, pp. 239ff.). When trouble comes, it generally occurs in distinguishing sequences of letters in given orders (e.g., *boat* from *baot*; *trial* from *trail*). Is this not a failure in, or rather a need to develop, the ability to integrate? Again, I doubt it. Perception of order requires perception of succession. Perceiving succession over time is a particularly good example of differentiation that improves with development. There is considerable evidence that temporal acuity develops in children; they become better at resolving information given over time, rather than at integrating it. The temporal relations for perception of phi movement provide one example. Younger children perceive movement rather than succession with a longer interval and a wider gap than do older children and adults. Another example is the effect of masking a visually presented target. The masking threshold—the temporal interval that must intervene between a target (a letter, say) and a mask (another letter or some figure like a grid or a dollar sign) in order to identify the target—has generally been found to be longer, the younger the child. I do not think that this is because he cannot remember the target. Rather, I think that events have to be differentiated, not integrated. Furthermore, perception of order requires ability to discriminate succession. In other words, differentiation of succession—including segmentation—is a prerequisite for pickup of order.

There is supporting but indirect evidence for this notion in studies of children's problems with segmentation when they begin to read. Words resist being broken down into sounds. Perhaps the same is true of printed letters in a string for younger children. We have recently initiated what I hope will be more focused experiments to study masking effects in second- and fifth-grade children to see whether such effects with letters and words are related to perception of order in words. Is confusion of order within visually presented words related to developing ability to detect temporal order or succession? In some sense, information for succession must be perceived, whether one reads letter by letter or not. Information processors would no doubt refer to short-term memory for letter order, but I would talk about perceptual pickup of order information—something that has to be differentiated, especially in the internal portions of words. Of course, there is not only order information in words, there is information about other structural relations too, and I want to turn to this, since it leads to the second important trend: increasing economy of information pickup.

Increasing Economy of Information Pickup

I think increasing economy comes about because the developing organism becomes more efficient in detecting and using relations that are present in the stimulus array. In general, there are two major ways of increasing the economy of extracting relevant information.

One is the detection and use of the smallest possible distinguishing feature that will permit a decision. It may sound as though relational information is not involved in detecting what some people think of as an element. But it must be remembered that it is not an element that is singled out. The differentiating process requires generalization and classification. The minimal information is relational—an abstraction of a common contrasting property that divides two sets. The two sets could be letters or artificial characters in a Sternberg type of task (Barron, 1975; Yonas, 1969) that are separable if some contrastive property is discovered; or they could be concepts that share many properties but differ critically in just one or two. It is *only* that one or two that will be retained for future classification (Vurpillot et al., 1966). Children tend to behave this way, as well as adults, but adults can accomplish a finer sifting—with word meanings, for instance.

The second way of increasing economy is the detection and use of superordinate structure that permits what has often been called "grouping information in larger units." This is a typical way of increasing economy in reading; a reader will deal with the information in the text in the largest units that are relevant for his task, if he is capable of it (Gibson & Levin,

1975). These units are not conglomerations of associated parts (whatever the parts might be—lines? letters?), but are generated by the various rule systems that characterize discourse, in this case written discourse, at all levels. There is order in the way the information is presented—within words, within sentences, and within passages of discourse.

There has been much talk of economical use of structure at the level of the word during the past decade and indeed at this symposium. I need hardly remind you that it takes as long to read a letter as a one-syllable word; that a word may be recognized at as short an exposure duration as a letter; that a letter *in* a word can (under some circumstances at least) be identified, with a short exposure, more accurately than the same letter alone; that it takes longer to identify a target letter in a word than to identify the word itself as a target; and so on.

Although we have far less research bearing on this question, there is reason to think that ability to treat words as units develops over a fairly long period while a child is learning to read. The earliest data I know of were collected by Hoffman in 1927 (reported in Woodworth, 1938, and Gibson & Levin, 1975). He compared the increase with grade level in the number of letters read correctly with tachistoscopic exposure of unconnected consonants, nonsense syllables, unfamiliar words, and familiar words. From the first to the eighth grades, there was only a slight rise in the number of randomly connected consonants and nonsense syllables read, but there was a large increase for words, especially familiar ones. The sharpest rise occurred between the first and third grades, a finding consistent with more recent data collected by me, my students, and my colleagues (Gibson, Osser, & Pick, 1963; Golinkoff, 1974; Rosinski & Wheeler, 1972).

None of our studies has covered a really wide age range, however, or compared more than two or three kinds of items (usually words, pseudo-words, and unpronounceable letter strings). I was pleased, therefore, to receive a copy of a very extensive study by Doehring (1976) comparing latencies of response to a number of kinds of verbal material, with different judgments, over a very broad age range.

I have chosen a few of Doehring's results (all typical) that make the point about growth of economical processing. When an auditory–visual match was to be made and latency recorded, children did not improve significantly after the first grade in matching single letters. But when four-letter words (presented visually) were to be matched to a sample presented auditorily, latency improved significantly to the middle of the second grade. When four-letter pronounceable syllables were presented, latency improved up to the ninth grade. The trends for purely visual matching were similar for the three kinds of material. The same trends were particularly strong for oral reading measured in mean latency in seconds per

Table 26.1
Examples of Orthographic Constraints within the English Monosyllable

Initial consonant cluster		Final consonant cluster
qu	/a/, /i/, /u/, /ae/	ck
br	/a/, /i/, /u/, /ae/	ng
scr	/a/, /i/, /u/, /ae/	pt
gl	/a/, /i/, /u/, /ae/	rd
fl	/a/, /i/, /u/, /ae/	nch
str	/a/, /i/, /u/, /ae/	ngth

syllable. The varying rates of progress for letters, words, and syllables had nothing to do with simple motor strategies of vocalizing, since picture naming over the same period showed no change at all in latency.

One further result deserves mention. Vellutino, Smith, Steger, and Kaman (1975) found that poor readers are frequently able to copy and name letters in words correctly, with tachistoscopic presentation. But the same words were often read incorrectly. The poor readers' performance on letter reproduction and naming approximated that of normal readers, although they were typically inferior to them in reading.

The fact is indubitable that most children *do* learn to extract information from text in larger units than the letter—both actual words and letter strings with structural constraints having to do with legal positions of consonant clusters and vocalic separation of consonants and clusters of them. Table 26.1 illustrates these constraints. The initial clusters are constrained to that position in a monosyllabic word or in a syllable, just as the final clusters are to their position. The vowel must be present in the syllable, and if there are both initial and final consonants, or consonant clusters, it must separate them. Any such arrangement, as indicated in the table, may be a word. Even if it is not a word, it can be pronounced and read like one. Now, do I not need the concept of integration to explain such learning? Do not children forge larger units by *associating* letters into blocks or chunks from originally smaller elements like single letters (sometimes called the "bottom-up" view)?

If a word has been integrated from letters, we must have "lost" the saliency of the incorporated letters, because a letter is perceived better when it is part of a word, if the word is exposed quickly. Several people have objected that this finding is due to redundancy; of course it is. The constraints that characterize a word as a word constitute first class, usable redundancy. At the same time, if one is asked to decide whether a given word or a given letter is present in a display, it is faster to detect a whole word than a letter (Johnson, 1975). The word does not decompose easily, for adults as well as young children, but for different reasons. Children must segment before they can observe order and constraints. They do not have the "pieces" to begin with. But after segmentation is possible, the constraints provide new structure. The word, or even a legal pseudo-word, has holistic properties.

How do I know that a word has holistic properties such that it resists segmentation? Numerous experiments on anagram solution provide very handy evidence. It is harder to break up a word to solve an anagram than to solve an anagram from the same letters presented in a random arrangement (Beilin & Horn, 1962; Ekstrand & Dominowski, 1965, 1968). High word frequency of the solution word may facilitate solution, as in the following examples:[2]

	Anagram	Solution Word
	sauce	cause
vs.	ceusa	cause
	bleat	table
vs.	bleta	table

On the other hand, high frequency of the anagram word may inhibit it. But the word–nonword effect holds despite varying frequency of either the anagram or the solution word (Ekstrand & Dominowski, 1968). "Pronounceable" anagrams, even though they are nonwords, are harder to solve than unpronounceable arrangements, so orthographic regularity as well as familiarity and meaning again contributes to a word's integrity as a unit (Dominowski, 1969). It has often been suggested that transitional probability, or bigram frequency, is a source of the word's unity (e.g., Mayzner & Tresselt, 1959, 1962), but transitional probability of letters and summed bigram frequency have been found to have only a little and sometimes no effect on anagram solution (Beilin & Horn, 1962; Dominowski, 1967; Stachnik, 1963). Since bigram counts where letter position is given consideration[3] are confounded with pronounceability and legality of orthography, a correlation with such a count would not be surprising—a bigram like *ck* in the fourth and fifth positions of such a word would have a pretty high frequency and at the same time accord with orthographic and phonological rules of English word structure. The sample of words used (and other variables such as frequency of the anagram in relation to the solution) would interact to make conflicting results possible, of course.

How early in the development of reading skill does a word exhibit strong unity, resisting fragmentation and rearrangement? Beilin (1967) gave three-, four-, and five-letter anagrams to subjects of four age groups (8, 10, 12, and 14 years). The difference in solution times for word as compared with nonsense anagrams was apparent for five-letter but not for three- or four-letter anagrams, but it did not reach significance until age 12. Along with the fact that the children were progressively able to solve any kind of anagram faster with increasing age, structural features of the word continued to become more prominent.

What are these features? In the first place, does a word have features? What is it that resists segmenting? Consider transitional probability first, although this is a letter-to-letter property rather than a property of the word as a whole. When other factors are controlled, summed bigram frequency as such does not prohibit the word inferiority effect for anagram solution. Neither does it account satisfactorily for the word superiority effect for tachistoscopic recognition of letter strings. Biederman (1966) found a slight effect of bigram (digram) frequency, taking letter position into effect (Mayzner–Tresselt count, 1965), with five-letter words, all of low word frequency. Some were words having typical English orthographic structure (e.g., *clang*, bigram count 203) and some were not (e.g., *gnome*, bigram count 15), so it may have been a higher level of structure that was actually effective. Gibson, Shurcliff, and Yonas (1970) compared the effects of pronounceability and sequential probability (as measured by four counts) on tachistoscopic recognition of pronounceable and unpronounceable pseudowords. Pronounceability had a strong predictive relationship to correct recognitions, but of the frequency counts, only the Mayzner and Tresselt (1965) bigram count did, and it was a far less effective predictor than pronounceability ratings. It stands to reason that there are structural variables in words that frequency counts (so far) have not captured.

What else characterizes a word? La Berge (1976) describes a model involving coalescing of features. If I understand him, he is thinking of the word's contour, or some kind of superordinate graphic information. I doubt that graphic information is very important in word "coalescence" (I prefer the term "unity" or "coherence"). Recent experiments by McClelland (1975) found evidence for the tachistoscopic word superiority effect despite scrambled type faces, making it unlikely that the visual outline of the word is necessary for the effect to occur. I am in agreement with McClelland that "knowledge of abstract properties of familiar stimuli, not just knowledge of specific featural configurations, can facilitate perception" (p. 42).

The effectiveness of structural properties in an experiment in some ways analogous to the word/letter experiments was demonstrated recently by Weisstein and Harris (1974). They showed an "object-superiority effect" for the detection of line segments. A single target line (one of four oblique lines) had to be detected when it appeared as part of a display containing the same eight context lines, variously arranged so as to produce a unified pattern of connected squares in a three-dimensional relationship, or a less unified, unclosed arrangement that appeared only partially or not at all three-dimensional. The target line was detected more accurately (with tachistoscopic exposure) when it was part of a configuration that looked unitary and three-dimensional. The effect does not contradict the notion that a highly coherent whole is hard to break up; it still may be. But detecting a given line in a "muddle" of context lines is much harder when the subject has a very short time to search. Weisstein and Harris (1974) suggest that "Perhaps recognition of both words and objects depends on more general processes that make use of structural rules and meaning to determine perception" (p. 754).[4]

It is these two relational properties of words—rule-like structure and meaning—that seem to me to be the ones that confer unity and coherence; that make them easily recognizable; that make them resist fragmentation; and that yet, when time is limited, make them easier ground for detecting a subordinate part than would a random arrangement of all those parts. They are abstract properties, not concrete, physical ones. The case for the structural rules is easy to make. English words have constraints that any monosyllabic word or any syllable in a multisyllabic one must obey. I have illustrated this point in Table 26.1. There must be a "vocalic center" (Hansen & Rodgers, 1968; Spoehr & Smith, 1973); there may be consonants or consonant clusters in either initial or final position. The letter may be constrained as to position. Indeed, nearly all consonant clusters in English are constrained (Fries, 1963). These constraints are a source of redundancy that contributes to ease of identifying even a pseudo-word, if the rules are obeyed. The rules apply both phonologically and orthographically. Invariance of the rules over phonology and orthography may also be important, but that question is still unsettled.

Orthography alone provides further useful rules in spelling patterns—contrastive groups of words that cover a large number of cases (see Fries, 1963, pp. 171ff.). An example is the shift in the value of any vowel when a succeeding consonant has an *e* added, as in the following examples:

pan—pane   con—cone   tin—tine
dun—dune   gem—gene

This principle, as well as others illustrated by Fries, makes individual association of letters as unnecessary as it would be uneconomical. The structure is generated by the rule. I do not need to appeal to a constructive process that integrates letter by letter. The reduction of information provided by these rules is as economical and as compulsively useful as the three-dimensional structure in the Weisstein and Harris experiment.

The orthographic structure of a word, it seems to me, is not "integrated"; I do not see how it can be and generalize the way it does to previously unseen but well-formed nonwords. The process of learning it must be akin to the way a child learns grammar, a kind of gradual abstraction. The knowledge itself is abstract, not a specific physical configuration. I am the more convinced of this by a series of experiments in which I tried to teach children about orthographic structure. None of them worked very well, including one in which we explained the rules. An abstraction has to be discovered for oneself. We can put the relevant information in the way—as we do when a child hears us talk while we provide the appropriate situational context—and hope that his endogenous motive to attend to new information, and the economy principle that leads him to reduce the information by abstraction and classification, will have their effect. Drill at least will get you nowhere, nor will M & Ms. Appropriately contrastive displays that prompt the generalizations implicit in orthography appear to be the most promising instructional aid.

The Meaning of Words

Now, what about meaning? This property of words distinguishes them from pseudo-words that are orthographically and phonologically legal, and many experiments have found that it contributes to the unity and coherence of the word, giving it an added advantage for recognition (Barron & Pittenger, 1974; Gibson, Bishop, Schiff, & Smith, 1964; Murrell & Morton, 1974), and an added disadvantage for fragmentation and recombination in anagrams. How meaning lodges itself in a word is still anybody's guess, but it is a cogent property of a spoken word very early, and makes difficult the beginning reader's task of considering the word as a phonetic object. My guess is that the meaning of a word is learned as part of a situational context in which it is invariant with an event of interest. "Here's a cookie" goes along with being offered a cookie, with all the affordances thereof. The meaning of a word is probably differentiated from both its linguistic and its situational context.

I have lately become unhappy with talk about meanings of individual words, because their derivation seems to me so obviously context dependent. But I shall describe briefly one more experiment in which three students of mine[5] studied the developmental course of abstraction of features of printed words, including meaning. This experiment was originally designed to illustrate what I have thought of as a third trend in development: the optimization of attention. It seems to me now that the phenomena that persuaded me at one time to consider such a trend as unique are well subsumed under the trend toward economy in extraction of information. I shall not argue for a third trend, therefore, but rather point out the cognitive economy and adaptiveness of increasing ability to attend readily and flexibly to those aspects of presented information that have most utility for the perceiver in his role as performer.

In several experiments with young children (Pick, Christy, & Frankel, 1972; Pick & Frankel, 1973) the subjects have been given tasks that required them to select one aspect of the information presented by some object, to the exclusion of the rest. The ability to abstract information in this way, and to change what is abstracted flexibly from one aspect to another as required, seems to increase with age. The experiment to be described made use of such a task, but words rather than objects constituted the displays from which several kinds of information—graphic, phonetic, or semantic—were to be abstracted. The subjects were children from the third and fifth grades and adults.

Supposing that children have the necessary knowledge of the graphic features, sound, and meaning of a word, do they nevertheless show progress in abstracting one of these characteristics from a given word when asked to compare it with another one? How efficiently can they select the aspect that is relevant and adapt themselves anew when asked to select a different aspect? Reading is always for a purpose, and we have generally assumed that active selection of wanted information is an important part of the development of reading skill. In this experiment, the selection process with words was investigated.

Slides were presented to the subjects portraying three words (projected on a small screen). One, a standard, was typed alone at the top center. Below it, one on the right and one on the left, were two other words. One of the other words resembled the standard by either *looking* like it, *sounding* like it (rhyming), or having a similar *meaning*. The second word was chosen as a possible distractor or else was neutral with respect to the standard. The subject was told before the slide appeared that he was to choose the word that looked (or sounded or meant) most nearly the same as the standard, and to press one of two buttons (on his right or his left, corresponding with the choice words) as soon as he had made his selection.

For example, a slide might appear in one of the following arrangements:

		cry				near				near		
high			weep	bear			close	bear			deer
		(A)				(B)				(C)		

The subject might be told before the slide (e.g., arrangement A) was projected, "Choose the word that means (or sounds) most like the top one"; or he might be told (e.g., arrangement B), "Choose the word that means (or looks) most nearly the same as the top one"; or (arrangement C) "Choose the word that looks (or sounds) most like the top one." A distractor was provided that looked or sounded like the standard if the subject was to select for meaning (cf. A or B); that looked or meant much the same if the subject was to select for sound (cf. A and C); and that sounded or meant much the same if the subject was to select for looks (cf. B and C). For each of the three tasks (looks, sounds, means), slides with neutral rather than distractor alternatives were also provided. A subject made judgments with respect to all these types of slides (nine in all: three tasks—looks, sounds, or means—and three types of distractor for each task).

Half the subjects in each age group were shown the slides for the three tasks in a mixed random order. Half were shown all the slides for each task in a block. We thought that the latter procedure, which did not require switching to a different aspect of the word from trial to trial, would be easier, particularly for the younger readers. Flexibility in this sense has increased with age in at least one other experiment (Pick & Frankel, 1973), although the materials used were different and the age range younger.

The results of this experiment, as regards main effects, were as expected. The second-grade children made most errors and were slower on every comparison than the two older groups, although errors were few overall. The fifth-grade subjects were slower than the adults. All the subjects were faster when the tasks were blocked, but, somewhat to our surprise there was a negligible interaction of blocking with age. Everyone found "switching" troublesome—but on the other hand everyone, including the second-graders, could do it. The "looks" task was easiest and the "means" task hardest. Judging synonymy is especially difficult for second-graders. The interaction of age × task was significant when "means" was compared with "looks" ($p < .01$) and when it was compared with "sounds" ($p < .01$).

The distractor items, compared with neutral items, increased decision times (e.g., it is harder to decide which word means the same as the standard when a third word is present that looks or sounds like it, than when the third word does not resemble it in any obvious way). The distractor effect held at all age levels. The younger children, however, were more distracted by a "looks like" distractor on the "sounds" task than were the older subjects. Oddly enough, the effect of distractors was not especially strong for them on the "means" task, probably because the task was so hard for them in general.

All in all, this experiment supports the hypotheses that one kind of information in a printed word can be abstracted and compared when a task requires it, and that the decision becomes more efficient with age. Random switching of the task was harder for the youngest subjects, but it was hard for everyone (even the adults commented on it). The most striking age differences showed up in length of decision time and in making the "means alike" decision. The second-grade children knew what the words meant, in the usual sense, and would have no trouble understanding them in an appropriate sentence context. The judgment of synonymy of two single words is difficult for them, however, both with and without a distractor present.

Skillful deployment of attention in extracting relevant verbal information evidently improves with age (as well as reading experience) and contributes to the economy of information pickup. I see no way of understanding this fact better, however, in the context of an information-processing stage analysis. I see instead the need for reexamining the concept of attention, and weighting heavily the role of the task assigned (either by an experimenter or by oneself). Perhaps attention is simply perceiving that information which is coincident with task demands. Skill then will vary greatly with the task, as it did in this experiment. Perceiving that something has utility for the task certainly does improve with age, but I doubt that we can understand this improvement better by inserting another stage in a processing chain and calling it "attention." The danger of homunculizing looms up, and with it comes the danger of pushing the problem further into obscurity rather than solving it.

Conclusion

And now, to come to a conclusion, or to put it more accurately, simply an end, am I not, in repulsing information processing, preventing myself from theorizing? Will my intention of describing what is learned in perceptual learning, and what the trends are in perceptual development, render me a mere collector of facts, a file cabinet for assorted odds and ends? I doubt it. It is the themes of atomism and construction that I have an aversion to. But I have a theme too, in Holton's (1975) sense. We all do— as scientists, we are as born and bred to seek them as Brer Rabbit the briar patch. What we have to fear is that those ideas that are easily tagged will deteriorate into "vogue words" and "vogue concepts" (Merton, 1975). Hardening them by mathematicizing them will only make things worse if they are wrong, since it will frighten the innocent into an uncritical respect for them.

My themes are that there is information in stimulation and that what we experience does not come in bits and particles (a theme I have obviously borrowed from James J. Gibson); that we should speak of learning and development in perception as differentiation rather than construction; that the relevant processes are more akin to discovery and abstraction than to association and integration; and that man evolved as a seeker of information, not an intellectual pauper who must build something to believe in, because there would be no truth otherwise.

Notes

1. Piaget, J. *The construction of reality in the child* (Translation by Margaret Cook). New York: Basic Books, 1954. P. 4.
2. Taken from Ekstrand and Dominowski (1968).
3. Letter position and word length are considered in a frequency count by Mayzner and Tresselt (1965).
4. The rules for unity of an object, or a pictured one, are by no means the same as the rules for words, of course. An object is perceived as having unity, I think, because it takes up space (is three-dimensional); because its parts move together when it moves, and stay together when the observer moves; because it has texture and substance different from the background; and because it has continuity of contours and surfaces. A drawing of a cube lacks many properties of a real object, but it still hangs together better than the array of discontinuous fragments.
5. Condry, S., McMahon, M., & Levy, A. A developmental investigation of extraction of graphic, phonetic and semantic information from words. (submitted for publication)

References

Barron, R. W. Locus of the effect of a distinguishing feature in a memory search task. *Memory and Cognition*, 1975, 3, 302–310.

Barron, R. W., & Pittenger, J. B. The effect of orthographic structure and lexical meaning on "same—different" judgments. *Quarterly Journal of Experimental Psychology*, 1974, 26, 566–581.

Beilin, H. Developmental determinants of word and nonsense anagram solution. *Journal of Verbal Learning and Verbal Behavior*, 1967, 6, 523–527.

Beilin, H., & Horn, R. Transition probability in anagram problem solving. *Journal of Experimental Psychology*, 1962, 63, 514–518.

Biederman, G. B. Supplementary report: Recognition of tachistoscopically presented five-letter words as a function of digram frequency. *Journal of Verbal Learning and Verbal Behavior*, 1966, 5, 208–209.

Chase, W. G., & Simon, H. A. The mind's eye in chess. In Chase, W. G. (Ed.), *Visual information processing*. New York: Academic Press, 1973. Pp. 215–281.

Doehring, D. G. The acquisition of rapid reading responses. *Monographs of the Society for Research in Child Development*. 1976, 41, Serial No. 165.

Dominowski, R. L. Anagram solving as a function of bigram rank and word frequency. *Journal of Experimental Psychology*, 1967, 75, 299–306.

Dominowski, R. L. The effect of pronunciation practice on anagram difficulty. *Psychonomic Science*, 1969, 16, 99–100.

Ekstrand, B. R., & Dominowski, R. L. Solving words as anagrams. *Psychonomic Science*, 1965, 2, 239–240.

Ekstrand, B. R., & Dominowski, R. L. Solving words as anagrams: II. A clarification. *Journal of Experimental Psychology*, 1968, 77, 552–558.

Fodor, J. A., Garrett, M. F., & Brill, S. L. Pi ka pu: The perception of speech sounds by prelinguistic infants. *Perception and Psychophysics*, 1975, 18, 74–78.

Fries, C. C. *Linguistics and reading*. New York: Holt, Rinehart & Winston, 1963.

Gibson, E. J., Bishop, C. H., Schiff, W., & Smith, J. Comparison of meaningfulness and pronounceability as grouping principles in the perception and retention of verbal material. *Journal of Experimental Psychology*, 1964, *67*, 173–182.

Gibson, E. J., & Levin, H. *The psychology of reading*. Cambridge, Mass.: MIT Press, 1975.

Gibson, E. J., Osser, H., & Pick, A. D. A study in the development of grapheme–phoneme correspondences. *Journal of Verbal Learning and Verbal Behavior*, 1963, *2*, 142–146.

Gibson, E. J., Shurcliff, A., & Yonas, A. Utilization of spelling patterns by deaf and hearing subjects. In H. Levin & J. P. Williams (Eds.), *Basic studies on reading*. New York: Basic Books, 1970. Pp 57–73.

Golinkoff, R. M. Children's discrimination of English spelling patterns with redundant auditory information. Paper presented at American Educational Research Association, Feb., 1974, New Orleans, La.

Hansen, D., & Rodgers, T. S. An exploration of psycholinguistic units in initial reading. In K. S. Goodman (Ed.), *The psycholinguistic nature of the reading process*. Detroit: Wayne State University Press, 1968. Pp. 59–102.

Holton, G. On the role of themata in scientific thought. *Science*, 1975, *188*, 328–334.

Johnson, N. F. On the function of letters in word identification: Some data and a preliminary model. *Journal of Verbal Learning and Verbal Behavior*, 1975, *14*, 17–29.

LaBerge, D. Perceptual Learning and Attention: In W. K. Estes (Ed.), *Handbook of Learning and Cognitive Processes*, Vol. 4. Hillsdale, N. J.: Lawrence Erlbaum Associates, 1976.

Lavine, L. O. Differentiation of letterlike forms in prereading children. *Developmental Psychology*. 1977, *13*, 89–94.

Mayzner, M. S., & Tresselt, M. E. Anagram solution times: A function of transition probabilities. *Journal of Psychology*, 1959, *47*, 117–125.

Mayzner, M. S., & Tresselt, M. E. Anagram solution times: A function of word transition probabilities. *Journal of Experimental Psychology*, 1962, *63*, 510–513.

Mayzner, M. S., & Tresselt, M. E. Tables of single-letter and digram frequency counts for various word-length and letter-position combinations. *Psychonomic Monographs* (Suppl.), 1965, *1*, 13–32.

McClelland, J. Preliminary letter identification in the perception of words and nonwords. Tech. Report No. 49, Center for Human Information Processing, University of California at San Diego, 1975.

Merton, R. K. Thematic analysis in science: Notes on Holton's concept. *Science*, 1975, *188*, 335–338.

Murrell, G. A., & Morton, J. Word recognition and morphemic structure. *Journal of Experimental Psychology*, 1974, *102*, 963–968.

Pick, A. D., Christy, M. D., & Frankel, G. W. A developmental study of visual selective attention. *Journal of Experimental Child Psychology*, 1972, *14*, 165–176.

Pick, A. D., & Frankel, G. W. A study of strategies of visual attention in children. *Developmental Psychology*, 1973, *9*, 348–357.

Rosinski, R. R., & Wheeler, K. E. Children's use of orthographic structure in word discrimination. *Psychonomic Science*, 1972, *26*, 97–98.

Spelke, E. Infants' recognition of moving faces. Paper presented at meeting of the American Psychological Association, Chicago, Ill., September, 1975.

Spoehr, K. T., & Smith, E. E. The role of syllables in perceptual processing. *Cognitive Psychology*, 1973, *5*, 71–89.

Stachnik, T. Transitional probability in anagram solution in a group setting. *Journal of Psychology*, 1963, *55*, 259–261.

Vellutino, F. R., Smith, H., Steger, J. A., & Kaman, M. Reading disability: Age differences and the perceptual deficit hypothesis. *Child Development*, 1975, *46*, 487–493.

Vurpillot, E., Lacoursière, A., de Schonen, S., & Werck, C. Apprentissage de concepts et différenciation. *Bulletin de Psychologie*, 1966, 252(XX), 1–7.

Weisstein, N., & Harris, C. S. Visual detection of line segments: An object-superiority effect. *Science*, 1974, 186, 752–755.

Woodworth, R. S. *Experimental psychology*. New York: Holt, 1938.

Yonas, A. The acquisition of information-processing strategies in a time-dependent task. Unpublished doctoral dissertation, Cornell University, Ithaca, N.Y., 1969.

Reading in Retrospect: Perception, Cognition, or Both?

Often nowadays when I talk to an audience about the ecological approach to perception, I am asked whether this approach has anything to say about cognition, or whether there must be a firm line drawn between perception and cognition with different principles applying. The first answer to this question is that perception *is* cognitive. Cognition has to do with knowing. The number one definition of cognition in my favorite dictionary (Random House) is "The act or process of knowing: perception." Many psychologists think of cognition exclusively as problem solving, reasoning, remembering, and so on, however. I like to point out that these processes begin with and depend on knowledge that is obtained through perception, which extracts information from arrays of stimulation that specify the events, layout, and objects of the world. The ecological approach holds that this process is a direct one, in that the information is picked up without the intermediary of secondary sources, like inference from past experience or from premises that are somehow inherited.

The reading process stands in an interesting relation to perception with respect to this question. Like perception, it has the function of extraction of information, and the information *does* specify something in the world. But reading is indirect in a way because that information is carried in text rather than in optic or acoustic arrays of stimulation specifying layout and events. Does that make it different, more cognitive?

Whether it does or not, we can look to see whether principles that characterize perception also characterize reading. The ecological approach to perception has three important principles that set it off from other theories of perception. We can ask whether these principles also apply to reading. The first of them has to do with *information*: there is information in arrays of energy available to our perceptual systems that specifies events, layout, and objects in the world. The information may specify permanent properties of the world, in which case it is *invariant* over transformations, and spread over time. This principle is quite distinct from theories that characterize stimulation as impoverished, nonspecific, and requiring supplementation. Perhaps we can carry this principle over to reading. Information is carried in text. It specifies language, which in turn specifies events, places, and so on in the world. There are indeed invariants in language. Although the rules for them are not the same as those that specify, for perception, something like the persisting properties of a place or an object, they can substitute for them and they are most certainly spread sequentially over time. One of the principal tasks of a perception psychologist is to describe the information specifying events in the world (see J. J. Gibson 1979, chapter on information). How is information in an ambient array able to specify the environment? A comparable task exists for the reading psychologist—what kinds of information are carried in text and how do they specify the world of places, objects, and events? There are more levels of correspondence to be described.

The second principle of the ecological approach is that information must be obtained by an actively seeking perceiver (J. J. Gibson 1966). Any teacher will agree that this principle applies to reading; mere mechanical decoding, converting a letter to sound, is worthless. The reader must be searching for what the text specifies, what it carries information about. One looks ahead for information that is foreshadowed.

What the text specifies can be likened to what is perceived. Here is the third principle unique to the ecological approach. What is perceived first and foremost are the affordances of events, places, and things. An affordance for perception can be thought of as the utility of some environmental resource for acting by an animal possessing the appropriate action system. Texts have affordances too, divers ones, for an organism possessing the active skills required for reading. The affordances branch out to all aspects of our lives in the case of reading. A text may afford finding out how to bake a Genevoise cake, or the telephone number to call a broker in San Francisco, or words and music for singing a hymn. The act of reading will be different, depending on the kind of information available, and part of learning to read is learning how to obtain most economically and use the kind of information in a text.

I did not try to compare reading with direct perception when I was engaged in reading research. But the connections were becoming apparent when Harry Levin and I wrote our book on reading. One chapter captures the approach more than the others, the one called "Learning from Reading." It emphasizes the functional aspects of the reading task—the extraction of relevant information, use of the information, and what kinds of information are extracted. It is a far cry from some of the models described in the book's final chapter, ones that depend on ludicrously complex diagrams with flow charts and boxes. The emphasis in the learning-from-reading chapter is on the acquisition of knowledge—what reading, like perception, is all about—a very cognitive process.

VI

Perceptual Development from the Ecological Approach (1972 to the present)

Introduction to Part VI

My years of research on the reading process culminated in the book *Psychology of Reading* (a title deliberately copied from Huey's book, published a half-century earlier). I always thought of this work as being a diversion from my concern with perceptual development, and in a sense a battle had been won. The stagnation in experimental research on reading was overcome and the field looked healthy and flourishing. I had another reason for moving on. I had finally acquired my own laboratory. I could at last take any direction of research I wished.

Since 1891, Cornell's laboratory of psychology had been situated in Morrill Hall, the oldest building on the Cornell Campus. The two top floors of this building had housed Titchener's laboratory, and they were still in use. The shop, the animals, the graduate students, and most of the lab space were on the top floor, very hot in summer and without even an elevator to haul up equipment and animals. For many years I had been obliged to work in someone else's laboratory, at first for lack of rank and support, and later for lack of space. A lot of the reading research was conducted in schools, but even so the situation was desperate. I was always quite successful in getting grants, but what to do with the equipment, the data to be stored, and personnel became more and more perplexing. I was not the only one with a space problem. My husband needed more laboratory space and so did others. One chairman after another fought the administration on the space problem. Finally, in 1967, the department was given temporary research space at the airport in a building formerly used for research by General Electric. Along with this compromise came a promise of a new building for psychology.

The space at the airport laboratory was good—lots of it, air conditioning, plenty of parking—but of course, it was inconveniently far from campus. In the end, only the department shop and the Gibsons and their graduate students moved out there. We had a number of graduate students and many visitors came from overseas and other universities, so we weathered the move without too much disruption and even enjoyed our rather exclusive club. It was a great day, however, when the new building was finally completed and everyone moved back together on campus, in 1972. The great advantage for me was that I was given the opportunity to plan my own laboratory. I chose to plan a laboratory for research on perception in infants, and I began switching my research priorities. Fortunately, a number of excellent graduate students were interested in working in this area.

There was a richness of problems to work on. No one had as yet examined any aspect of the new ecological approach in research with infants. I had become very interested in that approach as James Gibson worked it out and formulated the concepts needed to embrace a radically new way of thinking about perception. The ideas worked especially well, it seemed to me, for a behaviorally and developmentally oriented domain, such as perception in preverbal infants. The chance to pursue the new ideas and establish a new laboratory came none too soon, because I had to retire (formally, that is) in 1979. James Gibson died that same year, leaving me to extend his ideas to perception in infancy without his help (although I had the assistance of some very bright young colleagues). He did help plan one of the earliest experiments on perception of affordances in infants. This was an experiment on looming (Schiff, 1965), already studied in infants (Bower, Broughton, and Moore 1970, Ball and Tronick 1971), but we adapted it to ask a more specific question about perception of affordances for collision: will an infant detect the difference between approach of a closed contour that affords passing through (an aperture) and one that affords an abrupt stop (an obstruction or obstacle). One of the following papers describes the information provided in the experiment for differentiating the two cases.

The topics that I set out to study in the new infant laboratory included ones that were generating new research with adults, but they were presented so as to be appropriate for infants. They included: the perceptual pickup of invariants in an array of information; the perception of multimodally specified events; perception of affordances, and development of mobility. Affordances begged for attention, because that was the last important concept launched by my husband. There was very little research available as yet, and the concept was misunderstood and oversimplified by many people. In the course of research on infants' perception of the affordances of surfaces, I became interested in the concept of mobility in general and how it progresses. That also is a natural problem for the ecological approach, which stresses the inseparability of perception and action, and so our research was later extended to it (Gibson and Schmuckler 1989).

Research over these years and attempts with others to refine concepts of the ecological approach and carry it further have gradually had the effect of directing my theoretical concerns toward more epistemological questions. As a young scientist such questions concerned me very little. I am a natural behaviorist. But concentrating on what infants perceive and how they come to know the world forces one to confront the big epistemological questions (as Piaget had long been telling us). I was not content with Piaget's answers, so I have been attempting to formulate my own. Several of the papers that follow introduce these concerns. Perception as the foundation for knowledge of the world and the role of exploratory behavior as an active search for knowledge emerge as major themes in an ecological approach to development. Learning is again implicated, and a new path to perceptual learning unfolds.

27

The Senses as Information-Seeking Systems
Eleanor Gibson, James J. Gibson

This final section begins with two short newspaper essays written by invitation for the London Times Literary Supplement. *Together they present a confrontation of two radically opposed contemporary views of perception: the direct perception view of the ecological approach and the indirect perception view of Richard Gregory, spokesman for a traditional, concept-mediated approach to perception. Gregory, a prominent British psychologist, and a friend of many years standing, proposed the debate. The brief sparring puts the controversy in a nutshell, sometimes close to caricature, but the issues are drawn and the locus of disagreement is clear.*

Two issues stand out in these essays: where the action is, and where the information is. For the Gibsons, perception is itself an active, information-seeking process of searching ambient arrays of energy for information about the surrounding environment. For Gregory, who also claims to be an activist, the action is in a kind of thinking or problem-solving process following after perception, which for him is a passive intake of whatever energy happens to fall on receptors. For the Gibsons, the ambient array is rich in information that specifies layout, objects, and events in the world. For Gregory, only dregs or hints of information are available to perception, which must be supplemented by inference, piecing together the evidence with the aid of past experience, working like a detective or a solver of puzzles. How the past experience, which must itself have begun as impoverished, becomes meaningful is a problem and may leave the theorist with the disquieting belief that everyday perceptions are "imaginative constructions" or "fictions."

Gregory compares the Gibsons' position with B. F. Skinner's psychology, implying that it is an elementaristic, one-to-one S-R kind of position. What the ecological approach actually does is stress the interleaving and inseparability of perception and action. A perceptual system incorporates actions (e.g., head and eye movements, accomodation, etc. in the visual system), perception guides action,

(London) Times Literary Supplement, 1972, June 23, 711–712.

and action informs perception. In recent years the study of perception and action as an inseparable system has become a popular focus of research (see Developmental Psychology, *1989, No. 6). Gregory, on the other hand, stresses computer programs and the desirability of studying illusions rather than everyday behavior like guided locomotion. There is an implication that the direct perception approach neglects the tough "inside" problems of perception. But we think it is the people like Gregory who have given up on the problem, dismissing it by claiming that all we can know are illusions. The ecological view of perception comes head on with the problem in an attempt to account for our actually remarkably veridical ability to deal with the surfaces and substances, objects and events of the environment that we are, like it or not, obliged to cope with and use as a species and as individuals. It is our relations with the environment that we must perceive in order to behave successfully at all. For this, there must be information about what goes on, and we must obtain it in a current, up-to-date form as we continuously move through, and maintain, our relations with the environment. How we obtain this information from the very beginning is the question for a developmental approach.*

The first question a biologist asks in seeking to understand an organ is what adaptive function it serves in the evolution and survival of the species. The psychologist asks the same question, and the organs of sense are no exception. Indeed, it seems obvious that this is the first question to ask. Man and other animals are endowed genetically with equipment designed for the reception of stimuli from the environment around them. They are also endowed with the ability to learn from what they perceive. Hence there is both adaptation of the species in the course of its evolution and adaptation of an individual in the course of his life.

The answer to the question of function now seems clear. The sensory systems—the organs and their related activities—provide the means of attending to and getting information from the world surrounding the organism that must survive in it. He must find food, a mate, shelter, escape from predators and from environmental hazards. He must have information about objects that are edible, friendly, unfriendly, sexually exciting, and so on; about places that are safe for walking or flying, grazing or sleeping, and for their spatial layout; and about events of all sorts.

Information about the world comes from the world. None of us believes that this information is innately given. Richard Gregory would certainly agree that an animal is constantly interacting with his environment, taking in information, doing something, and getting fresh information from what he has done. What is the nature of the information he is getting? This is the question that has produced controversial answers.

There is a contradiction at the very heart of the existing theories of sense perception which can be expressed by the following two assertions: the senses *cannot* be trusted and the senses *can* be trusted. From the biological point of view it would seem that the senses *must* be trusted since they are all we have. How else is an observer to keep in touch with the environment? But everything we know about the physiology of the senses seems to show that the inputs of the sensory nerves are inadequate for keeping in touch with the environment, since they are nothing but signals touched off by stimuli. How to resolve this contradiction is the chief problem for understanding sense perception.

Existing theories try to resolve this contradiction by assuming either that the inputs of the sensory nerves are corrected by the brain, or that the corresponding sense impressions are interpreted by the mind. There are many such theories of correction, inference, interpretation, compensation, equilibration, organization and the like, all taking it for granted that the process of perception is some kind of operation on the deliverances of sense. But there is another way of resolving the contradiction that seems to us more promising. It is to assume that the inputs of the sensory nerves are merely incidental to the process of perception and that the useful senses are actually perceptual systems. These are systems which adjust the sense organs instead of just receiving stimuli; systems that have output as well as input; systems that explore the light and sound and pressure of the environment for the information contained. This is information about the sources of the stimulus energy, not merely signals.

Professor Gregory believes that there is "a cognitive element in perception." He is saying that one has to *know* something about the environment in advance before he can *perceive* it properly. But there is a dilemma here. Surely one cannot know anything about the environment *except* as he perceives it, or has perceived it.

The trouble comes from the long-standing assumption that the senses at birth can deliver nothing but meaningless signals over the sensory nerves, signals that have to be interpreted in the slow course of learning by association. On that assumption it follows that knowing must precede perceiving. But perhaps the long-standing assumption is wrong. We might assume instead that the senses, even at birth, are perceptual systems that pick up facts about the world. On the first assumption learning is a matter of supplementing the infant's bare sensations with memories. (But memories of what? Sensations?) On the second assumption learning is a matter of distinguishing the information, of discriminating not of associating. Bare sensations have no meaning until they have been enriched in some unknown way by past experience. But primitive perceptions have primitive meanings from the very outset of life.

Psychologists and physiologists who are of Professor Gregory's persuasion take it for granted that lights, sounds, chemicals, and contacts are mere stimuli for the receptors in the eyes, ears, nose, mouth, and skin, and they suppose that stimuli as such carry no information about their sources in the world. But we reject this doctrine and try to show that an array of light, for example, specifies the surfaces from which the light is reflected. At least it does so in the world outside the laboratory. Similarly, a natural flow of sound specifies the vibratory event from which it comes, a taste or an odor specifies the substance from which it emanates, and the sequence of pressures obtained by feeling an object specifies the object. The notion of *information* in stimulation is novel and unfamiliar, but it is the basis for a new theory of perception.

In life, the sea of stimulus energy in which an observer is immersed is always an array and always a flow. The stimuli as such, the pin-pricks of light or sound or touch, do not carry information about their sources. But the invariant properties of the flowing array of stimulation do carry information. They specify the objects of the world and the layout of its surfaces. They are invariants under transformation, non-change underlying change. Note that they are not in any sense pictures or images of objects and of layouts as so many psychologists have been tempted to think. Nor are they signals from the objects and surfaces of the environment like dots and dashes in a code. They are mathematical relations in a flowing array, nothing less.

The demonstration that a natural array of light specifies the surfaces from which the light is reflected, together with the layout and composition of these surfaces, depends on a new approach to optics, an approach that is ecological instead of physical. It begins with ambient light at a point of observation instead of radiant light from the source. It studies the structure and transformations of this ambient array instead of rays or waves or photon-paths. It treats the eye as an organ instead of a camera and rejects not only the doctrine that the retinal image is a picture but even the notion that it is an image, properly speaking.

The old theories of sense perception assumed that it consisted of the operations of the mind upon the data of sense. If this notion sounded too philosophical it could be made to sound more scientific by asserting that perception consisted of the processing by the brain of the signals arriving over the sensory nerves. This is the modern formula, but actually it is the same old theory. It still says that the act of perceiving is something that occurs wholly inside the head. The new theory that we advocate says that the act of perceiving occurs in a circular process from the sense organs to the brain then back to the sense organs, and so on. It involves exploration by the eyes of the whole array of light and exploration by the hands of the whole layout of surfaces around one. Man's delicately mobile postural system, which includes the eyes, head, hands, and body, is beautifully adapted for this activity.

Perception therefore does not have to be conceived as the interpreting of messages or the learning of the so-called "sensory code." It is the exploring of an array, the enhancing of available information, and the optimizing of its pickup. The eyes, for example, look around, focus their lenses on details of the world, and modulate the intensity of the light when the illumination is too high or too low. For listening, the head turns to equalize intensity of input to the two ears so as to point the head towards the source of sound.

The assertion that the information in stimulation specifies its sources in the world does not imply that this information is automatically picked up. It is available, but it may or may not be perceived. An observer must extract the information from the flowing array of stimulation. And he must often learn to do so. What is it that the human observer learns? We suggest that, beginning as an infant, he learns the distinctive features of objects, the layout of places in the environment, and the invariant features of events. A human observer also perceives representations of things and places and events, of course, and in that case the information coming from the picture or the television screen is essentially the same as it is when it comes from the environment. Finally, a human observer learns to extract information from the constituents of spoken and written language, but this is information of a quite different sort. It is *not* essentially the same as that which comes directly from the environment. The child's learning about the world from speech, and then from writing, is a much more complex process than learning about the world from what we call firsthand experience.

Here is a brief account of the development of perception of objects. The process begins in the newborn infant with visual attention to certain salient stimulus properties that carry information: motion, brightness contrast, and the kind of contrast provided by the edge of a surface in the world. The infant's attention is "caught" by these properties. The world he peceives, then, is not at all a "blooming, buzzing confusion," as William James put it, for he at least sees surfaces and edges. But this is only the beginning, since objects gradually become differentiated from one another by their distinctive features, that is, by attributes that render each object different from other objects. For example, babies differentiate human faces from non-faces in their environment very early, although it is doubtful that they perceive the relations between the features of a face before they are three months old, or thereabouts. Individual faces are not differentiated from one another until six months have passed. Other properties of an object such as its size and shape are differentiated within the first few months of life, before the baby can walk or even reach. There is no substance in the old notion that such visual attributes must gain their meaning from touching and grasping.

A human face, of course, has properties that are not constant over time as well as properties that are. The movement of the facial muscles produces different expressions that portend different events. Moreover a moving face usually produces sounds. Interestingly enough, an infant at twenty days perceives the voice as coming from the face—he does not seem to have to learn to connect these sensations by associating the sound with the sight.

An object comes to be perceived as permanent even when it is partially or entirely hidden by another object. If a screen is drawn in front of an object so that it is gradually concealed and then gradually revealed again, an infant soon learns that it has not gone out of existence and expects its reappearance. There is optical information for its continued existence and for its only having gone out of sight. This is not the same thing as remembering the object. Later on, when a child has learned names for familiar objects that he has distinguished from one another by their distinctive features, he knows things about objects that he can remember and think about, but perceptual differentiation is basic to this knowledge.

The differentiation of the features of the environmental layout also develops without having to be supplemented by knowledge. When a crawling infant is placed on a platform with a visual cliff on one side and a very shallow drop-off on the other side (but actually a glass surface of support on both sides) the infant will crawl to its mother over the shallow side but not over the deep side. Is this because it has "knowledge" that a cliff is dangerous? This seems unlikely. The baby has no past experience of falling and surely does not inherit racial memories of falling.

What about the perceiving of events? Events occur over time and are of many degrees of complexity, since a short episode may be embedded in a much longer episode. If perception were really based on single elementary sensations, each successive sensation would have to be somehow integrated for the total event to be perceived. Again, it seems that learning proceeds by differentiation, not by integration. For example, if an object approaches an observer on a collision course, he will blink or duck or dodge so as to mitigate or avoid the collision. The optical information for this imminent event is the progressive magnification of a silhouette in the field of view. Experiments consisting of the display of this information have been done with several species of animals and with human infants. The shadow of an object is cast on a translucent screen in front of the observer and its size is increased at an accelerating rate. The adult human observer perceives a virtual object approaching him. Turtles faced with this display pull their heads within their shells. Monkeys cry out and rush to the rear of the cage. Human infants, at two weeks, respond consistently with a backward jerk of the head and by raising the hands. A little later they differentiate between the information for an object on a collision course and that for an object on a non-collision course. This difference depends on the symmetry of magnification. A perception of this sort can hardly be a matter of successive sensations. It must be that optical motions of different kinds are distinguished from one another as perceptual development proceeds.

Different events involving motions are differentiated very early in life. The same animal that retreats from an approaching object may follow a retreating object. Baby chicks run away when they are faced with the optically expanding shadow on the screen, but they move towards an optically contracting shadow on the screen. This response to the diminishing shadow is related to the imprinting that occurs early in the life of a young bird such as a chick or duckling. It runs after a retreating mother and thus succeeds in staying with its protector and with its kind. And it demonstrates for us, incidentally, that two contrasting kinds of events are distinguished.

The early development of perception seems to us clearly to demonstrate the picking-up of information that is available in stimulation and not the supplementing of sensations by memories of past experience, or by some kind of knowledge. But, the reader may ask, what about symbols like words? They are perceived too. Aren't they at least a clear case of supplementing auditory sensations with an associated meaning?

The analysis of the information in a speech event tells us that it has three quite different kinds of information, all of which must be comprehended. There is the sound itself, the phonetic sequence, to be perceived. There is the syntactic information, the rule system that governs how words are put together. And there is semantic information, the "meaning." How does a child learn to pick up all this information? One thing seems certain—he does not simply learn by association. How then?

The first essential to this development is what the linguists call segmentation of the sounds of the speech system. Speech comes in a physically continuous flow, usually without the separation we seem to hear. This stream must be analysed. It is analysed at many levels, the lowest of which is considered to be the phoneme and the higher levels being syllables, words, phrases, etc. But phonemes themselves must be differentiated. They are differentiated from one another by sets of contrastive features. These distinctive features have a developmental sequence of their own, as the linguist Roman Jakobson has taught us. The first differentiation is between the optimal vowel and the optimal consonant, and development goes on from there in a series of ordered splittings.

It seems unquestionable that this process must be one of differentiation, not of association. The features cannot be associated with anything, since, as Jakobson said, they indicate mere "otherness." The same twelve pairs of contrastive features serve to differentiate, in various combinations, all the phonemes in human speech. The phonemes themselves are abstracted, by a process of analysis, for one cannot be heard alone, chopped out of a speech segment. Yet we do all differentiate it and acknowledge its constancy. We do not learn to perceive phonological features of speech, then, by adding something on.

The second essential in the learning of speech is grammar. No one has succeeded in accounting for a child's acquisition of grammar by an associative process. A child's first sentences are not copies of the sentences of adults, but they nevertheless follow rules of grammatical construction in accordance with the relations expressed, such as agent-action, agent-object, and action-object. What the child has learned appears to be the result of an inductive process—the extraction of relations from information presented to him in adult speech.

The third essential in learning speech is meaning. How do words come to have meaning for the child? By associating a word with a referent, like the word "kitty" with the animal referred to? This is the answer that used to be given, but it seems unlikely. Meaning in speech is not conveyed by single words, but always in a relational context. For example, when a child says "kitty all gone" or "here kitty" he is referring to an event in the world. The meaning of the event has been perfectly clear to him for some time. What he has succeeded in observing is the correspondence between the event itself and what someone said about it while it was occurring. Children begin by making predications about the immediate environment. Again, there seems to be an inductive process involved, an extracting of the relation between the two kinds of information, one in the event itself and the other in the spoken words.

By this brief survey of the development of perception we have tried to show that a child uses his "senses" in an active and adaptive way to extract information that is present in the ongoing flow of events in his environment. He does not use previous knowledge to interpret his sensations, or to supplement them. He could not do so, for he must begin by picking up this knowledge from what goes on around him. The pick-up comes from differentiating the complex, embedded, relational, dynamic structure of the world.

Seeing as Thinking: An Active Theory of Perception

Richard Gregory

Theories of perception—of what happens to bridge the extraordinary gap between sensory stimulation and our experience of external objects—have a long history, of astonishing variety. Speculation goes back to the beginning of recorded philosophy—and scientific work on perception escapes the philosophical questions and dilemmas only when it narrows inquiry by over-blinkering specialization. How we see remains essentially mysterious after a century of intensive experiment, on animals and on men, by such a variety of scientists that aims and communication can be lost between them. An adequate theory should include not only the favoured sense of sight but also: hearing, touch, hot and cold, taste, smell, balance and position of the limbs, the various kinds of pain; and tickle, from its irritation to sensuous pleasure and delirious laugh-making.

To the philosopher and the experimental scientist, it is how we see that offers the most exciting questions, with hearing the runner-up, for sight dominates by its giving us immediate external reality. By simply looking we seem to understand what we see. This close association between seeing and knowing makes the sense of vision attractive not only to philosophers but also to experimental psychologists and physiologists who hope to discover in the brain mechanisms serving our experience and knowledge of the world. By coming to understand how we see might we not at one stroke also discover how we think, remember, formulate hypotheses, appreciate beauty and—most mysterious—accept pictures and words as symbols, conveying not merely present reality but other realities distant in space and time? And if seeing involves all this, surely the net of understanding must be cast wide.

Perceptual theories form a spectrum—from *passive* to *active* theories. Passive theories suppose that perception is essentially cameralike, conveying selected aspects of objects quite directly, as though the eyes and brain are undistorting windows. The baby, it is supposed, comes to see not by using cues and hints to infer the world of objects from sensory data but by selecting useful features of objects available to it directly; without effort, information processing or inference. Active theories, taking a very different

(London) Times Literary Supplement. 1972, June 23, 707–708.

view, suppose that perceptions are constructed, by complex brain processes, from fleeting fragmentary scraps of data signalled by the senses and drawn from the brain's memory banks—themselves constructions from snippets from the past. On this view, normal everyday perceptions are not selections of reality but are rather imaginative constructions—fictions—based (as indeed is science fiction also) more on the stored past than on the present. On this view all perceptions are essentially fictions: fictions based on past experience selected by present sensory data. Here we should not equate "fiction" with "false." Even the most fanciful fiction as written is very largely true, or we would not understand it. Fictional characters in novels generally have the right number of heads, noses and even many of the opinions of people we know. Science fiction characters may have green hair and an exoskeleton—but is this novelty not a mere reshuffling of the pack of our experiences? It is doubtful if a new "card," suddenly introduced, could be meaningfully described or seen.

The passive paradigm may, at least initially, seem more acceptable as a scientific theory. It fits well with—and indeed essentially is—the familiar "stimulus/response" notion in which behaviour is described as controlled directly by prevailing conditions. This is also familiar in engineering: in most devices input directly controls output, and much emphasis is put on measuring input and output, and relating them by transfer functions or something equivalent, to describe the system. B. F. Skinner in his behaviourism claims to do much the same—to give at least a statistical account of the relationship between stimulus (input) and behaviour (output) in animals and men. An engineer would go on to suggest "models," of what the internal mechanisms might be, which transform inputs into the outputs. But, rather curiously, Skinner does not attempt to make this further step, and apparently distrusts it. He says remarkably little about brains, and at times denies memory and indeed all internal processes. His description is purely in terms of input-output relations, with emphasis on how the probability of certain kinds of behaviour is changed by environmental changes, especially "reinforcers."

Skinner himself has little interest specifically in perception, but passive theories of perception are in many ways similar. They have the same initial scientific credibility, but are (I believe) essentially incorrect. They deny that perception is an active combining of features stored from the past, building and selecting hypotheses of what is indicated by sensory data. On the active account we regard perceptions as essentially fictional. Though generally predictive, and so essentially correct, cognitive fictions may be wrong to drive us into error. On this active view, both veridical (correct-predictive) and illusory (false-predictive) perceptions are equally fictions. To perceive is to read the present in terms of the past to predict and control the future. This account is very different from the passive story implied by Skinner's behaviourism, and most ably propounded by James J. Gibson and Eleanor Gibson.

Why should one want to push all this stuff about "brain fictions" (as I do) when stimuli and responses are so easily observed, and so like the usual stuff of science? The essential reason is (I believe) very easily demonstrated, by common observation and by experiment. Current sensory data (or stimuli) are simply not adequate directly to control behaviour in familiar situations. Behaviour may continue through quite long gaps in sensory data, and remain appropriate though there is no sensory input. But how can "output" be controlled by "input" when there is no input? The fact is that sensory inputs are not continuously required or available, and so we cannot be dealing with a pure input-output system. Further, when we consider any common action, such as placing a book on a table (a favourite example of philosophers) we cannot test from retinal images the table's solidity and general book-supporting capabilities. In engineering terminology, we cannot monitor directly the most important characteristics of objects which must be known for behaviour to be appropriate. This implies that these characteristics are inferred, from the past. The other highly suggestive— indeed dominating—fact is that perception is predictive. In skills, there be zero delay between sensory input and behaviour. But how could there be zero delay, except by acting upon a predictive hypothesis? (Surrely J. J. Gibson's description of perceptions as selections from the available "ambient array" will not do; it would have to be a selection from a *future* "ambient array" for the passive account to work, but this evokes a metaphysics we cannot welcome. The significance of prediction in perception has been for too long almost totally ignored.

It is the fact that behaviour does not need continuous, directly appropriate sensory data that forces upon us the notion of inference from available sensory and brain-stored data. This account is very much in the tradition of the polymath nineteenth-century physicist and physiologist, Hermann von Helmholtz, who described perceptions as "unconscious inferences." This notion was unpalatable to later generations of psychologists, who were over-influenced by philosophers in their role—sometimes useful, but in this case disastrous—of guardians of semantic inertia: objecting to inference without consciousness. But with further data on animal perception, and computers capable of inference, this essentially semantic inhibition has gone. Curiously, though, the kinds of inference required for perception are remarkably difficult to compute.

The recent engineering-science of Machine Intelligence is finding heavy weather designing computer programs to identify objects from television camera pictures. The reason seems to be (apart from the very large and fast computers required to perform the operations serially) that the computer requires a vast amount of stored data of common object properties, with ready and rapid access. It requires, in short, what we have called "fictions" to augment and make use of data monitored from the world by its camera eye, and—in machines dealing with real objects—its touch probes. In short: we may think of perception as an engineering problem, but it is a highly atypical problem even for advanced computer engineering, and it requires a special philosophy which is unfamiliar in science, because only brains and to a limited extent computers are cognitive.

The notion that interpreting objects from patterns is a "passive" business must strike the computer programmer engaged on this problem, in Machine Intelligence, as an extremely unfunny joke. His problem is to devise active programs adequate even for perceptual problems solved by simple creatures, long before man came on the scene.

The notion of perceptions as predictive hypotheses going beyond available data is alien and suspect to many physiologists. Cognitive concepts appear unnecessary, even metaphysical—to be explained away by physiological data. Certainly more physiological data are needed, but will they tell us by what mechanisms the brain's hypotheses are mediated, or will the "brain fiction" notion drop out as unnecessary? Prediction is dangerous, but there are surely strong reasons for believing cognitive concepts to be necessary. In the first place, it is not surprising that special concepts should be required for brain research, because the brain is unique, in nature, as an information handling system. (Or at least it is on an active theory of brain function.) With the development of computers, we now have other information handling systems to consider: it is interesting to note that to describe computers, "software" concepts are adopted, similar to cognitive concepts. More basically, what are essentially cognitive concepts are very familiar in all the sciences, but hidden under a different guise—the *method* of science.

Generalizations and hypotheses are vital to organized science, for the same reasons they are essential for brains handling data in terms of external objects. Science is itself not "passive" in our sense, but puts up hypotheses for testing, and acts on hypotheses rather than directly on available data. Scientific observations have little or no power without related generalizations and hypotheses. Cognitive concepts are surely not alien to science, when seen as the brain's (relatively crude) strategies for discovering the world from limited data—which is very much the basic problem of all science. Scientific observations without hypotheses are surely as powerless as an eye without a brain's ability to relate data to possible realities— effectively blind.

The full power of human brain fiction is apparent when we consider how little current sensory information is needed, or is available, in typical situations. Here we do not need initially to consider particular experiments —and indeed the intentional simplifications and restrictions of the laboratory environment can make the point less obvious—that behaviour is generally appropriate to features of the world which are not continually available to the senses. When you trust your weight to the floor, or your mouth to the spoonful of food, you have not monitored the ground's strength or the food's palatability: you have acted on trust on the basis of the past. You have acted according to probabilities, based on generalizations from past events—and neither generalizations nor probabilities exist, except in your brain, for they are not properties of the world. Now suppose that you gave up acting on informed guesses and demanded continuously, direct selections of reality. How would you get on? Would you not avoid mistakes—never fall through rotten floor boards, never be upset by bad food—never be misled by going beyond the evidence? Yes, indeed, if there were sufficient evidence available. But the fact is that there is frequently no possibility, or time, for testing floorboards or food. They must be taken on trust—trust based on the past as stored in the brain.

We have arrived at questions which may be answered by experiment. We can measure performance, in the partial or total absence of sensory data, and establish whether and how far perception and behaviour continue to remain appropriate. We find that we can continue to drive or walk, or perform laboratory eye-hand tracking experiments, through gaps in sensory data: and not merely inertially, for we can make decisions and change our actions appropriately during data gaps. We must then be relying on internal data. This requires an internal fiction of the world—which in unusual situations may be false. If the situation is unfamiliar, or changes in unpredictable ways, then we should expect systematic errors, generated by false predictions. Errors and illusions thus have great importance for active theorists: they become obsessively used tools for discovering the underlying assumptions and strategies of the perceptual "computer" by which we infer—not always correctly—external objects from sensory data.

Looking at books written by passive and active theorists, we find an amusing difference between their indexes. Passive books devote much space to stimulus patterns, but very little to the phenomena of perception: spontaneous reversals in depth, changes into other objects, distortions, perceptual paradoxes in which the mind reels by being apparently confronted by logically impossible objects. Active theorists fill their books with examples of such phenomena, interpreting them in various ways, while the passive theorist ignores them, or writes them off as too trivial to concern him. But neither uncertainty nor ambiguity, neither distortion nor paradox, can be properties of objects: so how can we *perceive* uncertainties, ambiguities, distortions or paradoxes if perception is but a passive acceptance of reality? This simple though surely powerful argument is not raised or answered by passive theorists. By playing down the obvious phenomena of perception (such as illusions, found as children's puzzles) passive books may look academically safe—but at the cost of leaving out what is most interesting.

We may now return to the point that, although we regard brain function as physical, physical and engineering concepts are not adequate for describing some aspects—especially perception of objects. This only appears to be a metaphysical statement if an extreme reductionist view of science is adopted. This matter is controversial; there are eminent scientists who hold that knowledge of a hydrogen atom and the laws of quantum mechanics are sufficient to describe, in principle, any physical situation. Others hold that even common effects such as friction, heat, inertia or gravity (let alone brain function) could not in principle be described in these elementary terms. They hold that with increased complexity and organization new properties arise requiring new concepts to describe them. It would certainly be difficult to ascribe the notion of "cognitive fictions" to a hydrogen atom! (But it would be equally difficult to ascribe such concepts as servo-control, or even image-forming—so this is not a special objection to the "cognitive fiction" notion.)

There is a strong reason (apart from consciousness) why we wish to separate descriptions of aspects of brain function from physics. This is however a very tricky problem, easy to over-state and to misunderstand. Granted that brain activity is physical, we wish to hold that brain states representing information and problem-solving are not usefully described in terms of physical restraints. Consider the black marks (letters) on this page. They are physical (ink absorbed by paper), but their arrangement, surely, is not to be understood by the principles of physics. For this we must call upon English spelling and grammar, and upon the structure of what I am trying to say. In the vital respect of their order, they are free of the ink and paper of which they are made. If their order were determined directly by their material and its physical properties (as in crystal structure) then they could not serve as symbols. Being in this sense free of physical rstraints, and given receptive brains (or computers) then they can serve as symbols: to represent objects in other time and space, or abstractions which do not exist, in the sense that objects exist. This is true for all symbols: pictures, words, mathematical and musical notations, video and audio tapes, computer tapes. But symbols are powerless (or are just like any other objects) in the absence of brains or other information-handling systems. Evidently symbols must affect brains in some more or less lawful manner: but for this to be possible the relevant brain states must—like the typist's or compositor's characters—be free to adopt information storing and representing orders. So *they* must in this rather limited sense be free of physical restraint, though not quite isolated from the rest of the physical world for learning and perceiving to be possible.

The celebrated (and I believe essentially misleading) Gestalt theory of perception postulated physiological restraints to explain many visual phenomena, such as preference for, and distortion towards, figures of "simple" and "closed" form. Visual forms were supposed to be represented in the brain by similarly shaped electrical brain fields—circles by circular brain traces, presumably houses by house-shaped brain traces. These brain traces were supposed to tend to form simple and closed shapes, because of their physical properties: much as bubbles tend to become spheres, as this form has minimum potential energy. Now this implies that visual "organizations" and distortions are due to physical restraints and forces which will not in general be relevant to the logical problems the brain must solve to infer objects from sensory patterns and stored data. This is quite different from a cognitive account of perceptual distortions, and other phenomena which may be supposed to arise from misapplication of strategies quite apart from the physiology involved. Using a slide-rule, an error may be due to physical errors in the rule itself, or to misapplication of the rule for the problem in hand. This is exactly the distinction involved here, between physiological and cognitive errors.

We should expect physiological restraints to produce the same effects for any object situation (for example after-images, due to retinal fatigue, to any bright light). Misplaced strategy errors should, on the other hand, be related to the kind of perceptual inference, from sensory pattern to object, being carried out. So the point is that the physiology should only produce errors when it is exerting *general* restraints. We should not expect this except in abnormal situations, such as when the physiological "components" are driven beyond their dynamic range. Considering phenomena of perception, such as ambiguous, distorting, or paradoxical figures, do these figures upset the physiology, or select inappropriate strategies, to generate errors? In these cases, it seems to be the object significance of the figures which is relevant. So these phenomena seem quite unlike after-images—here it is not so much the physiology as the cognitive strategies which we need to discover. This needs a different (but still a "scientific") way of thinking, and powerful experimental techniques, to discover cognitive strategies and how they can mislead.

To separate errors due to physiological restraints from errors due to misplaced strategies surely has importance beyond understanding perceptual errors. The same distinction (between physiological and cognitive processes, and how either can go wrong) might be important for understanding mental illness. If schizophrenia is errors in the brain's strategies for developing hypotheses of external states of affairs, this should be understood not only in terms of biochemistry and physiology but also in terms of the strategies by which we normally cope with things. Perhaps this matter of strategies is hidden by the apparent ease with which we continually solve problems of the utmost difficulty to computer programmers: and which receive false answers when their programs are inappropriate. Seeing a table as something to support a book upon is to solve a problem so difficult it challenges the most advanced computer technology, and yet to us it is so simple that a passive theory of perception may seem plausible. This shows that passive theories may be so misleading as to hide aspects of brain function we must see clearly to understand not only perception but all mental processes and how they can go wrong.

Recent discoveries by physiologists, especially by electrical recording from single brain cells during controlled stimuli to the eyes, are so clearly important that they tend to dominate much current thinking about perception. The problem of how sensory patterns are interpreted in terms of objects tends to be ignored. The important physiological discovery is that certain stimulus patterns (lines of certain orientation, or movement, etc.) produce repeatable activity in specific brain cells. This discovery came as an unpalatable shock to passive theorists who tend to ignore brain function. To active theorists, it gives a clue to the kinds of data accepted for building object-hypotheses. One might think from this that passive theories would drop out, leaving the field of physiologists and active cognitive psychologists to work together in blissful harmony. Actually things are not quite like this: the physiological advance is so concrete, and clearly important, that many physiologists and cognitive psychologists feel that finding more feature analysers, and more abstract analysers, is the sole path we need to follow to understand vision. But is it? The physiological mechanisms being discovered relate to stimulus patterns only, and not recognition of objects as hypotheses. The physiological account thus remains passive, and so essentially inadequate, for the same reasons that cognitive passive accounts are inadequate.

The task ahead is to relate physiological processes not only to direct input-output links, as in reflexes, but also to the brain's logical and correlating activity endowing it with the power to predict. This will require further physiological data, and current techniques are providing extremely important new information so this will surely be available. Experiments on the phenomena of perception itself, in animals and in men—essentially on how patterns are interpreted as objects—has confusions (or at least impeding disagreements) in its philosophy, and a lack of powerful research techniques. Some of the most interesting clues are at present coming from studies of development of perception in babies. Early changes of the nervous system as a result of experience are now being discovered, which will perhaps help to tie up, or relate, physiology and cognition. Possibly the most fundamental and rigorous ideas are coming not from biology but from attempts to program computers to see and handle object-relations. It proves necessary to make the computers develop hypotheses and select the most likely, given the data from its glass eye.

There is more to this, for some computer programs designed to give "scene analysis" (recognizing objects from pictures by computer) assign alternative object probabilities to selected features in the picture: and then change these probabilities, according to probabilities assigned to other features of the scene. For example, a given shape may be a box or a building. If what is taken to be a hand is above it, then the probability of the box hypothesis will be increased and the building hypothesis decreased—for hands are generally too small and too low to be above buildings, but not above boxes. Now this gives interactions, due to conditional probabilities, which may generate visual effects in computers or brains quite like the old Gestalt phenomena, but for an entirely different reason. The reason is to be understood in terms of cognitive strategies or procedures for making effective use of data for deciding what objects are present in the scene.

In Machine Intelligence only precisely formulated theories are adequate: any gaps or errors in the theory show up as errors in the machine. At present machines perform only the simplest tasks, and are easily confused by shadows or small changes we scarcely notice.

Although the difficulties in Machine Intelligence demonstrate all too well how little we know, it now seems that we are beginning to understand ourselves—the inference-mechanisms of our humanity—by inventing adequate concepts for machines to infer objects from data, to perceive our world with their metal brains and human-devised programs. Is this science fiction? Yes—but like all fiction it may be largely true.

Philosophically, this is not the end of the matter. Behaviourism, with its related passive theories of perception, is unconcerned with what goes on between the senses and behaviour: indeed denies that anything goes on. This may be a legitimate expedient for focusing attention upon certain questions in behavioural research, but as a philosophy it is a kind of nihilism with a built-in contradiction. We are supposed to accept the behaviourist's writings as expressing his observations, thoughts, and judgments, which in these same writings he denies having. We are reminded of the poignant postcard received by Bertrand Russell saying: "I am a solipsist—why are there no other philosophers like me?"

28

Perception as a Foundation for Knowledge: Thoughts Inspired by Papers of Fraiberg and Bellugi

Eleanor J. Gibson

I include the brief set of remarks that follow because they illustrate the emergence of interest in questions about the origins of knowledge. The occasion was a symposium at Cornell organized as a memorial for Eric Lenneberg and it focussed on language. There were a number of invited speakers arranged on panels, one of which was composed of Selma Fraiberg, Ursula Bellugi, and Hermine Sinclair. I was asked, as one of the host faculty, to comment at the end of the panel on the three papers. Finding a common denominator was not easy, but I came up with one, the problem of reference, which arose often in the conference. Which comes first, the meaningful percept, or the linguistic symbol? In other words, what is the origin of the meanings in language, the things that we talk about?

These remarks were never published, although the speakers' papers were collected in a book, but my students were impressed with them. One student, Katherine Loveland, who had a major interest in language development, based her dissertation research on them. She liked the suggestion that the blind child's difficulty in achieving correct usage of the terms "you" and "I" was at least partly owing to lack of visual information for learning about what Piagetians call "coordination of perspectives." "You" and "I" refer to a speaker in a given place, and the words are interchangeable, as the roles are. Developmentally, learning about the stability of the layout whilst station-points are changing isn't accomplished until about two and a half years by even the sighted child. The blind child, unable to watch perspective transformations and occlusion-disocclusion as he moves around, is badly handicapped, lacking a prime source of information for the persistence of the layout along with changing views of it.

Loveland's research (1984) was a longitudinal developmental study of perspective-taking and achievement of correct usage of personal pronouns. She showed that knowledge of perspectives is always reached before consistently correct

Discussion prepared for the Lenneberg Symposium, Cornell University, Ithaca, N.Y., May 1976.

pronoun usage, usually shortly before it. This finding supports the notion of pre-
cedence of knowledge of events and features of the real world in the genesis of
linguistic reference. How else could it happen, anyway? The deprivation of the
blind child and its rather specific effects on language development are a persuasive
argument for it, as the following essay contends.

The Origin of Linguistic Meanings

Where do the meanings expressed in language come from? Like Eric
Lenneberg, I am of the opinion that linguistic meanings are rooted in the
perception of meaningful events in the world. And I would add, in the
accompanying proprioception of oneself in the world. Meanings are
anchored in knowledge obtained from perceiving the real world and thus
they derive from the meanings of *things, events,* and the *spatial layout.* It is
the latter, the spatial layout and the meanings it affords, that I am concerned with in the point I have chosen to elaborate. It is the juncture where
all three papers came together and struck a responsive chord in my own
thinking.

What Specifies the Self, and Especially, I?

I was impressed by Dr. Fraiberg's evidence that "A delay in the acquisition of self-reference pronouns and the concept 'I' is a unique problem for
the blind young child." Exactly what is it that is missing, perceptually, that
makes this meaning so elusive for a child who cannot see? What specifies
the self—*my*self—*I?*

I can think of a number of things that specify the self, and some of them
seem to be perfectly available, perceptually, to a blind child. What are they?
A useful specification of oneself must be invariant, relative to oneself. An
early incidence of such an invariant is the infant hearing himself cry, and
at the same time activating the peculiar breathing and vibratory patterns
that are contingent with it. Hearing the cry alone would not suffice—but
hearing a cry that is always contingent on unique breathing and activation of the vocal cords permits *control* of that activity; it affords self-
activation—pretty good information for oneself.

A little later, perhaps, as the child's use of arms and legs becomes agile,
all the kinesthetic information for lifting a limb can be experienced con-
tingently with feeling an object or a surface that is touched or struck—it
might be, in fact, one's own mouth that a thumb makes contact with. A
seeing infant can witness his hand come into view, contingent on activity
of the trunk and arm. But feeling the thumb get into the mouth and tasting
it is not a bad substitute. Neither is grasping something that results in

unique pressures and sounds, like crumpling paper. Preyer, (1890) discussing development of the "feeling of self," (his phrase) said an "important factor is *the perception of a change produced by one's own activity* ... an extremely significant day in the life of the infant is the one in which he first experiences the *connection of a movement executed by himself with a sense-impression following upon it,"* (p. 191 ff). Preyer thought this happened between the 45th and 55th week, when children do a lot of experimenting like shaking keys, opening and closing things, and pressing switches.

Many theorists have remarked, in the past, on the supposed difficulty of distinguishing one's self from the environment. Lest such a permanent confusion actually come to pass, nature has been extremely generous (especially to the sighted child) with means for discovering this distinction. A means often remarked on is the discovery of one's self in the mirror. A seeing child has the opportunity to move his arms, or grimace before the mirror, and to perceive a remarkable contingency in his reflection, information for one of the most interesting kinds of intermodal invariance. Preyer set the beginning of this discovery at about the 17th month. But he observed that there was a delay, after this, in the clear use of names, and especially the correct use of personal pronouns. "Many head-strong children," he said, "have a strongly marked 'I'-feeling without calling themselves anything but their names. These observations make it clear that the 'I' feeling, according to the facts given above, is present much earlier" (pp. 202–203 ff.).

One other invariant that we, as sighted persons, have always with us is the view straight ahead, the visual field. In the first place, even if we are sitting still, there is the frame provided by the nose and the eyebrows, always occluding the same area of the layout on either side. And if we move, the expansion pattern of the visual field that results has a motionless center—a beautiful, external, invariant reference point that exactly specifies the movement of the self. Since people don't remain fixed, like trees, they need movable invariants, and they have one.

But there is one trouble with all of these sources that specify the meaning of "myself." None of them seems to correspond perfectly with the use of the *word I. I* is not a name for me alone, it is a name for everybody.

What Perceptual Experience Corresponds with the Meaning of the Word I?

Either the hypothesis I began with, that verbal meanings derive from perceptually given experience, is wrong, or there must be something else that specifies *I*; and *you*, too, when *you* say the word *I!* To say that *I* is relative to oneself is not enough. It is relative to everyone. I think there is just one thing that is specific to this meaning, and that is the station point where the speaker is located. What is a station point, and how do we know about it?

A spatial layout, such as a room, has walls and furniture and a floor and light sources. Light—ambient light—bounces around in this layout, being reflected by everything there (J. J. Gibson 1966). An eye can be put in this room at any point, and it will have a view of the spatial layout from that standpoint, or as some would say, from that perspective. Some things in the room will be occluded and not be visible. But the observer who owns the eye can move to another station point, and then he may see what was occluded before. I cannot see what you see now, but I can move through the world taking adjacent points of observation at successive moments. I can see the same sequence of perspectives as you, and if they are "offset," we can both see the same layout of surfaces—an extended environment, some of whose surfaces are hidden at any one place and time. Perceiving the spatial layout surrounding one as objective, or, if you will, being able to take someone else's perspective or any perspective ("coordination of perspectives," in Piagetian terms), is an achievement that children eventually arrive at, and I propose that it is only then that the correct meaning of *I* and *you* is learned. They refer always and invariantly to the speaker's station point; *I* to *mine* when I am speaking, and *you* to *yours*, when I am; and vice versa when you are speaking.

There is considerable disagreement about when a child learns to perceive space objectively. Piaget and Inhelder set the time for development of "coordination of perspectives" between 7 and 9 years. Since their pioneer research, experimenters have been annually revising the age downward. Kosslyn, Pick, and Fariello (1974) found very convincing evidence that children had an objective scheme or cognitive map of an area in which they had just walked around locating toys at 4 years, although they had experienced only a fraction of the possible relations between points. Their investigation did not include younger subjects. Other experiments (Shantz and Watson 1971) have shown that 3-1/2 year olds realize that an array has more than one perspective.

If the hypothesis is correct that the meaning of *I* is defined by the speaker's station point, it is only too clear why a blind child should be handicapped. While an objective spatial layout and "coordination of perspectives" could eventually be obtained by blind but hearing speakers at different locations in an ambient echo-array, the accomplishment seems difficult. Comprehending the meaning of *I* would necessarily elude a blind child for some time.

If these arguments are correct, several things should follow. One concerns normal adult conversation. Indication of station points should substitute for *I*, or *you*, or *he* in an ordinary conversation. And so it does. We nod toward someone we are addressing, indicating *you*. We point to ourselves. We glance toward a third person indicating *he;* we even do this when the third person has recently left the scene by indicating where he stood, or had just been sitting. In the American Sign Language for the deaf, *you* and *I* are indicated by obvious gestures, and *he* by an orthogonal one. As Dr. Bellugi has told us, sign language makes very intricate use of space. I learned recently that when telling a story, a signer will often attempt to develop an imaginary stage or notion of setting, establishing the location of different persons and objects within the boundaries of this "signing space." The signer will then refer back to specific positions in this sign space in order to indicate relations between signs in a sentence. We saw something like that a few minutes ago when Dr. Frishberg signed "by my side" and "more than one."

We should expect then, should we not, that a deaf child would have relatively little trouble acquiring the personal pronouns, as compared to a blind child, if he grows up in a world of signers. (The answer to this question has to come from Dr. Bellugi.)

The *here* and *there* contrast (as Brown 1973, pointed out) is similar to the *I-you* contrast both in being relative and in relating to a station point in the spatial layout of surfaces. I would expect the two to be acquired at about the same time, for either a normal child or a blind child—later, of course, for the blind child.

How is the Verbal Meaning Learned?

Can one say anything about how the meaning of *I* is learned, in the sense of discovering its correspondence with all the specifications of the self? This is the question that touches on Dr. Sinclair's paper. Dr. Sinclair has emphasized regulatory mechanisms that establish an equilibrium, and especially, in the learning of language, the role of a disequilibrium or conflict that is resolved by the regulatory mechanisms in a new, superior equilibrium. Her example of the reversal of agent and patient, followed by ultimate understanding of what she terms the compensatory relation between them seems to me analogous to early confusions between *you* and *I*. Perhaps we can apply the notion of conflict to learning the meaning of *I*.

A disequilibrium or conflict should occur when a child first perceives that *I* is a name for everyone. He has already developed a concept of self, presumably on the basis of multimodal sources of information, such as contingencies of grasping and feeling a resultant pressure, shaking something and hearing resultant sounds, perceiving as he moves about the invariant for "straight ahead" in the expansion pattern, and a little later the invariance between his actions and the reflections of them in the mirror. The latter may then form a kind of "core" self-image, as Zazzo (1948) suggested, and the rest would be assimilated to it. A child's parents have communicated with him, at first referring to him and to themselves by name, but eventually by personal pronouns. His name belonged only to himself and might already have been assimilated to his concept of self. But how can he assimilate *you* and *I*? Is there a multitude of selves? There is a real conflict here that can only be resolved when he arrives at a concept of an objective spatial layout with movable station points.

The blind child may be slow in perceiving this conflict, since he has less rich information for developing a concept of self to start with, (lacking the mirror image, for instance); and he will also be slower in resolving the conflict, when he does perceive it, because he has so much less opportunity for developing "coordination of perspectives": for example, knowledge about objective space and the relations between station points in that space. The late development of mobility goes with visual deprivation, and enhances the retardation in discovering the spatial layout. *I* is where your eye is (a good reason for its use for *I* in hieroglyphic writing systems!).

What about a deaf child? He has excellent possibilities for developing a knowledge of the spatial layout and perspectives within it. He knows, if he is signed to, that the *eye* (the eye one sees with) goes with a station point and that reference to persons corresponds to the articulated use of space. But he doesn't *hear* the personal pronoun applied to *everybody*. Until he does, the disequilibrium or conflict can't occur, so as to push him to a superior way of dealing with his concept of himself and referring to it pronominally in words. He must, I think, learn to use self-reference via sign language very much sooner than he could do so via the word *I* even if he is being raised bilingually.[1]

Note

1. As it turns out (1989), the deaf child's achievement of correct pronoun usage in the spoken-written language is as difficult as for the hearing child, regardless of early signing.

References

Brown, R. *A first language. The early stages.* Cambridge, Mass.: Harvard University Press, 1973.

Gibson, J. J. *The senses considered as perceptual systems.* Boston: Houghton-Mifflin, 1966.

Kosslyn, S. M., Pick, H. L., and Fariello, G. R. Cognitive maps in children and men. *Child Development,* 1974, 45, 707–716.

Preyer, W. *The mind of the child. Part II. The development of intellect.* New York: D. Appleton and Co., 1890.

Shantz, C. U., and Watson, J. S. Spatial abilities and spatial egocentrism in the young child. *Child Development,* 1971, 42, 171–182.

Zazzo, R. Image du corps et conscience de soi. *Enfance,* 1948, 1, 29–43.

29

Perception of Invariants by Five-Month-Old Infants: Differentiation of Two Types of Motion

Eleanor J. Gibson, C. J. Owsley, J. Johnston

This was the first study undertaken after my return to research on infant perception. The highest priority topic at that time seemed to be information: how does dynamic information in an ambient optic array specify critical properties of objects in the world, and how early are infants capable of picking it up differentially? I chose rigidity-nonrigidity as an important property for investigation, because rigidity or elasticity of substance is a property with obvious utility for infants. It distinguishes surfaces that afford comfortable posture (rest) or locomotion, chewable things in the mouth, hard objects that afford gripping, and so on. The distinction is specified visually by a contrast in motion information over time (see paper 15 on rigid motion) and it is also specified multimodally, since haptic exploration yields information in patterns of mechanical resistance to pressure. Furthermore, the property is a persisting one and it is specified by information that is invariant over shapes, changes of source of pressure, observer position, etc., an example of perceptual constancy.

We chose habituation to a visual display as our method, combining it with a so-called "infant control" method (Horowitz et al. 1972). The latter method has the advantage that the infant may learn to shut off (control) the display by turning away its gaze. Times for habituation are rendered less random and more reliable with this procedure. The question of how to determine whether an infant detects an invariant property of substance was solved by using a generalization procedure. The same object was put through three different types of rigid motion for habituation. Following habituation, the infants were shown either a fourth type of rigid motion or a deforming elastic motion of the same object. If an infant generalized habituation to the new rigid motion, but not to the deforming motion, he must detect an invariant of information over the rigid motions.

Infants of five months gave reliable evidence of differentiating rigid from nonrigid motions over variations of presentation, so we concluded that they

Developmental Psychology, 1978, 14, 407–415. Copyright 1978 by the American Psychological Association. Reprinted by permission of the publisher.

were detecting invariance of a common property. Later experiments (not reprinted here) showed that invariance of substance was still perceived over a shape change, and that infants as young as three months detected the invariant information (Gibson et al. 1979). A final experiment in the series reversed the order of presentations, showing that habituation to varied deforming motions generalized and was perceived as contrasting with a rigid motion (Walker et al. 1980), so the contrast can be differentiated either way. The surfaces and substances of things in the world are bound to have varied affordances that must be differentiated for successful action, and informational invariants must specify them. Properties of substance are detected very early via at least one of these invariants, optical information for rigidity.

Five-month-old infants were habituated to three types of visually presented rigid motion, with duration of fixation as the dependent measure. After reaching a criterion of habituation, a fourth rigid motion (not habituated) and a deformation were presented. Dishabituation was significantly greater to the deformation than to the fourth rigid motion. Comparison with a no-change control condition showed a significant difference for deformation when it followed the fourth rigid motion. It was inferred that the infants detected the invariant property of rigidity and differentiated it from the deformation.

This experiment is the first of a series designed to investigate the infant's perception of invariants given through stimulus information.[1] It has long been known that human adults perceive objects in their environment as constant in size and shape, despite a changing optic array produced by movement of the observer from one observation point to another or by movement of the object itself in the surrounding spatial layout. As the observer moves, or as objects move in this layout, aspects of target objects are progressively occluded and revealed with consequent changes in the stimulus array that reaches the observer's receptors; yet the information generally remains adequate for the distal object to be apprehended for what it is. This story holds for many kinds of information presented in an ambient optic array. It probably also holds for information presented in an ambient acoustic array, although that has been less thoroughly investigated. We recognize voices despite noises enveloping them, distance, and variations in acoustic variables such as intensity and pitch caused by whispering, head colds, and shouting.

"Constancy" is only one example of the interesting and highly adaptive phenomena of human (and animal) cognition that we refer to as perception of invariants. Apprehension of "conservation" when a row of objects is lengthened (or shortened) is another, a phenomenon introduced to psychology by Piaget (1952); and so is perceived unity and persistence of an object when it is occluded and disoccluded, a phenomenon introduced by Michotte (Michotte, Thinès, & Crabbé, 1964). Permanence and objectivity of the spatial layout—the ground and sky around us and the arrangement of things in them with respect to one another and to us—has more recently been recognized as an important kind of invariant and is being studied under such rubrics as "perspective taking" and "cognitive maps."

Many of these phenomena have received some attention from developmental psychologists in studies with older children, for example, studies of size constancy in children between 5 and 12 years of age by Piaget and Lambercier (see Piaget, 1961). Investigation of perceived invariants in very early development has been scanty, except for a few studies of constancy in infants (e.g., Bower, 1964, 1966; Day & McKenzie, 1973). But before infancy is over, a child lives and acts in the world with apparent confidence. It seems unlikely that the surfaces and objects of the environment appear to shrink and expand as he moves or is moved, or as the objects move. Perception of invariants surely has a long developmental history, and one that begins early, perhaps with detection of some of the permanent properties of objects. It is this aspect of perceptual development that we have chosen to investigate, beginning with some simple properties of motion that carry information for invariant properties of things. The subjects in the experiment to be described were 5-month-old infants.

Specifically, we asked whether the motions in the stimulus array that are caused by movement of a rigid object provide information for an invariant property, even though the particular rigid motions differ. To answer this question, we compared perception of such motions with a motion of deformation that specifies elasticity in contrast to ridgidity to the adult perceiver (Fieandt & Gibson, 1959). For an infant to detect this information at an early age would be highly adaptive, since visual recognition of an object as rigid (unyielding to the touch if bumped into or fallen upon, for instance) versus elastic (yielding and potentially soft or even animate) could provide foreknowledge of the consequences of touching or collision. Knowledge of "affordances" given thus is one of the most useful achievements of perceptual development. Whether the affordance must be learned by association of the invariant given by motion with tactual and kinesthetic experiences given by pressure is a separate question. Our prediction was simply that young infants would distinguish a set of rigid motions, specifying the same invariant, from a motion of deformation.

The habituation paradigm was chosen. The essential procedure involved a repeated display of one type of motion for habituation, followed by a test for dishabituation with the other type. The infant's fixation was monitored, and looking time was used to determine habituation and to test for dishabituation when the new motion was introduced. In the classic paradigm, one infers that a rise in looking time at the test for dishabituation indicates that the subject has detected a change in the display. We were not interested in mere detection of any change of motion, however. The concern was whether something invariant was perceived in rigid motions, as a type, contrasted with deformation. The usual paradigm was modified, therefore, so that the infant was habituated not to one, but to three different rigid motions. At the end of the habituation sequence, half of the infants were presented with a fourth rigid motion and half with a deformation. If our prediction is correct, dishabituation should be significantly greater for the deformation, since new information is present in the array, whereas the fourth rigid motion still projects the same invariant property.

Method

Object and Motions Displayed

The object chosen to provide stimulus information for the two types of motion was a round disklike piece of foam rubber, 30 cm in diameter and 6.2 cm thick (see Figure 29.1). It was light yellow in color, dappled with black spots to provide some obvious color and texture variation.

The object could be manipulated so as to produce either rigid motion or deformation. All motions of the object were produced by an experimenter, whose fingers were inserted into 10 holes in the backside of the object. Four rigid motions were displayed: rotation in the frontal plane, rotation around the vertical axis, rotation around the horizontal axis, and looming (displacement to and fro on the axis perpendicular to the subject). The motions were cyclical and continuous. Each rigid motion embodied about 30° of displacement. The deformation consisted of a squeezing of the object by applying pressure with all 10 fingers and then releasing

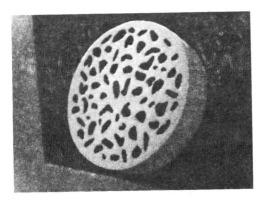

Figure 29.1
Object undergoing a rigid motion (rotation around the vertical axis).

it, producing a rippling (a "spongy" appearance) of its surface. The deformation was also cyclical and continuous.

Stimulus Information
In all four cases of rigid motion, the cross-ratios of surface elements remain invariant over time (Gibson, 1957; in press). This invariant relationship is information for the persistence of the object's surface structure. More simply stated, as the object undergoes rigid motion, any alignment of texture elements in the projected array remains aligned (Hay, 1966).

In deforming motion, the cross-ratios of the texture elements change over time. More simply stated, alignments of texture elements in the projected array do not remain aligned. The object's surface structure, rather than persisting, is continuously changing. The pattern of change, however, need not be random. In the present experiment, the pattern of change was quite regular in that there was a cyclical squeezing and releasing of the object.

Thus each type of motion can be described by a unique invariant relationship in the ambient optic array, which can serve as a basis for the motion's differentiation.

Subjects
Data from 24 full-term infants (mean age = 153 days; range: 131–179 days), half males and half females, are reported below. Data from 5 other infants could not be used because of the subjects' fussing. Subjects were obtained by sending letters to parents whose addresses were listed in the birth records of the local newspaper.

Apparatus
The subject was placed in an infant seat located in a rectangular curtained booth. 75.8 × 148.5 cm. He faced a plywood screen that had a 16 × 16 cm window that could be opened and closed by sliding a black cardboard screen across it. The object subtended an angle of 28°. It was displayed in the window in front of a black curtain. The experimenter who produced the object's motions stood behind the curtain, which entirely concealed her. She pushed her hands through an opening in the curtain, inserted her fingers into the finger holes in the object's back, and moved the object in a specified and carefully practiced routine for each of the five motions.

An observer watched the subject's eyes through a peephole below the window (diameter 1.9 cm) and depressed a button when the subject fixated the object. She was blind with respect to the particular routine being presented and to the experimental condition. The subject's fixation was recorded on a Harvard Apparatus recorder, located in a neighboring room and monitored by a second experimenter.

Experimental Design and Procedure
The experiment had a 2 × 2 × 2 × 2 factorial design: 2 between-group factors, order of presentation of motions in the posttest and sex, and 2 within-group factors, Posttest I versus Posttest 2 and type of motion presented in the posttest trials.

A habituation paradigm was used. The general procedure had three parts: a pretest, a habituation series, and a posttest. All 24 subjects were presented with three rigid motions in a consecutive fashion in the habituation series. The three rigid motions that a single subject observed were counterbalanced across subjects. The next motion in the sequence was presented when an infant looked away from the current display for 2 sec (Horowitz, Paden, Bhana, & Self, 1972). This routine was continued until a criterion of habituation was reached for each motion separately. The criterion for any subject was defined as one half of his first or second habituation exposure for that motion, whichever was longer. If the criterion for habituation was met for a certain motion, but was not yet reached for one or both of the other two motions, that motion was not dropped from the series. In other words, all three motions were presented until all had met their respective criteria.

When the criteria for habituation had been met, a posttest was presented that included a fourth rigid motion (the one that had not been seen in the habituation series) and the deformation. One group of 12 subjects saw the new rigid motion first, whereas the other 12 subjects saw the deformation first. The next motion in the posttest was presented when a subject looked away from the current display for 2 sec. The posttest was repeated, maintaining order of presentation. Males and females were divided evenly between the two groups.

A pretest was given before the habituation series. It was identical to the posttest, except that it was not repeated. In other words, it consisted of a single presentation of the fourth rigid motion followed by the deformation, or the reverse order, depending upon what group the subject was in. The purpose of the pretest was to determine whether one of the motions was intrinsically more interesting than the other.

Results

Subjects were generally attentive to the moving displays, but looking time varied considerably from one infant to another. Mean total looking time across trials to criterion was 153.70 sec ($SD = 110.37$). Mean duration of the first fixation was 18.98 sec ($SD = 14.17$). Mean duration of the last look before criterion was 6.05 sec ($SD = 10.31$). Mean number of trials to the final criterion was 11.13 ($SD = 3.18$).

The comparison of interest was between two difference scores: fixation time on the deformation minus the fixation time on the last trial of habituation compared to the fixation time on the fourth rigid motion minus the fixation time on the last trial of habituation. The means of these differences are presented in Figure 29.2, the two orders presented separately and the two tests within each order presented separately. Figure 29.2 indicates that for each order and for each test, differences in fixation on deformation were larger than differences in fixation on the fourth rigid motion.

Since the distributions of looking time on the criterion trial and on the posttest trials were positively skewed and since cell means were nonhomo-

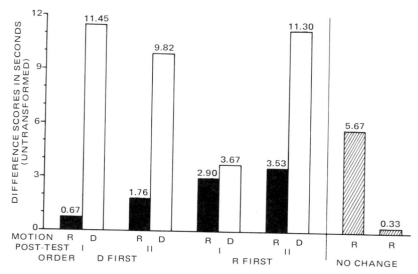

Figure 29.2

Mean differences in fixation time between trials following criterion and the trial just preceding. (Black columns indicate differences for the fourth rigid motion. White columns indicate differences for the deformation. Cross-hatched columns are differences in a no-change condition.)

geneous, log transformations, $\log(y = 1)$, were performed on all fixation times (see Winer, 1971, pp. 397–400). Transformed data are graphed in Figures 29.3 and 29.4. Backward habituation curves were plotted following Cohen's procedure (see Cohen & Gelber, 1975). The habituation trials are given negative numbers, since they are trials from criterion. All subjects are represented at the end of habituation, but as one reads to the left from the criterion trial the number of subjects decreases, owing to individual differences in number of trials to criterion. At least one half of the subjects are represented at each of the points plotted.

Primary Analyses

An analysis of variance was performed on the difference scores of the transformed data, the factors being Order × Sex × Posttest × Differential Increment in Fixation. There was no main effect of order, indicating that it made no difference which type of motion was presented first in the posttest. There was no main effect of posttest, indicating that both Posttests 1 and 2 revealed the same pattern of results. Nor was there a main effect of sex. The main effect of differential increment in fixation to the two motions was significant, $F(1, 20) = 9.69$, $p < .005$, with a greater incre-

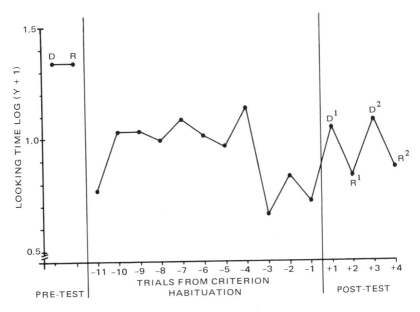

Figure 29.3
Backward habituation curve and pre- and posttests for subjects receiving deformation first in the pre- and posttests.

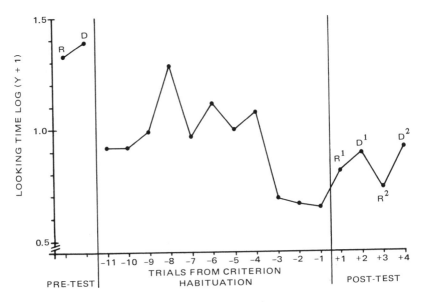

Figure 29.4
Backward habituation curve and pre- and posttests for subjects receiving rigid motion first in the pre- and posttests.

ment to deformation. Nineteen of 24 subjects showed this pattern. The other 5 looked longer at the fourth rigid motion.

The only significant interaction was between the sex, posttest, and differential increment factors, $F(1, 20) = 4.94$, $p < .04$; males showed a greater increase to rigid motion in Posttest 1 than in Posttest 2, while females showed a greater increase to rigid motion in Posttest 2 than in Posttest 1. Males showed a greater increase to deformation in Posttest 2 than in Posttest 1, while females showed the same magnitude of increase in both posttests.

An analysis of variance was also performed on the raw scores, despite the skewness of the distributions and the nonhomogeneity of variance. A similar pattern of results was obtained. The only main effect was the differential increment factor, $F(1, 20) = 5.16$, $p < .034$. There were no interactions.

It was possible to calculate the comparison of interest in another manner that increased the generality of the results. We averaged the duration (using transformed data) of the last three looks in habituation of any subject (thus including all three rigid motions to which he had been habituated) and subtracted that mean from the fixation time on the new rigid motion or on the deformation. A second analysis of variance was performed on these scores. The results were similar to the first analysis, with the only significant effect being the differential increment factor, $F(1, 20) = 9.87$, $p < .005$.

To investigate whether the significant differential increment in fixation might be due to the effects of only one or two of the rigid motions, two analyses of variance were performed. The factors were particular rigid motion and differential increment in posttest fixation. In the first analysis, the particular rigid motion that each subject received in his last look of habituation provided the levels of the motion factor. In the second, the particular rigid motion that was viewed in the posttest provided the levels of the motion factor. The two analyses yielded similar results. A significant main effect of differential increment in fixation again revealed a greater increment to deformation, $F(1, 20) = 6.89$, $p < .016$, in the first analysis, and $F(1, 20) = 8.66$, $p < .008$, in the second analysis. There was no main effect of particular type of motion, nor was there an interaction of it with the differential increment in fixation. Together, these results indicate that the differential increment in fixation time was not due to the overpowering effects of one or two rigid motions; rather, they contributed equally.

Was deformation intrinsically more interesting than rigid motion, thus accounting for longer fixation on it in the posttest? An analysis of variance was performed on the pretest fixation times, factors being type of motion (rigid vs. deformation) and order of presentation. There were no significant effects, indicating that the two types of motion were about equally effective in eliciting fixations before habituation. Thus the greater fixation increment to deformation in the posttest was due to the habituation experience and subsequent detection of new information in the display.

Habituation
Several questions might be asked concerning the time required for a subject to habituate, sometimes referred to as "rate of habituation." Since all subjects in this experiment were run to an established criterion (one half of their original looking time), we necessarily defined *rate* in terms of that criterion. Rate is accordingly defined as total fixation summed over trials until criterion is met. Findings were as follows. First, when a single rate was calculated across the three-motion series, a *t* test indicated that there were no sex differences. Second, there was no correlation between age (range: 131–179 days) and rate. Third, when rates were compared for order in the three-motions series, *t* tests showed no differences among the rates, for example, the third motion introduced was not habituated to more quickly than the first or second. Fourth, when a one-way analysis of variance was used to compare the rates of habituation to each of the four rigid motions, there was a significant effect of particular rigid motion. $F(3, 68) = 2.87$, $p < .05$. In order from fastest to slowest rates, the motions were looming, rotation around the vertical axis, rotation in the frontal plane, and rotation around the horizontal axis. Multiple comparisons were carried out using the Tukey (*b*) test. The only significant difference was between looming and rotation around the horizontal axis, $p < .05$, $df = 68$.

Comparison to No-Change Control Group
The experiment was designed so as to address the question of whether dishabituation to deformation would be relatively greater than dishabituation to the new rigid motion. Our results provided an affirmative answer. As an afterthought, we asked whether the amount of dishabituation to deformation and to the new rigid motion was greater than the increase that would be expected if no change of motion was introduced. Although a random assignment of subjects to groups at this date was impossible, 12 subjects (mean age = 152 days; range: 135–161 days) were run in a no-change control condition. Upon reaching criterion, instead of introducing the new motions in the posttest, these subjects were presented with the next two rigid motions of the habituation sequence, just as if subjects had not met criterion at all. It was expected that an increase in fixation on deformation would be significantly greater than an increase in fixation in the no-change posttest. The expectation regarding the fourth rigid motion was not so clear-cut. Significant dishabituation might occur if subjects detected the fourth rigid motion as being different from the previous three.

Continued habituation might occur if subjects perceived an invariant property as remaining in the array and if they were not sensitive to the change to a fourth rigid motion.

In evaluating the results, it should be noted that only Posttest I scores in the original experiment were relevant for comparisons between the no-change control posttest trials and the posttest trials in the original experiment. This is because only two test trials followed criterion in the no-change control condition.

Two difference scores were computed for each subject: The first difference score was the old rigid motion that was presented *first* in the posttest minus the last look in habituation. The mean difference score is displayed in Figure 2 as the first bar in the no-change condition. This difference score is properly compared to difference scores involving rigid motion and deformation. which also occurred first in Posttest 1. Note that the relevant deformation difference score (11.45 sec, $SD = 35.05$) is larger than the no-change difference score (5.67 sec, $SD = 11.08$), whereas the rigid motion difference score (2.90 sec, $SD = 8.71$) is smaller than the no-change difference score. Mann-Whitney U tests were computed, since distributions were not normal and variances were nonhomogeneous. Neither comparison was statistically significant, despite the apparent differences.

The second difference score computed for the no-change condition (the last bar in Figure 2) was the old rigid motion that was presented second in the posttest minus the last look in habituation. This difference score is properly compared to the difference scores involving the fourth rigid motion and deformation that occurred second in Posttest 1. Note that the deformation difference score (3.67, $SD = 5.05$) is larger than the no-change difference score (.33, $SD = 3.56$). A Mann-Whitney U test indicated that this difference was significant, $U = 114.5$, $p < .05$, two-tailed. The rigid motion difference score (.67, $SD = 11.27$) is slightly larger, but this difference is not statistically significant. Although the difference between the control group and the deformation was significant only when deformation was presented second in the posttest. the results are in the expected direction in both comparisons.[2]

Discussion

The results of the present experiment imply to us that 5-month-old infants are capable of perceiving rigidity of an object as an invariant property of that object. In contrast to a fourth rigid motion, a motion of deformation was perceived as different, presumably because it offered information about a new property of the object, that object being otherwise unchanged. Had the experiment merely found that the infants discriminated a single rigid motion from a motion of deformation (as an earlier pilot experiment did), there would be no grounds for concluding that an invariant property was detected. The four rigid motions all provide information for unchanging structure of the distal object. On the other hand, deformation provides information for changing structure, and a reversible, cyclic deformation of the kind displayed implies that the distal object is elastic. The experiment does not tell us whether elasticity, as such, would be perceived as invariant if other instances of it were provided, but it does imply that four motions specifying rigidity were perceived to have an invariant property. Whether that property can only be described in terms of proximal stimulus information, or can be referred to in distal terms as *rigidity* is a moot question.

Might there be other ways of interpreting the results? Several have been suggested to us. One interpretation, deriving from a constructivist view of perceptual development in which inference is considered an important process, might argue that the infants categorize the three rigid motions in the course of habituation and recognize the fourth one as a member of the newly acquired category (Bruner, 1973; Bryant, 1974). The flaw in this argument is a logical one; the infant must perceive some common property in order to form the category. If he is able to detect whatever specifies the property of rigidity in all four motions, he *is* perceiving an invariant property. Assuming a further process of categorization would be adding an unparsimonious theoretical superstructure.

Could one, under a kind of mediation stimulus–response view, assume that a response made to each of the three habituated motions "generalizes" to the fourth? The term *generalization* sounds plausible and innocuous; but there is again the problem of acquiring a mediating response that is the same for all four motions. What property underlies the generalization, if it is not the invariant that describes rigidity?

Could one, under a Piagetian umbrella, invoke a common scheme, constructed during viewing of the first three motions, to which the fourth is assimilated? This view seems to us the least likely of all, since (a) perception is assumed to be "figurative" at this age, a sequence of arrested "pictures" (Piaget, 1954, p. 4 ff; Piaget, 1971, pp. 248 ff), whereas the information for the invariant and its contrasting property are carried by motion; and (b) a scheme is defined as sensorimotor, and the motor aspect, especially one common to the four motions, would be extremely hard to identify. Piaget states that "groups of displacement," as these motions might be called, are "surely not perceived as such by the child," the child he referred to being less than 9 or 10 months of age (Piaget, 1954, pp. 97 ff.).

It will require further research to settle on any of these interpretations or to generate a better one. A related question, the role of motion as an object-defining property, also deserves investigation. Do unique motions enjoy the same privilege for object identification, as do static distinctive features (ones presumed to be used for distinguishing faces, for instance)? Are they perhaps used prior to static features for identifying properties of objects that have permanent affordances, if not for identifying the object itself? It is not at all unlikely that invariant properties of objects like rigidity and elasticity are detected well before objects themselves are identified on the basis of static distinctive features. We hope that experiments in progress will clarify these questions.

Finally, we return to a question posed earlier. Does detection of the invariant given by visually perceived rigid motions, as contrasted with deformation, lead the infant to expect that the object will feel rigid to the touch when pressed, in the first case, and feel yielding in the second? Must this expectation be acquired by association of the two experiences? Earlier in the century, it was generally accepted by Titchenerians and functionalists alike that the latter was the case. But in recent years, the doctrine that "the hand teaches the eye" has lost ground. Infants do not employ active touch to explore the feel of objects before 5 months after birth (see Gibson, 1969, pp. 359–362), yet they are capable of differentiating two types of visually presented motion that can afford information for rigidity and elasticity. To some of us, the visual information seems just as valid in its specification of rigidity as that given by feeling. Furthermore, multimodal redundant information that specifies the same property or the same object is frequently available to a perceiver. An intermodal experiment, performed as soon as an infant explores substances haptically by prodding or squeezing, may tell us whether the infant expects the visually rigid substance to feel rigid as well.

Notes

1. This research was supported in part by Training Grant 5T01 HD00381-05 from the National Institute of Child Health and Human Development; the Susan Linn Sage Fund of Cornell University; and National Science Foundation Grant BNS76-14942 to the first author.

   Thanks are due to Dale Klopfer for assistance in monitoring equipment and data analysis.

   A briefer version of this paper was presented at a meeting of the Society for Research in Child Development, New Orleans, March 1977.
2. The control−experimental comparisons were also computed using the log-transformed data. Since the log conversions rendered the distributions normal and the variances homogeneous, two-tailed t tests were carried out. The rigid motion difference scores did not differ from their corresponding no-change difference scores, both yielding t values at $p > .5$. When deformation was presented first, the deformation difference score did not significantly differ from the no-change difference score, $t(22) = 1.03$. $p < .32$, whereas when deformation was presented second, the deformation−no change comparison approached significance, $t(22) = 1.80$, $p < .086$.

References

Bower. T. G. R. Discrimination of depth in pre-motor infants. *Psychonomic Science*, 1964. 1, 368.

Bower, T. G. R. Slant perception and shape constancy in infants. *Science*, 1966, 151, 832–834.

Bruner, J. S. *Beyond the information given.* New York: Norton. 1973.

Bryant. P. E. *Perception and understanding in young children.* London: Methuen, 1974.

Cohen, L. B.. & Gelber. E. R. Infant visual memory. In L. B. Cohen & P. Salapatek (Eds.), *Infant perception: From sensation to cognition,* (Vol. 1). New York: Academic Press, 1975.

Day, R. H., & McKenzie. B. E. Perceptual shape constancy in early infancy. *Perception,* 1973, 2, 315–320.

Fieandt, K., & Gibson. J. J. The sensitivity of the eye to two kinds of continuous transformation of a shadow pattern. *Journal of Experimental Psychology,* 1959, 57, 344–347.

Gibson, E. J. *Principles of perceptual learning and development.* New York: Appleton-Century-Crofts, 1969.

Gibson, J. J. Optical motions and transformations as stimuli for visual perception. *Psychological Review,* 1957, 64, 288–295.

Gibson, J. J. The *ecological approach to visual perception.* Boston: Houghton-Mifflin, 1979.

Hay, J. C. Optical motions and space perception: An extension of Gibson's analysis. *Psychological Review,* 1966, 73, 550–565.

Horowitz, F. D., Paden, L., Bhana, K., & Self, P. An infant-control procedure for studying fixations. *Developmental Psychology,* 1972, 7, 90.

Michotte, A., Thinès, G., & Crabbé, G. Les compléments amodaux des structures perceptives. In A. Michotte & J. Nuttin (Eds.), *Studia Psychologica.* Louvain, France: Publications Universitaires de Louvain, 1964.

Piaget, J. *The child's conception of number.* London: Routledge & Kegan Paul, 1952.

Piaget, J. *The construction of reality in the child.* New York: Basic Books, 1954.

Piaget, J. *Les mécanismes perceptifs.* Paris: Presses Universitaires de France, 1961.

Piaget, J. *Perception and knowledge.* Edinburgh, Scotland: University of Edinburgh Press, 1971.

Winer, B. J. *Statistical principles in experimental design.* New York: McGraw-Hill, 1971.

30

Development of Knowledge of Visual-Tactual Affordances of Substance

Eleanor J. Gibson, Arlene S. Walker

The previous paper showed that rigidity-nonrigidity is distinguished by very young infants by means of optical information given in motion over time. Two questions arise. Do infants detect a meaning (affordance) for this property, or are they only discriminating a difference in stimulation, not a property of an object existing in the world outside them? Second, would they distinguish and recognize haptic information for the same property, that is, feel the difference, and recognize it as the same one, characterizing an external object? The two questions, one having to do with perceiving an affordance for action, the other having to do with multimodal information specifying the same property, are of great importance for the ecological approach. Information is not the same concept as stimulation striking a receptor surface: it is information for something, about something in the world. As such, it should be abstract, not tied to one sensory system. We would except to find generalization between bimodal presentations, even at an early age, denoting pick up of a property of an external object, not mere registering of input to a single receptor modality.

I have argued in other papers (Gibson 1983, on development of intermodal unity, and Walker-Andrews and Gibson 1986, on development of bimodal perception) that infants do not differentiate modalities as such at an early age. Information is amodal, rarely modality specific, and information for an external event may be specified by more than one perceptual system. The substance of an object, for example, may be specified visually, haptically, and even auditorily. Think of a steel bar, for instance—it looks hard and rigid, feels hard and cold, and has a metallic ring when struck. Information is conveyed over time and can have amodal, abstract properties together specifying the same affordance.

As adults we distinguish whether we recognize a substance by odor, sight, or feel, but it may be that young infants perceive the affordance of a substance without distinguishing the sensory quality (smell, vision, whatever) of the in-

Child Development, 1984, 55, 453–460.

formation that specified it, and only later come to differentiate particular sensory qualities, beginning around six months (Walker-Andrews and Gibson 1986). In any case, the paper reprinted here investigates whether a substantial property specified haptically is perceived as the same when specified visually by infants in the first year of life—at one month and at one year.

At the same time, we hoped to throw some light on whether an infant in distinguishing between a rigid and a nonrigid substance is detecting an affordance. If the baby detects the substance bimodally—that is, recognizes the substance visually after having felt it—does that tell us that the baby detects a meaning for it? It certainly indicates that the infant is perceiving a property of an object, something external to itself. If the infant has acted appropriately to the substance in haptic exploration of it, perhaps that is enough. We return later to the problem of perceiving affordances, and how it can be investigated experimentally.

Infants of 12 months were familiarized in the dark with an object of either a hard or an elastic (spongy) substance. Following 60 sec of manipulation, a visual preference test was given with simultaneous presentation of 2 films of identical objects, 1 moving in a pattern characteristic of a rigid object and 1 moving in a pattern characteristic of an elastic object. Infants handled the 2 substances differently in an appropriate manner and looked preferentially with more and longer first looks to the type of substance familiarized. A replication of this experiment with familiarization in the light yielded comparable results. A third experiment with 1-month- old infants allowed them to mouth objects of either a hard or a soft substance for haptic familiarization and then tested looking preferences with real objects moving rigidly or deforming. These infants looked longer at the object moving in a manner characteristic of the novel substance. The results, together, suggest that quite young infants detect intermodal invariants specifying some substances and perceive the affordance of the substance.

Previous research in this laboratory has shown that 3–5 month-old infants not only visually differentiate rigid motions from deforming ones but also detect optical information for rigidity that is invariant over different forms of rigid motion.[1] The symmetrical proposition is also supported by experimental evidence—that infants of 3 months detect optical information for elasticity of substance as invariant over a class of different deforming motions (Gibson, Owsley, & Johnston, 1978; Gibson, Owsley, Walker, & Megaw-Nyce, 1979; Walker, Gibson, Owsley, Megaw-Nyce, & Bahrick, 1980). Adults know that objects that feel hard and rigid when manipulated move so as to provide patterns of transformation (perspective transformations) that specify rigidity visually and that objects that feel spongy and elastic when manipulated can move in deforming patterns that specify elasticity visually. Visual recognition of these properties of substances is of great utility for development. For example, an elastic surface below affords jumping upon, but a hard one may afford breaking a leg. Chewable things can be seen to move in deforming patterns. Hard ones that might injure the mouth do not. Thus, information about the affordance of a substance is available to both haptic and visual pickup systems. When adults perceive the utility of this information for appropriate actions, we say that they have detected the affordance of the substance (E. J. Gibson, 1982; J. J. Gibson, 1979).

How early can infants obtain this knowledge about a useful intermodal invariant? Preliminary experiments extending over several years were instructive and informed us that manual exploration of a hidden object is extremely difficult to obtain before 10–12 months of age. For this reasons, the first two experiments to be reported were performed with subjects about 1 year old. The third experiment was performed with very young subjects (1 month), who explored haptically by mouth.

Experiment 1

This experiment employed a method adapted from Gottfried and Rose (1980) and Soroka, Corter, and Abramovitch (1979). The infants (12 months old) were presented with the objects to be manipulated in total darkness with only the object's location specified by a dot of luminescent paint. The infant's behavior was videotaped in infrared light and observed by an auxiliary experimenter on a TV screen in another room. This procedure allowed us to ask an important question for investigating the perception of affordances: When an infant makes an unexpected contact by touch with an unknown object, does exploratory behavior ensue that is appropriate for distinguishing objects of different substances, in one case rigid (hard), in the other elastic (yielding)?

Following manipulation of the object, we presented the infant, without its being moved or taken into the light, with motion picture films of two objects, side by side, one being moved in a pattern characteristic of a rigid object and one deforming in a pattern characteristic of an elastic object. Thus, optical information about the two substances was available, given solely by motion, since the two objects were otherwise identical. This procedure was designed to answer the question, Does the infant show, by preferential looking at one or the other of these films, that intermodal correspondence of substances can be recognized following exploratory handling of a substance in darkness?

Method

Subjects   The subjects were approximately 1 year old, ranging in age from 356 to 392 days. There were 18 boys and 14 girls. Numbers of boys and girls familiarized with the hard object were equal. For the soft object, there were 10 boys and six girls.

Apparatus   The infant sat on its mother's lap at a table 91 × 61 cm, facing a wooden frame the width of the table. A translucent screen (71 × 41 cm) was mounted in the frame 41 cm above the table. Motion pictures could be back-projected on this screen, which was at a comfortable eye height for the infants, as they looked up at it slightly. Mounted in the wood under the screen and 28 cm above the table's surface was the lens of a TV camera (General Electric infrared video camera CCTV). The camera was positioned so as to include the movements of the babies' hands and arms as well as their head and eyes. Two infrared lamps (Kodak Satellite filter no. 11) were positioned on opposite sides of the table below the screen. Behind the screen were mounted two 8 mm Bolex motion picture projectors arranged so as to project two films side by side on the screen. The objects filmed each cast an image approximately 17 cm in diameter on the screen. An experimenter sat at one side of the mother's chair, arranged so that she could place and remove objects in front of the infant and press the switch that started the two projectors. Small observation holes were cut in the wooden frame holding the screen at a comfortable height for observing the infant's eye movements. Button boxes were placed behind the screen for recording. When one was pressed, a pen on an event recorder in the next room was activated. A TV monitor in the next room was available for a second experimenter, who watched the infant on the screen and timed its hand movements with another button box. The times were accumulated on a digital clock. An intercom system permitted communication with the experimenter in the room with the infant.

Objects   The objects that the infant handled were in one case rigid (hard), made of wood with a thin coating of sponge rubber; in the other they were elastic (soft), cut from sponge rubber. Both objects were circular, $6\frac{1}{2}$ cm in diameter and $2\frac{1}{2}$ cm thick. In the center of each was a single dot of luminescent paint. A sufficient supply of these objects was constructed for two of either kind to be available to the infant throughout the first part of the experiment.

Motion picture displays   Two motion pictures were made. One was of a circular sponge rubber object (18.5 cm in diameter) being moved in a series of projective transformations characteristic of a rigid object; the other was of the same object being moved in a deforming pattern characteristic of a spongy object when pressure is applied to it (see Gibson et al., 1978). The objects were lightly spotted to provide some texture. They were filmed against a black background. The hand moving them was gloved in black, so that only the moving object was visible. The motions look to an adult typical of a rigid object in one case and a spongy, elastic one in the other. The objects filmed, it will be noted, were not identical with the objects actually handled.

Procedure   The infant sat on its mother's lap in the dimly lighted experimental room for about a minute, with a toy on the table before it, which it could pick up and manipulate. The lights were gradually dimmed to complete darkness, and the toy was removed. The experimenter then put two identical objects, either rigid (hard) ones or spongy (soft) ones, on the table, with the luminescent spots visible. Half the infants received hard objects and half received soft ones. The infant was left to itself to discover the objects and pick them up, the mother having been requested beforehand to sit as quietly as possible. If the infant did not pick up the objects in a few minutes, the experimenter moved the objects around slightly on the table so that the luminescent spots might catch the infant's attention. If the baby dropped or threw an object while handling it, the experimenter retrieved it or substituted another identical one. When the baby had manipulated one or the other object for a total of 60 sec, the experimenter watching the TV monitor signaled, and the experimenter in the room with the infant removed the objects and turned on the projectors. The films were projected for a total of 30 sec. Half the infants had the film depicting the familiarized substance on the right; half had it on the left. The observer watched the baby's eye movements, using a button box to transmit data to the event recorder, and indicated whether the infant was looking to the right or left side of the screen by pushing one of two buttons. The experimenter was behind the screen watching the baby's eyes and did not know to which side a film was projected. The two observers had been checked for reliability in previous experiments and achieved agreements above .90. The video camera also continued to photograph the infant, so eye movements could be checked on the tape.

Sixteen infants were familiarized with the hard objects and 16 with the soft ones, for a total of 32 subjects. Eight infants were run who did not complete the experiment or whose data were discarded—five because of failure to handle the objects, two because of fussiness, and one because of equipment failure.

Table 30.1
Frequency of Occurrence of Exploratory Manipulations, Experiment 1

	Presses	Throws/ Drops	Touches	Strikes	Mouths
Hard	50	26	31	40*	21
Soft	95*	61	60	9	13

*$p < .05$.

Results

Exploratory handling   Videotapes were examined for evidence of haptic exploratory behavior. A coding scheme was designed to include all the behaviors that we could distinguish. Two independent coders (not the authors), who had previously practiced on tapes of other experiments, viewed the tapes. The tapes were reviewed in cases of disagreement, and an agreement was reached. Some of the coded behaviors occurred very rarely or not at all (e.g., hands to parent or experimenter, passes from hand to hand, or holds both) and were dropped from the analysis. Other distinctions proved to be too fine. The categories were collapsed to yield five overall. Total frequencies for these five categories are entered in Table 30.1. "Presses" refers to gripping an object with adjustment of the fingers so as to apply pressure. Movement of the fingers against the object, with taut muscles, was the criterion. The grip was sometimes released and tightened in a cyclic fashion. "Touches," in contrast, refers to touching lightly or relaxed holding without gripping or changing pressure. "Strikes" refers to production of an impact on the table or on a second object.

To test differences in type of manipulation of the two substances, Mann-Whitney U tests were performed on each of the five categories. The differences were significant as follows: mouths, $U(16,16) = 99$, N.S.; throws/drops $U(16,16) = 81$, N.S.; touches, $U(16,16) = 79$, $p < .10$; strikes, $U(16,16) = 71$, $p < .05$; presses, $U(16,16) = 65$, $p < .02$ (all two-tailed). Frequency of striking was associated significantly with the hard object; pressing (squeezing) was associated with the soft one.

Looking preference   Twenty-three of the infants looked first to the film representing the familiarized substance, a significant preference by a binomial test, $p < .01$. Mean duration of the first look was 2.009 sec when it was familiar and .844 sec when it was novel, as portrayed in the bar graphs of Figure 30.1. An analysis of variance was run with group (soft or hard) × side (right or left) × preference, with duration of first look (familiar vs. novel) as the dependent measure. The main effect of duration was

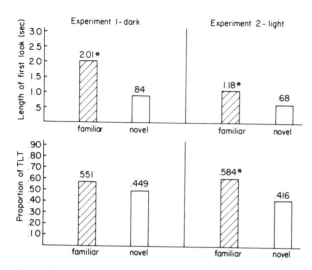

Figure 30.1
Mean length of first looks and proportion of total looking time for the familiar versus the novel object in Experiment 1 (familiarization in the dark) and Experiment 2 (familiarization in the light).

significant, $F(1,24) = 4.65$, $p < .0413$. No other main effects or interactions were significant.

When total looking time for the whole 30-sec test period was considered, 20 of the 32 infants showed a preference for looking at the familiarized substance. The mean proportion of time spent looking at the familiarized substance was .551 (SD = .186), as portrayed in Figure 30.1. This difference did not reach significance, $t(31) = 1.54$, $p < .134$. There were no significant effects of substance assigned for familiarization, sex of infant, or side of presentation.

Discussion
Both questions asked in the introduction have been answered in the affirmative. Infants given an opportunity to explore an object of unknown substance in darkness did exhibit diversified manual exploration. A spongy object was more often pressed or squeezed, a hard one more often struck on a resisting surface. Pressure on a spongy object leads to different consequences than pressure on a rigid object; striking a rigid object against a surface leads to different consequences than striking a spongy one. Thus, detection of different affordances was made possible, and different actions ensued. Then, when objects moving in differential patterns characteristic of the two substances were presented for visual comparison, the substances were distinguished by more first glances and longer first glances

at whichever substance had been familiarized by manual exploration, as if confirming what had been touched.

Why do these infants select the familiarized substance for the first look and look longer at it when it is the first look? A few babies did look at the novel substances first, as is almost bound to happen when films are suddenly flashed on in a dark room. If the head is turned to one side, the first glance is apt to fall there. But in these cases, the look was shorter, and the babies turned to the other object. Unimodal familiarization and preference tests (all visual, for example) have commonly shown a novelty preference on the preference test. If the baby recognizes the object as the same one, it should presumably select something novel to look at, the argument goes. The question arises whether infants familiarized haptically with an object in the light, so that they could see as well as feel it, would look preferentially at the film displaying a novel property. Experiment 2 was designed to answer this question by providing visual familiarization as well as a visual test.

Experiment 2

Subjects
The subjects were approximately 1 year old, ranging in age from 355 to 384 days. There were 17 boys and 15 girls. Numbers of boys and girls familiarized with the hard objects were equal. For the soft object, there were nine boys and seven girls. An additional eight infants' data were not included—five because of equipment failure, two because of crying, and one because the baby had Down's Syndrome.

Procedure
This experiment replicated the first as closely as possible, except that the infants were familiarized haptically with an object in a lighted room, so that they could see the object as well as handle it. Otherwise, the procedure was nearly identical. Thirty-two infants were given either two hard or two soft objects to manipulate, but in this case the lights were dimmed only slightly. Again, 16 infants were familiarized with the hard objects and 16 with the soft. Following 60 sec of manipulation by the infant (again timed by an experimenter watching the TV screen), the lights were dimmed further and the films were presented for 30 sec. Looking time was monitored as before.

Results

Exploratory handling   The infants' exploratory handling of the objects was coded by two observers. The useful categories of Experiment 1 were included and some others were added that were now pertinent because of the lighted environment. These included rotating and observing the object at the same time, and some unexpected ones such as turning to show the object to a parent (manipulation sometimes occurred while doing this). The manipulatory activity was considerably more varied and more frequent overall than in Experiment 1, as Table 30.2 shows. Perhaps because the babies were so busy looking at the object as they held it, the manipulatory behavior seems less informative. But pressing (squeezing) was vastly more frequent with the soft object, and the hard one was again struck against something more often, although the action was considerably more frequent in some of the babies than in others. Mann-Whitney U tests were computed, as follows: touches, $U(16,16) = 112$ N.S.; holds, $U(16,16) = 119$, N.S., holds and looks, $U(16,16) = 96$, N.S.; rotates and looks, $U(16,16) = 100$, N.S.; presses, $U(16,16) = 24$, $p < .0001$; throws/drops, $U(16,16) = 76$, $p < .06$; strikes, $U(16,16) = 92$, N.S.; mouths, $U(16,16) = 104$, N.S.; holds both, $U(16,16) = 111$, N.S.

Looking preference   Both the infants' first looks and the proportion of total looking time to the novel and familiar substances were examined. These are portrayed in bar graphs in Figure 30.1. When the direction and length of the infants' first looks were considered, the infants showed a familiar preference, as before: familiar, mean = 1.18 sec; novel, mean = .683 sec; $F(1,24) = 4.85$, $p < .038$. Twenty of the 32 first looks were directed toward the film of the familiarized substance. When total looking time was considered, 23 of the 32 infants showed a preference for the familiarized substance. The mean proportion of time spent looking at the familiarized substance was .584 (SD = .174), a significant proportion, $t(31) = 2.723$, $p < .01$.

Discussion

Familiarization in both Experiments 1 and 2 resulted in a preference for looking at the familiarized substance, when familiarization was haptic alone and when it was both haptic and visual. However one explains the direction of the preference, the evidence that there is one is convincing. Because it is about equally evident whether familiarization takes place in the dark or the light, we can infer that there is intermodal knowledge of some common properties of substances by 1 year of age. From these data, it is unclear whether infants can extract invariant information or whether they have associated haptic experience with visual experience in similar situations when both haptic and visual information were available. Finding that infants have intermodal knowledge of substance before they have gained control of opportunities for simultaneous manipulation and looking would

Table 30.2
Frequency of Occurrence of Exploratory Manipulations, Experiment 2

	Touches	Holds	Holds + Looks	Rotates, Looks	Presses	Throws/ Drops	Strikes	Mouths	Holds Both
Hard	28	24	48	67	29	14	72	58	11
Soft	32	22	41	47	131*	51	39	38	13

*$p < .0001$.

argue for the view that there may be direct detection of intermodal invariants without associative mediation. Experiment 3 addresses this point.

Experiment 3

This experiment was designed to provide as close a parallel as possible with the first one, but with much younger infants (about 1 month of age). Since manual exploration was out of the question, oral exploration provided the haptic experience for familiarization. We reasoned that infants of this age, while having experience of mouthing various substances, have not had the opportunity of simultaneously watching the patterns of movement produced by their mouthing. The experiment was in most cases performed in the homes of the subjects, rather than the laboratory, since parents were often reluctant to bring out such young infants. This change necessitated portable equipment and rather drastic differences in the display for testing preferential looking—for example, a display of real objects rather than films for the preference test.

Subjects

The subjects were 32 infants ranging from 26 to 45 days (median age, 30 days). Overall, 56 infants participated, 24 of whom did not complete the experiment because of sleeping or crying, or had to be eliminated because of equipment failure or experimenter error. Twenty-four of the infants were brought to the laboratory by their parents. The procedure was the same in these cases, except that the screens were built in and a Harvard Apparatus event recorder was used.

Apparatus and Procedure for Familiarization

The infant reclined at a comfortable angle in an infant seat, with foam rubber pads at each side of its head to keep it from inclining to one side. The seat was placed on the floor in a three-sided enclosure formed by portable black panels that screened off the room. The baby's mother was asked to insert the object for familiarization in the baby's mouth and hold it gently at one end until asked to withdraw it. There was no need to dim the light, since the mother's hand concealed the object from the infant's view. The mother kneeled behind the infant and was not visible. The rigid (hard) object was a cylinder of lucite 1 cm in diameter and 7.5 cm long. The elastic (soft) object was a stick of porous plastic of approximately, the same dimensions cut from a cellulose dish sponge (boiling rendered this object quite flexible as well as sterile). Half the babies received the hard object, and half received the soft one. The infants' mouthing was observed through a hole in one of the black panels and was timed by an observer.

When the infant had mouthed the object for 60 sec, the parent was asked to withdraw it.

Apparatus and Procedure for Visual Preference Test
The objects for display following familiarization were two cylinders of the same length as the familiarized object and 3 cm in diameter. One was constructed of foam rubber and was very pliable; the other was made of wood covered with a thin layer of the same foam rubber so that the two looked identical except when manipulated.

The screen directly in front of the infant had two slots through which an experimenter's hands could be thrust to provide the display. They were centered, side by side, 22 cm apart. The experimenter wore black gloves and was trained to manipulate the objects simultaneously so that the speed of movement was approximately equal. Both were gripped at either end of the long axis. One (the hard one) was rotated around the vertical and horizontal axes in arcs of about 15 degrees to provide a series of perspective transformations; the other was squeezed and released rhythmically. The moving display was approximately 27 cm from the infant's eyes, slightly above eye level. The test was divided in halves. For each infant, one half the time the familiarized object was displayed to the infant's right, the other half on its left. Each of these displays lasted 30 sec. Half the infants had the familiarized object presented first on the right, and the other half had it first on the left. The dual test was necessary to control for side bias, since at 4 weeks infants do not always have good head control.

Looking time to one side or the other was monitored by an experimenter concealed behind the screen, who watched the infant's eyes through a peephole in the screen. She pressed one of two button boxes while the infant's gaze was on one side or the other. Looking times were recorded on a portable Rustrak event recorder. In most cases, three experimenters were present; when only two were present, the observer was kept ignorant of either the substance of the familiarized object or the position of each object during the preference test.

Results
The results of interest in this experiment were the infants' looking preferences. When total looking time for the combined test periods was considered, the proportion of looking time for the novel substance was greater for 23 of the 32 infants (significant at $p < 0.1$ by a binomial test). The mean proportion of time spent looking at the novel substance was .605; at the familiar it was .395. This difference is significant, $t(31) = 2.915$, $p < .0066$. An analysis of variance with substance, side (right or left), test order (first or second), and sex as factors showed none of these factors to be signifi-

cant. Means for the groups familiarized on the soft or the hard substance show the same trend as the overall mean. For infants familiarized on the soft substance, mean proportion of time looking to the novel was .571; to the familiar it was .429. For infants familiarized to the hard substance, the mean proportion of looking to the novel was .639; to the familiar it was .361. Proportion of looking time to the novel substance was .553 on test 1; it was .666 on test 2.

The location and duration of first looks, although a very informative measure for older subjects, was not considered useful at this age because of possible side bias resulting from poor head control and long reaction times.

Discussion

These data support the conclusion that by 1 month infants may detect information for substance that is accessible intermodally, as indicated by the preference for looking at the novel display following oral haptic familiarization. It will be noted that the displays were identical in appearance except for type of motion, which was typical of the movement of a rigid object in one case and of a deformable one in the other. We were not able to obtain qualitative data on mouthing the two substances in this experiment, as we would have liked. There is evidence that babies do show some differentiation in oral exploration (Alegria & Noirot, 1982; Allen[2]), although it has not as yet been related to differences in substance.

General Discussion

All three experiments converge to show that intermodal information about substances, carried by differentiating motions, is picked up by infants, very likely by 1 month of age. But why did the older infants look preferentially at the familiar substance whereas the younger ones showed a preference for looking at the novel one? Many factors may constrain the preference (see Meltzoff, 1981). The explanation may rest in some developmental change. It has been suggested that very young infants show a familiar preference (Meltzoff & Borton, 1979), or that preference is related to duration of familiarization and that younger babies need more time to achieve familiarity (Rose, Gottfried, Melloy-Carminar, & Bridger, 1982). Neither of these explanations fits the present case. Perhaps older babies have a stronger tendency to unify multimodal experiences; Bahrick (in press) found that babies detected an intermodal invariant specifying substance (heard and seen) and looked preferentially at a film depicting the event just heard. Her subjects were 4 months old.

An alternative explanation should be considered. It has been suggested that similarity of the preference situation to the familiarizing one may affect the choice of familiar or novel (Rolfe & Day; 1981; Ruff, 1981). In Experiments 1 and 2, movies rather than real objects were presented for the visual preference test. The objects and their substances were not actually the same; they were pictured in a film raised slightly above the subject's eyes, whereas the felt object was a solid "thing" resting on the table. Both films were novel, but one offered the same invariant information for identifying a substance that feeling it could provide, and a tendency to unify two impressions, gained visually and haptically, was apparently strong. To put it another way, the infant detected an intermodal invariant, a very important accomplishment for economy of perceiving and eventual comprehension of an external world with permanent distinguishing properties of things. In Experiment 3, the visual display consisted of real solid objects of the same length and only slightly greater in diameter than the ones mouthed. There were no distinctive visual features except the motions, which were also relevant for the haptic experience and served to differentiate the substances in both cases. Motion is in any case very attractive to young infants. It seems reasonable to hypothesize that the novel motion caught their attention.

However the preference for a novel display versus a familiar display is to be explained, our experiments converge toward the conclusion that detection of intermodal invariant information for substances that are rigid or elastic is possible in young infants. It is likely that this information can be detected without previous association of unimodal experiences.

A final pair of questions arise that invite speculation: What is perceived? What is the nature of the correspondence when an intermodal invariant is detected? Gibson's (1979) ecological approach to perception hypothesizes that what is perceived, even very early in life, is the affordance of something, although exactly what affordances are perceived undoubtedly changes developmentally. Affordance refers to actions—what can be done with something. Is it, perhaps, the affordance of the substances that is perceived in unimodal presentations, either haptic or optical, that accounts for the correspondence we take for granted in normal multimodal perceiving?

Notes

1. We wish to thank Lorraine Bahrick and Ryan Bliss for their very active and creative participation in this research. Description of procedures that were tried and found unworkable are available in a previous report to the Spencer Foundation. We are also indebted to Janet Weinstein and Patty Phillips for coding of tapes and assistance in running subjects. This research was supported by a grant from the Spencer Foundation.
2. Allen, T. W. *Oral-oral and oral-visual object discrimination.* Paper presented at the third International Conference on Infant Studies, Austin, Texas, March 1982.

References

Alegria, J., & Noirot, E. On early development of oriented mouthing in neonates. In J. Mehler, M. Garret, & E. Walker (Eds.), *Perspectives on mental representation*. Hillsdale, N.J.: Erlbaum, 1982.

Bahrick, L. E. Infants' perception of substance and temporal synchrony in multimodal events. *Infant Behavior and Development*, in press.

Gibson, E. J. The concept of affordances in development: The renascence of functionalism. In W. A. Collins (Ed.), *The Minnesota symposia on child development*, Vol. 15: *The concept of development*. Hillsdale, N.J.: Erlbaum, 1982.

Gibson, E. J., Owsley, C. J., & Johnston, J. Perception of invariants by five-month-old infants: Differentiation of two types of motion. *Developmental Psychology*, 1978, 14, 407–415.

Gibson, E. J., Owsley, C. J., Walker, A. S., & Megaw-Nyce, J. Development of the perception of invariants: Substance and shape. *Perception*, 1979, 8, 609–619.

Gibson, J. J. The *ecological approach to visual perception*. Boston: Houghton Mifflin, 1979.

Gottfried, A. W., & Rose, S. A. Tactual recognition memory in infants. *Child Development*, 1980, 51, 69–71.

Meltzoff, A. N. Imitation, intermodal coordination, and representation in early infancy. In G. Butterworth (Ed.), *Infancy and epistemology*. Brighton: Harvester Press, 1981.

Meltzoff, A. N., & Borton, R. W. Intermodal matching by human neonates. *Nature*, 1979, 282, 403–404.

Rolfe, S. A., & Day, R. H. Effects of similarity and dissimilarity between familiarization and test objects on recognition memory in infants following unimodal and bimodal familiarization. *Child Development*, 1981, 52, 1308–1312.

Rose, S. A., Gottfried, A. W., Melloy-Carminar, P., & Bridger, W. H. Familiarity and novelty preferences in infant recognition memory: Implications for information processing. *Developmental Psychology*, 1982, 18, 704–713.

Ruff, H. A. Effect of context on infants' responses to novel objects. *Developmental Psychology*, 1981, 17, 87–89.

Soroka, S. M., Corter, C. M., & Abramovitch, R. Infants' tactual discrimination of novel and familiar tactual stimuli. *Child Development*, 1979, 50, 1251–1253.

Walker, A. S., Gibson, E. J., Owsley, C. J., Megaw-Nyce, J., & Bahrick, L. Detection of elasticity as an invariant property of objects by young infants. *Perception*, 1980, 9, 713–718.

31

The Concept of Affordances in Development: The Renascence of Functionalism

Eleanor J. Gibson

This paper is included because it marked an important occasion. The symposium took place in the fall of 1980, only a little more than a year after the publication of James Gibson's The Ecological Approach to Visual Perception. *That book presented the first lengthy discussion of the concept of affordances. The symposium was an opportunity to introduce the concept to developmental psychologists, relate it to its historical background, and show how it might profitably be applied to developmental research and theory. Here the paper has been drastically cut by removing the sections on the history of functionalism and the description of several other experiments so as to introduce only the concept itself and a major illustrative experiment.*

At the time the paper was written, no research at all had been published under the term "affordance," although earlier work existed that could be cited as relevant: most particularly, the work by Walk and myself on the visual cliff, which examined perception of the affordance of a surface of support by crawling infants and many other animals, and the work by William Schiff on perception of imminent collision, or "looming" (Schiff 1965). Schiff had observed responses to a looming shadow in a number of animals. A few years later, several experimenters observed responses to looming in human infants. The paper that follows describes an experiment performed by John Carroll and myself, the first undertaken exclusively in an effort to study perception of affordances. We sought to determine whether the avoidance response to a looming event was affected in an adaptive fashion when the looming object contained an aperture rather than constituting an obstruction. The distinction seemed to pose a truly diagnostic question as to whether the infants' action was guided adaptively by the event presented, indicating perception of the contrasting affordances. In recent years, more experiments have been performed on perception of affordances, and the questions asked have

In W. A. Collins (ed.), *The Concept of Development. The Minnesota Symposium on Child Psychology*, Vol. 15. Hillsdale, N.J.: L. Erlbaum, 1982, 55–81.

been formulated much more specifically to reflect the concept's reference to an animal-environment fit. There have been experiments on perception of apertures, in fact, asking whether an animal perceives the exact fit of the aperture in relation to its own size (Warren and Whang 1987, Palmer 1987). The concept of affordances has been sharpened and its theoretical value enhanced greatly by this later research, but I think the emphasis here on the functional nature of the concept and its place in psychology was important for its acceptance by many developmental psychologists.

It is a matter of common agreement among scientists that not many ideas are new. Physicists find new particles, evolutionary biologists and geneticists move toward new models of speciation and evolutionary change (Lewin 1980), but the discoveries and new views always have a past. Still, over the decades or at least centuries, science progresses, sometimes in spurts and sometimes slowly, to new understandings. Often, this happens because a way of viewing the phenomena of some scientific discipline, once discarded as worn out and unproductive, appears in a new light; reclothed and fresh, it points the way out of traps in which our thinking had become stalled and stereotyped, allowing us to take a naive look at what we are trying to understand, unfettered by paradigms that had slowly taken the place of the original problems.

My chapter focuses on a concept that is new and fresh, with great possibilities for offering insights into development. The concept is that of affordance, taken from a way of thinking about perception and the world to be perceived that was recently described by James Gibson in his last book, *The Ecological Approach to Visual Perception*. This way of thinking has a past in the early flourishing of a peculiarly American psychology, the psychology of functionalism, as opposed to the structuralism of the British empiricists and many German psychologists, which found its ultimate elaboration and also its nadir in Titchener's laboratory.

Functionalism declined in the finally fossilized and unproductive blind alley of S-R theory. But its earlier beginnings tie in remarkably well with modern notions of ecology and the mutual, reciprocal relations of living creatures and their environments. So does the concept of affordance.

> The *affordances* of the environment are what it *offers* the animal, what it *provides* or *furnishes*, either for good or ill. The verb *to afford* is found in the dictionary, but the noun *affordance* is not. I have made it up. I mean by it something that refers to both the environment and the animal in a way that no existing term does. It implies the complementarity of the animal and the environment. The antecedents of the term and the history of the concept will be treated later; for the present, let us consider examples of an affordance.

If a terrestrial surface is nearly horizontal (instead of slanted), nearly flat (instead of convex or concave), and sufficiently extended (relative to the size of the animal), and if its substance is rigid (relative to the weight of the animal), then the surface *affords support*. It is a surface of support, and we call it a substratum, ground, or floor. It is stand-on-able, permitting an upright posture for quadrupeds and bipeds. It is therefore walk-on-able and run-over-able. It is not sink-into-able like a surface of water or a swamp, that is, for heavy terrestrial animals. Support for water bugs is different (J. J. Gibson 1979, 127).

The description just given sounds like a physical description, and so it is. But notice that it is also relative to the animal. The properties that define the affordance have unity only "relative to the posture and behavior of the animal being considered." The mutuality of the affordances of the environment and the behavior of the animal is the essential thing. J. J. Gibson (1979) continues:

An important fact about the affordances of the environment is that they are in a sense objective, real, and physical, unlike values and meanings, which are often supposed to be subjective, phenomenal, and mental. But, actually, an affordance is neither an objective property nor a subjective property; or it is both if you like. An affordance cuts across the dichotomy of subjective-objective and helps us to understand its inadequacy. It is equally a fact of the environment and a fact of behavior. It is both physical and psychical, yet neither. An affordance points both ways to the environment and to the observer (p. 129).

Notice that the animal's behavior and perception are both involved here. The animal behaves in accordance with the affordances of the environment, and this depends on his perceiving them. We are at once concerned, as psychologists, with what he can do and also with what he can perceive. Acting appropriately implies perception of the affordances offered. As a developmental psychologist, a rather grand program immediately opens up before me: I need to find out what the environment offers in the way of affordances—how to describe them, what the appropriate behaviors are—and also whether and when they are perceived as affordances.

Perceiving an affordance implies perception that is meaningful, unitary, utilitarian, and continuous over time to the extent that environmental events that pertain to the observer may require. To what extent must young creatures (human or otherwise) learn to perceive them? And if they must learn, how is it done? Affordances are not invented or read into events by the perceiver. They are there to be perceived. A lever affords facilitation of moving something, even in the case of a small child who is as yet ignorant of its utility. He simply does not perceive its affordance. (Material deleted here.)

The Developmental Study of Affordances

Some affordances seem to be peceived, by some animals, without the necessity of learning of any kind. A newly hatched chick perceives the peckability of a bit of grain at once. Spalding's (1875) swallows perceived the open vistas for flight paths despite having been reared inside a small box. But as for human creatures, we know little or nothing about the development of perception of affordances. It has been fashionable for psychologists, in our recent past at least, to assume that all the meanings (in the sense of information for action) that I have been calling affordances must be learned through association with action, though there has been little agreement about how that might happen. Luckily, the present state of our technology for studying perceptual development in infancy is sufficient to permit us to pursue serious investigations of how perception of various affordances develops. The question I ask is this: Where there is invariant information that specifies an object, a place, or an event, and affords information for action, is the affordance detected by an infant? If so, when, and how does the perception of affordances develop? It makes sense to begin with affordances of events involving objects, surfaces, and properties like substance that seem to be basic for the young human creature. The direct way of asking the question is to choose a significant event for display, in which invariant information for the environmental event can be specified, and to see whether appropriate behavior ensues. Does the infant act in accord with the specified consequences (in the sense that the final trajectory of the ball is specified for the catcher earlier in the transforming flight path)?

A less-direct way of asking my question is to look for appreciation of intermodal relations in an event. Affordances have intermodal consequences that imply abstract relations. Knowledge of these, if it can be demonstrated, implies perceived meaning, not mere sensory processing of proximal stimuli. Evidence of this kind is more controversial, I admit.

The Affordance of a Surface of Support

About 20 years ago, Richard Walk and I devised an experimental setup that we dubbed a "visual cliff." We were set on investigating the detection of what we referred to as depth at an edge, and the method had two great advantages. The information for differentiating affordances (though it never occurred to us then to use that word) was easily specified, and the opportunity for behaving appropriately (or inappropriately) was available.

The cliff offers, as I would now put it, information for a solid surface of support for the animal on the near side, but not the far. The two surfaces are specified by optical information for gradients of texture, and by transformations in the ambient array when the animal moves its head or locomotes. Perspective transformations of the patterned texture specify that the surface is rigid, and the depth of the dropped surface on the far side is specified by occlusion of texture under the edge between the two as the perceiver moves his head. Information supplied by disparity gradients may also be available.

The main thing is that there is information for a surface that is "walk-on-able," that can be stepped on or crawled on, on one side, but for a place that does not afford support or affords falling off on the other. Precocial animals like chicks and baby goats have been shown to perceive these affordances at once, and so do rats that have been reared in the dark for an appreciable time. Human infants mostly perceive the affordance by the time they can locomote (crawl) on their own.

Whether human infants could perceive the depth at the edge before they were able to crawl was a moot question for some time. In an effort to answer it, Campos and his colleagues (Campos et al. 1978) decided to use a different measure of the baby's responsiveness, the change in its heart rate when it was placed on a Plexiglas surface and allowed to view a surface affording support directly under it, as compared with one 4-1/2 feet below. The notion was that if the baby perceived danger when there was no underlying surface of support, its heart rate should accelerate as compared with the "safe" side, indicating an emotion of anxiety. Infants under five months gave no indication of an accelerated heart rate, but, in fact, there was a relative deceleration, a change that is generally thought to accompany rapt attention in infants. Indication of acceleration began to appear only after about nine months, well after most infants respond appropriately in the cliff situation.

This disjunction of action and a presumed indicator of emotion underlines another aspect of affordances. They are not the attachment to a perception of feelings of pleasantness or unpleasantness. They are information for behavior that is of some potential utility to the animal. A road may afford crossing (if the lights are green), but it does not necessarily give one pleasure to observe this, especially if one does not wish to cross the road. I doubt that a mountain goat peering over a steep crag is afraid or charged with any kind of emotion; he simply does not step off. Many people do become afraid of heights at some point, but this fear is probably learned long after motor patterns for responding appropriately to surfaces of support have developed. This point has been clarified recently in some elegant research by Rader and her colleagues (Rader, Bausano, and Richards 1980).

Graspability and Palpability: Affordances of Objects

Objects and the substances they are made of have innumerable affordances, but one of the simplest ones to describe and to observe in an infant is graspability. An object of a certain size (not too big and not too small in relation to the infant's hands), not too far away for the length of the baby's arms, and having the property of substantiality—that is, more or less opaque and rigid—provides optical information in the ambient lighted array for graspability. Size, distance, and texture are optically specified in well-understood ways, as is opaqueness as contrasted with transparency. Optical information for rigidity is specified when slight movements of the object occur.

This information must be detected by an infant for an object's affordance of graspability to be observed. We can note that it has been when an infant reaches appropriately for an object and adjusts the shape of its hands during the reach so as to grasp it. There has been considerable research on reaching and grasping in recent years, with some disagreement as to the time of onset of successful reaching and grasping. But the evidence now is fairly conclusive that by three months or so, infants do not reach toward an object that is too far away or not of a graspable size. Field (1977) tested infants at two and five months with objects of varied sizes at variable distances. At two months, infants distinguished objects that were too far away from ones within reach by appropriate arm adduction (even when the retinal image was held constant). At five months, there was evidence of adjusted reaching for objects at variable distances. Bruner and Koslowski (1972) varied the size of objects presented to infants from two and a half to five months. Objects of graspable size were differentiated by different arm and hand movements by three months. Objects within reach but too large to grasp were approached with different hand and arm movements than ones of graspable size.

It is even more interesting to consider the affordance of a moving object. Infants are notoriously very interested in moving things and watch them attentively as neonates. But when are they perceived as something graspable, when the information of velocity and trajectory must be perceived, as well as that for size, substantiality, and so on? There is available some remarkable research on the baby as a catcher by von Hofsten and Lindhagen (1979). They presented seated infants beginning about fourteen weeks with an attractive moving object (a fishing lure). It was mounted on the end of a sort of boom that swung round on a pivot so that it came occasionally within the baby's reach. Infants successfully reached for and caught this object at about eighteen weeks, the same time that they had mastered reaching for stationary ones. Von Hofsten (1980) later analyzed the infants' arm movements during reaching, over the period from eighteen to thirty-six weeks of age. The movements improved in skill over this time, becoming more economical (fewer separate small movements) and more ballistic. But even at the beginning, the babies put a hand out to catch the object *not where it was seen at a given instant* but *where it would be*, predicting the object's trajectory. Later on, some of the infants used a hand to trail the object and chase it, speeding up for the catch, but I am most impressed by the earliest reaction, being ready for the catch in the right place at the right time. Von Hofsten's (1980) results imply a basic human capacity to coordinate one's behavior temporally with external events, as he says: "to foresee in one's actions future locations of moving objects." The timing consideration is overwhelming proof, it seems to me, of a perceived affordance.

Objects not only afford (or do not afford) grasping; they afford activities having to do with variable properties of the substance they are made of, properties discoverable by palpating but also potentially visible when the object is moved or palpated in appropriate ways. Of course, surfaces have substantial properties too, even when they are not surfaces of detached objects. Some substances afford walking on or pounding with or being pounded; others afford drinking or bathing; and others afford squeezing and all kinds of contact comfort. We refer to them by such terms as rigid, fluid, elastic, or spongy. Information for perceiving these substances visually, in particular the difference between rigid and elastic substances, is given only by motion. These are important properties of things at a very early age. The earliest activities of a baby include a lot of chewing and mouthing and, a little later, a lot of throwing and banging. I have been very interested in early differentiation of the affordance of rigid as contrasted with deformable elastic substances and with some young colleagues have done a number of experiments on their detection (Gibson, Owsley, and Johnston 1978; Gibson et al. 1979; Walker et al. 1981). (Material deleted here.)

Obstacles and Passages: Affordances of Events

There is an experimental situation, the so-called looming experiment, in which the perceived affordance is that of an imminent collision to be avoided. The information for this event was described by James Gibson thirty years ago when he suggested that optical information for the spatial layout consisted of spatiotemporal flow fields rather than a sequence of static retinal images (*Visual World*, 1950). In a paper on visually controlled locomotion (Gibson 1958), he wrote:

> Approach to a solid surface is specified by a centrifugal flow of the texture of the optic array. Approach to an object is specified by a

magnification of the closed contour in the array corresponding to the edges of the object. A *uniform* rate of approach is accompanied by an *accelerated* rate of magnification. At the theoretical point where the eye touches the object, the latter will intercept a visual angle of 180°; the magnification reaches an explosive rate in the last moments before contact. This accelerated expansion in the field of view specifies imminent collision, and it is unquestionably an effective stimulus for behaviour in animals with well-developed visual systems. In man, it produces eye blinking and aversive movements of the head, even when the stimulus is a harmless magnification of a shadow on a translucent screen (p. 188).

In 1965, Schiff published a monograph describing research on looming with several species of animal (monkeys, fiddler crabs, frogs, chicks, kittens, and an occasional human). The loom was produced with a shadow cast on a screen, and the inverse transformation, a minification of the shadow, was used as a control. The subjects all demonstrated some form of avoidance behavior, however different their visual and response systems, to the flow pattern of accelerated magnification.

Some years later, researchers began to study the sensitivity of human infants to optical information for impending collision. Bower, Broughton, and Moore (1970) reported that very young infants responded with avoidance behavior that included head withdrawal, eye widening, and raising the hands between the object and the face. Both a real approaching object and a magnified shadow were displayed. Ball and Tronick (1971) reported similar behavior in one-month-old infants with both types of display and compared the collision condition (symmetrical expansion) with an asymmetrical optical expansion pattern that provided information for a "miss" course. The infants in this case tracked the display to the side rather than exhibiting avoidance or withdrawing. But a differential heart rate, showing acceleration to the collision display and not to withdrawal, occurred only with older infants after eight months. Avoidance responses, in this case as well as with the cliff, are apparently not necessarily accompanied by physiological indicators of fear or anxiety.

Since that time, a number of experiments using more refined response measures have been performed with looming displays, and careful longitudinal comparisons have been made (reviewed by Yonas 1981). Yonas' own experiments on sensitivity to optical information for collision have made particular use of blinking, a response that can be very reliably observed, and have been extended to the study of preterm and postterm infants, as well as full-term ones (Petterson, Yonas, and Fisch 1980). The latter experiments provided evidence that maturation plays an important role in the development of the perceived affordance of optical information for impending collision. Defensive blinking to appropriate displays was advanced in postterm six-week-old infants as compared with full-term infants at six weeks.

Research of my own with John Carroll extends the usefulness of the concept of affordance in the analysis of how appropriate ways of acting develop in response to optical information about the layout of the environment. The paragraph I quoted from Gibson (1958) described the information for approach of an object as "magnification of the closed contour in the array corresponding to the edges of the object." But this is only part of the story. There are obstacles with which one may collide, but there are also paths that open up and afford locomotion through a passageway. In both cases, there are contours or edges, but the affordance for locomotion varies with the presence or absence of other information. Quoting Gibson (1958) again:

> In short, the lay of the land, the jumping-off places, the interspaces, barriers and obstacles, as well as the level stretches, are given by the geometry of the optic array. Depending on the locomotor capacities of the animal, this terrain provides definite possibilities or impossibilities for crawling, walking, climbing and the like. And if the animal can discriminate the textural variables it can discriminate among potential paths for locomotion. A potential path is a stretch of surface extending away from the animal which affords the kind of locomotion for which the animal is equipped. A barrier or obstacle is a surface which does not afford locomotion (p. 192).

This description emphasizes the role of textural variables, but Gibson had not yet combined this variable with information deriving from flow patterns produced as a creature moved forward along a path or toward an obstacle, or as an obstacle or a contour around an opening moved toward him/her. What is the optical information for approaching an opening that has to be steered through, as opposed to an obstacle with the same contours that will bar locomotion and afford collision? According to Gibson (1979), when an opening is to be entered, movement toward it is accompanied by "opening up of a vista," by "magnification or gain of structure inside the contour and not loss outside" (p. 234). As a barrier is approached (or an obstacle approaches one), it occludes more and more of the background structure until it is lost entirely at 180°.

Our experiment undertook to contrast these two situations with infants as subjects. Do infants, before they achieve independent locomotion of any kind, differentiate between a path ahead that provides an opening vista and might afford passage from an obstacle that progressively occludes more and more of the background structure, even as its own textured structure is magnified? To put it another way, if a rectangular contour is approaching or approached by an animal, when is it perceived as affording a barrier that makes stopping obligatory and when is it perceived as a vista, an opening, or aperture that affords passing through? What is the information for the affordance in either case, and when is the affordance detected?

We chose to present the two situations in the form of something moving toward the infant, as is done in the looming experiment. An obstacle or an aperture of the same measurements was moved toward the stationary subject. The optical flow pattern of accelerated expansion of the contour as it approached is the same as if the infant approached it, and deletion or accretion of background structure would also be the same. The optical expansion pattern of the contour of the obstacle and of the aperture would be identical to one another. Panels providing an obstacle or an aperture condition were moved toward an infant in approach trials and were moved away in withdrawal trials. The infants' behavior was recorded on videotape, and pressure of the subject's head against a foam rubber headrest was measured. The subjects in this experiment were approximately three months old.

The infant sat at the rear of a booth surrounded by curtains on three sides, all textured with the same pattern. A flat table extended in front of the subject. At the far end of the booth could be placed either of two movable panels, both covered with the same textured material as the walls of the booth, so that, when flush with the rear wall, they covered it and tended to fade into it. Movement of either panel resulted in optical information for edges at the contours of the obstacle or the opening. The panels were supported on invisible carts that were moved toward or away from the subject by an unseen experimenter, at a constant velocity. A panel's approach trip began at the rear wall and ended just short of the infant's face. The movement of the panel lasted approximately six seconds.

Each infant took part in four conditions of the experiment: (1) ten trials with the obstacle approaching (Obstacle Approach); (2) which were alternated with ten trials with the obstacle withdrawing; and (3) ten trials with the aperture approaching (Aperture Approach); (4) alternated with ten trials with the aperture withdrawing. The order of the main condition (obstacle or aperture) was alternated from one subject to the next.

The results indicated that these infants definitely differentiated between the two approach conditions, although no infant cried or became alarmed as the obstacle approached (this finding agrees with all the more recent research on looming, which the obstacle condition resembled in its arrangements). The results of change in head pressure are especially interesting. We calculated a mean curve of head pressure change for every infant in all four conditions, and also a composite group curve for each of the four

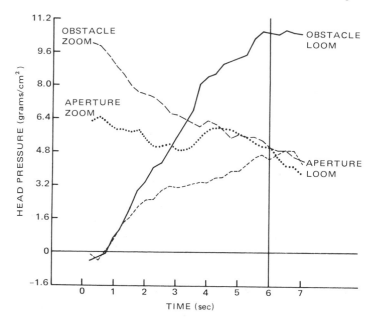

Figure 31.1

conditions. The group curves may be seen in the figure. Approach trials in both main conditions are grossly different from withdrawal trials, with positive slopes for approach (increasing pressure of the head against the headrest) and negative slopes for withdrawal, where the infants' postures relaxed and backward head pressure was released. However, curves for the two approach conditions differ from one another. Head pressure increases very rapidly in the "Obstacle Approach" condition, rising steeply until the cessation of the panel's movement. In the "Aperture Approach" condition, head pressure increases for the first three seconds of the panel's movement and then shows little change. Typically, infants in this condition seemed to track the top edge of the opening upward at first, but, as it came closer, they turned their heads toward a side of the opening.

Regression coefficients were calculated for the slopes of each of the four mean curves for all the individual infants, and these bear out the group trends. For example, the coefficient of the positive slope for "Obstacle Approach" is higher than for "Aperture Approach" for twelve of the sixteen infants. In an analysis of variance peformed on these coefficients, the effect of approach condition was significant ($p = <.018$), but the interaction of condition and order was not, so the two conditions differed no matter which came first.

Differences in head pressure are only part of the story, however. A more complex pattern of behaviors differentiated the two approach conditions. The videotapes of each infant were analyzed and coded for a number of different behaviors. Behaviors that differed significantly and reliably in frequency of occurrence (more frequent for the obstacle's approach) were reaching toward the panel, excited movement, arms up, head turned to avoid, anticipation, frowning, and head withdrawal. Blinking came close to significance. Two behaviors, head turning to track and passive interest, were noted significantly more often as the aperture approached. Reaching and touching were especially notable as the obstacle approached, frequently with pressure exerted on the surface of the obstacle. The beginning of the reach more often resembled the "placing" response of a kitten extending its forepaws as it is moved toward a surface, than a defensive response of hands raised before the face.

Altogether, the patterns of behavior and the differences appeared to be appropriate indicators of the affordances of the two situations, approach of an impassable surface or obstacle in one case and a vista or passageway in the other. Potential paths for and barriers to locomotion may be differentiated early in life, before self-initiated locomotion has begun. (Material deleted here.)

Conclusion

Development is best viewed in the context of an organism in a relationship of mutuality with its environment. Perception serves the function of keeping an animal in touch with the information in its environment about affordances for actions, like going places and making use of surrounding objects in ways that serve its needs. Evolution of the species has done a lot to provide an individual with the means for accomplishing this, but in the development of an individual, we need to study the way these means are refined by ongoing differentiation of perceived affordances, of actions, and the way the two are related.

A functionalist perspective keeps in mind the utility of actions for supporting a creature's needs. But the creature, human in the case that interests me most, is at once an actor and a perceiver. He cannot act adaptively without perceiving the affordances of his habitat. But on the other hand, he cannot perceive effectively without acting. We are, even as infants, active seekers of information, and as we perform actions, we put ourselves in a position to obtain more information. The flow of perceiving and acting is continuous and unbroken.

This point brings me to another, very important, facet of a functionalist view. It shuns atomism in any form. It does not seek components or final particles of any kind, whether stimuli, or sensations, or memory traces, or responses. The flow of information around us that our environs provide is continuous, and the things that are specified, the surfaces and places and people, are unitary and meaningful. It is the meanings that we need to extract. The complementarity of the animal and its environment is a whole and must be studied as such. The more we try to decompose this complementarity by looking for elements, the more likely we are to sacrifice the meanings we are looking for.

It is a sort of corollary of these points that we should try to study development in the most lifelike possible surroundings. That does not mean that we should shun the laboratory, but rather that we should make conditions of our experiments as much like real ones as possible. The research I have been describing seems to me to do that by attempting to simulate real situations without sacrificing control. I have already alluded to the program of research that this perspective encourages. The study of affordances of the things and places of the world, how they are perceived and lead to action is the way to proceed. Primitive affordances in the young infant are being studied, and some appear to be tuned in innately, but perception is bound to action, and most affordances must be detected in the course of action. New actions become possible, as development progresses, and thus new information for affordances is continually becoming available.

The old functionalists were essentially pragmatists, and at one point this pragmatism led to formulation of the goal of psychology as the prediction and control of behavior. I have never liked this slogan, because it was not clear who was going to do the controlling. It is control of one's own behavior that is important. Behavior occurs in an environment, and adaptive control requires perceiving the affordances of that environment.

References

Ball, W. A., and Tronick, E. Infant responses to impending collision: Optical and real. *Science*, 1971, 171, 818–820.

Bower, T. G. R., Broughton, M. M., and Moore, M. K. Infant responses to approaching objects: An indicator of response to distal variables. *Perception and Psychophysics*, 1970, 9, 193–196.

Bruner, J. S., and Koslowski, B. Visually prepared constituents of manipulatory action. *Perception*, 1972, 1, 3–14.

Campos, J. J., Hiatt, S., Ramsay, D., Henderson, C., and Svejda, M. The emergence of fear on the visual cliff. In M. Lewis and L. Rosenblum (Eds.), *The development of affect*. New York: Plenum, 1978.

Dewey, J. The reflex arc concept in psychology. *Psychological Review*, 1896, 3, 357–370.

Field, J. Coordination of vision and prehension in young infants. *Child Development*, 1977, 103, 48–57.

Garcia, J. Tilting at the paper windmills of Academe. *American Psychologist*, 1981, 36, 149–158.

Gibson, E. J., Carroll, J., and Ferwerda, J. Differentiation of an aperture as contrasted with an obstacle under conditions of optical motion. In *Final Report to the Spencer Foundation*. August 1, 1980.

Gibson, E. J., Owsley, C. J., and Johnston, J. Perception of invariants by 5-month-old infants: Differentiation of two types of motion. *Developmental Psychology*, 1978, 14, 407–415.

Gibson, E. J., Owsley, C. J., Walker, A., and Megaw-Nyce, J. Development of the perception of invariants: Substance and shape. *Perception*, 1979, 8, 609–619.

Gibson, J. J. *The perception of the visual world*. Boston: Houghton-Mifflin, 1950.

Gibson, J. J. Visually controlled locomotion and visual orientation in animals. *British Journal of Psychology*, 1958, 49, 182–194.

Gibson, J. J. *The ecological approach to visual perception*. Boston: Houghton-Mifflin, 1979.

Heidbreder, E. *Seven psychologies*. New York: Century, 1933.

Hofsten, C. von. Predictive reaching for moving objects by human infants. *Journal of Experimental Child Psychology*, 1980, 30, 369–382.

Hofsten, C. von. and Lindhagen, K. Observations on the development of reaching for moving objects. *Journal of Experimental Child Psychology*, 1979, 28, 158–173.

Hruska, D., and Yonas, A. Developmental changes in cardiac responses to the optical stimulus of impending collision. *Paper presented at the meeting of the Society for Psychophysiological Research*, St. Louis, October 1971.

James, W. *Principles of psychology*. New York: Holt, 1890.

Johansson, G., von Hoftsten, C., and Janssen, G. Event Perception. *Annual Reviews of Psychology*, 1980, 31, 27–63.

Koffka, K. K. *Principles of Gestalt psychology*. New York: Harcourt, 1935.

Köhler, W. *The mentality of apes*. New York: Harcourt, 1925.

Lewin, R. Evolutionary theory under fire. *Science*, 1980, 210, 883–887.

Murchison, C. *Psychologies of 1930*. Worcester, Mass.: Clark University Press, 1930.

Petterson, L., Yonas, A., and Fisch, R. O. The development of blinking in response to impending collision in preterm, full-term, and postterm infants. *Infant Behavior and Development*, 1980, 3, 155–165.

Rader, M., Bausano, M., and Richards, J. E. On the nature of the visual-cliff avoidance response in human infants. *Child Development*, 1980, 51, 61–68.

Ryan, T. A. Dynamic, physiognomic, and other neglected properties of perceived objects: A new approach to comprehending. *American Journal of Psychology*, 1938, 51, 629–650.

Schiff, W. The perception of impending collision: A study of visually directed avoidant behavior. *Psychological Monographs*, 1965, 79 (Whole No. 604).

Spalding, D. A. Instinct and acquisition. *Nature*, 1875, 12, 507–508.

Spelke, E. Infants' intermodal perception of events. *Cognitive Psychology*, 1976, 8, 533–560.

Spelke, E. *Intermodal exploration by 4-month-old infants: Perception and knowledge of auditory-visual events*. Ph.D. thesis, Cornell University, 1978.

Spelke, E. Perceiving bimodally specified events in infancy. *Developmental Psychology*, 1979, 15, 626–636.

Tolman, E. C. *Purposive behavior in animals and men*. New York: Century, 1932.

Walker, A. S. *The perception of facial and vocal expressions by human infants*. Ph.D. thesis, Cornell University, 1980.

Walker, A., Gibson, E. J., Owsley, C. J., Megaw-Nyce, J., and Bahrick, L. Detection of elasticity as an invariant property of objects by young infants. *Perception*, 1980, 9, 713–718.

Yonas, A. Infants' responses to optical information for collision. In R. N. Aslin, J. Alberts, and M. Peterson, (Eds.), *Sensory and perceptual development: Influences of genetic and experiential factors*, 1981.

32

Detection of the Traversability of Surfaces by Crawling and Walking Infants

E. J. Gibson, G. Riccio, M. A. Schmuckler, T. A. Stoffregen, D. Rosenberg, J. Taormina

This paper records the results of a program of experiments on perception of the affordance of a surface with regard to locomotion—in other words, its traversability. The method is directly descended from my old studies with the visual cliff; this time, we built what we referred to as walkways, with interchangeable surfaces. The particular affordance investigated has to do with substance—what the surface is made of—and so is also related to the previous investigations of detecting rigidity of objects optically and haptically. A new question is introduced that has to do with the concept of affordances—that is, the influence of the particular action to be performed in relation to the environmental property that is required to support it. The concept of affordance holds that the utility of an environmental support must be relative to the structure and dynamic properties of the organism involved in an interaction with the environment. The shoulder width of a walker, for example, would define the minimal width of an aperture so as to afford passing through it; the weight of an animal would limit the surfaces that might bear it; and its manipulatory action system would determine whether it could pick up berries or hold a spoon. Likewise, the level of development of an animal of a given species would constrain the affordance of environmental supports for certain actions such as jumping, even when the species at maturity is capable of such an interaction.

Whether an animal perceives the affordances for acting appropriately, in agreement with both environmental and organismic constraints, is a question for research (see Newell [1986] for a useful discussion of constraints on development of perception and action). It is also essential to ask what the information for the affordance is, and how the animal picks up that information (if it does). We asked these questions with regard to infants in early stages of locomotion, comparing infants who were only capable of crawling with infants who had begun to walk.

Journal of Experimental Psychology: Human Perception and Performance, 1987, 13, 4, 533–544.
Copyright 1987 by the American Psychological Association. Reprinted by permission of the publisher.

Walking requires maintaining bipedal balance, which is a difficult task on a pliant surface. We asked whether walkers would distinguish between rigid, highly supportable surfaces and deformable ones, and whether they explored the surfaces actively to obtain information about their properties. Do walkers differ from crawlers, perform actions that crawlers do not, given a newly available means of locomotion that sets new constraints? Are they aware of the capabilities, or lack of them, of their own systems, in relation to the supportability of a surface to be traversed?

Many experiments were performed over a period of five years. Some experiments not reported here have to do with other features of the surface, such as its opacity and its integrity as regards "holes." Others have to do with possible use of secondary sources of information like the opportunity to watch a toy or a tool performing on a surface so as to indicate the surface's supportability. Some of these experiments are reported briefly in Gibson and Schmuckler (1989). The major outcome of all these experiments was the evidence of active spontaneous exploration on the part of infants and use of it in an adaptive fashion to capitalize on the affordances the environment offers.

In four studies we investigated the perception of the affordance for traversal of a supporting surface. The surface presented was either rigid or deformable, and this property was specified either optically, haptically, or both. In Experiment 1A, crawling and walking infants were presented with two surfaces in succession: a standard surface that both looked and felt rigid and a deforming surface that both looked and felt nonrigid. Latency to initiate locomotion, duration of visual and haptic exploration, and displacement activity were coded from videotapes. Compared with the standard, the deforming surface elicited longer latency, more exploratory behavior, and more displacement in walkers, but not in crawlers, suggesting that typical mode of locomotion influences perceived traversability. These findings were replicated in Experiment 1B, in which the infant was presented with a dual walkway, forcing a choice between the two surfaces. Experiments 2, 3A and B, and 4A and B investigated the use of optical and haptic information detecting traversability of rigid and nonrigid surfaces. Patterns of exploration varied with the information presented and differed for crawlers and walkers in the case of a deformable surface, as an affordance theory would predict.

How does anyone decide whether an unfamiliar surface stretching ahead over the ground is safe for travel by foot, by car, by ski, or by any other mode of transportation?[1] Particularly, how does a young member of the human species, newly ready to undertake self-initiated and self-propelled locomotion, detect the properties of a surface that make it safe to traverse? Is adult tuition necessary? Reinforcement by trial and error? Or is information for traversable properties detected, and if so, when does this occur? What is the relation between perception and action in the novice perceiver–actor?

The questions relate to the concept of affordance (E. J. Gibson, 1982; E. J. Gibson, 1984; J. J. Gibson, 1979). According to Gibson (1979), what is perceived first and foremost is utility for action—what an event or the layout of the environment or an object offers for doing something, either for good or ill. The concept refers to the unique relation between the potential actions of an animal and some aspect of its environment such as a place (e.g., a cave, which may be entered and will afford shelter), an object (e.g., a stone, which may be grasped or hurled), or an event (e.g., a wave, which may be "ridden" or may engulf an animal). Objects, places, and events that provide support for adaptive actions for some animals may not for others of different size, bodily structure, and organic requirements. The relation is an ecological one, the result of the evolution of an animal in a given niche. The relation is real, not simply "in the eye of the beholder," and it may not be perceived by the animal. In some instances, perception of an affordance may be innate, in the sense that the animal detects information for it in an optical or other array and acts appropriately in a way characteristic of its species (e.g., defensive or avoidance activities of many animals in response to a "looming" object or shadow); but it may be learned, as would be the affordance of a tool for prodding something out of reach or for operating as a lever. The information for an affordance is twofold: There must be information specifying properties of the thing perceived and also information about relevant capacities and structural constraints of the perceiver. A good example that has been studied experimentally is the affordance of stair-height for climbing (Warren, 1984). To perceive the optimal stair-height, the perceiver must detect not only information for the height of the riser but also the constraints imposed by his or her own stature. This apparently is done so well that the relation can be described mathematically and is predictive for an adult climber of stairs. In the experiments to be described, two classes of subjects were observed: infants capable of crawling but not walking and infants capable of walking. Bipedal locomotion, as compared with crawling on four limbs, imposes constraints that may change the affordance of a surface for traversal. We were interested to know whether infants whose motor development had attained bipedal locomotion acted differently than ones capable of crawling only, depending on a surface's affordance for traversability. Will they perceive surface properties differently, in relation to their affordance for an action of which they are newly capable?

The information available for perceiving the traversability of surfaces is potentially manifold. There may be optical information for a surface's rigidity or elasticity and for discontinuities such as holes or obstacles. The degree of rigidity and weight-bearing properties of a surface's substance may be detected haptically by exploring the surface with a hand or with a foot or a tool. Events that we witness, such as impact of an object striking a potential surface of support, can provide dynamic optical and acoustical information about the traversability of a surface. In a familiar situation most of us rely heavily on barely attended optical information for guiding locomotion, but in a strange place or under unusual climatic conditions, we actively obtain information from all the available sources.

In this research we investigated perception of traversability in infants making independent trips in an unfamiliar environment. The overall plan was to put young ambulatory infants in a novel situation where surfaces varying in properties defining traversability or nontraversability stretched between the infant and a customary objective (a parent). We observed the infant's spontaneous behavior before embarking on a trip over the surface, including latency to leave a starting position, the exploratory behavior (both visual and haptic), and the displacement (evasive or playful) behavior that occurred, as well as the manner of locomotion once the trip was undertaken. Both crawling and walking subjects were observed when presented with surfaces having different affordances for walking as compared with crawling.

The rigidity of a surface—its resistance to deformation—was chosen as the property to be focused on in the experiments to be reported.[2] This property was of particular interest for several reasons. It can be specified both optically and haptically, permitting an analysis of what information specifying an affordance is used. Earlier research (Gibson, Owsley, & Johnston, 1978; Gibson, Owsley, Walker, & Megaw-Nyce, 1979; Gibson & Walker, 1984) showed that even precrawling infants can discriminate differences in rigidity of objects that can be mouthed or handled. Here we asked whether the affordance of rigid and nonrigid surfaces was detected with respect to locomotion. The following experiments systematically vary the deformability of a surface, the sources of information that specify its deformability, and the locomotor development of the infant subjects. We asked whether the infants differentiated these surfaces behaviorally in both exploratory and executive actions, whether they employed appropriate means of detecting the relevant information, and whether an infant's locomotor development (crawling or walking) was related to differential behavior on surfaces specifying rigidity versus nonrigidity. We reasoned that maintaining upright posture and walking would be difficult on a deforming surface (weight must be supported and balance maintained on one foot as the other is lifted and moves forward), whereas it would be feasible on a rigid surface. Crawling, with four limbs to support the weight as the infant progressed, would be feasible on both types of surface. A baby capable of walking was expected to detect the surface's affordance for maintaining balance and moving ahead bipedally, in contrast to one capable only of crawling.

We were especially concerned to observe the infants' exploratory activities when confronted with these surfaces, in addition to their hesitation or lack of it in traversing them. Exploratory behavior of infants in handling and examining objects has been studied and is relatively skillful in infants of the ages we observed (Palmer, 1985; Ruff, 1982, 1984), but we know little about it in the case of a surface to be traversed by an ambulatory infant.

Experiment 1A

Two surfaces were selected for the basic experiment. One (to be termed the *rigid* surface) presented both optical and haptic information for rigidity; the second (to be termed the *deforming* surface) presented both optical and haptic information for non-rigidity. It was hypothesized that (a) infants would tend to embark upon the surface presenting information for good traversability more readily than the one not specifying that affordance, (b) that exploratory behavior would take place and delay embarkation on a surface specifying poor traversability, (c) and that locomotor development would be linked to exploration and detection of traversability of the surface.

General Method

Subjects   Subjects included 16 crawlers and 16 walkers. Ages ranged from 8 to 14 months for crawlers (M age = 10.25 months) and from 10 to 21 months (M age = 14.44 months) for walkers. Two infants did not yield usable data, due to temperamental problems, experimenter error, and/or because they refused to cross either surface, in which case they were replaced. Only babies who could walk at least 10 steps independently were classified as walkers. Subjects were located through birth notices in the local newspaper, letters of explanation were sent to the parents, and finally, telephone calls were made to solicit participation.

Apparatus   Walkways were constructed to hold different experimental surfaces (see Figure 32.1). A walkway was sturdily built of wood, 222 × 104 cm in length and width. Frames at 85 cm above the floor held the experimental surfaces, which could (with one exception) be removed and replaced. A superstructure was built above the frames that held the surfaces. The superstructure on the two long sides had strong, large-meshed nets stretched along the sides for the infants' protection. At one end (the starting position), a low wooden fence padded with foam rubber formed a backing. Curtains hung behind the fence to conceal an experimenter. The

Figure 32.1
Model of the walkway. (The baby's mother stands at the open end; an experimenter stands behind the closed curtains at the entrance. CU = curtain; SP = starting platform; CN = canopy; N = protective nets; VS = variable surface.)

opposite end of the walkway was open. The infant's parent stood at this end. A platform 2 cm high extended 38 cm so as to conceal the experimental surface at the starting position. This starting platform was covered with burlap and was always the same. Over the superstructure was hung an artificial ceiling made of black cloth. The purpose of the ceiling was to permit control of lighting from the sides or below the surfaces. The walkways were built in the center of a large room. On the far side of the walkway was video equipment for monitoring the experiment.

Surface   The *rigid* surface (R) of heavy plywood was covered with a textured, opaque fabric of white, crosshatched by a regular geometric pattern of brown diagonal lines, presenting excellent optical contrast. It stretched tautly over the plywood, presenting an unwrinkled, firm appearance and feeling hard to the touch. Both optical and haptic information for a rigid surface was available, given an actively exploring baby. Manual exploration would provide haptic information, and head movements while looking would provide perspective transformations of the geometrical pattern.

The *deforming* nonrigid surface (W) was constructed of a waterbed covered with the same patterned fabric as the rigid, textured surface (R). It was agitated by an unseen experimenter when it was presented to the infant, giving a "wavy" appearance. The surface yielded to application of pressure, so both haptic and optical information for nonrigidity was available.

Design and procedure   Each infant was presented, once only, with both surfaces, alternating order over subjects. The baby was encouraged to play until it appeared to be comfortable and at ease. The parent then placed him or her on the starting platform in a sitting position, facing the far end. An experimenter remained standing behind the infant, concealed by curtains, while the parent walked to the far end and faced the infant. If the baby did not look immediately at the parent, the experimenter pointed to direct the baby's gaze. The parent was requested to smile at the baby silently for 30 s. After 30 s, if the infant was still on the platform, the parent was signaled to call the baby and urge him or her to come. After 60 s, the parent was signaled to take down a concealed toy (a red plastic ring holding a bunch of metal keys), shake the toy, and continue to urge the baby to come. If the baby still remained on the starting platform after 120s, the trial was terminated. During the procedure on the walkway, the infant was continuously videotaped.

Treatment of results   Because our major data consisted of video-tapes of the infants' behavior in a relatively free situation, it was necessary to develop a procedure for coding behavior from the tapes that was reliable and yet captured the essence of activity that might inform us about the child's perception of surface properties and detection of their affordances. We were particularly concerned with the child's activities before leaving the platform—for example, whether the child simply implored help from the parent or whether the child engaged in his or her own information gathering or testing. Performances of both kinds occurred, but study of the tapes of a pilot study made it clear that the latter kind of activity was more frequent and most likely to prove enlightening for a study of how affordances are detected. Four major categories of activity were adopted: (a) latency to leave the starting platform, beginning when the parent appeared and ending when the child had three limbs off the platform; (b) accumulated duration of visual exploration (scanning over the surface) before leaving the platform; (c) accumulated duration of haptic exploration before leaving the platform (touching the surface was counted as haptic exploration only when accompanied by looking); and (d) *displacement*, a term borrowed from ethological research, to which the present research bears a strong relation methodologically. *Displacement* designates behavior directed away from the "problem" confronting the infant. The child was occasionally playful (playing with the protective nets and rubber bumpers) but often was evasive (e.g., attempting to part the rear curtains and "escape" from the situation). The category of displacement did not include behavior directed exclusively at the parent, such as holding out arms toward her or him, pointing at the surface and looking at the parent, vocalizing with apparent intent to communicate, and so forth.

All tapes were coded independently by two coders, who practiced on pilot tapes before starting to code. Because the behaviors we were concerned with were very easy to observe, training offered no problem. A coder watched the tape over and over, stop-watch in hand, and summed the time an infant spent in the various categories to be coded. When detailed activities were to be coded (such as types of haptic activity, which could be idiosyncratic with respect to a surface), a check list was available. Correlation coefficients were run separately for the four categories to determine interrater reliability. They ranged from .946 to .996.

Results

Mode of locomotion   Of the 16 walkers, 14 crossed the rigid surface to the parent, 9 crawling and 5 walking.[3] Twelve crossed the waterbed surface, all 12 crawling. Of the 16 crawlers, 13 crossed the rigid surface and 11, the waterbed.

Latency to initiate locomotion   Histograms (see Figure 32.2) show the mean latencies to initiate locomotion on the two surfaces. Each pair represents the same subjects. Walkers took relatively longer to initiate locomotion on the waterbed than on the rigid surface, but crawlers did not. Analysis of variance indicated an $F(1, 28)$ of 2.116, $p = .157$, for the main effect of surface. The interaction of surface and motor development was not significant, $F(1, 28) = 1.709$, $p = .202$.

Visual exploration   The mean accumulated time spent in visually exploring the surfaces is graphed in Figure 32.2. There was considerably more visual exploration of the waterbed than of the rigid surface—more than three times as much by the walkers. Analysis of variance indicated a significant

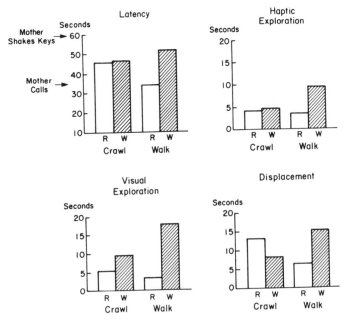

Figure 32.2
Responses of crawlers and walkers to a rigid textured plywood surface (R) compared with a texture deforming surface (W) in Experiment 1A.

main effect of surface, $F(1, 28) = 10.797$, $p = .003$. The Surface × Motor Development interaction was near significance, $F(1, 28) = 3.175$, $p = .086$.

Haptic exploration   The walkers spent more than twice as much time in haptic exploration of the waterbed surface as of the rigid surface, but there was no difference for crawlers. Differences were not statistically significant, however, for surface, $F(1, 28) = 2.308$, $p = .140$, nor was there an interaction with motor development, $F(1, 28) = 1.652$, $p = .209$. There were large individual differences, but some walkers felt the surface intently and in a distinctive manner, pushing it with both hands and putting considerable weight on it. Watching them on the tapes gives the inescapable impression that they were "trying it out." Haptic exploration was coded by two observers for differential use of hands and feet, and type of action. Comparisons across surfaces suggest that there may have been some differentiation by type of haptic exploration. Exploration with the feet was rare, but it did occur with half the walkers on the waterbed (not at all with crawlers, however). Feeling or rubbing the surfaces occurred with more than half of all babies, both walkers and crawlers, and was about the same for the two surfaces. Patting the surface was fairly frequent, but less so on the waterbed. On the other hand, more pushing (putting weight on the surface with both hands) occurred with the waterbed.

Displacement and evasive behavior   The mean time spent in displacement behavior can be compared in Figure 32.2. The waterbed elicited more displacement and evasive behavior in walkers, but less, if anything, in crawlers. Analysis of variance indicated no main effect of surface, $F(1, 28) = 0.727$, $p = .401$, but a very significant interaction between surfaces and motor development, $F(1, 28) = 9.107$, $p = .005$.

Multivariate analysis   In view of the suggested disparity between crawlers and walkers on the waterbed compared with the rigid surface on several measures, a multivariate analysis of variance was performed including all four of the measures. For crawlers considered separately as a group, the four variables taken together did not differentiate the two surfaces, $F(4, 27) = 1.55$, $p = .215$. But for the walkers, the four variables differentiated the two surfaces significantly, $F(4, 27) = 3.59$, $p = .018$. When the two groups (crawlers vs. walkers) were compared, they were differentiated significantly by this analysis, $F(4, 25) = 3.06$, $p = .035$.

The four dependent measures made various contributions to the differences found in the multivariate analyses of variance. Canonical discriminant analyses were run to examine the predictive value of the four measures in differentiating the rigid surface from the waterbed for walkers. Visual exploration made the largest contribution (structure coefficient = .686), displacement was next (structure coefficient = .551), haptic exploration third (structure coefficient = .490), and latency made the smallest contribution (structure coefficient = .324).

The predictive value of the four measures for differentiating walkers from crawlers on the waterbed/rigid comparison showed the heaviest weighting for displacement (structure coefficient = .84), visual exploration second (.54), haptic exploration third (.43) and latency fourth (.41). Displacement may indicate the presence of conflict when a mother tries to entice her child onto an apparently unsafe surface; the waterbed surface evidently looked uninviting to walkers, but not to crawlers.

Discussion

With respect to our first question, whether the surfaces are differentiated behaviorally, the results suggest a qualified yes. As we had expected, the rigid surface, which we adopted as a standard, tended to have a shorter latency for initiation of traversal and elicited a moderate amount of visual and haptic exploratory behavior and displacement activity, as compared with a nonrigid surface (the waterbed) in the case or the walkers. The crawlers, on the other hand, did not differentiate these two surfaces except by somewhat longer visual exploration. This difference is not surprising for an affordance theory, because the waterbed surface affords adequate support for crawling but not for walking. Walking infants differentiated this affordance from that of the rigid surface by all four of our measures, with the difference in age groups supported by a significant multivariate analysis.

Experiment 1B

In this experiment we sought to replicate the trends just observed with a different method. The apparatus was converted to a double-walkway choice situation. A second walkway was built parallel to and joining the original one, and the starting platform was placed centrally and lengthwise, partially straddling the surface of both walkways. A strip of wood (2 in. × 4 in., 5.08 cm × 10.16 cm) continued to the end of the walkways, making a slight (but not impassible) barrier between the two. The baby had to choose one surface or the other in leaving the starting platform, thus giving us a new measure of perceived relative traversability. The parent stood in the center, opposite the baby. Because there was a supporting post exactly in the center between the two walkways, the parent was asked to play a kind or peekaboo, alternating the head from side to side. Otherwise, the procedure followed that of the first experiment. The rigid textured surface was on the baby's right and the waterbed surface on its left. The waterbed was gently agitated as before. There were 32 new subjects;

16 crawlers (*M* age = 11.28 months; range = 9–13) and 16 walkers (*M* age = 13.81 months; range = 11–18). This choice was presented to each subject only once.

Results

Only the walkers (13 out of 16) showed a preference for the rigid surface over the waterbed ($p = .01$ by a binomial test). Seven crawlers chose the rigid surface, 6 chose the waterbed, and 3 did not cross in the 2-min interval. Of 3 walkers who chose the waterbed, none walked. Of the 13 who chose the rigid surface, 7 walked. These results provide converging evidence to support the trends observed in Experiment 1A.

Latencies for leaving the platform are consistent with the ratios of choices; that is, for walkers, latency for choosing the rigid side was short, but for the waterbed side was long. For example, the mean latency for all the walkers who chose the rigid over the waterbed was only 9.5 s, whereas it was 31.3 s for the few (3) who chose the waterbed. For the crawlers, the case was different; times were no longer (in fact, slightly less) for those who chose the waterbed than for those who chose the rigid surface (55.5 s compared with 64.0 s). Times spent in exploration and displacement behavior tended to be shorter, on the whole, than in earlier experiments, probably due to the availability of an attractive alternative. They showed no particular trend.

There was a potential side bias in the W/R (waterbed/rigid) choice, because the waterbed could not be alternated from left to right. For this reason, the W/R condition was repeated with a new group of 16 walkers, with the ends of the walkways reversed so that left–right relations were transposed. Again, there was a preference for the rigid surface (12 out of 16 subjects, $p = .0384$). These results support the findings of Experiment 1A and lead us to conclude that there is evidence for a difference in perceived affordances of a deforming, nonrigid surface, depending on the infants' locomotor development. The walkers perceived the waterbed as a surface that did not afford walking, but the crawlers did not.

Experiment 2

The question of what information the walkers were using to detect the property of nonrigidity was our next focus of investigation. The waterbed presented both optical and haptic information for a deforming surface. The babies could have relied on either of these sources alone. It might be suspected (Hatwell, 1985) that they were making little use of haptic information, even though most of them did actively explore the surface manually. We sought to test the hypothesis that only optical information was effective by covering the waterbed with a Plexiglas surface. It could still be agitated by an unseen experimenter, so that optical information specifying deformation would remain available, but the surface to be traversed would be firm to the touch, thus contradicting the optical information for deformability. Experiment 2 was designed to test this condition.

The experiment was conducted with single walkways, and each infant was presented once with both the waterbed condition (W_R) and the textured rigid condition (R); order alternated from subject to subject. The waterbed was covered with the same fabric as in the standard rigid condition, but the Plexiglas was laid over it, with a space of about 4 cm between the surface of the waterbed and the Plexiglas to allow for deformations of the waterbed. (To an adult with a hand placed on the Plexiglas, the depth difference was intermodally detectable). Plexiglas was also laid over the rigid surface so that the control and experimental surfaces would not differ in slipperiness or reflectance.

The subjects of this experiment were 24 walkers (M age = 15.69 months; range = 11.5–20 months). No crawlers participated, because they had not responded differently to the waterbed and the rigid surface in the earlier studies.

Results
Of the 24 subjects, all 24 crossed the rigid surface, and 22 the waterbed surface when Plexiglas covered them. The same number of infants (7) walked across the two surfaces. They were the same individuals. It would seem that these infants perceived the same affordance for the two surfaces, unlike the previous experiments where no infant walked on the waterbed.

Analyses of variance were performed separately for the four measures, comparing the waterbed surface and the patterned rigid surface. Differences were not significant for any of the four measures, $F(1, 22) = 0.527$, $p = .476$, for latency; $F(1, 12) = 1.304$, $p = .266$, for haptic exploration; $F(1, 22) = 2.156$, $p = .156$, for visual exploration; and $F(1, 22) = 0.643$, $p = .431$, for displacement.

Results for latency, exploration, and displacement are shown in Figure 32.3, along with the data for the comparable conditions in Experiment 1, where the waterbed was not covered by Plexiglas. Data for each experiment are presented in mean difference scores for ease of comparing across experiments. For each infant, its score on the textured rigid surface was subtracted from its score on the deforming surface. The textured rigid surface in each experiment thus served as a comparison surface, so that each child could be its own control. The histograms represent the mean differences for each experiment. Positive values indicate that the measure for the experimental condition exceeded that for the standard (rigid) condition.

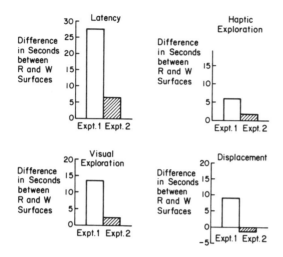

Figure 32.3
Comparison of Experiment 1A—waterbed (W) and rigid (R) surfaces—with Experiment 2—waterbed (W_p and rigid (R_p) surfaces under Plexiglas. (Values plotted are mean difference scores [W−R] and [W_p−R_p]. All subjects are walkers.)

A multivariate analysis of variance was performed on the differences between the standard and comparison surfaces within the two experiments. When the four variables were pooled as predictors in the analysis, the conditions in the two experiments were significantly differentiated, $F(4, 33) = 4.34$, $p = .006$. A canonical discriminant analysis yielded structure coefficients of .75 for displacement, .63 for visual exploration, .33 for latency, and .33 for haptic exploration, the first two having the strongest predictive value.

The comparison between the means of the two experiments does not support a visual dominance hypothesis, that optical information—in this case, for deformability—will determine the perceived affordance and override competing haptic information. The infants apparently detected the rigidity of the Plexiglas surface covering the waterbed by haptic testing and were capable of using the haptic information. However, it is possible that self-initiated change or nonchange in the optic array (change in the case of Experiment I and no change in this experiment) is perceived as a consequence of haptic activity and is attended to as a particularly informative event for discovering the affordance of a surface. It is also the case that haptic and optical information are contradictory in this experiment. The next experiment adopted the strategy of varying optical information without placing it in conflict with haptic. In it we investigated the perception of a surface's affordance when optical information was reduced while haptic information was still available.

Experiment 3A

In this experiment, optical information for a surface's affordance for travers-ability was manipulated by presenting a walkway with a textureless sur-face. Black matte velveteen covered a plywood surface. Lighting was such that no texture was discernible to an adult eye, nor were there any non-homogeneities in reflection. Because inhomogeneity of texture is a major condition for specifying a surface (Gibson, Purdy, & Lawrence, 1955), this surface presented little optical information for either rigidity or nonrigidity. It was contrasted with the textured rigid surface used as a standard in the previous experiments. Because both surfaces were hard to the touch, haptic information could be obtained for their rigidity in each case. The textured surface provided good optical information, whereas the black velveteen textureless surface did not.

The two surfaces were presented in a single walkway, one at a time, following the procedure of Experiment 1A. Subjects were 16 crawlers and 16 walkers; mean age was 10.25 months for crawlers (range = 8–14 months) and 14.63 months for walkers (range = 12–20 months). Five other infants were not included for reasons of experimenter error, refusal to embark on any surface, or temperamental problems.

Results

Mode of locomotion   All 16 walkers crossed the patterned rigid surface, and 14 crossed the black velveteen surface. They crossed the two surfaces walking an equal number of times (6 on each). Fourteen of the 16 crawlers crossed each of the two surfaces.

Latency to initiate locomotion   Figure 32.4 presents histograms for mean latencies to initiate locomotion on the two surfaces. Both crawlers and walkers took longer to embark on the black velveteen surface than on the textured surface. Analysis of variance showed a significant effect of surface, $F(1, 28) = 5.092, p = .032$, but no interaction of surface with motor devel-opment, $F(1, 28) = 0.020, p = .890$.

Visual exploration   Despite the longer latencies for embarking on the black velveteen surface, it elicited no more (in fact, rather less) visual exploration than did the textured surface. This finding suggests that relative optical inhomogeneity (visually perceptible texture) triggers visual attention and exploration. Attention to inhomogeneity as opposed to homogeneity has often been documented by looking-preference experiments with infants (Berlyne, 1958; Fantz, 1958; Karmel, 1969). Analysis of variance indicated

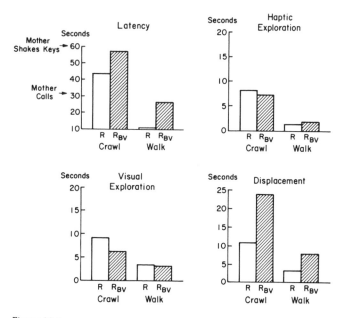

Figure 32.4
Responses of crawlers and walkers to a surface offering good optical and information for rigidity (R) compared with a surface offering good haptic information but poor optical information (RBV).

no difference between the two surfaces, $F(1, 28) = 1.662$, $p = .208$, nor any developmental interaction, $F(1, 28) = 1.72$, $p = .288$.

Haptic exploration   As was the case with visual exploration, the histograms in Figure 4 show that the black velveteen surface elicited no more haptic exploration than did the patterned surface. Analysis of variance indicated no difference between surfaces, $F(1, 28) = 0.028$, $p = .896$, nor any developmental interaction, $F(1, 28) = 0.441$, $p = .512$.

Displacement   Mean times spent in displacement activities on the two surfaces are presented in Figure 32.4. The times for the black velveteen surface exceeded those for the patterned surface. Analysis of variance indicated a significant difference between the two surfaces, $F(1, 28) = 5.926$, $p = .022$. The interaction with motor development was not significant, $F(1, 28) = 1.290$, $p = .266$.

These results suggested, on the basis of longer latencies to embark and greater displacement activity, that the black velveteen surface was unattractive compared with the patterned surface, but there was no indication whatsoever of a difference based on age or motor development. We sought replication of these findings in the next experiment.

Experiment 3B

In this experiment, subjects were presented with the dual walkway to force a choice between the black velveteen surface on plywood and the textured surface on plywood. The procedure was in every way comparable to Experiment 1B. Thirty-two new subjects participated, 16 crawlers (M age = 10.47 months; range = 7.5–15.5) and 16 walkers (M age = 13.94 months; range = 10–17). The side on which the black velveteen surface was presented was alternated from right to left from one subject to the next.

Results

Both crawlers and walkers tended to choose the textured rigid surface in preference to the black velveteen one. Crawlers chose the patterned surface in 15 cases (p = .0003 by a binomial test). Walkers chose it in 11 (p = .0592), while 4 chose the black velveteen surface. Latencies to leave the platform were rather long but followed the same pattern as the patterns of choice: Crawlers choosing the textured surface had a mean of 53.13 s, while those choosing the black velveteen had a mean of 72.5 s; walkers choosing the textured surface had a mean of 30.25 s, while those choosing the black velveteen had a mean of 67.8 s. Times spent in haptic exploration were not long and did not favor either surface. Of the walkers, 6 of the 11 who chose the patterned surface walked on it. Of the 4 who chose the black velvet surface, I walked.

The findings of this experiment support the conclusions drawn in Experiment 3A. Lack of optical information for traversable properties of a surface both delayed locomotion and led to the choice of an alternative surface. The black velveteen surface was clearly unattractive, compared with the patterned surface. Differences in mean age and in motor development of the subjects made no difference, however. The reason for shunning the black velveteen surface was not, therefore, that it was perceived as not affording walking. In fact, a number of the walkers did walk on it (the same number as on the patterned surface in Experiment 3A). There was no information specifying that it was "unwalkable." It would seem, rather, that the ambiguity of the optical information led to indecision (witness the increase in displacement activities). Lack of visually perceptible "surfaciness" apparently leads to wariness in engaging in visually guided locomotion in any form. The role of haptic information was apparently small in this situation. Why? In the next experiments, we varied the kind of haptic information available while retaining the black textureless covering.

Experiment 4A

The last experiments left many questions about the information for traversability and how it is used. Our original hypothesis was that infants would explore a surface actively, obtaining haptic information as well as optical information about the surface's properties. Experiment 2 led us to think that walkers, at least, do so because a rigid transparent cover over the deforming waterbed changed the pattern of results. Yet the babies explored the black velveteen, textureless surface only slightly, and most hesitated to embark on it, despite its rigidity. It is the case that any pressure applied to the rigid surface, whatever its cover, yields no optical consequences (no event-like visible change). Might optical consequences become important, when static optical information is impoverished (as it was in Experiments 3A and s)? Would optical consequences lead to enhanced haptic exploration? Experiment 4A was designed to test this possibility. The waterbed was covered with the black velveteen fabric so that optical information was poor unless haptic exploration was engaged in. The waterbed was presented without agitation (no waves) so that optically it resembled the surface presented in Experiment 3A, when the black velveteen covered plywood. But if the subject applied pressure to it with haptic testing, the surface would ripple and produce inhomogeneities that were easily visible (there were shadows and changes in reflectance, revealing the deforming motion).

Experiment 4A presented this black velveteen surface over a waterbed, without agitation, on a single walkway. Each subject was run with the textured surface over plywood also so that the design was exactly comparable to Experiment 3A. The subjects were 16 crawlers (M age = 9.78 months; range = 9−11.5) and 16 walkers (M age = 14.66 months; range = 13−19 months).

Results

All of the walkers crossed the rigid surface; 14 of the 16 crossed the waterbed. They differentiated the two surfaces by their mode of locomotion. Ten of the 16 walkers walked to their mothers on the rigid surface; 4 attempted to stand up on the waterbed (but didn't walk). Fifteen of the crawlers crossed the rigid surface; 14 crossed the waterbed.

Results for this experiment, accompanied by similar measures for Experiment 3A, are presented in Figure 32.5. The histograms represent mean differences between the textureless black velveteen surface and the comparison, textured, rigid, control surface for each infant, to make possible comparison across experiments. The results are of interest both across experiments (comparison with Experiment 3A), and for a comparison between crawlers and walkers in Experiment 4A.

When Experiments 4A and 3A are compared, it may be seen that the underlying waterbed, despite its lack of optical texture, elicited more ex-

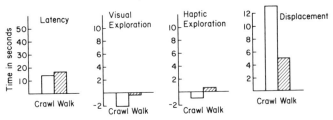

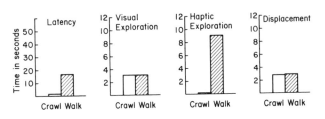

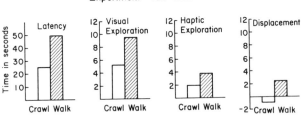

Difference Scores

Figure 32.5
Patterns of exploration with varying haptic and optical information. (All surfaces were covered with black velveteen. In Experiment 3A, black velveteen covered plywood. In Experiment 4A, black velveteen covered a motionless waterbed [no waves]. In Experiment 4B, black velveteen covered an agitated waterbed [waves]. Values are mean difference scores.)

ploratory activity. The difference is most apparent for haptic exploration in the case of the walkers. Visual exploration rose noticeably for both walkers and crawlers. Even a minimal amount of haptic pressure resulted in ripples appearing on the surface, and this optical motion evidently attracted the attention of both groups of infants. The walkers, however, greatly increased the haptic activity and showed increased latency to initiate locomotion, though not more than in Experiment 3A. The crawlers did not increase their latency to embark; in fact, it was less than in 3A. The black textureless surface was apparently less inhibiting to them when some rippling changed the surface. Displacement activity occurred moderately, but was considerably less than in Experiment 3A.

This condition resulted in very large individual differences. The great variability may be attributed to the fact that the surface, unless prodded, provided the same information as the black velveteen over plywood. Haptic activity produced rippling and optical inhomogeneity, but there was a wide range in the time spent in haptic exploration; the range was from 2 s to 115 s in walkers, and from 0.5 s to 44 s in crawlers. Statistical comparison of this condition with the black velveteen over plywood condition, because of this variability, did not yield very significant differences. A multivariate analysis gave nearly significant differences for surface, $F(4, 57) = 2.26$, $p = .07$; and developmental status, $F(4, 57) = 2.41$, $p = .06$. The interaction was not significant. Nevertheless, the pattern of differences looks different for crawlers and walkers and is in line with expectations based on earlier results with the waterbed.

These results suggest that the optical consequences of haptic exploratory activity may constitute important information for detecting properties of a surface for traversability. Overall, crawlers looked at the surface longer in this condition than in Experiment 3A, when no ripples had appeared, but they were not deterred in locomotion by information about the surface's nonrigidity. Walkers, on the other hand, engaged in increased haptic activity, when the underlying surface was a waterbed than when it was rigid, looked longer at the consequences of their activity, and took longer to embark on the surface. Was it really the optical consequences of the haptic activity that were informative for them? We tried to push this question further in the next experiment.

Experiment 4B

In this experiment, the waterbed covered with black velveteen was again compared with the rigid textured surface exactly as in Experiment 4A, except that the waterbed was agitated by an unseen experimenter as in Experiment 1A. Waves were apparent on the otherwise textureless surface upon its presentation to the infant. Subjects were new groups of 16 crawlers (M age $= 10.09$ months; range $= 7-16$ months) and 16 walkers (M age $= 14.72$ months; range $= 9\ 1/2-20$ months).

Results

Results are presented in Figure 32.5, Experiment 4B. The most interesting comparisons are for visual and haptic exploration across the three experiments. When the black surface was presented with waves, visual exploratory activity rose, compared with both the other experiments, particularly in the case of walkers. Haptic exploration, though greater than for the textureless rigid surface, was much reduced for walkers compared with the waterbed presented without waves. The range of time spent in haptic activity in this condition was 0-24 s, with 9 walkers spending less than 5 s. Patterns of exploration have changed from the "no waves" to the "waves" condition. For the walkers, preponderance of visual or haptic exploration has traded. When the optical information for deformation was already good, haptic activity that would produce the information was relatively low; when it was poor, haptic activity that would produce it rose. For the crawlers, the trade-off is not apparent. Looking simply increased when there was something to look at. A multivariate comparison of this condition with the black velveteen over plywood yielded a significant difference for surfaces, $F(4, 57) = 6.85$, $p = .0001$.

The differences ascribable to developmental status showed up again in this condition, although the interaction overall did not attain significance. Walkers showed greater increases in all the behaviors coded than did crawlers, as earlier waterbed results led us to expect. An analysis of variance for latency difference scores yielded a significant difference for walkers, $F(1, 30) = 5.340$, $p = .028$. The same comparison was not significant for crawlers, $F(1, 30) = 0.435$, $p = .515$. Exploratory behavior increased in both cases, as expected, but overall it increased more for walkers.

Fourteen of the crawlers crossed the rigid patterned surface, and 12 crossed the waterbed. Fifteen of the walkers crossed the rigid patterned surface, but only 9 crossed the waterbed. Eight of the 16 walkers in this experiment walked to their mothers on the rigid texture control surface. Two tried to stand on the waterbed but fell. One, after 14 s of haptic exploration, stood up, balanced with arms outstretched and feet wide apart for 90 s, and then carefully walked to his mother (amid applause)—the only one of our many subjects to manage this feat.

General Discussion

As infants become capable of independent locomotion, most actively seek information about an unfamiliar terrain ahead of them that must be traversed to reach a goal. They examine the terrain both visually and haptically, the amount and type of exploration varying with properties of the surface to be traversed, the information specifying these properties, and the child's locomotor development. In line with the concept of affordances, we interpret these results as indicating that infants perceive the traversability of surfaces in relation to the mode of locomotion (crawling or walking) characteristic of their developmental stage and that they do so by actively detecting optical and haptic information that specifies traversability.

Are we, in fact, justified in this interpretation? Four separate experiments confirmed the difference between walkers' and crawlers' responses to the waterbed; unlike crawlers, walkers tended to hesitate longer before crossing it, to choose a rigid, patterned surface as an alternative when a choice was offered, to engage in more exploratory activity when confronted with the waterbed, and to divert their attention away from it to a greater extent. In all four experiments, more walked on the rigid surface than on the waterbed, whereas there was no distinction in mode of locomotion in the black velveteen standard comparisons. But walkers are, in general, older than crawlers. Is this difference in approaching a nonrigid surface due simply to a few months' difference in age? Walking and age are so tightly correlated that we could not, with the number of subjects available to us, separate the two groups while holding age constant, though there was occasional overlapping. Furthermore, mode of locomotion is a dichotomous variable. But age as such is not a causal variable—only biological and cognitive processes and constraints that develop with age could be. The variables that we coded might reflect such constraints. Latency in many tasks decreases with age (although in the case of the waterbed, latency increased). Active exploration might increase with age, and diversion of attention away from the "central" task also might, under some circumstances. Because all of these variables are graded ones, it was possible to correlate them with age.

Using the data from Experiment I A, we ran correlations between age and all four of the coded measures on both the rigid and the waterbed surfaces, for crawlers alone, for walkers alone, and for the two groups pooled, making 24 correlations in all. Of these, only 5 were significant, all of them occurring for the waterbed surface. Two of these were for the walkers alone: with latency, $r = .36$, $p < .05$; with visual exploration, $r = .54$, $p < .001$. Two were for the pooled groups: visual exploration, $r = 34$, $p < .01$; displacement, $r = .26$, $p < .01$. One was for crawlers alone, with haptic exploration, $r = .31$, $p < .05$. Among 24 correlations, a few low but significant ones might be expected to occur at random. The only impressive one of these is the correlation for the walkers with visual exploration, which seems to make good sense in terms of the affordance hypothesis; the older walkers may have learned to engage in more extensive visual examination of a surface in motion as they gained more experience in balancing on two legs. The lack of any correlation between age and exploratory activity on the other surface suggests (a) that development of exploratory activity overall has reached basic competence by the ages tested in this experiment, as we might expect from earlier studies of object exploration, and (b) that differences depend on other factors, such as the task, physical characteristics of the subject, and the situation encountered (in this case a nonrigid surface encountered by subjects characterized by two different modes of locomotion).

During the period of growth between crawling and walking, human infants are presumably developing increasing communicative competence. It was possible, in our experiments, that some infants would watch the parent and solicit reactions or "cues" (Sorce, Emde, Campos, & Klinnert, 1985), despite the fact that the parent was instructed to smile and to urge the infant in a positive way for all the surfaces presented. For this reason, a coding system was devised for what we termed *communicative behavior*. There were three major categories: negative behavior, positive behavior, and commenting. Negative behavior included vocalizations (e.g., saying no), whining or crying while looking at the parent, shaking the head, and stretching out arms toward the parent, as if requesting to be picked up. Only behavior while the infant was on the platform was included (very little occurred during traversal of a surface). Positive behavior included positive vocalizations, such as playful sounds, giggling, and babbling, waving arms and legs, rocking, and smiling. Commenting was any vocalization or pointing that drew the parent's attention to the surface while observing the parent's reaction. These latter gestures were infrequent but unmistakeable. The infants did not appear to be seeking the parent's advice (the parent was, after all, urging them to come), but calling attention to some feature of the surface.

These behaviors were coded for all subjects and all surfaces in Experiments 1A and 3A. The differences between the rigid textured surface and the other two (the textured waterbed and the black velveteen over plywood) were small and insignificant, indicating the relative noninformativeness of this kind of behavior compared with behavior directed toward exploring the surface or with displacement. Frequency of communicative behavior did not differentiate the surfaces, not did the quality of it, that is, whether it was positive or negative in affective tone. It appeared from these data that communicative behavior in this situation is more likely attributable to characteristics of the individual infant. Differences between crawlers and walkers were apparent only in a few instances of words (e.g., saying no) in walkers. They were not related to a particular surface.

Could the difference between crawlers and walkers be interpreted in terms of familiarity and novelty? Recent research on infants has generally capitalized on a preference for attending to a novel display rather than a highly familiar alternative or for attending again (dishabituating) to a novel display after repeated presenation has led to habituation of another. Infants' reactions to places also show preferential exploration of new territory (Rheingold & Eckerman, 1969; Ross, Rheingold, & Eckerman, 1972; Ross, 1974). We designed the present research to capitalize on the predilection to attend to something novel by constructing special walkways and by selecting all the surfaces presented to be ones with which our subjects would be unfamiliar (unlike any in their homes or the usual places visited), so as to elicit attention to them. The fact that order effects were consistently found, even though not significant in any one experiment, supports the notion that this happened. But unfamiliarity as such seems insufficient to explain the difference between crawlers and walkers on the waterbed. Parents were asked whether their child was familiar with a waterbed, and when this was the case, the infant was run in a different condition. Rigid and nonrigid surfaces are in a sense familiar (e.g., a hard piece of furniture as opposed to human flesh or a pillow), but a new one must be identified by available information—whether optical, haptic, or other—and this process may require exploration and observation of its informative consequences. However unfamiliar, there were few indications that the waterbed elicited fear in either group of infants; rather, the visual attention seemed to indicate interest in the wavy appearance.

It might be argued that cognitive ability increases between 10 and 14 months of age and somehow has produced an attitude of greater caution or wariness in the older infants. This suggestion cannot easily be refuted and can be made more than plausible by considering how cognitive processes might interact with changes caused by maturation of a new action system. That achievement of locomotion plays a pervasive role in development has been suggested by other authors (Acredolo, 1978; Campos & Bertenthal, 1984; Gustafson, 1984). But as Gustafson pointed out, it may not be considered a cause apart from the experiences it produces. Bipedal locomotion, especially in its early stage, produces unique experiences having to do with maintaining equilibrium (an active process, even in adults). Every stagger or waver produces optical flow patterns that control activities essential to maintaining balance while engaged in locomotion, especially on a "compliant" surface (Lee & Aronson, 1974; Lee & Lishman, 1975; Stoffregen, Schmuckler, & Gibson, in press). These experiences undoubtedly have two further consequences: (a) to enhance visual attention to the stability of the surface of support and (b) to make the infant aware of his or her own physical structure and action system. Both consequences can be seen in our videotapes where a walker, having observed the waterbed in the choice experiment, monitors his or her steps and the floor with great care in advancing even on the firm side of the double walkway. This behavior, along with manual exploration of a surface, contributes to the process of learning an affordance not hitherto appreciated, or even relevant for the crawler. Infants learn about the capacities of their own action system in relation to environmental supports. Another way of saying this is that the crawlers may be quite able to discriminate the difference between a rigid and a deforming surface (as other research has indeed suggested) but do not relate the distinction to the action system that involves locomotion. The onset of walking and the constraints imposed by bipedal locomotion lead to discovery of the relevance of rigidity of surfaces for controlling stance and locomotion.

In the case of the black velveteen surface on a rigid base, both crawlers and walkers showed longer latencies and greater displacement activity than on the patterned rigid surface. Should this result be interpreted as perception of an affordance? Might the results be interpreted as a case of misperceiving the surface as specifying depth and thus engaging in avoidant behavior, as in the case of the visual cliff (Gibson & Walk, 1960; Walk & Gibson, 1961)? There are some distinct differences between the two cases. In the case of the cliff, there is a transparent surface through which the floor, at a depth of (about) 4 ft (122 cm) below, can be clearly seen. There is ample optical information for depth at an edge, a "falling-off" place. Infants in this situation engage in a large amount of manual exploratory behavior, as we observed in preliminary experiments with a transparent surface on the walkway, although the optical information proved compelling. But the black velveteen surface has no information to specify a falling-off place. There is information for some kind of a surface, because it is continuous and bounded on all four sides, but the absence of texture and inhomogeneities impoverishes optical information for properties of the surface. The result seems best interpretable as wariness in embarking on a surface where optical specification of properties of the surface is weak, whatever the mode of locomotion.

The issue of visual dominance over haptic information that comes up in these experiments is a classic and lively one. A seeing adult does appear to depend more heavily on visual information for guidance than on haptic; the hand is used more often as an "executive organ" than as a perceptual one (Hatwell, 1985). Adults are nevertheless capable of using it for obtaining information, and so are infants by the second half of the first year. The hand may be used in the service of the eye to produce optical consequences. It may be that (when vision is available) haptic exploration waits on visual, requiring inhomogeneity in the optic array to be elicited, and that the haptic activity that ensues is particularly useful if it produces secondary optical consequences, such as visible deformation. But complex patterns of exploration evolve in the course of development, often involving every kind of information available. Consider the patterns of exploratory behavior in a 10-month-old infant handed a bell. The baby looks at the object, reaches for it, brings it to his mouth for haptic exploration, pulls it out and looks at it again, shakes it and listens to the sound, and so forth. This pattern is remarkably well coordinated and maximally informative about the properties of the object. It is instructive to compare this highly effective pattern of exploring objects with patterns of exploring a surface. A surface cannot be picked up, put in the mouth, and transferred from hand to hand. But as we have seen, there is, as in object exploration, a kind of canonical pattern, integrated and multimodal. It is not properly described as stimulation of two receptive systems; it is, rather, an active, coordinated pattern, and it varies depending on the kind and amount of information available in the scene. As in object exploration, the pattern is flexible and is varied to explore potential affordances, tending to optimize the information available. Haptic exploration especially varies from delicate brushing to a strong two-handed push. A third point stands out: The exploratory pattern is obviously in the service of action, as the walkers' differentiation of rigid and deformable surfaces tells us, and it results in a kind of perceptual learning. There is no overall role of dominance for haptic or optical information. Both are actively obtained, but circumstances alter the role of the two, both for obtaining the information and in its control over action. Experiments 4A and B showed an exchange in the frequency of haptic and visual exploration; haptic was more prominent when no "waves" were simply presented to the infant, but visual exploration was more prominent when they were. When the black velveteen surface was rigid (Experiment 3A), exploration of both kinds was at a minimum. There was little to look at, and haptic exploration had no optical consequences. Control of action, however much dependent on results of information getting, is a different problem, and it is closely linked to perceived affordances for executive action, such as going somewhere either on all fours or else on two legs. In the case of a visual cliff with no visible surface at the perceiver's feet, the affordance for crossing is negative. (This is true even for most adults, however knowledgeable they may be about the presence of Plexiglas.) In the case of an optically impoverished, opaque, rigid surface, hesitation is the usual case, but eventually locomotion ensues. In the case of a deforming surface, both optical and haptic information is sought, but action is controlled in relation to motor development and affordance for the type of action. Rather than engaging in speculation over dominance, it seems more profitable to study just how exploratory activity develops and how its consequences are used under varied circumstances for controlling action.

The picture this research suggests of the maturing infant confronted with a novel surface is one of a creature prepared (perhaps through evolutionary history) to attend to a surface that must be traversed; to explore it actively, both visually and haptically, depending on the information available; to observe the consequences of self-initiated exploration; and to detect in this way its affordances for locomotion in a particular mode. It suggests that perception, exploration, and action are closely intertwined in development. The theory of affordances highlights the interconnection of these capacities and thus provides a valuable perspective on development.

Notes

1. This research was supported in part by National Science Foundation Grant BNS-8209856 and National Institute of Child Health and Human Development Grant 1RO1HD 17207-02 to Cornell University and the first author. The authors are greatly indebted to Ulric Neisser, Nancy Rader, Elizabeth Spelke, and James Cutting, all of whom gave invaluable advice.
2. Other properties, such as extension and continuity, are investigated in further experiments.
3. The number of walkers on the rigid surface might have been greater if infants had not all been placed on the platform seated (whether or not they wished to stand), because there was no handhold to pull up on when rising.

References

Acredolo, L. P. (1978). Development of spatial orientation in infancy. *Developmental Psychology*, 14, 224–234.

Berlyne, D. E. (1958). The influence of the albedo and complexity of stimuli on visual fixation in the human infant. *British Journal of Psychology*, 56, 315–318.

Campos, J. J., & Bertenthal, B. I. (1984). The importance of self-produced locomotion in infancy. *Infant Mental Health Journal* 5, 160–171.

Fantz, R. L. (1958). Pattern vision in young infants. *Psychological Record* 8, 43–47.

Gibson, E. J. (1982). The concept of affordances in development: The renascence of functionalism. In W. A. Collins (Ed.), *The concept of development* (Vol. 15, pp. 55–81). (The Minnesota Symposium in Child Psychology). Hillsdale, NJ: Erlbaum.

Gibson, E. J. (1984). Perceptual development from the ecological approach. In M. E. Lamb, A. L. Brown, & B. Rogoff (Eds.), *Advances in developmental psychology* (Vol. 3, pp. 243–286). Hillsdale, NJ: Erlbaum.

Gibson, E. J., Owsley, C. J., & Johnston, J (1978). Perception of invariants by five-month-old infants: Differentiation of two types of motion. *Developmental Psychology*, 14, 407–415.

Gibson, E. J., Owsley, C. J., Walker, A. S., & Megaw-Nyce, J. S. (1979). Development of the perception of invariants: Substance and shape. *Perception* 8, 609–619.

Gibson, E. J., & Walk, R. D. (1960). The "visual cliff" *Scientific American*, 202(4), 64–71.

Gibson, E. J., & Walker, A. S. (1984). Development of knowledge of visual–tactual affordances of substance. *Child Development*, 55, 453–460.

Gibson, J. J. (1979). *The ecological approach to visual perception*. Boston: Houghton-Mifflin.

Gibson, J. J., Purdy, J., & Lawrence, L. (1955). A method of controlling stimulation for the study of space perception. The optical tunnel. *Journal of Experimental Psychology*, 50, 1–14.

Gustafson, G. E. (1984). Effects of the ability to locomote on infants' social and exploratory behaviors: An experimental study. *Developmental Psychology* 20, 397–405.

Hatwell, Y. (1985, July). *Motor and cognitive function of the hand*. Paper presented at the meeting of the International Society for the Study of Behavioral Development, Tours, France.

Karmel, B. Z. (1969). The effect of age, complexity, and amount of contour on pattern preferences in human infants. *Journal of Experimental Child Psychology, 7,* 339–354.

Lee, D. H., & Aronson, E. (1974). Visual proprioceptive control of standing in infants. *Perception & Psychophysics, 15,* 529–532.

Lee, D. H., & Lishman, J. (1975). Visual proprioceptive control of stance. *Journal of Human Movement Studies, 1,* 87–95.

Palmer, C. (1985). *Infants' exploration of objects: Relations between perceiving and acting.* Unpublished dissertation, Institute for Child Development, University of Minnesota, Minneapolis, MN.

Rheingold, H. L., & Eckerman, C. O. (1969). The infant's free entry into a new environment. *Journal of Experimental Child Psychology, 8,* 271–283.

Ross, H. S., Rheingold, H. L., & Eckerman, C. O. (1972). Approach and exploration of a novel alternative by 12-month-old infants. *Journal of Experimental Child Psychology, 13,* 85–93.

Ross, H. S. (1974). The influence of novelty and complexity on exploratory behavior in 12-month-old infants. *Journal of Experimental Child Psychology, 17,* 436–451.

Ruff, H. (1982). The role of manipulation in infants' responses to invariant properties of objects. *Developmental Psychology, 18,* 682–691.

Ruff, H. (1984). Infants' manipulative exploration of objects: Effects of age and object characteristics. *Development Psychology, 20,* 9–20.

Sorce, J. F., Emde, R. N., Campos, J., & Klinnert, M. D. (1985). Maternal emotional signaling: Its effect on the visual cliff behavior of 1-year-olds. *Developmental Psychology, 21,* 195–200.

Stoffregen, T A., Schmuckler, M. A., & Gibson, E. J. (in press). Use of central and peripheral optical flow in stance and locomotion in young children. *Perception.*

Walk, R. D., & Gibson, E. J. (1961). A comparative and analytical study of visual depth perception. *Psychological Monographs, 75*(No. 15).

Warren, W. H. (1984). Perceiving affordances: Visual guidance of stair climbing. *Journal of Experimental Psychology: Human Perception and Performance, 10,* 683–703.

33

Exploratory Behavior in the Development of Perceiving, Acting, and the Acquiring of Knowledge

Eleanor J. Gibson

The last paper that I include has to do with the biggest issue, the origins of knowledge. The terms perception and learning were introduced many centuries ago as ways of talking about this issue. How do we know about the world? How does the knowledge we presume to have of it get into our heads? Philosophers first asked these questions (and still do). Developmental psychologists would seem to have a special obligation to formulate researchable hypotheses, not just broad theories, to address the questions as scientists. There have always been two camps among psychologists, those who favor a rationalist approach, believing human creatures to be endowed with some form of knowledge or principles about the world they are going to encounter, and those who favor a more empirical approach. The former group has an obligation to provide a theory of how innately given constraints could come about and operate, and the latter has an obligation to show how learning about the world could occur.

Most psychologists today would insist that we now know better than to draw a sharp line between nativists and empiricists because both have something to say. Nevertheless, the difference in emphasis is still very strong, the nativists prompted often by the Cartesian arguments of Chomsky, and the empiricists by fresh evidence that the development of the nervous system is strongly affected by early encounters with the world.

I favor the empiricist camp in that I want to show how infants can obtain knowledge about the world, use it in interactions with the environment, and thereby enrich their knowledge further. But to do this, I have to be a nativist too. I have to accept what I think are facts: that an infant comes equipped with the systems needed to find out what goes on in the world; that all infants are spontaneously motivated to do so; and that ontogenetic development is a spiral of maturing systems (perceptual, motor, neural), and give and take with the world. All the ingredients are essential, so the total system we have to deal with is an

Excerpts from *Annual Review of Psychology*, vol. 39, 1988, 1–41. Reproduced, with permission, from the Annual Review of Psychology, Vol. 39, © 1988 by Annual Reviews Inc.

animal-environment system. Evolution—the development of the species—lies behind this, the operation of a similar spiral. What I do not accept is that a "theory" of the world comes ready-made. Constraints on the kind of theory that an animal will form do exist, however, in the size, powers, and perceptual systems that the species has evolved as a biomechanical, sentient being. Functions that are required to survive and thrive in a given niche are provided for and must run their course in a developmental interchange with the world.

A few years ago I was invited to prepare an article for the Annual Review of Psychology on any topic I chose. I chose development of exploratory activity because I think the origins of learning about the world and of the early development of cognition are to be found there. Exploratory activity is perceiving and acting literally rolled into one—a perceptual search, embodied in information-seeking action. This view leads to testable hypotheses about acquisition of knowledge by infants as yet without speech: for example, that emergence of manual exploratory activity leads to acquiring knowledge about objects (Eppler 1990), or that emergence of bipedal locomotion leads to testing properties of surfaces of support, resulting in knowledge about the larger layout (Gibson et al. 1987).

Implications for Perception, Action, and Cognition

The point of view of this essay is functional, in the old sense, but also in a modern sense that incorporates systems theory. I assume that both information about the environment and action occur over time in a sequence related by some common factor. A sequence of acts termed exploratory will have some outcome and will not be random. It will have a perceptual aspect, a motor aspect, and a knowledge-gathering aspect.

Why is exploratory behavior implicit in perception, in fact an essential part of it? The old view of perception was that "input" from stimuli fell upon the retina, creating a meaningless image composed of unrelated elements. Static and momentary, this image had to be added to, interpreted in the light of past experiences, associated with other images, etc. Such a view of perception dies hard, but die it must. There is no shutter on the retina, no such thing as a static image. Furthermore, perceiving is active, a process of *obtaining* information about the world (J. J. Gibson). We don't simply see, we look. The visual system is a motor system as well as a sensory one. When we seek information in an optic array, the head turns, the eyes turn to fixate, the lens accommodates to focus, and spectacles may be applied and even adjusted by head position for far or near looking. This is a point long emphasized by functional psychologists such as Dewey and Woodworth. It was developed in detail by Gibson—e.g., in his experiments on active touch. These adjustments of the perceptual system are often, especially in early life, exploratory in nature because the young creature is discovering optimal means of adjustment. But they may be exploratory even in a skilled observer, because they are used to seek information. We live in interaction with a world of happenings, places, and objects. We can know it only through perceptual systems equipped to pick up information in an array of energy, such as the optical array. Furthermore, time is required for the adjustment of the perceptual system, for the monitoring of the information being acquired, and for the scanning required by most perceptual systems to pick up information (perceiving an object by touching, for example, or locating a sound source through hearing). Information, accordingly, is picked up over time. Thus if a stable world is to be discovered, there must be temporal invariants of some kind that make constancy of perception possible. I take for granted that perceptual acts extend over time. Perceiving and acting go on in a cycle, each leading to the other.

Perception occurs over time and is active. Action participates in perception. Active adjustments in the sensory systems are essential. But action itself may be informative, too. Information about things and events exists in ambient arrays of energy. Actions have consequences that turn up new information about the environment. They also provide information about the actor—about where he is, where he is going, what he is doing. All actions have this property; but it is useful to distinguish *executive* action from action that is *information-gathering*. We tend to think of some perceptual systems and the activities that go on within them as primarily information-gathering. The visual and auditory systems, in particular, seem to have little or no executive function. (There are exceptions. The eyes, for example, are used socially in an executive fashion to signal approbation, displeasure, surprise and so on.) Some systems, on the other hand, have on the surface a primary executive function, such as the haptic systems of the mouth and of the hand. The mouth is used for tasting and testing for substantial properties as well as for sucking, eating, and speaking. The hand is used for examining textures, substantial properties of objects, shape, and location, as well as for holding, carrying, and lifting. Because executive functions like lifting can be informative, the distinction between exploratory and executive actions has sometimes been questioned. But it is a useful distinction for a developmental approach. The possibilities of executive action are minimal in very young infants, but research in recent years has made it clear that exploratory activities are available and are used in functional ways even in the newborn.

Executive actions, such as reaching, grasping, and locomotion, have their own role in perceptual and cognitive development because they change the affordances of things and places, providing new occasions for information-gathering and for acquiring knowledge about what Tolman referred to as the "causal texture" of the environment. Cognition, I suggest, rests on a foundation of knowledge acquired as a result of early exploration of events, people, and things. As the baby's perceptual systems develop, exploratory activities are used to greater and greater advantage to discover the affordances that are pertinent to each phase of development. As new action systems mature, new affordances open up and new "experiments on the world" can be undertaken, with consequences to be observed.

The active obtaining of information that results from the spontaneous actions of the infant is a kind of learning. To say that learning occurs only when actions are repeatedly "reinforced" is to blind ourselves to the most important kind of learning that underlies our accumulation of knowledge about the world and ourselves. Spontaneous self-initiated actions have consequences, and observation of these is supremely educational. Affordances of things generally have to be learned, with the aid of the perceptual systems and exploratory behavior. External reinforcement plays a small role, if any. Intellectual development is built on information-gathering, and this is what young creatures (not only human ones) are predestined to do. They have structures, action patterns, and perceptual systems that are either ready to start doing this at birth or grow into it in a highly adaptive sequence during the first year (in human infants). These activities continue as play through the preschool years and as deliberate learning in later life, but the serious role they fill is most obvious as they are coming into being. Cognition begins as spontaneous exploratory activity in infancy. Piaget said this long ago. But now research puts a new face on the story.

The Course of Exploratory Development: An Overall Perspective

A baby is provided by nature with some very helpful equipment to start its long course of learning about and interacting with the world. A baby is provided with an urge to use its perceptual systems to explore the world; and it is impelled to direct attention outward toward events, objects, and their properties, and the layout of the environment. A baby is also provided with a few ready-to-go exploratory systems, but these change and develop as sensory processes mature and as new action systems emerge. There is an order in this development that has interesting implications for cognitive growth. As new actions become possible, new affordances are brought about; both the information available and the mechanisms for detecting it increase.

Exploratory development during the first year of life occurs as a sequence of phases that build the infant's knowledge of the permanent features of the world, of the predictable relations between events, and of its own capacities for acting on objects and intervening in events. The three phases that I am about to suggest are not stages, in a Piagetian sense. They overlap, change is not "across the board," and absolute timing varies tremendously from one infant to another. They depend heavily in at least one case on growth in anatomical structure. Nevertheless, an order is apparent that gives direction to development and makes clear how perceptual and action systems cooperate in their development to promote cognitive growth.

The first phase extends from birth through about four months. During this phase the neonate focuses attention on events in the immediate visual surround, within the layout commanded by its limited range of moving gaze. Sensory capacities and exploratory motor abilities are geared to this task, and some serendipitous possibilities for preliminary learning about features of the grosser layout exist. Visual attention to objects is minimal, but discovery of some basic properties of objects is made possible by visual attention to motion and by the active haptic system of mouthing. Sounds accompanying events are attended to. It is most impressive that these early exploratory systems, rudimentary as they seem, appear well coordinated.

The second phase, beginning around the fifth month, is a phase of attention to objects. Development of the manual exploratory system makes reaching and grasping possible. By the same time visual acuity has increased, and stereoscopic information for depth is available. Objects, though presented in a static array, can be explored and their affordances and distinctive features learned.

The third phase, beginning around the eighth or ninth month, expands attention to the larger layout, which can only be explored as the baby becomes ambulatory. Spontaneous, self-initiated locomotion makes possible discovery of properties of the extended environment around corners, behind obstacles, and behind oneself. Affordances of places for hiding, escaping, and playing are open for investigation. Watching a two-year-old on a playground is a revelation of attention to affordances of things like swings, ladders, bridges, and ropes.

After the first year, other phases might be identified—e.g., exploring devices that have complicated affordances like mirrors, and tools that must be carried to other objects as well as manipulated. Research is still scanty in this area. There is also the whole domain of speech development, in which exploratory activity plays an extensive role during the first year. This domain I reluctantly leave to the experts.

(Here follow sections on the three phases of exploration, with presentation of the relevant available research. They are omitted from this excerpt.)

Exploration in the Service of Acquiring Knowledge

The Grounding of Knowledge

In the final accounting, what is the significance of exploratory activity and its perceptual consequences? May it not be the essential ingredient for building a foundation of knowledge about the world? Or does intelligence emerge as a separate force that pulls action—even exploratory activity—along behind it? I have not discussed the latter idea at all, but the notion that intelligence develops and action somehow follows along has been fairly prevalent during the so-called cognitive revolution. Beliefs about and representations of the world and the self presumably come first, and actions follow after them. This notion is clearly opposed to the points I have been trying to make. Perhaps knowledge eventually becomes a system of representations and beliefs about the world (and oneself as an inhabitant of it), but it seems to me that representations and beliefs must be grounded by detection of the surfaces, events, and objects of the layout—the "stuff" of knowledge must somehow be obtained from the world. Furthermore, as living beings we act in the world and necessarily interact with the events and furnishings of the layout surrounding us. Our knowledge cannot consist of general abstract properties alone but must relate to the affordances for action that the world provides, not only in general beliefs but also in intimate everyday situations whose ever-changing circumstances demand great flexibility. I have been trying to show that the young organism, as it grows, has the capability to discover what the world affords and what to do about it. The foundations of the organism's knowledge evolve in an orderly fashion, with something new around the corner in each phase in a kind of spiralling evolution. What kind of knowledge could result, other than flexible means of interaction?

Predications About the World
The knowledge that results from learning affordances for action through exploratory activity and observation of its consequences is, in the beginning, probably entirely utilitarian. Meanings may be confined to situations where interactions are occurring and then can reoccur. It seems to me that this utilitarian, early, simple knowledge constitutes the beginning of ability to make predications about the world. For example, objects rest on a ground (but can be lifted from it, if they are the right size and substance). Ground is always underneath them. Some things are in front of other things. Things can be bumped into. Things can move in the surrounding layout. Some things make sounds. Some of these things are responsive (can eventually be categorized as animate). One can oneself control these responses by one's own actions (cooing, smiling). These are simple examples, but with expanding exploratory and action systems they may become much more elaborate as means available through grasping, manipulation, and later locomotion open up new possibilities of learning affordances.

Controlled manipulation accompanied by increasingly mature capabilities of visual observation provides a mechanism for differentiating affordances and qualitative properties of things and thus furnishes the material for categorizing, yielding more refined and more general predications. Locomotion with ensuing exploration of places and territories firms up incomplete knowledge and makes possible predications about the objectivity and permanence of the layout and the moveability of oneself and others. Events, both external and self-perpetrated, present the opportunity for learning about consequences of movement, impact, and applying pressures, and thus provide the foundation for discovering causal relations.

I am not suggesting that predications of the kind I have illustrated have been formulated as anything like verbal propositions. Rather, knowledge has been attained that can function as a basis for further categorization and inference. Learning a vocabulary and a syntax for verbal representation of predications and events is an achievement that presupposes knowledge (something to talk about). It may well have rules of its own, but I doubt that these rules determine or even select what the infant first attends to and discovers about its early environment. I see little profit for the scientist in arguments about the mental representation of knowledge that cannot be talked about, but I think it must be conceded that such knowledge exists, even in adults, and certainly in the preverbal child.

Other questions—e.g., how knowledge is organized—are well worth asking and have a good chance of being answered. An important one has to do with the generalizability of knowledge, sometimes referred to as "domain specificity." After an infant has discovered an affordance pertaining to one action system, will it transfer appropriately across action systems? Is the affordance of a substance detected by mouthing detected as the same when the hands become active in exploring it? Is the differentiation of an aperture and an obstacle by a three-month-old in a looming situation generalized immediately to guiding locomotion by a crawler? I doubt that such transfer is automatic in early life, because new action systems bring new affordances, and some exploratory practice with them seems essential. But the role of practice would diminish as maturation winds down. Proliferation of tasks, however, increases as possibilities of action increase, bringing new opportunities for generalization. So do tasks proliferate with social expectations of caretakers, and these may engender a new kind of domain specificity as "training" by society begins. Still more affordances must be learned and the question of flexibility of generalization over domains can reappear on a new level.

Ontogenesis of Perceptually Based Knowledge
The course of development of perceptually based knowledge (knowledge based on exploratory perceptual systems) is an orderly one, as I have tried to show. As the phases of development evolve in the individual, with a focus in each phase, there is a progressive fanning out. New exploratory systems develop and new action systems emerge, making new tasks (e.g.,

carrying something somewhere) possible. Still, one sees evidence of earlier phases foreshadowing the later ones, as in the case of the aperture-obstacle distinction. The process does not look like disconnected shoots growing out in different directions, but rather like a spiralling course, an echoing of earlier abilities of affordance detection plus strengthened opportunities for discovering new meanings. Perhaps a system of meanings begins its evolution thus.

Differentiation is the key process in the kind of development I have been describing—differentiation of organs of both perception and action, and differentiation of perceived affordances. But the process is always related to the environment—its resources and its constraints. In the case of the looming experiment in the three-month-old, the information in the optical array, an expanding occluding contour increasing at an accelerated rate, has the affordance of imminent collision, calling for such avoidance behavior as the child can muster (head retraction, raising of hands). When a crawler's own locomotion produces an expansion pattern of an object in its path, the information has the affordance of potential imminent collision, but not in the same way, because the crawler can stop or detour. Furthermore, the information, while similar, is not the same. In the case of the approaching object, the expansion pattern characterizes only a part of the total array; but in the case of the infant's advance by way of its own locomotion, the expansion encompasses the total array. The cases call for differentiation, and yet they are closely related; the consequences of failing to perceive the affordance are the same because important environmental conditions are the same. The system that must be referred to for understanding the organization of perceived affordances is not the child's own organism alone, despite its manifold relations between perceptual and action systems, but an organism-environment system. Understanding behavioral and cognitive development requires consideration of both as reciprocal entities, a requirement for both the developing child and the psychologist.

Epilogue: Prospects for a New Approach to Perceptual Learning

Where has this wandering journey led, if anywhere? One might ask this question about the field, of experimental psychology as a whole, as I knew it in the thirties and forties. Its face has changed remarkably to the extent that many who would once have been the rising generation of first-rate experimental psychologists are on the verge of casting off the term, leaving "psychologist" for the clinicians, and rebaptizing themselves "cognitive scientist." They seek the company of other scholars and see their field as interdisciplinary, but the favored companions are now the computer scientists, philosophers, and linguists. The cognitive revolution really turned things around. My own subfields of perception and learning are scarcely recognizable. Only a few hardy perception psychologists still study perception of the real world rather than small displays on computer screens. As for learning, only acquisition of expertise by adults studying something like math seems to be of concern.

I go along with this trend to only a small extent. I'm happy enough to dissociate myself from the clinicians, and I want companions in other disciplines. But I want to associate with the biologists, the people concerned with evolution, the ecologists, and the people studying development. It is the focus on development that deserves the center of the stage, in my opinion, and with it the realization that we are animals living in an environment that we evolved in. We behave in it more or less adaptively to survive. We occupy a niche, like other animals. Descartes was wrong; we are not a sublime species set apart by reason to rule the world and the lower orders (although I admit that humans have done a lot to spoil things for the other species).

Where do I see a path ahead, then? The path I see has been foreshadowed in many ways, as developmental milestones in behavior are, too. That is the way evolution works. The path started with the functional psychology that was so typically American, and flourished for awhile in the learning theories of the thirties and forties. Behaviorism was an important part of the climate for many years, but not Watsonian behaviorism, because it made too many extravagant claims and rested on too few facts. The behaviorist theories of Hull, Tolman, and Skinner were the ones that gained acceptance and followers. But, except for the hard-core Skinnerians, most of that sturdy movement collapsed with the cognitive revolution of the sixties, leaving only a few legacies.

Not all of the foundation of functionalism collapsed, nor all interest in learning. At the same time that many psychologists were being impressed with artificial intelligence and reading Chomsky's review of Skinner's *Verbal Behavior*, a few other more biologically oriented psychologists were uncovering revolutionary facts about animal learning. Unwelcome as the news was to journal reviewers (Garcia, 1981), it turned out that under some circumstances an animal was "conditioned" in one trial; that the "conditioned stimulus" could precede the "reinforcement" by many hours; and that *what* can be learned is specific to the species, its habitat and way of life (Garcia, McGowan, and Green 1972).

A new generation of learning theorists and experimenters has grown up, giving rise to an ecologically oriented learning theory (Bolles and Beecher 1988; Johnston and Pietrewicz 1985). These people study what animals learn naturally under real-life circumstances—foraging for food, staying clear of predators, developing the means of communication. The new approach is rooted in ecology and evolution, and it does not seek to classify behavior as either innate *or* learned. It studies learning during development, instead—not in the adult, but in the growing animal as it learns to survive in its appropriate niche (Johnston 1985).

This approach to learning has not yet been applied to learning in humans, but it is time to do so. The ecological approach to perception has been bearing fruit in studies of development of perception in infants. I believe renewed study of learning in infants, in ecologically natural and appropriate circumstances, is called for and can be profitably combined with study of early perceptual development.

I now see my earlier theory of perceptual learning, published in 1969, as flawed by its concentration on learning by an adult or a child who is already a competent speaker of a language. Learning begins long before any language is available, and before much of any action is. Here is the real role for perceptual learning, and what a lot must go on in just the months before a child can navigate on its own or speak a single word!

Experiments with infants already exist that can be assimilated to this view, showing that infants learn even before performatory actions are possible, making optimal use of their perceptual systems. I describe a few cases of early learning that seem ecologically relevant to a baby's development in a human environment. The examples chosen by no means exhaust the field, but they serve to illustrate its promise. I have selected four cases: (1) learning to recognize faces; (2) learning about bimodal specification of an event; (3) learning about properties of an environmental support; and (4) learning about control of an environmental event by one's own action. Others would be ecologically equally relevant, such as phonological perception or turn-taking in communicative interaction with a caretaker, but as yet there are no studies with infants that tell us much about the kind of learning that goes on. Actually, very few studies tell us a lot about it, but the ones that follow are suggestive.

How early recognition of a human face begins has been a question of interest for a long time, and it inspired a number of studies before very good methods of observing infant perception and learning were achieved. In my 1969 book, I devoted most of a chapter on development of object perception to perception of faces because there was considerable research on it (and nothing much else except perception of checkerboards). I summed it up as follows:

> Development takes the course of first responding discriminatively with crude compulsory fixation on high contrast edges or spots in the field. Then follows gradual extraction of distinctive features of the oft-presented face object, differentiated as individual features only. Later comes noticing of invariant relations between features such as the two eyes in a given orientation in the head; later still, the array of features characterizing a real face as distinct from a dummy's or from schematic drawings is distinguished, with no one feature any longer dominant. Eventually, the unique feature pattern characterizing a particular face is selectively responded to.

I now think that this is all wrong. There have been twenty years of research on infants' perception of faces since 1969. Most of it has been done with photographs, drawings, or schematic faces. Take a brief look at it. Following the lead of ethologists, a number of psychologists thought babies might have a primitive native attention to a human face pattern as a kind of "releaser." In experiments by Fantz (1963) and others, babies were shown schematic drawings of faces to see what they attended to most. Babies preferred to look at the displays with more information, or higher contrast, or certain spatial frequency characteristics until four months or so, when a preference was found for a "face pattern" (a preference for a properly arranged face vs. a scrambled one). Fagan (1979) summarized many studies by himself and others. Certain features seemed to be more important than others (such as hairline and eyes, contrasted with mouth and nose). At five months, specific photographs of subjects of different sex and ages were discriminated (e.g., a man's face paired with a woman's or either of these paired with a baby's). The photographs needed to be upright for this discrimination. Only at seven months did infants recognize a familiarized face and distinguish it from an unfamiliar one when tested with different poses, such as a profile or three-quarter view, following a full face. At seven months, infants could also discriminate photographs on the basis of sex when different photographs were used in the test, providing that several same-sex ones were used in familiarization before the test. Two quite similar faces could be discriminated, provided that several views of the same face were presented during familiarization. Fagan concluded that facial recognition was present at seven months. He thought that this ability was not exclusively for faces but extended to other abstract patterns. This conclusion is correct, I think, for the material employed— two-dimensional, static drawings or photographs. But I suspect that these findings apply only to pictorial perception and give us no basis for a theory of perceptual learning in infants.

It is a notable fact that pictorial perception (that is, getting information *about* something from a picture) has been found to mature at about seven months by other psychologists for other domains. Yonas (e.g., Yonas et al. 1986) found that information for distance or depth in pictures was not extracted until about seven months; Schmidt and Spelke (1984) have a similar finding for Gestalt laws of organization in patterns. Of those so-called laws, only common fate, involving motion, functions to insure perception of unity in earlier infancy. The others may operate in pictorial perception, but not before seven months or later.

Learning to recognize features of faces portrayed in photographs or drawings does not tell us what happens in the kind of perceptual learning involved in looking at real faces. Quite soon after birth (48 hours), infants prefer to look at the live faces of their own mothers (Bushnell et al. 1989). Furthermore, soon after birth they can imitate a facial gesture of another person, particularly when the mouth is implicated. What are babies perceiving then? Perhaps what they perceive is an affordance, having to do with a face in a context that is part of an act of communication. Faces are *not* just visual patterns; they appear as part of an event, one including touch and odors and sounds as well, and the event implies some interaction with another person. At three months, babies are distressed by their mother's immobile, unreactive faces (Tronick et al. 1978). If babies are presented with movies or videotapes of a person behaving in a happy fashion or a distressed fashion, they can identify the appropriate event with a sound track that corresponds to it well before seven months (Walker 1982).

Does the baby form an association between modal or other aspects of an event when it is only a few hours old? I doubt it. All the aspects are already together in a natural context for the baby to observe, as it uses the limited exploratory and communicative skills it possesses. I think all the aspects are simply perceived as one event to begin with, without analysis into features or modally specific experiences. We started with the wrong end of the stick. Feature analysis and separation by modes comes later, perhaps with pictorial perception. What is perceived first is the unanalyzed affordance of an event in which a caretaker and the baby are actors. This event involves a kind of interpersonal relation sometimes referred to as "protocommunication" (Trevarthen 1979). The mother's voice and facial gestures are prominent in this event and are clearly responded to by the baby with coos and its own facial gestures. Babies distinguish their mothers' voices from others at birth (DeCasper and Fifer 1980). This differentiation may enhance attention to the facial gestures uniquely synchronized with the vocal information, a unified multimodal event. Recognizing faces begins here with multimodal specification of a person having a unique communicative affordance for an infant.

Learning about multimodal specification of an event is my second case. What kind of learning, if any, is involved? A number of experiments have been performed showing that infants between four and seven months may perceive bimodal information specifying an event as belonging together, united in the same event. A method for demonstrating this competence was devised by Spelke (1976). Infants (aged four months) are shown moving pictures of two events. Both events are filmed with sound tracks providing the appropriate context. For example, one event in a Spelke experiment was a woman shown playing peek-a-boo, making appropriate exclamations as she smiled and covered and uncovered her eyes. The other was a hand tapping out a rhythm on a little percussion instrument. Babies were shown the films of these two events side by side, but only one sound track was played, centered between the two films. The babies' eye-movements were monitored for a looking preference. In a number of experiments babies have been found to show a preference for looking at the event with bimodal specification, perceiving, it would seem, a unified event.

Careful examination of all the research of this kind by Marion Eppler (1990) has shown, however, that not all the experiments agree in this finding. Positive results often favor slightly older babies (five to seven months); and positive results with younger infants (about four months) have been found most consistently when a person's face, animated and conversing, was portrayed. Do infants learn about bimodal specification? If so, do they detect bimodal invariance, abstract information specifying the event? Or are the two modes of information associated by being experienced contiguously? It is reasonable that bimodal specification of persons should come earliest, for the first events that infants are engaged in are social, whereas they are engaged with events involving objects somewhat later, increasingly as manual exploration develops enough for objects to afford actions on them. Some kind of perceptual learning appears to take place. What kind?

Lorraine Bahrick (1988) has addressed this question directly in an experiment with three-month-old infants. The infants were given an opportunity for perceptual learning by familiarizing them with two visible and audible events, one at a time, and then assessing the conditions of familiarization that actually resulted in learning.

Four groups of infants were given two minutes of familiarization training with the two event films. One film depicted a hand shaking a clear plastic bottle containing one very large marble. The other depicted a hand shaking a similar bottle containing a large number of very small marbles. The four familiarization conditions varied in their pairings of film and sound track, as to whether the track was synchronous with the film or not. Only *one* condition (one group of infants) was familiarized with films paired with their appropriate, synchronized sound track. A fifth (control) group was familiarized with films of irrelevant events. Following familiarization, an intermodal preference test was given all groups, with the two films presented side by side, and a single, centered sound track played.

Results of this experiment showed that learning did occur as a result of familiarization, resulting in a preference for watching the film specified by its appropriate sound track, but *learning was confined to only one group*, the one given familiarization with the appropriate, synchronous pairing of sight and sound. Equal opportunity for association with an inappropriate sound track did not lead to a preference for that combination in the intermodal test.

This ingenious experiment tells us that experience with events may be important for knowledge of bimodal invariance of specification; some kind of learning does go on, since the control groups of three-month-old infants showed no bimodal preference. It also tells us that the kind of learning that happens is not based on sheer association, since groups receiving inappropriate pairing showed no evidence of learning.

What is happening then, when this kind of perceptual learning occurs? It may be differentiation of the two modes of specification and detection of an abstract invariant specifying the same affordance. Evidently, opportunities to look and listen to varied kinds of events are important for this kind of learning to occur. That it is specific to any particular event seems unlikely, for Bahrick found that older infants (over six months) showed preferences in her experiment that indicated knowledge of intermodal specification without prior familiarization with that particular event. There is other evidence that differentiation of modal specification begins around six months (Walker-Andrews and Gibson 1986). It may be boosted by onset of manual exploration and the consequent opportunities for self-initiated events implicating objects and providing multimodal information while they are manipulated.

What Bahrick's experiment tells us explicitly, I think, is that association of intermodal experiences is not a mechanism that results in knowledge of intermodal specification of an event. The mechanism, if that word is to be used, must be one of differentiation of multimodal information and detection of an abstract invariant, probably one specifying an affordance, such as creating a particular kind of noise.

I have made many references now to affordances, that is, the relationship between a creature like a human infant and a way of acting that is appropriate to both the environmental opportunities offered and the potential (organismic, dynamic, etc.) of the actor. An affordance must be perceived for appropriate action to ensue. Affordances change as an infant develops and new potentials such as emerging action systems arise. Here is a prime case for perceptual learning. The infant must detect the information specifying both the required environmental supports and its own capabilities and, above all, the relation between them, a kind of abstract relational invariant.

My third case of learning is of this kind, learning about properties of an environmental support needed for realization of some action, in this case locomotion. Emergence of locomotor systems occurs naturally during development and requires learning about new capacities and their limits as well as detecting what the environment provides for putting them to use. My example is research on the affordance of a surface of support for the actions of crawling and walking. Babies capable of self-produced locomotion observe surfaces that may or may not afford support and tend to avoid those that look or feel as though they do not. Richard Walk and I (Walk and Gibson 1961) found, for example, that few crawling infants will move out on a transparent surface even though it is actually firm and solid to the touch. They expect that a surface of support should provide good optical information for solidity. We did not at that time investigate how they came to expect this, but in recent years, my colleagues and I (Gibson et al. 1987) have investigated properties of surfaces perceived as necessary for walking by very young walkers (see chapter 32). In contrast to crawlers, they explored a surface for its affordance for maintaining an upright posture and supporting bipedal locomotion.

I think that emergence of a new action system, such as walking, instigates exploratory activity, resulting in learning about properties of environmental supports implicated in the activity and also about capacities of the actor's body, its competence or "effectivity." Spontaneous exploration has the immediate result of producing consequences. Observation of these consequences is the key to perceptual learning in development.

Learning that involves self-controlled exploration with observation of its consequences has been shown to occur very early in infants. Learning about consequences of one's own action leads to control of events in the surrounding environment. The baby detects information that specifies an action performed by itself, and something happening in the world contingent with it. Such cases were described 100 years ago by Preyer (1881), later by Piaget (1952), and in recent times by followers of Skinner, who refer to them as operant conditioning. Several examples have been well-researched in recent years. Non-nutritive sucking on an empty nipple, attached to a pressure transducer, so as to trigger some environmental event when appropriate pressure is applied, is by now a classic technique for studying phonetic discrimination by young infants (Eimas et al. 1971). Mouthing is an exploratory activity engaged in by infants soon after birth. If a tool (the nipple in this case) is provided with appropriate attachments, babies learn to operate it to produce environmental contingencies such as a tape recorder playing bits of human speech, even single syllables (BA or PA). The baby discovers the consequence of its action, its predictability, and its own control over the event. Siqueland and DeLucia (1969) found that babies quickly learn to produce another kind of contingent event, pictures displayed by a slide projector. If the pictures were varied, babies continued to act to obtain them for long periods.

One of the most interesting of these experiments was done by Kalnins and Bruner (1973). A movie was projected before the infant subject, and the nipple and transducer arranged so that sucking would control the focus of the film. If the babies engaged in high amplitude sucking at a regular rate, the film was kept in focus, otherwise it was blurred. The babies provided with this arrangement quickly learned to use it, as long as blur was avoided, and stopped when the focussing mechanism was detached. The babies learned, in short, to use a tool to optimize their exploratory activity. When sucking resulted in blur, the rate dropped almost at once.

A string tied to a baby's wrist or ankle has been used frequently to demonstrate how infants learn to act to produce an environmental consequence. Rovee and Rovee (1969) tied a ribbon to a baby's ankle, with the other end attached to a mobile overhanging the crib in which it lay. Babies quickly learned to kick the leg to make the mobile turn. Babies in a control group were given the same display, but it was not contingent on their own kicks. They fussed, looked away, and cried after a short time, while babies allowed to control the moving display cooed and smiled (Rovee-Collier and Capatides 1979).

Results similar to these have been obtained (Lewis, Sullivan and Brooks-Gunn 1985) with a string tied to the baby's wrist and the other end hitched to a switch that operated a slide projector and a tape recorder that played a song from Sesame Street. Babies in both an experimental and a control group were videotaped and their facial expressions coded afterward in relation to their activity. The babies in the experimental group exhibited intense interest as they discovered the consequences of their arm pulls, and accelerated their arm pulling. Babies in the control group fussed.

What is learned in these cases? The babies are observing the consequences of an action of their own and learning a causal relationship in an event sequence. They are discovering what a given action in a specific context affords. The emotional accompaniments of this learning suggest that there is great satisfaction in discovering predictability, and in control of an event by one's own action. Can we dismiss these cases of learning to control an event as mere cases of operant conditioning? I think not. The essence of learning is the exploratory activity, instigated entirely by the infant, and used appropriately for searching for information. It is not mere repetition followed by reinforcement. An infant's behavior is modulated to test out effects of action or nonaction. For example, cessation of an interesting consequence (by intervention of an experimenter, for instance) does not result in a neat curve of extinction. It is more likely to result in a burst of action, not unlike what an adult driver does when his car suddenly refuses to start. Bower (1989) presents a detailed description of an infant's exploratory activity as the experimenter introduces changes in the consequences of the baby's actions. The aptness of the spontaneous behavior that ensues for revealing the underlying "causal texture" of the events going on and the baby's own relation to them is remarkable.

The old mistake was to start with static displays in formulating a theory of perceptual learning. Letters, numbers, and even photographs of human faces are not the natural occasions for study of human perceptual learning in its beginnings. The baby necessarily learns by perceiving, and what he has to perceive are complex, multimodal events that often involve his own activity. This activity is limited to start with—looking, mouthing, kicking. Big changes occur when a baby begins to grasp and manipulate objects, and still more take place with the advent of mobility. When we study learning in relation to this development it takes on a new look.

A human infant seeks information about its environment, actively searching a surrounding ambient array of energy, often instigated by the advent of a new action system—a naturally developing one, or in some of the examples above, one rigged for the infant by an experimenter. Exploratory activity, spontaneous and self-initiated rather than fortuitously supplied, has the effect of testing the reliability of consequences following the activity. Observation of the relationship between one's own action and the consequent events is a powerful means for perceptual learning. This is not association, in the old sense. Events are associated in the causal texture of the environment, and a human infant learns by observing the predictable relations.

Are we going to find the answer to learning in "connectionism"? I doubt it, because it appears to neglect properties of behavior that stand out even in infants—its directedness, its flexibility with changing context, in short its functional character and adaptiveness. In any case, neural underpinnings of perceptual learning in infants can wait their turn, while we turn our attention again to what it is that preverbal infants learn, using the biologists' methods of good naturalistic observation and experimental methods that are now available to discover what an infant perceives. Whatever name we choose to give it now, psychology still has a domain in its own right. And so has perception—we perceive to learn, as well as learn to perceive.

References

Anderson, G. J., 1989. Perception of three-dimensional structure from optic flow without locally smooth velocity. *Journal of Experimental Psychology: Perception and Performance*, 15:363–371.

Arnoult, M. D., 1953. Transfer of predifferentiation training in simple and multiple shape discrimination. *Journal of Experimental Psychology*, 45:401–409.

Bahrick, L. E., 1988. Intermodal learning in infancy: Learning on the basis of two kinds of invariant relations in audible and visible events. *Child Development*, 59:197–209.

Ball, W. A., and Tronick, E., 1971. Infant responses to impending collision: Optical and real. *Science*, 171:818–820.

Bass, M. J., and Hull C. L., 1934. The irradiation of a tactile conditioned reflex in man. *Journal of Comparative Psychology*, 17:47–65.

Bishop, C. H., 1964. Transfer effects of word and letter training in reading. *Journal of Verbal Learning and Verbal Behavior*, 3:215–221.

Bishop, C. H., 1976. Orthographic structure, word recognition, and reading. Ph.D. dissertation, Cornell University.

Blake, R. R., and Ramsay, G. V., 1951. *Perception: An approach to personality.* New York: Ronald Press.

Bloomfield, L., 1942. Linguistics and reading. *Elementary English Review*, 19:128–130.

Bolles, R. C., and Beecher, M. D., 1988. *Evolution and learning.* Hillsdale, NJ: Erlbaum, Associates.

Boring, E. G., 1933. *The Physical Dimensions of Consciousness.* New York: Century.

Bower, T. G. R., 1989. *The Rational Infant: Learning in Infancy.* New York: W. H. Freeman & Co.

Bower, T. G. R., Broughton, M. M., and Moore, M. K., 1970. Infant responses to approaching objects: An indicator of response to distal variables. *Perception and Psychophysics*, 9:193–196.

Bushnell, I. W. R., Sai, F., and Mullin, J. T., 1989. Neonatal recognition of the mother's face. *British Journal of Developmental Psychology*, 7:3–15.

Campos, J. J., Langer, A. and Krowitz, A., 1970. Cardiac response on the visual cliff in prelocomotor infants. *Science*, 170:196–197.

Changeux, J. P., Heidmann, T., and Patte, P., 1984. Learning by selection. In *The Biology of Learning* ed. P. Marler and H. S. Terrace, 115–133. Berlin: Springer-Verlag.

Condry, S. M., McMahon-Rideout, M., and Levy, A. A., 1979. A developmental investigation of selective attention to graphic, phonetic, and semantic information in words. *Perception and Psychophysics*, 25:88–94.

DeCasper, A. J., and Fifer, W. P., 1980. Of human bonding: Newborns prefer their mothers' voices. *Science*, 208:1174–1176.

Dewsbury, D. A., 1989. Comparative psychology, ethology, and animal behavior. *Annual Review of Psychology*, 40:581–602.

Eimas, P. D., Siqueland, E. R., Jusczyk, P. and Vigorito, J., 1971. Speech perception in infants. *Science*, 171:303–306.

Eppler, M., 1990. Perception and action in infancy: Object manipulation skills and detection of auditory-visual correspondence. Ph.D. dissertation, Emory University, Atlanta.

Epstein, W., 1982. Percept-percept couplings. *Perception*, 11:75–83.

Fagan, J. F. III, 1979. The origins of facial pattern recognition. In (Eds.), *Psychological Development from Infancy: Image to Intention* ed. Bornstein, M. H. and Kessen, W. 83–113. Hillsdale, NJ: Erlbaum Associates.

Fantz, R. L., 1965. Ontogeny of perception. In *Behavior of Non-human Primates*, ed. A. M. Schrier, H. F. Harlow, and F. Stollnitz, 365–403. New York: Academic Press.

Frances, R., 1962. *Le développement perceptif*. Paris: Presses Universitaires de France.

Gallistel, C. R., 1989. Animal cognition: The representation of space, time and number. *Annual Review of Psychology*, 40:155–189.

Garcia, J., 1981. Tilting at the paper mills of academe. *American Psychologist*, 36:149–158.

Garcia, J., McGowan, B. K. and Green, K. F., 1972. Biological constraints on conditioning. In M. E. P. Seligman and J. L. Hager (Eds.), *Biological boundaries of learning*, New York: Appleton-Century-Crofts.

Garner, W. R., 1979. Letter discrimination and identification. In *Perception and its development*, ed. A. D. Pick, 111–144. Hillsdale, NJ: Erlbaum Associates.

Gibson, E. J., 1953. Improvement in perceptual judgments as a function of controlled practice or training. *Psychological Bulletin*, 50:401–431.

Gibson, E. J., 1959. A re-examination of generalization. *Psychological Review*, 66: 340–342.

Gibson, E. J., 1963. Perceptual development. In *Child Psychology*, ed. H. W. Stevenson, J. Kagan, and C. Spiker, 144–195. 62nd Yearbook National Society for Study of Education, Chicago, Ill.: Univ. of Chicago Press.

Gibson, E. J., 1969. *Principles of Perceptual Learning and Development*. New York: Appleton-Century-Crofts.

Gibson, E. J., 1983. Development of knowledge about intermodal unity: Two views. In *Piaget and the foundations of knowledge*, ed. L. S. Liben, 19–41. Hillsdale, NJ: Erlbaum Associates.

Gibson, E. J., 1987. What does infant perception tell us about theories of perception? *Journal of Experimental Psychology: Human Perception and Performance*, 13:515–523.

Gibson, E. J., and Gibson, J. J., 1950. The identifying response: A study of a neglected form of learning. Abstract in *American Psychologist*, 7:276.

Gibson, E. J., and Guinet, L., 1971. The perception of inflections in brief visual presentations of words. *Journal of Verbal Learning and Verbal Behavior*, 10:182–189.

Gibson, E. J., and Levin, H., 1975. *The Psychology of Reading*. Cambridge, MA: MIT Press.

Gibson, E. J., and Olum, V., 1960. Experimental methods of studying perception in children. In *Handbook of Research in Child Development*, ed. P. H. Mussen 311–373. New York: Wiley.

Gibson, E. J., Owsley, C. J., Walker, A. S., and Megaw-Nyce, J., 1979. Development of the perception of invariants: Substance and shape. *Perception*, 8:609–619.

Gibson, E. J., Riccio, G., Schmuckler, M. A., Stoffregen, T. A., Rosenberg, D., and Taormina, J., 1987. Detection of the traversability of surfaces by crawling and walking infants. *Journal of Experimental Psychology: Perception and Performance*, 13:533–544.

Gibson, E. J., and Schmuckler, M. A., 1989. Going somewhere: An ecological and experimental approach to development of mobility. *Ecological Psychology*, 1:3–25.

Gibson, E. J., Shurcliff, A., and Yonas, A., 1970. Utilization of spelling patterns by deaf and hearing subjects. In *Basic Studies on Reading*, ed. H. Levin and J. P. Williams, 57–73. New York: Basic Books.

Gibson, E. J., and Walk, R. D., 1960. The "visual cliff." *Scientific American*, 202:64–71.

Gibson, E. J., Walk, R. D., Pick, H. L., and Tighe, T. J., 1958. The effect of prolonged exposure to visual patterns on learning to discriminate similar and different patterns. *Journal of Comparative and Physiological Psychology*, 51:584–587.

Gibson, E. J., Walk, R. D., and Tighe, T. J., 1959. Enhancement and deprivation of visual stimulation during rearing as factors in visual discrimination learning. *Journal of Comparative and Physiological Psychology*, 52:74–81.

Gibson, E. J., and Yonas, A., 1966. A developmental study of the effects of visual and auditory interference on a visual scanning task. *Psychonomic Science*, 5:163–164.

Gibson, J. J., 1929. The reproduction of visually perceived forms. *Journal of Experimental Psychology*, 12:1–39.

Gibson, J. J. ed., 1947. Motion picture testing and research. Report No. 7 in Army Air Forces Aviation Psychology Program Research Reports. U.S. Government Printing Office, Washington, D.C.

Gibson, J. J., 1950. *Perception of the Visual World*. Boston: Houghton-Mifflin.

Gibson, J. J., 1957. Optical motions and transformations as stimuli for visual perception. *Psychological Review*, 64:288–295.

Gibson, J. J., 1966. *The Senses Considered as Perceptual Systems*. Boston: Houghton-Mifflin.

Gibson, J. J., 1979. *The Ecological Approach to Visual Perception*. Boston: Houghton-Mifflin. Reprint, Hillsdale, NJ: Erlbaum Associates, 1986.

Harnad, S., 1987. *Categorical Perception*. New York: Cambridge University Press.

Hatfield, G., and Epstein, W., 1985. The status of the minimum principle in the theoretical analysis of visual perception. *Psychological Bulletin*, 97:155–186.

Hebb, D. O., 1937. The innate organization of visual activity: I. Perception of figures by rats reared in total darkness. *Journal of Genetic Psychology*, 51:101–126.

Hebb, D. O., 1949. *The Organization of Behavior*. New York: Wiley.

Hebb, D. O., 1980. In *A History of Psychology in Autobiography, Vol. VII*, ed. R. C. Atkinson, J. Freedman, G. Lindzey, and R. F. Thompson, 273–303. San Francisco: W. H. Freeman.

Hilgard, E. R., and Marquis, D. G., 1940. *Conditioning and Learning*. New York: Appleton-Century.

Horowitz, F. D., Paden, L., Bhana, K., and Self, P., 1972. An infant-control procedure for studying fixations. *Development Psychology*, 7:90.

Hubel, D. H., and Wiesel, T. N., 1959. Receptive fields of single neurons in the cat's striate cortex. *Journal of Physiology*, 148:574–591.

Huey, E. B., 1908. *Psychology and Pedagogy of Reading*. New York: Macmillan.

Hull, C. L., 1929. A functional interpretation of the conditioned reflex. *Psychological Review*, 36:498–511.

Hull, C. L., 1935. The conflicting psychologies of learning—a way out. *Psychological Review*, 42:491–516.

Hymovitch, B., 1952. The effects of experiential variations on problem solving in the rat. *Journal of Comparative and Physiological Psychology*, 45:313–321.

Itard, J., 1894. *Rapports et mémoires sur le Sauvage de L'aveyron*. Paris. Trans. by G. & M. Humphrey as *The Wild Boy of Aveyron*. New York: Appleton-Century-Crofts, 1962.

James, W., 1890. *The Principles of Psychology*. New York: Henry Holt.

Johansson, G., 1950. *Configurations in Event Perception*. Uppsala: Almkvist and Wiksell.

Johnston, T. D., 1985. Conceptual issues in the ecological study of learning. In *Issues in the ecological study of learning*, ed. Johnston, T. D., and Pietrewicz, A. T., 1–24. Hillsdale, NJ: Erlbaum Associates.

Johnston, T. D., and Peitrewicz, A. T., 1985. *Issues in the Ecological Study of Learning*. Hillsdale, NJ: Erlbaum Associates.

Kalnins, I. V., and Bruner, J. S., 1973. The coordination of visual observation and instrumental behavior in early infancy. *Perception*, 2:307–314.

Köhler, W., 1925. *The Mentality of Apes*. New York, N.Y.: Harcourt Brace & Co.

Kosslyn, S. M., 1989. Components of high-level vision: A cognitive neuroscience analysis. Technical Report, Air Force Office of Scientific Research, Bolling Air Force Base, Washington, D.C.

Lashley, K. S. and Russell, J. T., 1934. The mechanism of vision. XI. A preliminary test of innate organization. *Journal of Genetic Psychology*, 45:136–144.

Lavine, L. O., 1977. Differentiation of letterlike forms in prereading children. *Development Psychology*, 13:89–94.

Lewis, M., Sullivan, M. W., and Brooks-Gunn, J., 1985. Emotional behavior during the learning of a contingency in early infancy. *British Journal of Developmental Psychology*, 3:307–316.

Logvinenko, A. D., 1988. Russian translation of J. J. Gibson, *The Ecological Approach to Visual Perception*. Moscow.

Loveland, K., 1984. Learning about points of view: Spatial perspective and the acquisition of I/you. *Journal of Child Language*, 11:535–556.

Marr, D., 1982. *Vision: A Computational Investigation into the Human Representation and Processing of Visual Information*. San Francisco: W. H. Freeman & Co.

Melzack, R., and Scott, T. H., 1957. The effects of early experience on the response to pain. *Journal of Comparative and Physiological Psychology*, 50:155–161.

Miller, N. E. and Dollard, J., 1941. *Social Learning and Imitation*. New Haven: Yale University Press.

Mowrer, O. H., 1947. On the dual nature of learning: A re-interpretation of "conditioning" and "problem-solving." *Harvard Educational Review*, 17:102–148.

Newell, K. M., 1986. Constraints on the development of coordination. In *Motor development in children: Aspects of coordination and control*, ed. M. G. Wade and H. T. A. Whiting, 341–360. Dordrecht: Martinus Nijhoff.

Palmer, C., 1987. The specificity of infant locomotion through apertures varying in width. Paper presented at the International Conference on Event Perception and Action, Trieste, Italy, August 1987.

Piaget, J., 1952. *The Origins of Intelligence in Children*. New York: International Universities Press.

Pick, A. D., 1965. Improvement of visual and tactual form discrimination. *Journal of Experimental Psychology*, 69:331–339.

Preyer, W., 1881. The mind of the child. Pt. II. The development of the intellect. New York: Appleton & Co.

Riesen, A. H., 1947. The development of visual perception in man and chimpanzee. *Science*, 106:107–108.

Robinson, E. S., 1932). *Association Theory Today*. New York: Appleton-Century.

Romanes, G. J., 1889. *Mental Evolution in Man: Origin of Human Faculty*. London: Kegan Paul, French.

Rosinski, R. R., 1977. Picture-word interference is semantically based. *Child Development*, 48:643–647.

Rosinski, R. R., Golinkoff, R. M., and Kukish, K. S., 1975. Automatic semantic processing in a picture-word interference task. *Child Development*, 46:247–253.

Rovee, C. K., and Rovee, D. T., 1969. Conjugate reinforcement of infant exploratory behavior. *Journal of Experimental Child Psychology*, 8:33–39.

Rovee-Collier, C. K., and Capatides, J. B., 1979. Positive behavioral contrast in 3-month-old infants on multiple conjugate reinforcement schedules. *Journal of the Experimental Analysis of Behavior*. Vol. 32, 1 : 15−27.

Rumelhart, D. E., and McClelland, J. L. (Eds.), (1986). *Parallel Distributed Processing: Explorations in the Microstructure of Cognition*. Vol. 1, *Foundations*. Cambridge, MA: MIT Press.

Schiff, W., 1965. The perception of impending collision: A study of visually directed avoidant behavior. *Psychological Monographs, 79* : 604.

Schmidt, H., and Spelke, E. S., 1984. Gestalt relations and object perception in infancy. Paper presented at the meeting of the International Conference on Infant Studies, New York.

Senden, M. von, 1932. *Raum und Gestaltauffassung bei Operierten Blindgeborenen*. Kiel, Germany. Trans. by P. Heath as *Space and Sight*. London: Methuen & Co., 1960.

Siqueland, E. R., and DeLucia, C. A., 1969. Visual reinforcement of nonnutritive sucking in human infants. *Science*, 165 : 1144−1146.

Society for Research in Child Development (1970). *Cognitive Development in Children*. Chicago, IL: University of Chicago Press.

Spelke, E. S., 1976. Infants' intermodal perception of events. *Cognitive Psychology*, 8 : 553−560.

Sternberg, S., 1967. Two operations in character recognition: Some evidence from reaction-time measurements. *Perception and Psychophysics*, 2 : 45−53.

Stevens' Handbook of Experimental Psychology 1988. 2nd ed. eds. R. Atkinson, R. Herrnstein, G. Lindzey, and D. Luce. New York: Wiley.

Thompson, W. R., and Heron, W., 1954. The effects of restricting early experience on the problem-solving capacity of dogs. *Canadian Journal of Psychology*, 8 : 17−31.

Tighe, T. J., and Shepp, B. E., 1983. *Perception, Cognition, and Development: Interactional Analyses*. Hillsdale, NJ: Erlbaum Associates.

Trevarthen, C., 1979. Communication and cooperation in early infancy: A description of primary intersubjectivity. In *Before Speech*, ed. M. Bullowa, 321−341. New York: Cambridge University Press.

Tronick, E. Z., Als, H., Adamson, L., Wise, S., and Brazelton, T. B., 1978. The infant's response to entrapment between contradictory messages in face-to-face interaction. *Journal of the American Academy of Child Psychiatory*, 17 : 1−13.

Ullman, S., 1979. *The Interpretation of Visual Motion*. Cambridge, MA: MIT Press.

Walk, R. D. and Gibson, E. J., 1961. A comparative and analytical study of visual depth perception. *Psychological Monographs*, No. 519, Vol. 75, No. 15.

Walk, R. D., Gibson, E. J., Pick, H. L., and Tighe, T. J., 1958. Further experiments on prolonged exposure to visual forms: The effect of single stimuli and prior reinforcement. *Journal of Comparative and Physiological Psychology*, 51 : 483−487.

Walker, A. S., 1982. Intermodal perception of expressive behaviors by human infants. *Journal of Experimental Child Psychology*, 33 : 514−535.

Walker, A., Owsley, C. J., Megaw-Nyce, J., Gibson, E. J., and Bahrick, L. E., 1980. Detection of elasticity as an invariant property of objects by young infants. *Perception*, 9 : 713−718.

Walker-Andrews, A. S., and Gibson, E. J., 1986. What develops in bimodal perception? In *Advances in infancy research*, Vol. 4 ed. Lipsitt, L. P. and Rovee-Collier, C., 171−181. Norwood, NJ: Ablex Publishing Co.

Wallach, H., and T. O'Connell, D. N., 1953. The kinetic depth effect. *Journal of Experimental Psychology*, 45 : 205−217.

Wertheimer, M., 1923. Untersuchungen Zur Lehre von der Gestalt, II. *Psychologische Forschung*, 4 : 301−350.

Warren, W. H., Jr., and Whang, S., 1987. Visual guidance of walking through apertures. *Journal of Experimental Psychology: Human Perception and Performance*, 13 : 371−383.

Washburn, M. F., 1908. *The Animal Mind*. New York: Macmillan.

Weiss, P. A., 1970. Whither life science. *American Scientist*, 58 : 156–163.

Wickens, D. D., 1939a). A study of voluntary and involuntary finger conditioning. *Journal of Experimental Psychology*, 25 : 127–140.

Wickens, D. D., 1939b. The simultaneous transfer of conditioned excitation and conditioned inhibition. *Journal of Experimental Psychology*, 25 : 332–338.

Woodworth, R. S., 1938. *Experimental Psychology*. New York: Holt.

Yonas, A. W., and Gibson, E. J., 1967. A developmental study of feature-processing strategies in letter discrimination. Paper presented at Eastern Psychological Association, Boston, MA.

Yonas, A., Granrud, C. E., Arterberry, M. E., and Hanson, B. L., 1986. Infants' distance perception from linear perspective and texture gradients. *Infant Behavior and Development*, 9 : 247–256.

Zinchenko, V. P., 1966. Perception as action. In *Proceedings of the 28th International Congress of Psychology* 64–73, Symposium 30. Moscow.

Author Index

Subject Index